NEW JAPA

NEW

JAPAN

SOLO

Eiji Kanno
Constance O'Keefe

KODANSHA INTERNATIONAL
Tokyo • New York • London

Originally published in 1985 as *Japan Solo*, by Nitchi Map-Publishing Co., Ltd., Tokyo, Japan.

Revised edition published in Japan by the Japan National Tourist Organization (JNTO) Staff Association in cooperation with Kodansha International Ltd., and in the U.S. by Warner Books under the title *Japan Solo*.

Third edition published by Kodansha International Ltd., 17-14 Otowa 1-chome, Bunkyo-ku, Tokyo 112, Japan in cooperation with the Japan National Tourist Organization Staff Association.

Maps by Eiji Kanno.

Photos and illustrations courtesy of the Japan National Tourist Organization: Tourist Associations of Aichi, Aomori, Ehime, Fukushima, Gifu, Hiroshima, Ishikawa, Iwate, Kagawa, Kanagawa, Kochi, Kyoto, Mie, Miyagi, Nagano, Nagasaki, Nara, Osaka, Shimane, Shizuoka, Tokyo, Wakayama, and Yamaguchi.

Distributed in the United States by Kodansha America, Inc., 114 Fifth Avenue, New York, N.Y. 10011, and in the United Kingdom and continental Europe by Kodansha Europe Ltd., 95 Aldwych, London WC2B 43F. Published by Kodansha International Ltd., 17-14 Otowa 1-chome, Bunkyo-ku, Tokyo 112, and Kodansha America, Inc.

Copyright © 1985 by Eiji Kanno. Second edition copyright © 1988 and third edition copyright © 1994 by Eiji Kanno and Constance O'Keefe. All rights reserved.

Printed in Japan.

94 95 96 10 9 8 7 6 5 4 3 2 1

ISBN 4-7700-1739-1

Library of Congress Cataloging-in-Publication Data

Kanno, Eiji
  New Japan Solo / Eiji Kanno and Constance O'Keefe,
  -- Expanded & updated 3rd. ed.
      p. cm.
  Rev. ed. of: Japan solo.
  Includes index.
  ISBN 4-7700-1739-1
  1. Japan--Guidebooks. 2. Japan--Maps. I. O'Keefe, Constance.
  II. Kanno, Eiji. Japan solo. III. Title.
  DS805.2.K37 1993
  915.204'49--dc20   93-26595

A Foreword from the President of the Japan National Tourist Organization

Our former colleagues, Eiji Kanno and Constance O'Keefe, have once again updated their comprehensive guide, *New Japan Solo*, now in its third edition. Since the guide book was first published in 1985, it has indeed proven to be *the* indispensable source book for independent travelers to Japan.

This third edition features all new maps, expanded information on travel destinations and additional details on public transportation. The more than 200 maps offer regional, district, municipal and neighborhood perspectives, permitting foreign tourists to have greater travel independence. An added component of the book addresses the travel interests of those attending international meetings and conventions in Japan, as well as business people, academics and scientists visiting the country. Information of special interest to foreigners residing in Japan is also provided. We at JNTO are pleased that our former colleagues have emphasized these additional areas in their book.

JNTO operates Tourist Information Centers (TICs) in downtown Tokyo, Kyoto and at New Tokyo International Airport in Narita, as well as its toll-free Japan Travel-Phone service, which offers English language assistance to foreign visitors every day of the year. JNTO also assists the International Tourism Center of Japan with its Welcome Inn Reservation Service, and has lent a helping hand to local tourist information offices throughout Japan. We are proud that *New Japan Solo*, with its proven track record, provides another service for foreign visitors to Japan that originated with JNTO.

We believe that tourism is a passport to peace, and that people-to-people contact is one of the surest ways to bring all of us closer together in today's global community. *New Japan Solo*, the best guidebook that we have come across, can be your passport to Japan and your introduction to the Japanese people, who truly constitute the greatest attraction Japan has to offer international travelers.

I wish you a very warm welcome to Japan.

Akira Niwa
President
Japan National Tourist Organization
August 1993

A Message from Japan Railways

JR is pleased that the number of foreign visitors to Japan using Japan Rail Passes is increasing every year. We believe that Rail Passes offer foreign visitors to Japan excellent value and unequalled access to every corner of the country. *New Japan Solo* is unique in its emphasis on transportation, and on traveling as the Japanese travel. The authors are quite correct to emphasize the benefits of Japan Rail Passes and travel on the extensive JR system. The maps in the guide book provide excellent information on rail lines and the text provides details on how to use trains and combine routes, along with details on travel time, schedules and fares. With a Japan Rail Pass and a copy of *New Japan Solo*, foreign visitors to Japan have the means to experience Japan as fully as possible. The hustle and bustle of the big cities and the splendor of Japan's cultural treasures as well as the local flavor of the seemingly remotest areas are all accessible.

JR is pleased with the publication of this revised edition of *New Japan Solo*. We look forward to welcoming you aboard JR trains for your exploration of Japan.

Kenichi Shimura
Director
JR Group New York Office
August 1993

Contents

LIST OF MAPS

Preface to the Third Edition

In the second edition of this book, we expanded the scope of *New Japan Solo* beyond the "Golden Route," to include information on all parts of Japan. We have provided even wider coverage in this third edition, with the travel interests of four types of travelers in mind. First, of course, is the tourist from overseas, traveling on a Rail Pass and discovering the freedom and pleasures of exploring Japan independently. For those attending international conferences, we have covered Japan's new convention facilities, as well as nearby, easily accessible, tourist attractions. We have also added information on family destinations and on resorts that are likely to be of most interest to foreign residents in Japan, including appealing locales off the beaten track. Finally, with Japan's growing internationalization, business travelers are increasingly visiting such cities as Osaka and Nagoya in addition to Tokyo. We have therefore expanded our suggestions for one-day and half-day excursions from these major cities.

We have again walked and walked *and walked* in order to check the itineraries we recommended in previous editions as well as to develop new ones. All the maps in this edition—a total of more than 200—are new. They provide overviews of the regions described in the text and information on intra- and inter-city transportation. There are also more detailed city maps, indicating downtown areas, tourist attractions, train stations, bus stops, major hotels, restaurants, shops and landmarks.

Because we are still strong advocates of traveling as the Japanese travel—on the trains—we have included a great deal of detailed information on this nation's train systems: the various JR companies and other smaller, regional railroads. Emphasis is on JR trains, because we believe that Japan Rail Passes provide the best bargain available for foreign tourists in Japan. The names of train lines are indicated on the maps and the text explains how to use them (including suggestions on making connections between various lines). The text also includes information on travel times between cities and fares for the trips described.

Japan today is much more accessible to the foreign tourist, especially those speaking English, than it was a decade ago. An improved and expanded tourist information system at various locations throughout the country supplements the TIC (Tourist Information Center) offices of JNTO in Tokyo, Kyoto and at the New Tokyo International Airport in Narita. There are also now a great many bilingual signs, with English added where there used to be only Japanese. Things have improved so much that "no English whatsoever" is now the exception rather than the rule. This does not mean, however, that our observations in earlier editions about the state of spoken English in Japan are no longer true. We therefore still include "Conversation Cards" at the back of the book that are designed for you to obtain immediate results in situations (usually involving transportation) where you need exact information and specific assistance.

Once again, we owe a debt of gratitude to our families and friends, in both Japan

14

and the United States. We are, as always, dependent on their support and assistance. And once again, we are grateful for the many suggestions, comments and constructive criticisms we have received from readers of previous editions.

Eiji Kanno
Constance O'Keefe
September 1993

INTRODUCTION
Remarks, Details and Survival Tips

HOW TO USE THIS BOOK AND ITS MAPS

The destinations introduced in this guide are arranged in rough geographical order starting at Tokyo and moving west to Kyoto, and then southwest to Kyushu. Areas north of Tokyo (Hokkaido and Tohoku) are placed at the end of the book. In this guidebook, Japan is divided into ten regions as follows (in the order of introduction):

(1) Kanto (Tokyo plus surrounding destinations),
(2) Joetsu & Shin-etsu (destinations along the JR Joetsu Shinkansen, plus mountain areas to the northwest of Tokyo),
(3) Chubu (the central part of the main island, with Nagoya being its center),
(4) Kansai (Osaka, Kyoto and Nara, plus surrounding destinations),
(5) Sanyo (the western part of the main island, facing the Inland Sea),
(6) San-in (the western part of the main island, facing the Japan Sea),
(7) Shikoku (Japan's fourth largest island),
(8) Kyushu (Japan's southernmost and third largest island, plus Okinawa),
(9) Hokkaido (Japan's northernmost and second largest island), and
(10) Tohoku (the northern part of the main island of Honshu).

We've walked every one of the suggested itineraries in this book. There is a regional map at the beginning of each chapter outlining the locations of major cities and resorts and the region's transportation network. The text that follows explains each destination in detail and is coordinated with

more detailed walking tour maps. If a city is large (such as Tokyo, Osaka and Kyoto) and divided into several districts, we have placed an area map at the beginning of the section. Use the area map to understand the intra-city transportation network and to locate the downtown and tourist attractions, etc. that are explained in detail. More detailed maps of each district, to be used for walking tours, follow, and are, again, coordinated with the text. We suggest that you use the regional maps first to locate your destinations and plan inter-city transportation. Then proceed to the area maps and locate downtowns, places of interest, etc. and get an idea of the intra-city transportation network. Once you understand how an area is laid out in general terms, proceed to the more detailed walking tour maps on the pages that follow. They are much easier to use than the big city maps.

SAFETY AND SECURITY

Japan is one of the safest countries in the world. Robberies are very rare and impersonal violent crime is virtually unknown. It is because Japan is so safe that we can wholeheartedly encourage you to travel there on your own.

GEOGRAPHY AND POPULATION

The Japanese archipelago stretches 3,000 km (1,860 miles) from northeast to southwest along the eastern coast of the Asian Continent. The country has four major islands (from north to south: Hokkaido, Honshu, Shikoku and Kyushu), and about 4,000 small islands. The total area of

Japan is about 378,000 square km (146,000 square miles). Although it is one and a half times the size of the U.K., it is only one-twenty-fifth the size of the U.S., and the whole country is only about the size of the state of California. Three-fourths of Japan is mountainous and covered with forests. The highest peak is Mt. Fuji (3,776 m or 12,388 feet). Japan's other high mountains are grouped in the middle of the main island of Honshu and form the "Japan Alps." Several volcanic ranges that run through the islands of Japan have created a unique topography and account for the large number of hot-springs located throughout the country.

Only 15% of the land is arable, and residential areas account for only 3% of the total land of the country.

Some 123 million people (roughly half the population of the U.S.) are crowded onto these mountainous islands. Post-war industrialization and housing shortages have resulted in incredibly high population density in all of the major cities. Eleven cities have populations in excess of one million. They are Tokyo, Yokohama, Osaka, Nagoya, Sapporo, Kobe, Kyoto, Fukuoka, Kawasaki, Hiroshima and Kita-Kyushu. Thirty-one cities have populations of 400,000-900,000. The nation's capital,

MAP 2   Relative Size of Japan to the U.S.

Tokyo, has about 8 million people within its city limits, and an additional 3.6 million in its suburbs. Yokohama, the second largest city, with a population of 3.2 million, is located only 29 km (18 miles) from Tokyo. Between these two giant cities is Kawasaki, the nation's ninth largest city, with a population of 1.2 million. These three cities form the world's largest megalopolis.

CLIMATE

The map of Japan (Intro Map 2) is overlaid on a map of the East Coast of the United States, at the same latitude, to facilitate comparisons. The climate of Japan is similar to that of the East Coast of the United States. Japan has four distinctively different seasons. Spring begins in March (April in northern Honshu and Hokkaido) and lasts until the middle of June. Plum and peach blossoms appear in March, heralding the blooming of the cherry trees in early April and Japan's annual spring time love affair with these beautiful blossoms. The first cherry blossoms appear in the southern part of Kyushu around March 20. The "Cherry Blossom Frontier" then moves gradually to the northeast. Full bloom in the Kyoto/Osaka and Tokyo areas is usually around April 5. The northern part of Japan is in full bloom by the middle of April. The cherry trees are easily affected by slight changes in temperatures, and the period of full bloom varies slightly from year to year. With warm temperatures and stable weather, April and May are very comfortable months for traveling in Japan. This comfortable weather usually continues until the second week of June, when the rainy season sets in.

Summer begins with the rainy season. With the exception of Hokkaido, high humidity and temperatures, along with occasional showers, prevail over the entire country. This is not an ideal season for traveling, but many landscaped gardens are said to look most attractive during a shower or just after a rainfall. The rainy season usually ends in the middle of July. Hot yet stable weather lasts until late August or early September. Areas of high altitude, such as Hakone, Nikko, Koyasan, the Japan Alps and Mt. Asozan, are pleasantly cool throughout the summer. September is typhoon season, but most of these storms remain at sea with only about three or four a year coming ashore. Severe damage is rare.

Autumn is marked by occasional quiet showers in late September and early October. After this short rainy period, Japan has a two-month-long period of stable, comfortable weather, with brilliant blue skies and pleasant temperatures. Japan's scenic beauty reaches its peak in the middle of November, when the country is bedecked with the intense hues of the autumn leaves.

Winter begins with cold western winds blown in by Siberian high pressure systems. The areas along the Japan Sea Coast and the mountainous areas of the interior receive heavy snowfalls throughout the winter, and become winter sports paradises. Even though walking tours are often difficult in these areas in winter, the rugged snow-covered mountains are scenes of magnificent natural beauty. Most areas on the Pacific coast, especially those southwest of Tokyo, have clear skies and low humidity. Temperatures are mild and seldom fall below freezing. In these areas of the Pacific coast, winter is really not at all a bad time for sightseeing.

LANGUAGE

Pronunciation Hepburn romanization is used throughout this book because we believe it is the easiest system for foreigners who want to pronounce Japanese words correctly. There are only five vowels in Japanese — **a** (pronounced like "ah"), **i** ("i" of itch), **u** ("oo" of food), **e** ("e" of bet), and **o** (pronounced like "oh"). Consonants are pronounced as in English (if in doubt, you should use a hard rather than a soft sound).

Japanese is a language of syllables, not

Average Temperatures in Major Cities

Month		Tokyo		Kyoto		Fukuoka		Sapporo	
		F	C	F	C	F	C	F	C
January	High	49	10	48	9	49	10	30	-1
	Low	33	1	32	0	36	2	16	-9
	Average	41	5	39	4	42	6	23	-5
February	High	50	10	49	10	51	10	32	0
	Low	34	1	33	1	37	3	17	-9
	Average	42	5	40	5	44	6	24	-4
March	High	55	13	56	13	57	14	38	4
	Low	40	4	37	3	41	5	24	-4
	Average	47	8	46	8	49	10	31	0
April	High	65	18	67	20	66	19	52	11
	Low	50	10	47	9	50	10	35	2
	Average	57	14	57	14	58	14	43	6
May	High	73	23	76	24	74	23	64	18
	Low	58	15	56	13	57	14	45	7
	Average	65	18	65	18	65	18	54	12
June	High	78	25	81	27	79	26	70	21
	Low	65	18	64	18	65	18	53	12
	Average	71	22	72	22	72	22	61	16
July	High	84	29	88	31	87	31	77	25
	Low	72	22	73	23	74	24	62	16
	Average	77	25	79	26	80	27	68	20
August	High	87	31	91	33	89	32	79	26
	Low	75	24	74	23	75	24	63	18
	Average	80	27	82	28	81	27	70	21
September	High	80	27	83	28	82	28	71	22
	Low	68	20	67	19	68	20	54	12
	Average	73	23	74	23	74	23	62	17
October	High	70	21	73	23	73	23	61	16
	Low	57	14	55	13	56	13	42	6
	Average	63	17	63	17	64	18	51	11
November	High	62	17	63	17	64	18	47	8
	Low	47	8	44	7	47	8	32	0
	Average	54	12	53	11	55	13	39	4
December	High	58	12	53	12	54	12	35	2
	Low	38	3	36	2	40	4	23	-5
	Average	45	7	44	6	47	8	29	-2

individual letters. The five vowels are separate syllables. All other syllables combine the vowels with a consonant or a consonant blend, e.g., **Na, ri, ta, ryo,** and **shi.** Except for occasional doubling of consonants between syllables (e.g., Jakkoin), virtually the only exception is **n,** which can be a syllable all by itself. The name of the Japanese city Sendai has four syllables: **Se-n-da-i.** To pronounce it correctly be sure to pronounce each separate syllable. Even long words like Amanohashidate become manageable when you separate them thusly: **A-ma-no-ha-shi-da-te.** Remember that each Japanese vowel counts as a separate syllable and that long vowels in Japanese count as two syllables. For example, Tokyo and Osaka are each four syllable words: **To-o-kyo-o** and **O-o-sa-ka.**

Japanese makes no distinction between singular and plural nouns or pronouns, or between present and future tenses. Many English sounds — such as "c", "f", "v", and especially the difference between "r" and "l", are very difficult for Japanese to say; it is also difficult for them to distinguish these sounds when they hear them. Bear this in mind when conducting conversations. Speak slowly and distinctly, and be patient.

As we emphasize below, communications problems, especially difficulties with spoken language, still inhibit the interaction of many Japanese with foreigners. Just as it will be difficult for Japanese to understand English, especially when it involves sounds they have difficulty pronouncing themselves, so will it be difficult for you to understand spoken Japanese words or have your use of Japanese words understood, unless you familiarize yourself with proper pronunciation of Japanese. These pronunciation tips are, therefore, not just an academic exercise. Japanese simply won't understand you if you inquire about a destination and don't pronounce its name with a fair degree of accuracy. Likewise, you will be much more likely to understand Japanese when they respond to your inquiries or even Japanese announcements (especially on public transportation) if your expectation of what you will hear corresponds to how Japanese speakers will pronounce it.

If your pronunciation of Japanese is accurate enough, it will actually be better for you, if asking for help, to just pronounce your Japanese destination properly with a questioning intonation rather than inserting the Japanese word in the middle of an English sentence. Thus, you are more likely to be understood if you just say "Kinkakuji?" **(Ki-n-ka-ku-ji)** rather than "Would you please direct me to the Temple of the Golden Pavilion?" or "Is Kinkakuji this way?" Properly pronounced Japanese words are much easier for Japanese to understand. And Japanese words buried in the middle of English sentences, especially if not pronounced perfectly, will just sound like more English to Japanese people. The response is likely to be an embarrassed shake of the head and an apologetic "No English" **(No-o In-gu-ri-shu).**

Japanese Suffixes There is often great confusion on how to handle Japanese suffixes when translating into English. For example, "Kiyomizudera" is usually translated as Kiyomizu Temple ("Kiyomizu" is the name of the temple, and "dera" means temple), while "Nanzenji" is usually translated Nanzenji Temple ("Nanzen" is the name of the temple, and "ji" is another suffix that means temple). To avoid this kind of confusion, this text leaves all Japanese suffixes attached, and adds explanatory English nouns. Therefore, Kiyomizudera is translated as Kiyomizudera Temple, and Nanzenji as Nanzenji Temple. Nagoyajo (the castle - *jo* - in the city of Nagoya) is Nagoyajo Castle, and Asozan (an active volcano in Kyushu) is Mt. Asozan. The only exception is Fujisan because the mountain is already world famous as "Mt. Fuji." To impress the Japanese you meet, delete the explanatory

English word and use the full Japanese name. The suffixes will also be helpful when you complete the Conversation Cards.

With the increase of foreign residents as well as foreign visitors, many cities have started posting English names on street signs. In Japanese a street is usually called "-dori," e.g., Chuo-dori, Harumi-dori, Karasuma-dori and Hanamikoji-dori. There is no general rule for the proper English translation — street, avenue or boulevard — to be added to the street names. Unless one particular word is already in use, we use "Street" as the English explanatory word for the full Japanese name, e.g., Chuo-dori Street, Harumi-dori Street, Karasuma-dori Street, etc. If you see a street sign that says "Chuo-dori Avenue" or "Karasuma-dori Avenue," where we have used "Chuo-dori Street" or "Karasuma-dori Street," don't worry — they are the same. It simply means that local officials selected "Avenue" (rather than "Street") as the English explanatory word. There will never be two different streets with the same Japanese name (and with different English explanatory words) in the same neighborhood. Another possibility of confusion with streets is that (as with temple names), local officials sometimes drop the Japanese suffix ("-dori") on English street signs. In such cases, we might have used "Chuo-dori Street" but the street signs may say "Chuo Street" or "Chuo Avenue;" "Karasuma-dori Street" in this book can be "Karasuma Street" or "Karasuma Avenue." Pay attention to the Japanese name — for example, Chuo, Harumi, Karasuma. When asking a direction to a certain street, your best bet is to use the full Japanese name only (Chuo-dori, Karasuma-dori, etc.) with a questioning intonation. This is much easier for Japanese to understand than "Chuo Street?" or "Karasuma-dori Avenue?"

Japanese Names We write Japanese names Western style, with the family name last. This is the reverse of Japanese style.

Thus, it's Eiji KANNO for this text, while in Japan it is KANNO Eiji. We have chosen this method because Japanese (unlike Chinese) generally reverse their names themselves for contacts outside Japan. Other examples are Eishiro ABE (although we left the name of the museum exhibiting this famous paper maker's work as it is in Japanese because that's what the Museum itself did when it translated its name — thus, ABE Eishiro Memorial Museum); Shoji HAMADA, the famous Mashiko potter; and Ieyasu TOKUGAWA, the first Tokugawa Shogun.

CONVERSATION CARDS

This book includes nine Conversation Cards. Several copies of each card are attached at the back of this book so you can tear them out and use them while traveling. Remember to **print** your questions clearly on the cards. Handwriting is not easy for Japanese to read. Here are details on the Conversation Cards:

1. Looking for train and subway stations.
Card 1 - Where is the following train/subway station?

Circle either train or subway and fill in the name of the station and the name of the line you are looking for.

You shouldn't have much difficulty finding train stations. However, in some huge complexes that house several different lines — including JR, city subways, and other railways — you will need to use this card to locate the station for the particular line you want.

🚃 STATION	下の電車の発車ホーム番号を教えてください		
	Where is the following train /subway station? (Circle either train or subway and fill in the name of the station and the name of the line.)		
	Circle either one	路線名 Line Name	駅名 Destination
1	Train 電車　Subway 地下鉄		
2	電車　地下鉄		
3	電車　地下鉄		
4	電車　地下鉄		
5	電車　地下鉄		

2. Purchasing tickets for subways and short-distance commuter trains.

Card 2 - How much is the fare to the following station?

Fill in the name of your destination and the name of the line you want to take.

Tickets for subways and short-distance commuter trains are sold in vending machines. Because Japanese train and subway fares vary with the distance traveled, and because the fare tables are often written only in Japanese, you will probably use this Card frequently to make sure that the ticket you're purchasing is for the proper amount.

TICKET	下の電車の発車ホーム番号を教えてください	
	How much is the fare to the following station? (Fill in the name of your destination and the name of the line you want to take.)	
	路線名 Line Name	目的駅 Destination
1		
2		
3		
4		
5		

3. Looking for train platforms.

Card 3 - What is the number of the platform for the following train to the destination listed below?

Fill in the name of the line, the name of the train you plan to take, and the name of your destination. If the train is a local on a long distance line and does not have a name, write "Donko." If the train is a commuter line, leave the train name blank.

The best person to show this card to is the railway employee at the entrance gate. For long distance trains, railway employees sit at the entrance gate to punch tickets. For commuter trains, however, most of the entrance gates are automated and no attendants are available at the gate areas. You'll have to ask a passerby. Show your ticket along with Card 3.

PLATFORM	下の電車の発車ホーム番号を教えてください		
	What is the platform number for the following train to the destination listed below? (If the train is a local and does not have a name, write "Donko" in the train name column.)		
	路線名 Line Name	電車名 Train Name	目的駅 Destination
1			
2			
3			
4			
5			

4. Purchasing a reserved ticket.

Card 4 is designed so that you can easily fill in all the information necessary to purchase a reserved seat ticket.

Present the completed card to the clerk at the ticket window. If you don't know the train name, leave it blank. The ticket clerk will select an appropriate train according to the departure time you are requesting. If you have a Japan Rail Pass, there is no charge for seat reservations. Fill out the form and present it together with your Japan Rail Pass.

RESERVATION	座席指定申込書 Application for reserved seats						If you have a Rail Pass, you can request reservations for JR trains free of charge. Show the Pass with this form. Your Rail Pass cannot be used for pre-reserved seats.	
乗車日 Date of Trip	月 (month)	日 (date)	人数 No. of Pass.	大人 Adults	枚	子供 Children	枚	
出発駅 Departure		Station	目的駅 Destination				Station	
座席の種類 Class of Seat (check either one)	□グリーン車 First Class		□普通車 Coach Class			□禁煙席 Nonsmoking section, if available		
第一希望 First Choice	電車名 Train Name				出発時間 Dep. Time	時 (hour)	分 (minute)	
第二希望 Second Choice	電車名 Train Name				出発時間 Dep. Time	時 (hour)	分 (minute)	
第三希望 Third Choice	電車名 Train Name				出発時間 Dep. Time	時 (hour)	分 (minute)	

5. Looking for a bus or streetcar stop.

Card 5 - Where is the stop for the bus (or streetcar) going to the following stop?

Circle either streetcar or bus and fill in the name of your destination.

BUS STREETCAR	下の行先の市電またはバス乗場を教えてください	
	Where is the stop for the streetcar (or bus) going to the following destination? (Circle either streetcar or bus and fill in the name of your destination.)	
	Circle either one	目的駅 Destination
	Streetcar 市電　Bus バス	
1	市電　バス	
2	市電　バス	
3	市電　バス	
4	市電　バス	
5	市電　バス	

6. Asking about the arrival of your train, bus or streetcar at your destination (for use while on the train, bus or streetcar).

Card 6 - I am going to the following place. Please let me know when we near the destination.

Fill in the name of your destination and show the card to a fellow passenger.

6 私は下の目的地まで行きます 目的地が近づいたら教えてください		
DESTINATION I am going to the following place. Please let me know when we near the destination. (On the train, streetcar or bus) (Fill in the name of your destination and show the card to a fellow passenger.)		
1		6
2		7
3		8
4		9
5		10

7. Instructions for taxis.

Card 7 - Please take me to the following place.

Fill in the name of your destination.

We recommend that you pick up a brochure, a sheet of letterhead, a match box or something else with the name of your hotel in Japanese before you go out. Showing taxi drivers one of these is the easiest way to communicate in this situation.

7 下の目的地まで行ってください		
TAXI Please take me to the following place. (For a taxi driver) (Fill in the name of your destination.)		
1		7
2		8
3		9
4		10
5		11
6		12

8. Checking baggage

Card 8 - Where are the coin lockers or a short-term baggage check room?

Train stations have either coin lockers (usually 200-300 yen per day) or a short-term baggage check room with an attendant (very rare nowadays). The standard size coin lockers can accommodate only carry-on size bags. Though most train stations are also equipped with larger size coin lockers (400-500 yen per day), only a few have lockers large enough to accommodate large suitcases of international travelers.

We suggest arranging separate baggage transfers between major cities, while you travel with just a smaller carry-on bag. If you don't travel light, you will have many difficulties, not only finding places to check your baggage but also managing large station staircases and long passageways (which

are usually crowded), storing your bags on the trains and buses, and fitting them into relatively smallish taxi trunks. Travel light is the rule in Japan.

8 BAGGAGE 手荷物一時預り所 または コインロッカーを 教えてください
Where are the coin lockers or a short-term baggage check room?

9. One more important question.

Card 9 - Where is a rest room?

All train stations, department stores and most tourist destinations have rest rooms. In a city, you can use rest rooms in hotels or in office buildings (They are not locked). As a last resort you can always take a rest at one of the millions of coffee shops.

9 REST ROOM お手洗の場所を 教えてください
Where is a rest room?

TRAVEL PHONE

The most convenient information service for you while traveling in Japan is the toll-free Travel Phone. This toll-free telephone service is operated by Japan National Tourist Organization (JNTO) to provide travel information free of charge, from 9:00 AM to 5:00 PM daily. Outside of Tokyo and Kyoto, you can call either 0120-222-800 (for information on Eastern Japan) or 0120-444-800 (for information on Western Japan). In Tokyo you can reach the Tourist Information Center at 3502-1461 (a ten yen call), and in Kyoto you can reach the Information Center by calling 371-5649. To use the toll free number, pick up the receiver of a green or yellow phone (there is no dial tone until you insert money), insert a 10 yen coin, and then dial. You will be connected to an Information Center and your 10 yen will be returned at the end of your call.

GOOD-WILL GUIDE

This volunteer program was launched by JNTO to help visitors get past the language barrier. More than 24,000 Japanese have registered with JNTO or with local governments as volunteer good-will guides. They wear distinctive blue badges and are happy to give directions and answer questions in English.

WHAT TO PACK

Clothes Japan is located in the North Temperate Zone and has four distinct seasons. Jackets or sweaters are generally enough in the spring and autumn, but don't forget to take something heavier if you're making a trip to a mountain area, or to Tohoku and Hokkaido. Summer is hot and humid and only very light clothes are needed. In winter, you will need a light overcoat or raincoat with a liner and warmer clothes in the north or in the mountains. Casual clothes are fine for sightseeing, but Japanese usually get dressed up when they're going out to shop or to eat, so you'll probably want to be a little more formal yourself on these occasions.

Supplies at Japanese hotels and ryokan Japanese people travel very light because essential travel amenities are provided by the hotels and *ryokan* in Japan. A fresh *nemaki* (sleeping robe) is provided every night. They are **not** giveaways. If you want to keep one as a souvenir, ask the hotel or *ryokan* clerk if it's possible to buy one. Towels, soap, shampoos, washcloths, razors, combs, toothbrushes and toothpaste are standard supplies at all regular accommodations. If you are staying at inexpensive accommodations (where the charge is less than 13,000 yen for a twin room at a West-

ern-style hotel, or less than 10,000 yen per person for a Japanese room plus two meals), these items will not necessarily be supplied (but you'll always be able to purchase them at such places, often from vending machines).

Shoes Bring a pair of comfortable shoes for your walking tours. Don't expect to be able to buy shoes in Japan. It'll probably be impossible to find any to fit. Because you have to take your shoes off when you enter most temples and shrines (some days you might feel that this is one of your major sightseeing activities), socks are indispensable, especially in the winter, when the wooden corridors of these old, unheated buildings are very chilly.

Medicines Japan's medical services and facilities meet the highest international standards. If you have prescription medicines you should be sure to pack them. Hotels can help with emergencies. A few drugstores in large cities stock wide varieties of American and European over-the-counter remedies. Japanese drugstores (which feature green crosses on their signs) offer a dazzling variety of Japanese patent medicines, most of which are likely to be a complete mystery to you.

Electrical products Electric current in Japan is 100 volts. Fifty cycles is the standard in Tokyo and to the northeast, and 60 cycles in Nagoya, Kyoto, Osaka and areas to the southwest. Most electrical products used by North American travelers, such as electric shavers and hair dryers, will just run a little slower than they do at home. More sensitive devices won't work properly unless they are adjusted.

Others Japanese always carry tissue paper and handkerchiefs because public toilets often don't have toilet paper or hand towels. These items are always available at newsstands in train stations.

SHOPPING AND MONEY

Tax Free Shopping Foreign visitors to Japan can avoid taxes by patronizing the authorized stores that display "Tax-Free" signs. Be sure to carry your passport with you because the store clerks have to complete special forms and attach them to the passport. These forms are collected by Customs officials when you leave Japan. Tax free shopping is available in major department stores, hotel arcades and other tourist locations. The tax exemptions vary from 5 to 40 percent, and the items available include precious and semi-precious gems, pearls, electronic goods, watches and cameras.

Currency The Japanese currency is the yen. There are three kinds of bills — 1,000 yen, 5,000 yen and 10,000 yen — and six kinds of coins — 1 yen (aluminum), 5 yen (brass), 10 yen (copper), 50 yen, 100 yen and 500 yen (all nickel/silver). Banks at international airports are open for all arriving flights. You can also convert foreign currency into Japanese yen at banks, hotels and other established tourist facilities that display an "Authorized Money Exchanger" sign. There is no currency black market in Japan. The conversion rate is always a bit more advantageous at banks than at other locations. There are no restrictions on reconversion of unused yen to other currencies. You can also take up to 5 million yen out of Japan. The Japanese yen constantly fluctuates against foreign currencies. As of mid-1993, major currencies conversion rates are as follows:

one Australian dollar = 73 yen,
one British pounds = 160 yen,
one Canadian dollar = 82 yen,
one French franc = 18 yen,
one German mark = 62 yen,
one Hong Kong dollar = 13 yen,
one Indian rupee = 3.70 yen,
one New Zealand dollar = 60 yen,
one Singapore dollar = 66 yen,

¥10,000

¥5,000

¥1,000

¥500   ¥100

¥50   ¥10

¥5   ¥1

one Korean won = 0.13 yen,
one Swiss franc = 72 yen,
one Taiwan dollar = 4 yen,
one Thai baht = 4.25 yen,
one U.S. dollar = 104 yen.

Credit Cards Credit cards are becoming more and more popular in Japan. Major credit cards, such as American Express, Mastercard, Visa and Diners Club, are accepted at major tourist facilities, including hotels, restaurants and souvenir shops. Less expensive establishments are less likely to accept credit cards.

Travelers' Checks Travelers' checks are accepted at established tourist facilities. But inexpensive shops and restaurants usually do not accept them. You should exchange your travelers' checks for Japanese yen at banks.

Cash Though credit cards have become much more popular in recent years, Japan is still pretty much a cash society. Because it is safe to do so, people usually carry relatively large amounts of cash, and prefer cash to credit cards or checks.

SERVICE CHARGES AND TAX

Personal tipping is not customary in Japan. Instead of tipping, a 10-15% service charge is automatically added to your bill at most major restaurants and accommodations. Many inexpensive restaurants do not add a service charge. The few porters who do work at airports and train stations charge a standard per piece fee of about 300-500 yen.

A 3% consumption tax is levied on sales of goods and services. Some stores include this 3% consumption tax in ticket prices, while others omit the tax from price tags (and add 3% tax at the register).

If the charge at an accommodation is less than 15,000 yen per person per night, only the 3% consumption tax is levied. If the charge is 15,000 yen or more, an additional 3% tax is added as well.

WATER, FOOD AND DRINKS

Water Tap water is safe everywhere in Japan.

Food Food (even what's sold by street vendors) is also safe.

Drinks A variety of soft drinks, including international and Japanese brands, are available, but diet soft drinks with saccharine are banned in Japan. One hundred percent fruit juice is hard to find. Major hotels have refrigerators in every room so guests always have easy access to cold beer and soft drinks, but anything you take from one of these refrigerators will be very expensive. Inexpensive hotels usually have vending machines for soft drinks and beer. Prices are tolerable, but still higher than prices in the stores. You might want to consider buying beverages and taking them to your room (see below). Alcoholic beverages are not unusually expensive, but this does not mean that they are cheap. If you drink alcohol regularly you should purchase some at an airport duty-free shop before you leave your own country. You can bring in up to three regular-sized bottles of any kind of alcoholic beverage duty free. All hotels supply guests with hot water or some method of boiling water, along with green tea bags. You can, of course, use the water and the cups for coffee or regular tea if you carry your own instant coffee or tea bags.

Take Out A variety of take out foods and canned soft drinks and alcoholic beverages are sold in basements of department stores. There are also many different American fast food chains and take out *sushi* shops in major cities. If you feel like relaxing in your hotel room but don't want to spend the money for room service, you should buy food and beverages at these places. Many housewives shop for dinner for their families at the department store basements, which have a wide selection at inexpensive prices. Even if you don't intend to buy anything, a visit to one of these establishments is worth it just for the experience.

Morning Service If you don't want a big breakfast at your hotel, find a coffee shop nearby. Most serve a "morning service" special for around 500 yen. See the Restaurant Chapter below for more details.

TABLE MANNERS

At all but the most prestigious and expensive Japanese restaurants, you are generally expected to seat yourself.

As soon as you are seated you'll be presented with an *oshibori* — a hot towel (cold in summer). Use it to clean your hands. Most restaurants provide disposable chopsticks (*waribashi*); pull them apart at the top. If you ask for a knife, fork or spoon, don't be surprised if they're not available. Don't eat soup with a spoon. In Japan it's proper to "drink" your soup. Pick up the bowl and drink the broth; use your chopsticks for the contents. Expect to hear Japanese slurping as they eat — especially soup and noodles. Slurping is **good** manners in Japan, and demonstrates one's appreciation.

USEFUL HINTS

Rest Rooms In real emergencies, you can always stop in a coffee shop. You'll probably find it well worth the cost of a cup of coffee or soft drink. In cities, department stores and hotels are a good idea. All train stations have rest rooms but they are almost always dirty; often they are inside the ticket barriers (another advantage for holders of Japan Rail Passes, who have unlimited access to all JR trains and platforms — for whatever the reason). Rest rooms in office buildings are not locked. Public rest rooms are not clean, but will do in emergencies. Not all public facilities have toilet paper or paper towels. You can buy toilet paper at train station newsstands and it's generally a good idea to carry tissues and handkerchiefs with you. The Japanese sometimes use the British "W.C." to indicate facilities.

You will encounter many Western-style toilets in Japan, but if you're traveling as the Japanese travel, you're sure to come across Japanese-style toilets. Japanese style requires squatting rather than sitting. It's supposed to be better for you, and it's certainly cleaner. Once you get used to it you might find that you prefer it.

Baggage Handling Trains in Japan are not equipped to accommodate the big bags of international travelers. Train stations in Japanese cities are generally very large

and have many staircases and underground passages connecting the various platforms and entrances/exits, but it's almost impossible to find a porter. It's torture trying to lug big bags through these huge, confusing and often very crowded stations. Plan a separate baggage transfer between major cities such as Tokyo and Kyoto. Baggage transfers can be easily arranged at your hotel or *ryokan*. It's faster between major cities (1-2 days), and takes more time (3-4 days) between small cities. The baggage delivery costs somewhere between 800 yen and 2,500 yen, depending on the zone, the distance and the weight. Even if you plan to travel extensively, consider arranging several side trips using large transportation centers as bases. There are more details in the Transportation Chapter below. Virtually every train station in Japan has coin lockers and the larger stations offer a range of sizes of lockers. The coin lockers typically costs 200-300 yen for up to 24 hours. You'll be able to check your sensible small bag as you tour the sites of a particular destination. In some tiny stations, if the lockers won't accommodate your bags, the station master or a local merchant will usually keep them for you for a modest fee.

Traffic on the Left As in the U.K., traffic on the left is the rule in Japan. Not only automobiles, but also trains and subways run on the left. Be careful when you're waiting for a train at a local station or for a bus on an empty street. If you don't think about it, you're likely to wait on the right hand side facing your destination!

Japan has the largest number of cars per square foot in the world. Because traffic is so heavy, pedestrian bridges and underground passages are quite commonplace. Use the facilities and cross only at intersections. Don't jaywalk. Japanese tend to obey traffic signals, and drivers aren't prepared for pedestrians who don't.

Why Tourists Shouldn't Drive in Japan There are several reasons why we recommend that foreigners travel on the trains rather than by car. Although there are many more bilingual road signs than there used to be, you're bound to have some difficulty if you can't read Japanese. Secondly, many Japanese cities were laid out during the feudal era, with streets arranged in complicated patterns for strategic, defensive purposes. Even for Japanese it is not easy to get around in these cities by car. Thirdly, renting a car costs far more than taking trains. Even though the rentals themselves are not too expensive, gas costs about double what it does in the U.S., and tolls are extremely expensive. For example, the one-way toll from Tokyo to Kyoto is about the same as the Shinkansen fare for the same distance. The last and best reason is that trains are much faster than cars. For example, the Shinkansen takes less than three hours to make the trip from Tokyo to Kyoto, but driving the same distance usually takes eight hours, even on the expressway. In big cities and popular tourist destinations it is not easy to find parking spaces. Even if you have experience driving on the left, there's no guarantee that you'll enjoy driving in Japan. Experiencing the efficiency and punctuality of public transportation should be part of your discovery of Japan.

NATIONAL HOLIDAYS

January 1: New Year's Day

Only January 1 is a legal holiday, but government offices and corporations are closed from December 29 through January 3.

January 15: Adults' Day

February 11: Founding of the Nation Day

March 21: Vernal Equinox Day

April 29: Green Day

May 3: Constitution Day

May 5: Children's Day

Most Japanese take a long break at this time of year, bridging these three holidays with the weekends before or after them. As a result, the period from April 28 through May 6, called "Golden Week," is the period of the largest movement of people throughout the country.

September 15: Respect for the Aged Day

September 23: Autumn Equinox Day

October 10: Health Sports Day

November 3: Culture Day

November 23: Labor Thanksgiving Day

December 23: Emperor's Birthday

BUSINESS HOURS

Department Stores are open from 10:00 AM to 6:00 PM (6:30 PM on Saturdays and Sundays). They are closed once a week on a weekday. Closing days differ from store to store, so in major cities at least one store is open on any given weekday.

Smaller Stores are usually open from 10:00 AM to 8:00 PM (some stay open until 10:00 PM). They usually close once a week or once every two weeks, on a weekday.

Banks are open from 9:00 AM to 3:00 PM on weekdays. Banks at the international airports are open for all arrival flights year round.

TIME DIFFERENCE

All of Japan is in a single time zone. Japanese standard time is nine hours ahead of GMT, 14 hours ahead of New York, 15 hours ahead of Chicago and 17 hours ahead of Los Angeles. If it is 7:00 AM in New York it is 9:00 PM in Japan (plus 14 hours). If it is 4:00 PM in Los Angeles, it is 9:00 AM the next day in Japan (plus 17 hours).

When you travel to Japan from the U.S. you lose one day (arriving in Japan the following day). When you return from Japan to the U.S., you gain one day (arriving in the U.S. on the same day — usually even "before" you left Japan!).

Japan does not switch to daylight savings time in the summer. Japan is generally an early-to-bed, early-to-rise country. A good general rule for sightseeing is "Get started early." Many tourist attractions are open by 8:00 or 8:30 in the morning. The tour buses with hordes of Japanese tourists usually get a later start, so the best time to see popular places is often early in the morning. Tourist attractions also tend to close rather early — between 4:00 and 5:00 PM. In addition, many places open slightly later and close earlier in the winter. It is an almost universal custom not to admit any more visitors to a tourist attraction in the last half hour before closing, and this rule is enforced strictly.

POSTAL SERVICES

Mail boxes in Japan are red. You can buy stamps in your hotel or at local post offices. 〒 is the symbol for the Japanese Post Office.

TELEPHONE SERVICE WITHIN JAPAN

Public phones in Japan usually have two slots, one for 10 yen coins and another for 100 yen coins. A local call costs 10 yen for the first one minute. The cost of a long distance call varies depending on the city you call. If you have no idea about the cost of a long distance call you want to make, insert several 100 yen coins. Unused coins will be returned after your call.

Telephone cards. Public phones are designed to accept telephone cards, which are sold at newsstands in train and subway stations. If you need to make many telephone calls, especially long distance calls, from public phones, you should purchase a 500 yen or a 1,000 yen telephone card. Pick up the receiver of a green public phone and insert your telephone card in the slot. The unused yen amount remaining on the card is displayed electronically on a small screen on the telephone. While you are making a call, the machine automatically deducts the charge. When you finish a call your card will be returned from the slot. Many companies and organizations distribute specially designed telephone cards as a form of PR or advertising. NTT also issues special telephone cards in commemoration of certain events. They are becoming collectors' items! Telephone cards are also an important source of revenue for NTT, because they are prepaid. NTT makes pure profit on the ones collectors keep in "mint" condition, and on the many that are lost before all of their value is deducted. To assuage those who have complained, NTT now issues cards worth 1,050 yen to those purchasing 1,000 yen cards.

International Telephone Service In major Japanese cities, international telephone calls can be arranged at your hotel. Further information is available from KDD (International Telegram and Telephone Company) at (03) 3270-5111. (When you call from Tokyo you don't have to use the (03) area code.) Several other international carriers serve Japan and advertise heavily in international tourist locations. You should be able to use any service familiar from home. It is always best, if possible, to avoid placing calls from hotel rooms. Hotels typically add very large service charges on top of the normal charge for telephone service, especially international telephone service.

PLACES OF WORSHIP

Large Japanese cities have a selection of churches, synagogues and other places of worship. Check with the concierge at your hotel.

ENGLISH NEWSPAPERS

Four English language newspapers are published daily in Japan — three in the morning and one in the evening. They are sold at newsstands in large metropolitan train stations and at major hotels. International news magazines (usually Asian editions) are also sold at major hotels and bookstores.

MASSAGE SERVICE AT ACCOMMODATIONS

Japanese masseuses are renowned (justifiably) for their skill. Massages can be arranged at most accommodations — Western-style hotels as well as Japanese inns. The charge is around 3,000-5,000 yen for 30-45 minutes.

GUIDES AND HIRED CARS

If you plan to sightsee using a car and a guide, you'll have to hire a chauffeur-driven car and guide separately: these two services are completely separate in Japan. The standard charge for a tourist guide is 25,000-30,000 yen per day. You'll have to pay for the guide's transportation. If you take a guide on an overnight trip, you'll also have to pay for the guide's accommodations and meals as well. The cost of a chauffeur-driven car varies from city to city. A typical rate is about 5,000 yen per hour, and varies depending on the distance you travel. A guide and a hired car can be arranged for at your accommodations. You can also make arrangements through the Japan Guide Association. About 1,000 active licensed guides belong to the association. Phone: (03) 3213-2706.

ABOUT THE JAPANESE

Archeological discoveries have confirmed that the Japanese archipelago was inhabited as long as 10,000 years ago. Contrary to the belief popular in Japan that the "Yamato race" is monotribal, recent studies indicate that the Japanese are a mixture of various Asian races, including Mongolians, Chinese, Koreans and Southeast Asians, who inhabited Japan before it split away from the continent. Even after the Japanese islands floated away from the Asian mainland, many Asian peoples, especially Koreans and Chinese, emigrated to Japan, adding new strains to Japanese native stock and creating the "Japanese" as they are today. Because of the country's geographical location off the Asian continent, and because of its 250-year long isolation from the outside world in the 17-19th centuries, Japan became an unusual monoculture country. This isolationist tradition and lack of cultural diversity is why Japanese still have the "monotribe" belief. The myth that the Japanese are a monotribal people who conquered the uncivilized inhabitants of their islands still persists and is an important part of the view most Japanese have of themselves and of their nation. It was used to fan the flames of the nationalism that consumed Japan in the period between the Meiji Restoration and the end of World War II.

Japan is located only 176 km (110 miles) from the Korean peninsula. Throughout its history, this proximity to the continent has enabled Japan to import advanced culture and technologies from various Asian countries, especially China. At the same time, the roughness of the Japan Sea and the primitive equipment and rudimentary navigational techniques of ancient times kept Japan relatively free from military and political interference by other countries. Japan created its own unique culture, based on the imports from the continent, adopting and "Japanizing" them, much as it has done in the modern era with its adoptions and modifications of Western cultures and technologies. Since the War, the "monoculture" has begun to diversify. Japan's minorities, including Koreans whose families have resided in Japan for several generations as well as more recent foreign arrivals, Asian and South American temporary workers, are adding new influences. Japan is, for the first time, having to deal with some strains of multiculturalism.

Religion Japan's native religion is Shinto. Because it originated in the daily life of the people during the primitive era, all sorts of natural objects and phenomena were considered gods or the work of gods. A naturalistic religion, it does not involve belief in any specific creator and has no scriptures. After the Meiji Restoration in 1868, Shinto was designated the national religion. The new government, organized in the name of the emperor, portrayed the Shinto gods as progenitors of the imperial family as a means of legitimating the power of the throne. After World War II Shinto lost its official status.

Buddhism was introduced into Japan in the 6th century. It deeply influenced the philosophical life of the Japanese, introducing for the first time the belief in eternal life. Buddhism first spread among the aristocrats, and was used as the spiritual base of the unified nation. Zen is one of Buddhism's sects and was especially popular with the military classes. It emphasized serenity of mind and freedom from worldly desires, to be achieved not through the study of scripture, but rather through the practice of meditation. A number of Buddhist groups are active today, and most of them have, either

formally or informally, a substantial influence on political affairs.

But neither Buddhism nor Shintoism has much real influence on the every day life of today's Japanese. In Japan, religion is usually regarded as merely the provider of social ceremonies. Ceremonies related to birth, coming of age, and marriage are usually performed according to Shinto rites, while those related to death utilize Buddhist rites. Most Japanese do not think it at all unusual to be involved with more than one religion.

Christianity, introduced in the middle of the 16th century, but then banned during the period of Japan's isolation, was reintroduced after the Meiji Restoration. Despite great missionary efforts and the establishment of many useful Christian social institutions, such as hospitals and schools, neither Catholicism nor Protestantism has attracted many adherents. The total number of Christians is estimated to be around 1 million.

Airport Transportation

NARITA AIRPORT
(New Tokyo International Airport)

Refer to Intro Map 3. There is no truly pleasant way to get from Narita International Airport to downtown Tokyo. Our best advice is to pay attention to the information presented below and choose carefully. If you are going to endure a trip from Tokyo's too small, too remote "new" international airport, you might as well be sure not to spend too much as well.

There are several means of public transportation between Narita Airport and the city of Tokyo.

There are two terminal buildings at Narita Airport. All transportation listed below is

available from both terminals. When you take a bus or a train to the airport, be sure to check to find out which terminal the airline you're taking uses.

I. Airport Limousine Bus

This is the most popular and the easiest way to get to Tokyo, if you have large bags. The Airport Limousine Bus information and ticketing counter is located in the arrivals lobby right outside the Customs Hall. There is a huge orange English sign. This company operates several bus routes:

(1) Between Narita Airport and Tokyo City Air Terminal (TCAT)

This is the main Airport Limousine Bus

MAP 3   Tokyo: Airport Transportation

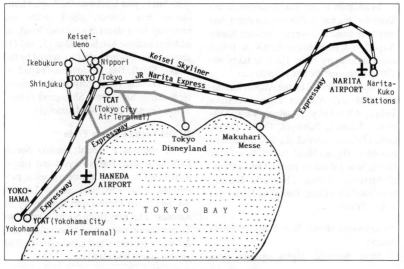

route. Buses operate about every 15 minutes. The ride takes 70-90 minutes, and the fare is 2,700 yen. From TCAT, most hotels are within a 1,500-3,000 yen taxi ride (10-20 minutes). At TCAT, the buses arrive on the third floor. Escalators take you down to the baggage claim area on the ground floor. Plenty of taxis are always waiting at the TCAT exit.

(2) Between Narita Airport and Tokyo Station

A direct bus from the airport to Tokyo Station (Yaesu or eastern side) operates every 15-20 minutes. The ride takes about 90 minutes, and the fare is 2,800 yen.

(3) Between Narita Airport and the Shinjuku District

There are direct buses twice an hour on this route. The buses stop at Shinjuku Station, the Keio Plaza Hotel, the Century Hyatt Hotel, the Tokyo Hilton, and the Shinjuku Washington Hotel. The ride takes about 2 hours and the fare is 2,900 yen.

(4) Between Narita Airport and Major Hotels in Tokyo

In addition to the special service to the Shinjuku area hotels, there is also direct Airport Limousine Bus service between Narita Airport and other major hotels in Tokyo about once every hour. The ride takes 90-120 minutes, and the fare is 2,900 yen.

The hotels served by the Airport Limousine Bus are: Akasaka Prince, Akasaka Tokyu, ANA Tokyo, Asakusa View, Diamond, Edmont, Fairmont, Ginza Tokyu, Grand Palace, Imperial, Kayu Kaikan, Metropolitan, Miyako Hotel Tokyo, New Otani Hotel, New Takanawa Prince, Okura, Pacific Meridien, Palace, Shimbashi Daiichi, Sunshine City Prince, Takanawa Prince and Tokyo Prince.

(5) Between Narita Airport and Haneda Airport

Most domestic flights operate from Haneda Airport ("Old" Tokyo International Airport). The two airports (Narita and Haneda) are connected by Airport Limousine Bus service every 20-30 minutes, from morning to night. The ride takes 90-100 minutes and the fare is 2,900 yen.

(6) Between Narita Airport and Yokohama, Chiba and Urayasu

When you are traveling to Japan for international conventions and exhibitions, your destinations might be one of these three cities (instead of downtown Tokyo).

There are buses between Narita Airport and these three cities. See Metropolitan Tokyo section for more details — Yokohama, Chiba (Makuhari Messe) and Urayasu (Tokyo Disneyland).

II. Airport Shuttle Bus

This second company (with a name frustratingly similar to the first) operates direct buses about once an hour to major hotels in Tokyo. It too has an information and ticketing counter in the arrivals lobby at Narita Airport (not far from the Airport Limousine Bus counter). If you cannot find a convenient bus to your hotel with the Airport Limousine Bus service, check with this company for a direct bus to your hotel. In addition to those hotels listed at (3) and (4) above, the following hotels are served by the Airport Shuttle Bus: Atagoyama Tokyu Inn, Ginza Dai-ichi Hotel, Miyako Inn Tokyo, New Sanno, Shiba Park, Shinagawa Prince, Tokyo Grand and Tokyo Marunouchi.

III. JR Narita Express Train

JR operates a special nonstop Narita Express between Narita Airport and Tokyo Station. At the airport the train stops at two stations — No. 1 terminal and No. 2 terminal. The Narita Express runs about every 30 minutes. The ride from Narita Airport to Tokyo Station takes about 60 minutes. Fare: 2,890 yen for coach, and an additional 1,220 yen for green (first class) car.

Narita Express trains run beyond Tokyo Station to three other important terminal stations — Shinjuku and Ikebukuro in Tokyo, and Yokohama.

Between JR Shinjuku Station and Narita Airport (via Tokyo Station), the trains run about every 30-60 minutes. The ride takes about 80 minutes. Fare: 3,050 yen for coach, and an additional 1,220 yen for green (first class) car.

Between JR Ikebukuro Station and the airport (via Shinjuku and Tokyo Stations), only several trains run each day. The ride takes about 85 minutes and the fare is 3,050 yen for coach and an additional 1,220 yen for green car.

Between JR Yokohama Station and the airport (via Tokyo Station), the trains run about every 30-60 minutes. The ride takes about 90 minutes. Fare: 4,100 yen for coach and an additional 1,220 yen for green.

If you are headed for other cities in Japan from Narita Airport without staying in Tokyo, or heading for Narita Airport from cities outside Tokyo, the JR Narita Express is an ideal method of transportation. Tokyo Station provides direct connections to/from the four Shinkansens (Tokaido-Sanyo, Joetsu, Tohoku and Yamagata).

Allow a plenty of time (at least 30 minutes) for your train connection at Tokyo Station.

When you are traveling light for a short business trip, the JR Narita Express is the quickest and most comfortable method of travel to downtown Tokyo. You can even keep appointments on the day of arrival in Tokyo.

If you have large bags, however, we do not recommend the Narita Express. Upon arrival at Tokyo Station you must carry your bags through a maze of long passageways to the taxi stand. If you add the cost and the time of a taxi ride to your hotel, the Airport Limousine Bus is definitely cheaper and may be quicker. Even if you are using a Japan Rail Pass, we recommend the Airport Limousine Bus if you have big bags.

The Narita Express has reserved seats only. The trains are very crowded, especially in tourist seasons. Be prepared to wait through one or two departures until seats for the trip from Narita Airport to Tokyo are available. No reservations are accepted from overseas because of the uncertainties of flight arrivals. If you plan to use the Narita Express when you depart from Tokyo, request reservations as soon as you arrive in Japan.

IV. Keisei Line Skyliner Train

The Keisei Electric Railways operates special deluxe trains between Narita Airport (both terminals) and Keisei-Ueno Station in Tokyo. Like the JR Narita Express, Keisei has stations in the basement of each terminal building of the airport. The train is called the Skyliner, and runs about every 40 minutes. The ride takes one hour, and the fare is 1,740 yen. In Tokyo, the Skyliner also stops at Nippori Station. Because Nippori Station is also served by the JR Yamanote Loop Line, it may be easier for you to take this train to/from Nippori. Keisei-Ueno Station is about 5-minute walk from JR Ueno Station.

Keisei Skyliner is as quick a method of transportation as the JR Narita Express. This is the cheapest and most convenient method for travelers with small bags. If you have large suitcases, we don't recommend the Skyliner for the same reasons we don't recommend tha JR Narita Express.

V. Taxis

Taxis are plentiful at Narita Airport, and the drivers are quite willing to take you the long distance to your hotel in Tokyo, but the ride costs about 20,000-25,000 yen.

HANEDA AIRPORT
("Old" Tokyo International Airport)

I. Airport Limousine Bus between Narita and Haneda Airports

See above.

II. Airport Limousine Bus between Haneda Airport and Hotels in Tokyo

The following hotels are served by the Airport Limousine Bus: Akasaka Prince, Akasaka Tokyu, ANA Tokyo, Century Hyatt, Keio Plaza, Metropolitan, New Otani, Shinjuku Washington, Sunshine City Prince and Tokyo Hilton. The buses run about once every hour and the ride takes 50-60 minutes (The fare is 1,000 yen).

III. Monorail between Haneda Airport and Hamamatsucho Station

There is frequent monorail service between Haneda Airport and Hamamatsucho Station in Tokyo (a 15-minute ride; 300 yen). Hamamatsucho Station is on the JR Yamanote Loop Line.

IV. Taxis

A taxi trip from Haneda Airport to any major Tokyo hotel will cost about 5,000 yen.

OSAKA AIRPORT

Refer to Intro Map 4.

Osaka Airport functions as the gateway to three major cities in the Kansai district — Osaka, Kyoto and Kobe. There is no train service between Osaka Airport and these three cities, but airport buses are available. Taxis are plentiful at the airport, but they are not recommended if you are headed for Kyoto.

Kansai International Airport is under construction on a manmade island in Osaka Bay. Construction is a little behind the original schedule, and the opening of the new airport is expected toward the end of 1994.

I. To and From Kyoto

Airport Bus: There is service between

MAP 4   Osaka: Airport Transpotation

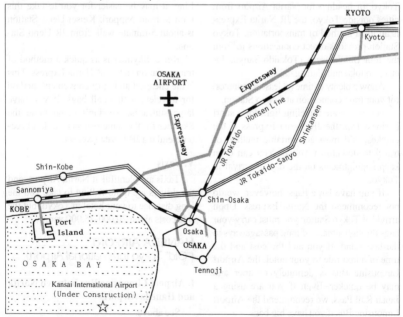

MAP 5 Major Airports in Japan

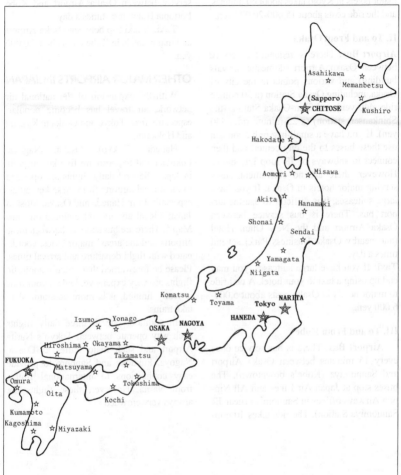

Osaka Airport (from the Domestic Arrivals Building — 200 meters or 660 feet from International Arrivals Building) and Kyoto Station (Hachijo-guchi or the southern side of the station) three times an hour each way from early in the morning till late at night. The ride takes about one hour and the fare is 890 yen.

In addition, hourly buses operate between Osaka Airport and major hotels in Kyoto. The ride takes 60-100 minutes, and the fare is 890 yen to 950 yen depending on the hotel. The hotels in Kyoto served by the Airport Limousine Bus are: ANA Kyoto, International Kyoto, Kyoto Hotel, Kyoto Grand, Kyoto Tokyu, Miyako Hotel, New Miyako, and New Hankyu.

Taxi: A taxi trip from Osaka Airport to major hotels in Kyoto takes about 60 minutes, and the ride costs about 15,000-20,000 yen.

II. To and From Osaka

Airport Bus: There is frequent bus service between Osaka Airport (domestic arrivals building) and various points in the city of Osaka, including Osaka Station (a 30 minute ride; 440 yen) and Shin-Osaka Station (the Shinkansen station) (a 25-minute ride; 340 yen). If you have a small bag only, you can use these buses to the city center, and then connect to subways or JR loop line trains. However, there are no convenient buses serving major hotels in Osaka. If you have large suitcases, it is difficult to use the airport bus. There is bus service between Osaka Airport and the New Otani Hotel (and nearby Osaka Business Park) several times a day.

Taxi: If you have large suitcases, you may end up using a taxi to your hotel. A taxi ride to major hotels in Osaka costs about 5,000-6,000 yen.

III. To and From Kobe

Airport Bus: There is bus service once every 15 minutes between Osaka Airport and Sannomiya (Kobe's downtown). The buses stop at Japan Air Lines and All Nippon Airways offices in Sannomiya (near JR Sannomiya Station). The ride takes 40 minutes and the fare is 720 yen. There is bus service between Osaka Airport and Kobe Portopia Hotel three times a day.

Taxi: A taxi trip between Osaka Airport and major hotels in Kobe costs about 10,000 yen.

OTHER MAJOR AIRPORTS IN JAPAN

With the expansion of the national air network, air travel has become popular, especially from Tokyo and Osaka to Kyushu and Hokkaido.

Haneda (Tokyo), Osaka, Nagoya, Fukuoka and Sapporo are five key airports in Japan. Several daily flights are operated to most local airports from these key cities, especially from Haneda and Osaka. Most of Japan's local airports are pictured on Intro Map 5. There are bus services between these airports and the areas' major cities, coordinated with flight departure and arrival times. Please be forewarned that Japan's domestic flights are very expensive. Unless your time is really limited, it is more economical to take trains.

In addition, one to three daily flights each way operate between Tokyo's Narita Airport and such major cities as Osaka, Nagoya, Fukuoka and Sapporo to provide easy connections to international flights from Narita. However, these flights are always very crowded.

Entrance Requirements

PASSPORTS

All foreign visitors must have valid passports to enter Japan.

VISAS

In principle, foreign visitors need to obtain Japanese visas prior to their departure for Japan. You can apply for visas at Japanese Consular Offices (or Japanese Embassies) abroad. Depending on the type of visas, you will need to submit certain documents to the Japanese authorities. Please check with the nearest Consulate (or Embassy) for details.

On a reciprocal basis, certain nationalities are exempted from obtaining visas for tourist visits to Japan.

The following are the major countries with reciprocal visa exemption agreements with Japan, as of date of publication. Please check with the nearest Japanese Consular Office or JNTO.

1. Visa exemption for a maximum stay of up to 6 months: Austria, Germany, Ireland, Liechtenstein, Mexico, Switzerland, and the United Kingdom.*

2. Visa exemption for a maximum stay of up to 3 months: Argentina, Bahamas, Bangladesh, Barbados, Belgium, Canada, Chile, Colombia, Costa Rica, Cyprus, Denmark, Dominican Republic, El Salvador, Finland, France, Greece, Guatemala, Honduras, Iceland, Iran, Israel, Italy, Lesotho, Luxembourg, Malaysia, Malta, Mauritius, the Netherlands, New Zealand, Norway, Pakistan, Peru, Portugal,* San Marino, Singapore, Spain, Surinam, Sweden, Tunisia, Turkey, Uruguay, and the U.S.A.

JAPANESE EMBASSY AND CONSULATES GENERAL IN THE U.S.A.

Embassy of Japan, Washington, D.C.
Tel: (202) 939-6700

Consulates General of Japan

1. Anchorage, AK: (907) 279-8428
2. Atlanta, GA: (404) 892-2700
3. Boston, MA: (617) 973-9772
4. Chicago, IL: (312) 280-0400
5. Honolulu, HI: (808) 536-2226
6. Houston, TX: (713) 652-2977
7. Kansas City, MO: (816) 471-0111
8. Los Angeles, CA: (213) 624-8305
9. New Orleans, LA: (504) 529-2101
10. New York, NY: (212) 371-8222
11. Portland, OR: (503) 221-1811
12. San Francisco, CA: (415) 777-3533
13. Seattle, WA: (206) 682-9107

CUSTOMS

The following can be brought into Japan duty free:

– Up to three regular sized bottles of alcoholic beverages.

– Twenty packs of cigarettes (400 cigarettes), or 100 cigars, or 500 grams of pipe, powdered or chewing tobacco.

– Two ounces of perfume.

* Holders of British passports issued in British colonial territories (such as Hong Kong) are required to obtain Japanese visas.

* Holders of Portuguese passports issued in present or former Portuguese colonial territories need to obtain Japanese visas.

– In addition to the items listed above, souvenirs whose combined market value is less than 200,000 yen.

The following cannot be brought into Japan under any circumstances:
– Illegal drugs, including marihuana (Don't try it; you'll be in big trouble!). Properly labeled prescription drugs are fine.
– Pornographic books, pictures, films and other items.

OTHER REQUIREMENTS

Vaccinations are not required unless you are visiting Japan after traveling in an affected area.

Security checks at Japanese airports are rather strict. You're likely to be frisked at the entrance gates to the departure wings.

There is no departure tax per se at Japanese airports. However, if you leave Japan from Narita (New Tokyo International) Airport, a 2,000 yen "airport utility charge" will be imposed. The tickets are sold in the vending machines right before you descend to the departure immigration office. You should remember to reserve 2,000 yen in cash so you can pay this charge.

AIRLINES

In addition to Japan Airlines and All Nippon Airways, the flag carriers of most nations serve Japan. From the United States, American Airlines, Continental Airlines, Delta Airlines, Northwest Airlines and United Airlines provide service between virtually all major U.S. cities and Tokyo (Narita Airport) and Osaka.

MAJOR EMBASSIES IN TOKYO

Algeria	3407-7900	Malaysia	3476-3840
Argentina	5420-7107	Mexico	3581-1131
Australia	5232-4111	Morocco	3478-3271
Austria	3451-8281	Nepal	3705-5558
Bangladesh	3442-1501	Netherlands	
Belgium	3262-0191		5401-0411
Brazil	3404-5211	Nigeria	5721-5391
Canada	3408-2101	Norway	3440-2611
Chile	3452-7561	Pakistan	3454-4861
China	3403-3380	Peru	3406-4240
Colombia	3440-6451	Philippines	3496-2731
Cuba	3716-3112	Portugal	3400-7907
Czech Republic		Romania	3479-0311
	3400-8122	Russia	3583-4224
Slovak Republic		Saudi Arabia	
	3400-8122		3589-5241
Denmark	3496-3001	Singapore	3586-9111
Egypt	3770-8021	South Africa	
Ethiopia	3718-1003		3265-3366
Finland	3442-2231	Spain	3583-8531
France	5420-8800	Sri Lanka	3585-7431
Germany	3473-0151	Sudan	3476-0811
Ghana	3710-8831	Sweden	5562-5050
Greece	3403-0871	Switzerland	
Hungary	3798-8801		3473-0121
India	3262-2391	Tanzania	3425-4531
Indonesia	3441-4201	Thailand	3441-7352
Iran	3446-8011	Turkey	3470-5131
Iraq	3423-1727	Uganda	5493-5690
Israel	3264-0911	United Kingdom	
Italy	3453-5291		3486-1750
Jordan	3580-5856	U.S.A.	3224-5000
Kenya	3723-4006	Venezuela	3409-1501
Korea	3452-7611		

Transportation Within Japan

SOME ADVICE - HOW TO USE JAPANESE COMMON SENSE

Trains are the most convenient and efficient method of travel in Japan. Most Japanese cities are conveniently linked by the Japan Railways (JR) network. In the larger cities and major resort areas, other private railways provide parallel and supplementary service.

All long distance trains (whether JR or other private railways) have reserved seats. To make your trip as comfortable as possible you should make reservations for the long distance trains as soon as you arrive in Japan. If you are not able to make reservations, don't worry because most long distance trains also have nonreserved cars. For example, the "Hikari" Shinkansen, between Tokyo and Osaka via Nagoya and Kyoto, has 16 cars, five of which are nonreserved. On the slower "Kodama" Shinkansen on the same line, 11-13 cars out of the 16 are nonreserved.

At least one nonreserved car and one reserved car on most long distance trains are nonsmoking cars. The number of nonsmoking cars has been increasing gradually. Smoking is prohibited on all short-distance and commuter trains.

Japanese trains are not designed to accommodate the large suitcases and bags that many international travelers use. Except in the green car (first class) of the Shinkansen, there is no space for luggage other than on the overhead rack (though there is sometimes some space behind the last seat in a car). The JR Narita Express (special trains connecting downtown Tokyo and Narita Airport) has space for luggage, of course. On regular long distance trains, if you must carry your large bags with you, you can leave them outside the door of the car. They will be safe (Japan really is as safe as all the promotional materials claim). If you feel uneasy, go to the door whenever the train stops at a station. This won't be too much of a bother because long distance trains only stop at major stations. Small and medium sized bags can be stowed on the overhead racks. You cannot keep your large bags in the passage between seats. On long distance trains, the aisles must be clear for the food service carts that attendants push through, selling beverages and snacks.

It is customary in Japan to arrange separate delivery of large bags between your hotels in major cities. When planning your itinerary, consider the most effective use of baggage delivery between the major cities you are visiting. For example, if you plan a

MAP 6 Tokaido-Sanyo Shinkansen

JR TOKAIDO-SANYO SHINKANSEN

Shin-Shimonoseki • *Shin-Iwakuni* • *Tokuyama* • *Higashi-Hiroshima* • *Shin-Onomichi* • *Shin-Kurashiki* • *Fukuyama* • *Mihara* • *Nishi-Akashi* • *Aioi*

HAKATA • KOKURA • OGORI • HIROSHIMA • OKAYAMA • HIMEJI • SHIN-KOBE • OSAKA • KYOTO

Tokyo–Central Japan–Kyoto–Inland Sea—Tokyo route, you should:

(1) Arrange baggage delivery from your Tokyo hotel to your Kyoto hotel.
(2) Travel to Central Japan (typically 3-4 nights) with only a small bag.
(3) Upon arrival in Kyoto repack your bags. Arrange separate baggage delivery from your Kyoto hotel to your Tokyo hotel.
(4) Travel to Inland Sea (typically another 3-4 nights) with only a small bag. Then return to Tokyo. All your bags are now at your Tokyo hotel ready for your departure from Japan.

See "Useful Hints" section above for more information on baggage delivery.

During the following period, trains are very crowded. Avoid them. When we say **avoid**, we mean it. These are major holiday

and home visit periods, and most Japanese take a family vacation or travel back to their original home towns for big family get-togethers. The inter-city trains at these times look something like the famous rush hour subways of Tokyo - the ones where professional pushers cram everyone into the car! Pick another time or stay in a major tourist destination such as Tokyo or Kyoto. Stay off the trains.

- New Year's Holiday (Dec. 29 - Jan. 3)
- Golden Week (April 29 - May 5)
- Obon Period (August 12-18)

JAPAN RAILWAYS (JR)

As with most of the passenger railways in the world, the Japanese National Railways (JNR) suffered massive deficits for years. In an attempt to rationalize the industry, the Japanese Diet passed a law to privatize the JNR and split it into six regional passenger railway companies. The law went into effect on April 1, 1987, and JNR was split into the following six companies:

(1) Japan Railways (JR) Hokkaido,
(2) JR Eastern Japan (Tokyo and northern Honshu),
(3) JR Tokai (central Honshu),
(4) JR Western Japan (Kyoto/Osaka and western Honshu),
(5) JR Shikoku, and
(6) JR Kyushu.

Privatization so far has been successful, and most of the new JR companies are financially healthy. In addition, the good news for passengers is that long distance trains, even if operated jointly by several JR companies, run as if they were still operated by one company. Fares are calculated for the through train ride, not for each company's segment. Best of all, the Japan Rail Pass is also administered jointly, and can be used on trains of each of the six companies, as if there were still one nationwide railway company.

Types of JR Trains

1. Shinkansen

Popularly known as the bullet trains. Because all the English signs in the JR stations refer to these as "Shinkansen" rather than "bullet train," "Shinkansen" is used throughout this book when referring to this super express train. Only major cities have stations on the Shinkansen lines, in some cases separate from the stations for other lines, because the Shinkansen runs on its own special tracks.

There are now four Shinkansen lines operating in Japan:

(1) West-bound from Tokyo (Tokaido-Sanyo Shinkansen)

This Shinkansen runs between Tokyo (Tokyo Sation) and Fukuoka (Hakata Station) via such major cities as Nagoya, Kyoto, Osaka (Shin-Osaka Station), Kobe (Shin-Kobe Station), Okayama and Hiroshima. Most foreigners have this line in mind when they refer to the Shinkansen. Most of the popular destinations (and gateways to popular resorts) are located on this line. Intro Map 6 pictures all the stations on the Tokaido-Sanyo Shinkansen.

There are three types Shinkansens operating on this line.

"**Nozomi**" is a special business express. "Nozomi" Shinkansens are not covered by Japan Rail Passes. This new train enables business travelers in the Tokyo/Yokohama area to take day trips to Osaka, and Osakans to make day trips to the capital area. This all-reserved train connects Japan's three largest cities — Tokyo (Tokyo Station), Yokohama (Shin-Yokohama Station), and Osaka (Shin-Osaka Station) — in 2 hours and 30 minutes. Eventually, "Nozomi" Shinkansens will operate at hourly intervals.

"**Hikari**" and "**Kodama**" are conventional Shinkansen trains. Hikaris make fewer stops.

All "**Hikari**" trains stop at the stations pictured with black circles on Intro Map 6. There are only 8 stations over the distance of 1,176 km (735 miles). Some "Hikari" trains stop at several more stations, which are pictured with white circles with dots on Intro Map 6. Travel time between major

FARES BETWEEN MAJOR STATIONS ON THE TOKAIDO-SANYO SHINKANSEN

To /From	Tokyo	Nagoya	Kyoto	Shin-Osaka	Okayama	Hiroshima
Tokyo		10,380 yen (366.0 km)	12,970 yen (513.6 km)	13,480 yen (552.6 km)	16,050 yen (732.9 km)	17,700 yen (894.2 km)
Shin-Yokohama	2,620 yen (28.8 km)	8,770 yen (337.2 km)	12,350 yen (484.8 km)	13,170 yen (523.8 km)	15,740 yen (704.1 km)	17,400 yen (865.4 km)
Odawara	3,570 yen (83.9 km)	8,530 yen (282.1 km)	11,530 yen (429.7 km)	12,040 yen (468.7 km)	14,920 yen (649.0 km)	17,190 yen (810.3 km)
Atami	4,000 yen (104.6 km)	8,220 yen (261.4 km)	11,320 yen (409.0 km)	11,830 yen (448.0 km)	14,720 yen (628.3 km)	16,360 yen (789.6 km)
Mishima	4,310 yen (120.7 km)	7,910 yen (245.3 km)	10,590 yen (392.9 km)	11,530 yen (431.9 km)	14,720 yen (612.2 km)	16,360 yen (773.5 km)
Shizuoka	6,060 yen (180.2 km)	6,060 yen (185.8 km)	9,770 yen (333.4 km)	10,380 yen (372.4 km)	13,480 yen (552.7 km)	15,740 yen (714.0 km)
Hamamatsu	7,910 yen (257.1 km)	4,720 yen (108.9 km)	7,910 yen (256.5 km)	8,530 yen (295.5 km)	12,040 yen (475.8 km)	14,720 yen (637.1 km)
Nagoya	10,380 yen (366.0 km)		5,340 yen (147.6 km)	6,060 yen (186.6 km)	10,380 yen (366.9 km)	13,170 yen (528.2 km)
Maibara	11,830 yen (445.9 km)	3,410 yen (79.9 km)	3,240 yen (67.7 km)	4,720 yen (106.7 km)	8,530 yen (287.0 km)	11,830 yen (448.3 km)
Kyoto	12,970 yen (513.6 km)	5,340 yen (147.6 km)		2,680 yen (39.0 km)	7,190 yen (219.3 km)	10,590 yen (380.6 km)
Shin-Osaka	13,480 yen (552.6 km)	6,060 yen (186.6 km)	2,680 yen (39.0 km)		5,750 yen (180.3 km)	9,770 yen (341.6 km)
Shin-Kobe	14,000 yen (589.5 km)	7,500 yen (223.5 km)	3,180 yen (75.9 km)	2,760 yen (36.9 km)	5,340 yen (143.4 km)	9,560 yen (304.7 km)
Himeji	14,920 yen (644.3 km)	8,220 yen (278.3 km)	5,050 yen (130.7 km)	3,570 yen (91.7 km)	3,570 yen (88.6 km)	7,910 yen (249.9 km)
Okayama	16,050 yen (732.9 km)	10,380 yen (366.9 km)	7,190 yen (219.3 km)	5,750 yen (180.3 km)		5,750 yen (161.3 km)
Shin-Kurashiki	16,050 yen (758.1 km)	10,590 yen (392.1 km)	7,910 yen (244.5 km)	7,190 yen (205.5 km)	2,710 yen (25.2 km)	5,030 yen (136.1 km)
Shin-Onomichi	17,190 yen (811.3 km)	11,830 yen (445.3 km)	8,530 yen (297.7 km)	7,910 yen (258.7 km)	3,410 yen (78.4 km)	3,570 yen (82.9 km)
Hiroshima	17,700 yen (894.2 km)	13,170 yen (528.2 km)	10,590 yen (380.6 km)	9,770 yen (341.6 km)	5,750 yen (161.3 km)	
Shin-Iwakuni	18,520 yen (935.6 km)	13,690 yen (569.6 km)	11,530 yen (422.0 km)	10,380 yen (383.0 km)	7,190 yen (201.7 km)	2,870 yen (41.4 km)

To /From	Tokyo	Nagoya	Kyoto	Shin-Osaka	Okayama	Hiroshima
Ogori	19,660 yen (1,027.0 km)	14,920 yen (661.0 km)	12,970 yen (513.4 km)	12,040 yen (474.4 km)	8,530 yen (294.1 km)	5,030 yen (132.8 km)
Kokura	20,690 yen (1,107.7 km)	16,050 yen (741.7 km)	14,000 yen (594.1 km)	13,480 yen (555.1 km)	10,380 yen (374.8 km)	7,190 yen (213.5 km)
Hakata	21,300 yen (1,175.9 km)	17,190 yen (809.9 km)	14,920 yen (662.3 km)	14,310 yen (623.3 km)	11,830 yen (443.0 km)	8,530 yen (281.7 km)

NOTES:
(1) The above fares are for coach class reserved seats on "Hikari" and "Kodama" Shinkansen during the regular seasons.
(2) A 200 - yen peak season surcharge will be added during the spring, summer and winter school recesses and during Golden Week. There will be 200 yen discount during off seasons.
(3) Unreserved seat coach class fare is 500 yen less than those listed above.
(4) There is a surcharge for the faster "Nozomi" Shinkansen.
(5) Green Car (first class) fares are 40 - 50 % higher than those of coach class.

cities is as follows: Tokyo (17 minutes) Shin-Yokohama (60 minutes) Shizuoka (60 minutes) Nagoya (45 minutes) Kyoto (16 minutes) Shin-Osaka (15 minutes) Shin-Kobe (40 minutes) Okayama (50 minutes) Hiroshima (60 minutes) Kokura (20 minutes) Hakata. In other words, the ride from Tokyo takes about 2 hours to Nagoya, about 3 hours to Kyoto/Osaka, about 5 hours to Hiroshima, and about 7 hours to Hakata. Some "Hikari" trains run from Tokyo all the way to Hakata, while others terminate at Osaka, Okayama or Hiroshima. Between Tokyo and Osaka, "Hikari" trains run about once every 7-10 minutes. Between Osaka and Okayama, they run about once every 10-15 minutes, and between Okayama and Hakata about once every 30 minutes.

"Kodama" Shinkansens stop at all the stations pictured on Intro Map 6. One type of "Kodama" runs between Tokyo and Shin-Osaka (Tokaido Shinkansen portion), and the other runs between Shin-Osaka and Hakata (Sanyo Shinkansen portion). The "Kodama" is comparatively slower, but it runs from Tokyo to Nagoya (366 km or 229 miles) in 2 hours and 50 minutes, to Kyoto (514 km or 321 miles) in 3 hours and 55 minutes, and to Osaka (553 km or 346

miles) in 4 hours and 15 minutes. From Osaka the ride on the "Kodama" takes 40 minutes to Himeji (92 km or 57 miles), 70 minutes to Okayama (180 km or 113 miles), 2 hours and 25 minutes to Hiroshima (342 km or 214 miles), and 4 hours and 10 minutes to Hakata (623 km or 390 miles). If the "Hikari" trains are crowded, "Kodama" trains should still be fast enough for your trip.

(2) Japan Sea-bound from Tokyo (Joetsu Shinkansen)

This train runs from Tokyo (Tokyo Station) to Niigata on the Japan Sea Coast. Destinations introduced in this book along this line are Harunasan (Kanto Destinations section of Kanto Chapter), Mt. Tanigawadake, Niigata and Sado Island (Joetsu & Shin-etsu Chapter). You may also use this line for your visit to Hagurosan (Tohoku Chapter).

The faster "Asahi" trains stop only at major stations, and connect Tokyo with Niigata (334 km or 209 miles) in 2 hours. The slower "Toki" trains stop at all 11 stations on the line, and travel the same distance in 2 hours and 25 minutes. Because the travel time is not much different between the two types of trains, you can choose either, depending on your departure time. At least one "Asahi" and one "Toki" operates every hour.

(3) North-bound from Tokyo (Part I)
(Tohoku Shinkansen)

This line connects Tokyo with Morioka. Thanks to this Shinkansen, Tohoku has become an easily accessible destination from Tokyo. The faster "**Yamabiko**" trains stop at only several stations between Tokyo and Sendai, such as Utsunomiya, Koriyama and Fukushima. Between Sendai and Morioka they stop at all the stations. The ride from Tokyo takes 50 minutes to Utsunomiya (110 km or 69 miles), 1 hour and 30 minutes to Fukushima (273 km or 171 miles), about 2 hours to Sendai (352 km or 220 miles), 2 hours and 40 minutes to Ichinoseki (445 km or 278 miles), and 3 hours and 30 minutes to Morioka (535 km or 334 miles). "Yamabiko" Shinkansens run about once every 30 minutes.

The slower "**Aoba**" runs only between Tokyo and Sendai, stopping at all of the 11 stations along the line. The ride from Tokyo takes 60 minutes to Utsunomiya, 2 hours to Koriyama, 2 hours and 15 minutes to Fukushima, and 2 hours and 50 minutes to Sendai. "Aoba" Shinkansens run about once every hour. Again, for tourists, the travel time difference between these two trains is negligible.

(4) North-bound from Tokyo (Part II)
(Yamagata Shinkansen)

This is the first of the "Mini Shinkansens" that JR is constructing to secondary cities. "**Tsubasa**" Shinkansens run on the Tohoku Shinkansen track between Tokyo and Fukushima (in most cases attached to "Yamabiko" Tohoku Shinkansens). At Fukushima Station, the "Tsubasa" branches off onto the conventional JR Ou Honsen Line's tracks (which have been modified for the Yamagata Shinkansen's new car specifications) to Yamagata, the last stop. The Yamagata Shinkansen is thus different from the three other Shinkansens, which have their own separate tracks. More details are explained in the Tohoku Chapter.

2. Limited Express Trains & Express Trains

These are long distance trains that operate on regular tracks. Limited expresses use fancier and more spacious cars and make fewer stops than expresses. The extra charges are higher for limited expresses than for expresses. In Japan, where most people are looking for speed and comfort, many express trains have been replaced by limited expresses.

3. Local Trains

Local trains operate on the same tracks as the limited expresses and the expresses, but over comparatively short distances. The distances and schedules are designed to meet the everyday needs of the people in each region. These trains are convenient for traveling around in the larger cities, or for making side trips from these larger cities. Only a basic fare is required on this type of train. Whenever tours or itineraries involve local trains, details are explained in the text.

Classes of Service

There are two classes of service, first class and coach class, on Shinkansen trains, limited express trains, most express trains, and some local trains. There's an extra charge for the Green Car (the name JR gives its first class cars).

Directions to a JR Reserved Ticket office.

Sleeping berth service is available on some long distance night trains. However, sleeping berth charges (quite expensive) are not covered by Japan Rail Passes and the berths are generally not big enough for most foreigners.

Fare Systems

Although we highly recommend Japan Rail Passes, we have also included some JR fare information. JR fares are very complicated. There are four types of trains and two classes of service. At the end of each Chapter (or, in the case of the Kanto Chapter, at the end of the Tokyo Core, Metropolitan Tokyo and Kanto Destinations sections of the Chapter) we have inserted a Chart with information on JR fares and the lines to be used between various cities. Each Chart shows fares between the major destination stations described in the text. The price quoted is for the type of train most typically used between the two points, i.e., for longer distances, the prices quoted assume travel on limited express trains. All long distance train prices quoted on these charts also assume reserved seats. Using non-reserved seats will generally reduce the total price by about 500 yen. Please also note that first-class Green Car travel usually costs 40-50% more than the coach fares listed on the Charts. Actual Green Car surcharges depend on the distances travelled. Thus, the

Charts serve as benchmarks. They should also give you a good idea of how much money you're saving if you have a Japan Rail Pass. We have also included the most important of these Charts above, in the Tokaido-Sanyo Shinkansen section. It lists Shinkansen fares between major Pacific coast cities.

For all non-JR trains that we recommend, fares are listed in the text when we introduce the trains.

How to Purchase and Use Tickets

If you are using a Japan Rail Pass, skip this section and proceed to the next section (Japan Rail Pass).

Reserved seats. You can make reservations and purchase tickets at JR stations. Because there are no English-speaking clerks at the ticket windows except in a few of the largest stations, Conversations Card 4 will help you purchase tickets. In large JR stations there are special *Midori-no-Madoguchi* "Reserved Ticket" offices that are distinguishable by their green signs. If the station does not have a green ticket office, you can purchase both reserved-seat tickets and nonreserved-seat tickets at the regular ticket windows.

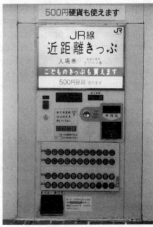

Nonreserved seats for longer distance trains. Purchase tickets at regular ticket windows. At larger stations, vending machines often sell even long distance nonreserved train tickets.

Commuter train tickets. Because the fares are low, these tickets are usually sold in vending machines. (A JR station without vending machines means a really remote rural area.) Fares, which vary with the distance traveled, are usually listed only in Japanese (though English fare boards are becoming popular in larger stations in key cities). If you cannot figure out the fare, write the name of your destination on Conversation Card 2 and show it to a Japanese passerby.

Ticket check. When you go through the entrance gate, your ticket will be punched. On long distance trains, this check is usually done by station clerks. In the case of commuter trains, this ticket check is now managed by machines. At the entrance, you have to insert your magnetized ticket in the slot at the front of the gate. The ticket is checked magnetically and the bar across the entrance retracts if the ticket is valid. Pick up your ticket from the slot on the other side of the barrier. Keep the ticket with you. At your destination, you again insert your ticket into the machine. You can then exit, but the ticket does not come out this time. You have to buy a new ticket for each trip. If the ticket you bought was for less than the required amount, an alarm bell will sound and a station clerk will arrive on the scene to settle the difference with you.

JAPAN RAIL PASS

For foreign visitors to Japan, the Japan Railways companies, working as a single entity, make available the specially discounted Japan Rail Pass. The Pass entitles the bearer to unlimited travel on the entire combined JR rail, bus and boat system.

Eligibility A Japan Rail Pass voucher can be purchased by any foreign tourist visiting Japan on a tourist visa or a transit visa. If you are exempted from obtaining a Japanese visa, you are considered a tourist, and are eligible to use a Japan Rail Pass. Holders of diplomatic, student or business visas cannot use Japan Rail Passes. A Japan Rail Pass cannot be purchased in Japan. The Pass (actually a voucher that you exchange for a pass once you arrive in Japan) must be obtained before you leave for Japan.

Types of Japan Rail Passes and Prices There are two types of Japan Rail Passes — ordinary and first class (Green Car) passes. One week, two week and three week passes are available at the following prices:

Type	7 days	14 days	21 days
Coach	27,800 yen	44,200 yen	56,600 yen
Green	37,000 yen	60,000 yen	78,000 yen

How to Purchase a Japan Rail Pass A voucher for a Japan Rail Pass can be purchased from your travel agent. If your agent doesn't know about Japan Rail Passes, ask your nearest JNTO office for Japan Rail Pass outlets in your area.

Exchange of a Voucher for a Pass Upon arrival in Japan, you can exchange your voucher for a Pass at the JR Travel Service Center in any of the following JR stations throughout Japan (they are open from 10:00 AM to 6:00 PM): Fukuoka (Hakata Station), Fukushima, Hiroshima, Kagoshima (Nishi-Kagoshima Station), Kobe (Sannomiya Station), Kokura, Kumamoto, Kyoto, Misawa, Nagoya, Niigata, Osaka (Osaka Station and Shin-Osaka Station), Sapporo, Sendai, Shimonoseki, Tokyo (Ikebukuro Station, Shibuya Station, Shinjuku Station, Tokyo Station and Ueno Station), Tsukuba, Yamagata, and Yokohama.

If you land in Japan at Narita Airport, however, we definitely recommend that you change your voucher for your pass at the JR counter or the JR Travel Service Center in the airport. The JR counter, which is open from 7:00 AM to 9:00 PM daily, is located on the concourse of the arrivals lobby just outside the Customs Hall. The JR Travel Service Center is located in the concourse connecting the arrivals lobby and the JR Narita-Kuko Station.

When you exchange your voucher specify the date on which you'd like your pass to start running. Depending on the type of pass you have, your pass will be valid for 7, 14 or 21 consecutive days.

Seat Reservations The Japan Rail Pass entitles its holder to make seat reservations for ordinary cars or green cars (depending on the type of Pass). Plan your long distance train rides in advance and request seat reservations when you exchange your voucher. As a matter of fact, you can request seat reservations at any JR station while you are traveling in Japan. There's no additional charge for seat reservations. If you change your schedule while you are traveling, you can change your reservations at any of the JR stations, or just abandon your reserved seat and take a nonreserved seat on another train. Sleeping berths (all reserved) are not covered by the Japan Rail Pass. An additional surcharge will be collected if you request sleeping berth reservations.

Dining Cars and Catering Services Most long-distance trains have either a dining car or a buffet car. In addition, there are vendors on every long-distance train who walk up and down the aisles with baskets or carts (keep your legs out of the aisle!). You can buy sandwiches, box lunches, whiskey, beer, soft drinks, and even local souvenirs from these vendors.

Rest Rooms On long-distance trains almost every other car has a rest room.

OTHER PRIVATE RAILWAYS

JR covers the entire country. Other private railways usually operate commuter trains in large cities and deluxe tourist trains from large cities to nearby resorts. In this guide we describe them when we believe they are more convenient than JR trains. Even in these situations we have also introduced parallel JR service, if it exists, for the convenience of Japan Rail Pass holders. As with JR, reserved-seat tickets are sold at the ticket windows and commuter train tickets are sold in vending machines.

SUBWAYS

There are subways in Tokyo, Yokohama, Nagoya, Kyoto, Osaka, Kobe, Hakata, Sapporo and Sendai. Tickets are sold in vending machines. Subway stations are equipped with automatic entrance and exit gates, similar to the JR automated gates for commuter trains (see above). During rush hours (8:00-9:00 AM, 5:30-6:30 PM), Tokyo subways, as well as all the other commuter trains, really are as horribly crowded as everyone says. It's probably best to avoid them during these hours.

BUSES AND STREETCARS

Buses are especially important means of public transportation in Kyoto, Nara and most smaller cities. Streetcars provide tourists with convenient and inexpensive transportation in Hakodate, Hiroshima, Matsuyama, Kochi, Kagoshima, Kumamoto, Nagasaki, Okayama and Sapporo. This book provides detailed information in the city sections on the bus networks and streetcar systems. Both streetcars and buses are usually operated by a driver only, and you are required to deposit the exact fare into the box near the driver when you get off. Many local bus systems charge only one flat fare, but others operate on a zone fare system. When you get on, make sure to check to see if there's machine that issues *seiri-ken,* or fare zone tickets. If there is, be sure to take one. When you're ready to get off the bus, match the number on your *seiri-ken* ticket with the number on the fare board posted at the front of the bus (usually above the driver's seat) to determine your fare, and deposit the *seiri-ken* along with your fare as you exit the bus. If you don't have a *seiri-ken* ticket to surrender, you may be charged the maximum fare possible for the route. Make sure you have a good supply of 100, 50 and 10 yen coins. If you don't have the exact amount, use the coin changer near the driver's seat (usually part of the fare box). Coin changers usually accept 500 and 100 yen coins, and most even make change for 1,000 yen bills.

Don't hail taxis as a matter of course. Follow our suggestions and you will not only save money but also have many additional experiences available only when you travel as the Japanese do.

TAXIS

Taxis are plentiful all over Japan, even in remote towns and tourist destinations. If you follow the suggestions in this book, you will probably only need to use them a few times. Taxis wait at designated taxi stands in front of train stations. They are also available at major bus terminals and tourist spots. In larger cities, taxis also cruise to pick up passengers. Empty taxis can be recognized by the red light in front of their wind shields. Fares vary slightly from city to city. The average basic fare is 600 yen for the first 2 km (1.25 miles), and 80 yen for each additional 400 m (a quarter mile). From 11:00

PM to 5:00 AM a 20% surcharge is added. The maximum number of passengers is four. Taxi trunks can only accommodate one or two suitcases. The left hand side rear doors on all taxis are operated by the driver. When a taxi stops for you, wait for the door to open, and once you're inside wait for it to be closed. Keep your hands to yourself or you'll find your fingers closed inside the door! When you arrive at your destination, pay the exact amount shown on the meter (no tipping) and wait again for the door to open. When you get out you should just walk away. Don't worry about the door. Neither the right-hand side front nor rear doors are automatic.

BICYCLES

In some destinations, rental bicycles offer the most convenient means of transportation to explore the area. When this is the case, we suggest bicycles and include information on where to rent them.

ROPEWAYS AND CABLE CARS

Because Japan is quite mountainous, many tourist destinations offer ropeway and cable car rides. We use these terms as the Japanese do. **Ropeway** always means passenger compartments (varying in size from gondolas that can accommodate 50 persons to individual seats) suspended from cables that run between supporting towers. **Cable Car** always means a railway propelled (usually up mountains) by means of an underground cable (like San Francisco's cable cars)

Accommodations

INTRODUCTION

In 1949, the Japanese Diet passed a special law to encourage construction of high quality accommodations suitable for foreign guests. The law provided low cost government loans for construction of hotels or *ryokan* (Japanese inns) that met official standards; facilities that met the standards were registered with the government. Since then many facilities have benefitted from this law. The number of government-registered hotels has increased from 30 to more than 600, and registered *ryokan* increased from 2 to over 1,600. Today the Japan Hotel Association and the Japan Ryokan Association represent the operators of Japan's top hotels and *ryokan*. Most member hotels have 300-1,000 rooms, and member *ryokan* generally have 15-100 rooms.

But that's not the entire story. Most of these new accommodations, eager for the prestige and profits connected with an international clientele, made their best efforts to welcome foreign guests. Many had good experiences and are still capitalizing on their international contacts. But others were discouraged by the inevitable problems — language barriers, differences in customs, no-shows, etc. — and gradually grew reluctant to accept foreign guests. Some just decided it would be less trouble and more profitable to cater to Japanese guests. Because the average occupancy rate in Japanese accommodations — of all types — is quite high, the domestic market can be quite enough just on its own for many accommodations, especially for *ryokan* in hotspring resorts. Most *ryokan* in hotsprings, as well as many *ryokan* in popular tourist destinations, will not accept single occupancy guests on weekends and in peak tourist seasons. Even double occupancy is sometimes rejected on weekends when the facilities are filled with Japanese groups.

Accommodations are introduced in each city and resort, classified into three categories — deluxe, first class, and standard. For hotels, another category — business hotels — is added as the least expensive class.

In recent years the value of the Japanese yen has risen markedly, and most foreign currencies have lost value against the yen. Even though yen prices of accommodations have risen only modestly, the prices expressed in foreign currencies have jumped up, due to the value of the yen. To respond to requests by foreign tourists looking for affordable accommodations, many owners of inexpensive *ryokan* and *minshuku* formed an association and introduced reasonable accommodations in early 1980's. Now supported by the International Tourism Center (a nonprofit foundation), these accommodations are organized as the Welcome Inn Group. In addition to *ryokan* and *minshuku*, the Welcome Inn Group includes business hotels, pensions and *kokumin shukusha*. Member properties are generally small and their service is not at the level of international standards. They are best suited to the budget-minded and small groups of family members or friends. These accommodations are introduced in the city and resort sections that follow, classified as "Welcome Inns."

Each accommodation listing includes price information. The price quoted takes into account service charges and taxes. In this we differ from most other listings, which generally do not include such charges, even though all accommodations add them to your bill automatically. Hotels add a 10 percent service charge and *ryokan* add 10-15 percent. The Japanese government, too, is quite diligent about collecting its share — an additional 3 percent consumption tax for all accommodations, plus 3% extra tax if your charge is 15,000 yen or more per person per night. We believe that our approach gives you a much more realistic idea of what accommodations will really cost you.

RESERVATIONS

There are about 90,000 accommodations of various types throughout Japan, ranging from five-room *minshuku* (small family-run inns) to giant deluxe hotels with more than 1,000 rooms. Almost all of them are crowded during the spring (from the middle of March to the end of May), summer (from the middle of July to the end of August) and autumn (October and November) tourist seasons, and the New Year's holidays (from December 29 through January 3). If you are traveling during the busy seasons, you should absolutely make reservations well in advance. Under any circumstances, making reservations in advance will make your life far easier.

It is possible, nevertheless, to travel in Japan without reservations. Hotel and *ryokan* reservation offices are located in major train stations. Though the clerks probably won't speak English, they should be able to help you find an accommodation for the night. Needless to say, conveniently located, reasonable accommodations sell first. If you try to make reservations at the last minute, especially during the busy seasons, you may end up staying at a rather expensive accommodation or one that is inconveniently located.

For many foreign tourists in Japan the most important task of each day is visiting the reservations office in the train stations to find a place to stay for the night. "Keep your itinerary flexible" sounds like good advice, but doing so is not necessarily enjoyable. Careful advance planning is especially important when you are traveling extensively in a limited time period. We think it's best not to waste valuable sightseeing and leisure time trying to find places to stay.

Another tip to coordinate your reservations is to use hotels in the same chain at your various destinations. Hotels in these chains introduce clients to each other. For example, if you stay at a property of the Tokyu Inn Chain in Tokyo, you can request reservations at your hotel for other Tokyu Inn Chain properties, e.g., Kyoto Tokyu Inn, Osaka Tokyu Inn, Matsue Tokyu Inn, etc. The following are the major hotel chains in Japan, classified by category:

1. Deluxe and First Class Hotel Chains

(1) ANA Hotel Chain: Fukuoka, Hakodate, Hiroshima, Kanazawa, Kyoto, Matsuyama, Niigata, Okinawa, Osaka, Sapporo, Tokyo, Ube, Yamagata, etc.

(2) Miyako Hotel Chain: Fukuoka, Kanazawa, Kyoto, Nagoya, Nara, Okinawa, Osaka, Tokyo, Yokkaichi, etc.

(3) New Otani Hotel Chain: Chiba (Makuhari Messe), Fukuoka, Kobe, Nagaoka, Osaka, Saga, Sapporo, Tokyo, Tottori, Yokohama, etc.

(4) Okura Hotel Chain: Ito, Karuizawa, Kobe, Niigata, Sapporo, Tokyo, etc.

(5) Prince Hotel Chain: Furano, Hakone, Hikone, Karuizawa, Kyoto, Lake Towada-ko, Naeba, Narita, Nikko, Oiso, Sapporo, Shimoda, Tokyo, Yokohama, etc.

(6) Tokyu Hotel Chain: Fukuoka, Hakuba, Kagoshima, Kanazawa, Kyoto, Nagasaki, Okayama, Okinawa, Osaka, Sapporo, Sendai, Shimoda, Tokyo, Yokohama, etc.

2. Standard and Business Hotel Chains

(7) Chisan Hotel Chain: Fukuoka, Hiroshi-

ma, Kobe, Koriyama, Nagoya, Okayama, Osaka, Sapporo, Sendai, Tokyo, Yokkaichi, etc.

(8) Hotel Rich Chain: Fukuoka, Hakodate, Kyoto, Morioka, Nagoya, Niigata, Sapporo, Sendai, Takamatsu, Yokohama, etc.

(9) Hotel Sunroute Chain: Akita, Aomori, Fukushima, Ichinoseki, Morioka, Nagoya, Nara, Okayama, Sapporo, Sendai, Shizuoka, Tokyo, Toyama, and Urayasu (Tokyo Disneyland), etc.

(10) Tokyo Daiichi Hotel Chain: Akita, Fukuoka, Kochi, Kofu, Kyoto, Nagoya, Okayama, Osaka, Sendai, Takamatsu, Tokyo, Toyama, Tsuchiura, Tsukuba, Tsuruoka, etc.

(11) Tokyu Inn Chain: Asahikawa, Fukushima, Hiroshima, Iwaki, Kagoshima, Kobe, Kokura, Kumamoto, Kushiro, Kyoto, Matsue, Matsumoto, Nagoya, Narita, Niigata, Obihiro, Osaka, Saga, Sakata, Sapporo, Shimonoseki, Takamatsu, Tokyo, Tokushima, Toyama, Wakayama, Yamagata, etc.

(12) Washington Hotel Chain: Fukushima, Hachinohe, Kagoshima, Kobe, Koriyama, Matsue, Miyazaki, Nagano, Nagasaki, Nagoya, Niigata, Sapporo, Sendai, Takamatsu, Tokyo, Toyama, Utsunomiya, etc.

The Welcome Inn Reservation Center offers free reservation service for visitors to Japan. Reservations are accepted by mail or fax from overseas at the International Tourism Center of Japan, in close cooperation with JNTO, the Japan National Tourist Organization. Because these accommodations are not registered with international hotel representations, travel agents abroad, and even travel agents in Japan, generally cannot make bookings for these properties. There are certain restrictions for bookings through the International Tourism Center. Ask for more details on the reservation procedures from JNTO's overseas offices. Upon arrival in Japan you can request reservations for Welcome Inn Group properties at JNTO's Tourist Information Centers in Tokyo, Kyoto and at Narita Airport.

SELECTING ACCOMMODATIONS

When selecting accommodations, you should pay attention not only to the rates but also to the locations. Even if you find inexpensive accommodations, you might end up spending your savings on taxis if they can't be reached easily by public transportation or on foot.

We suggest alternating Western style hotels and Japanese style *ryokan* during your trip. Even if you think you're not really interested in a *ryokan*, we think you should try one for a night or two. They are usually small; you can expect personalized service; and they'll give you closer contact with Japanese people and an idea of traditional Japanese lifestyle. If you are especially attracted by the idea of staying in a *ryokan*, allocate more nights to staying in them. We do, nevertheless, suggest that you occasionally choose a Western style hotel. The contrast will be interesting, and the familiar surroundings might well be soothing in a certain sense. It is important to remember that *ryokan* rates usually include two meals (dinner and breakfast the next morning). Staying in *ryokan* precludes you from eating out and exploring on your own. We especially recommend Western style accommodations in large cities that have good varieties of restaurants.

HOTELS

Hotel rates quoted here are based on Tokyo prices, which are the most expensive in Japan. You can expect rates 10-20% lower at hotels in other Japanese cities.

Deluxe and First-Class Hotels
(24,000 yen and up for a twin room)

Hotels in this category are designed to

serve foreign visitors and Japanese VIPs. In polls of the world's best hotels, many of them have ranked near the top. They are usually quite big and have fancy lobbies, large meeting and banquet rooms, and a variety of boutiques and shops. Most of the hotels in this category have more than 500, and some as many as 1,500-2,000 rooms. Travel agencies have offices in these hotels to assist guests in making travel arrangements. In Tokyo and Kyoto, pick- up service for English guided tours is usually available from these hotels. Top hotels in this category maintain special "business service salons" to provide foreign business people with information, assistance and secretarial services. A variety of restaurants, bars and lounges are located in these hotels. Most of the hotels in this category have representative agencies and/or their own sales offices in the United States and other foreign countries to accept overseas reservations.

Standard Hotels
(18,000-24,000 yen for a twin room)

Hotels in this category are usually smaller (100-500 rooms) and do not have luxurious lobbies designed to impress. They generally don't tailor their services to foreign visitors. However, each of these hotels has English-speaking employees and foreign guests should be able to communicate. Typical features of these hotels include several restaurants, coffee shops and a bar. Most of these hotels use representative agencies to book reservations abroad.

Business Hotels
(18,000 yen and less for a twin room)

It is rather difficult to separate lower class Standard Hotels from good Business Hotels. We have separated them based on their primary target customers and their affiliation with the Japan Hotel Association. Business Hotels were developed to provide Japanese businessmen with convenient, inexpensive accommodations. They usually

have 100-300 rooms. Because their primary target customer is single travelers, most of their rooms are singles at reasonable rates (6,000 - 10,000 yen). Their rates for double rooms are not as inexpensive as those for single rooms, and the number of the rooms of this type is rather limited (typically only 10-20% of the total rooms). Double rooms usually cost 15,000-18,000 yen. (In many cases, the cost for one twin room is similar to that of two single rooms.) Triple use of a room is often very difficult due to the small size of rooms in these hotels. If you are traveling as a couple, you might not save much by staying at business hotels. All the fancy elements of most hotels, such as spacious lobbies, room service, and even bellboys, are often non-existent. Rooms are smallish, but each has its own pre-fab bath unit (the tubs aren't really big enough for most foreigners, but taking showers should be fine). Though some business hotels have several restaurants, most of them have only one or two restaurants that do double or triple duty — as coffee shops in the morning, or bars at night. The staff usually does not speak English, but standard check-in and check-out procedures shouldn't cause any problems.

RYOKAN

Over 80,000 of Japan's 90,000 accommodation facilities can be classified as *ryokan*. The name "ryokan" covers a wide variety of Japanese-style facilities, from the very expensive to the very economical. Common features of *ryokan* are:

— the number of rooms at each property is very small — usually 20-40 rooms;

— guest rooms have *tatami* mat floors — you have to remove your shoes at the entrance of the property, or, in some cases, at the entrance to your room;

— instead of beds, *futon* mattresses are spread on the floor (and folded away in closets during the day);

— meals (dinner and breakfast the next day)

are included in the rate, and the menu, which is selected by the chef rather than the guest, varies with the season;

— the entrance is locked up at night (usually after 11 PM); and

— single occupancy guests are often rejected, especially on weekends and at peak tourist seasons.

Facilities and services vary greatly depending on price.

There are no accommodations deserving the name "ryokan" in large business cities, such as Tokyo, Yokohama, Osaka and Nagoya. The best places to try a *ryokan* stay is either historic cities, such as Kyoto, Takayama, Kanazawa and Hagi, or hotspring resorts, such as Hakone, Izu and Beppu.

Traditional Deluxe Ryokan
(40,000 yen and up for two persons with breakfast and dinner)

These distinguished *ryokan* represent traditional, refined Japanese values, and their service is geared to individual clients. Due to the high cost of maintaining these

properties, many owners have replaced their traditional small buildings with more space-efficient large buildings. Thus, the number of *ryokan* in this category is decreasing. Staying at a *ryokan* in this category can be an extremely intimate and memorable way to experience Japanese hospitality. Meals are genuine Japanese *kaiseki* multi-course cuisine, usually served in your room. Private bathrooms and air-conditioning are standard.

Modern Deluxe Ryokan
(40,000 yen and up for two persons with breakfast and dinner)

These *ryokan* combine Japanese tradition with western convenience. The buildings are usually modern concrete structures, and public space is similar to a regular hotel. However, the guest rooms are authentic Japanese style, and meals are authentic Japanese cuisine. Private bathrooms and air-conditioning are standard. A number of *ryokan* in this category are located in famous hotspring resorts and are often the best available in the area.

First-Class Ryokan

(30,000-40,000 yen for two persons with breakfast and dinner)

These *ryokan* have similar facilities and services to the above Modern Deluxe *Ryokan*, but are more modest in facilities and cuisine. These *ryokan* offer a good chance to experience Japanese life-style at less cost. Private bathrooms and air-conditioning are standard.

Standard Ryokan

(20,000-30,000 yen for two persons with breakfast and dinner)

These *ryokan* are popular among young Japanese and are often used for school excursions and small group tours. They are in modest concrete buildings or wooden houses. Meals are simple and similar to those eaten by Japanese in daily life. Private bathrooms are rather exceptional and communal bathrooms may be shared with other guests. In many cases there are no big differences between standard *ryokan* and Welcome Inn Group member properties, though the latter often only have a few rooms.

Welcome Inn Group Ryokan and Minshuku

(10,000-16,000 yen for two persons with breakfast and dinner)

These *ryokan* are similar to regular hous-

es. Meals are simpler, and common baths are shared by all the guests. They are probably most comparable to cheap bed-and breakfast type accommodations. Many of them will accept guests on a "room only" basis (no meals). These are not the places to experience "traditional" Japan, but you can expect a more friendly attitude and at home atmosphere.

Minshuku are small, family-operated accommodations. The Welcome Inn Group includes some *minshuku*. *Minshuku* are not common in larger cities. They were originally developed to provide extra accommodations in resort areas during busy seasons. Most *minshuku* are remodeled private homes, and the rooms are usually smaller than those of regular *ryokan*.

Shukubo

Shukubo are temple lodgings. Their facilities are very similar to those of standard *ryokan*. There are two distinct differences:

— the lodgings are attached to temples, and located in the temple precincts; and

— the meals served are vegetarian. The best place to experience *shukubo* is Koyasan. There are about 50 accommodations available in Koyasan, and they are all temple lodgings.

Restaurants and Pubs

A number of restaurants and pubs are introduced in this guidebook. All of them are clearly pictured on the detailed maps. We simply haven't had enough space to include detailed information on restaurants in smaller cities. You can always find inexpensive and reasonable restaurants in the downtown areas of such cities and prestigious and expensive restaurants in the good hotels.

In this chapter, we would like to give you some useful hints on eating in Japan.

Breakfasts There are a number of alternatives to start your day.

The easiest but the most expensive way is to have breakfast at your hotel. An American breakfast typically costs somewhere between 1,500 yen and 2,800 yen, depending on the class of the hotel. Most hotels in Japan serve breakfasts buffet-style. When you start your day a little late, it is not bad idea to invest in a big hotel breakfast and skip lunch.

Most coffee shops serve a "morning service" special for 400-500 yen. The special consists of coffee or tea, toast, an egg (usually hard boiled), and a small salad or a piece of fruit. In Japan, where a cup of coffee costs 300-400 yen, this "morning service" special is a great deal, and especially popular among white collar workers. You should be able to find coffee shops near your hotel or around train/subway stations easily.

Stand-up noodle counters in larger train/subway stations and underground passageways are another Japanese breakfast place. Though some such shops serve Chinese-style *ramen* noodles, the majority of them serve only Japanese-style *soba* and *udon* noodles. The simplest soup noodle typically costs around 300 yen. You can add a raw egg and/or vegetable *tempura* as extra toppings for an extra charge of 80-100 yen per item. You will see busy commuters crowding these shops, finishing their breakfasts in just a few minutes.

Fast food chains, including such popular American names as McDonald's, Wendy's, Kentucky Fried Chicken and Dunkin' Donuts, also serve breakfasts. Menus are similar to those back home, but prices are a little more expensive: typically 300-500 yen. You will be surprised at the popularity these foreign shops have achieved in Japan in a short period of time.

Lunches Noodle counters, coffee shops and fast food chains (see above) are also available for light lunches.

Even American fast food chains have been Japanized and, in addition to their regular foods, serve "Japan Special" menus — such as *katsu curry* (a bowl of rice topped with pork cutlet and curry) and *rice burger* (a hamburger sandwiched in rice patties instead of bread). You may like these "exotic" foods. Many coffee shops serve light lunches, such as sandwiches and spaghetti at reasonable prices (500-1,000 yen). Japanese love these establishments, especially for afternoon breaks, because customers are never hurried along. You might come to appreciate them too because they are good places to sit down, relax and rest your feet when you're tired. Coffee is still considered a bit of an exotic luxury in Japan. It is expensive (300-400 yen), and you don't get automatic refills. If you order tea you have to ask for milk or it will come with lemon. Many coffee shops are pretty utilitarian affairs, with rather standardized decor, but some have decors worthy of the exotic beverage they serve. Coffee shops always have tea, coffee, "cake-sets" — tea or coffee plus a piece of fancy cake — ice creams and light snacks. In the evening coffee shops are popularly used as meeting places for dating couples.

If you are traveling on a train during lunch time, your best bet is to buy a box lunch (*bento*). You can buy *bento* in most large train stations, and, in the case of the JR Shinkansen and other long distance trains, on the train itself. Attendants wheel carts through the trains selling several kinds of *bento* (800-1,500 yen) and sandwiches, as well as coffee, tea, beer, *sake*, and other canned drinks. Contents of *bento* vary from town to town, and often include local specialties. One of the treats Japanese enjoy when travelling is sampling these local specialties. The divided containers usually have a few portions of fish or meat along with vegetables, rice and Japanese pickles.

Noodle shops are the most popular lunch places for Japanese. Most of the noodle shops specialize in either Chinese-style *ramen* noodles or Japanese-style *soba* and *udon* noodles. Prices range from 400 yen to 1,000 yen, depending on toppings. These restaurants also serve curry rice and *donburi-mono* (rice bowl dishes) for heavier lunches. *Donburi-mono* dishes are served atop a large bowl of rice. *Katsudon*, the most typical, is deep-fried pork cutlet and egg atop rice; *oyakodon* is chicken and egg atop rice; *gyudon* is beef and onion atop rice; *chukadon* is mixed vegetables and pork atop rice; and *unadon* is broiled eel atop rice. The first four range in price from 500-800 yen, and unadon is usually more expensive (1,200-2,000 yen). At rather expensive restaurants, the *-don* suffix becomes *-ju*, and your meal is served in an attractive lacquer box, instead of a simple ceramic bowl. The prices go higher accordingly.

In business districts, most restaurants, not only reasonable restaurants but also many expensive ones, serve special lunch menus for local white collar workers. These "specials" are always good buys and range in price from 800 to 1,500 yen.

Dinners Most of the restaurants in the inexpensive to reasonable price range serve the same menus at the same prices for both lunch and dinner. Incidentally, these restaurants do not take a break between lunch and dinner. Once they open at around 11:00 AM for lunch, they stay open until they close (around 10:00 PM). When you want a simple dinner, these restaurants are recommended.

When you want a dinner on the rather expensive side, there are a great number of restaurants serving a variety of meals, from authentic Japanese (including *sushi*, *tempura*, *sukiyaki*, *shabu-shabu*, and the luxurious *kaiseki* course dinner), to Western (French, Italian, Spanish, Swiss, German, Greek, Russian and Mexican), and Asian (Chinese, Thai, Indian and Indonesian). Many of these restaurants are listed in this guidebook. If you are looking for top notch, you can easily find these establishments by consulting your hotel conceirge.

Pubs There usually is a remarkable difference in the clientele of Japanese-style and Western-style pubs (and wine houses). The former are usually used by groups of business colleagues, while the latter are often used by couples on dates. Beer halls occupy a middle ground. The atmosphere of Western-style pubs is not too different from those you're used to at home. But if you go to a Japanese pub, you'll see lots of differences. First, you will find that the majority of the customers are male (although the number of women patrons has increased in recent years). Secondly, you will find that Japanese drink a lot - you'll sometimes be convinced that Japan is a nation of alcoholics. Thirdly, you will find that many of the drinkers are engaged in conversations that seem quite intense. In the Japanese business world (which is also the most important community for the majority of people), it is considered rather uncouth to express one's opinion too clearly or to object to another's proposal openly. So after work Japanese business people often go drinking with their office colleagues. Over drinks, they discuss differences of opinion, seek compromises, and sound each other out before presenting proposals formally. Thus, pubs are places where a great deal of business is conducted, and a great many decisions made, before even the preliminary memos begin to make the rounds in the office. Pubs are also important places for younger employees, because it is only in such establishments that they are free to ease their frustrations in the workplace by criticizing their "untalented" bosses. Such behavior, "under the influence," is viewed as a necessary safety valve, and involves no adverse consequences for those whose tongues are loosened by alcohol.

It is rather difficult to clearly separate Japanese pubs from Japanese restaurants. Many Japanese restaurants add appetizer-type small dishes to accompany drinks to their evening menu. Even in restaurants much more alcohol is consumed than in regular Western restaurants.

In this book restaurants are classified into the following categories: Inexpensive Restaurants; Reasonable Restaurants; Moderate Restaurants; and Expensive Restaurants.

Inexpensive Restaurants. These are restaurants where most items on the menu are 500-1,000 yen. Noodle restaurants are good examples of this category. In addition to the noodles, these restaurants also serve curry rice and *donburi* rice bowl menus.

They offer the same menus at the same prices for both lunch and dinner. Many of them promote drinking by adding appetizer-style small dishes to their evening menus.

Reasonable Restaurants. There are a variety of restaurants in this category, including Japanese, Western, Chinese, Indian, etc. They use more elaborate furniture and interior design, and the atmosphere is more pleasant. Typical dinner menus cost somewhere between 1,500-3,000 yen. Even supposedly expensive meals, such as *sushi* and *tempura* are available in this price range, if you order a set menu. If you order appetizer *sashimi*, and eat *sushi* or *tempura* a la carte, your bill will be easily 5,000-10,000 yen. Even for beef steaks, there are a number of restaurants serving one steak dish for around 3,000 yen (portions are small and the beef is not *Kobe* beef, of course).

Moderate Restaurants. These restaurants serve set dinners for 3,000-6,000 yen. They have pleasant atmospheres, the menus are varied and imaginative and the quality of the food served is quite good. At Western restaurants, in addition to the main dish, a set menu meal will typically include an appetizer, soup, and a cup of coffee. Most beef dishes, such as steaks, *shabu-shabu*, *sukiyaki*, and Korean barbecue are served at the restaurants in this category. Please be forewarned that beef portions are rather smallish.

Expensive Restaurants. This category includes restaurants that serve dinners at more than 6,000 yen (usually well over 10,000 yen). Many big name *kaiseki* restaurants, steak houses (Kobe beef), *sushi*, *tempura*, *sukiyaki* and *shabu-shabu* (Matsuzaka beef) specialists belong to this category. Their excellent reputations reflect both their food and their service. Even at these places, as long as you order a set menu dinner, it won't cost you a fortune. They do have rather "reasonable" set menu dinners around

5,000-8,000 yen. If you start ordering extra appetizers for your drinks, as Japanese usually do, or eat dinner a la carte, your bill can go up quite high. These establishments are usually patronized by business people on expense accounts and by international travelers. In addition to those we have mentioned by name, all restaurants in major hotels belong to this category. Probably the most expensive restaurants are those featuring *Kyoto Kaiseki* (a full course Japanese dinner in traditional Kyoto style). It is not unusual that one dinner costs 30,000-40,000 yen per person at these places. If you are interested in tasting a *kaiseki* dinner, we recommend that you stay at a deluxe traditional *ryokan* in a historic citiy, such as Kyoto, Nara, Kanazawa or Kurashiki, where a *kaiseki* dinner is included in the price.

Most Japanese use these deluxe restaurants only on special occasions, such as wedding anniversaries, alumni reunions or very classy dates. Unless you are the kind of person who always stays at the Four Seasons in New York and who always eats meals at the hotel, you won't want to make a habit of patronizing these restaurants. "Expensive" means "expensive" (with an exclamation point)!

Most restaurants, either inexpensive or expensive, have display cases out front with plastic models of the dishes they serve. If you have trouble making yourself understood you can always walk the waiter or waitress out front with you and just point to what you want. Many "fashionable" Western restaurants post their menu, instead of plastic models, in the display cases, like European and American restaurants. If you do not see either plastic models or menus outside the restaurant, it is better to keep looking for another restaurant.

The following are typical popular menus:
- **Donburi-mono** 丼物 , or rice bowl dishes, are explained above (see Lunches above).
- **Noodles** 麺類 . *Ramen*, *soba* and *udon*

are all varieties of Japanese noodles. They are usually served in large bowls, with soup broth and a choice of toppings such as scraps of meat or seafood, vegetables, seaweed and Japanese condiments. Cold *mori-soba* is available year round (and popular as an after drink food). Cold *ramen* is usually served in summer time only. Spaghetti is also quite popular, too. Due to its foreign cachet, spaghetti usually costs slightly more than other noodles.

- **Curry Rice** カレーライス . This is a unique Japanese concoction. It's cheap, and it fills you up for 600-1,000 yen. But don't expect to be reminded in way of Bombay, if you eat curry at regular Japanese restaurants (typically noodle restraurants). Real Indian curry cuisine is also very popular in Japan. There are a number of Indian restaurants with Indian Chefs. Prices at these "exotic" restaurants are a little more expensive.
- **Tempura** 天婦羅 is deep-fried seafood and vegetables. It usually includes shrimp, white fish, squid, eggplant, green pepper and onion. A special dipping sauce is also

served. A set menu *tempura* lunch or dinner usually costs 1,000-2,000 yen. At tempura specialty restaurants, if you eat a la carte, the costs can be astronomical.

● *Sukiyaki* すき焼 is probably the Japanese dish most popular with foreigners. Thinly sliced beef, and vegetables, tofu and Japanese vermicelli are cooked in an iron pan in a special broth. Raw egg is used as a dip. A *sukiyaki* lunch or dinner costs around 3,000-5,000 yen. You may wish to order extra slices of beef (1,000-2,000 yen more).

● *Shabu-shabu* しゃぶしゃぶ is a close relative of *sukiyaki*. A brass pot with a chimney in its center is placed on the table. Thinly sliced beef and ingredients similar to those used for *sukiyaki* are prepared on a large tray. Guests dip these ingredients into the boiling water in the pot for a few seconds to cook them, and then eat them after dipping them again in a special sauce that is served separately. The price of *shabu-shabu* is similar to that of *sukiyaki*.

● *Sushi* 寿司 is a Japanese culinary innovation. Various types of thinly sliced raw fish are served atop small rice patties. Fish and vegetables are also rolled up with rice in seaweed wrappers. A set menu *sushi* lunch or dinner usually includes about 10 pieces of *sushi* and costs about 1,000-2,000 yen. A la carte orders at *sushi* counters are usually substantially more than the set menu meals. Be ready to pay a minimum of 5,000 yen.

● *Kaiseki* 懐石 is an authentic Japanese full course dinner. The meal usually consists of about 10 different courses, and features the

Kaiseki

delicacies of the season. The best way for foreign tourists to try a *kaiseki* meal in a relaxed atmosphere is to stay at a deluxe traditional *ryokan* in a traditional city like Kyoto, as mentioned above. *Ryokan* in cheaper categories seldom serve this type of full course Japanese dinner. A simplified *kaiseki* lunch, which is served at many moderate to expensive Japanese restaurants, is a good compromise (3,000-5,000 yen).

The following are typical side dishes served at Japanese pubs as accompaniments to drinks:

● **Robatayaki** 炉端焼 . In any given area, the *robatayaki* pubs are usually the most popular. A variety of seafood, meats and vegetables are arranged in front of the counter where guests are seated. You can order whatever you want to have broiled on the hearth. Because you can just point, the language barrier is no problem. Each item costs around 500 yen.

● *Yakitori* 焼鳥 is barbecued chicken shish kebob. This is one of the most popular snacks, especially with alcoholic beverages.

● *Sashimi* さしみ is thinly sliced raw fish.

Yakitori

Unlike *sushi*, where the raw fish is served atop small rice patties, *sashimi* is just the slices of fish. Another popular side dish with drinkers.

● *Nabemono* 鍋物 means "things cooked in an earthen bowl." Various ingredients and broth bases are used in the different versions of this popular dish, and its name varies with the ingredients used. *Chankon-abe*, for example, was concocted by sumo wrestlers. It uses fish, chicken and vegetables. Another *nabemono* dish — *Ishikarin-abe* — uses salmon and vegetables. *Nabemono* dishes are a special treat on cold winter nights.

For many Japanese, eating and drinking at pubs is a substitute for dinner. After drinking, people will order *onigiri* おにぎり (rice balls that contain small pieces of broiled salmon, cod roe or pickled plums), or *ochazuke* お茶漬 (green tea poured over a bowl of rice and topped with broiled salmon, cod roe or pickled plums).

Sashimi and Nabemono

Brief History of Japan

PRE-HISTORIC ERA

About 10,000 years ago when the level of the sea rose at the end of the 4th Ice Age, the Japanese archipelago separated from the Asian Continent. According to first century Chinese documents, at that time there were more than 100 small tribal communes scattered about Japan. Large tombs, which date from the 4th century, have been found in many parts of Japan, and giant ones are located in Nara and Osaka. This supports the theory that of the many small "nations" led by powerful families at this time, the most powerful "nation" was located in the Nara-Osaka area. The establishment of what can be considered the first unified nation of Japan was achieved in the 5th century, in Nara.

ASUKA ERA
(End of the 6th century to the end of the 7th century)

Buddhism was introduced to Japan in the middle of the 6th century and provided a common spiritual basis for organization of centralized political and social systems. Horyuji Temple in the Ikaruga area of Nara was constructed around the end of the 6th century. Even though its original designs were changed slightly when the Temple was reconstructed in 670 after a fire, its scale and grandeur testify to the power and influence Buddhism had acquired in such a short period of time. The first Japanese Constitution, the "Seventeen Article Constitution," was promulgated by Regent Shotoku.

FUJIWARA ERA
(End of the 7th century to 710)

A large scale capital was constructed in Fujiwara (south of Nara) in 694. An aristocracy was established along with a sophisticated tax collection network that extended to virtually every corner of the country. The East Tower of Yakushiji Temple in Nara is the symbol of the cultural achievements of this era. Its balanced beauty has been described as "frozen music."

NARA ERA (710-794)

Japan's first permanent capital was constructed in Nara (a little to the west of the center of the modern city) in 710. The imperial court sent cultural missions to China to master the advanced science and culture of the Asian continent. During this era, art treasures of India and Persia as well as those of China were brought back to Japan. Throughout this period, Buddhism, protected by the imperial family and the powerful aristocrats, grew in influence. The Great Buddha at Todaiji Temple in Nara, cast in 752, symbolizes this influence. The powerful Buddhist priests eventually extended their activities beyond the spiritual world and became involved in political affairs. Emperor Kammu moved the capital to Kyoto in order to rid the court of their influence.

HEIAN ERA (794-1192)

The new capital in Kyoto was completed in 794, and about this time, leading priests, among them Kukai and Saicho, began a reform movement within Buddhism. As part of their pursuit of spiritual purification, they opened training centers for priests in isolated mountain areas. Koyasan and Hieizan were locations of two of these new monasteries. For hundreds of years Kyoto continued to prosper, and the city's imperial and aristocratic families enjoyed political and economic power. They were also the leaders, along with the priests, of cultural activities. In the 12th century, economic development in the rural areas resulted in new power for local military leaders. The Taira family, based in western Japan, and the Minamoto family, based in the east, were the two most influential military powers of their time. Under the leadership of Kiyomori, the Taira family won major battles against the Minamotos, and then began its ascent up the ladders of political power at the imperial court. Kiyomori became the prime minister, and members of the family occupied other important government posts. Kiyomori's daughter, Empress Kenreimon-in, bore Emperor Takakura a son who grew up to be Emperor Antoku. The Taira's prosperity, however, did not last long. After the death of Kiyomori, the reorganized Minamoto force sparked revolts against the Tairas. After three major victories in the Inland Sea area, Yoritomo Minamoto seized power. The rapid rise to power and equally rapid downfall of the Tairas have long symbolized what the Japanese regard as one of history's greatest lessons — that prosperity is like a bubble on the surface of the water, easily formed and just as easily broken, lost and forgotten. While the Taira family prospered in Kyoto, an autonomous government flourished in Hiraizumi, in the northern part of Japan's main island. The Fujiwara family, leaders of this local government, were also patrons of high culture, as symbolized by the Konjiki-do (Golden Hall) at Chusonji Temple and the Heavenly Garden of Motsuji Temple. After 100 years of prosperity, the Fujiwaras too were destroyed, by Yoritomo Minamoto.

KAMAKURA ERA (1192-1333)

Learning his lesson from the rapid deterioration of the Taira military spirit once the family joined the imperial court, Yoritomo established Japan's first independent military government. He made Kamakura, far from the ruined imperial court of Kyoto, his capital. The simple and straightforward warrior spirit of the Minamoto family became the social norm, and the austere strictures of the Zen School of Buddhism gained countless adherents.

After the assassination of the third Minamoto shogun, the political power of the Kamakura Shogunate fell into the hands of the Hojos, the family of Yoritomo's wife. In 1274, and again in 1281, the Mongolians, who had established the Yuan Dynasty in China, tried to attack Japan. These unsuccessful assaults were made at Fukuoka, in Kyushu, the southernmost island. Though the Kamakura Shogunate successfully defended the nation, the economic difficulties caused by the wars weakened its leadership. Emperor Godaigo rallied dissatisfied warrior leaders from all parts of the nation and defeated the Shogunate forces in 1333. This new imperial government only survived for three years, and another military leader, Takauji Ashikaga, established a new Shogunate in 1336, this time in Kyoto.

MUROMACHI AND AZUCHI MOMOYAMA ERAS (1336-1603)

Though the Ashikagas centered their government in the Kyoto area, their rule over rural areas did not last long. The financial power of local military leaders allowed them to remain independent of the Ashikaga Shogunate and to set up their own feudal systems. Beginning with the middle of the 15th century, there were frequent civil wars among local feudal lords who sought to expand their territory. The Ikko sect of Buddhism played an influential role in these wars, especially in the central part of the Japan Sea coast area. Members of this sect defeated the feudal lord in Kanazawa and established an autonomous government that endured for as long as 100 years. The famous Gold and Silver Pavilions in Kyoto were constructed by Shoguns of the Ashikaga family and are the representative historic relics of the era. Flower arranging, tea ceremony and the Noh drama also date from this era.

In the second half of the 16th century, Nobunaga Oda, a minor feudal lord and brilliant military strategist from Gifu, near Nagoya, conquered neighboring lords and emerged as one of the nation's greatest military powers. In 1573, Nobunaga attacked Kyoto and defeated the Ashikaga Shogunate. After victories over other influential feudal lords, Nobunaga was on the brink of unifying the nation when he was assassinated in 1582 by his retainer, Mitsuhide Akechi. Another powerful retainer, Hideyoshi Toyotomi, a mere farmer's son who had risen to a position of power, crushed Mitsuhide's rebel force, and then went on to complete the establishment of a centralized government. In the period of peace that began with the end of the 16th century, all sorts of cultural pursuits flourished; it was a particularly rich and lavish era in the history of Japanese art. The gorgeous paintings of Kano School are representative of the work of this era. Prototypes of modern kabuki and the *bunraku* puppet dramas also developed at this time.

The reign of the Toyotomi family did not last long. After the death of Hideyoshi, a top retainer of the Toyotomis, Mitsunari Ishida, and a most influential feudal lord, Ieyasu Tokugawa, vied for power, and their struggle divided the other feudal lords. The two forces had a final decisive battle at Sekigahara, between Kyoto and Nagoya, in 1600, and Ieyasu's victory led to the establishment of a new Shogunate in Edo (modern Tokyo) in 1603.

Toward the end of the period of civil war, Christianity was introduced on Kyushu island. Because the Christian missionaries accompanied the European traders who brought advanced technologies and foreign products into the country, Nobunaga Oda allowed them to act freely, and the new religion spread, especially in Nagasaki and other trading centers of western Kyushu. Some of the feudal lords of that area became Christians and even sent envoys to Rome. It is estimated that Christianity quickly gained 700,000 adherents. But because the new religion was especially popular among the poor farmers who suffered most from the heavy taxes and rigid caste system of the Shogunate, it was not acceptable to either Hideyoshi or Ieyasu. Christianity was officially forbidden by the Tokugawa Shogunate in 1613. The bloody battle at Shimabara near Nagasaki between the Christian farmers and the army of the shogun sealed the tragic fate of Christians in Japan at this time.

EDO ERA (1603-1868)

The third Tokugawa shogun, Iemitsu, closed all the ports of Japan, except Nagasaki, in 1639. His intentions were to shut out Christianity, and, at the same time, to monopolize foreign trade. Only Dutch and Chinese traders with no connections to missionaries were allowed to trade at a secluded area in Nagasaki. This isolationist period, which continued for over 200 years, until 1854, was also the longest peaceful era in Japanese history. By the middle of the 18th century, the population of Edo had increased to one million, the largest in the world at that time. Economic progress allowed even the common people to engage in cultural activities, and *ukiyo-e* (woodblock prints) and *haiku* (short stylized poems) achieved great popularity.

By the middle of the 19th century, the rigid feudal system had become an obstacle to development of a modern economy. Despite their low social status, the merchants had real economic power and became underground supporters of a new, freer social system. In 1853, Commodore Perry of the United States brought his fleet to Uraga, near Yokohama, and demanded the opening of Japanese ports for the supply of commodities to foreign fleets, and for international trade in general. The advanced technological level of the West that Perry and his sailors demonstrated helped make the people aware of the need for change. After civil wars between the conservative Shogunate forces, and those who wanted a new order (these included members of the imperial family and the innovative feudal lords of western Japan), the 15th Tokugawa shogun, Yoshinobu, returned the reins of government to Emperor Meiji. This historic event of 1868 is referred to as the Meiji Restoration.

MODERN ERA
(Meiji, Taisho, Showa and the current Heisei Eras 1868-)

The new imperial government aggressively took the initiative in importing Western culture, technology and social structures. Japan's new government also invested heavily in and promoted industrialization. Despite the many changes that accompanied this modernization, the nation's traditional, unequal social structure survived. Sovereignty rested with the Emperor and, ultimately, he possessed all power. Only aristocrats could be members of the House of Chancellors and only men who paid taxes above a certain level were eligible to vote for members of the House of Representatives (Women gained the right to vote in 1925). After the tragedy of World War II, a genuine democratization took place in Japan under a new Constitution. The emperor was declared to be merely symbolic of the spirit of the nation. Elected officials, wielding all political power, ushered in a period marked by unparalleled efforts and crowned by achievement of genuine social equality and phenomenal economic growth and success.

KANTO REGION

関東

Except for the approximately 100 years of the Kamakura Era (13th century), the Kanto Region was Japan's less developed area, and the Kansai (Kyoto/Nara/Osaka) Region prospered as the nation's political, economic and cultural center. The Kanto became the nation's focal point when Ieyasu Tokugawa established his Shogunate in Edo (Tokyo) in 1603. After the Meiji Restoration in 1868, the capital was officially moved to Tokyo, and since that time, the Kanto has developed into one of the world's largest and most advanced urban areas.

Tokyo is Japan's New York, Washington, Chicago, Los Angeles and San Francisco all rolled into one. It is the seat of Government, the nation's business capital and the center for international finance, education, communications, transportation and fashion. It is a giant magnet for the Japanese people, and one in every three of them now live in the Kanto Region. Its fast pace, its population density, its drastic space limitations and its astronomical real estate prices make New York seem relatively slow, empty, spacious and reasonably priced. Be prepared for an encounter with fast-moving urban life of the future.

We have divided the Kanto Region into three zones as described below.

I. Tokyo Core

Tokyo consists of the 23 urban wards (*ku*) and its suburbs. These 23 wards are similar to the five boroughs of New York City. The area including the 23 wards is generally considered "Tokyo City," though there is no official or administrative unit so named. There is neither a Mayor of Tokyo nor a Tokyo City Council. The Governor of Tokyo is the chief of Tokyo Prefecture (the administrative equivalent of New York State). Each ward has its chief administrator and its own council. We describe twelve interesting districts of "Tokyo City," focusing on the areas inside and immediately outside the JR Yamanote Loop Line. This is the area generally considered "Tokyo," just as Manhattan, for non-residents, is "New York." The area contains Japan's central government offices, major corporate headquarters, financial institutions, shopping and fashion centers, fabulous (and expensive!)

MAP 1   Outline of Kanto

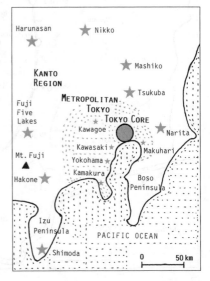

nightlife zones, and several areas of historic and cultural interest.

II. Metropolitan Tokyo

This area includes the suburbs of Tokyo administered with the central core of the city, as well as satellite cities in neighboring Kanagawa, Saitama and Chiba Prefectures. Most of the residents of these areas commute to the Tokyo Core. Each of these areas is struggling to create its identity as an independent community. These areas feature several large projects developed to attract international meetings and conferences. You

are most likely to visit these areas if you attend such a conference or a trade show. There are also several attractions that work as half-day or full-day excursions from Tokyo Core. Six areas are described in detail: (1) Yokohoma; (2) Kamakura; (3) Kawasaki; (4) Chiba (Makuhari Messe); (5) Urayasu (Tokyo Disneyland); and (6) Kawagoe.

III. Kanto Destinations

There are several important and exciting tourist destinations along the border of the Kanto Region. These places are ideal for long full-day excursions or overnight trips

MAP 2 Tokyo Core

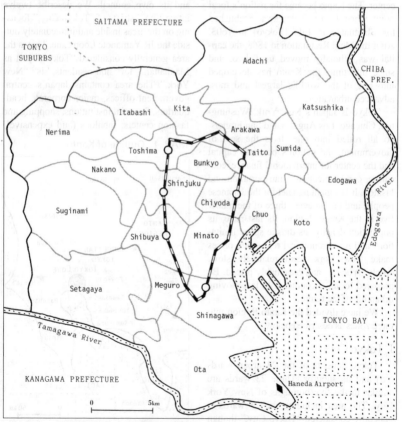

from Tokyo. Izu Peninsula actually belongs to the Chubu Region, but we introduce Izu in this chapter. Izu Peninsula is more easily accessible from Tokyo, and is generally considered an oasis for Tokyoites. We describe the following nine destinations: (1) Hakone; (2) Izu Peninsula; (3) Fuji Five Lakes; (4) Nikko; (5) Mashiko; (6) Tsukuba; (7) Narita; (8) Boso Penisnula; and (9) Mt. Harunasan and Ikaho Onsen.

Tokyo Core 都心

As explained in the introduction to Kanto, "Tokyo City" consists of 23 urban wards. But what people usually mean when they say "Tokyo" is the area inside and just outside the JR Yamanote Loop Line, an area 7 km (4.5 miles) from east to west and 12 km (7.6 miles) from north to south. Most places you're likely to visit in Tokyo (hotels, business contacts and places of interest) are likely to be in one of the following nine wards (*ku*): Chiyoda, Chuo, Minato, Shinagawa, Shibuya, Shinjuku, Toshima, Bunkyo and Taito. Kanto Map 3 compares the central part of Tokyo with Manhattan and should give you a good idea of the size of the city. Tokyo is much newer than most Japanese cities. Its real development only began in 1603 when Ieyasu Tokugawa, the first Tokugawa shogun, selected the town then known as Edo as headquarters of his military government. During the 265-year reign of the Tokugawas, Edo functioned as the nation's administrative center even though Kyoto, the home of the emperors, remained the nominal capital. After the Imperial forces regained power in 1868 (the Meiji Restoration), Edo officially became the capital and was renamed Tokyo (eastern Kyoto or eastern capital). Emperor Meiji moved to Tokyo and established his court in what had been the Shogun's Edojo Castle. Unlike the Tokugawa Shogunate, which had kept the nation isolated from the rest of the world, the new government aggressively imported advanced Western technology and scientific knowledge and worked to develop modern industries. Tokyo was devastated in World War II, but was rebuilt quickly (and, some say, haphazardly). Today it is an ultra-modern city rushing toward the 21st century. The Tokyo area has a population of 11,632,000. It is the nation's political, economic, commercial, financial, education, communications and entertainment capital.

MAP 3
Relative Size of Tokyo to New York

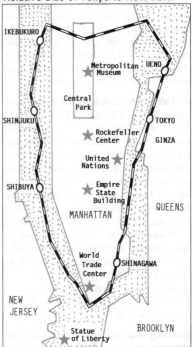

TOKYO DISTRICT BY DISTRICT

It is often said that Tokyo is a combination of several "cities within the city." We have selected twelve of the most interesting districts. They are listed here in the order in which they are introduced in the text that follows (all references are to Kanto Map 4):

1. Asakusa   (upper right) is famous for its Sensoji (Kannon) Temple. It is one of the few areas that preserves the nostalgic atmosphere of Tokyo's old *shitamachi* downtown.

2. Ueno   (upper right) is the cultural capital of Tokyo. The Tokyo National Museum, Metropolitan Festival Hall, the Zoological Garden and other cultural facilities are located in spacious Ueno-Koen Park. Nearby Ameya-Yokocho Shopping Street is a kitchen for Tokyoites and a good place to understand the daily lifestyle of Tokyo's people.

3. Ginza and Hibiya   (middle right). Ginza is Tokyo's Fifth Avenue: it has huge department stores, elegant shops, a variety of restaurants and expense-account-only bars and night clubs. Hibiya features many movie houses and theaters. The Tsukiji Central Fish Market is also in this area.

4. Tokyo Station and Vicinity   (middle right). Tokyo Station is JR's largest train station, with four Shinkansens (Tokaido-Sanyo, Joetsu, Tohoku and Yamagata), many long distance trains and a number of commuter trains. Marunouchi and Otemachi (western side of Tokyo Station) are the nation's business center and home of the headquarters of many major Japanese corporations. The Imperial Palace is to the west of Marunouchi. On the eastern side of Tokyo Station are Yaesu and Nihombashi, Tokyo's financial district and home of the Tokyo Stock Exchange. Tokyo City Air Terminal (TCAT), the terminus of the Airport Limousine Bus to/from Narita Airport, is also in this area.

5. Shinjuku   (middle left) is home of the Tokyo Metropolitan Government and is Tokyo's new "downtown." Shinjuku Station, used by more than 3 million every day, is Japan's largest commuter terminus. Western Shinjuku is home of most of the city's skyscrapers. Eastern Shinjuku has two faces — one as a fashionable shopping center with department stores, specialty shops and restaurants; and the other as a bustling night-time risque playground that is especially attractive to the young.

6. Ikebukuro   (upper left) is one of Tokyo's largest shopping and nightlife areas. But because most of its habitues are commuters from Saitama Prefecture (who are roughly the equivalent of the "bridge and tunnel" crowd of New York City), Ikebukuro has also been considered rather second-rate. Sunshine City, one of Tokyo's tallest buildings, has the city's best observatory.

7. Shibuya   (middle left), another commuter terminus, was once known for its inexpensive shops, restaurants and pubs. Now this area is known for its fashionable shopping and entertainment.

8. Harajuku and Aoyama   (middle left). Harajuku, home of Meiji Jingu Shrine, is also a fashion center for teenagers. Aoyama is an adult fashion center that boasts of famous name shops and boutiques. National Stadium and Jingu Baseball Stadium are not far from Aoyama. Omote-sando Boulevard, which connects Aoyama with Harajuku, is a lovely tree-lined promenade, and an ideal place for a leisurely stroll.

9. Akasaka and Kasumigaseki (middle center). Akasaka is a world famous night spot with an astonishing concentration of high-class restautants and other entertainment facilities. Kasumigaseki is the political and administrative center of Japan. Most government offices are located in Kasumigaseki, and the Diet Building in nearby Nagatacho.

MAP 4 Outline of Tokyo's Core

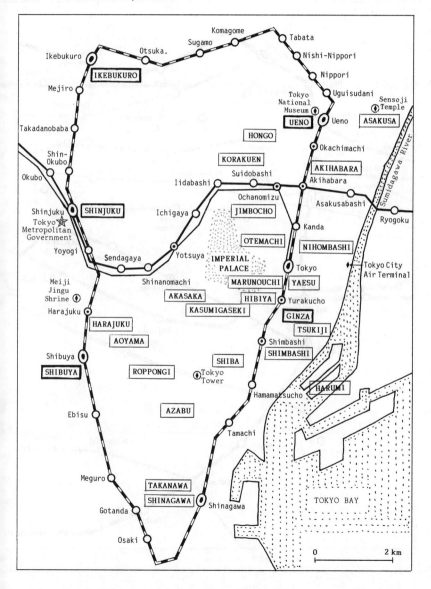

MAP 5 Tokyo's Transportation Network

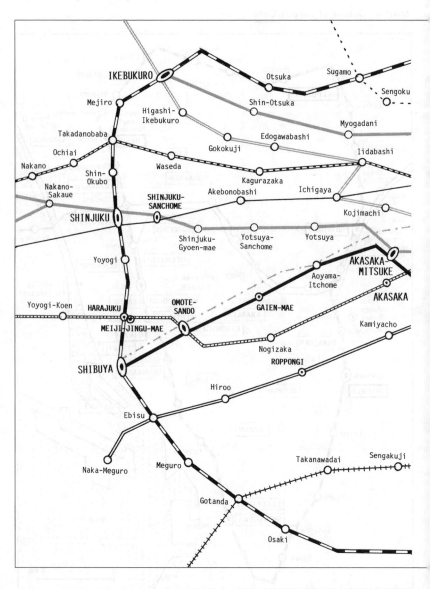

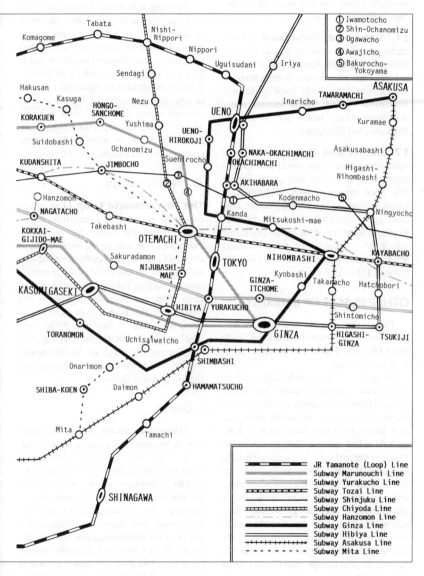

Legend (top right):
① Iwamotocho
② Shin-Ochanomizu
③ Ogawacho
④ Awajicho
⑤ Bakurocho-Yokoyama

Line legend:
- JR Yamanote (Loop) Line
- Subway Marunouchi Line
- Subway Yurakucho Line
- Subway Tozai Line
- Subway Shinjuku Line
- Subway Chiyoda Line
- Subway Hanzomon Line
- Subway Ginza Line
- Subway Hibiya Line
- Subway Asakusa Line
- Subway Mita Line

10. Roppongi (middle center) is another high-class night spot, popular with the relatively young and with many of the foreign residents of Tokyo.

11. Shiba and Shinagawa (lower center) are in the southern part of the city. This area is still, for the most part, a residential area (very prestigious). Shiba is home to Tokyo Tower, the World Trade Center and Shibarikyu Garden. Azabu features many embassies. Many hotels are located in Takanawa and Shinagawa.

12. Kanda and Korakuen (upper right). Akihabara is the world famous discount paradise for electronic goods. Jimbocho, once synomous with bookstores, is losing its status as Japan's book center. Discount sports shops are taking over the area. Korakuen is the site of the Tokyo Dome (the "Big Egg" — Japan's first indoor stadium) and Korakuen Playground. Nearby Hongo is home of Tokyo University.

OTHER PLACES OF INTEREST

Harumi (lower right), an artificial island, is the site of the Tokyo International Trade Show Grounds. This exhibition venue is not far from the Ginza.

Ryogoku (middle right) is the site of Kokugikan (National Martial Arts Hall), home of professional sumo wrestling. There are six official sumo tournaments each year, each lasting for fifteen days. Three of them are held in Kokugikan in Tokyo (in January, May and September). The others are held in Osaka (in March), in Nagoya (in July) and in Fukuoka (in November). Nowadays more and more sumo wrestlers hail from Hawaii and Micronesia. These foreign wrestlers have achieved high status in Japan and helped to popularize this uniquely Japanese sport abroad. Akebono, a Hawaiian wrestler, became the first foreign-born Grand Champion in 1993.

TOKYO'S TRANSPORTATION NETWORK

To transport millions of commuters from suburban areas to the city, Tokyo has developed extensive railway and subway networks. For tourists, however, many of them have little value. To avoid confusion and to give you a clear idea of which of Tokyo's public transportaiton facilities will be useful to you, only one essential JR line and ten essential subway lines are pictured on Kanto Map 5. Note that this map is not drawn to scale. In relationship to its north-south axis, the east-west axis is twice the size it should be.

JR (Japan Railways)

The JR Yamanote Loop Line (green cars or silver cars with green stripes): The line surrounds the central part of Tokyo. There are 29 stations on the loop. All trains stop at all stations. It takes about one hour to make the trip around the loop. All important stations, such as Tokyo, Yurakucho, Shinagawa, Shibuya, Shinjuku, Ikebukuro and Ueno are on this loop line. In most JR stations, the name of this line, "Yamanote Line" and the direction of the train, e.g., "for Shibuya and Shinjuku" or "for Shimbashi and Tokyo" are written in both Japanese and English on many signboards.

Subways

Entrances are clearly marked "subway" in both Japanese and English. At large stations, such as Shinjuku, Ginza and Otemachi, long underground passages connect the platforms of the various lines. There are also signs in English on every subway platform. Tokyo subway maps and fare boards show each line with a different color, and the trains themsleves are painted to coordinate. If you ever have difficulty finding the subway you want, you should go back to the surface and walk to the approximate location of the station as pictured on the map.

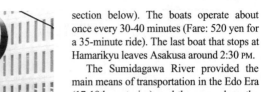

section below). The boats operate about once every 30-40 minutes (Fare: 520 yen for a 35-minute ride). The last boat that stops at Hamarikyu leaves Asakusa around 2:30 PM.

The Sumidagawa River provided the main means of transportation in the Edo Era (17-19th centuries), and the areas along the river were, at that time, the most prosperous in the city. The center of Tokyo moved west only with the development of the railroad and other surface transportation. The view from the boat is not particularly noteworthy, but the ride is an interesting way to see the face this huge city never shows to the casual tourist.

The private Tobu Railways operates special trains from Tobu-Asakusa Station (in the Matsuya Department Store building, middle right, Kanto Map 6) to Tobu-Nikko. See the Nikko Chapter below.

Sensoji Temple 浅草寺 (Upper center, Kanto Map 6)

Kaminarimon Gate is the entrance to the main approach to the Temple. Gods of Wind and Thunder stand in niches on both sides of the Gate, and a 3.3 m (11 foot) red lantern hangs from it. Both sides of the main approach, called Nakamise-dori Street, are lined with souvenir shops decorated with colorful small lanterns. Shin-Nakamise Shopping Arcade is lined with modern stores, restaurants and traditional souvenir shops. At the western end of the arcade are many movie houses and other theaters reminiscent of the old Asakusa. The Rox building is the center of this entertainment section of Asakusa. Hanayashiki Playland (upper center) is a family amusement park.

Kappabashi-dori Street 合羽橋商店街 (Extreme left)

Both sides of this street are lined with shops selling various restaurant products such as lacquerware, pottery, small decorative objects (lanterns, umbrellas), *noren* (entryway curtains) and traditional Japanese

ASAKUSA 浅草

Asakusa has prospered as a temple town throughout Japanese history. Sensoji Temple (popularly known as Asakusa Kannon Temple) is the oldest temple in Tokyo. Until recently Asakusa was also the entertainment center of Tokyo, and was especially famous for comedy and "all girl" revues. Though tastes in entertainment have changed, and the city's pleasure districts now have new locations, Asakusa stubbornly preserves the nostalgic atmosphere of the traditional *shitamachi* downtown of the common people.

For transportation to Asakusa, take either the Ginza or the Asakusa subway line. You can also take a boat. We recommend it if you plan to visit Hamarikyu as well as Asakusa. The boat operates between Asakusa and Hinode Pier (10 minutes walk from Hamamatsucho Station on the JR Yamanote Line) via Hamarikyu. Boats do not stop at Hamarikyu on Monday because the Garden is closed on Monday (See Ginza

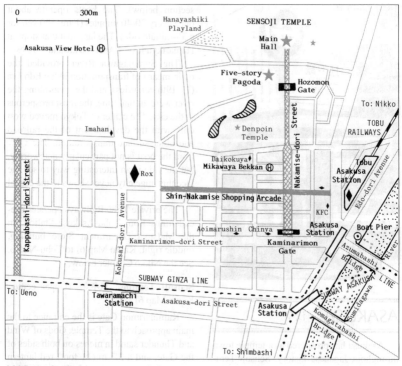

MAP 6 Asakusa

paintings as well as the menu stands of traditional Japanese restaurants and the plastic food models used in many modern Japanese restaurants and coffee shops. Though the primary clients of these stores are restaurant owners, retail sales to the general public are also made. The southern part of Kappabashi is especially interesting. Exploring here you'll find many items much more interesting than ordinary souvenir shop wares.

Restaurants in Asakusa

Try authentic Japanese cuisine in this nostalgic downtown. Each of the following are in the moderate price range. Chinya (middle center) is famous for *sukiyaki* and *shabu-shabu*. Aoimarushin (middle center) is famous throughout Japan as *the* restaurant

for *tempura*. The higher up you go in this seven-story restaurant, the better the facilities become, and the higher the prices go. Daikokuya (middle center) is another famous traditional *tempura* restaurant. Imahan (upper left) is another big-name *sukiyaki* restaurant.

UENO 上野

Ueno Station is one of Tokyo's largest terminals. The JR Joetsu, Tohoku and Yamagata Shinkansens, which originate at Tokyo Station, also stop here on their way out of the metropolis. Other northbound long distance JR trains originate here. You can reach Ueno on the JR Yamanote Loop

Line, and the Ginza and Hibiya subway lines.

Ueno-Koen Park 上野公園

Ueno-Koen Park is a spacious wooded area to the west of Ueno Station. Several museums, a concert hall, Ueno Zoo and other cultural institutions are located there.

Tokyo National Museum 東京国立博物館 (upper right, Kanto Map 7) consists of the following halls: **The Main Hall**, which houses Japanese fine and applied arts; **The Gallery of Oriental Antiquities**, which features historical and artistic objects of China, India and other Asian countries; **The Hyokeikan Gallery**, which specializes in Japanese archeological relics; and **The Gallery of Horyuji Treasures**, which contains the priceless Buddhist treasures of Nara's Horyuji Temple. Hours: 9:00 AM to 4:30 PM. Closed on Mondays. The Gallery of Horyuji Treasures is open only on Thursdays. Even on Thursdays, if it is rainy or very humid, the Gallery may be closed in order to protect the fragile relics. Admission: 360 yen.

Ueno Zoo 上野動物園 (upper center) is home to about 8,300 animals from all over the world. The most popular animals here are the pandas presented by the Chinese government. A monorail connects the Aquarium with the main grounds. Hours: 9:30 AM to 4:00 PM. Closed on Mondays. Admission: 400 yen.

The National Science Museum 国立科学博物館 (upper right) is the Japanese version of New York's Natural History Museum. Hours: 9:00 AM to 4:30 PM. Closed on Mondays. Admission: 360 yen.

The National Museum of Western Art 国立西洋美術館 (upper right) contains carvings and statues, many of them by Rodin, as well as a number of paintings of the French Impressionist school. Hours: 9:30 AM to 5:00 PM. Closed on Mondays. Admission: 360 yen.

Metropolitan Festival Hall 東京文化会館 (middle right) is the mecca for classical music concerts, operas and ballet performances.

The Metropolitan Art Museum 東京都美術館 (upper center) is mainly used for exhibitions of the works of younger Japanese artists.

Toshogu Shrine 東照宮 (upper center) was built in 1627 to honor the spirit of Ieyasu Tokugawa, the first Tokugawa Shogun. The structure is painted vermilion and decorated with gold foil and numerous carvings. Both sides of the approach are lined with many stone lanterns. Hours: 9:30 AM to 5:00 PM. Admission: 200 yen.

Shinobazu-no-ike Pond 不忍池 (middle center): On your way down to the hill to Shinobazu-no-ike Pond, you will pass through numerous small red *torii* gates that lead to the precincts of Hanazono Jinja Shrine. On an island in the center of the pond stands a small hall called Bentendo. This hall contains the image of Benzaiten, the goddess of wealth. We assume that paying one's respects can only be a good idea!

Shitamachi Museum 下町博物館 (lower center): This small two-story museum was founded in 1980 thanks to the efforts of the people of the Ueno area. It features various objects used in the daily life of the people in the late 19th and early 20th centuries. Reconstructed buildings, including a modest residence, a merchant's showroom and a candy shop, are on display, along with related utensils. Visitors can get an idea of the lost life of the *Edokko* (children of Tokyo) who lived in the traditional *shitamachi* downtown. Hours: 9:30 AM to 4:30 PM. Closed on Mondays. Admission: 200 yen.

Ameya-Yokocho Street アメヤ横町
(Lower right)

The area wedged between the JR Yamanote tracks and Chuo-dori Street (under which the Subway Ginza Line runs) is Ueno's main shopping district. Matsuzakaya Department Store is the largest and most

MAP 7 Ueno

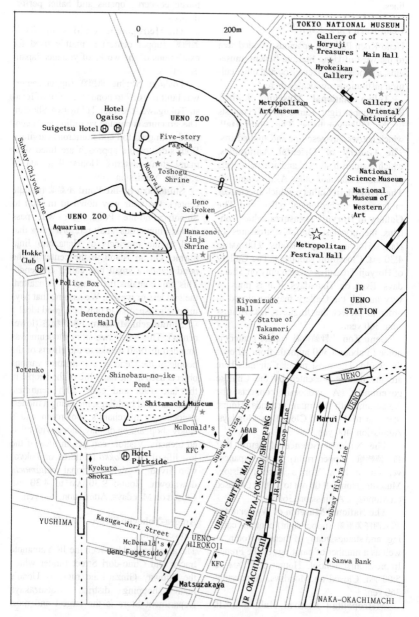

TOKYO NATIONAL MUSEUM

Gallery of Horyuji Treasures

Main Hall

Hyokeikan Gallery

Gallery of Oriental Antiquities

Metropolitan Art Museum

National Science Museum

National Museum of Western Art

Metropolitan Festival Hall

0   200m

Hotel Ogaiso
Suigetsu Hotel

UENO ZOO

Five-story Pagoda

Monorail

Toshogu Shrine

Ueno Seiyoken

Hanazono Jinja Shrine

UENO ZOO
Aquarium

Subway Chiyoda Line

Hokke Club

Police Box

Bentendo Hall

Kiyomizudo Hall

Statue of Takamori Saigo

JR UENO STATION

UENO

UENO

Marui

Totenko

Shinobazu-no-ike Pond

Shitamachi Museum

McDonald's

ABAB

Subway Ginza Line

UENO CENTER MALL

AMEYA-YOKOCHO SHOPPING ST

JR Yamanote Loop Line

Subway Hibiya Line

KFC

Hotel Parkside

Kyokuto Shokai

YUSHIMA

Kasuga-dori Street

McDonald's
Ueno Fugetsudo

UENO HIROKOJI

KFC

Matsuzakaya

JR OKACHIMACHI

Sanwa Bank

NAKA-OKACHIMACHI

prestigious business in the area. Ameya-Yokocho Shopping Street is a narrow lane along the west side of the elevated JR tracks between Ueno and Okachimachi Stations (lower center). The area was originally developed as a wholesale market for candies and snacks. *Ameya* means candy store, and *Yokocho* meals narrow lane. Nowadays, the shopping street is lined with about 400 retail discount stores that sell food, clothing, jewelry, sporting goods, etc. The area always has a festive atmosphere, especially in the late afternoon, when housewives crowd the shops to purchase what they need for the family dinner. Walk down the crowded alley to experience something of the casual, everyday life of the people of Tokyo.

Restaurants

Ueno Seiyoken (middle center) opened right after the Meiji Restoration in 1868 and introduced Western cuisine to Japan. The grill is located in a quiet corner of Ueno-Koen Park and overlooks Shinobazu-no-ike Pond. Rather expensive, but quality is excellent. Totenko (middle left): This eight-story Chinese restaurant is proud of its fantastic view of Shinobazu-no-ike Pond and the thickly wooded Ueno-Koen Park. The 7th floor grill serves a fine lunch (moderate). Ueno Fugetsudo (lower center) is famous for its *kasutera* sponge cake (which is retailed all over Japan). You can enjoy this famous delicacy in the first-floor cafe. The second floor serves Western food, such as

beef stew and salmon steak (moderate). Immediately to the west of Ameya-Yokocho Street is **Ueno Center Mall** (lower center), a discount shopping center featuring a wide variety of consumer goods. It is also the home of a large number of inexpensive restaurants.

GINZA AND HIBIYA
銀座・日比谷

Ginza literally means silver mint. The area was so named when the Tokugawa Shogunate built its mint here in 1612. Instead of minting silver coins, the area now collects millions and millions of yen every day from the customers who patronize its many stores, restaurants and bars. No one visiting Tokyo should skip the Ginza. It is Tokyo's Fifth Avenue, Champs Elysees and Regent Street. You can reach the Ginza easily from every part of Tokyo: on the JR Yamanote Loop Line (Yurakucho Station); on the Marunouchi, Ginza and Hibiya subways lines (Ginza Stations); on the Subway Yurakucho Line (Ginza-Itchome Station); and on the Subway Asakusa Line (Higashi-Ginza Station). Refer to Kanto Map 8.

Outline of District

The Ginza 銀座 is a rectangular area sandwiched between Sotobori-dori Street (which runs parallel to the JR Yamanote Loop Line tracks) on the northwest and Showa-dori Street on the southeast (under which the Subway Asakusa Line runs). The area is divided into eight long rectangular zones by narrower street that run perpendicular to these boundaries; these narrow blocks are numbered 1-chome through 8-chome. The center of the Ginza is the large intersection made by Chuo-dori Street and Harumi-dori Street. The famous round building (San-ai) and clock tower are located at this intersection. Many department stores and specialty shops line Chuo-dori Street. The department stores include Melsa,

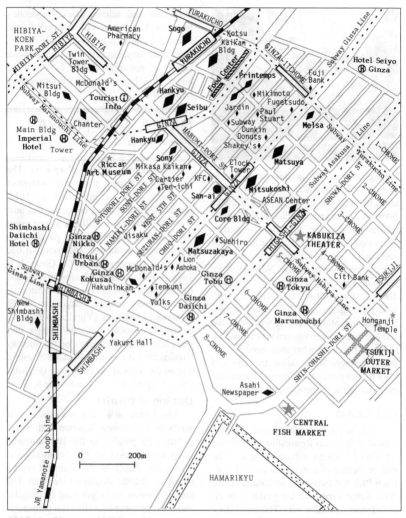

MAP 8 Ginza and Hibiya

Matsuya, Mitsukoshi and Matsuzakaya. Noteworthy specialty shops include Mikimoto (upper center), which is world famous for its pearls, and famous foreign establishments such as Paul Stuart (upper center) and Cartier (middle center), as well as Ginza Hakuhinkan (middle left), which specializes

in toys. Chuo-dori is always crowded with window shoppers. The area is closed to traffic on Saturdays (3:00 PM to 6:00 PM) and on Sundays (12 noon to 6:00 PM).

To the northwest of the Ginza is **Yurakucho** 有楽町 (around the JR Yurakucho Station), with many modern office buildings, as well as other department stores, including Printemps, Seibu, Hankyu (2 stores) and Sogo.

Hibiya 日比谷 is a theater and restaurant district. Many foreign airlines have offices in this area. American Pharmacy (upper left) sells a wide variety of Western over-the-counter medicines. International Arcade is near the Imperial Hotel, under the elevated JR tracks. It houses a number of small boutiques and shops that sell everything from traditional handicrafts to the newest electronics. It is rather expensive and is touristy to the extreme, but undeniably convenient for those with little time to spare. **Hibiya-Koen Park** (upper left) is an oasis for the *Ginzakko* (Ginza native and habitues). Spacious gardens are arranged around a large pond, and the Park contains an open-air concert hall, a public hall and a library. A French restaurant named Matsumotoro is Tokyo's version of "Tavern on the Green" in New York's Central Park. To the north of Subway Hibiya Station is the Outer Garden of the Imperial Palace. See the Tokyo Station and Vicinity section below.

There are extensive underground passages linking the subway and rail stations. It is possible to walk underground all the way from Subway Hibiya Station (upper left, Kanto Map 8) to Subway Higashi-Ginza Station (middle right). The underground passageways house many inexpensive restaurants and coffee shops.

Tourist Information Center (T.I.C.)
(Upper left, Kanto Map 8)

The Japanese government's free Tourist Information Center is located on Harumi-dori Street near the elevated JR tracks. This is one of the three T.I.C.'s operated by the Japan National Tourist Organization (the others are located at Narita Airport and in Kyoto). JNTO's toll-free travel phone is answered at the Tokyo and Kyoto T.I.C.'s. T.I.C. can arrange Home Visits. Hours: 9:00 AM to 5:00 PM. Closed on Saturdays and Sundays.

Kabukiza Theater 歌舞伎座 (Middle right, Kanto Map 8)

The kabuki drama has a four hundred year history. Of the many traditional Japanese theater arts (kabuki, noh, *kyogen*, *bunraku* and *gagaku*), kabuki is probably the most accessible for foreigners. It is famous for its colorful stage settings and stylized acting style. There are no actresses in kabuki plays, and the female impersonators are among the most renowned of kabuki actors. Matinees start at 11:00 AM, and evening performances at 5:00 PM. Admission ranges from 2,500 yen to 16,000 yen. You can rent an English language "Earphone-guide." Reservations can be made through your hotel or you can call the Kabukiza Theater at 3541-3131.

Kabuki is also often presented at the **National Theater (Kokuritsu Gekijo)** 国立劇場 in Kasumigaseki (See the Akasaka and Kasumigaseki section below; upper center, Kanto Map 14). Telephone: 3265-7411. Kabuki is also presented occasionally at **Sunshine Theater** サンシャイン劇場 in Ikebukuro (See the Ikebukuro Section below; middle right, Kanto Map 11 — in Cultural Hall in the Sunshine City Complex). Telephone: 3987-5281.

If you want to sample noh, you should check with JNTO's T.I.C. Tokyo has more than a dozen small noh theaters that offer occasional performances of this classic theater art.

Museums in the Area

Riccar Art Museum リッカー美術館 (upper left, Kanto Map 8) is famous for its collection of *ukiyo-e*, Japanese wood-block prints. Hours: 11:00 AM to 6:00 PM. Closed on Mondays. Admission: 400 yen.

Idemitsu Museum 出光美術館 (a 2-minute walk north of Yurakucho Station — outside the upper center of Kanto Map 8) is located on the ninth floor of its building. The museum specializes in Japanese and Asian (mostly Chinese) antiquities, and is especially renowned for its collection of pottery and ceramics. Hours: 10:00 AM to 5:00 PM. Admission: 500 yen.

Restaurants

A number of small restaurants are located on the second floor of Yuraku Food Center near JR Yurakucho Station (under the expressway). They feature all sorts of cuisines, from Japanese and Chinese, to Italian and Continental, at very reasonable prices. You can also find a number of reasonable restaurants in the basement of the Kotsu Kaikan Building (upper center, Kanto Map 8).

Tenkuni (middle center, Kanto Map 8) and Ten-ichi (middle center) are prestigious and expensive *tempura* restaurants. Jardin (upper center) serves moderately priced French home-style food. Suehiro and Volks (both middle center) are famous for their reasonable steaks. Maison de France and Totenko are located in Twin Tower Building (upper left). The former is a famous, moderately-priced French restaurant, and

the latter a moderate Chinese restaurant. Lion (middle center) is a beer hall-style restaurant with an extensive menu. Mikasa Kaikan (middle center) houses several famous restaurants: Haruna is an excellent French restaurant and Yamato is a steak and seafood restaurant (both expensive). Maharao, which serves reasonable Indian food, is in the basement of the Mitsui Building (upper left), which also has a number of other restaurants that cater to the lunchtime office worker crowd. Ashoka (lower center) is another Indian restaurant with higher prices.

If you're on a lavish expense account and want to sample Tokyo's best, visit the Imperial Hotel. All of the hotel's many restaurants are top-notch: Fountainbleu features exquisite French cuisine; Kitcho and Nadaman are authentic Japanese restaurants that serve traditional *kaiseki* multi-course meals; Nakata is famous for *sushi*; and Peking serves excellent Chinese food.

TSUKIJI 築地

Tsukiji Central Fish Market 築地中央卸売市場 (lower right, Kanto Map 8): This wholesale market handles all the fish and meat consumed in the Tokyo area. Because the overwhelming volume of trade is in fish and fish products, it is popularly called the Central Fish Market. The business between the fishermen and the wholesalers is conducted early in the morning, between 5:20 AM and 6:00 AM. From 6:00 AM to 9:00 AM the market is crowded with purchasers from retail stores and restaurants. The many small restaurants in the market serve *sushi*, *tempura*, *noodles*, etc. The restaurants are busy, noisy, no-frills affairs, but the food is excellent and they are inexpensive. The Market is closed on Sundays and holidays, on August 15 and 16, and for the New Year's Holidays.

Tsukiji Outer Market 築地場外市場: Small shops that sell fish, other foodstuffs and various consumer products crowd the

narrow lanes near the Central Fish Market. The Outer Market is for members of the general public who want small quantities of the freshest food and other inexpensive items. This is one of the two best places to learn about what goes home in shopping baskets to the kitchens of typical Tokyoites, with Ameya-Yokocho being the other (See Ueno section above).

HAMARIKYU 浜離宮 (Lower center, Kanto Map 8)

This Garden was built about 335 years ago at the order of Tsunashige Matsudaira, a feudal lord. Later, it was ceded to the sixth Tokugawa shogun, Ienobu, who used it for duck hunting. After the Meiji Restoration the Garden became the property of the Imperial Household Agency and was used for outdoor parties for the nobles and for receptions for foreign guests of honor. General Ulysses S. Grant, the 18th President of the United States, was entertained here when he visited Japan. Later, the Garden was given to the Tokyo Metropolitan Government and opened to the public. Hours: 9:00 AM to 4:30 PM. Closed on Mondays. Admission: 200 yen. Shimbashi is the JR Yamanote Loop Line station closest to Hamarikyu Garden (800 m or 0.5 miles).

Boats from Hamarikyu Garden pier to Asakusa operate about once every 30-40 minutes. See Asakusa Section above.

TOKYO STATION AND VICINITY   東京駅周辺

Tokyo Station (middle center, Kanto Map 9) is the central point for all transportation in Japan. Four JR Shinkansen Lines originate here: Tokaido-Sanyo Shinkansen, Joetsu Shinkansen, Tohoku Shinkansen and Yamagata Shinkansen. It is also the terminus for JR long distance trains to all points west of Tokyo and to the Boso Peninsula. In addition, it is served by the JR Narita Express, which connects the international airport with downtown in one hour (thus making it possible to connect directly to the airport from cities outside Tokyo and the Kanto Region). Note that the terminus for the JR Keiyo Line is about 500 m (1,640 feet) from the central terminal building (there is an underground passageway). The JR Keiyo Line connects Tokyo with Makuhari Messe International Convention and Exhibition Center and Tokyo Disneyland. In addition, the JR Yamanote Loop Line, the JR Keihin-Tohoku Line, the JR Chuo Line and the Subway Marunouchi Line provide local transportation links with other parts of Tokyo. The Station itself and its underground passageways are huge, sprawling and unbelievably complex. It is impossible to draw an understandable map of the Station, and it is easy to get lost. The Station is, however, well marked with many signs in English, and you should be able to find your way around if you are careful and patient. It is nevertheless wise to leave yourself extra time to navigate the Station.

MARUNOUCHI AND OTEMACHI
丸の内・大手町

Marunouchi 丸の内 is the area sandwiched between the Imperial Palace moats and the JR lines. Before it was developed, the area was known as Mitsubishi Meadow,

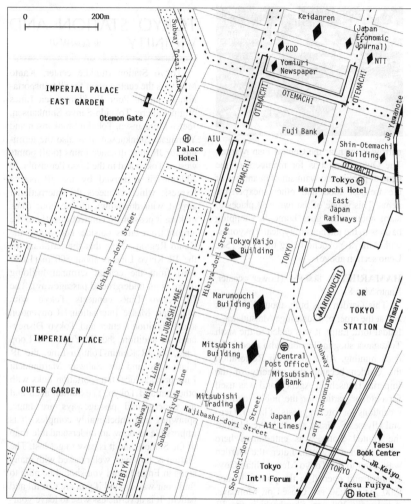

MAP 9 Tokyo Station and Vicinity

and it is now home to many corporate headquarters, especially those of the Mitsubishi conglomerate. For tourists, Marunouchi is really nothing more than rows of modern office buildings. But it is the place to observe Japan's business elite in their natural habitat. A large construction project is under way at the former venue of the Tokyo

Metropolitan Government (which is now in Shinjuku). The area will be a new international meeting and exhibition center called **Tokyo International Forum**.

Otemachi 大手町 is the home of Keidanren (Japanese Federation of Economic Organizations) (upper center), Japan's most powerful business, finance and commerce

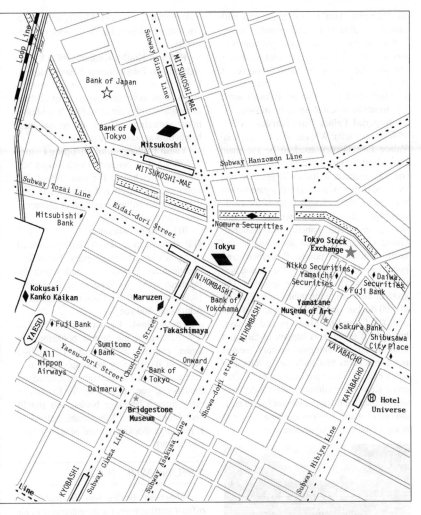

organization. It is widely considered the driving force of Japan's economic juggernaut. Otemachi is also a communications center. It is the home of Yomiuri Shimbun, the world's largest newspaper, Nikkei Shimbun (Japan Economic Journal), and KDD and NTT, Japan's telecommunications giants.

IMPERIAL PALACE 皇居

Imperial Palace Outer Garden 皇居外苑 (lower left, Kanto Map 9). This part of the Imperial Palace compound is actually closer to and more easily accessible from Subway Hibiya Station (See Ginza and Hibiya Section above). The Outer Garden (often called the "Imperial Plaza") is a spacious park with numerous pine trees and pebble-covered pedestrian paths. The area is popular with tourists, both Japanese and foreign, during the daytime, and with amorous couples in the evening. If you are a camera fan, the shot of Nijubashi Bridge with the Palace's turret and moats behind it is not to be missed.

Imperial Palace East Garden 皇居東御苑 (upper left). What is now the Imperial Palace East Garden used to be the main grounds of Edojo Castle. Otemon Gate was the main entrance to the castle grounds, and even today most visitors use this gate to visit the East Garden. Though most of the castle buildings were lost to repeated fires, the garden grounds still contain the Hundred-Guard Office, huge old stone walls, and neatly maintained ponds, flowerbeds and pine trees. The stone base of the donjon is at the northeastern end of the grounds. The grounds are open to the public from 9:00 AM to 4:00 PM, but visitors are not admitted after 3:00 PM. Closed on Mondays and Fridays, but open if those days happen to fall on a holiday. At the entrance visitors receive numbered cards that have to be turned in when exiting. There are three gates — Otemon, Kita-Hanebashimon (west side, outside of map) and Hirakawamon (north side, outside of map). Visitors can enter and exit at any of the three. Admission free.

YAESU 八重洲

The upper floors of the east (Yaesu) side of Tokyo Station house the Daimaru Department Store. Yaesu is the area to the east of Tokyo Station. As with Marunouchi, modern office buildings line both sides of wide streets.

Kokusai Kanko Kaikan 国際観光会館, right next to Tokyo Station, houses information offices of local prefectural governments. Free travel brochures (most of them in Japanese only) are available. In addition, many prefectural offices sell typical local handicrafts at reasonable prices.

Yaesu Underground Shopping Center 八重洲地下街 is connected with Tokyo Station and stretches to the east. About 200 stores and reasonable restaurants are located in this huge, confusing and rather characterless underground village.

Bridgestone Museum ブリヂストン美術館 (lower center, Kanto Map 9) is owned by Japan's largest tire company. The collection features Western art and works by Japanese artists in Western style. Hours: 10:00 AM. to 6:00 PM. Closed on Mondays. Admission: 500 yen.

Yaesu Book Center 八重洲ブックセンター, one of the largest bookstores in Japan, contains as many as 1.5 million books in its six-story building. There is a coffee shop on the mezzanine. Closed on Sundays. If you are looking for English or other foreign language books, you should visit Maruzen (See Nihonbashi, below) or Kinokuniya Bookstore (See Shinjuku Section below).

NIHONBASHI 日本橋

Nihonbashi Bridge was the traditional official starting point for measurement of all roads and travels in Japan during the Edo Era. For example, the distance on the Tokaido Road from Tokyo to Kyoto was measured from Nihonbashi Bridge, and all journeys were described and understood in terms of their distance from this ground zero starting point. Nihonbashi Bridge was the first of the famous fifty-three "stages" of the old Tokaido Road that connected Tokyo and

Kyoto. These stages were immortalized in the famous woodblock print series by the *ukiyo-e* master Hiroshige.

Modern Nihonbashi is a financial center, and functions as Japan's Wall Street. The neighborhood is home to the headquarters of the Bank of Japan, the national bank (upper center, Kanto Map 9) and the Bank of Tokyo, the country's largest international bank (upper center). Nihonbashi is also home to the headquarters of Japan's largest securities firms: Nomura, Nikko, Yamaichi and Daiwa (all middle right). **The Tokyo Stock Exchange** 東京証券取引所 (middle right) is open to visitors. Hours: 9:00 AM to 11:00 AM and 12:30 PM to 3:00 PM, Monday-Friday. Admission free. A visit to the Stock Exchange is quite interesting just in terms of the opportunity to witness the hurly-burly of trading. It is also interesting in light of the recent history of the Exchange, which was the source of controversy when foreign firms complained about the many difficulties they encountered listing their stock on the Exchange. The Exchange is in the process of trying to rehabilitate itself in the eyes of individual investors and the public at large in the wake of the scandal of the early 90's when it was discovered that securities houses had covered the losses of their largest and most influential corporate and institutional investors.

Nihonbashi is also home to three venerable department stores: Mitsukoshi (upper center), Tokyu (middle right) and Takashimaya (middle right). Visits to this area, where Japan's first department stores opened about a century ago, are a family tradition with many Tokyoites on special occasions. Nihonbashi is also the home of Maruzen (middle right), a bookstore with a very large inventory of foreign language books.

Yamatane Museum of Art 山種美術館 (middle right, Kanto Map 9) features Japanese style paintings from the Meiji through Heisei Eras. The collection was assembled by the late Chairman of the Yamatane Secu-

rities Company. Hours: 10:00 AM to 5:00 PM. Closed Mondays. Admission: 600 yen.

SHINJUKU   新宿

In the last twenty years, Shinjuku has undergone the most drastic changes of any area of Tokyo. Western Shinjuku used to be nothing more than a sleepy small town whose only claim to fame was that it was the location of the reservoirs that provided millions of Tokyoites with their water. But starting with the completion of Keio Plaza Hotel, more than a dozen skyscrapers have been constructed in the area. In 1991, the Tokyo Metropolitan Government moved its offices from Marunouchi to Western Shinjuku. This reflects the movement of Tokyo as a whole to the west, with new development in that direction and the most fashionable residential areas, such as Setagaya-ku Ward, now on train lines west from Shinjuku. Eastern Shinjuku was once famous for its inexpensive nightlife. It featured thousands of small bars, restaurants, snack shops and more dubious establishments. With the advent of urban development in the western suburbs of Tokyo and the new development of Western Shinjuku, the character of Eastern Shinjuku has changed; it is now rather more respectable and more expensive. It is generally considered one of the best of Tokyo's "downtowns," after, of course, the Ginza.

Shinjuku Station is the largest commuter terminal in Japan. Over three million commuters pass through it every day. In addition to the JR Yamanote Loop Line, the JR Chuo Line, the Marunouchi and Shinjuku subway lines provide transportation from Shinjuku to other parts of Tokyo Core. The JR, Seibu, Keio and Odakyu Railway Companies all operate commuter trains from Shinjuku to the outlying suburbs and satellite cities of Kanagawa and Saitama Prefectures. Odakyu operates special deluxe tourist trains from

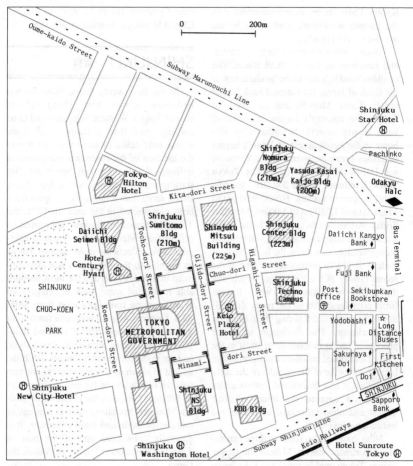

MAP 10 Shinjuku

Shinjuku to the Hakone area. See Hakone Section below. Seibu operates the Seibu Shinjuku Line to Kawagoe. See Kawagoe Section below. In addition, JR long distance trains (Chuo Line) leave from Shinjuku, providing transportation to Matsumoto and the areas in the vicinity of the Japan Alps. The JR Narita Express trains (about once an hour) originate at Shinjuku, passing through Tokyo Station on their way to the airport.

Like Tokyo Station, Shinjuku Station is a huge and potentially confusing complex of interlocking stations of the various train companies and subway lines with shopping malls and department stores such as Odakyu Halc, Odakyu Department Store, Keio Department Store, Lumine and My City on the top floors. An underground passage runs from Shinjuku-Sanchome subway station to Shinjuku Station and from there to Shinjuku Chuo-Koen Park. Again, there are a large number of signs in English, but you should

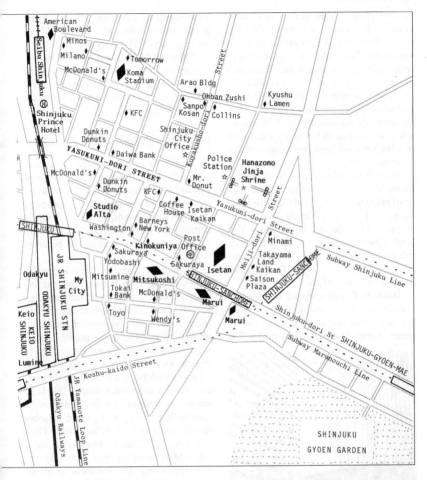

be alert and it will take care and patience not to get lost. In recent years, relatively large numbers of homeless people have begun living in the station precincts and many underground passages.

WESTERN SHINJUKU 西新宿

The skyscrapers of this new urban center include: Shinjuku Mitsui Building (225 m, 738 feet); Shinjuku Center Building (223 m, 732 feet); Shinjuku Sumitomo Building (210 m, 689 feet); Shinjuku Nomura Building (210 m, 689 feet); and Yasuda Kasai Kaijo Building (200 m, 656 feet). The new Tokyo Metropolitan Government Office towers over the entire district at 243 m (797 feet). Opened in 1991 and designed by the famed architect Kenzo Tange, this massive structure, like the medieval European cathedrals that inspired its design, is intended to impress, dominate and display the power of the establishment. There is a special elevator to the 45th floor observatory (at 240 m). Hours: 10:00 AM to 6:00 PM (8:00 PM on weekends). Closed Mondays. All of the skyscrapers have restaurants in their basements and on their top floors. Those in the basements are generally reasonable, while those on the top floors are more expensive. The Shinjuku NS Building has over 30 reasonable restaurants on its top floors, and is your best bet for good food plus good views at reasonable prices.

Togo Seiji Museum　東郷青児美術館：About 100 works of Seiji Togo, a great master of paintings of young girls, are displayed on the 42nd floor of Yasuda Kasai Kaijo Building. This Museum also displays Van Gogh's Sunflowers. It has an observatory gallery overlooking the Shinjuku area. Hours: 9:30 AM to 5:00 PM. Closed Mondays. Admission: 500 yen.

Discount Camera Shops: Tokyo's two leading discount camera shops, Yodobashi and Doi are located near the station (lower center, Kanto Map 10). They also sell a

wide variety of other consumer electronic goods, such as Nintendos, personal and laptop computers, CD players, watches, etc.

Shinjuku Chuo Koen　新宿中央公園　or Shinjuku Central Park, is a popular jogging route for those staying at the area's hotels. The Park is an oasis for Shinjuku's amorous couples in the evening.

EASTERN SHINJUKU　東新宿

Everything new under the rising sun, especially everything new with young people, makes its debut in Eastern Shinjuku. If the behavior of young people is a barometer of future social trends, Eastern Shinjuku is certainly the place to get an idea of where Japanese society is headed, for better or worse.

There are two distinct areas in Eastern Shinjuku. The southern part, from Yasukuni-dori Street south, is a shopping and restaurant area. There are three large department stores: Isetan, Mitsukoshi and Marui as well as many elegant specialty shops. Kinokuniya carries a large number of foreign books, many of them in English. Sakuraya and Yodobashi are two more discount camera and electronics shops. The large number of American fast food chains in the area might surprise you. There are a number of restaurants in the area, and Saison Plaza and Takayama Land Kaikan (middle right, Kanto Map 10) are occupied entirely by various restaurants. The basement of Studio Alta (middle center) also houses a number of reasonable restaurants.

The second area is **Kabukicho**, which lies to the north of Yasukuni-dori Street. Koma Stadium, a popular music concert hall, is the center of Kabukicho. The area contains more drinking places than restaurants, and innumerable discos, snack shops, trysting places and porn palaces. It is estimated that Kabukicho's population during the daytime is only 3,000, but that its nighttime population swells to an astonishing

400,000. It crackles with the energy of the young people who throng its streets. It is seductive, tawdry, vulgar and exciting. In recent years an increasing number of workers in the many small shops are foreigners, often temporary workers from other Asian countries. Many of Kabukicho's patrons are now likewise non-Japanese. Kabukicho trades in desires, and the veils that usually mask human emotions are torn aside here. Scams and bunco schemes are the norm rather than the exception. The area is not particularly dangerous, but alertness and caution are advisable, especially late at night. **Hanazono Jinja Shrine** 花園神社 (middle right) is the home of an antique flea market on the second and third Sundays of each month.

　　Shinjuku Gyoen Garden 新宿御苑 (lower right). With huge Japanese and West-ern gardens, Shinjuku Gyoen Garden is an oasis for busy city people. With 1,900 cherry trees, the Garden is crowded with thousands of cherry blossom lovers in early April. Hours: 9:00 AM to 4:30 PM. Closed on Mondays. Admission: 160 yen.

IKEBUKURO   池袋

　　Ikebukuro is one of the largest terminals in Tokyo. In addition to the JR Yamanote Loop Line, it is served by the Marunouchi and Yurakucho subway lines and three commuter train lines from the Tokyo suburbs and Saitama Prefecture. There are a number of different department stores and shopping and nightlife zones within the neighborhood, but because Ikebukuro is a com-

MAP 11 Ikebukuro

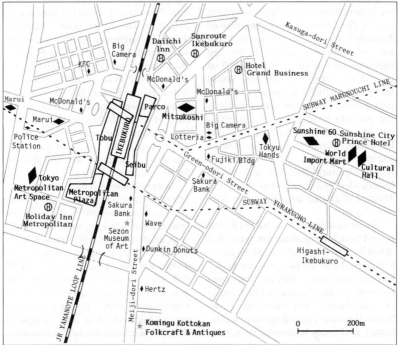

muters' center, it lacks the prestige of the Ginza and the panache of Shinjuku. What you'll find here is the lifestyle of the common people rather than the rich and famous. Accordingly, prices in general are cheaper than those of central Tokyo.

Ikebukuro Station is sandwiched between Seibu and Parco Department Stores on the east, and the Tobu Department Store (and its annex — Metropolitan Plaza), Japan's largest department store, on the west. Mitsukoshi Department Store is just a few minutes east of the station.

Komingu Kottokan　古民具骨董館 (Folkcraft & Antiques Hall) (lower center, Kanto Map 11) is a ten-minute walk south from the Station. It is a sort of headquarters for most of Japan's antique dealers. More than 50 dealers are located in this building. Many of the country's antique flea markets are operated by these dealers.

Sunshine City　サンシャインシティ　is the name of Ikebukuro's urban development project. The 240 m (787 foot) **Sunshine 60 Building** is one of Japan's tallest buildings and its observatory commands the best panoramic view of Tokyo. Hours: 10:00 AM to 8:30 PM. Admission: 620 yen. **World Import Mart Building** contains a permanent exhibition of international products imported into Japan, as well as a planetarium, an aquarium, and a branch of Mitsukoshi Department Store. Many foreign national tourist boards also have offices in this building. **The Cultural Hall** next to the World Import Mart Building houses the Orient Museum (Egyptian antiquities) and Sunshine Theater.

On the western side of Ikebukuro Station is the **Tokyo Metropolitan Art Space** 東京 芸術劇場 , the home of the Metropolitan Orchestra. There are two branches of Big Camera in the area — they are camera and electronic goods discounters like those in the Shinjuku area. The eastern side of the Station is generally considered more sophisticated, while many believe that the western side of the Station is primarily the domain of bar hoppers and drinkers.

SHIBUYA　渋谷

You can reach Shibuya on either the JR Yamanote Loop Line or the Ginza or Hanzomon subway lines. Shibuya is also the terminus for several private commuter lines: the Tokyu Toyoko (Tokyo-Yokohama) Line; the Shintamagawa Line; and the Inogashira Line.

As a large terminal where suburbanites transfer from commuter trains to city transportation, Shibuya has a great many shopping, eating and drinking establishments. Shibuya is also one of Tokyo's leading fashion centers, thanks to two conglomerates: Seibu and Tokyu. In addition to a huge department store (with two connected buildings) bearing its name, Seibu also developed three Parco (Part I to Part III) fashion complexes (middle center, Kanto Map 12). Tokyu, in addition to its main department store (middle left), opened Tokyu Plaza near the Station (lower center), Tokyu Hands, a do-it-yourself store (middle center) and Tokyu Bunka Kaikan Hall (lower right). Other fashion retailers include: Marui, Shibuya 109 and Loft (middle center). All of these fashion palaces have restaurants and coffee shops in their basements and on their top floors. Restaurants and bars also line Shibuya Center-gai Street.

Denryokukan 電力館 (Electric Energy Museum) (upper center) was built by Tokyo Gas Company to educate the electronic generation about the energy source so essential to its lifestyle. Hours: 10:30 AM to 6:30 PM. Closed Wednesdays. Admission free. **Tobacco & Salt Museum**　たばこと塩の博 物館 (upper center) is probably the only museum of its kind in the world, and is a remnant of the days when one Government agency monopolized all trade in Japan in these two seemingly unrelated commodities.

Especially interesting are the numerous packages collected from all over the world. The fourth floor displays woodblock prints featuring smoking. Hours: 10:00 AM to 6:00 PM. Closed on Mondays. Admission: 100 yen.

NHK 日本放送協会 (Japan Broadcasting Corporation) (upper left). This working broadcasting center has a special 600 m (2,000 foot) tour path through the main building that leads visitors past several studios and panel displays featuring popular programs of the past. Sound effects and film

MAP 12 Shibuya

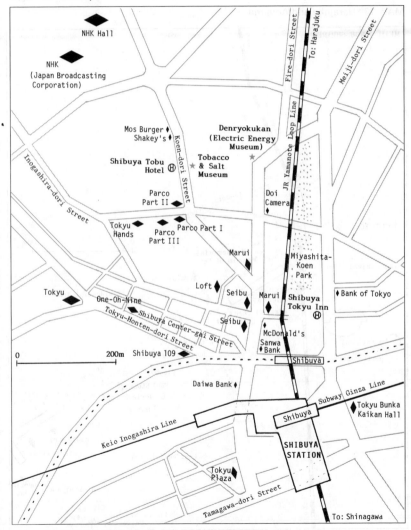

techniques are demonstrated. Displays are only in Japanese, but if you're interested in broadcasting, you will probably still enjoy seeing the workings of this popular contemporary industry. Hours: 9:00 AM to 5:00 PM. Closed irregularly. Admission free. **NHK Hall** is usually used for recording NHK

variety and music shows. It is also the home of the celebrated NHK Philharmonic Orchestra.

If you continue your walk to the north, you will soon arrive in Harajuku. See Harajuku and Aoyama Section below.

MAP 13   Harajuku and Aoyama

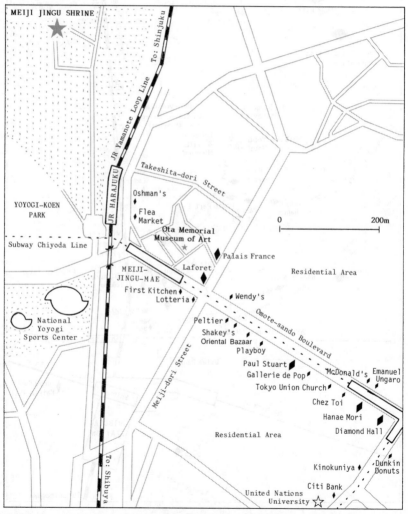

HARAJUKU AND AOYAMA 原宿・青山

Harajuku and Aoyama are fashionable sophisticated, internationalized neighborhoods considered Tokyo's fashion leaders.

Harajuku is also home of Meiji Jingu Shrine and National Yoyogi Sports Center.

HARAJUKU 原宿

Meiji Jingu Shrine 明治神宮 (upper left, Kanto Map 13) is dedicated to Emperor Meiji, who was responsible for Japan's

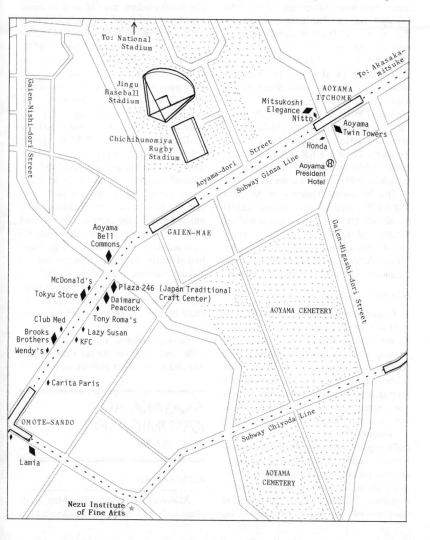

modernization. The present buildings were reconstructed in 1958. The Shrine grounds provide the people of Tokyo with a refuge from the concrete welter. Hours: 9:00 AM to 5:00 PM. Admission to the Treasure House: 200 yen. Admission to the Garden free.

National Yoyogi Sports Center 国立代々木競技場 (middle left): The two indoor arenas here were constructed for the 1964 Olympic Games. The unique designs of these arenas still fascinate visitors. You can enter the large arena if it is not in use. Hours: 10:00 AM to 4:00 PM. Admission free.

Teenager Fashion Streets: The area bounded by Takeshita-dori Street on the north, Omote-sando Boulevard on the south, Meiji-dori Street on the east and JR Harajuku Station on the west (middle left) is home to countless small boutiques and fashion shops. There is a full time Flea Market in front of the Station that deals exclusively in trinkets and cheap fashion items.

Ota Memorial Museum of Art 太田記念美術館 (middle left) houses 12,000 woodblock prints of famous artists such as Sharaku and Hiroshige. The exhibits change periodically. Hours: 10:30 AM to 5:30 PM. Closed Mondays, and from the 25th through the end of each month. Admission: 500 yen.

AOYAMA 青山

Omote-sando Boulevard 表参道 is lined with lovely gingko trees and is probably the most beautiful street in Tokyo. After crossing Meiji-dori Street, you'll see Oriental Bazaar (lower center), a large vermilion colored Chinese style building that houses a shop selling Chinese and Japanese antiques and souvenirs. Once you've passed this store, you are officially in Aoyama.

Aoyama 青山 is a residential area especially popular with artists, professionals and foreign residents. Many designer boutiques and fashionable shops serve this elite clientele. Fashions here are sophisticated and cosmopolitan. Hanae Mori's sleek glass showcase for her exquisite designs is on Omote-sando Boulevard, along with foreign stores such as Play Boy, Paul Stuart, Chez Toi and Ungaro. Major attractions on Aoyama-dori Street (middle center) are Brooks Brothers, Carita Paris and Aoyama Bell Commons, as well as the rib house Tony Roma's. Japan Traditional Craft Center is located on the second floor of the Plaza 246 Building. Handicraft products from all parts of Japan, including lacquerware, pottery, silk clothing and accessories, are displayed and sold here.

Nezu Museum of Fine Arts 根津美術館 (lower center): This jewel-box museum houses about 8,000 works of art from Japan and other parts of Asia. The collection includes several National Treasures. Hours: 9:30 AM to 4:30 PM. Closed on Mondays and for the entire month of August. Admission: 500 yen.

Jingu-gaien Park 神宮外苑 (upper right): Literally the Outer Garden of Meiji Jingu Shrine. Omote-sando Boulevard was originally designed as the main approach connecting the Shrine and this Outer Garden. The Park contains the **National Stadium** 国立競技場 , the main site for the 1964 Tokyo Olympic Games and still the nation's most prestigious sports center, **Jingu Baseball Stadium**, the home of the professional Yakult Swallows, and other sports facilities. The area, with its countless gingko trees, provides refreshing promenades and is especially beautiful in autumn when the leaves turn yellow.

Passing Aoyama, you can continue to walk northwest on Aoyama-dori Street. Akasaka is only about a 10-minute walk.

AKASAKA AND KASUMIGASEKI
赤坂・霞が関

AKASAKA 赤坂

Akasaka (middle left, Kanto Map 14) is, along with the Ginza, one of Tokyo's most sophisticated night spots. Because the area is patronized primarily by politicians and bureaucrats busy hatching plots and strategies, by businessmen on company expense accounts, by high society people, and by foreign VIP's visiting Tokyo, prices are generally quite high. The Marunouchi and Ginza subway lines serve Akasakamitsuke Station and the Subway Chiyoda Line stops at Akasaka Station.

Suntory Museum サントリー美術館 (upper left) houses about 2,000 traditional Japanese art objects, including paintings, lacquerware, glassware and women's ornaments. A tea-house is attached to the museum, and, if it's not occupied by a group you can enjoy real tea-ceremony powdered green tea there for an extra 300 yen. Hours: 10:00 AM to 5:00 PM (7:00 PM on Fridays). Closed on Mondays. Admission: 700 yen (500 yen on Sundays and holidays).

Hie Jinja Shrine 日枝神社 (middle left): The entrance is marked by a big *torii* gate. At the end of the street, steep stone steps are lined with numerous small red *torii* gates. Watch your head! This authentic shrine is quite impressive, and the precincts are unexpectedly quiet despite the shrine's location right next to the bustling play town.

Akasaka Fudo Hall 赤坂不動 (upper left). Although the Hall itself is only a small structure housing an image of the god Fudo, the narrow path leading to the hall is illuminated by small lanterns, and is especially exotic and romantic in the evening.

Restaurants and Night Spots

Tamachi-dori and **Hitotsugi-dori** Streets are crowded with all sorts of restaurants, pubs, discos and pachinko pinball parlors. **Misuji-dori Street**, located between them, is a rather quiet street that is home to many extremely expensive Japanese-style restaurants. These restaurants have private rooms that are used for business negotiations and VIP entertaining. *Geisha* are often called to these establishments to enhance the

party atmosphere. Stay away from these places unless you are invited by Japanese business associates. They are much too expensive for anyone not on a very generous expense account.

Belle Vie Akasaka is a shopping and restaurant building. The restaurants are all moderate and serve everything from spaghetti to *sushi*. The Taj is an authentic Indian restaurant (reasonable). Volks is a reasonable steak restaurant. Hai Whan is famous for its Chinese-style seafood dishes and is expensive. Seoul is a Korean barbecue restaurant (moderate). Manos serves Russian dishes (reasonable). Inakaya is a moderate Japanese-style pub. Ten-ichi is a famous expensive *tempura* restaurant. Kushinobo serves Japanese-style shishkebob (moderate). TBS Kaikan houses three famous expensive restaurants: Zakuro (*sukiyaki* and *shabu-shabu*); Granata (Italian); and Shido (French).

KASUMIGASEKI 霞が関

Most governmental ministries and agencies are concentrated in Kasumigaseki and the National Diet is in neighboring Nagatacho. The area can be reached easily by many subways.

The wide street in front of the Ministry of Foreign Affairs (middle center, Kanto Map 14) is lined with a number of cherry trees. Japan's National Flower blooms in early April to announce the beginning of a new fiscal year to the area's elite bureaucrats.

Government of Japan

Japan's modern government, established after World War II, is based on the new Constitution, which was promulgated on November 3, 1946 and came into effect six months later. Under the new Constitution, the emperor, who had held sovereign power, became a symbol of the State, and sovereign power was vested in the people. Three independent governmental branches, the legisla-

MAP 14 Akasaka and Kasumigaseki

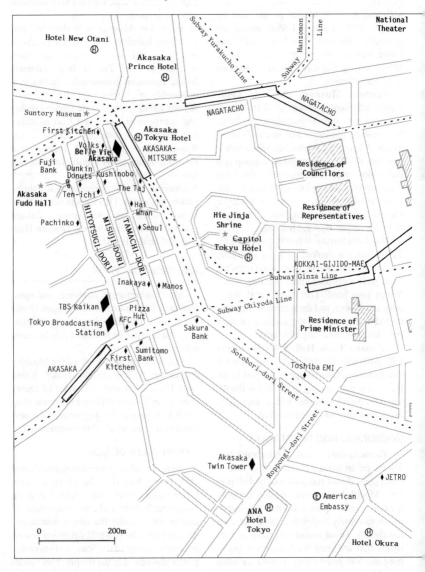

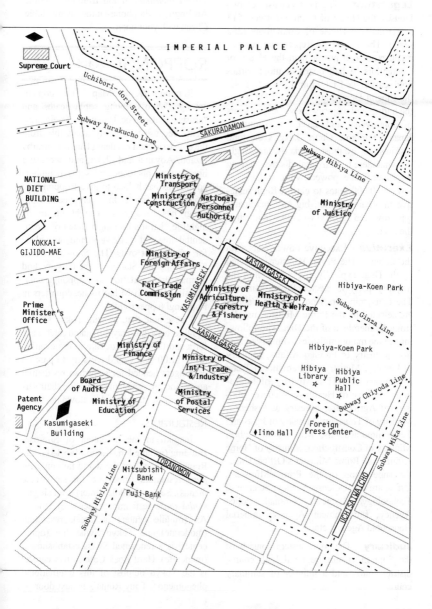

IMPERIAL PALACE

Supreme Court

Uchibori-dori Street

Subway Yurakucho Line

SAKURADAMON

Subway Hibiya Line

NATIONAL DIET BUILDING

Ministry of Transport

Ministry of Construction

National Personnel Authority

Ministry of Justice

KOKKAI-GIJIDO-MAE

Ministry of Foreign Affairs

KASUMIGASEKI

Fair Trade Commission

Ministry of Agriculture, Forestry & Fishery

Ministry of Health & Welfare

Hibiya-Koen Park

Subway Ginza Line

Prime Minister's Office

KASUMIGASEKI

Hibiya-Koen Park

Ministry of Finance

Ministry of Int'l Trade & Industry

Hibiya Library

Hibiya Public Hall

Subway Chiyoda Line

Board of Audit

Ministry of Education

Ministry of Postal Services

Patent Agency

Kasumigaseki Building

Iino Hall

Foreign Press Center

Subway Mita Line

TORANOMON

Mitsubishi Bank

Fuji Bank

UCHISAIWAICHO

Subway Hibiya Line

tive, the executive and the judiciary, operate on checks-and-balances principles.

Legislature The Diet consists of two Houses, the House of Representatives (513 seats) and the House of Councillors (252 seats). The House of Representatives has much more real power than the House of Councillors. A half dozen or more parties hold seats in the Diet. From 1955 until 1993, the Liberal Democratic Party ("LDP") was the undisputed majority party. Despite years of controversy and several decisions by Japan's Supreme Court, Japan's electoral districts are, by most standards, amazingly gerrymandered, with rural districts having disproportionate power: while it takes as few as 50,000 votes to elect a Representative in a rural district, big city candidates typically need 150,000 votes to win a seat in the Diet.

Executive Executive power rests with the Cabinet. The Prime Minister is elected by the Diet. Typically, the chairman of the majority party is elected Prime Minister. The other ministers who form the Cabinet are selected by the Prime Minister, usually from the members of the Diet. The following are the major ministries: Ministry of Justice; Ministry of Foreign Affairs; Ministry of Finance; Ministry of International Trade & Industry ("MITI"); Ministry of Education; Ministry of Health & Welfare; Ministry of Agriculture, Forestry & Fisheries; Ministry of Transport; Ministry of Posts and Telecommunications; Ministry of Labor; Ministry of Construction; Ministry of Home Affairs; and Prime Minister's Office. Under the supervision of the Prime Minister's Office are the: Defense Agency; Science & Technology Agency; National Police Agency; Environment Agency; Imperial Household Agency, etc.

Judiciary The court system consists of the Supreme Court, regional high courts, district courts and a number of summary courts.

National Theater (upper center) stages traditional Japanese theatricals, such as kabuki, *bunraku* and noh, from time to time. An English "Earphone-Guide" is available. Check with your hotel.

ROPPONGI 六本木

Roppongi (Kanto Map 15) is popular among Tokyo's young sophisticates and "artists." It also appeals to many foreign residents because it is easily accessible from the embassies and residential areas in nearby Azabu, Aoyama and Shiba, and because a liberal atmosphere pervades the neighborhood. This has helped to give Roppongi an international flavor. In recent years, Roppongi has become so caught up in its nightlife, that it's no longer much of a residential area, but it is a very enjoyable place for urban night owls. The Subway Hibiya Line (Roppongi Station) is the only method of mass transportation to Roppongi. Incidentally, Japan IBM has its headquarters in Roppongi (upper right).

Please note that, as with Tokyo's other nightlife areas, it is very difficult to catch a cab for a short distance ride late in the evening (after 11:00 PM). Cab drivers try to pick up passengers headed for suburban residential areas, and are reluctant to provide their services to those staying at downtown hotels.

Restaurants

Inagiku in the basement of Sunroser Building (middle left, Kanto Map 15) is the Roppongi branch of the world famous *tempura* restaurant (moderate for set course menus). Seryna (middle center) is an elegant *shabu-shabu* restaurant (expensive). Double Ax (middle center) is Greek restaurant (moderate) and Tokyo Swiss Inn (upper center) is a renowned Swiss establishment (moderate). Hard Rock Cafe (lower center) is the Tokyo outpost of this international phenomenon. Tony Roma's is next door —

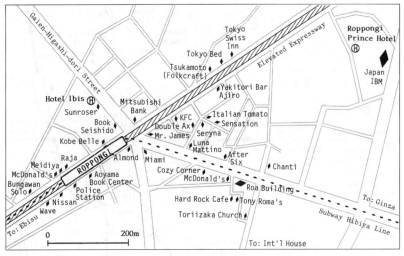

MAP 15 Roppongi

another branch of the U.S. rib house. Roa Building (lower center) houses a large number of restaurants and pubs. Kobe Belle (middle left) is a steak restaurant (expensive). Raja (lower left) is an Indian restaurant and Bungawan Solo (lower left) is Indonesian (both reasonable).

SHIBA AND SHINAGAWA 芝・品川

Hamamatsucho Station on the JR Yamanote Loop Line is the terminus of the monorail that connects the city with Tokyo's Haneda Airpot (domestic flights). The monorail ride between Haneda and Hamamatsucho takes only 16 minutes. Fare: 300 yen. The southern part of Tokyo is basically a residential zone for the well-to-do. A number of hotels and embassies are located in the area. See the Entrance Requirements section of the Introduction Chapter above for a list of Tokyo embassies.

SHIBA AND HAMAMATSUCHO
芝・浜松町

World Trade Center 世界貿易センター (152 m or 498 feet) (upper right, Kanto Map 16) rises next to Hamamatsucho Station. The 40th floor observatory, "Seaside Top," provides a panoramic view of Tokyo. Hours: 10:00 AM to 8:00 PM. Admission: 600 yen. A number of inexpensive restaurants are housed in the basement of the building.

Shibarikyu Garden 芝離宮 : This Garden was built about 300 years ago as part of the private residence of Tadaatsu Okubo, a top shogunate official. After the Meiji Restoration, the Garden belonged to the imperial family for a time, and then was given to the Tokyo Metropolitan Government. Its oddly shaped pine trees are especially delightful. Hours: 8:00 AM to 4:30 PM. Closed on Monday. Admission: 100 yen.

Hinode Pier 日の出桟橋 , from which boats operate for Asakusa via Hamarikyu (see Asakusa section above), is a ten-minute walk east of Hamamatsucho Station and is located just outside the northeast corner of

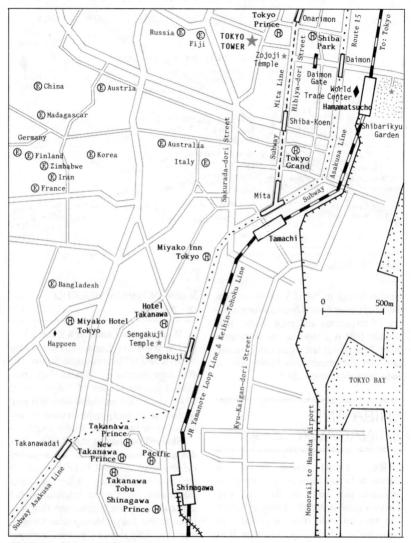

MAP 16 Shiba and Shinagawa

Kanto Map 16.

Tokyo Tower 東京タワー (upper center): The Tower itself is 333 m (1,093 feet) tall, and with the completion of Tokyo's many new skyscrapers, its observatories have lost some of their appeal. But the Special Observatory, located at an altitude of 250 m (820 feet) is still the highest point in Tokyo and commands an extensive view of the city and Tokyo Bay. Hours: 9:00 AM to

9:00 PM in summer (8:00 PM in spring and fall; and 6:00 PM in winter). Admission: 720 yen to the Main Observatory; 520 yen additional for admission to the Special Observatory.

Zojoji Temple 増上寺 (upper center): This temple prospered during the Edo Era as one of the family temples of the Tokugawa shogun. Though most of the buildings were lost during World War II, the artistic structures of the Main Gate to the temple and Nitenmon Gate, now located in the grounds of the Tokyo Prince Hotel, remain intact. There are statues of fierce guardians in niches next to the gates.

The area between Hamamatsucho and Shinagawa Stations west of the JR tracks is known as **Azabu** and **Takanawa**. Although there has been increasing commercial development, the area is still basically residential. It has a large number of embassies and a fair number of foreign residents.

SHINAGAWA 品川

Shinagawa (lower center, Kanto Map 16) is one of the largest hotel districts in Tokyo. The area is easily accessible on the JR Yamanote Loop Line.

Sengakuji Temple 泉岳寺 (lower center): This temple is linked to one of the most famous stories of Japanese history, the loyalty and revenge saga of the "Forty-seven *Ronin*." In the early 18th century, Naganori Asano, the lord of a small fiefdom in an area near modern Himeji, was ordered by the shogun to supervise the reception of an imperial messenger. Unsure of the intricacies of the protocal involved, Lord Asano sought the advice of Yoshinaka Kira, chief protocol officer of the Shogunate. The proud and arrogant Kira insulted Asano so deeply that the rural lord drew his sword and wounded Kira. Because he committed this offense in Edojo Castle, the stronghold of the shogun, Lord Asano was executed by means of an order to commit suicide. He was buried in Sengakuji Temple in Edo. Upon his death, his family was disinherited and his lands seized by the Shogunate. The Asano family retainers, including the samurai, were left unemployed. In these circumstances, samurai would normally have sought employment by other fuedal lords. But forty-seven of the Asano samurai remained loyal to the memory of their lord and secretly planned revenge. They patiently waited until the time when the guard on Yoshinaka Kira became lax. After more than a year had passed, these *ronin*, masterless samurai, attacked Kira's Edo residence on a snowy evening, killed the high official, and took his head to the cemetery at Sengakuji to present it to their Lord. These forty-seven *ronin* then turned themselves in to the Shogunate and awaited their fate. Like their Lord, they were ordered to commit suicide. After their deaths, they were all buried in the cemetery of Sengakuji. Even the Shogunate that ordered them to their deaths honored them with elaborate tributes. This story evokes admiration in the Japanese for the steadfast loyalty of the retainers and their courage in embracing their noble fate. Their story has been told again and again, in kabuki and *bunraku* plays, in popular novels and in movies and TV dramas. It is still one of the most celebrated events of Japanese history and every contemporary Japanese has grown up on this story.

KANDA AND KORAKUEN
神田・後楽園

The old downtown district of Kanda and vicinity still holds some interest even though the area has undergone a great deal of change and redevelopment.

AKIHABARA　秋葉原

Akihabara (middle right, Kanto Map 17) is world famous as Japan's bargain basement for electrical and electronic products. When you arrive in Akihabara you'll be confronted with a confusing jumble of colorful signs inviting you to sample the various wares of this electronic bazaar. The area is always bustling with bargain hunters, and the streets always have a bit of the air of a festival. With the increase in discount shops in other parts of Tokyo, Akihabara is no longer the only place with a wide variety of electronic goods.

Transportation Museum 交通博物館 (lower right) illustrates the development of air, land and ocean transportation, with special emphasis on trains, and is very popular with the young. Hours: 9:30 AM to 5:00 PM. Closed on Monday. Admission: 300 yen.

Kanda Myojin Shrine 神田明神 (middle center) is famous for its Kanda-Matsuri Festival (May 14-16). In addition to the procession of miniature shrines, formally dressed *geisha* girls participate in the parade.

JIMBOCHO　神保町

Traditionally, Japan has absorbed advanced cultures, science and technology by way of written documents, from China and other Asian countries in olden times, and from European countries and the U.S. in modern times. The Japanese love of books developed as a result of these experiences, and still endures even though TV and other audio-visual media have, in recent years, dimished what used to be the overwhelming popularity and power of the written word. Jimbocho (lower center, Kanto Map 17) used to be a scholars' and students' area, and was especially famous for its new and used bookstores. Many of the area's colleges and universities have moved to the suburbs, and the bookstores that lined Yasukuni-dori Street have been replaced, in many instance, with sporting goods shops and fashion boutiques. **Sanseido** and **Shosen Grande** (lower center) are still among Tokyo's largest bookstores. They specialize in new editions of Japanese books. The neighborhood also still has a few small bookstores along Yasukuni-dori Street that specialize in calligraphy, woodblock prints, maps and other printed documents.

KORAKUEN AND HONGO
後楽園・本郷

Korakuen (upper left, Kanto Map 17) is a huge complex sandwiched between Subway Marunouchi Line Korakuen Station and the JR Chuo Line Suidobashi Station. The complex includes Japan's first covered stadium, Tokyo Dome (the "Big Egg"), which is home to the Tokyo Giants and the Nippon Ham Fighters, two professional baseball teams. Korakuen Playland, adjacent to Tokyo Dome, is a paradise for Tokyo kids. Bowling alleys, an ice skating rink, an off-track-betting parlor and a boxing gymnasium are also part of the complex.

Tokyo University is located in Hongo, a five-minute walk from the Subway Marunouchi Line's Hongo-Sanchome Station. "Todai," as it is nicknamed, is still far and away Japan's most prestigious and influential educational institution. It is, and is likely to continue to be, the traditional training ground of all of Japan's elite — its high ranking bureaucrats, politicians and business leaders.

Koishikawa Korakuen Garden 小石川後楽園 (upper left): This Garden was first constructed by one of Ieyasu Tokugawa's sons in 1626, and cultivated, added to and renovated by successive generations of the Tokugawas. It is a large garden arranged on Chinese principles and is designed for pleasurable strolls. It now belongs to the Tokyo Metropolitan Government. Hours: 9:00 AM to 5:00 PM. Admission: 200 yen.

Kitanomaru-Koen Park 北の丸公園 (Lower left)

Originally part of Edojo Castle, this Park is now home to several museums and public facilities. **Budokan Hall** 武道館, built as a competition hall for martial arts events, is now also used for concerts, boxing matches and large musical events. **The Science Museum** 科学技術館 is always crowded with school children. The exhibits are not particularly interesting for adults, but this is a good place to get an idea of how the scientific education of Japanese children is organized and conducted. Hours: 9:30 AM to 4:50 PM. Closed during New Year's holidays.

On the southern rim of the Park (outside of map) are located the **National Museum of Modern Art - Craft Gallery** 国立近代美術館工芸館, the **National Museum of Modern Art** 国立近代美術館 and the **National Archives** 国立公文書館.

Yasukuni Jinja Shrine 靖国神社 (lower left) enshrines the spirits of 2.5 million soldiers who died in the wars since the Meiji Restoration. The Shrine has been controversial for a long time. Left-wing political groups have accused the conservative parties of disregarding the tragedy these wars brought to the nation and of trying to revitalize Japanese militarism by putting too much emphasis on this Shrine and the chauvinism they say it encourages. In spite of all this, the Shrine grounds are famous as one of the best places in Tokyo to enjoy cherry blossoms in early April.

HOTELS IN TOKYO

1. Deluxe Hotels

Akasaka Prince Hotel (upper left, Kanto Map 14). 761 rooms. Single (28,000 yen -) & Double (40,000 yen -). Add: 1-2, Kioicho, Chiyoda-ku, Tokyo. Tel: (03) 3234-1111.

ANA Hotel Tokyo (lower left, Kanto Map 14). 903 rooms. Single (36,000 yen -) & Double (40,000 yen -). Add: 1-12-33, Akasaka, Mintato-ku, Tokyo. Tel: (03) 3505-1111.

Capitol Tokyu Hotel (middle left, Kanto Map 14). 459 rooms. Single (33,000 yen -) & Double (39,000 yen -). Add: 2-10-3, Nagatacho, Chiyoda-ku, Tokyo. Tel: (03) 3581-4511.

Century Hyatt Hotel (middle left, Kanto Map 10). 800 rooms. Single (35,000 yen -) & Double (39,000 yen -). Add: 5-15-8, Nishi-Shinjuku, Shinjuku-ku, Tokyo. Tel: (03) 3349-0111.

Hotel Edmont (middle left, Kanto Map 17). 446 rooms. Single (18,000 yen -) & Double (28,000 yen -). Add: 3-10-8, Iidabashi, Chiyoda-ku, Tokyo. Tel: (03) 3237-1111.

Four Seasons Hotel (upper center, Kanto Map 18). 286 rooms. Single (40,000 yen -) & Double (44,000 yen -). Add: 2-10-8, Sekiguchi, Bunkyo-ku, Tokyo. Tel: (03) 3943-2222.

Hotel Grand Palace (middle left, Kanto Map 17). 467 rooms. Single (29,000 yen -) & Double (32,000 yen -). Add: 1-1-1, Iidabashi, Chiyoda-ku, Tokyo. Tel: (03) 3264-1111.

Imperial Hotel (upper left, Kanto Map 8). 1,059 rooms. Single (38,000 yen -) & Double (44,000 yen -). Add: 1-1-1, Uchisaiwaicho, Chiyoda-ku, Toyo. Tel: (03) 3504-1111.

Keio Plaza Hotel (middle left, Kanto

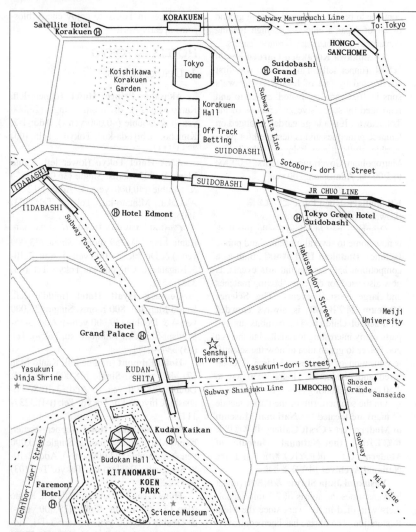

MAP 17 Kanda and Korakuen

Map 10). 1,500 rooms. Single (29,000 yen -) & Double (31,000 yen -). Add: 2-2-1, Nishi-Shinjuku, Shinjuku-ku, Tokyo. Tel: (03) 3344-0111.

Miyako Hotel Tokyo (middle left, Kanto Map 16). 498 rooms. Single (26,000 yen -) & Double (31,000 yen -). Add: 1-1-50, Shiroganedai, Minato-ku, Tokyo. Tel: (03) 3447-3111.

Hotel New Otani (upper left, Kanto Map 14). 1,612 rooms. Single (32,000 yen -) & Double (38,000 yen -). Add: 4-1, Kioicho,

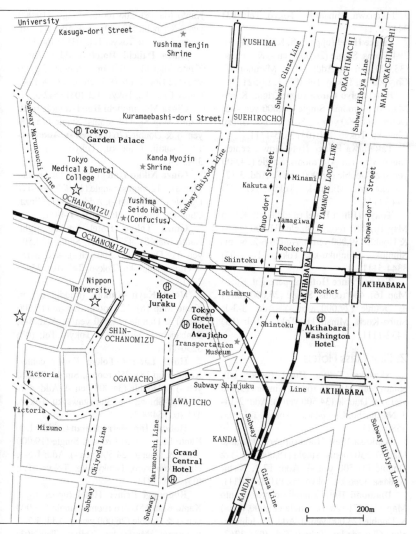

Chiyoda-ku, Tokyo. Tel: (03) 3265-1111.

New Takanawa Prince Hotel (lower center, Kanto Map 16). 946 rooms. Single (25,000 yen -) & Double (33,000 yen -). Add: 3-13-1, Takanawa, Minato-ku, Tokyo. Tel: (03) 3442-1111.

Hotel Okura (lower center, Kanto Map 14). 883 rooms. Single (38,000 yen -) & Double (44,000 yen). Add: 2-10-4, Toranomon, Minato-ku, Tokyo. Tel: (03) 3582-0111.

Hotel Pacific Meridien (lower center, Kanto Map 16). 954 rooms. Single (25,000 yen -) & Double (29,000 yen -). Add: 3-13-

3, Takanawa, Minato-ku, Tokyo. Tel: (03) 3445-6711.

Palace Hotel (upper left, Kanto Map 9). 394 rooms. Single (26,000 yen -) & Double (33,000 yen -). Add: 1-1-1, Marunouchi, Chiyoda-ku, Tokyo. Tel: (03) 3211-5211.

Hotel Seiyo Ginza (upper right, Kanto Map 8). 80 rooms. Single (56,000 yen -) & Double (68,000 yen -). Add: 1-11-2, Ginza, Chuo-ku, Tokyo. Tel: (03) 3535-1111.

Takanawa Prince Hotel (lower center, Kanto Map 16). 416 rooms. Single (24,000 yen -) & Double (28,000 yen -). Add: 3-13-1, Takanawa, Minato-ku, Tokyo. Tel: (03) 3447-1111.

Tokyo Hilton Hotel (middle left, Kanto Map 10). 807 rooms. Single (31,500 yen -) & Double (39,000 yen -). Add: 6-6-2, Nishi-Shinjuku, Shinjuku-ku, Tokyo. Tel: (03) 3344-5111.

Tokyo Prince Hotel (upper right, Kanto Map 16). 484 rooms. Single (26,000 yen -) & Double (27,000 yen -). Add: 3-3-1, Shiba-Koen, Minato-ku, Tokyo. Tel: (03) 3432-1111.

2. First Class Hotels

Akasaka Tokyu Hotel (upper left, Kanto Map 14). 535 rooms. Single (23,500 yen -) & Double (34,500 yen -). Add: 2-14-3, Nagatacho, Chiyoda-ku, Tokyo. Tel: (03) 3580-2311.

Asakusa View Hotel (upper left, Kanto Map 6). 350 rooms. Single (18,000 yen -) & Double (32,500 yen -). Add: 17-1, Nishi-Asakusa, Taito-ku, Tokyo. Tel: (03) 3847-1111.

Diamond Hotel (middle center, Kanto Map 18). 471 rooms. Single (15,000 yen -) & Double (23,000 yen -). Add: 25, Ichiban-cho, Chiyoda-ku, Tokyo. Tel: (03) 3263-2211.

Fairmont Hotel (middle center, Kanto Map 18). 210 rooms. Single (15,000 yen -) & Double (23,000 yen -). Add: 2-1-17, Kudan-Minami, Chiyoda-ku, Tokyo. Tel: (03) 3262-1151.

Ginza Tobu Hotel (middle center, Kanto Map 8). 206 rooms. Single (19,000 yen -) & Double (33,000 yen -). Add: 6-14-10, Ginza, Chuo-ku, Tokyo. Tel: (03) 3546-0111.

Ginza Daiichi Hotel (middle center, Kanto Map 8). 801 rooms. Single (22,500 yen -) & Double (28,000 yen -). Add: 8-13-1, Ginza, Chuo-ku, Tokyo. Tel: (03) 3542-5311.

Ginza Marunouchi Hotel (middle right, Kanto Map 8). 114 rooms. Single (15,000 yen -) & Double (26,000 yen -). Add: 4-1-12, Tsukiji, Chuo-ku, Tokyo. Tel: (03) 3543-5431.

Ginza Nikko Hotel (middle left, Kanto Map 8). 112 rooms. Single (17,000 yen -) & Double (29,000 yen -). Add: 8-4-21, Ginza, Chuo-ku, Tokyo. Tel: (03) 3571-4911.

Ginza Tokyu Hotel (middle right, Kanto Map 8). 437 rooms. Single (23,500 yen -) & Double (33,500 yen -). Add: 5-15-9, Ginza, Chuo-ku, Tokyo. Tel: (03) 3541-2411.

Hotel Kayu Kaikan (middle center, Kanto Map 18). 127 rooms. Single (15,500 yen -) & Double (24,500 yen -). Add: 8-1, Sanbancho, Chiyoda-ku, Tokyo. Tel: (03) 3230-1111.

Hotel Laforet Tokyo (lower center, Kanto Map 18). 250 rooms. Single (28,000 yen -) & Double (34,000 yen -). Add: 4-7-36, Kita-Shinagawa, Shinagawa-ku, Tokyo. Tel: (03) 5488-3911.

Holiday Inn Metropolitan (middle left, Kanto Map 11). 818 rooms. Single (19,000 yen -) & Double (24,500 yen -). Add: 1-6-1, Nishi-Ikebukuro, Bunkyo-ku, Tokyo. Tel: (03) 3980-1111.

Roppongi Prince Hotel (upper right, Kanto Map 15). 216 rooms. Single (23,000 yen -) & Double (26,000 yen -). Add: 3-2-7, Roppongi, Minato-ku, Tokyo. Tel: (03) 3587-1111.

Royal Park Hotel (middle right, Kanto Map 18). 450 rooms. Single (24,500 yen -) & Double (32,500 yen -). 2-1-1, Nihon-bashi-Kakigaracho, Chuo-ku, Tokyo. Tel: (03) 3667-1111.

Shiba Park Hotel (upper right, Kanto

Map 16). 400 rooms. Single (16,500 yen -) & Double (23,500 yen -). Add: 1-5-10, Shiba-Koen, Minato-ku, Tokyo. Tel: (03) 3433-4141.

Shimbashi Daiichi Hotel (middle left, Kanto Map 8). 1,106 rooms. Single (13,000 yen -) & Double (19,000 yen -). Add: 1-2-6, Shimbashi, Minato-ku, Tokyo. Tel: (03) 3501-4411.

Shinjuku Prince Hotel (upper center, Kanto Map 10). 571 rooms. Single (18,000 yen -) & Double (20,000 yen -). Add: 1-30-1, Kabukicho, Shinjuku-ku, Tokyo. Tel: (03) 3205-1111.

Sunshine City Prince Hotel (middle right, Kanto Map 11). 1,166 rooms. Single (16,500 yen -) & Double (23,500 yen -). Add: 3-1-5, Higashi-Ikebukuro, Bunkyo-ku, Tokyo. Tel: (03) 3988-1111.

Hotel Takanawa (middle center, Kanto Map 16). 132 rooms. Single (21,000 yen -) & Double (31,000 yen -). Add: 2-1-17, Takanawa, Minato-ku, Tokyo. Tel: (03) 5488-1000.

Tokyo Marunouchi Hotel (middle center, Kanto Map 9). 210 rooms. Single (16,000 yen -) & Double (28,000 yen -). Add: 1-6-3, Marunouchi, Chiyoda-ku, Tokyo. Tel: (03) 3215-2151.

Yaesu Fujiya Hotel (lower center, Kanto Map 9). 377 rooms. Single (15,000 yen -) & Double (24,500 yen -). Add: 2-9-1, Yaesu, Chuo-ku, Tokyo. Tel: (03) 3273-2111.

3. Standard & Business Hotels

Akihabara Washington Hotel (middle right, Kanto Map 17). 238 singles (10,500 yen -) & 66 doubles (19,000 yen -). Add: 1-8-3, Sakumacho, Chiyoda-ku, Tokyo. Tel: (03) 3255-3311.

Aoyama President Hotel (upper right, Kanto Map 13). 153 singles (15,000 yen -) & 57 doubles (19,000 yen -). Add: 2-2-3, Minami-Aoyama, Minato-ku, Tokyo. Tel: (03) 3497-0111.

Asakusa Vista Hotel (upper right, Kanto Map 18). 114 singles (8,300 yen -) & 22 doubles (14,000 yen -). Add: 2-2-9, Kotobuki, Taito-ku, Tokyo. Tel: (03) 3842-8421.

Atagoyama Tokyu Inn (middle center, Kanto Map 18). 165 singles (12,000 yen -) & 103 doubles (17,000 yen -). Add: 1-6-6, Atago, Minato-ku, Tokyo. Tel: (03) 3431-0109.

B & B Kiba (middle right, Kanto Map 18). 127 singles (10,000 yen -) & 156 doubles (17,000 yen -). Add: 2-1-1, Kiba, Koto-ku, Tokyo. Tel: (03) 3642-0011.

Chisan Hotel Hamamatsucho (lower center, Kanto Map 18). 272 singles (11,000 yen -) & 32 doubles (18,000 yen -). Add: 1-3-10, Shibaura, Minato-ku, Tokyo. Tel: (03) 3452-6511.

Daisho Central Hotel (upper left, Kanto Map 18). 111 singles (7,500 yen -) & 85 doubles (14,000 yen -). Add: 1-27-7, Takadanobaba, Shinjuku-ku, Tokyo. Tel: (03) 3232-0101.

Gajoen Kanko Hotel (lower left, Kanto Map 18). 36 singles (12,000 yen -) & 52 doubles (21,000 yen -). Add: 1-8-1, Shimo-Meguro, Meguro-ku, Tokyo. Tel: (03) 3491-0111.

Hotel Grand Business (upper center, Kanto Map 11). 234 singles (6,700 yen -) & 50 doubles (10,800 yen -). Add: 1-30-7, Higashi-Ikebukuro, Toshima-ku, Tokyo. Tel: (03) 3984-5121.

Grand Central Hotel (lower right, Kanto Map 17). 98 singles (8,000 yen -) & 59 doubles (12,200 yen -). Add: 2-2, Kanda-Tsukasacho, Chiyoda-ku, Tokyo. Tel: (03) 3256-3211.

Harumi Grand Hotel (middle right, Kanto Map 18). 200 rooms. Single (14,000 yen -) & Double (21,000 yen -). Add: 3-8-1, Harumi, Chuo-ku, Tokyo. Tel: (03) 3533-7111.

Hotel Hokke Club Ikenohata (middle left, Kanto Map 7). Under Construction.

Holiday Inn Tokyo (middle right, Kanto Map 18). 64 singles (18,000 yen -) & 55 doubles (26,000 yen -). Add: 1-13-7,

MAP 18 Hotels in Tokyo

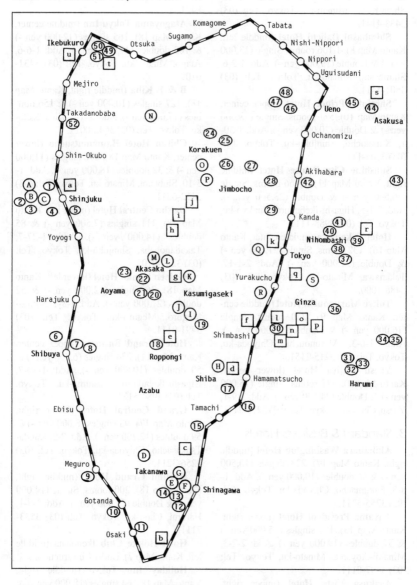

DELUXE HOTELS

(A) Tokyo Hilton Hotel
(B) Century Hyatt Hotel
(C) Keio Plaza Hotel
(D) Miyako Hotel Tokyo
(E) New Takanawa Prince Hotel
(F) Hotel Pacific Meridien
(G) Takanawa Prince Hotel
(H) Tokyo Prince Hotel
(I) Hotel Okura
(J) ANA Hotel Tokyo
(K) Capitol Tokyu Hotel
(L) Akasaka Prince Hotel
(M) Hotel New Otani
(N) Four Seasons Hotel
(O) Hotel Edmont
(P) Hotel Grand Palace
(Q) Palace Hotel
(R) Imperial Hotel
(S) Hotel Seiyo Ginza

FIRST-CLASS HOTELS

a Shinjuku Prince Hotel
b Hotel Laforet Tokyo
c Hotel Takanawa
d Shiba Park Hotel
e Roppongi Prince Hotel
f Shimbashi Daiichi Hotel
g Akasaka Tokyu Hotel
h Diamond Hotel
i Hotel Kayu Kaikan
j Fairmont Hotel
k Tokyo Marunouchi Hotel
l Ginza Nikko Hotel
m Ginza Daiichi Hotel
n Ginza Tobu Hotel
o Ginza Tokyu Hotel
p Ginza Marunouchi Hotel
q Yaesu Fujiya Hotel
r Royal Park Hotel
s Asakusa View Hotel
t Sunshine City Prince Hotel
u Hotel Metropolitan

STANDARD HOTELS & BUSINESS HOTELS

(1) Star Hotel Tokyo
(2) Shinjuku New City Hotel
(3) Shinjuku Washington Hotel
(4) Hotel Sunroute Tokyo
(5) Shinjuku Park Hotel
(6) Shibuya Tobu Hotel
(7) Shibuya Tokyu Inn
(8) Aoyama Shanpia Hotel
(9) Gajoen Kanko Hotel
(10) Hotel Royal Oak Gotanda
(11) New Otani Inn Tokyo
(12) Shinagawa Prince Hotel
(13) Takanawa Keikyu Hotel
(14) Takanawa Tobu Hotel
(15) Miyako Inn Tokyo
(16) Chisan Hotel Hamamatsucho
(17) Tokyo Grand Hotel
(18) Hotel Ibis
(19) Atagoyama Tokyu Inn
(20) Hotel Yoko Akasaka
(21) Mar Lord Inn Akasaka
(22) Akasaka Shanpia Hotel
(23) Aoyama President Hotel
(24) Satellite Hotel Korakuen
(25) Suidobashi Grand Hotel
(26) Tokyo Green Hotel Suidobashi
(27) Hotel Juraku
(28) Tokyo Green Hotel Awajicho
(29) Grand Central Hotel
(30) Mitsui Urban Hotel Ginza
(31) Mariner's Court Tokyo
(32) Harumi Grand Hotel
(33) Tokyo Hotel Urashima
(34) B & B Kiba
(35) Tokyo Sunny Side Hotel
(36) Ginza Capital Hotel
(37) Holiday Inn Tokyo
(38) Hotel Universe Nihombashi Kayabacho
(39) Kayabacho Pearl Hotel
(40) Tokyo City Hotel
(41) Hotel Gimmond Tokyo
(42) Akihabara Washington Hotel
(43) Ryogoku Pearl Hotel
(44) Asakusa Vista Hotel
(45) Hotel Towa Ueno
(46) Hotel Park Side
(47) Hotel Hokke Club Ikenohata
(48) Hotel Ogaiso
(49) Hotel Grand Business
(50) Daiichi Inn Ikebukuro
(51) Hotel Sunroute Ikebukuro
(52) Daisho Central Hotel

Hatchobori, Chuo-ku, Tokyo. Tel: (03) 3553-6161.

Hotel Ibis (middle left, Kanto Map 15). 107 singles (13,000 yen -) & 76 doubles (21,500 yen -). Add: 7-14-4, Roppongi, Minato-ku, Tokyo. Tel: (03) 3403-4411.

Hotel Juraku (middle right, Kanto Map 17). 154 singles (9,100 yen -) & 72 doubles (14,500 yen -). Add: 2-9, Kanda-Awajicho, Chiyoda-ku, Tokyo. Tel: (03) 3251-7222.

Kayabacho Pearl Hotel (middle right, Kanto Map 18). 238 singles (8,200 yen -) & 30 doubles (14,000 yen -). Add: 1-2-5, Shinkawa, Chuo-ku, Tokyo. Tel: (03) 3553-2211.

Mar Lord Inn Akasaka (middle center, Kanto Map 18). 159 singles (8,900 yen -) & 103 doubles (15,000 yen -). Add: 6-15-17, Akasaka, Minato-ku, Tokyo. Tel: (03) 3585-7611.

Mariner's Court Tokyo (middle right, Kanto Map 18). 42 singles (9,500 yen -) & 40 doubles (14,000 yen -). Add: 4-7-28, Harumi, Chuo-ku, Tokyo. Tel: (03) 5560-2525.

Mitsui Urban Hotel Ginza (middle left, Kanto Map 8). 177 singles (12,500 yen -) & 76 doubles (22,000 yen -). Add: 8-6-15, Ginza, Chuo-ku, Tokyo. Tel: (03) 3572-4131.

Miyako Inn Tokyo (middle center, Kanto Map 16). 184 singles (11,500 yen -) & 192 doubles (16,500 yen -). Add: 3-7-8, Mita, Minato-ku, Tokyo. Tel: (03) 3454-3111.

New Otani Inn Tokyo (lower left, Kanto Map 18). 206 singles (11,500 yen -) & 150 doubles (23,000 yen -). Add: 1-6-2, Osaki, Shinagawa-ku, Tokyo. Tel: (03) 3779-9111.

Hotel Parkside (lower center, Kanto Map 7). 39 singles (9,300 yen -) & 52 doubles (16,500 yen -). Add: 2-11-18, Ueno, Taito-ku, Tokyo. Tel: (03) 3836-5711.

Hotel Royal Oak Gotanda (lower left, Kanto Map 18). 90 singles (8,000 yen -) & 29 doubles (15,000 yen -). Add: 1-9-3, Nishi-Gotanda, Shinagawa-ku, Tokyo. Tel: (03) 3492-5111.

Ryogoku Pearl Hotel (upper right, Kanto Map 18). 217 singles (7,300 yen -) & 54 doubles (13,000 yen -). Add: 1-2-24, Yokozuna, Sumida-ku, Tokyo. Tel: (03) 3626-3211.

Satellite Hotel Korakuen (upper left, Kanto Map 17). 136 singles (9,500 yen -) & 106 doubles (15,000 yen -). Add: 1-15-8, Koishikawa, Bunkyo-ku, Tokyo. Tel: (03) 3814-0202.

Shibuya Tobu Hotel (middle center, Kanto Map 12). 100 singles (13,000 yen -) & 99 doubles (22,000 yen -). Add: 3-1, Udagawacho, Shibuya-ku, Tokyo. Tel: (03) 3476-0111.

Shibuya Tokyu Inn (middle right, Kanto Map 12). 95 singles (16,000 yen -) & 127 doubles (23,500 yen -). Add: 1-24-10, Shibuya, Shibuya-ku, Tokyo. Tel: (03) 3498-0109.

Shinagawa Prince Hotel (lower center, Kanto Map 16). 1,016 singles (10,500 yen -) & 257 doubles (16,000 yen -). Add: 4-10-30, Takanawa, Minato-ku, Tokyo. Tel: (03) 3440-1111.

Shinjuku New City Hotel (lower left, Kanto Map 10). 244 singles (8,600 yen -) & 129 doubles (14,500 yen -). Add: 4-31-1, Nishi-Shinjuku, Shinjuku-ku, Tokyo. Tel: (03) 3375-6511.

Shinjuku Park Hotel (middle left, Kanto Map 18). 164 singles (6,800 yen -) & 35 doubles (11,800 yen -). Add: 5-27-9, Sendagaya, Shibuya-ku, Tokyo. Tel: (03) 3356-0241.

Shinjuku Washington Hotel (lower left, Kanto Map 10). 843 singles (11,000 yen -) & 457 doubles (17,500 yen -). Add: 3-2-9, Nishi-Shinjuku, Shinjuku-ku, Tokyo. Tel: (03) 3343-3111.

Shinjuku Star Hotel Tokyo (upper center, Kanto Map 10). 100 singles (8,200 yen -) & 114 doubles (16,300 yen -). Add: 7-10-5, Nishi-Shinjuku, Shinjuku-ku, Tokyo. Tel: (03) 3361-1111.

Suidobashi Grand Hotel (upper center, Kanto Map 17). 166 singles (8,000 yen -) & 50 doubles (14,000 yen -). Add: 1-33-2, Hongo, Bunkyo-ku, Tokyo. Tel: (03) 3816-2101.

Hotel Sunroute Ikebukuro (upper center, Kanto Map 11). 96 singles (9,000 yen -) & 48 doubles (16,500 yen -). Add: 1-39-4, Higashi-Ikebukuro, Toshima-ku, Tokyo. Tel: (03) 3980-1911.

Hotel Sunroute Tokyo (lower center, Kanto Map 10). 388 singles (12,500 yen -) & 153 doubles (17,000 yen -). Add: 2-3-1, Yoyogi, Shibuya-ku, Tokyo. Tel: (03) 3375-3211.

Takanawa Tobu Hotel (lower center, Kanto Map 16). 112 singles (15,500 yen -) & 75 doubles (23,500 yen -). Add: 4-7-6, Takanawa, Minato-ku, Tokyo. Tel: (03) 3447-0111.

Takanawa Keikyu Hotel (lower center, Kanto Map 18). 132 singles (12,000 yen -) & 32 doubles (20,000 yen -). Add: 4-10-8, Takanawa, Minato-ku, Tokyo. Tel: (03) 3443-1211.

Tokyo City Hotel (middle right, Kanto Map 18). 210 singles (8,000 yen -) & 57 doubles (12,500 yen -). Add: 1-5-4, Nihonbashi-Hashimotocho, Chuo-ku, Tokyo. Tel: (03) 3270-7671.

Tokyo Grand Hotel (upper right, Kanto Map 16). 88 singles (15,000 yen -) & 67 doubles (22,000 yen -). Add: 2-5-3, Shiba, Minato-ku, Tokyo. Tel: (03) 3454-0311.

Tokyo Green Hotel Awajicho (middle right, Tokyo Map 17). 171 singles (7,000 yen -) & 36 doubles (12,600 yen -). Add: 2-6, Kanda-Awajicho, Chiyoda-ku, Tokyo. Tel: (03) 3255-4161.

Tokyo Green Hotel Suidobashi (middle center, Kanto Map 17). 243 singles (7,500 yen -) & 71 doubles (13,000 yen -). Add: 1-1-16, Misakicho, Chiyoda-ku, Tokyo. Tel: (03) 3295-4161.

Tokyo Hotel Urashima (middle right, Kanto Map 18). 627 singles (7,500 yen -) & 300 doubles (14,000 yen -). Add: 2-5-23, Harumi, Chuo-ku, Tokyo. Tel: (03) 3533-3111.

Tokyo Sunny Side Hotel (middle right, Kanto Map 18). 168 singles (7,500 yen -) & 106 doubles (13,800 yen -). Add: 2-3-12, Toyo, Koto-ku, Tokyo. Tel: (03) 3649-1221.

Hotel Towa Ueno (upper right, Kanto Map 18). 118 singles (10,500 yen -) & 32 doubles (23,500 yen -). Add: 5-5-6, Higashi-Ueno, Taito-ku, Tokyo. Tel: (03) 5828-0108.

Hotel Universe Nihonbashi Kayabacho (lower right, Kanto Map 9). 116 singles (7,800 yen -) & 38 doubles (12,600 yen -). Add: 2-13-5, Nihonbashi-Kayabacho, Chuo-ku, Tokyo. Tel: (03) 3668-7711.

Hotel Yoko Akasaka (middle center, Kanto Map 18). 165 singles (9,000 yen -) & 32 doubles (16,000 yen -). Add: 6-14-12, Akasaka, Minato-ku, Tokyo. Tel: (03) 3586-4050.

4. Welcome Inns

Akasaka Shanpia Hotel (5 minute walk from Akasaka Station on the Subway Chiyoda Line). 232 Western rooms. Add: 7-6-13, Akasaka, Minato-ku, Tokyo. Tel: (03) 3586-0811.

Aoyama Shanpia Hotel (5 minute walk from Shibuya Station on the JR Yamanote Loop Line). 135 Western rooms. Add: 2-14-15, Shibuya, Shibuya-ku, Tokyo. Tel: (03) 3407-2111.

Hotel Asakusa Mikawaya (5 minute walk from Asakusa Station on the Subway Ginza Line). 17 Japanese & 5 Western rooms. Add: 2-7-11, Hanakawado, Taito-ku, Tokyo. Tel: (03) 3844-7757.

Asia Center of Japan (5 minute walk from Aoyama-Itchome Station on the Subway Ginza Line). 172 Western rooms. Add: 8-10-32, Akasaka, Minato-ku, Tokyo. Tel: (03) 3402-6111.

Daiichi Inn Ikebukuro (1 minute walk from Ikebukuro Station on the JR Yamanote Loop Line). 139 Western rooms. Add: 1-42-

8, Higashi-Ikebukuro, Toshima-ku, Tokyo. Tel: (03) 3986-1221.

Hotel Gimmond Tokyo (2 minute walk from Kodenmacho Station on the Subway Hibiya Line). 220 Western rooms. Add: 1-6, Nihombashi-Ohdenmacho, Chuo-ku, Tokyo. Tel: (03) 3666-4111.

Ginza Capital Hotel (1 minute walk from Tsukiji Station on the Subway Hibiya Line). Add: 3-1-5, Tsukiji, Chuo-ku, Tokyo. Tel: (03) 3543-8211.

Hotel I. B. A. Ikebukuro (8 minute walk from Ikebukuro Station on the JR Yamanote Loop Line). 60 Western rooms. Add: 3-10-7, Higashi-Ikebukuro, Toshima-ku, Tokyo. Tel: (03) 5396-5555.

Kikuya Ryokan (8 minute walk from Tawaramachi Station on the Subway Ginza Line). 8 Japanese & 1 Western rooms. Add: 2-18-9, Nishi-Asakusa, Taito-ku, Tokyo. Tel: (03) 3841-6404.

Resort Hotel Yushima (3 minute walk from Yushima Station on the Subway Chiyoda Line). 61 Western & 9 Japanese rooms. Add: 2-15-13, Yushima, Bunkyo-ku, Tokyo. Tel: (03) 3835-1551.

Ryokan Katsutaro (5 minute walk from Nezu Station on the Subway Chiyoda Line). 7 Japanese rooms. Add: 4-16-8, Ikenohata, Taito-ku, Tokyo. Tel: (03) 3821-9808.

Ryokan Mikawaya Bekkan (3 minute walk from Asakusa Station on the Subway Ginza Line). 12 Japanese rooms. Add: 1-31-11, Asakusa, Taito-ku, Tokyo. Tel: (03) 3843-2345.

Ryokan Sansuiso (5 minute walk from Gotanda Station on the JR Yamanote Loop Line). 9 Japanese rooms. Add: 2-9-5, Higashi-Gotanda, Shinagawa-ku, Tokyo. Tel: (03) 3441-7475.

Ryokan Seifuso (5 minute walk from Iidabashi Station on the Subway Yurakucho Line). 15 Japanese & 1 Western rooms. Add: 1-12-15, Fujimi, Chiyoda-ku, Tokyo. Tel: (03) 3263-0681.

Sawanoya Ryokan (7 minute walk from Nezu Station on the Subway Chiyoda Line). 12 Japanese rooms. Add: 2-3-11, Yanaka, Taito-ku, Tokyo. Tel: (03) 3822-2251.

Shimizu Bekkan (5 minute walk from Hongo-Sanchome Station on the Subway Marunouchi Line). 17 Japanese rooms. Add: 1-30-29, Hongo, Bunkyo-ku, Tokyo. Tel: (03) 3812-6285.

Suigetsu Hotel/Hotel Ogaiso (10 minute walk from Ueno Station on the JR Yamanote Loop Line). 85 Western rooms & 54 Japanese rooms. Add: 3-3-21, Ikenohata, Taito-ku, Tokyo. Tel: (03) 3822-4611.

Suzuki Ryokan (1 minute walk from Nippori Station on the JR Yamanote Loop Line). 15 Japanese rooms. Add: 7-15-23, Yanaka, Taito-ku, Tokyo. Tel: (03) 3821-4944.

JR FARES BETWEEN MAJOR STATIONS IN TOKYO CORE
(The JR Yamanote Loop Line)

To / From	Tokyo	Shinjuku	Ueno
Tokyo		250 yen (17.4 km)	150 yen (3.6 km)
Yurakucho	120 yen (0.8 km)	250 yen (16.6 km)	150 yen (4.4 km)
Shinagawa	160 yen (6.8 km)	190 yen (10.6 km)	190 yen (10.4 km)
Shibuya	190 yen (14.0 km)	150 yen (3.4 km)	250 yen (17.6 km)
Harajuku	250 yen (15.2 km)	120 yen (2.2 km)	250 yen (18.8 km)
Shinjuku	250 yen (17.4 km)		190 yen (13.5 km)
Ikebukuro	190 yen (12.3 km)	150 yen (4.8 km)	160 yen (8.7 km)
Ueno	150 yen (3.6 km)	190 yen (13.5 km)	
Akihabara	120 yen (2.0 km)	250 yen (15.1 km)	120 yen (1.6 km)

Metropolitan Tokyo 首都圈

Here we introduce Tokyo suburbs and satellite cities in Tokyo's neighboring prefectures of Kanagawa, Saitama and Chiba. All references are to Kanto Map 19. Six cities are introduced below: Yokohama (middle center), Kamakura (lower center), Kawasaki (middle center), Chiba (Makuhari Messe near Kaihin-Makuhari Station; middle right), Urayasu (Tokyo Disneyland near Maihama Station; middle right) and Kawagoe (upper left). In addition, sketches of other major cities are included here:

1. Tokyo Suburbs

Hachioji (middle left) is located at the western end of the Tokyo suburbs. With its 20 universities and several research institutions, this former farm village is rapidly becoming Tokyo's educational center. Its current population is 455,000; it is the largest city in the Tokyo suburbs. About 40 minutes by Keio Honsen Line from Shinjuku and about one hour by JR Chuo Line from Shinjuku.

Machida (middle left) is the home of Tama New Town, a seemingly endless development of high-rise *danchi* apartment buildings. Machida is also the home of several universities. Its population stands at 347,000. About 40 minutes on the Odakyu Line from Shinjuku.

Fuchu (middle left). Population 204,000. Home of large Toshiba and NEC factories. Fuchu is also the home of Japan's most important racetrack, where the Japan Cup race is held every November. Horses from around the world compete in this major race. You can reach the racetrack by taking the Keio Line from Shinjuku to Higashi-Fuchu (25 minutes) and transferring there to the

special train to Keibajo (racetrack) (2 minutes).

Chofu (middle left) prospered as a post town in the Edo era. It has always been a good residential area; in recent years, real estate prices headed for the stratosphere. It is a 20-minute Keio Line ride from Shinjuku. Population 190,000. Chofu is the home of Jindaiji Temple, which is famous for its noodles.

Tama Dobutsu Koen Zoo (middle left) is located in Hino City. This is the largest zoo in the Tokyo area, and is a good destination for family excursions. Hino is also the home of the Hino Motor Company. Population 161,000. It is about a 40-minute ride on the Keio Line from Shinjuku to Takahata-Fudo, and another three minutes on the Keio Dobutsuen Line to the Zoo. Incidentally, Takahata-Fudo Temple (a two-minute walk from Takahata-Fudo Station) has an impressive five-story pagoda.

Tachikawa (middle left) prospered as a military base after World War II. The base was returned to the municipality of Tachikawa several years ago. Local officials are actively pursuing new development. Population: 153,000. A 40-minute ride from Shinjuku on the JR Chuo Line.

Musashino (Kichijoji Station is the city's transportation center: middle left) is just outside Tokyo Core. Musashino is becoming a second Shinjuku — a commercial, financial and entertainment center. Population: 134,000. An 18-minute trip from Shinjuku on the JR Chuo Line.

Fussa (upper left) is the home of Yokota U.S. Air Force Base. Its population is 58,000. It is a 15-minute ride on the JR Oume Line from Tachikawa.

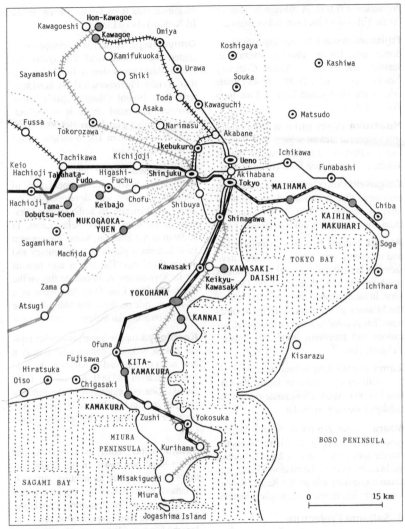

MAP 19 Outline of Metropolitan Tokyo

2. Kanagawa Prefecture

Sagamihara (middle left) is a university and manufacturing city on the Tokyo/Kanagawa border. NEC and Mitsubishi Heavy Industries have large factories here. Population 526,000.

Yokosuka (lower center) is where U.S. Admiral Perry appeared in 1854 with his "Black Ships" and demanded the contact that changed Japanese history. Yokosuka is also the Pacific home of the 7th Fleet of the U.S. Navy. There is huge U.S. military base.

Population 437,000. A 80-minute ride on the JR Yokosuka Line from Tokyo Station.

Fujisawa (lower left) is an expensive residential area. The city also has several universities and an Isuzu Motor Company factory. Population 348,000. A 48-minute ride on the JR Tokaido Honsen Line from Tokyo Station.

Hiratsuka (lower left) is another expensive residential area on Sagami Bay. Population 244,000. A 60-minute ride on the JR Tokdaido Honsen Line from Tokyo Station.

Chigasaki (lower left), once a resort with exclusive villas, is now a bedroom community. Population 203,000. A 56-minute ride from Tokyo on the JR Tokaido Honsen Line.

Atsugi (middle left) is a manufacturing and university city. Sony and Nissan have factories here. Population 193,000. About a one-hour ride from Shinjuku on the Odakyu Line. In recent years Atsugi, with the help of the Ministry of Posts and Telecommunications, has decided to focus on telecommunications and transform itself into "Atsugi Telecom Town."

Zama (middle left) is headquarters of all U.S. military operations in Japan. Population 111,000. About a 50-minute ride on the Odakyu Line from Shinjuku.

Miura (lower center) is Japan's biggest tuna fishing fleet port. Miura promotes marine sports and is one of Japan's leading yacht racing centers. Population 53,000. It is about a one-hour trip on the Keihin Kyuko Line from Shinagawa to Misakiguchi Station.

3. Saitama Prefecture

Kawaguchi (upper center) has a large number of small foundries. It is Saitama's largest city with a population of 436,000. A 25-minute ride from Tokyo Station on the JR Keihin-Tohoku Line.

Urawa (upper center) is the capital of Saitama Prefecture. Population 417,000. A 50-minute ride from Tokyo Station on the JR Keihin-Tohoku Line.

Omiya (upper center) is a transportation center: the Tohoku (and Yamagata) and Joetsu Shinkansens stop at JR Omiya Station. Taisho Pharmaceuticals is headquartered here. Bonsai Village, Japan's bonsai wholesale and retail center, is on the outskirts of Omiya. Population 403,000. About a one-hour ride from Tokyo Station on the Keihin-Tohoku Line.

Tokorozawa (upper left) is a typical commuters' town with a population of 300,000. The city was developed by the Seibu conglomerate. Its Seibu Baseball Stadium is the home of the Seibu Lions. In addition to the Stadium, Seibu Amusement Park features a playland, golf courses and indoor ski slopes. The area is also famous for its Sayama tea. A 30-minute trip on the Seibu Chichibu Line from Ikebukuro or a 35-minute ride on the Seibu Shinjuku Line from Seibu Shinjuku Station

Koshigaya (upper center) is another typical Tokyo bedroom community. It was a post town on the road to Nikko in the Edo Era. Population 283,000. It is on the Tobu Isezaki Line (an extension of the Subway Hibiya Line) and is about a 35-minute ride from the Ginza stop on the Subway Hibiya Line.

Souka (upper center) is another former Nikko Road post town. In the feudal era, this area was popular for hunting parties. It is famous for its *sembei* rice crackers, and is the home of a Pentel factory. Population 204,000. Like Koshigaya, it is on the Tobu Isezaki Line; it takes about 30 minutes to reach Souka from the Ginza.

4. Chiba Prefecture

Funabashi (upper right), once a leading port, is now another bedroom community. There are a large number of heavy industry factories along Tokyo Bay here. It is about a

25-minute ride on the JR Sobu Line from Tokyo Station. Population 525,000.

Matsudo (upper right) is a former post town on the road to Mito. Today it has a population of 450,000 and is a university and manufacturing city. It is on the JR Joban Line, and is a 20- minute ride from Ueno.

Ichikawa (upper right) is a residential city for commuters. Population 428,000. It is a 20-minute ride from Tokyo on the JR Sobu Line.

Kashiwa (upper right) is located on the Tonegawa River and was once the area's water transportation center. With a population of 304,000, the city is now another Tokyo bedroom community. It is a 30-minute ride on the JR Joban Line from Ueno.

Ichihara (middle right) is a golf paradise for space-starved Tokyoites. It has more than 25 golf courses. It is also the home of the Furukawa Electric Company, Mitsui Petroleum and Mitsui Shipbuilding. It is about a one-hour ride on the JR Uchibo Line from Tokyo Station to Goi, Ichihara's main train station.

YOKOHAMA 横浜

In the feudal era Yokohama was a small farming and fishing village. In the middle of the 19th century, when the Tokugawa Shogunate reluctantly abandoned its policy of isolation and opened several Japanese ports to Western traders, Yokohama was selected as one of them. At that time, nearby Kanagawa was the main port in the area, but it was too busy a place for the authorities to be able to adequately protect the Western traders against assassins, so the Shogunate had a new port constructed at Yokohama, which was a rather isolated place. Yokohama was the only place the western traders were allowed to live and work. Moats were constructed to make the area unassailable, and check-points were set up to keep out the fanatics who wanted no foreigners in the country. The area inside the moats was Kannai (Inside the Checkpoints), while the rest of the area was called Kangai (Outside the Checkpoints). After the Meiji Restoration, the new imperial government emphasized international trade. Yokohama grew rapidly and became Japan's largest port. Today Yokohama is Japan's second largest city with a population of 3,211,000. Kannai became the center of the new city. Once Yokohama was opened to the Western traders, many Chinese also took up residence in the city and today part of Kannai is a bustling Chinatown. Kannai is a living display of Japanese, Western and Chinese cultures, and has an exotic and rather cosmopolitan air quite different from that of other Japanese cities.

Outline of the City

Kannai (lower center, Kanto Map 20) is still the city's heart, with municipal and prefectural government buildings (including Yokohama City Hall). The area around Yokohama Station (left center) has, in the last decade or so, been the site of a great deal of development, and is now a shopping and transportation center. Between the two is an area now receiving a great deal of attention from developers. Following an ambitious "Harbor City of the Future" plan, Yokohama has embarked on construction of Minato Mirai 21 ("**MM 21**"), which will eventually include: "Pacifico Yokohama パシフィコ横浜," an international exhibition, convention and hotel complex; "Landmark Tower," Japan's tallest building (296 m; 971 feet); a preservation area with traditional brick buildings; museums; "Yokohama Cosmo World," a playland; restaurants; office buildings; and condominiums. Sakuragicho Station is the gateway to Pacifico Yokohama. The road from Sakuragicho Station to Pacifico Yokohama is a covered people mover (moving pedestrian path). With this project, Yokohama, as Japan's

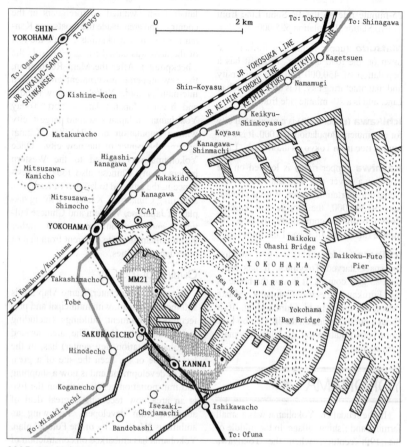

MAP 20 Yokohama

second largest but oft-ignored city, is trying to establish an independent identity for itself. The area around Shin-Yokohama Station (upper left) is emerging as an office building and hotel center.

Transportation

Kannai, Yokohama and Shin-Yokohama are connected by the city's subway line. A boat (the "Sea Bass") connects the Yokohama Station area, MM 21 and Kannai. The boats operate about once an hour in each

direction, and the ride from the Yokohama Station area to MM21 takes 10 minutes, and another 15 minutes to Kannai (Yamashita-Koen Park Pier). Fare: full trip 500 yen; 300 yen for each segment).

From Tokyo, Shimbashi and Shinagawa Stations, you can take either the JR Keihin-Tohoku Line or the JR Yokosuka Line to Yokohama. The JR Keihin-Tohoku Line also serves Kannai (the JR Yokosuka Line does not).

There are two ways to reach Narita Airport from Yokohama. First, the JR Narita Express operates about once an hour from Yokohama Station to Narita via Tokyo Station. The ride takes about one and a half hours and the fare is 4,100 yen. Second, the Airport Limousine Bus leaves for Narita from Yokohama City Air Terminal (YCAT) (about a 10-minute walk from Yokohama Station). The trip takes about two hours and the fare is 3,300 yen.

Places of Interest in Kannai

Isezaki Mall 伊勢佐木モール (middle left; Kanto Map 21) is a lovely traffic-free pedestrian mall with good shops and restaurants. It is home to Matsuzakaya and Marui Department Stores.

Bashamichi Street 馬車道 (middle left)

is paved in part with bricks. Some of the buildings in this area still have the flavor of the late 19th and early 20th centuries in Japan.

Kanagawa Prefectural Museum 神奈川県立博物館 (upper left) is a Western-style building topped with a dome. The first floor of the Museum features nature displays, the second floor archaeology, and the third sculpture and painting of medieval and modern times. Hours: 9:00 AM to 4:00 PM. Closed on Monday. Admission: 200 yen.

Monument of Japan-U.S. Friendship Treaty 日米和親条約締結の地碑 (upper center). In 1854, Japan ended its more than 200 year long period of isolation by signing the first treaty of friendship with the United States. This monument commemorates this historical event.

MAP 21 Kannai

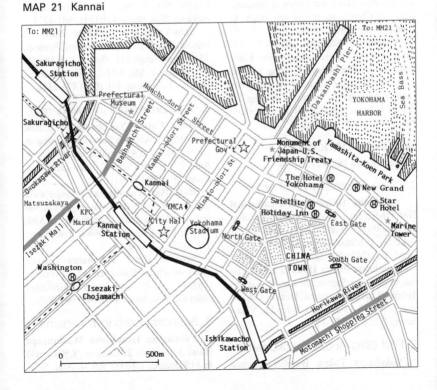

Yamashita-Koen Park 山下公園 (upper right) is a green oasis for Yokohama's citizens. The Park features water fountains and a Statue of the Goddess of Water presented to Yokohama by its sister city, San Diego.

Marine Tower マリンタワー (middle right) (106 m; 347 feet) was built in 1961 to commemorate the 100th anniversary of the opening of Yokohama Port. Its Observatory is at an altitude of 100 m (328 feet). If the weather permits, visitors can enjoy a panoramic view in all directions, even as far as Mt. Fuji. Hours: 10:00 AM to 9:00 PM (10:00 PM in summer; 7:00 PM in winter). Admission: 700 yen.

Chinatown 中華街 (lower right) sits within four gates. Its main street stretches from East Gate to North Gate. More than 160 Chinese restaurants are located in Chinatown. Prices are generally more expensive than the Chinatown prices you might be used to in the United States.

Yokohama Stadium 横浜スタジアム (middle center) is the home of the Yokohama Taiyo Whales, a professional baseball team. It also is the venue for a number of international sports events, including the annual U.S. college football all-star exhibition game in early January.

ACCOMMODATIONS

(Refer to Kanto Map 21)

1. Deluxe Hotels in Yokohama

Yokohama Grand Inter-Continental Hotel (adjacent to MM21). 600 rooms. Single (29,000 yen -) & Double (34,000 yen -). Add: 1-1-1, Minato-Mirai, Nishi-ku, Yokohama. Tel: (045) 223-2222.

Yokohama Prince Hotel (3 minutes by car from Isogo Station on the JR Keihin-Tohoku Line). 441 rooms. Double (38,500 yen -). Add: 3-13-1, Isogo, Isogo-ku, Yokohama. Tel: (045) 751-1111.

2. First Class Hotels in Yokohama

Yokohama Tokyu Hotel (1 minute walk from Yokohama Station). 212 rooms. Single (21,000 yen -) & Double (28,000 yen -). Add: 1-1-12, Minami-Saiwai, Nishi-ku, Yokohama. Tel: (045) 311-1682.

Shin-Yokohama Prince Hotel (2 minute walk from Shin-Yokohama Station). 1,002 rooms. Single (16,000 yen -) & Double (21,000 yen -). Add: 3-4, Shin-Yokohama, Kita-ku, Yokohama. Tel: (045) 471-1111.

The Hotel Yokohama (middle right). 168 rooms. Double (24,500 yen -). Add: 6-1, Yamashitacho, Naka-ku, Yokohama. Tel: (045) 662-1321.

Hotel New Grand (middle right). 201 rooms. Double (33,000 yen -). Add: 10, Yamashitacho, Naka-ku, Yokohama. Tel: (045) 681-1841.

Holiday Inn Yokohama (middle right). 188 rooms. Single (21,000 yen -) & Double (23,500 yen -). Add: 77, Yamashitacho, Naka-ku, Yokohama. Tel: (045) 681-3311.

Shin-Yokohama Kokusai Hotel (3 minute walk from Shin-Yokohama Station). 154 rooms. Single (11,000 yen -) & Double (20,000 yen -). Add: 3-18-1, Shin-Yokohama, Kita-ku, Yokohama. Tel: (045) 473-1311.

3. Standard Hotels in Yokohama

Hotel Cosmo Yokohama (7 minute walk from Yokohama Station). 111 singles (10,500 yen -) & 45 doubles (19,500 yen -). Add: 2-9-1, Kita-Saiwai, Nishi-ku, Yokohama. Tel: (045) 314-3111.

Hotel Rich Yokohama (5 minute walk from Yokohama Station). 98 singles (12,500 yen -) & 106 doubles (22,500 yen -). Add: 1-11-3, Kita-Saiwai, Nishi-ku, Yokohama. Tel: (045) 312-2111.

Satellite Hotel Yokohama (middle right). 46 singles (9,000 yen -) & 55 doubles (15,000 yen -). Add: 76, Yamashitacho, Naka-ku, Yokohama. Tel: (045) 641-0202.

4. Business Hotels in Yokohama

Yokohama Isezakicho Washington Hotel (lower left). 280 singles (8,500 yen -) & 117 doubles (16,000 yen -). Add: 5-53,

Chojamachi, Naka-ku, Yokohama. Tel: (045) 243-7111.

Star Hotel Yokohama (middle right). 7 singles (9,500 yen -) & 112 doubles (15,000 yen -). Add: 11, Yamashitacho, Naka-ku, Yokohama. Tel: (045) 651-3111.

Fuji View Hotel Shin-Yokohama (3 minute walk from Shin-Yokohama Station). 140 singles (8,500 yen -) & 54 doubles (16,000 yen -). Add: 2-3-1, Shin-Yokohama, Kita-ku, Yokohama. Tel: (045) 473-0021.

KAMAKURA 鎌倉

The first military government in Japanese history was established in Kamakura by Shogun Yoritomo Minamoto in 1192. Before the Minamoto family seized control of the country, the Taira family, another powerful military clan (which the Minamotos destroyed) had already played an influential role in the imperial government in Kyoto. The Minamotos made history by establishing a government independent, both geographically and structurally, from Kyoto. The second and third Minamoto shogun were assassinated, and political power shifted to the family of Yoritomo's wife, the Hojos. Succeeding generations of the Hojo family installed puppet shogun, reserving for themselves the powerful office of Regent. The military government of Kamakura lasted until 1333. During these 141 years, Kamakura prospered as Japan's political, economic and religious center. Zen Buddhism was especially popular among the samurai class, and flourished here in the stronghold of the shogun.

Japan was attacked by the forces of the Yuan Dynasty of China twice, in 1274, and again in 1281. The Kamakura government, led by Regent Tokimune Hojo, successfully defeated the Mongolian invaders, thanks in part to fortuitous typhoons (*Kamikaze*, or Divine Wind), but these wars caused the Kamakura Shogunate great financial diffi-

culties. The local lords whose military support had made the victories possible expected recognition, gratitude and hard cash in return for their contributions, and felt that the Shogunate was not supplying any of them. Emperor Godaigo capitalized on this situation, rallying these dissatisfied lords to his cause. With their support, the imperial forces defeated the Kamakura forces and the Emperor was restored to political power in 1333. The Emperor's ascendancy was, however, very short lived, and in 1336, the Ashikaga family seized power and established a new Shogunate.

After the fall of the Hojos, Kamakura never reappeared on the historical scene. Today, its many carefully preserved cultural relics testify to the glory the area enjoyed in the medieval era.

Outline of the Area

As pictured on Kanto Map 19, Kamakura (lower center) is located about 48 km (30 miles) southwest of Tokyo. Foreign tour groups usually skip this city or visit only the Great Buddha. But Kamakura is definitely worth exploring, and has much more to offer. This once prosperous feudal city is now an expensive high class residential area with a population of 176,000. It is on a direct train line from Tokyo and is an ideal day excursion from the capital.

Transportation to Kamakura

The JR Yokosuka Line operates between Tokyo (Tokyo, Shimbashi and Shinagawa Stations) and Kurihama via Ofuna, Kita-Kamakura, Kamakura and Yokosuka. The ride to Kita-Kamakura takes between 50 and 60 minutes, depending on the Station in Tokyo from which you leave. It's an additional three minutes to Kamakura. On the way to Kamakura, you can see a 25 m (82 foot) statue of a Kannon from the right-hand side of the train. She looks down a hill near Ofuna Station. As the train leaves Ofuna, we recommend that you turn back to get a good look.

Suggested Itinerary

Kamakura's major temples and shrines are located between Kita-Kamakura and Kamakura Stations. A walking tour is the ideal way to visit these places.

The Great Buddha and Hasedera Temple are located near Hase Station (lower left, Kanto Map 22) on the Enoden (the Enoshima Dentetsu) Line. This line originates at Kamakura Station; Hase is the third stop, and the ride from Kamakura takes only five minutes. The fare between Kamakura and Hase is 170 yen for the 5-minute ride.

The full day walking tour starts from Kita-Kamakura Station as explained below. If you want to see just the highlights of Kamakura, take a train to Kamakura Station and visit Tsurugaoka Hachimagu Shrine, Hasedera Temple, and finally the Great Buddha.

Engakuji Temple 円覚寺 (Upper center)

Engakuji Temple was built in 1282 to honor the victims of the wars against the Mongolian invaders. In the Kamakura of the time, Engakuji was second in importance only to Kenchoji Temple, and, at the peak of its prosperity, its precincts contained more than 50 minor temples and other buildings. Even though most of the original buildings were lost in fires, the reconstructions preserve the atmosphere of a powerful Zen temple. What might be the original Shariden Hall (National Treasure) still stands, and is Engakuji's most important historical relic. You can't go through the gate in front of Shariden, but you can get a glimpse of part of this famous building. The gardens of Butsunichian and Obaiin are open to the public. Obaiin is the mausoleum of Tokimune Hojo and has a well-maintained garden located at the foot of a steep cliff. Japanese powdered tea is served in the garden of Butsunichian. If you are interested in tasting real Japanese tea ceremony tea (it's green and bitter!),

Butsunichian is a good place to enjoy it in a casual atmosphere. The entrance to Butsunichian is a small wooden door. Hours of Temple precincts: 8:00 AM to 5:30 PM (4:00 PM in winter). Admission: 200 yen (extra charge for green tea).

Tokeiji Temple 東慶寺 (Upper center) (optional)

Tokeiji Temple was a convent until the Meiji Restoration, and was popularly known as the "Divorce Temple." In the feudal era, women were not allowed to initiate divorces, no matter how cruel their husbands. A special law promulgated by the wife of Tokimune Hojo designated Tokeiji Temple as the place where unhappily married women could seek refuge as a last resort. Once a woman escaped into the Temple's precincts, no one was allowed to remove her. The Temple still has something of the atmosphere of a peaceful and refined sanctuary, and the Temple's gardens are filled with the flowers of the season. Hours: 8:30 AM to 5:00 PM (4:00 PM in winter). Admission: 50 yen. The Treasure House in the Temple's precincts is open from 10:00 AM to 3:00 PM. Closed on Mondays. Admission: 300 yen.

Jochiji Temple 浄智寺 (Upper center) (optional)

Kamakura-kaido Street is the main road connecting Kita-Kamakura and Kamakura. The traffic is always heavy and there's only a narrow sidewalk — be careful!

The entrance to Jochiji Temple is at the top of a long moss-covered stone stairway. The unique gate houses a temple bell on its second floor. All of the Temple's magnificent original buildings were destroyed by fires over the course of history, and the present buildings were constructed about 50 years ago. There is a neatly trimmed garden behind the Main Hall. Statues of the Seven Gods of Fortune stand at the northern end of the precincts. Hours: 9:00 AM to 4:30 PM. Admission: 100 yen.

MAP 22 Kamakura

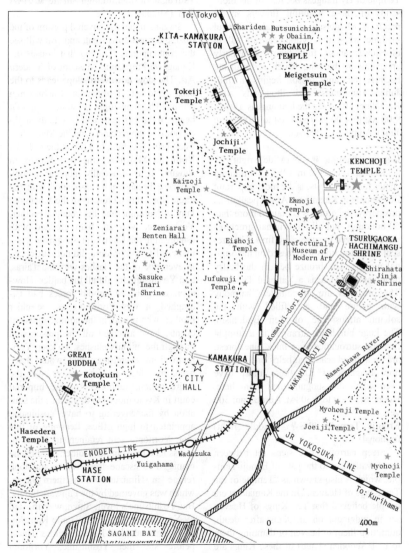

To: Tokyo

KITA-KAMAKURA STATION

Shariden Butsunichian Obaiin

★ ★ ★

★ **ENGAKUJI TEMPLE**

Meigetsuin Temple

★

Tokeiji Temple ★

Jochiji Temple ★

KENCHOJI TEMPLE ★

Kaizoji Temple ★

Ennoji Temple ★

Zeniarai Benten Hall ★

Eishoji Temple ★

Prefectural Museum of Modern Art ★

TSURUGAOKA HACHIMANGU SHRINE ★

Shirahata Jinja Shrine

Sasuke Inari Shrine ★

Jufukuji Temple ★

Komachi-dori St.

WAKAMIYA-OJI BLVD

Namerikawa River

GREAT BUDDHA

★ Kotokuin Temple

KAMAKURA STATION

☆ **CITY HALL**

Myohonji Temple ★

Joeiji Temple ★

Hasedera Temple ★

ENODEN LINE

Wadazuka

Yuigahama

HASE STATION

JR YOKOSUKA LINE

Myohoji Temple ★

To: Kurihama

0   400m

SAGAMI BAY

Meigetsuin Temple 明月院 (Upper right) (optional)

Meigetsuin Temple is known as the Temple of Hydrangeas because of the thousands of these beautiful flowers in its precincts. Meigetsuin is especially beautiful in June when the hydrangeas are all in bloom. Japanese find them particularly appealing in the rain, which is fortunate, because the rainy season begins in mid-June. Thousands and thousands visit Kamakura just to see the hydrangeas. Hours: 9:00 AM to 4:00 PM (6:00 AM to 6:00 PM in June). Admission: 200 yen.

Kenchoji Temple 建長寺 (Middle right)

Kenchoji, erected in 1253 as a training center for Zen priests, is the most important Zen temple in Kamakura. At the peak of its prosperity, the grounds contained more than 50 buildings, but all the original structures were destroyed in successive fires. The present reconstructions were based on the original models. The bronze bell in the belfry near Sanmon Gate is a National Treasure. The precincts are in complete harmony with nature and are filled with the solemn atmosphere of Zen Buddhism. The huge buildings, arranged in a straight line and surrounded by a thick pine forest, are on a grand scale that helps one imagine how magnificent Kamakura must have been when the shogun ruled from here. Hours: 8:30 AM to 4:30 PM. Admission: 300 yen.

Ennoji Temple 円応寺 (Middle right) (optional)

Steep narrow stone steps set between stone walls lead to the gate of Ennoji Temple, which is also known as "Temple of the Ten Kings of Heaven." In the Kamakura era people believed that Ten Kings of Heaven sat in judgment on all souls after death, admitting them to heaven or damning them to hell. Wooden statues of these Kings are housed in this small Temple. Unless you are especially interested in sculpture, you should skip this Temple. Hours: 9:00 AM to 4:00 PM. Admission: 100 yen.

Tsurugaoka Hachimangu Shrine 鶴ガ岡八幡宮 (Middle right)

Passing under the covered portion of the road, the street turns right, and you will see the contemporary building that houses the Kanagawa Prefectural Museum of Modern Art. The slow downward slope leads to the back gate of Tsurugaoka Hachimangu Shrine. The long flight of stone steps that begins at the *torii* gate leads you to the highest point of the precincts and the Main Hall. The Shrine was built in 1180 at the order of Yoritomo Minamoto, the first Kamakura shogun. It is especially popular among Japanese because it is associated with the tragic story of two brothers of the Minamoto family, Yoritomo and his younger brother, Yoshitsune, who are both credited with establishing the Kamakura Shogunate. As a matter of fact, Yoritomo did not participate in even one of the clashes with the Tairas, and Yoshitsune fought all the battles. However, once the Minamoto forces had triumphed, it was Yoritomo, as the elder brother, who would, in the normal course of events, have assumed all the power won through the military clashes. To keep Yoritomo from exercising what would have been, in effect, absolute power over the entire nation, supporters of the imperial court in Kyoto moved to destabilize the situation by maneuvering to have Yoshitsune appointed to high office. Learning of this plot, Yoritomo sent retainers to Kyoto to assassinate his younger brother. Yoshitsune managed to escape from Kyoto and took refuge in Hiraizumi in northern Japan, which was governed by the Fujiwara family. But Yoshitsune's lover, Shizu, was arrested by Yoritomo's force and taken to Kamakura. Because she had been a famous dancer before she met Yoshitsune, Yoritomo ordered Shizu to entertain him and his wife. Enduring the humiliation, Shizu made the forced performance an emotional expression of her love for Yoshitsune and her anxiety about his fate in his remote exile. Maiden Hall, located at the foot of the stone steps to the Main Hall, is where Shizu danced 800 years ago. Incidentally, Yoshitsune and the Fujiwaras were destroyed by forces dispatched from Kamakura in 1189; with this there remained no challengers to Yoritomo, who established the Kamakura Shogunate. Hours: 8:00 AM to 5:30 PM. Admission to the grounds is free. **The Treasure House 宝物館** displays artistic and historical objects related to Zen Buddhism. Hours: 9:00 AM to 4:00 PM. Closed on Mondays. Admission: 100 yen. Shirahata Jinja Shrine, also located here, was built to honor Yoritomo and Sanetomo, the first and the third Kamakura shogun.

Wakamiya-oji Boulevard 若宮大路 (Middle right)

Wakamiya-oji Boulevard leads to Tsurugaoka Hachimangu Shrine from Kamakura Station. In the stretch that runs between the two huge *torii* gates, one at the southern end of the Shrine precincts and the other near McDonald's, there is a pedestrian path in the central part of the boulevard. Cherry trees on both sides of the path make this approach to the Shrine especially beautiful in early April when the pale pink flowers are in bloom. During the New Year's Holidays the boulevard is thronged with visitors because millions of Japanese visit this Shrine to make their New Year's Resolutions. There are many souvenir shops and restaurants along the boulevard.

Komachi-dori Street 小町通り (Middle right)

Komachi-dori Street is a narrow street parallel to Wakamiya-oji Boulevard on its west. This street represents the modern face of Kamakura with many (perhaps too many) restaurants, souvenir shops, coffee shops and boutiques. Komachi-dori Street and Wakamiya-oji Boulevard have a number of souvenir shops with good inventories of bamboo products and *Kamakura-bori*, a special Kamakura craft. (Carved wooden items lacquered and relacquered many times in either black or vermilion.) You can also find Japanese dolls and antiques in Kamakura.

To Hase The Enoden Line's Kamakura Station is at the western side of the JR station. It is easier to find the ticket vending machines and the entrance if you go around the JR station.

Hasedera Temple 長谷寺 (Lower left)

The first thing you see upon entering the precincts of Hasedera Temple is a lovely garden. Stone steps lead to the main grounds of the Temple. On the way, you will see hundreds of small stone images of *jizobosatsu* (God of Travelers and Children). The colorful pinwheels attached to each image were placed there by grieving parents of stillborn babies and children who died young. Unlike most temples in Kamakura, which open their precincts but not their interior halls to the public, Hasedera Temple allows visitors inside both its Amida Hall and Kannon Hall. After looking at just the exteriors of temple buildings, the encounters you will have here with the images of many Buddhas and other Gods is very impressive. Especially important is the 9 m (30 foot) tall Eleven-Faced Kannon housed in Kannon Hall. This golden image was carved in 721 and is the tallest wooden statue in Japan. Another group of stone *jizobosatsu* images stands at the western end of the grounds. One more attraction of this Temple is the marvelous view of Sagami Bay from the southern part of the grounds. Hours: 8:00 AM to 5:00 PM (4:30 PM in winter). Admission: 200 yen.

Great Buddha 鎌倉大仏 (Lower left)

The Great Buddha, the main object of worship at Kotokuin Temple, is popular worldwide, and attracts visitors all year round. The 11.3 m (37 foot) tall bronze image was cast in 1252. It is Japan's second largest statue (the largest is the Great Buddha of Todaiji Temple in Nara). This Buddha was originally housed in a wooden hall, which was swept away by a tidal wave in 1495. Since then the Buddha has sat in the open air. There's an entrance to the interior of the statue at the right side of its base (as you face the Buddha). Steep ladders go up to a small window at the top of the back of the statue. Hours: 7:00 AM to 4:00 PM. Admission: 150 yen. Additional 20 yen admission to the interior of the statue.

To Kamakura Station A bus to Kamakura Station stops right in front of the grounds of the Great Buddha. You can also walk back to Hase Station and take an Enoden train to Kamakura.

Hotel in Kamakura

Kamakura Park Hotel (12 minute walk from Hase Station on the Enoden Line). Standard. 41 rooms. Double (15,500 yen -). Add: 33-6, Sakanoshita, Kamakura. Tel: (0467) 25-5121.

KAWASAKI 川崎

Sandwiched between Japan's largest and second largest cities (Tokyo and Yokohama — See Kanto Map 23), Kawasaki truly gets no respect. It first developed as Tokyo's heavy industry center. Kawasaki is actually Japan's ninth largest city, with a population of 1,153,000. The city is bordered by the

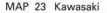

MAP 23 Kawasaki

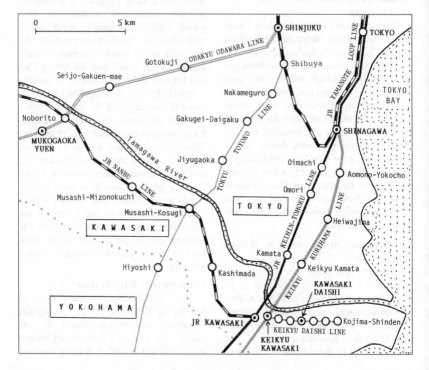

Tamagawa River on the north. It stretches a long distance from east to west. The downtown is centered around JR Kawasaki Station (lower center), which is served by the JR Keihin-Tohoku Line. We recommend two Kawasaki attractions for side trips from Tokyo.

Kawasaki Daishi Temple 川崎大師 (Lower right, Kanto Map 23)

You can reach this Temple on the Keikyu Kurihama train from Shinagawa, switching at Keikyu Kawasaki Station to the local Keikyu Daishi Line. Kawasaki Daishi Station is the third stop from Keikyu Kawasaki. The ride from Shinagawa to Keikyu Kawasaki Station takes about 15 minutes on an express. Fare: 190 yen. Keikyu Kawasaki to Kawasaki Daishi is a five-minute trip. Fare: 110 yen. Kawasaki Daishi Temple, officially Heikenji Temple, is one of the most popular New Year's destinations for Tokyo, Yokohama and Kawasaki residents. More than one million people visit it each New Year's Eve to welcome in the New Year and make their resolutions. The Temple is only a five-minute walk from the train station (see Kanto Map 24). The main approach is lined with colorful souvenir shops that sell the roly-poly *daruma* dolls so popular in Japan. It is customary for Japanese to purchase a *daruma* and color in one of its blank eyes, making a wish and trusting the *daruma* to help it come true. When it does, the second eye is colored in, often at official celebrations. You may have seen pictures of Japanese politicians celebrating victory in such a fashion.

Nihon Minka-en (Japan Open-Air Folkhouse Museum) 日本民家園

Nihon Minka-en is near Mukogaoka-Yuen Station (upper left, Kanto Map 23) on the Odakyu Line. The ride to Mukogaoka-Yuen Station from Shinjuku takes about 20 minutes. Fare: 200 yen. A monorail in front of the train station will take you to Mukogaoka-Yuen Playland (outside of Kanto Map 25), a good family destination for Tokyo residents. Nihon Minka-en (Japan Open-Air Folkhouse Museum) (lower left) is about a 15-minute walk from the Station. It is a museum of more than 20 traditional homes assembled here by the city of Kawasaki in an effort to preserve these relics of the past. These lovely old residences, in various Japanese architectural styles, are laid out in a quiet wooded area. Walking around here is enjoyable as well as educational. Hours: 9:30 AM to 4:30 PM. Closed Monday. Admission: 300 yen.

MAP 24 Kawasaki Daishi Temple

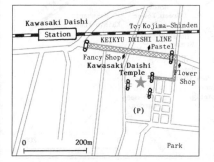

MAP 25 Nihon Minkaen

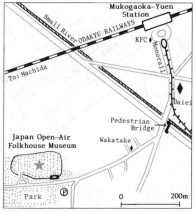

CHIBA (MAKUHARI MESSE)
千葉(幕張メッセ)

Chiba City (middle right, Kanto Map 19) is the capital of Chiba Prefecture. The city has a population of 821,000. It first developed as the northernmost outpost of the Tokyo-area industrial zone. Located between New Tokyo International Airport (Narita) and Tokyo Core, Chiba, in recent years, has emphasized its international links and its attractions as a venue for international meetings and events. **Makuhari Messe** is a convention, meeting and business office complex near Kaihin-Makuhari Station (middle right), in the eastern corner of Chiba City.

Transportation to Makuhari Messe
Kaihin-Makuhari Station is only a 37-minute ride from Tokyo on the JR Keiyo Line. Please note that the Keiyo Line platform is about 500 m (1,670 feet) from the main building of Tokyo Station (There is an underground passage). Airport Buses connect all Makuhari hotels (see below) with Narita Airport. For those used to difficult transportation from Narita into Tokyo, this is an almost unbelievably short ride. The trip takes only about 30 minutes, and the fare is 830 yen.

Makuhari Messe 幕張メッセ

The heart of Makuhari's new development is Makuhari Messe (Kanto Map 26), which features an International Exhibition Hall, an International Conference Hall, an Event Hall and a Central Plaza. The twin towers of the World Business Center house offices, and a good selection of restaurants. Many additional highrise office buildings are under construction on the northern side of the JR Keiyo Line tracks. Makuhari is targeting high tech companies as tenants for these

MAP 26 Makuhari Messe

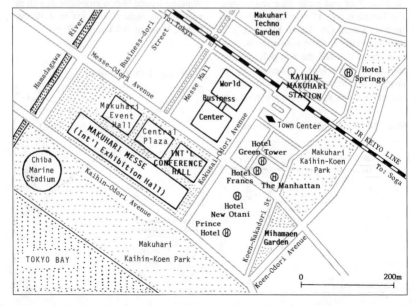

office buildings. Already, Japan IBM, NTT, Canon, Seiko, Fujitsu, Sharp and Tokyo Gas have offices in Makuhari. With its easy access from Narita Airport as well as its train connections to downtown Tokyo, Makuhari Messe has already met some of its goals and has been chosen as the venue for important international exhibitions and meetings. With this prime location and its superior facilities, it seems impossible for Makuhari not to achieve its goal of becoming Japan's preeminent international meeting and event venue.

Mihamaen Garden 見浜園 (lower right), a Japanese-style "stroll" garden has been laid out in Makuhari Kaihin-Koen Park, to give foreign visitors a taste of traditional Japanese garden arts.

Chiba Marine Stadium 千葉マリンスタジアム (middle left) is the home of the Chiba Lotte Marines, a professional baseball team.

Hotels Around Makuhari Messe

(Refer to Kanto Map 26)

Makuhari Prince Hotel (lower center). Deluxe. 1,001 rooms. Single (17,500 yen -) & Double (35,000 yen -). Add: 2-3, Hibino, Mihama-ku, Chiba. Tel: (043) 296-1111.

Hotel New Otani Makuhari (lower center). 418 rooms. Opening in September, 1993. Add: 2-2, Hibino, Mihama-ku, Chiba.

The Manhattan (middle center). Deluxe. All suite hotel (131 rooms). Double (44,500 yen -). Add: 2-10-1, Hibino, Mihama-ku, Chiba. Tel: (043) 275-1111.

Hotel Springs Makuhari (upper right). First Class. 110 singles (13,000 yen -) & 88 doubles (23,000 yen -). Add: 1-11, Hibino, Mihama-ku, Chiba. Tel: (043) 296-3111.

Hotel Green Tower (middle center). First Class. 135 singles (11,500 yen -) & 66 doubles (22,500 yen -). Add: 2-10-3, Hibino, Mihama-ku, Chiba. Tel: (043) 296-1122.

Hotel Francs (middle center). First Class. 155 singles (12,000 yen -) & 81 doubles (21,000 yen -). Add: 2-10-2, Hibino, Mihama-ku, Chiba. Tel: (043) 296-2111.

Toyoko Inn Chiba Makuhari (10 minutes by taxi from Makuhari Messe). Business. 192 singles (6,000 yen -) & 24 double (9,000 yen -). Add: 131, Shinminato, Mihama-ku, Chiba. Tel: (0472) 42-1045.

URAYASU (TOKYO DISNEYLAND)
浦安(東京ディズニーランド)

Urayasu, a city built on landfill, has a current population of 113,000. This Tokyo bedroom community's only distinction has been its selection as the site of Tokyo Disneyland. Tokyo Disneyland was the first Disney venture outside the United States. It is wildly popular. It is *the* leisure destination in Japan. Hours: 10:00 AM to 6:00 PM (9:00 AM to 10:00 PM on weekends and in "prime tourist season" in summer). Closed on an irregular, unscheduled basis. Admission prices vary. A basic one day "passport" costs 4,400 yen. Tokyo Disneyland is extremely crowded, especially during school vacations. For information, call (0473) 54-0001.

Transportation

Maihama is the name of the train station

MAP 27 Tokyo Disneyland

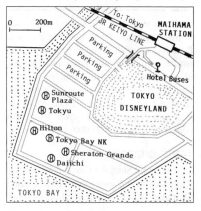

for Tokyo Disneyland (middle right, Kanto Map 19). It is only a 16-minute ride from Tokyo Station on the JR Keiyo Line. Airport Buses operate between area hotels and Narita Airport. The ride takes 70 minutes, and the fare is 2,200 yen.

Hotels around Tokyo Disneyland
(Refer to Kanto Map 27)

Sheraton Grande Tokyo Bay (lower center). Deluxe. 665 rooms. Double (35,000 yen -). Add: 1-9, Maihama, Urayasu. Tel: (0473) 55-5555.

Tokyo Bay Hilton (middle left). Deluxe. 728 rooms. Double (34,000 yen -). Add: 1-9, Maihama, Urayasu. Tel: (0473) 55-5000.

Tokyo Bay Hotel Tokyu (middle left). Deluxe. 700 rooms. Double (29,500 yen -). Add: 1-7, Maihama, Urayasu. Tel: (0473) 55-2411.

Daiichi Hotel Tokyo Bay (lower left). Deluxe. 412 rooms. Double (41,000 yen -). Add: 1-8, Maihama, Urayasu. Tel: (0473) 55-3333.

Sunroute Plaza Tokyo (middle left). First Class. 471 rooms. Double (21,000 yen -). Add: 1-6, Maihama, Urayasu. Tel: (0473) 55-1111.

KAWAGOE   川越

Kawagoe (upper left, Kanto Map 19) is a former Saitama Prefecture castle town. Because of its strategic importance at the gateway to Tokyo, the Tokugawa shoguns always made sure that members of their family were assigned to rule Kawagoe. Kawagoe is now a commercial center as well as a Tokyo bedroom town. Its current population stands at 299,000.

Transportation

The Seibu Shinjuku Line links Kawagoe (Hon-Kawagoe Station) with Tokyo's Seibu Shinjuku Station. The ride takes one hour

and the fare is 420 yen. The Tobu Tojo Line also connects Kawagoe and Tokyo (Ikebukuro Station). The ride takes about 40 minutes and the fare is 400 yen.

Places of Interest

Kawagoe's main attraction is **Kitain Temple** 喜多院 (upper right, Kanto Map 28). The Temple was erected in 830. The current buildings are 1638 reconstructions. Part of the main building was moved here from Edojo Castle. The Temple has a pagoda and a small Toshogu Shrine. Gohyaku-Rakan (Five Hundred Disciples of Buddha) is an impressive array of more than 500 stone statues in the Temple grounds. Hours: 9:00 AM to 4:30 PM. Closed Monday. Admission to the main building and Gohyaku Rakan grounds: 400 yen.

Kawagoe's main shopping street is called Sun Road (shaded on Kanto Map 28). The shopping district extends from Seibu Hon-Kawagoe Station to the JR (and Tobu) Kawagoe Station. You can savor typical Tokyo satellite city lifestyle strolling on this bustling street.

Former Hatsukarijo Castle (in northeastern part of the city; outside Map 28) has been converted to the city's sports complex.

Kawagoe is also famous for Kawagoe Matsuri Festival. On October 14-15, twenty Shrine floats parade through the narrow alleys and streets of the city. They are especially impressive when lit with lanterns at night.

Hotels in Kawagoe
(Refer to Kanto Map 28)

Kawagoe Prince Hotel (upper floors of Hon-Kawagoe Station, middle center). First Class. 105 rooms. Double (22,500 yen -). Add: 1-22, Shintomicho, Kawagoe. Tel: (0492) 27-1111.

Kawagoe Tobu Hotel (lower center). Standard. 63 singles (8,000 yen -) & 40 doubles (14,000 yen -). Add: 29-1, Wakitacho, Kawagoe. Tel: (0492) 25-0111.

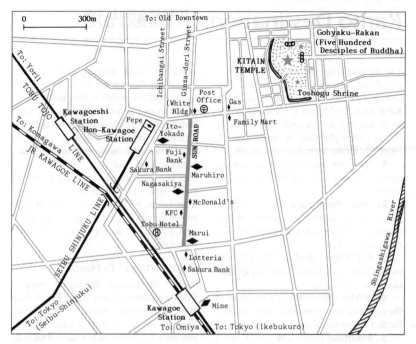

MAP 28 Kawagoe

JR FARES BETWEEN TOKYO STATION
AND MAJOR STATIONS IN METROPOLITAN TOKYO

To/From	Tokyo	Remarks
Yokohama	440 yen	JR Keihin-Tohoku Line (28.8 km)
Kannai	530 yen	JR Keihin-Tohoku Line (31.8 km)
Kamakura	880 yen	JR Yokosuka Line (51.0 km)
Kaihin-Makuhari	530 yen	JR Keiyo Line (31.7 km)
Maihama	210 yen	JR Keiyo Line (12.7 km)

Kanto Destinations 関東観光地

The outlying areas and resorts of Kanto are introduced here, divided into the nine sections listed below (all map references are to Kanto Map 29). Most of the destinations can be visited in a day excursion from Tokyo, but an overnight visit is recommended, especially for the hotspring destinations.

1. Hakone (middle left) is a mountain resort with hotsprings and Mt. Fuji observatories.

2. Izu Peninsula (lower left) is famous for a variety of hotsprings, marine scenery and fresh seafood. Details on Shimoda are included.

3. Fuji Five Lakes (middle left) is an area of great natural beauty and has spectacular views of Mt. Fuji.

4. Nikko (upper center) is the home of the elaborate and impressive mausoleum of the first Tokugawa Shogun.

5. Mashiko (upper center) is Kanto's leading pottery center.

6. Tsukuba (middle center) is Japan's official R&D city, and is home to a large number of educational institutions.

7. Narita (middle right) is home of New Tokyo International (Narita) Airport, and is also famous for its Shinshoji Temple and the National Museum of Japanese History.

8. Boso Peninsula (middle right) is an easily accessible recreation area for Tokyoites.

9. Harunasan and Ikaho Onsen (upper left) are popular hotspring resorts.

HAKONE 箱根

Hakone is a National Park and mountain resort about 80 km (50 miles) southwest of Tokyo. Volcanic activity is responsible for the area's beautiful, complex topography.

The many "hells" emitting steam and sulphur fumes found amid the 1,300 m (4,300 foot) mountains testify to the great geological forces still at work underfoot. The calm surface of Lake Ashinoko reflects the symmetrical figure of Mt. Fuji as it rises 3,776 m (12,399 feet) northwest of the Lake. Japanese think this is one of the world's most beautiful natural sights, and we're sure you'll agree. Hakone is easily a day trip from Tokyo, but if you have a night to spare and linger in this hotspring resort, you'll treat yourself to an experience you won't soon forget.

Transportation to Hakone

The JR Kodama Shinkansen stops at Odawara Station (lower right, Kanto Map 30). The faster Nozomi and Hikari Shinkansens do not stop at Odawara. The ride from Tokyo Station to Odawara takes 41 minutes. You also have to use the Kodama if you visit Hakone from the Kansai Region (Osaka and Kyoto) or the Chubu Region (Nagoya). From Odawara, it takes 2 hours and 15 minutes to Nagoya, an additional one hour to Kyoto and 16 more minutes to Osaka.

The Odakyu Railways operates frequent service between Shinjuku Station in Tokyo and Odawara Station, including a special limited express train called the "Romance Car," which features attendants and luxurious seating. Most Romance Cars go beyond Odawara to Hakone-Yumoto Station (middle right) but some terminate at Odawara. The Romance Car operates about once every 30 minutes from Shinjuku, and the ride to Odawara takes one hour and 20 minutes (Fare: 2,300 yen), and the ride to Hakone-Yumoto takes one hour and 30 minutes (Fare: 2,780 yen). It is highly advised that you buy your return ticket before you leave Shinjuku. Romance Cars are all-reserved

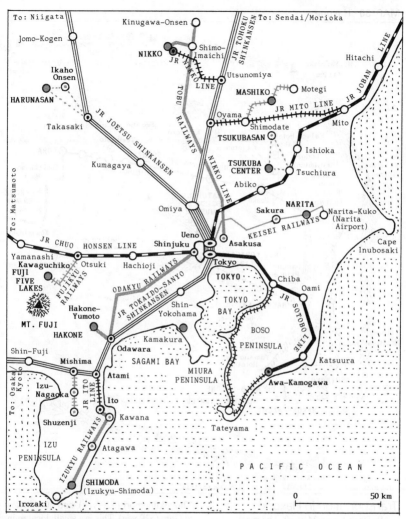

MAP 29 Outline of Kanto Region

trains. If there are no seats available on the Romance Cars, you can take one of Odakyu's regular express trains, which are designed for commuters. They operate about once every 30 minutes. The ride to Odawara Station takes about 1 hour and 50 minutes (750 yen). All of these express trains originate and terminate at Odawara Station. You can transfer at Odawara or Hakone-Yumoto from the Odakyu Line to the Hakone Tozan Testsudo Line, which connects Odawara and Gora (passing through Hakone-Yumoto on the way).

MAP 30 Hakone

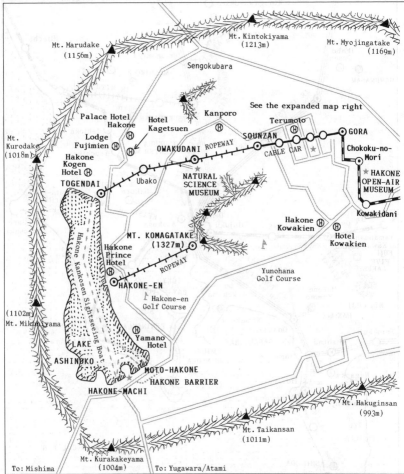

Transportation in Hakone

Refer to Kanto Map 30. The most exciting way to reach Lake Ashinoko is to use the Hakone Tozan Tetsudo Line from Odawara to Gora (upper center). The Hakone Tozan Tetsudo Line operates from Odawara Station about once every 20 minutes. There are ticket windows near the entrance to the tracks of the Tozan Tetsudo Line. The trip takes 46 minutes to Chokokunomori (520 yen), and 50 minutes to Gora (520 yen). This is a small, local train that climbs the steep mountains. After the train leaves Hakone-Yumoto Station, it switchbacks several times. Famous Hakone accommodations, the Fujiya Hotel and Naraya Ryokan, are near Miyanoshita Station (middle center). From Gora, you take a cable car to Sounzan (9 minutes; 290 yen) and a ropeway from Sounzan to Togendai

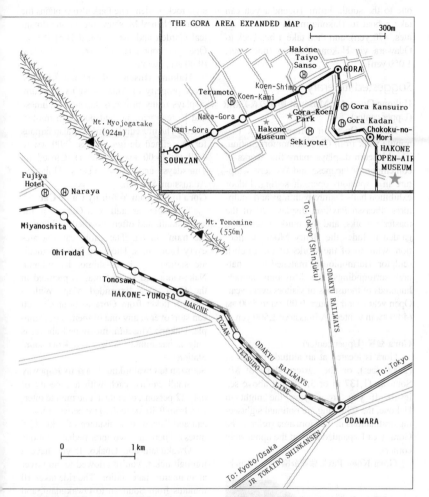

THE GORA AREA EXPANDED MAP

0   300m

Hakone
Taiyo
Sanso   GORA

Koen-Shimo
Terumoto   Koen-Kami   Gora Kansuiro

Naka-Gora   Gora-Koen   Gora Kadan
                 Park   Chokoku-no-
Kami-Gora   Hakone   Mori
             Museum   HAKONE
SOUNZAN   Sekiyotei   OPEN-AIR
                                        MUSEUM

Mt. Myojogatake
(924m)

Fujiya
Hotel   Naraya

Miyanoshita   Mt. Tonomine
                               (556m)
Ohiradai

Tonosawa

HAKONE-YUMOTO

                                                To: Tokyo (Shinjuku)
                                                ODAKYU RAILWAYS

                          HAKONE TOZAN TETSUDO ODAKYU RAILWAYS LINE
                                                To: Tokyo

0   1 km
                                                ODAWARA

                          To: Kyoto/Osaka
                          JR TOKAIDO SHINKANSEN

(middle left; 28 minutes; 1,180 yen) with an intermediate stop at Owakudani. If you go this way, you can visit the Open-Air Museum and Owakudani "Hell" on the way to the Lake. Unless you are really afraid of heights and ropeways, we definitely recommend that you follow this route. If you don't want to take the ropeway trip between Sounzan and Togendai, your alternative is to take a bus from Odawara to Togendai (one hour;

1,100 yen). The bus terminal at Odawara Station is in front of the main exit (southern side of the station). The bus to Togendai operates from stop No. 4 every 15-20 minutes. Stop No. 3 is for the bus to Hakone-machi (lower. left), at the southern side of Lake Ashinoko; it operates every 10-15 minutes. These two buses run on the same route until they reach Miyanoshita (middle center), then branch off, one to the north and one to the south. From Togendai you can take a boat to Hakone-machi (30-40 minutes; 870 yen), and then take a bus back to Odawara via Hakone-Yumoto (one hour; 1,050 yen).

Suggested Itinerary

Hakone Open-Air Museum 彫刻の森美術館 (Upper center)

Hakone Open-Air Museum is a two minute walk from Chokokunomori Station. The Museum displays many fine works of contemporary Japanese and Western sculpture in a spacious open-air setting. Indoor exhibition halls feature paintings and sculptures. Picasso Pavilion displays 20 of the master's works, and the outdoor sculpture garden includes the Henry Moore Collection, with 26 of the works of the English sculptor. Harmoniously matched to its natural surroundings, the Museums attracts hundreds of thousands of visitors every year. Open year round. Hours: 9:00 AM to 5:00 PM (4:00 PM in winter). Admission: 1,500 yen.

Gora 強羅 (Upper center)

Gora is located at an altitude of 600 m (2,000 feet), on the eastern slope of Mt. Sounzan (1,137 m or 3,730 feet above sea level). If you are staying the night in Hakone, the following are optional sightseeing destinations in the Gora area (refer to the Gora Area Expanded Map at the upper right corner):

Gora-Koen Park 強羅公園 is a French-

style rock garden. The Park also contains the Hakone Natural Museum, the Alpine Botanical Garden and the Tropical Bird House. Open year round. Hours: 9:00 AM to 5:00 PM (9:00 PM in winter).

Hakone Museum of Art 箱根美術館, a sister property of Atami's MOA Museum, displays many priceless Japanese, Chinese and Korean ceramic and porcelain masterpieces. The museum's garden is also famous for its refined design. Hours: 9:00 AM to 4:30 PM (4:00 PM in winter). Closed on Thursdays and New Year's Holidays. Admission: 800 yen.

Gora to Sounzan 早雲山 by Cable Car

The cable car station in Gora is in the same small, and often crowded building as the train station. The cable car operates every 15 minutes. There are four intermediate stations — Koen-shimo, Koen-kami, Naka-Gora and Kami-Gora, as pictured in the Gora Area Expanded Map. With a through ticket from Gora to Sounzan you can stop over at any one of them. For example, Hakone Museum, mentioned above, is only a one-minute walk from Koen-kami Station.

Sounzan to Owakudani 大湧谷 by Ropeway

Small cabins, each with a capacity of only 12 persons, operate at one minute intervals from 9:30 AM to 4:00 PM between Sounzan and Togendai, a distance of 4 km (2.5 miles). There are two intermediate stations — Owakudani and Ubako. If you have a through ticket, you're allowed to stop over at an intermediate station. The ride takes 10 minutes from Sounzan to Owakudani, and an additional 18 minutes from Owakudani to Togendai. The highlight of the ropeway ride is when it passes over Owakudani Valley just before it arrives at the Owakudani Station. Far below you can see steam escaping from the rugged mountains. We recommend that you get out at Owakudani Station.

The top floor of the Owakudani Station houses a restaurant that commands a grand view of Hakone National Park. If the weath-

er permits, you can see Mt. Fuji rising above the lower mountains to the northwest. Unfortunately, the menu at this restaurant is not nearly as special as the view. Lunches range from 1,000-4,000 yen.

Owakudani Natural Science Museum 大湧谷自然科学博物館 , a modern three-story building near the station, displays various objects featuring the history, flora and fauna of Hakone. Open year round. Hours: 9:00 AM to 4:30 PM. Admission: 400 yen.

Owakudani Natural Exploration Path 大湧谷自然探勝路 goes through volcanic "hells." The circular path is 680 m (0.4 miles) long, and the walk takes about 30 minutes. At the entrance to the Path, a vendor sells black eggs cooked in one of the "hells": the yolks are hard, the whites are soft, and the shells are black. Try one if you're interested in volcanic cuisine.

Owakudani to Togendai 桃源台 by Ropeway

Continue your ride to Togendai via the ropeway. Because Owakudani is the highest point on the route, the cabin descends slowly toward Lake Ashinoko. The view of the Lake beneath your feet is breathtaking.

Togendai. This is where your visit to Hakone will begin if you skip the ropeway and take the bus from Odawara to Togendai.

Togendai to Hakone-machi 箱根町 by Boat

Togendai Pier is only a few minutes walk from the ropeway station. Boats leave every 30-40 minutes, and all boats that originate at Togendai go to Hakone-machi. Most boats go to Hakone-machi first and then to Moto-Hakone, but a few stop at Moto-Hakone first, and then continue to Hakone-machi. The cruise takes 30 to 40 minutes. Buy your ticket in the terminal before boarding at Togendai Pier. Fare: 870 yen (regular — second class); 1,180 yen (green — first class).

Hakone-machi (lower left). If you have time before you return to Odawara (or Hakone-Yumoto) to catch your train, you should visit **Hakone Barrier** 箱根関所跡 , a brief walk from the boat pier. Follow the path along the lake to Hakone Barrier. In the Edo era, the main road between Tokyo and Kyoto (the "Tokaido" so vividly illustrated in Hiroshige's wood-block prints) ran through Hakone. To keep the minor feudal lords from rebelling, the Tokugawa shogun forced the lords' wives to live in Edo, and the lords themselves had to make formal, compulsory visits to the city every other year. These trips to Edo costs the lords a great deal because they traveled in grand processions accompanied by hundreds of retainers. The financial burden was even heavier for those lords unfriendly to the Tokugawas because they had been assigned to areas far away from Edo. At Hakone Barrier, the shogun checked on the number of guns the lords took into the Edo area. The Barrier also served as a checkpoint on the route out of Edo, ensuring that none of the wives would be able to escape. The build-

ings here are reconstructions. Open year round. Hours: 9:00 AM to 4:30 PM. Admission: 200 yen. If you have additional time, cross the modern road. On the other side, you can walk on a preserved portion of the old "Tokaido". A short hike here, along the old cryptomeria-lined road, is a pleasant break from more organized sightseeing activities.

Back to Odawara (or Hakone-Yumoto) by Bus
The bus stop is in front of the souvenir shop/restaurant at the Pier, and there's a ticket office inside.

Hakone-en 箱根園 and Mt. Komagatake 駒ガ岳 (Middle left)

Though not included in our suggested itinerary, Hakone-en is another major attraction in Hakone. Located on Lake Ashinoko near the Hakone Prince Hotel, Hakone-en is a recreation complex that includes an aquarium, and facilities for barbecuing, archery, swimming, golf and tennis. A ropeway operates between Hakone-en and the summit of Mt. Komagatake (1,327 m or 4,354 feet). The mountain top observatory commands a graceful view of Mt. Fuji over Lake Ashinoko. There is an ice skating rink near the observatory.

ACCOMMODATIONS
(Refer to Kanto Map 30)

1. Hotels in Hakone

Hakone Prince Hotel (middle left). Deluxe. 294 rooms. Cottage (28,000 yen -) & Double (35,000 yen -). Add: 144, Moto-Hakone, Hakonemachi. Tel: (0460) 3-7111.

Palace Hotel Hakone (upper left). First Class. 98 rooms. Single (21,000 yen -) & Double (26,000 yen -). Add: 1245, Sengoku-bara, Hakonemachi. Tel: (0460) 4-8501.

Yamano Hotel (lower left). First Class. 93 rooms. Double (22,500 yen -). Add: 80, Moto-Hakone, Hakonemachi. Tel: (0460) 3-6321.

Fujiya Hotel (middle center). First Class. Double (23,500 yen -). Add: 359,

Miyanoshita, Hakonemachi. Tel: (0460) 2-2211.

Hotel Kowakien (middle center). First Class. 194 rooms. Double (23,500 yen -). Add: 1297, Ninotaira, Hakonemachi. Tel: (0460) 2-4111.

Yumoto Fujiya Hotel (2 minute walk from Hakone-Yumoto Station). Standard. 88 rooms. Double (19,000 yen -). Add: 256, Yumoto, Hakonemachi. Tel: (0460) 5-6111.

Hotel Kagetsuen (middle left). Standard. 59 rooms. Double (14,000 yen -). Add: 1244-2, Sengokubara, Hakonemachi. Tel: (0460) 4-8621.

2. Ryokan in Hakone

Naraya (middle center). Deluxe. 15 rooms. 40,000 yen & up per person. Add: 162, Miyanoshita, Hakonemachi. Tel: (0460) 2-2411.

Kanporo (upper left). Deluxe. 19 rooms. 40,000 yen & up per person. Add: 1251, Sengokubara, Hakone-machi. Tel: (0460) 4-8551.

Terumoto (upper center). First Class. 50 rooms. 18,000 yen & up per person. Add: 1320, Gora, Hakonemachi. Tel: (0460) 2- 3177.

Hakone Kowakien (middle center). First Class. 352 rooms. 15,000 yen & up per person. Add: 1297, Ninotaira, Hakonemachi. Tel: (0460) 2-4111.

Hakone Kogen Hotel (middle left). First Class. 52 rooms. 15,000 yen & up per person. Add: 164, Moto-Hakone, Hakonemachi. Tel: (0460) 4-8595.

3. Welcome Inns in Hakone

Moto-Hakone Guest House (about 50 minutes by bus from Odawara Station). 5 Japanese rooms. Add: 103, Moto-Hakone, Hakonemachi. Tel: (0460) 3-7880.

Ivy Square Club (about 50 minutes by bus from Odawara Station). 5 Western rooms. Add: 160, Moto-Hakone, Hakonemachi. Tel: (0460) 4-6776.

Fuji-Hakone Guest House (about 50 minutes by bus from Odawara Station). 7 Japanese rooms. Add: 912, Sengokubara, Hakonemachi. Tel: (0460) 4-6577.

IZU PENINSULA 伊豆半島

Izu Peninsula (Kanto Map 31) is a wide area stretching 60 km (37 miles) from north to south and 33 km (20 miles) from east to west. A number of hotspring resorts are scattered across the peninsula, along the sea coast and in quiet valleys. Many people visit Izu to stay at a hotspring, to relax away from busy city life, and to enjoy the excellent fresh seafood served there. If you want to combine a stay in a hotspring with sightseeing, the following is a typical two-day itinerary from Tokyo:

Day 1. Tokyo/Shimoda

Several direct limited express trains called "Odoriko" run between Tokyo Station and Izukyu-Shimoda Station. Many of them are special trains with panoramic windows to enhance passengers' enjoyment of the trip along the coast. The ride takes about 3 hours. The train runs on the JR Line between Tokyo and Ito, and then on the Izukyu Line between Ito and Izukyu-Shimoda. Japan Rail Passes are good for the JR portion only. Fare for the entire trip is 6,150 yen. If you have a Japan Rail Pass you will only have to pay 3,070 yen. Another alternative for those with Japan Rail Passes is to take the Kodama Shinkansen from Tokyo to Atami, and switch there to the Izukyu Line. Afternoon sightseeing in Shimoda and Cape Irozaki, overnight in Shimoda.

Day 2. Shimoda/Shuzenji/Tokyo

Take a pleasant bus ride from Shimoda to Shuzenji across the picturesque Amagi mountains (a 2 hour ride). On the way, if you wish, you can visit Inoshishimura (Boar Park) and Joren-no-taki Falls. At Inoshishi-

MAP 31 Izu Peninsula

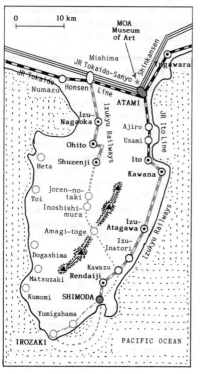

mura, trained boars and badgers perform a show. The Park and the Falls are just a 15-minute walk from each other. From Shuzenji you can take a direct train back to Tokyo Station (2 hours and 20 minutes). The trains run on the Izu-Hakone Tetsudo Line tracks between Shuzenji and Mishima, and JR tracks between Mishima and Tokyo. Japan Rail Passes are good for the JR portion only. The fare for the entire trip is 4,470 yen; with a Japan Rail Pass, the fare is only 670 yen. If you have a Japan Rail Pass, you can also take the Izu-Hakone Tetsudo Line to Mishima, and connect there to the Kodama Shinkansen for the trip back to Tokyo. If you plan to go west, e.g., to Kyoto, you can take the westbound Kodama from Mishima.

ATAMI 熱海

(Upper right, Kanto Map 31)

Only a 50-minute ride on the Kodama Shinkansen from Tokyo, Atami is the largest resort in Izu. Atami literally means "hot sea;" it is famous all over Japan for its hotsprings and its casual, relaxed pace. Thanks to its proximity to Tokyo, over 10 million people visit this city of 47,000 every year. There are several famous and authentic ryokan here, as well as many large hotels/*ryokan* catering to groups.

MOA Museum MOA美術館 is located on the steep hills above Atami Station. Buses run frequently from Platform No. 4 at the Bus Terminal in front of Atami Station (Fare: 120 yen). There is an *i* Information Office located in the Travel Service Center in JR Atami Station. If you purchase your Museum admission ticket at the Travel Service Center, it will cost you only 1,300 yen. If you purchase your admission ticket at the Museum itself, it will cost you 1,500 yen. The MOA Museum is a large complex owned by a religious organization. The Museum exhibits priceless paintings, pottery and other art objects, some of which are National Treasures. Before you reach the galleries with the art works, you have to ascend several long escalators; during the course of the journey to the galleries, you will also have the opportunity to view a laser show. Hours: 9:30 AM to 4:00 PM. Closed Thursday.

1. Hotels in Atami

New Fujiya Hotel (5 minutes by taxi from Atami Station). First Class. 316 rooms. 78 singles (12,000 yen -), 82 doubles (24,000 yen -) & 128 Japanese rooms (26,000 yen -). Add: 1-16, Ginzacho, Atami. Tel: (0557) 81-0111.

Chateautel Akanezaki (15 minutes by taxi from Atami Station). 300 rooms. 147 doubles (23,500 yen-) & 117 Japanese rooms (23,500 yen -). Add: Akane, Kamitaga, Atami. Tel: (0557) 67- 1111.

2. Ryokan in Atami

Atami Sekitei (5 minutes by taxi from Atami Station). Deluxe. 40 rooms. 50,000 yen & up per person. Add: 6-17, Wadacho, Atami. Tel: (0557) 81-7191.

Kajikaso Warakutei (8 minutes by taxi from Atami Station). Deluxe. 20 rooms. 40,000 yen & up per person. Add: 17-62, Nishiyamacho, Atami. Tel: (0557) 81-5223.

Taikanso (10 minute walk from Atami Station). Deluxe. 45 rooms. 40,000 yen & up per person. Add: 7-1, Hayashigaokacho, Atami. Tel: (0557) 81-8137.

Kiunkaku (7 minutes by taxi from Atami Station). Deluxe. 34 rooms. 40,000 yen & up per person. Add: 4-2, Showacho, Atami. Tel: (0557) 81-3623.

3. Welcome Inn in Atami

Atami Village (15 minutes by taxi from Atami Station). 26 Japanese rooms. Add: 21-7, Umezonocho, Atami. Tel: (0557) 81- 8295.

ITO 伊東

(Upper right, Kanto Map 31)

Ito is another large hotspring resort along the picturesque sea coast. Its population stands at 73,000. There is an *i* Information Office located in the Travel Service Center in JR Ito Station.

Saboten-Koen Park サボテン公園 (Cactus Park), located on pleasant Mt. Omuroyama, has several huge pyramidal greenhouses and features 5,000 cactuses transplanted from around the world. Buses operate between Ito Station and Saboten-Koen frequently. The ride takes about 35 minutes. Fare: 620 yen.

Kawana (middle right, Kanto Map 31) is the southern part of Ito, and the home of an elaborate resort hotel complex. It is often the venue for small political gatherings and international business meetings. The complex features an excellent golf course overlooking the Pacific as well as tennis courts, swimming pools, etc.

1. Hotels in Ito

Kawana Hotel (15 minutes by taxi from Ito Station). Deluxe. 140 rooms. Double (28,000 yen -). Add: 1459, Kawana, Ito. Tel: (0557) 45-1111.

Hotel Southern Cross (15 minutes by taxi from Ito Station). First Class. 67 rooms. Double (23,500 yen -). Add: 1006, Yoshida, Ito. Tel: (0557) 45-1234.

2. Ryokan in Ito

Yonewakaso (5 minutes by taxi from Ito

Station). Deluxe. 18 rooms. 40,000 yen & up per person. Add: 2-4-1, Hirono, Ito. Tel: (0557) 37-5111.

Nagoya (1 minute walk from Ito Station). Deluxe. 14 rooms. 30,000 yen & up per person. Add: 1-1-18, Sakuragaoka, Ito. Tel: (0557) 37-4316.

Hotel Sun Hatoya (5 minutes by taxi from Ito Station). First Class. 198 rooms. 27,000 yen & up per person. Add: 572-12, Yukawa-Kataiwa, Ito. Tel: (0557) 36-4126.

Hotel Juraku (7 minutes by taxi from Ito Station). First Class. 102 rooms. 25,000 yen & up per person. Add: 281, Oka, Ito. Tel: (0557) 37-3161.

ATAGAWA 熱川

(Middle right, Kanto Map 31)

There are several large ryokan in Atagawa. Many retreats owned by companies and associations are also located here. All of the accommodations described below have hotspring swimming pools (available year round).

Atagawa Banana-Wanien 熱川バナナ・ワニ園 (Banana and Crocodile Park) is in front of Izu-Atagawa Station, and features more than 400 crocodiles gathered from all over the world. Several huge greenhouses in the Park contain tropical plants.

Ryokan in Atagawa

Atagawa Yamatokan (10 minute walk from Izu-Atagawa Station). First Class. 60 rooms. 20,000 yen & up per person. Add: 986-2, Naramoto, Izucho. Tel: (0557) 23-1126.

Atagawa Daiichi Hotel (8 minute walk from Izu-Atagawa Station). First Class. 58 rooms. 18,000 yen & up per person. Add: 1267-2, Atagawa, Izucho. Tel: (0557) 23-2200.

Atagawa View Hotel (10 minute walk from Izu-Atagawa Station). First Class. 56 rooms. 18,000 yen & up per person. Add: 1271, Naramoto, Izucho. Tel: (0557) 23-1211.

SHIMODA 下田

(Lower center, Kanto Map 31)

Shimoda prospered as early as the Edo Era as an intermediate port for trade ships between Tokyo and Osaka. In 1854 the Japan- U.S. Friendship Treaty was signed here. Townsend Harris, the first U.S. Consul General to Japan, arrived in Shimoda two years later. The shogun selected Shimoda as the location for the first permanent foreign Consulate on Japanese soil primarily because of its remoteness from the capital and the seat of power. Shimoda's history, together with its beautiful location, have made it a favorite venue for high level international meetings, especially U.S.-Japan bilateral consultations. The population of Shimoda is only 30,000.

A Japan-U.S. Friendship Treaty Monument 開国記念碑 (lower center, Kanto Map 32) in Shimoda-Koen Park commemorates these historical events. The beautiful Park has extensive pedestrian paths. U.S. President Jimmy Carter visited the Park and the Monument in 1979.

Ryosenji Temple 了仙寺 (middle left) is where the Treaty was actually signed on May 25, 1854. Townsend Harris' Consulate was established at another temple, Gyokusenji, which is located in the eastern part of the city (outside Kanto Map 32).

Other lovely shrines and temples are at the foot of the hills on the northern edge of the downtown portion of the city (upper center). They include Hachiman Jinja Shrine, Hofukuji Temple, and Kaizenji Temple.

A ropeway near Izukyu-Shimoda Station climbs to **Mt. Nesugatayama** 寝姿山. Ropeway fare: 820 yen roundtrip. The observatory at the top of the mountain is a bit of a tourist trap but commands a panoramic view of Shimoda Port and the Pacific Ocean.

Cape Irozaki 石廊崎 is at the southern tip of Izu Peninsula (lower center, Kanto Map 31). We suggest that you take a bus

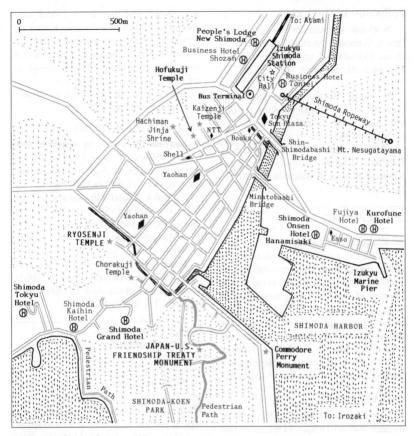

MAP 32 Shimoda

from Izukyu-Shimoda Station to Irozaki Todai (Lighthouse), the last stop (a 50-minute ride). Fare: 840 yen. A promenade to the Lighthouse passes a huge "Jungle Park" greenhouse. The Lighthouse stands on a steep cliff overlooking the Pacific Ocean. We suggest you take a boat from Irozaki for the return trip to Shimoda (a 40-minute ride). Fare: 1,350 yen. In Shimoda, the boat arrives at Izukyu Marine Pier (middle right, Kanto Map 32). A twenty minute harbor cruise also operates from Izukyu Marine Pier. Boats leave about once an hour and the fare is 800 yen.

ACCOMMODATIONS
(Refer to Kanto Map 32)

1. Hotels in Shimoda

Shimoda Prince Hotel (outside the map. 10 minutes by taxi from Izukyu-Shimoda Station). Deluxe. 86 rooms. Double (28,000 yen–). Add: 1547-1, Shirahama, Shimoda. Tel: (0558) 22-2111.

Shimoda Tokyu Hotel (lower left). First Class. 93 rooms. Double (18,500 yen -). Add: 5-12-1, Shimoda. Tel: (0558) 22-2411.

2. Ryokan in Shimoda

Seiryuso (5 minutes by taxi from Izukyu-Shimoda Station). Deluxe. 33 rooms. 35,000 yen & up per person. Add: 2-2, Kawauchi, Shimoda. Tel: (0558) 22-1361.

Kurofune Hotel (middle right). First Class. 69 rooms. 27,000 yen & up per person. Add: 3-88, Kakizaki, Shimoda. Tel: (0558) 22-1234.

Shimoda Grand Hotel (lower left). Standard. 72 rooms. 17,000 yen & up per person. Add: 3-21-1, Shimoda. Tel: (0558) 22-1011.

SHUZENJI 修善寺

(Middle center, Kanto Map 31)

Shuzenji is a prestigious traditional hot-spring resort. Most accommodations are located about 2 km (1.2 miles) to the west of Shuzenji Station, in a long narrow valley along the Katsuragawa River. Shuzenji was famous as long ago as the 9th century. The second Kamakura shogun, Yoriie, was assassinated here in 1204. The Treasure House of Shuzenji Temple displays historic objects related to the Kamakura Shogunate.

Ryokan in Shuzenji

Yagyu-no-sho (10 minutes by taxi from Shuzenji Station). Deluxe. 14 rooms. 48,000 yen & up per person. Add: 1116-6, Shuzenji. Tel: (0558) 72-4126.

Arai Ryokan (10 minutes by taxi from Shuzenji Station). 41 rooms. 25,000 yen & up per person. Add: 970, Shuzenji. Tel: (0558) 72-2841.

Hotel Katsuragawa (5 minutes by taxi from Shuzenji Station). First Class. 91 rooms. 22,000 yen & up per person. Add: 860, Shuzenji. Tel: (0558) 72-0810.

IZU-NAGAOKA 伊豆長岡

(Upper center, Kanto Map 31)

Izu-Nagaoka is another famous hot-spring town. The Hojo family, which captured the political power of the Kamakura Shogunate after the assassination of the third Minamoto Shogun, was originally from this town. The observatory of Mt. Katsuragiyama, which can be reached by ropeway, has a panoramic view of the Amagi mountains, Mt. Fuji, and the Pacific Ocean.

Ryokan in Izu-Nagaoka

Sanyoso (5 minutes by taxi from Izu-Nagaoka Station). Deluxe. 20 rooms. 45,000 yen & up per person. Add: 270, Domanoue, Izu-Nagaoka. Tel: (0559) 48-0123.

Nagaoka Sekitei (10 minutes by taxi from Izu-Nagaoka Station). Deluxe. 19 rooms. 40,000 yen & up per person. Add: 55, Minami-Onoue, Izu-Nagaoka. Tel: (0559) 48-2841.

Kona Hotel (5 minutes by taxi from Izu-Nagaoka Station). Deluxe. 12 rooms. 30,000 yen & up per person. Add: 31, Kona, Izu-Nagaoka. Tel: (0559) 48-1225.

WEST COAST OF IZU PENINSULA 伊豆西海岸

Izu's west coast is less developed. There are only a few hotels and *ryokan*, and *minshuku* are the main accommodations in the area. If you live in Japan and want to spend a slightly longer affordable vacation in a marine resort, this area will be an ideal destination. Frequent bus service is available from Shuzenji Station to major towns on the western coast, such as Toi (60 minutes, 1,300 yen), Dogashima (1 hour and 40 minutes, 1,920 yen) and Matsuzaki (1 hour and 50 minutes, 2,020 yen). Buses are also available between Izukyu-Shimoda Station and Matsuzaki (55 minutes, 1,110 yen), and Dogashima (60 minutes, 1,220 yen).

FUJI FIVE LAKES 富士五湖

Fuji Five Lakes (Kanto Map 33) is the area to the north of Mt. Fuji, scattered in wild forests. Kawaguchiko is the center of the area, and most of the accommodations in the area are located on the southeastern shore of Lake Kawaguchiko (Funazu District). A bus runs from Kawaguchiko Station to the fifth grade of Mt. Fuji. Many retreats owned by companies and colleges are located in the Lake Yamanakako area. The other three lakes — Saiko, Shojiko and Motosuko — are less developed. Unless you drive, visiting all five of the lakes is very difficult. We suggest that you relax in the beautiful natural setting, enjoying the magnificent view of Mt. Fuji. The area is an ideal overnight destination from Tokyo. Even a full day excursion from Tokyo is possible if you visit only the Lake Kawaguchiko area.

LAKE KAWAGUCHIKO 河口湖

To get to Kawaguchiko from Tokyo, you have to take two trains: first a limited express train on the JR Chuo Honsen Line from Tokyo's Shinjuku Station to Otsuki (1 hour; fare 2,850 yen), and then a Fujikyu Line train from Otsuki to Kawaguchiko (50 minutes; fare 1,110 yen).

There is direct bus service from Shinjuku Station in Tokyo to Lake Kawaguchiko. The bus platforms are in the Long Distance Bus Terminal on the western side of Shinjuku Station (lower center, Kanto Map 10). The bus trip takes 2 hours and the fare is 1,520 yen.

Tenjozan Observatory 天上山展望台. The ropeway station is a 15-minute walk from Kawaguchiko Station (middle right, Kanto Map 34). The gondola brings you up to the top of Mt. Tenjozan (1,104 m. or 3,622 feet) in just three minutes. Fare: 620 yen round trip. The observatory commands a great view of Mt. Fuji to the south and Lake Kawaguchiko below.

MAP 33 Fuji Five Lakes

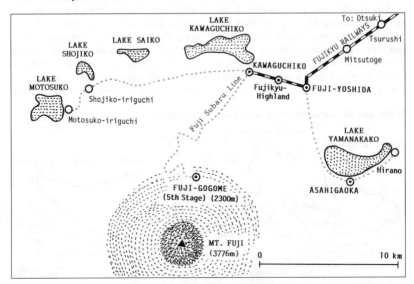

Sightseeing Boat. A 30-minute sightseeing boat around Lake Kawaguchiko leaves from near the ropeway station and operates frequently. Fare: 900 yen. Mt. Fuji viewed beyond the blue water of the lake appears in a new and quite impressive guise.

OTHER LAKES

You can visit the other four lakes by bus from Kawaguchiko Station. If you must choose only one of them, we suggest that you visit Lake Motosuko. **Lake Motosuko** 本栖湖 (middle left, Kanto Map 33) is located at the westernmost end of the five lakes area. The bus ride from Kawaguchiko Station takes about one hour (fare: 1,170 yen). The bus runs through Aokigahara Wild Forest, with a view of Mt. Fuji from time to time. Lake Motosuko is the deepest of the five lakes (138 m) and has the clearest water.

Lake Yamanakako 山中湖 (Kanto Map 35) is the largest of the five lakes. The bus ride from Kawaguchiko Station takes about 35 minutes (fare: 730 yen) (Asahigaoka is the bus stop for Lake Yamanakako). A 40-minute sightseeing boat operates from the pier near the bus stop (fare: 900 yen). You can enjoy a grand view of Mt. Fuji from yet another angle. There is also frequent bus service between Lake Yamanakako (Asahigaoka and Hirano stops) and Tokyo's Shinjuku Station. The trip takes about 2 hours and the fare is 1,760 yen.

Fuji-Gogome 富士五合目. If you want to see Mt. Fuji from closer up, you should take a bus from Kawaguchiko to Fuji-Gogome (the 5th grade of Mt. Fuji). The hour drive through the wild forests (called the "Fuji Subaru Line") is refreshing and thrilling. Fare: 1,610 yen. There are restaurants and souvenir shops at the Fuji-Gogome Terminal. The bus operates from April 5 through November 8.

Please note that there is bus service once a day in each direction between Fuji-Gogome and Tokyo's Shinjuku Station via the Chuo Expressway (about a 3 hour ride; fare: 2,160 yen).

Fujikyu Highland 富士急ハイランド (upper center, Kanto Map 33) is an amusement and sports complex, located in front of Fujikyu-Highland Station. The playland contains all sorts of amusement facilities, from a merry-go-round to double-loop jet roller coasters. If you are travelling with children, this is an ideal place for family activities, while still enjoying a great view of Mt. Fuji. The playland is also popular in winter, when its five ice skating rinks are open. The area has very stable weather, and Mt. Fuji appears with its snow-covered graceful shape in a clear blue sky. The buses between Shinjuku and Lake Yamanakako and between Shinjuku and Lake

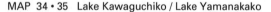

MAP 34 • 35 Lake Kawaguchiko / Lake Yamanakako

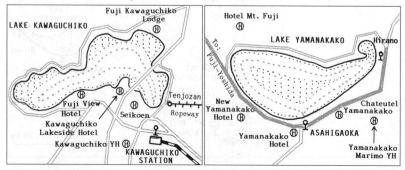

Kawaguchi-ko both stop at Fujikyu Highland.

ACCOMMODATIONS

1. Hotels near Lake Kawaguchiko

Fuji View Hotel (middle center, Kanto Map 34). Standard. 45 Western & 31 Japanese rooms. Double (22,000 yen -). Add: 511, Katsuyamamura, Yamanashi Prefecture. Tel: (0555) 83-2211.

Highland Resort (in front of Fujikyu-Highland Station). First Class. 157 rooms. Double (21,000 yen -). Add: 5-6-1, Fuji-Yoshida. Tel: (0555) 22-1000.

Hotel Regina Kawaguchiko (3 minutes by taxi from Kawaguchiko Station). Standard. 64 rooms. 19,000 yen & up per person (with 2 meals). Add: 5239-1, Funatsu, Kawaguchikomachi. Tel: (0555) 73-2771.

2. Ryokan near Lake Kawaguchiko

Maruei Hotel (7 minutes by taxi from Kawaguchiko Station). First Class. 51 rooms. 20,000 yen & up per person. Add: 498, Kodachi, Kawaguchikomachi. Tel: (0555) 72-1371.

Hotel Kogetsukan (5 minutes by taxi from Kawaguchiko Station). First Class. 48 rooms. 13,000 yen & up per person. Add: 4016, Funatsu, Kawaguchikomachi. Tel: (0555) 72-1180.

Kawaguchiko Daiichi Hotel (7 minutes by taxi from Kawaguchiko Station). Standard. 59 rooms. 12,000 yen & up per person. Add: Asakawa, Kawaguchikomachi. Tel: (0555) 72-1162.

Kawaguchiko Hotel (5 minutes by taxi from Kawaguchiko Station). Standard. 50 rooms. 12,000 yen & up per person. Add: 197, Funatsu, Kawaguchikomachi. Tel: (0555) 72-1313.

3. Hotels near Lake Yamanakako

Hotel Mount Fuji (upper left, Kanto Map 35). First Class. 80 rooms. Double (21,000 yen -). Add: 1360-83, Yamanaka, Yamanakakomura. Tel: (0555) 62-2111.

Yamanakako Hotel (middle center, Kanto Map 35). First Class. 71 rooms. Double (21,000 yen -). Add: 506-296, Yamanaka, Yamanakakomura. Tel: (0555) 62-2511.

Chateutel Yamanakako (middle right, Kanto Map 35). First Class. 23 rooms. 12,000 yen & up per person (with 2 meals). Add: 506-215, Hirano, Yamanakakomura. Tel: (0555) 62-2231.

New Yamanakako Hotel (middle left, Kanto Map 35). Standard. 62 rooms. Double (17,000 yen -). Add: 352-1, Yamanaka, Yamanakakomura. Tel: (0555) 62-2311.

4. Welcome Inns in the Fuji Five Lakes Area

Friendly Inn People (15 minutes by taxi from Kawaguchiko Station). 8 Western rooms. Add: 2123-14, Oishi, Kawaguchikomachi. Tel: (0555) 76-6069.

Hotel Sunnide Village (15 minutes by taxi from Kawaguchiko Station). 13 Japanese & 3 Western rooms. Add: 2549-1, Oishi, Kawaguchikomachi. Tel: (0555) 76-6004.

Lake Yamanaka Inn (2 minute walk from Asahigaoka bus stop, middle center, Kanto Map 35). 7 Japanese rooms. Add: 506, Asahigaoka, Yamanakakomura. Tel: (0555) 62-0218.

NIKKO 日光

Nikko (Kanto Map 36), a small city with a population of only 20,000, is located about 128 km (80 miles) north of Tokyo. Its excellent reputation as a tourist attraction is well deserved; in just a one-day excursion from Tokyo, visitors can enjoy both the great natural beauty of Lake Chuzenjiko and Kegon-no-Taki Falls, and the impressive cultural artifacts of the magnificent Toshogu Shrine.

Nikko's history as a sacred region began in 782 when a priest named Shodo erected Shihonryuji Temple (the original of today's

Rinnoji Temple). Shihonryuji prospered as a training center for priests of the Tendai sect, and at its peak the precincts were filled with more than 300 minor temples and other buildings. But the temple went into serious decline when Hideyoshi Toyotomi completed the unification of Japan at the end of the 16th century. Because its congregation had supported his opponent during the civil wars, the great Hideyoshi seized the manors that had been held by the Temple. Nikko began to regain the prominence of its glorious past when, at the suggestion of the priest Tenkai, an adviser to the Tokugawas, it was selected in 1617 as the site of the mausoleum of Ieyasu Tokugawa, the first Tokugawa shogun. Toshogu Shrine was completed in 1636 at the order of the third Shogun, Iemitsu. No expense was spared. It is estimated that the Tokugawas expended the equivalent of 300 million of today's dol-

lars in erecting this memorial. Master artisans, including architects, sculptors and painters all worked together to achieve the splendor of Toshogu Shrine, which is a living memorial to the high artistic standards and achievements of 17th century Japan.

Transportation in Nikko

There are two ways to get to Nikko, either directly by the Tobu Nikko Line, or on JR (which involves two trains — the Tohoku Shinkansen and the JR Nikko Line). The Tobu Line is more convenient and less costly, except for those with Japan Rail Passes. Note that Nikko can also be included at the end of a trip to Tohoku.

1. Tobu Nikko Line

The Tobu Nikko Line operates between Tobu-Asakusa Station and Tobu-Nikko Station. Asakusa is easily accessible from most

MAP 36 Nikko

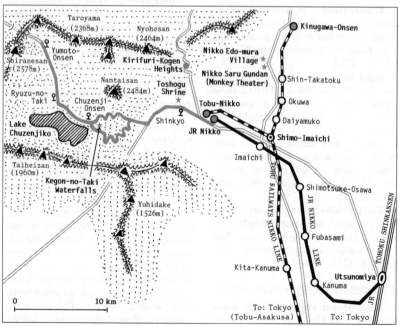

places in Tokyo via the Subway Ginza Line. The exact location of Tobu Asakusa Station, which is beneath the Matsuya Department Store, is pictured on Kanto Map 6 (middle right). The ticket office is on the first floor and the platforms on the second. Two types of trains leave frequently for Nikko: Limited Expresses and Rapid Service Trains. The Limited Express is a specially designed deluxe train, with amazing luxury touches *and* waitress service. The Limited Express trip takes one hour and 45 minutes and the fare is 2,530 yen (reserved seats only). Advance reservations are recommended during high season and on weekends. The Rapid Service Train is a regular commuter train and has only nonreserved seats. The Rapid Service trip takes two hours and ten minutes and the fare is 1,270 yen.

2. Japan Railways

There is no direct JR train to Nikko from Tokyo. The fastest way to reach Nikko by JR is the combination of the Tohoku Shinkansen (either the fast "Yamabiko" or the slower "Aoba") from Tokyo Station or Ueno Station in Tokyo to Utsunomiya (about one hour), and the JR Nikko Line from Utsunomiya to JR Nikko Station (a 40-minute commuter train trip). JR Nikko Station is only a few minutes walk to Tobu Nikko Station (middle center, Kanto Map 36).

Outline of Nikko

As pictured on Kanto Map 36, Nikko's major cultural and historical attractions are located in the vicinity of **Toshogu Shrine** (upper center). The area's natural wonders are on the eastern side of **Lake Chuzenjiko** (middle left). The train stations are at an altitude of about 600 m (2,000 feet), the surface of the Lake at 1,269 m (4,163 feet), and Mt. Nantaisan at 2,484 m (8,150 feet). "Nikko" thus encompasses not only a wide area but also an area with great differences in altitude. To facilitate the flow of traffic on the mountainous roads of the area, special one-

way toll roads have been constructed to and from the Lake. The southern road, No. 2 Iroha-zaka Slope, is used for the west-bound traffic up to the Lake, while the northern road, No. 1 Iroha-zaka Slope, is used for the east-bound traffic back down from the Lake. "Iroha" is the name of the 48 character Japanese syllabic alphabet. The roads were so named because of their many (but not exactly 48) hairpin curves.

In addition, **Kinugawa-Onsen** (upper right), which is very popular with Tokyoites who want to escape the big city, might be of interest to foreign residents in Japan. Tobu Railways trains run frequently between Tokyo (Tobu-Asakusa Station) and Kinugawa-Onsen. There are a number of large *ryokan* in the hotsprings. Nearby are **Nikko Edo-mura Village** 日光江戸村, a reconstructed Edo Era town that boasts various performances and demonstrations, including one of *ninja* arts, and **Nikko Saru Gundan** 日光猿軍団 (Monkey Theater), which features a half-hour show by a troupe of more than 30 monkeys. There is frequent bus service from Kinugawa-Onsen Station to Nikko Edo-mura Village and Nikko Saru Gundan.

Nikko also has two popular ski resorts: **Kirifuri-Kogen Heights** (upper center) and **Yumoto-Onsen** (upper left). Yumoto-Onsen is especially popular due to its hotsprings.

There is an *i* Information Office in Tobu-Nikko Station.

Suggested Itinerary

Nikko Station to Chuzenji-Onsen by Bus
Nikko buses have both Japanese and English signs, and there are even some announcements on the buses in English. To get to Chuzenji-Onsen take a bus headed for either Chuzenji-Onsen or Yumoto-Onsen. At the JR Nikko Station, the bus for Chuzenji-Onsen uses stop No. 2, and the bus for Yumoto-Onsen uses stop No. 3. Departure times of the buses are coordinated with the arrival times of the JR Nikko Line trains.

If you plan to visit only the Toshogu

Shrine area, you can also take the bus headed for Nishi-Sando, from stop No. 5. Nishi-Sando stop is pictured at the lower left of Kanto Map 38.

There's a bus ticket office in the Tobu-Nikko Station (don't buy a Japanese tour "course" ticket; tell the attendant your destination). The bus for Chuzenji-Onsen uses stop No. 2, and the bus for Yumoto-Onsen uses stop No. 1. The trip to Chuzenji-Onsen takes about 45-50 minutes and the fare is 1,050 yen.

The bus for Nishi-Sando uses stop No. 9. The trip to Nishi-Sando takes 6 minutes and the fare is 280 yen.

CHUZENJI-ONSEN AREA

(Kanto Map 37)

Chanokidaira 茶ノ木平 (1,618 m, 5,308 feet) commands a great view of Lake Chuzenjiko and the 2,500 m (8,200 feet) mountains surrounding the Lake. To reach the observatory, take a ropeway from Chuzenji-Onsen (a short 6-minute ride). Hours: 9:00 AM to 5:00 PM. Roundtrip ropeway fare: 820 yen. You can also hike in the Chanokidaira Botanical Garden behind the ropeway station.

A sightseeing boat operates on the Lake every hour from the Boat Pier (middle center). The cruise takes 55 minutes. Fare: 900 yen.

The Observatory of Kegon-no-Taki Waterfalls 華厳ノ滝展望台 (middle right) is reached by an elevator, which is only a five-minute walk from Chuzenji-Onsen Bus Stop. The dynamic 99 m (325 foot) waterfalls are known as the best in Japan. The Falls are especially impressive in the spring when the snow melts and the run off from the Lake swells the Falls far beyond their normal size. Admission: 520 yen.

Chuzenji-Onsen to Nishi-Sando Catch a bus headed for Nikko Station at either Chuzenji-Onsen or Kegon-no-Taki bus stop. These buses run about once every 30 minutes, and the ride to Nishi-Sando (lower left, Kanto Map 38) takes about 30 minutes.

TOSHOGU SHRINE AREA

(Kanto Map 38)

Toshogu Shrine, Futarasan Jinja Shrine and Rinnoji Temple (and its Taiyuinbyo) are the attractions in this area. Purchase the combination admission ticket 二社一寺共通券 (750 yen), which gives you access to most areas of the shrines and the temple. You will, however, have to pay additional admissions to see some of the special treasures, as explained below.

Taiyuinbyo 大猷院廟 (Middle left)

Taiyuinbyo is the mausoleum of Iemitsu

MAP 37 Lake Chuzenjiko

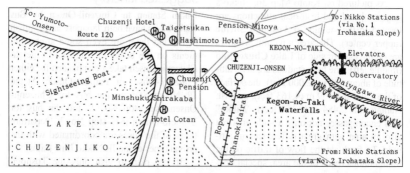

Tokugawa, the third Shogun, who established the strong, isolationist government that ruled Japan for 250 years. The mausoleum was built in 1653. Compared to the lavish, colorful Toshogu Shrine, this complex is small and modestly decorated, but it harmonizes beautifully with its natural setting and reflects the careful attention the architects obviously paid to the complex. Most of the buildings are National Treasures or Important Cultural Properties. Hours: 8:00 AM to 5:00 PM (4:00 PM in winter). The Combination Ticket gives you access to all the buildings on the grounds of Taiyuinbyo.

Futarasan Jinja Shrine 二荒山神社 (Upper left)

Futarasan Jinja Shrine is only a short walk northeast from Taiyuinbyo. Until Toshogu Shrine was constructed, Futarasan Jinja Shrine, dedicated to the god of Mt. Futarasan (or Mt. Nantaisan), was the center of Shintoism in Nikko for about 800 years.

The present main buildings were donated in 1619 by the second Tokugawa Shogun. The old cedar trees that surround the precincts contribute to the sacred and solemn atmosphere of the Shrine. Hours: 8:00 AM to 5:00 PM (4:00 PM in winter). The Combination Ticket gives you access to all the buildings in the Shrine precincts.

Toshogu Shrine Treasure House 東照宮 宝物館 (Middle center) (Optional)

The Treasure House contains about 250 artistic and historical objects, of which approximately 60-70 are displayed in turn. The treasures include samurai armor, swords, paintings, portraits of Tokugawa shogun, etc. Hours: 8:30 AM to 4:30 PM (4:00 PM in winter). Admission: 500 yen.

Toshogu Shrine 東照宮 (Upper center)

Passing under a huge *torii* gate on the Omote-Sando Path, you will see **Five-Story Pagoda** 五重塔 on your left. The original was destroyed by fire and the present pago-

MAP 38 Toshogu Shrine

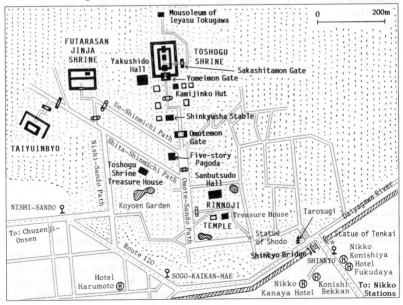

da was built in 1818. **Omotemon Gate** 表門 is the main and the only entrance to the Shrine. Two Deva Kings stand in the niches at the sides of the vermilion gate. The 66 carvings on the Gate presage what is waiting inside the Shrine precincts.

Three buildings on the right-hand side of the path are warehouses for the costumes and equipment used each spring and fall for the Festival of the Procession of the Warriors (May 18 and October 17). The side of the **Shinkyusha** 神厩舎 (Stable for Sacred Horses) features eight carvings that depict the life of monkeys (as an allegory of human existence). The second scene is the famous "hear-no-evil, see-no-evil, speak-no-evil" monkeys. On the side of **Kamijinko** 上神庫 are two rather strange carvings of elephants. (When Tanyu Kano, a master painter of the Kano School, drew the original design, elephants were unknown in Japan; the artist had only read about them, and you will see that his imagination was applied liberally.) Passing through the *torii* gate, you will see **Yomeimon Gate** 陽明門 (National Treasure) at the top of the stone steps. The 11 m (36 foot) tall gate is entirely covered with more than 400 carvings painted brilliant shades of gold, vermilion, blue, and green. **Corridors** 回廊 (National Treasures) stretch in both directions from Yomeimon Gate and surround the main buildings (National Treasures). On the western side of the Yomeimon Gate is **Yakushido (Honchido) Hall** 薬師堂, which is famous for the dragon painting on its ceiling. The original building was lost to fire in 1961 and the present one was completed in 1963. The dragon was painted from the original design by Nampu Katayama, a modern master. If you clap your hands under the head of the dragon, the resulting echo is said to be the sound of the dragon roaring. Additional admission: 200 yen. Each of the main buildings of the Shrine boasts of its own carvings; especially famous is the Sleeping Cat (very small) in the East Corridor. You can see it on the upper left-hand side as you cross the East Corridor toward Sakashitamon Gate. The mausoleum of Ieyasu Tokugawa is located to the north of Toshogu Shrine at the end of the long stone stairway. Additional admission charge for the Sleeping Cat Corridor and the Mausoleum: 430 yen.

Rinnoji Temple 輪王寺 (Lower center)

Walking down Omote-Sando Path you will come to the impressive **Sanbutsudo Hall** 三仏堂 of Rinnoji Temple on your left. Until the 17th century, most religious activity in Nikko took place in this Temple. Even though the glory days of the Temple, when thousands of priests were housed in its precincts, vanished with Hideyoshi Toyotomi's suppression, the Temple still plays a leading role for Buddhism in the Nikko area. The Sanbutsdo Hall contains three Buddha images. (Entrance to this Hall is included in the basic Combination Ticket.) Sorinto Tower is an impressive golden construction decorated with 24 golden bells. Rinnoji Temple Treasure House and its lovely attached garden require an additional 250 yen admission price.

To Nikko Station When you emerge from the Temple precincts, you will see a statue of the priest Shodo. Stone steps lead you down to the main street. On the northern side of the main street stands "Tarosugi," a huge cedar tree. About 15 years ago, the Ministry of Construction insisted that Tarosugi be cut down in order to facilitate the flow of traffic. This venerable giant was spared only after a long court battle between the Temple and the Ministry. As you cross Daiyagawa River, look to your right to see the "Shinkyo" (Sacred Bridge). On the other side of the Daiyagawa River stands a statue of the priest Tenkai. The stop for buses to Nikko Station is in front of Nikko Koni-shiya. Most buses go to Tobu-Nikko Station first, and then to the JR Station. Some of them terminate at Tobu-Nikko Station, but the JR Station is only a few minutes walk from Tobu Station.

ACCOMMODATIONS

1. Hotels in Nikko

Nikko Prince Hotel (on the northern shore of Lake Chuzenjiko). First Class. 92 rooms. Double (24,000 yen -). Add: 2485, Chugushi, Nikko. Tel: (0288) 55-0661.

Nikko Lakeside Hotel (on the northern shore of Lake Chuzenjiko). First Class. 98 rooms. Double (21,000 yen -). Add: 2482, Chugushi, Nikko. Tel: (0288) 55-0321.

Nikko Kanaya Hotel (lower right, Kanto Map 38). First Class. 90 rooms. Double (16,000 yen -). Add: Kami-Hatsuishimachi, Nikko. Tel: (0288) 54-0001.

2. Ryokan in Nikko

Hotel Harumoto (lower left, Kanto Map 38). Standard. 22 rooms. 12,000 yen & up per person. Add: 5-13, Yasukawacho, Nikko. Tel: (0288) 54-1133.

Konishi Bekkan (lower right, Kanto Map 38). Standard. 24 rooms. 12,000 yen & up per person. Add: 1115, Kami-Hatsuishimachi, Nikko. Tel: (0288) 54-1105.

Hotel Fukudaya (lower right, Kanto Map 38). Standard. 37 rooms. 13,000 yen & up per person. Add: 1036, Kami-Hatsuishimachi, Nikko. Tel: (0288) 54-0389.

Nikko Konishiya Hotel (lower right, Kanto Map 38). 26 rooms. 10,000 yen & up per person. Add: 1030, Kami-Hatsuishimachi, Nikko. Tel: (0288) 54-1101.

3. Welcome Inns in Nikko

Aizuya Ryokan (12 minute walk from Nikko Stations). 15 Japanese rooms. Add: 928-Naka-Hatsuishimachi, Nikko. Tel: (0288) 54-0039.

Pension Turtle (7 minute walk from Sogo-Kaikan-mae bus stop, lower center, Kanto Map 38). 6 Western & 3 Japanese rooms. Add: 2-16, Takumicho, Nikko. Tel: (0288) 53-3168.

4. Ryokan in Kinugawa Onsen Hotsprings

Kinugawa Kanaya Hotel (3 minute walk from Kinugawa-Onsen Station, upper right, Kanto Map 36). Deluxe. 48 rooms. 40,000 yen & up per person. Add: 1394, Ohara, Fujiwaramachi. Tel: (0288) 77-2121.

Kinugawa Grand Hotel (8 minute walk from Kinugawa-Onsen Station). First Class. 100 rooms. 20,000 yen & up per person. Add: 1021, Ohara, Fujiwara-machi. Tel: (0288) 77-1313.

Kinugawa Royal Hotel (10 minute walk from Kinugawa-Onsen Station). Standard. 125 rooms. 15,000 yen & up per person. Add: 1426, Ohara, Fujiwaramachi. Tel: (0288) 77-2111.

MASHIKO 益子

Mashiko-yaki pottery dates back to the Nara Era (the 8th century). The modern success of *Mashiko-yaki* began in 1853 when Keizaburo Otsuka started production of everyday potteryware in this small town. *Mashiko-yaki* was elevated to the level of art by Shoji Hamada, and was introduced worldwide by Bernard Leach, an English potter. More than 150 kilns are located in the peaceful farm town of Mashiko. Many of them are indicated with stars on Kanto Map 39. Mashiko has a population of only 25,000.

Transportation to Mashiko

Refer to Kanto Map 29. You can take the JR Tohoku Shinkansen ("Aoba" trains only) from either Tokyo Station or Ueno Station in Tokyo or a commuter train on the JR Tohoku Honsen Line from Ueno Station to Oyama. The Shinkansen takes 45 minutes and the regular train takes one hour and 15 minutes. Switch at Oyama to the JR Mito Line (local trains only) to Shimodate (a 25-minute ride). At Shimodate, switch to a Mouka Railways train headed to Motegi.

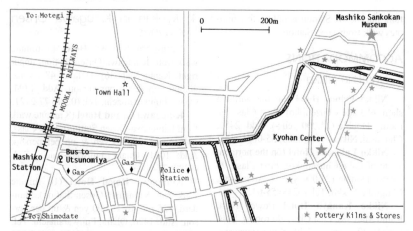

MAP 39 Mashiko

Mashiko is about halfway to Motegi, a 45-minute ride (fare 640 yen).

You can also visit Mashiko on your way to or from Nikko. There is convenient bus service between Mashiko Station and Tobu-Utsunomiya Station (about 1,500 m or 1 mile from JR Utsunomiya Station). The ride takes 70 minutes and the fare is 1,100 yen.

There are a large number of reasonable Western-style hotels in Utsunomiya, and we recommend that you spend a night there if you plan a trip that includes Mashiko as well as Nikko.

Attractions in Mashiko

Kyohan Center 共販センター (lower right). This large complex is operated jointly by the potters of Mashiko. It functions not only as a shop but also as a museum, displaying both old and new products of Mashiko.

Mashiko Sankokan Museum 益子参考館 (upper right). This is the workshop where Shoji Hamada devoted his life to developing *Mashiko-yaki* into one of the most popular artistic potteries. The workshop was converted into a Museum to display Hamada's works along with photographs of the master potter. Mr. Hamada was named one of Japan's first Living National Treasures. All displays in the Museum have English explanations.

Hotels in Utsunomiya

Utsunomiya Tobu Hotel Grande (3 minute walk from Tobu-Utsunomiya Station). First Class. 102 singles (10,000 yen -) & 46 doubles (20,000 yen -). Add: 5-12, Honcho, Utsunomiya. Tel: (0286) 27-0111.

Hotel New Itaya (5 minute walk from JR Utsunomiya Station). Standard. 182 singles (6,000 yen -) & 43 doubles (12,000 yen -). Add: 2-4-6, Odori, Utsunomiya. Tel: (0286) 35-5111.

Kanto Chisan Hotel Utsunomiya (1 minute walk from JR Utsunomiya Station). Business. 176 singles (7,500 yen -) & 27 doubles (12,500 yen -). Add: 3-2-3, Ekimae-dori, Utsunomiya. Tel: (0286) 34-4311.

Utsunomiya Washington Hotel (5 minute walk from Tobu-Utsunomiya Station). Business. 122 singles (6,500 yen -) & 51 doubles (12,000 yen -). Add: 4-11, Honcho, Utsunomiya. Tel: (0286) 21- 3111.

TSUKUBA 筑波

First targeted as Japan's Science City in the late 1970's, Tsukuba has grown in stature with every passing year. Tsukuba Science Expo was held here in 1985. The city, with a growing population that now stands at 138,000, is home to universities, research institutes and corporate and governmental research organizations. The major institutions are listed below. The numbers on the Kanto Map 40 correspond to those on the list. Tsukuba is the venue of many smaller academic scientific meetings and seminars.

TSUKUBA RESEARCH AND EDUCATION INSTITUTIONS

1. University of Tsukuba
2. Tsukuba College of Technology
3. University of Library and Information Science
4. Tsukuba Laboratories, National Research Institute for Metals
5. National Institute for Research in Inorganic Materials
6. Mechanical Engineering Laboratory
7. Tsukuba Space Center
8. Agency of Industrial Science and Technology; National Research Laboratory of Metrology; National Chemical Laboratory for Industry; Fermentation Research Institute; Research Institute for Polymers and Textiles; Geological Survey of Japan; Electrotechnical Laboratory; and Industrial Products Research Institute
9. Aerological Observatory; Meteorological Instruments Plant; Meteorological Research Institute
10. National Research Institute for Pollution and Resources
11. The National Institute for Environmental Studies
12. National Food Research Institute
13. Secretariat of Agriculture, Forestry and Fisheries Research Council
14. National Institute of Animal Health
15. National Institute of Agroenvironmental Sciences
16. Japan International Cooperation

MAP 40 Tsukuba

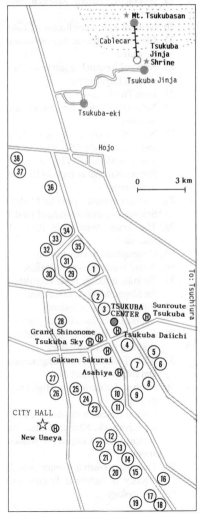

Agency; Japan International Agricultural Training Center; Tsukuba Life Science Center (Riken); and Japan Construction Method and Machinery Research Institute

17. National Institute of Animal Indutry
18. Forestry and Forest Products Research Institute
19. Nippon Agricultural Research Institute
20. National Agriculture Research Center
21. National Institute of Agrobiological Resources
22. National Research Institute of Agricultural Engineering
23. Fruit Tree Research Station
24. National Center for Seeds and Seedlings
25. National Institute of Sericultural and Entomological Science
26. Tsukuba Medicinal Plant Research Station, National Institute of Hygienic Sciences
27. Tsukuba Primate Center for Medical Science, National Institute of Health
28. The Japan Automobile Research Institute
29. Geographical Survey Institute
30. Public Works Research Institute
31. Tsukuba Institute, Japan Foundation for Shipbuilding Advancement
32. Building Research Institute
33. National Education Center Annex
34. Center for Better Living, Tsukuba Building Pests Laboratory
35. NTT Tsukuba Field Engineering Development Center
36. National Laboratory for High Energy Physics
37. Central Research Institute for Feed and Livestock, National Federation of Agricultural Cooperative Associations
38. Tsukuba Research Center No. 2, Agency of Industrial Science and Technology

Transportation to Tsukuba

From Tokyo, you can reach Tsukuba via a JR Joban Line Limited Express Train called the "Hitachi." This train operates frequently and the trip to Tsuchiura Station takes about 50 minutes. There is frequent bus service from the western side of Tsuchiura Station to Tsukuba Center (middle center, Kanto Map 40). The trip takes about 25 minutes, and the fare is 430 yen. An *i* Information Office is located on the second floor of Tsuchiura Station, just outside the exit gate from the train tracks. There is another *i* Information Office in Tsukuba Center.

Side Trip from Tsukuba If you have extra time during your stay in Tsukuba, we recommend that you visit Tsukuba Jinja Shrine and Mt. Tsukubasan, at the northern end of the city. There is bus service from Tsukuba Center (middle center) to Tsukuba-eki (upper center). The ride takes about 40 minutes and the fare is 620 yen. Another bus from Tsukuba-eki to Tsukuba Jinja operates frequently; the ride takes 12 minutes and the fare is 180 yen. Tsukuba Jinja Shrine is dedicated to the Shinto gods *Izanagi* and *Izanami*, the mythological progenitors of the Japanese islands and the imperial family. A cable car behind the Shrine will take you to the summit of Mt. Tsukubasan. The trip takes 8 minutes and costs 930 yen roundtrip. From this height, you will have what everyone agrees is the best view of the entire Kanto plain. There is a revolving observatory and hiking path around the summit.

ACCOMMODATIONS

(Refer to Kanto Map 40)

1. Hotels in Tsukuba

Tsukuba Daiichi Hotel (middle center). Standard. 171 rooms. Single (11,000 yen -) & Double (17,000 yen -). Add: 1, Azuma, Tsukuba. Tel: (0298) 52-1112.

Hotel Sunroute Tsukuba (middle

right). Business. 51 singles (7,000 yen -) & 14 doubles (13,000 yen -). Add: 1145-3, Hanamuro, Tsukuba. Tel: (0298) 52-1151.

Tsukuba Sky Hotel (middle center). Business. 42 singles (7,000 yen -) & 26 doubles (12,500 yen -). Add: 283-1, Onozaki, Tsukuba. Tel: (0298) 56-5111.

Hotel Grand Shinonome (middle center). Business. 46 singles (7,000 yen -) & 22 doubles (12,500 yen -). Add: 488-1, Onozaki, Tsukuba. Tel: (0298) 56-2211.

Gakuen Sakurai Hotel (middle center). Business. 46 singles (6,000 yen -) & 22 doubles (12,000 yen -). Add: 8-7, Higashi-Arai, Tsukuba. Tel: (0298) 51-3011.

2. Hotels in Tsuchiura

Tsuchiura Tobu Hotel (3 minute walk from JR Tsuchiura Station). Standard. 60 singles (8,500 yen -) & 16 doubles (15,000 yen -). Add: 6-5, Yamatocho, Tsuchiura. Tel: (0298) 23-2111.

Tsuchiura Daiichi Hotel (1 minute walk from JR Tsuchiura Station). Standard. 48 singles (8,000 yen -) & 18 doubles (14,000 yen -). Add: 1-8-26, Minatocho, Tsuchiura. Tel: (0298) 22-4111.

NARITA　成田

Narita (population 86,000) is the home of the New Tokyo International Airport (Narita Airport). For most tourists, Narita is nothing more than the city they pass through to get to Tokyo. However, the area contains two important and interesting tourist attractions — Shinshoji Temple (upper center, Kanto Map 41) and the National Museum of Japanese History, which is in nearby Sakura City (lower left).

These two places are worth visiting from Tokyo if you have an extra day. They are especially recommended for those who must spend a night in Narita while waiting for a connecting flight to other countries. Starting from Narita Airport, you need three hours to visit Shinshoji Temple. You need six hours to visit both the Temple and the Museum.

Shinshoji Temple 新勝寺 (Kanto Map 42). Shinshoji Temple is located about a 15-minute walk from both the JR Narita Station and the Keisei-Narita Station, which are only about 150 m (492 feet) away from each

MAP 41 Narita

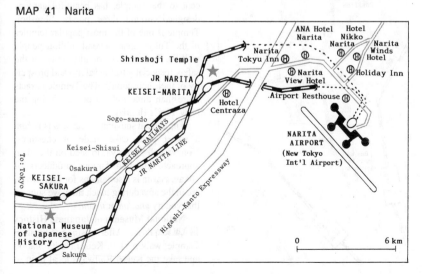

other. Bus service is available between Narita Airport and JR Narita Station (the bus stop is marked on Kanto Map 42). If you visit Narita from Tokyo, you can take a Keisei Line commuter train from Nippori Station (which is also served by the JR Yamanote Loop Line) to Keisei-Narita Station (about a 60-minute ride; fare 940 yen), or the JR Sobu Line Rapid Service train called "Airport Narita" (from Tokyo Station to JR Narita Station — 70 minutes).

MAP 42 Shinshoji Temple

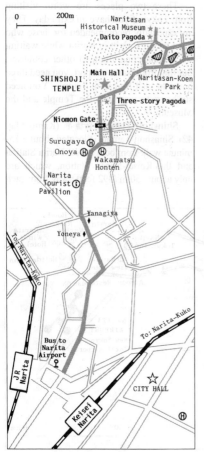

In 939, when the social status of samurai or soldiers was still low despite their service to the aristocracy, a Kanto samurai, Masakado Taira, organized a rebellion against the reign of the imperial court in Kyoto. Though the rebellion was suppressed and Masakado was killed in 940, the uprising presaged the rise of samurai power. The original Shinshoji Temple was built at the order of Emperor Sujaku during the rebellion. He hoped that his act of piety would result in his ultimate triumph. The gods were evidently pleased with his offering. The Temple was moved to the present location in 1705. The entrance to the main approach (shaded on Kanto Map 42) to Shinshoji Temple is marked by an arch. The main approach is lined on both sides with souvenir shops, restaurants and stores. There is also an *i* Information Office on the main approach called the "Narita Tourist Pavilion." There are several *ryokan* near the Niomon Gate that put up the many pilgrims who come to the Temple from all over Japan. The huge precincts include a number of impressive buildings, including the Main Hall, a three-story pagoda, and Daito Pagoda. Naritasan-Koen Park, adjacent to the Temple, has beautiful gardens designed around three ponds. Shinshoji Temple is one of the most popular temples in the Tokyo area. Several million people visit the Temple year round to pray for the safety (especially traffic safety) and prosperity of their households. The Temple attracts more than three million people during the New Year's Holiday.

The special souvenir of the area is *yokan*, a sweet paste cake made of chestnuts. Yoneya and Yanigiya, located on the main approach, are two famous producers of yokan. Narita is also famous for eels. If you are in the area during lunch time, we suggest that you try *unadon* or *unaju*.

National Museum of Japanese History 国立歴史博物館 . After visiting Shinshoji Temple, walk back to Keisei Narita Station and take the Keisei Railways local train to

Keisei-Sakura Station, the fourth stop (lower left, Kanto Map 41). This trip takes about 13 minutes and the fare is 240 yen. The Museum is a 15-minute walk (or 5-minute taxi ride from the Station).

The Museum was established by the Japanese Government in 1981 to introduce Japanese history to both Japanese and foreign visitors. Housed in an unexpectedly large structure, built on the former site of Sakurajo Castle, the Museum contains four galleries. Each gallery displays miniature reproductions of characteristic buildings of various stages of Japanese history. Authentic cultural artifacts are displayed.

The first gallery features the period from pre-history (7,500 B.C.) through the establishment of central power in Nara (the 8th century). The reproduction of Japan's first permanent capital in Nara may especially interest the visitor.

The second gallery features the period from the Heian Era to the Azuchi-Momoyama Era (the 16th century). Especially interesting are the contrasts of a Heian Era aristocrat's mansion and a civil war period samurai mansion. The first encounter of the Japanese with Western civilization is also featured here. The third gallery features the Edo Era. A reproduction of a typical Edo downtown depicts the people's life in the feudal era. The gallery also offers information on the folk culture that flourished in this era.

The fourth and last gallery features the contemporary life of the Japanese people in various parts of the archipelago. Hours: 9:30 AM to 4:30 PM. Closed Mondays, except for National Holidays that fall on Mondays (and then closed Tuesdays). Also closed New Year's Holidays. Admission: 400 yen.

Hotels in Narita
(Refer to Kanto Map 41)

Narita Winds Hotel (upper right). First Class. 84 singles (17,500 yen -) & 224 dou-bles (22,500 yen -). Add: 560, Tokko, Narita. Tel: (0476) 33-1111.

ANA Hotel Narita (upper right). First Class. 142 singles (18,500 yen -) & 257 doubles (24,500 yen -). Add: 68, Horinouchi, Narita. Tel: (0476) 33-1311.

Holiday Inn Tobu Narita (upper right). First Class. 112 singles (17,500 yen -) & 131 doubles (22,000 yen -). Add: 320-1, Tokko, Narita. Tel: (0476) 32-1234.

Hotel Nikko Narita (upper right, Kanto Map 41). First Class. 326 singles (17,500 yen -) & 201 doubles (28,000 yen -). Add: 500, Tokko, Narita. Tel: (0476) 32-0032.

Narita View Hotel (upper right). First Class. 128 singles (16,500 yen -) & 368 doubles (26,000 yen -). Add: 700, Kosuge, Narita. Tel: (0476) 32-1111.

Narita Tokyu Inn (upper right). First Class. 96 singles (16,000 yen -) & 308 doubles (25,000 yen -). Add: 31, Oyama, Narita. Tel: (0476) 33-0109.

Narita Airport Resthouse (upper right). Standard. 50 doubles (11,500 yen -) & 150 doubles (17,000 yen -). Add: Narita Airport, Narita. Tel: (0476) 32-1212.

Hotel Centraza Narita (upper center). Standard. 130 singles (12,500 yen -) & 132 doubles (19,000 yen -). Add: 1-1-5, Hiyoshidai, Tomisato-cho. Tel: (0476) 93-8811.

Note: Except for Hotel Centraza Narita, which is located in downtown Narita, all the other hotels are located in or near the airport. Complimentary bus service is provided from time to time between the airport terminal building and each hotel.

BOSO PENINSULA
房総半島

The Boso Peninsula arches around the eastern side of Tokyo Bay. A number of resorts have been developed here, especially along the Pacific Ocean coast, for Tokyoites. The area is still seldom visited by foreign tourists. The Boso area has a number of government-subsidized accommodations ("Kokumin-shukusha") that are especially appropriate for affordable family travel. We recommend them for foreign residents in Tokyo.

Transportation to Boso Peninsula

Three JR lines run to Boso. Each of them operates Limited Express Trains. The JR Sobu Honsen Line connects Tokyo Station with Choshi (upper right, Kanto Map 43). Limited Express Trains called "Suigo" operate several times a day. The ride from Tokyo to Choshi takes two hours and 15 minutes. The JR Sotobo Line connects Tokyo Station and the Pacific Side of the

Boso Peninsula, terminating at Awa-Kamogawa (lower center). Limited Express Trains called "Wakashio" operate about once every hour. The ride from Tokyo takes about two hours. The JR Uchibo Line connects Tokyo Station and the Tokyo Bay side of the Boso Peninsula, terminating at Tateyama (lower left). Limited Express Trains called "Sazanami" operate about once an hour. The ride from Tokyo Station takes about two hours. Local trains on the JR Uchibo Line connect Awa-Kamogawa and Tateyama (lower left) in about 45 minutes. The JR Togane Line connects the JR Sobu Honsen Line and the JR Sotobo Line (from Naruto to Oami) (upper center) in 20 minutes.

MAP 43 Boso Peninsula

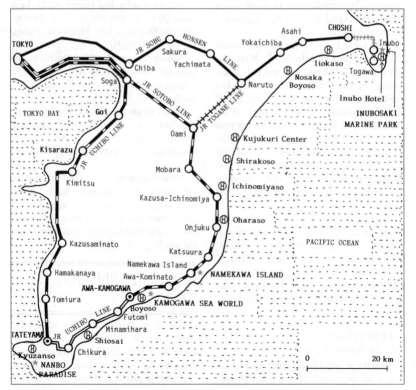

Places of Interest

Kamogawa Sea World 鴨川シーワールド (lower center). With its rugged coast line, Awa-Kamogawa is famous for its picturesque marine scenery, and is often called the "Matsushima of Boso." Kamogawa Sea World is five minutes by bus from Awa-Kamogawa Station. This large complex contains several pavilions and outdoor pools, featuring a number of sea animals from around the world. Open year round. Hours: 9:00 AM to 5:00 PM. Admission: 2,200 yen.

Nearby **Namekawa Island** 行川アイランド features a bird show with flamingo dances and peacocks and guinea hens, as well as a small zoo and swimming pools. Open year round. Hours: 9:00 AM to 5:00 PM (4:30 PM in winter). Admission: 1,550 yen.

Tateyama is the principal city of the southern Boso Peninsula. Its population is 55,000. **Nanbo Paradise** 南房パラダイス (lower left) is 40 minutes by bus from JR Tateyama Station. Flowers bloom here earlier than anywhere else in the Kanto Region. This amusement complex includes: greenhouses, flowerbeds, "Butterfly Pavilion," and "Singapore Orchid House." It is a very popular family destination throughout the year, especially in March with Tokyoites tired of winter.

Cape Inubosaki 犬吠崎 (upper right) has steep cliffs that climb out of the Pacific Ocean. The contrast of the white of Inubosaki Lighthouse and the blue of the Pacific has always been a popular theme for camera buffs and painters. You can take the Choshi Denki Tetsudo Railways from Choshi to Togawa (a 20-minute ride; fare 270 yen). The inside of the Lighthouse is open to the public, and the observatory commands a dynamic view of the ocean. Hours: 8:30 AM to 4:00 PM. Closed Mondays and when the weather is inclement. Admission:100 yen. Inubosaki Marine Park is an aquarium near the Lighthouse. Incidentally, Choshi, a city

of 87,000, is the fishing center of northern Kanto. The city's Fish Market might be of interest to those with extra time.

1. Ryokan in Awa-Kamogawa

Kamogawa Grand Hotel (10 minute walk from Awa-Komogawa Station). Deluxe. 58 Japanese & 58 Western rooms. 25,000 yen & up per person. Add: 820, Hiroba, Kamogawa. Tel: (04709) 2-2111.

Kamogawakan (5 minutes by taxi from Awa-Kamogawa Station). First Class. 75 rooms. 20,000 yen & up per person. Add: 1179, Nishimachi, Kamogawa. Tel: (04709) 3-4111.

Kamogawa Sea World Hotel (5 minutes by taxi from Awa-Kamogawa Station). First Class. 76 rooms. 18,000 yen & up per person. Add: 1464-18, Higashicho, Kamogawa. Tel: (04709) 2-2121.

2. Ryokan in Cape Inubosaki

Hotel New Daishin (5 minute walk from Inubo Station). Standard. 45 rooms. 13,000 yen & up per person. Add: 10292, Inubosaki, Choshi. Tel: (0479) 22-5024.

Inubosaki Kanko Hotel (10 minute walk from Inubo Station). Standard. 50 rooms. 12,000 yen & up per person. Add: 10293, Inubosaki, Choshi. Tel: (0479) 23-5111.

3. Ryokan in Tateyama

Tateyama Seaside Hotel (5 minutes by taxi from Tateyama Station). Standard. 123 rooms. 13,000 yen & up per person. Add: 2544-1, Shirahama, Shirahamacho. Tel: (0470) 22-0151.

Note: There are a number of People's Lodges in Boso Peninsula. They are marked on Kanto Map 43. If you live in Japan, try them as destinations. Facilities at People's Lodges are similar to standard/first class ryokan, but they are less expensive (usually around 8,000 yen per person with 2 meals). They are very popular and crowded. Make reservations as far in advance as possible.

HARUNASAN 榛名山

This destination is recommended for those living in Japan. About 40,000 years ago, Harunasan was one big mountain. After a series of volcanic eruptions that blew the mountain apart, a caldera lake formed, surrounded by several surrounding peaks. The area is a popular summer vacation destination. When the Lake is frozen in winter, it is crowded with ice fishermen in pursuit of smelt.

Transportation to Harunasan

The JR Joetsu Shinkansen (both "Asahi" and "Toki") from Tokyo stops at Takasaki

(a one-hour trip) (Lower right, Kanto Map 44-A). From the western side of Takasaki Station take a Lake Harunako-bound bus. The trip takes one and a half hours, and the fare is 1,200 yen.

Lake Harunako is shown on Kanto Map 44-B. Restaurants and souvenir shops are concentrated near the bus stop on the southern side of the Lake. A newly constructed high-rise condominium mars the view of the Lake and the mountains. You can rent a boat if you want to make direct exploration of the Lake. Horse-drawn carriages will take you from Lake Harunako Bus Terminal to the Ropeway Station (you can easily walk this distance). The Ropeway takes you to the

MAP 44-A, B, C Harunasan and Ikaho Onsen

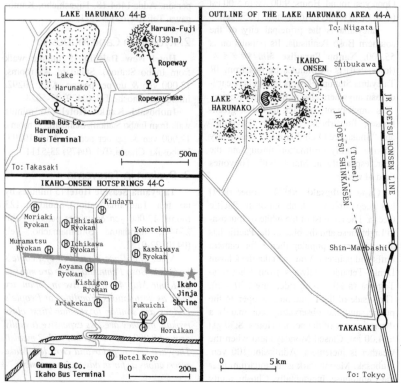

summit of Mt. Haruna-Fuji in three minutes (roundtrip fare: 750 yen). There is a grand view of the Lake from the top of this mountain. If you are making a day excursion from Tokyo, walk back to Lake Harunako Bus Terminal, and trace your route back to Tokyo. If, however, you want to stay overnight in a hotspring, you should take a bus from Ropeway-mae stop (Kanto Map 44-B) to Ikaho-Onsen bus terminal (upper center, Kanto Map 44-A).

For details on Ikaho-Onsen, see Kanto Map 44-C. Buses from the Lake Harunako area terminate at Ikaho Bus Terminal (lower left), which is located at the lowest point of the hilly Ikaho-Onsen Hotspring area. **Ikaho Jinja Shrine** 伊香保神社 (middle right) is located at the highest point, and many *ryokan* are tucked into the hillsides. The stone steps of the main approach to the Shrine (shaded on the map) are lined with souvenir shops, restaurants and bars. This area has the festive but slightly tawdry atmosphere of a typical Japanese hotspring resort. The northern end of the hotspring area (outside the map) has a ropeway that will take you to **Ikaho Highland** 伊香保ハイランド, which has an observatory and an ice skating rink. The trip takes four minutes and costs 600 yen roundtrip.

To return to Tokyo, you can take a bus from the Ikaho Bus Terminal (lower left, Kanto Map 44-C) to Takasaki (lower right, Kanto Map 44-A). The trip takes one hour and 15 minutes, and the fare is 1,050 yen. Then take the JR Joetsu Shinkansen from Takasaki back to the city. A less expensive alternative is to take a bus from the bus terminal near the Ropeway Station (outside Kanto Map 44-C) to JR Shibukawa Station (upper right, Kanto Map 44-A). The trip takes 30 minutes, and the fare is 520 yen. From Shibukawa, take the JR Joetsu Line Limited Express (the "Tanigawa" or the "Kusatsu") back to Tokyo's Ueno Station.

Ryokan in Ikaho-Onsen Hotsprings
(Refer to map 44-C)

Kishigon Ryokan (middle center). First Class. 78 rooms. 20,000 yen & up per person. Add: 48, Ikahomachi. Tel: (0279) 72-3105.

Hotel Kindayu (upper center). First Class. 62 rooms. 18,000 yen & up per person. Add: 19, Ikahomachi. Tel: (0279) 72-3232.

Moriaki Ryokan (upper left). Standard. 77 rooms. 13,000 yen & up per person. Add: 60, Ikahomachi. Tel: (0279) 72-2601.

JR FARES BETWEEN MAJOR STATIONS IN THE KANTO REGION

1. JR FARES BETWEEN TOKYO STATION AND MAJOR STATIONS

To / From	Tokyo	Remarks
Odawara	3,570 yen (83.9 km)	JR Tokaido-Sanyo Shinkansen
Atami	4,000 yen (104.6 km)	JR Tokaido-Sanyo Shinkansen
Ito	4,300 yen (121.5 km)	JR "Odoriko" limited express
Mishima	4,310 yen (120.7 km)	JR Tokaido-Sanyo Shinkansen
Oyama	3,870 yen (80.6 km)	JR Tohoku Shinkansen
Utsunomiya	4,710 yen (109.5 km)	JR Tohoku Shinkansen
Nikko	5,330 yen (154.1 km)	JR Tohoku Shinkansen & JR Nikko Line
Choshi	4,000 yen (133.9 km)	JR Sobu Line limited express
Awa-Kamogawa	4,000 yen (132.5 km)	JR Sotobo Line limited express
Tateyama	4,000 yen (128.9 km)	JR Uchibo Line limited express
Takasaki	4,710 yen (105 km)	JR Joetsu Shinkansen

2. JR FARE BETWEEN SHINJUKU STATION & OTSUKI STATION

To / From	Shinjyuku	Remarks
Otsuki	2,890 yen (77.5 km)	JR Chuo Honsen Line limited express

3. JR FARE BETWEEN UENO STATION & TSUCHIURA STATION

To / From	Ueno	Remarks
Tsuchiura	2,520 yen (66 km)	JR Joban Line limited express

JOETSU AND SHIN-ETSU REGION

上信越

Major mountain chains separate the Pacific coast and the Japan Sea coast. Their presence makes for radically different weather on Japan's two "sides." The Japan Sea side has heavy snowfalls in winter, while the Pacific coast enjoys dry weather. Severe winter weather and inconvenient transportation from Tokyo have combined to slow industrial development of the Japan Sea area, even though the chemical and pharmaceutical industries have grown rapidly there in recent years.

Three Japan Railways (JR) long distance lines run through this district, along the valleys and through the tunnels, connecting Tokyo with major cities on the Japan Sea coast via scenic inland cities. This district is roughly divided into three areas as listed below.

1. Joetsu Area (Along the JR Joetsu Shinkansen)

Refer to Joetsu and Shin-etsu Map 1. The Joetsu Shinkansen runs from Tokyo to Niigata, crossing Mt. Tanigawadake via the Shin-Shimizu tunnel. Thanks to heavy snowfalls in the winter, there are a number of ski resorts along the line. The snow in this area is rather wet. For skiers, there's no comparison to the powder of the Japan Alps area or Hokkaido. However, thanks to the easy access from Tokyo via the fast Joetsu Shinkansen, these resorts are popular destinations for Tokyoites. You can enjoy skiing even in a day trip from Tokyo. During the non-snow season, the area offers good hiking trails and pleasant overnight stays at hotsprings.

(1) Mt. Tanigawadake and nearby Minakami Onsen hotsprings (middle center) are the most scenic tourist destinations along the Joetsu Shinkansen. (2) Niigata (upper center), the terminal of the Joetsu Shinkansen, and a major port for trade with Russia, and (3) Sado Island (upper center) are also introduced in this Chapter.

2. Shin-etsu Area (Along the JR Shin-etsu Honsen Line)

The JR Shin-etsu Honsen Line runs from Tokyo's Ueno Station to Naoetsu (middle center) on the Japan Sea, skirting Mt. Asamayama, Shiga-Kogen Heights, and the Myoko mountains. These mountains, too, are sites of a number of ski resorts, many of which also feature hotsprings. Nagano will host the 1998 Winter Olympic Games, and many of the area's ski resorts and ice rinks will become Olympic venues. We describe the following three destinations along the Shin-etsu Honsen Line: (1) Karuizawa (middle center), a famous (summer) mountain resort for the Japanese establishment; (2) Komoro (middle center), a small castle town with a magnificent view of Mt. Asayama, an elegantly-shaped active volcano; and (3) Nagano (middle center), the capital of Nagano Prefecture and home of the sacred Zenkoji Temple.

3. The Japan Alps Area (Along the JR Chuo Honsen Line)

The JR Chuo Honsen Line runs from Tokyo's Shinjuku Station to Matsumoto, through narrow valleys that lie between the Yatsugatake mountains to the east and the

MAP 1 Outline of Joetsu and Shin-etsu

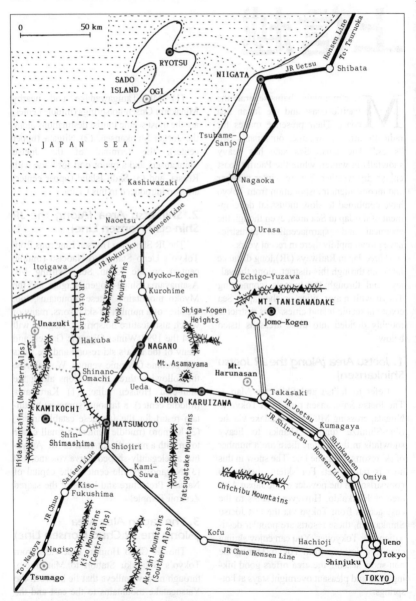

Southern Japan Alps to the west. The JR Oito Line extends from Matsumoto to Itoigawa (middle left) on the Japan Sea, along the eastern foot of the Northern (main) Japan Alps. There are many fine ski resorts along the JR Oito Line, some of which will also be used for the 1998 Olympics. If you are a mountain fan, this area should be your first priority.

In this Chapter, we describe (1) Matsumoto (lower left), a castle town and gateway to the Japan Alps; (2) Kamikochi (lower left), a lovely valley deep in the heart of the Japan Alps; and (3) the Northern Alps (Ushiro-Tateyama portion of the Hida Mountains) (middle left) along the JR Oito Line.

Matsumoto is also easily accessible from Nagoya via the JR Chuo Saisen Line. Matsumoto and Nagano (in the Shin-etsu Area) are connected by the JR Shinonoi Line (an extension of the JR Chuo Saisen Line from Matsumoto to Nagano), and can be combined in one itinerary.

The Kurobe-Tateyama Alpine route, a scenic cross-Alps sightseeing route starting at JR Shinano-Omachi Station (middle left), is described in the Chubu Region Chapter.

4. Other Major Cities in the Area

Nagaoka (upper center) is located at the intersection of the JR Joetsu Shinkansen and the JR Hokuriku Honsen Line. The city is leading the Shinanogawa Technopolis project, targeting at developing the area into a high-tech industry center. Population: 184,000.

Kofu (lower center) is the capital of Yamanashi Prefecture, with a population of 199,000. In the feudal era the city prospered as the main castle town of the powerful Takeda family, but lost all of its historic legacies in World War II.

Ueda (middle center), a castle town of the Sanada family, is now promoting research institutes and laboratories in its Ueda Research Park. Population: 119,000.

TRANSPORTATION IN THE JOETSU AND SHIN-ETSU REGION

The JR Joetsu Shinkansen runs between Tokyo (Tokyo Station) and Niigata, which is on the opposite side of the country, on the Japan Sea. Most of the Joetsu Shinkansen trains also stop at Ueno Station in Tokyo. There are eleven stations on the 334 km (209 mile) long Joetsu Shinkansen Line — Tokyo, Ueno, Omiya, Kumagaya, Takasaki, Jomo-Kogen, Echigo-Yuzawa, Urasa, Nagaoka, Tsubame-Sanjo and Niigata. There are two types of Shinkansen trains on this line. The faster "Asahi" trains run about once an hour, and stop only at major stations, such as Takasaki, Echigo-Yuzawa, and Nagaoka. The ride from Tokyo to Niigata takes only two hours. The slower "Toki" trains also run about once every hour and stop at all stations. The ride from Tokyo to Niigata takes about two and a half hours. Because the time difference is only 30 minutes between the two types of Shinkansen, when you plan to travel from Tokyo to Niigata, you can simply think of the JR Joetsu Shinkansen as operating about once every 30 minutes. Please note, however, that when you travel to Jomo-Kogen (for Mt. Tanigawadake), you must take the "Toki" Shinkansen.

The JR Shin-etsu Honsen Line connects Tokyo (Ueno Station) with Naoetsu on the Japan Sea coast. Most limited express trains on this line (called "Asama") run between Tokyo's Ueno Station and Nagano (about once every hour). Only two or three trains a day run the whole length of the Shin-etsu Honsen Line (between Ueno and Naoetsu). The ride on the Asama from Ueno Station takes about two hours to Karuizawa, two hours and ten minutes to Komoro, and two hours and fifty minutes to Nagano.

Limited express trains (called "Azusa") on the JR Chuo Line run between Tokyo's Shinjuku Station and Matsumoto via Kofu about once every hour. Several of the Azusa trains run beyond Matsumoto onto the JR

Oito Line to Shinano-Omachi Station (the end of the Tateyama-Kurobe Alpine Route described in the Chubu Region Chapter). The ride from Shinjuku to Matsumoto takes two hours and 45 minutes. Local trains also run on the JR Oito Line, originating at Matsumoto Station.

Along the JR Joetsu Shinkansen 上越新幹線沿線

MT. TANIGAWADAKE & MINAKAMI ONSEN
谷川岳・水上温泉

(Refer to Joetsu and Shin-etsu Map 2)

Transportation to Mt. Tanigawadake

You can take the Joetsu Shinkansen from Tokyo to Jomo-Kogen (lower center). The ride takes 70 minutes on the slower "Toki" train. Alternatively, you can take a limited express train (called "Tanigawa") on the JR Joetsu Line from Ueno to Minakami (middle center). The train operates about once every two hours, and the ride takes 2 hours and 15 minutes. The bus to the Tanigawa-Ropeway terminus (middle center) runs about once every 40-60 minutes, and the ride takes 25 minutes from Minakami Station and 55 minutes from Jomo-Kogen Station. When you take the bus from Jomo-Kogen, you may have to change buses at Minakami Station (there are only a few direct buses a day from Jomo-Kogen to Tanigawa-Ropeway).

Tanigawa Kyudo Path 谷川旧道 (Upper center)

Because of heavy snow in the area in the winter, the Tanigawa mountains have precipitous cliffs and snowy ravines despite their relatively low heights (1,978 m or 6,490 feet above sea level), and the mountains are very popular with rock climbers.

Tanigawa Kyudo Path, starting at Tanigawa-Ropeway bus terminus, is an extension of the bus road from Minakami. It is well paved. Once the road was used only by the vehicles of the Park Office, and private cars and commercial vehicles were prohibited beyond the bus terminus. Unfortunately, to promote more tourists to the area, private cars are now allowed access to this road as far as to the entrance to Ichinokura Ravine. They are a bit of a nuisance as you walk on this supposedly quiet scenic path. The road is closed from November until the end of May because of the danger of snow avalanches. The path curves as it hugs the mountainside. Forty minutes from the bus terminus you will see Machiga, the first ravine. Machiga Ravine マチガ沢 is broad and rises gradually towards Mt. Tanigawadake. Forty minutes from Machiga you will reach Ichinokura Ravine 一ノ倉沢. This ravine is quite precipitous. Looking up at the cliffs rising sharply into the sky, you can understand why Ichinokura is a favorite destination for rock climbers, and also why this threatening ravine has taken more than 500 young lives.

Ropeway to Tenjindaira 天神平 (Middle center)

Returning to the bus terminal, take the ropeway to Tenjindaira. Small cabins operate frequently to halfway up Mt. Tanigawadake. The ride takes only 10 minutes (1,800 yen roundtrip). Tenjindaira is a chal-

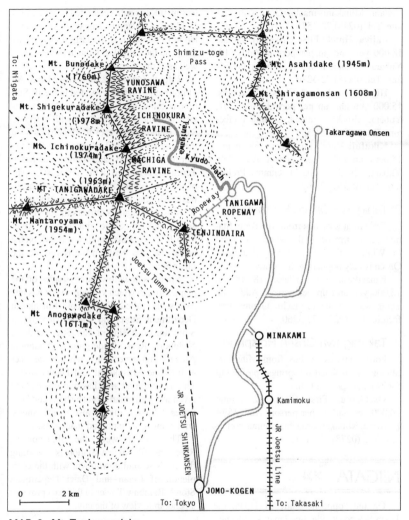

MAP 2 Mt. Tanigawadake

lenging ski ground proud of its long season — from the end or November until the middle of May. There's a panoramic view of the nearby mountains. In summer, a leisurely stroll will give you a chance to enjoy the mountain flowers. You can return via the same route from either Minakami or Jomo-Kogen.

ACCOMMODATIONS (Ryokan)

1. Minakami Onsen Hotsprings

The largest hotsprings of the area, around Minakami Station.

Hotel Juraku. First Class. 200 rooms. 18,000 yen and up per person. Add: 665,

Yubara, Minakami-machi, Gunma Prefecture. Tel: (0278) 72-2521

Fujiya Hotel. First Class. 81 rooms. 18,000 yen and up per person. Add: 719, Yubara, Minakami-machi, Gunma Prefecture. Tel: (0278) 72-3270.

Higaki Hotel. First Class. 116 rooms. 15,000 yen and up per person. Add: 701, Yubara, Minakami-machi, Gunma Prefecture. Tel: (0278) 72-2552.

Kikufuji Hotel. First Class. 38 rooms. 15,000 yen and up per person. Add: 750, Yubara, Minakami-machi, Gunma Prefecture. Tel: (0278) 72-3020.

2. Tanigawa Onsen Hotsprings

Ten minutes by bus from Minakami Station. A quiet resort in the woods. Adjacent to White Valley Ski Resort, Tanigawa Onsen is very popular in the winter.

Kinseikan. First Class. 18 rooms. 12,000 yen and up per person. Add: 544, Tanigawa, Minakami-machi, Gunma Prefecture. Tel: (0278) 72-3260.

3. Takaragawa Onsen Hotsprings

Forty minutes by bus from Minakami Station. An isolated hotsprings spa famous for its large open-air baths.

Osenkaku. First Class. 52 rooms. 16,000 yen and up per person. Add: 1899, Fujiwara, Minakami-machi, Gunma Prefecture. Tel: (0278) 75-2121.

NIIGATA 新潟

On the "opposite" side of Japan, the Japan Sea coast side, lies Japan's *Yukiguni*, Snow Country. Transformed by the mounds of snow that bury it in winter, and blessed with uniformly pleasant weather in summer, this remote area is famous for tranquility conducive to contemplation. Its hearty people are direct and open in a way you won't often encounter in the rarified atmosphere of most Japanese cities. It was this area that

Yasunari Kawabata celebrated in his famous 1947 novel *Yukiguni*. Niigata, with a population of 476,000, is the largest city in this area, and the capital of Niigata Prefecture as well as of the "Snow Country."

Refer to Joetsu and Shin-etsu Map 3. An *i* Information Office is located in the JR Station, near the Bandaiguchi Exit. Most tourists visit Niigata in conjunction with a trip to Sado Island (below), or to Hagurosan (See the Tohoku Chapter). Please note that the pier for the boats to Sado Island (Sado Kisen Terminal) is located in the northeastern part of the city (upper right). There is frequent bus service between JR station and the pier.

Most of Niigata's attractions for visitors are located across the Shinanogawa River from JR Niigata Station (lower right), on the island that lies between the River and the Japan Sea.

Niigata's downtown area (shaded on the map), through which virtually every bus line passes, is called Furumachi. Mitsukoshi Department Store and Daiwa Department Store are on Nishibori-dori Street and the Nishibori Rosa Underground Shopping Area runs underneath it. There are entrances at both the Mitsukoshi and Daiwa stores. The underground area has two wings: "6th Avenue" is all smart, stylish shops and boutiques. "7th Avenue" is also mostly shops, with a few restaurants and snack bars.

The area between the Shinanogawa River and JR Niigata Station is becoming the city's second downtown, with the completion of Isetan and Daiei Department Stores. Rainbow Tower in this area provides a panoramic view of the city.

Transportation in Niigata

The best way to get around Niigata is on the city's buses. There's a bus terminal in front of JR Niigata Station, to your left as you emerge from the station. Because so many buses originate at the Station, it's probably a good idea to use Conversation Card 5 here.

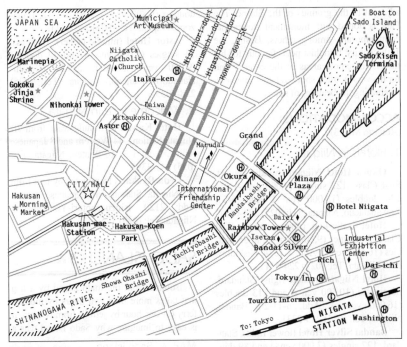

MAP 3 Niigata

Hakusan-mae Station (middle left) is the terminal of the area's commuter line, and is no use for tourists.

Places of Interest

Hakusan-Koen Park 白山公園 (lower left). Catch the bus bound for Hakusan-Koen-mae stop at the JR Station. The Park, located in the city's cultural zone, contains Hakusan Jinja Shrine, which was established in the 10th or 11th century, and a spectacular garden. Take some time to walk around the garden: it has two ponds, one with a curved bridge, and the second with an arbor overhead. In the spring, the garden's beautiful lotus, wisteria and azalea blooms make it especially attractive.

Nihonkai Tower 日本海タワー (upper left) (optional). This observatory is 2.4 km (1.5 miles) from Niigata Station — 10 minutes by bus. Catch the bus bound for Nihonkai-Tower-mae stop from the Station. When you get off the bus walk back the way the bus was traveling to the entrance. Hours: 9:00 AM to 5:00 PM (10:00 AM to 4:00 PM in winter). Admission: 300 yen. The Tower features exhibits from Niigata's sister cities. The Tower, which revolves, is 62.6 m (191 feet) tall, and boasts a 360 degree view. The Japan Sea lies to the North and the West, and the city itself to the East and South.

Gokoku Jinja Shrine 護国神社 (upper left) (optional). You can walk the short distance from Nihonkai Tower to the Shrine. Through the large concrete *torii* gate, there is a long, paved approach to the Shrine, lined with wind-bent pines and a great many monument stones. If you visit the Shrine, we suggest that you also wander through **Nishi-Kaigan-Koen Park** 西海岸公園, which is adjacent to the grounds of the Shrine. The Park is dotted with monument stones that commemorate, among others, Basho, the 17th century Buddhist poet, famous for his travels to remote areas of the country and for his verses, often short and epigrammatic, celebrating the beauties of nature.

ACCOMMODATIONS
(Refer to Map 3)

1. Hotels in Niigata

Okura Hotel Niigata (middle center). First Class. 122 singles (9,000 yen -) and 174 doubles (18,000 yen -). Add: 6-53, Kawabatacho, Niigata. Tel: (025) 224-6111.

Hotel Italia-ken (upper center). First Class. 50 singles (9,500 yen -) and 36 doubles (16,500 yen -). Add: 7-1574, Nishiboridori, Niigata. Tel: (025) 224-5111.

Hotel Niigata (middle right). Standard. 66 singles (10,500 yen -) and 113 doubles (16,000 yen -). Add: 5-11-20, Bandai, Niigata. Tel: (025) 245-3331.

Bandai Silver Hotel (lower right). Standard. 127 singles (7,000 yen -) and 89 doubles (15,000 yen -). Add: 1-3-30, Bandai, Niigata. Tel: (025) 243-3711.

Hotel Rich Niigata (lower right). Business. 81 singles (5,800 yen -) and 22 doubles (13,000 yen -). Add: 2-1-21, Higashi-Odori, Niigata. Tel: (025) 243-1881.

Niigata Tokyu Inn (lower right). Business. 198 singles (7,500 yen -) and 111 doubles (15,000 yen -). Add: 1-2-4, Benten, Niigata. Tel: (025) 243-0109.

Niigata Washington Hotel (lower right). Business. 219 singles (7,500 yen -) and 84 doubles (15,000 yen -). Add: 1-1, Sasaguchi, Niigata. Tel: (025) 243-7311.

Niigata Minami Plaza Hotel (middle right). Business. 157 singles (5,700 yen -) and 33 doubles (11,500 yen -). Add: 3-1-1, Bandai, Niigata. Tel: (025) 241-3730.

Niigata Dai-ichi Hotel (lower right). Business. 211 singles (5,000 yen -) and 80 doubles (9,800 yen -). Add: 1-3-12, Hanazono, Niigata. Tel: (025) 243-1111.

Astor Hotel (middle center). Business. 53 singles (5,000 yen -) and 32 doubles (9,000 yen -). Add: 289-2, Higashi-Nakadori-Nibancho, Niigata. Tel: (025) 228-4033.

2. Welcome Inns in Niigata

Hotel Kawai. (2 minute walk from JR Niigata Station). 44 Western and 8 Japanese rooms. Add: 1-3-10, Benten, Niigata. Tel: (025) 241-3391.

Ueda Ryokan (15 minutes by taxi from JR Niigata Station). 10 Japanese rooms. Add: 2120, Ishizuechotori-Yonnomachi, Niigata. Tel: (025) 225-1111.

SADO ISLAND 佐渡

Isolated from the main island by a trip that takes more than two hours by modern ferry (or one hour by jetfoil) from Niigata, it is easy to imagine why Sado Island was a

MAP 4 Sado Island

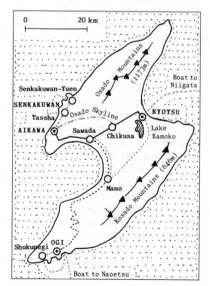

place of exile in the middle ages and a prison colony during the Edo Era. With an area of 1,885 square km (857 square miles), Sado Island is the fifth largest of Japan's islands. One of the most famous of the early residents of Sado Island was Emperor Juntoku, who lost out in a 1221 attempt to wrest control from the Kamakura Shogunate (which was in fact controlled by hereditary regents of the Hojo family). Regent Yoshitoki Hojo banished the Emperor to Sado, where he lived until his death in 1242. Another famous medieval era resident of Sado Island was Nichiren, the founder of the still popular Buddhist sect (which reduces essentials of religious observance to chanting *Namu-Myo-Ho-Renge-Kyo*). Nichiren was exiled on Sado Island from 1271 until 1274.

Sado Island is at its best between April and October, and winter visits are really not recommended. The weather is harsh, the crossings from Honshu can be quite rough, bus services on the island are severely reduced, and once the autumn equinox has passed, the sun sets quite early, limiting the time available for sightseeing. In other seasons, Sado is a delightful change of pace from the larger islands. The beauty of the island's majestic mountains and spectacular coastline make it ideal for those who really want to get off the beaten path. The simple and direct warmth of the country people adds to the pleasure of the experience.

Transportation to Sado Island

Refer to Joetsu and Shin-etsu Map 4.

MAP 5 Ryotsu

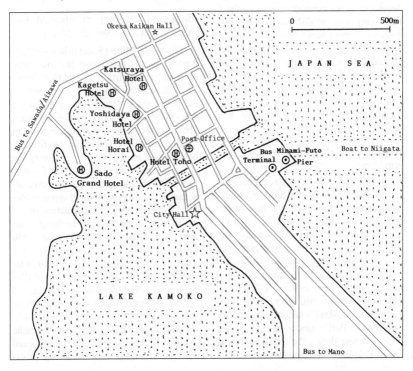

Aside from flights from Niigata to Ryotsu, Sado Island's capital city, the only transportation to Sado Island is by water. The main ferry line connects Niigata and Ryotsu (middle right). Ferry boats operate five times a day between the two ports. The ride takes two hours (1,780 yen - 5,340 yen depending on the class). Jetfoils operate on the same route more frequently (about once every hour). The fare is higher — 5,460 yen each way. A supplemental ferry and jetfoil service (about five times a day) is available between Naoetsu (mainland) and Ogi (lower left), a town on the southern coast of Sado Island.

Transportation on Sado Island

Buses are the only means of mass transportation. Taxis are also plentiful at major terminals, such as Ryotsu, Aikawa and Ogi. An extensive bus network covers the island. Fares vary with the distance traveled. Frequency of service varies from route to route, and with the season. We recommend that you ask for a bus schedule at the Ryotsu port building or any of the other bus terminals. Ask for a *teiki* bus 定期バス schedule (so you won't get the schedule for the regularly scheduled Japanese-language only tour buses).

Ryotsu 両津 (Refer to Joetsu and Shin-etsu Map 5)

Ryotsu is Sado Island's capital and largest city. It also has the most accommodations, and its status as the hub of the island's transportation system makes it the most convenient starting point for day tours of the island. The city is dominated by Kamoko Lake, which is 17 km (10.6 miles) wide and connected to the Japan Sea by a narrow inlet. Many of the city's *ryokan* boast lake-view rooms. Ryotsu is also the home of Sado Island's famous Okesa Odori Folkdance. Performances are presented every evening during the tourist season at Okesa Kaikan Hall (upper center).

Suggested Itinerary on Sado Island

Day 1. Ryotsu to Aikawa

Refer to Joetsu and Shin-etsu Map 4. The bus from Ryotsu to Aikawa runs about once every 30 mintues. The ride takes about one hour (670 yen). As the bus traverses the island you begin to realize that you're really out in the country. Sado Island has two parallel mountain chains, one in the northwest (Osado mountains) and the other in the southeast (Kosado mountains), with a fertile farmland plain between the two. The bus crosses the island on the plain, and the mountains are visible in the distance. The bus makes a terminal-type stop at Sawada Bus Station after it rambles through the town of Sawada. Stay put; it'll continue to Aikawa shortly. The Ryotsu-Aikawa trip takes about 1 hour and 15 minutes.

Places of Interest in Aikawa 相川
(Refer to Joetsu and Shin-etsu Map 6)

Old Gold Mine (Sodayu-ko) 佐渡金山 (upper right). Take a short taxi ride from Aikawa bus terminal to the Old Gold Mine. The Aikawa taxi company is right next to the bus terminal. Because the route to the Old Gold Mine from the town of Aikawa is uphill, we recommend that you take a taxi to the mine, and walk back. Gold was first discovered on Sado Island in 1601. During the Edo Era, this mine, Japan's most famous, reached the height of its prosperity. Aikawa at the time had a population of approximately 100,000. (Today, the population of the entire island is 80,000, and declining.) The mine's tunnels covered 400 km (250 miles) — the distance between Aikawa and Tokyo — and some of them extended as far as 600 m (1,969 feet) below sea level. The mine was worked by prison slave labor, and served as a major source of revenue for the Tokugawa Shogunate. Some mining is still done here on a small scale. Today the mine is primarily a living museum. Dioramas and mechanical models demonstrate the privations of the lives of the miners, who dug many of the old tunnels with only hammers and chisels. The path through the display area winds down through the tunnels of the mine, and if you look closely you can still see a few traces of gold and silver in the walls. Hours: 8:00 AM to 6:00 PM. Admission: 600 yen.

If you walk back to Aikawa from the Old Gold Mine, you might want to stop at the following, all of which are optional: **Sado Hangamura Museum** 佐渡版画村美術館 (Woodblock Print Museum) is located in a beautiful old wooden building, and has a lovely garden with twisted pines in front of it. It displays the works of members of local woodblock print clubs. Recommended only for devotees of woodblock prints. Hours: 9:00 AM to 5:00 PM. Closed December through February. Admission:

300 yen. **Aikawa Museum** 相川郷土博物館 displays Edo period maps, pictures, scrolls and everyday items, including implements used for mining. The second floor has woven goods, and the third, pottery. Hours: 8:30 AM to 5:00 PM. Closed on Sundays in January and February. Admission: 300 yen. Near the Aikawa Bus Terminal there are several *Mumyoyaki* pottery shops. *Mumyoyaki* is a distinctive (and expensive) red-hued pottery made with clay from the Gold Mine.

Aikawa to Senkakuwan 尖閣湾 (outside Map 6 to the north; please see Map 4). Buses from Aikawa to Tassha operate about once an hour (a 15-minute ride). When the weather is good, you can take a 40-minute boat trip from Tassha that circles Senkakuwan Bay for a close-up view of the spectacular coast and its exotic rock formations.

MAP 6 Aikawa

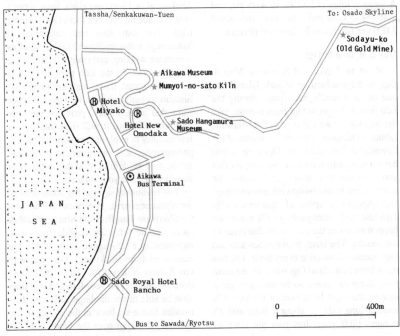

This trip is, in our opinion, the biggest attraction of the Aikawa area.

Osado Skyline Drive 大佐渡スカイライン (middle center, Joetsu and Shin-etsu Map 4) (optional). The only public transportation available on the Osado Skyline, which runs through the mountains between Aikawa and Chikusa, is on Japanese tour buses. The Skyline Tour Route starts from Ryotsu and stops at Aikawa, Senkakuwan and the Old Gold Mine before returning to Ryotsu. Japanese tours are notorious for their superficiality and rushed atmospheres; plus you won't be able to understand the explanations of the tour guide — but these tours are the easiest way to get around the Aikawa area and might be worth it for the skyline route. You can catch a bus back to Ryotsu in Chikusa. The April-November Japanese sightseeing bus schedule is as follows (from Ryotsu back to Ryotsu): Morning tour (8:20 AM to 11:45 AM), and Afternoon tours (12:30 PM to 4:05 PM; and 2:40 PM to 6:20 PM). The tour costs about 3,000 yen (each tour is slightly different).

Day 2. Ryotsu to Ogi

Refer to Joetsu and Shin-etsu Map 4. Ogi, on the southern tip of Sado Island, was one of the island's main ports during the Edo period. To get to Ogi from Ryotsu, take the bus for Aikawa and get off at Sawada (about 40 minutes, 480 yen). Transfer at the Sawada bus terminal to the Ogi Line. If you have a wait between buses, we suggest that you visit the tiny temple just across the street. It has lovely woodwork and carvings, and captures a spirit of quintessentially Japanese rustic tranquility you'll never just happen across in the more crowded areas of the country. The buses between Sawada and Ogi operate about once every hour. The bus route from Sawada to Ogi runs, for the most part, along the coast, so be sure you get a seat on the right hand side of the bus. It's another long ride — about 1 hour and 15 minutes (800 yen). Just past the town of

Takazaki, you'll be able to see Sado Island's most famous fantastic rock formation, Benten-iwa, which has a miniature shrine dedicated to the goddess Benten.

Places of Interest in Ogi 小木
(Refer to Joetsu and Shin-etsu Map 7)

Ogi (upper right) is most famous for a unique form of transportation — its tubs. These tubs, or *taraibune*, can easily accommodate three or more people. Rent your tub at the *taraibune* port, to your right as you exit from the Ogi Bus Terminal. If you have time to spare in Ogi, we suggest that you explore Shiroyama-Koen Park. A quiet shrine, Kisaki Jinja, stands at its foot, and the path behind it leads you up a hill. The paths in the park are punctuated with pavilions for picnicking, and observatories with great views of the Japan Sea.

Ogi to Shukunegi 宿根木 (lower left). The Shukunegi Line bus connects Ogi and Shukunegi (a 15-minute ride). Boat service is also available between them (a 20-minute trip). You can also rent *taraibune* at Shukunegi, a tiny traditional town. All of its houses are wooden, and many are more than 200 years old. In the Edo period it was a center of export trade, and the people of Shukunegi built many of the Japanese-style ships that in those days provided the only link with Honshu. It will only take you a few minutes to explore the town. If you're a photographer and interested in traditional Japan, this is definitely a day when you should remember your camera.

The traditional sightseeing attractions of the Shukunegi area, **Iwayasan** 岩谷山 and the **Shiawase Jizo Buddha Statue** 幸福地蔵 (both middle left) are outside the town. Iwayasan is a 15-minute walk along the main road from Shukunegi. On your way you'll pass a beautiful, large traditional thatched building on your left, and will then soon be able to see the large Shiawase Jizo Buddha Statue set back in the woods in the distance, towering over the fields. Stay on

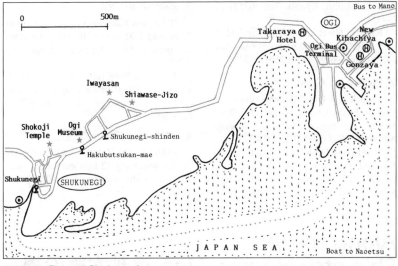

MAP 7 Ogi and Shukunegi

the road until you see a brown wooden post on your left. The sign has characters but also says "400 m." Turn there off the road and onto the gravel path. Follow the path through the fields, keeping to the right when it forks, and you'll arrive at Iwayasan. The temple entrance is marked by two stone statues, and by another sign that says "200 m" and points in the direction of the Shiawase Jizo Buddha Statue. Visit Iwayasan first. Go through the lantern entrance and up the steps. At the top there is a circular area ringed with tiny Buddha statues. The clearing also has huge trees, the biggest of which is in front of the cave that houses the temple. Numerous tiny statues of Buddhas line the cave, and seven very old images of Buddha are also carved right into its walls. When you leave Iwayasan, continue on the path, following the "200 m" sign to the Shiawase Jizo Buddha Statue. The Shiawase Jizo stands 17.5 m (58 feet) tall. This temple, appropriately enough for the "Happiness Buddha," is a thoroughly cheerful place. There's a smaller, seated laughing Buddha

to the right of the big statue, and huge tubs (*taraibune*-type) are scattered around the temple area. One of the tubs has even been given a roof and turned into a mini-temple: Walk straight away from the statue back to the road. There's a bus stop nearby where you can catch a bus back to Ogi (a 10-minute ride).

ACCOMMODATIONS

1. Ryokan in Ryotsu

Sado Grand Hotel (middle left, Map 5). First Class. 89 rooms. 15,000 yen and up per person. Add: 4918-1, Kamo-Utashiro, Ryotsu. Tel: (0259) 27-3281.

Yoshidaya Hotel (middle center). First Class. 52 rooms. 15,000 yen and up per person. Add: 261, Ebisu, Ryotsu. Tel: (0259) 27-2151.

Hotel Toho (middle center). Standard. 31 rooms. 12,000 yen and up per person. Add: 224, Ebisu, Ryotsu. Tel: (0259) 27-6131.

Hotel Horai (middle center). Standard. 28 rooms. 12,000 yen and up per person.

Add: 262 Ebisu, Ryotsu. Tel: (0259) 27-2141.

Kagetsu Hotel (upper left). Standard. 26 rooms. 10,000 yen and up per person. Add: 262, Ebisu, Ryotsu. Tel: (0259) 27-3131.

2. Ryokan in Aikawa

Sado Royal Hotel Bancho (lower left, Map 6). First Class. 82 rooms. 15,000 yen and up per person. Add: 58, Shimoto, Aikawacho, Sado. Tel: (0259) 74-3221.

Hotel New Omodaka (middle center). Standard. 36 rooms. 10,000 yen and up per person. Add: 12, Nishisaka, Aikawacho, Sado. Tel: (0259) 74-3175.

3. Ryokan in Ogi

Hotel New Kihachiya (upper right, Map 7). Standard. 38 rooms. 10,000 yen and up per person. Add: Ogi-machi, Sado. Tel: (0259) 86-3131.

Takaraya Hotel (upper right). Standard. 17 rooms. 10,000 yen and up per person. Add: 280-1, Ogi-machi, Sado. Tel: (0259) 86-3165.

4. Welcome Inn in Ryotsu

Sado Seaside Hotel (5 minutes by taxi from Ryotsu Port). 12 Japanese rooms. Add: 80, Sumiyoshi, Ryotsu. Tel: (0259) 27-7211.

Along the JR
Shin-etsu Honsen Line 信越本線沿線

KARUIZAWA 軽井沢

With the development of the Nakasendo Road in Edo Era, Karuizawa prospered as a post town. At its peak over 200 ryokan were located here to cater to travelers on Nakasendo. After the Meiji Restoration, when the nation's traffic shifted heavily to the Tokaido Road along the Pacific coast, Nakasendo lost its importance and Karuizawa became just a small town with a few inns.

Karuizawa's value as a summer resort was discovered by an Scottish priest, Alexander Show, in the middle of the Meiji Era. Its cool, dry weather in summer, coupled with its scenic beauty throughout the year, attracted foreign diplomats, aristocrats, politicians, business executives, novelists, artists, and even the imperial family. Karuizawa soon became a "villa" town for the establishment. The Mikasa Hotel was built in 1904 and functioned as a salon for the rich and famous. Emperor Akihito played tennis with Empress Michiko in Karuizawa before they married. They still visit Karuizawa periodically and enjoy tennis. Foreign dignitaries are often invited here for casual meetings.

In recent years, many resorts have been built in the area, which has changed the area's elite character quite a bit. However, except for a summer time wave of youngsters flooding the area's boutiques and restaurants, the original villa area (called "Kyu-Karuizawa" or Old Karuizawa) still remains largely the home of the establishment. Many villas, which cost 100-200 million yen, sit quietly in thick larch forests, isolated from the masses. Most of the area's hotels are proud of their world class standard, and they cost as much as deluxe hotels in downtown Tokyo.

Refer to Joetsu and Shin-etsu Map 8. Karuizawa's main street, Mikasa-dori Street (shaded on the map), extends to the north from Karuizawa Station. There are several rental cycle shops near the station. Temporary "fashionable" shops line the street in summer to squeeze some yen from youngsters from Tokyo. In other seasons, the street is rather quiet. The main shopping street (shaded on the map, branching off from Mikasa-dori Street) is called Karuizawa Ginza. Famous Tokyo boutiques and restaurants have branches here. Karuizawa Ginza really is like Tokyo's Ginza (or rather Roppongi) in the summertime, with the hustle and bustle of youngsters (mostly from the Tokyo area). The rest of Karuizawa is covered with larch trees.

If you are fortunate enough to visit Karuizawa, be sure to enjoy a leisurely stroll

MAP 8 Karuizawa

(or cycling) in the area near Manpei Hotel (upper right), Hotel Kashimanomori (upper left), and the northern extension of Mikasa-dori Street. If you don't have such an opportunity, you can still enjoy the beauty of the graceful Mt. Asamayama through the train window on the JR Shin-etsu Honsen Line.

Hotels in Karuizawa

(Refer to Joetsu and Shin-etsu Map 8)
Note: Prices are much higher in summer peak season.

Karuizawa Prince Hotel (lower center). Deluxe. 895 rooms. 28,000 yen and up per room. Add: Kyu-Karuizawa, Karuizawa-machi, Nagano Prefecture. Tel: (0267) 42-1111.

Manpei Hotel (upper right). Deluxe. 84 rooms. 21,000 yen and up per room. Add: 925 Karuizawa, Karuizawa-machi, Nagano Prefecture. Tel: (0267) 42-1234.

Hotel Otowanomori (middle center). Deluxe. 49 rooms. 20,000 yen and up per room. Add: Kyu-Karuizawa, Karuizawa-machi, Nagano Prefecture. Tel: (0267) 42-7711.

Hotel Kashimanomori (upper left). Deluxe. 50 rooms. 20,000 yen and up per room. Add: Hanareyama, Karuizawa-machi, Nagano Prefecture. Tel: (0267) 42-3535.

Mar Lord Inn Karuizawa (middle right). First Class. 41 rooms. 20,000 yen and up per room. Add: 1178 Karuizawa, Karuizawa-machi, Nagano Prefecture. Tel: (0267) 42-8444.

KOMORO 小諸

Komoro's first castle was built at the present site in the middle of the 16th century at the order of Shingen Takeda, a powerful feudal lord who governed the area during the civil war period. Most of the buildings have been lost and only gates and rock walls stand today.

If you have a few extra hours during

your trip on the JR Shin-etsu Honsen Line, we recommend that you make a stop at Komoro to visit the castle grounds and enjoy a stroll through the town's historic streets. Refer to Joetsu and Shin-etsu Map 9.

Komorojo Castle Grounds 小諸城址 (left half) are located on the western side of the JR tracks. There is an underground passage beneath the railroad tracks to Sannomon Gate. **Chokokan Museum** 徴古館 displays swords, armor, hanging scrolls and other castle treasures. **Toson Memorial Hall** 藤村記念館 exhibits memorials of Toson Shimazaki, a Meiji-era novelist. Cross the bridge to the northern corner of the castle grounds. **Folklore Museum** 郷土博物館 , housed in a modern building, displays everything relevant to Komoro. **Koyama Keizo Art Museum** 小山敬三美術館 features paintings by Koyama, a famous artist from Komoro. Return to the main grounds and ascend to the donjon grounds. The three-story donjon was destroyed long ago by lightening. Kaiko Jinja Shrine, as well as a few restaurants, stand on the site of the donjon. Cross another bridge to proceed to the southern side of the grounds, which is now used for a small zoo. A 400-yen admission gains you entry to all parts of the castle grounds. Hours: 9:00 AM to 5:00 PM. Open daily from April to October. Closed Wednesdays from November to March.

Komoro's downtown spreads to the east of Komoro Station. Modernization is taking place even in this small city of 44,000, especially along Chuo-doro Street. There are many old buildings on the northern side, along Kitaguni Kaido (an old post road). Otemon Gate (upper center) was once the main entrance to Komorojo Castle. Shiokawa House is the former residence of *shoya* (a village chief of the feudal era). Otsuka Sake Breweries has an impressive structure from the Edo era. Yorozuya is an antique shop in an antique house, and Yamatoya is a 150-year old paper shop.

ACCOMMODATIONS

(Refer to Joetsu and Shin-etsu Map 9)

1. Hotels in Komoro

Komoro Grand Castle Hotel (5 minute walk from Komoro Station). Standard. 53 singles (7,400 yen -) and 31 doubles (14,700 yen -). Add: 1-1-5, Kojo, Komoro. Tel: (0267) 22-8000.

Komoro Station Hotel (middle center).

MAP 9 Komoro

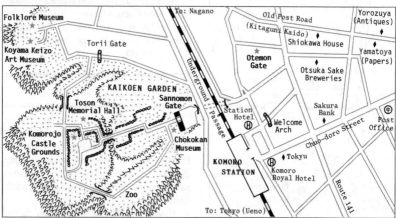

Business. 28 singles (6,000 yen -) and 10 doubles (11,000 yen -). Add: 1-1-7, Aioi-cho, Komoro. Tel: (0267) 22-4831.

Komoro Royal Hotel (lower center). Business. 21 singles (6,200 yen -) and 17 doubles (9,900 yen -). Add: 1-3-1, Aioicho, Komoro. Tel: (0267) 22-6633.

2. Welcome Inn in Komoro

Nakadana Onsen Ryokan (5 minutes by taxi from Komoro Station). 13 Japanese rooms. Add: Nakadana, Kojo-ku, Komoro. Tel: (0267) 22-1511.

NAGANO 長野

Nagano, with a population of 346,000, is the capital of Nagano Prefecture. The city is located in a valley surrounded by 2000 m (6,560 foot) high mountains. Nagano has been selected as the host of the 1998 Winter Olympic Games. Nagano Station is served by the JR Shin-etsu Honsen Line (about 3 hours from Tokyo's Ueno Station) and the JR Chuo Saisen Line (about 3 hours from Nagoya Station). Nagano Dentetsu Railways originates at Nagano to Yudanaka, a hotspring resort and a gateway to the famous Shiga Heights ski grounds.

Refer to Joetsu and Shin-etsu Map 10. The city's downtown extends to the north from Nagano Station (lower center). Three department stores — Tokyu, Sogo and Daiei — are the core of this commercial zone. Many old buildings are located on the northern part of Chuo-dori Street. They sell local specialties and Buddhist utensils.

Zenkoji Temple 善光寺 (upper center) is located at the northern end of Chuo-dori Street. The Temple was erected in the 8th century, when Buddhism in Japan was not yet divided into many sects. Even today, Zenkoji does not belong to any particular sect, and attracts millions of worshippers regardless of their sects. The main approach

starts at the Niomon Gate. The path is paved by rocks and lined with a number of souvenir shops and restaurants. The area has always a bit of a festive atmosphere. Before Sanmon Gate, six *jizo* statues sit on the right. *Jizo* is a guardian of children and travelers. The Treasure House is on the left. The Main Hall of Zenkoji Temple (National Treasure) is a massive wooden structure, Japan's third largest (after Nara's Great Buddha Hall and Yoshinoyama's Zaodo Hall - both in Kansai Chapter). The interior of the Main Hall is open from 9:00 AM to

MAP 10 Nagano

4:30 PM (4:00 PM in winter) (optional). Admission: 300 yen. Zenkoji's main statue is open to the public only once every 7 years. A three-story pagoda, built in 1970, stands in the northwestern corner of the precincts.

Shinano Art Museum 信濃美術館 (upper right) is located in a park next to the Temple. The Museum features products by local Nagano artists. Special exhibitions are held several times a year. **Higashiyama Kaii Gallery** 東山魁夷館 is an annex of the Shinano Art Museum. The famous Japanese artist, Kaii Higashiyama, donated more than 600 of his works to Nagano Prefecture. The 2-story Gallery was constructed in 1990 to preserve his works. The Gallery displays about 60 paintings at a time. The Museum and the Gallery are open from 9:00 AM to 5:00 PM. Closed Wednesday. Admission: 350 yen for both.

Hotels in Nagano

(Refer to Joetsu and Shin-etsu Map 10)

Hotel Nagano Kokusai Kaikan (middle left, Map 10). Standard. 36 singles (8,500 yen -) and 27 doubles (15,500 yen -). Add: 576, Kencho, Nagano. Tel: (0262) 34-1111.

Nagano Washington Hotel (lower center). Business. 141 singles (7,400 yen -) and 40 doubles (15,000 yen -). Add: 1177-3, Kami-Chitosecho, Nagano. Tel: (0262) 28-5111.

Hotel Nagano Avenue (lower center). Business. 189 singles (7,700 yen -) and 21 doubles (14,000 yen -). Add: 2-8-5, Minami-Chitosecho, Nagano. Tel: (0262) 23-1123.

Hotel New Nagano (lower center). Business. 105 singles (6,200 yen -) and 19 doubles (12,000 yen -). Add: 828, Minami-Chitosecho, Nagano. Tel: (0262) 27-7200.

Nagano Palace Hotel (lower center). Business. 28 singles (5,500 yen -) and 15 doubles (10,000 yen -). Add: 1326, Minami-Sekidocho, Nagano. Tel: (0262) 26-2221.

Along the JR Chuo Honsen Line 中央本線沿線

MATSUMOTO 松本

Matsumoto is located in a small valley, flanked by the Japan Alps on the west (3000 m or 9800 feet) and Utsukushigahara Heights (2000 m or 6560 feet) on the east. The city prospered in the feudal era under the reign of the Ishikawa family.

Today, Matsumoto is the second largest city of Nagano Prefecture with a population of 196,000. Matsumoto is the terminal of the JR Chuo Honsen Line (from Tokyo's Shinjuku Station) and the most popular gateway to the Japan Alps (See Kamikochi section below). Matsumoto is also linked to Nagoya by the JR Chuo Saisen Line. Thus it is easy to incorporate this area in a Tokyo - Matsumoto (Japan Alps) - Nagoya - Kyoto itinerary. If you travel through this area, save a half day to explore this historic city, especially Matsumotojo Castle. If you can stay overnight in Matsumoto, enjoy a stroll through the city's lovely downtown streets. Refer to Joetsu and Shin-etsu Map 11.

Matsumotojo Castle 松本城 (upper right), completed in 1614 after the civil war period, has never been the venue of actual battles. The Castle is one of Japan's oldest still standing today (National Treasure). Surrounded by moats, the donjon and turrets are a not-to-be missed shot for camera fans. The donjon is 5 stories outside and 6 stories inside. You can climb to the top floor of the donjon for a panoramic view of the city and the surrounding mountains. Hours: 8:30 AM to 4:30 PM. Closed during New Year's Holidays only. Admission: 500 yen, including the admission to Japan Folklore Museum in the castle grounds.

Downtown Matsumoto. Koen-dori Street runs to the east from Matsumoto Station (shaded on the map, lower left to middle center). Many souvenir shops and restaurants are located in this area. The area around Nakamachi-dori Street (shaded on the map, middle right) has many restaurants and pubs. The station area caters to tourists, and the Nakamachi area caters to Matsumoto people.

MAP 11 Matsumoto

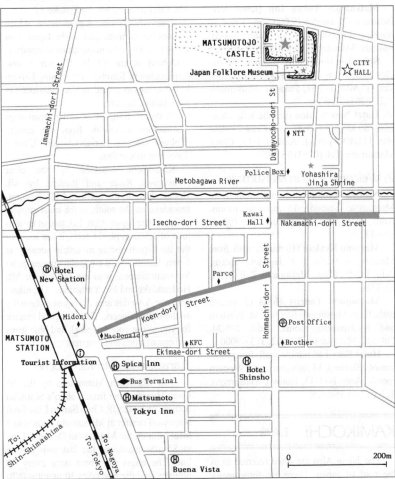

An *i* Information Office is adjacent to Matsumoto Station.

ACCOMMODATIONS
(Refer to Joetsu and Shin-etsu Map 11)

1. Hotels in Matsumoto

Hotel Buena Vista (lower center, Map 11). First Class. 200 rooms. Singles (12,000 yen -) and Doubles (20,000 yen -). Add: 1-2-1, Honjo, Matsumoto. Tel: (0263) 37-0111.

Matsumoto Tokyu Inn (lower left). Business. 79 singles (9,000 yen -) and 76 doubles (15,000 yen -). Add: 1-3-21, Fukashi, Matsumoto. Tel: (0263) 36-0109.

Spica Inn (lower left). Business. 54 singles (6,600 yen -) and 43 doubles (12,000 yen -). Add: 1-2-31, Fukashi, Matsumoto. Tel: (0263) 32-6000.

Hotel New Station (middle left). Business. 80 singles (6,100 yen -) and 23 doubles (11,400 yen -). Add: 1-1-11, Chuo, Matsumoto. Tel: (0263) 35-3850.

2. Welcome Inns in Matsumoto

Nishiya Ryokan (8 minute walk from Matsumoto Station). 15 Japanese rooms. Add: 2-4-12, Ote, Matsumoto. Tel: (0263) 33-4332.

Marumo Ryokan (10 minute walk from Matsumoto Station). 8 Japanese rooms. Add: 3-3-10, Chuo, Matsumoto. Tel: (0263) 33-3586.

Matsumoto Tourist Hotel (5 minute walk from Matsumoto Station). 96 Western and 8 Japanese rooms. Add: 2-4-24, Fukashi, Matsumoto. Tel: (0263) 33-9000.

Hotel Ikkyu (8 minute walk from Matsumoto Station). 14 Japanese and 5 Western rooms. Add: 1-11-13, Honjyo, Matsumoto. Tel: (0263) 35-8528.

KAMIKOCHI   上高地

The Japan Alps are often referred to as the roof of Japan. There are three major mountain ranges in the Japan Alps - from north to south: the Hida mountains or the Northern Alps; the Kiso mountains or the Central Alps; and the Akaishi mountains or the Southern Alps. The Northern Alps have the most precipitous and scenic mountains, and the phrase "Japan Alps" usually refers to this area. The highest peak of the Northern Alps is Mt. Hodakadake (3,190 m or 10,466 feet), and there are several other mountains that top 3,000 meters, such as Mt. Tateyama and Mt. Yarigatake.

Tateyama-Kurobe Alpine Route, which crosses the northern part of the Japan Alps using a variety of transportation methods, is explained in the Chubu Chapter below. Exploration of Kurobe Gorge, using Unazuki hotsprings as a base, is also introduced in the Chubu Chapter.

In this section, we describe Japan Alps destinations accessible from the eastern (Tokyo) side — Kamikochi and Ushiro-Tateyama mountains.

Kamikochi, bisected by the clear Azusagawa River and flanked by Mt. Hodakadake on the north and Mt. Kasumisawadake on the south, is the most popular valley in the Japan Alps. Located at an altitude of 1,500 m (4,921 feet), it has some of the most picturesque mountain scenery in Japan. Kamikochi is a popular starting point for mountaineers who are headed for Mt. Hodakadake and Mt. Yarigatake. The hikers who also love this area dress just as casually as the mountaineers. This is a good chance for you to use your knapsack and blue jeans and casual shirts and sweaters.

Transportation to Kamikochi

You can reach Matsumoto by the JR Chuo Honsen Line from Tokyo's Shinjuku Station, or by the JR Chuo Saisen Line from Nagoya. Transfer at Matsumoto Station to a local train on the Matsumoto Dentetsu Line to Shin-Shimashima, the last stop on the line. The trains run about once every 40 minutes, and the ride takes 30 minutes (670 yen). Buses operate to various parts of the Japan Alps from the terminal in front of Shin-Shimashima Station. Matsumoto Dentetsu buses run between Shin-Shimashima and Kamikochi about once every hour. The trip takes 1 hour and 15 minutes, and the fare is 2,000 yen. Due to heavy snow in the area, the buses operate from early May until early November. No commercial vehicles are allowed beyond Kamikochi Bus Terminal (middle center, Joetsu and Shin-etsu Map 12).

Kamikochi Hiking

In Kamikochi you can enjoy a stroll along the crystal-clear Azusagawa River and relish the beautiful view of the rugged mountains, which are covered by snow most of the time. Kappabashi Bridge (middle center) with Mt. Hodakadake in the background

MAP 12 Kamikochi

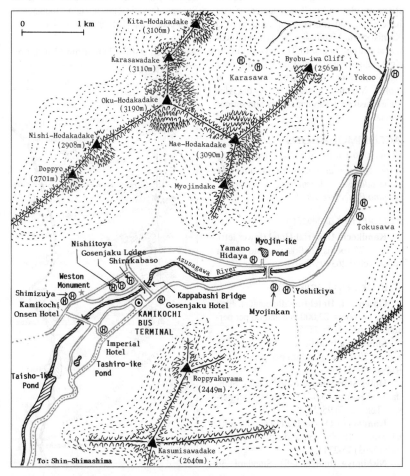

is snapped by hundreds of thousands of camera fans every year.

Weston Monument (middle left) is dedicated to Sir Weston, an Englishman, who introduced the sport of mountaineering into Japan.

Taisho-ike Pond was created by debris and lava from nearby Mt. Yakedake (still active). The view of Taisho-ike with the Alps towering in the distance has long been popular with painters.

The roads running along the Azusagawa River are flat and well maintained. If you have time, you can enjoy a stroll beyond Kamikochi to Myojin-ike Pond (middle center, about one hour), to Tokusawa (middle right, another hour), and to Yokoo (upper right, one more hour). The road ends at Yokoo. Mountain paths leading to the Alps are exclusively for mountaineers and serious hikers.

ACCOMMODATIONS

(Refer to Joetsu and Shin-etsu Map 12)

Note: All the accommodations have the same address — Kamikochi, Azumi-mura, Nagano Prefecture 390-15.

1. Hotel in Kamikochi

Kamikochi Imperial Hotel (lower left). Deluxe. 75 rooms. 29,000 yen and up per room. Tel: (0263) 95-2001.

2. Ryokan in Kamikochi

Gosenjaku Hotel (middle center). First Class. 31 rooms. 23,000 yen and up per person. Tel: (0263) 95-2111.

Shimizuya (middle left). First Class. 38 rooms. 20,000 yen and up per person. Tel: (0263) 95-2121.

Hotel Shirakabaso (middle left). Standard. 55 rooms. 15,000 yen and up per person. Tel: (0263) 95-2131.

Kamikochi Onsen Hotel (middle left). 61 rooms. 15,000 yen and up per person. Tel: (0263) 95-2311.

Nishiitoya (middle left). Standard. 30 rooms. 12,000 yen and up per person. Tel: (0263) 95-2206.

USHIRO-TATEYAMA MOUNTAINS 後立山連峰

The JR Oito Line runs from Matsumoto to Itoigawa on the Japan Sea coast, parallel to the Ushiro-Tateyama mountains of the Japan Alps. Several "Azusa" trains run beyond Matsumoto onto the Oito Line, to Shinano-Omachi (lower right, Joetsu and Shin-etsu Map 13) or to Hakuba (upper

MAP 13 Ushiro-Tateyama Mountains

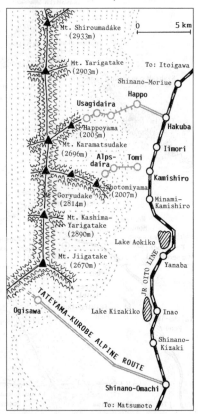

right). There are a number of ski resorts that boast of long slopes, powder snow, and magnificent views of the Japan Alps along this route. In summer some of them continue to operate their gondolas and chair lifts for tourists who want to see the Japan Alps from higher altitudes. In this section we describe the two best such observatories of the Japan Alps. If you start from Matsumoto, you can visit one of the two observatories and easily return to Tokyo (or Nagoya) on the same day.

Happo Ridge 八方尾根

One of Japan's best ski slopes is on Happo Ridge. We believe that Happo will be the venue of some of the alpine ski competitions in the 1998 Olympic Games. Hakuba is the station for Happo Ridge. Hakuba is reached from Matsumoto in one hour by limited express train, or one hour and 20 minutes by rapid service train.

There is frequent bus service between Hakuba Station and Happo (a 5-minute ride, 170 yen). There are hotels, pensions and *ryokan* in the Happo district.

Happo ropeway station is near the bus terminal. The ropeway brings you to Usagidaira in 8 minutes (1,400 yen roundtrip). Transfer to a chair lift from Usagidaira to Kurobishidaira, a 10-minute ride (310 yen roundtrip). The view of the Ushiro-Tateyama mountains is fantastic. If you are a good walker, and if weather permits, you can walk along a clear path on Happo Ridge to higher points. But remember that you are in the Japan Alps and that (with sudden changes in the weather) the temperature can easily fall below freezing, even in summer.

Tomi Ridge 遠見尾根

Tomi Ridge is also a popular ski resort in winter. Kamishiro on the JR Oito Line is the station for Tomi Ridge. The train ride from Matsumoto is about 20 minutes shorter to Kamishiro than to Hakuba (See above).

Tomi ropeway station is about 20-minute walk from Kamishiro Station. Many pensions and *minshuku* are located in the small village of Kamishiro and neighboring Iimori. The gondola brings you up to Alps-daira in 8 minutes (1,200 yen roundtrip). You can connect to a chair lift at Alps-daira, to reach Jizo-no-Atama, the highest point you can reach without hiking. The grand view of the Ushiro-Tateyama mountains rises like a screen. The mountains are especially beautiful when covered by snow.

JR FARES BETWEEN MAJOR STATIONS IN THE JOETSU AND SHIN-ETSU REGION

1. ALONG THE JR JOETSU SHINKANSEN and JR JOETSU LINE

To/Fromh	Tokyo	Ueno	Remarks
Jomo-Kogen	5,640 yen (151.6 km)	5,440 yen (148.0 km)	JR Joetsu Shinkansen
Minakami		5,030 yen (160.5 km)	JR Joetsu Line limited express
Niigata	10,080 yen (333.9 km)	9,880 yen (330.3 km)	JR Joetsu Shinkansen

2. ALONG THE JR SHIN-ETSU HONSEN LINE (Based on limited express trains)

To/From	Ueno	Nagano
Ueno		6,580 yen (217.2 km)
Karuizawa	4,720 yen (142.3 km)	2,890 yen (74.9 km)
Komoro	5,440 yen (164.7 km)	2,560 yen (52.5 km)
Nagano	6,580 yen (217.2 km)	

3. ALONG THE JR CHUO HONSEN LINE and THE JR OITO LINE

To/From	Shinjuku	Matsumoto	Remarks
Shinjuku		6,580 yen (225.1 km)	Limited express
Matsumoto	6,580 yen (225.1 km)	1,860 yen (38.6 km)	Limited express
Shinano-Omachi	7,300 yen (263.7 km)		Limited express
Kamishiro		1,090 yen (60.7 km)	Local Train
Hakuba	7,920 yen (290.8 km)	2,310 yen (65.7 km)	Limited express

CHUBU REGION

中部

The Chubu Region is the vast area between Tokyo and Kyoto, the modern and traditional capitals. You can easily include some of the Chubu Region destinations in a standard Tokyo-Kyoto itinerary to add interest. We divide the region into five districts (Refer to Chubu Map 1):

1. Nagoya and Vicinity
(Middle center)

Nagoya, the castle town of the Tokugawas, is Japan's third most important business center (after Tokyo and Osaka). It is also the transportation center of the Chubu Region. All destinations in the region are linked to Nagoya by train.

Toyota is the home of the world famous automobile manufacturer. Although the city doesn't have much in the way of traditional tourist attractions, you might be interested in a visit to the ultra-modern factory.

Seto. If you are interested in pottery, you can visit Seto in a half-day excursion from Nagoya.

Inuyama, a castle town on the peaceful Nagaragawa River, is an easy one-day (or a rushed half-day) excursion from Nagoya; we recommend it if you have extra time in Nagoya.

Tsumago, a historic post town on the old Nakasendo Road, can be the destination of a full-day excursion from Nagoya or can be included as a stop on the way from Nagoya to Joetsu and Shin-etsu Region destinations, such as Matsumoto or Nagano. Tsumago's attractions are similar to those of Takayama (historic feudal-era streets and houses). If you visit Takayama (detailed below), you should skip Tsumago.

2. Ise-Shima National Park
(Lower left)

Ise-Shima National Park is located to the south of Nagoya. Ise is the site of Ise Jingu

MAP 1 Outline of Chubu

Shrine, Japan's most important Shinto shrine. Ise-Shima National Park features several scenic beach resorts, such as Toba and Kashikojima. Ise-Shima is also conveniently connected with Kyoto and Osaka by train. You can visit this area in a full-day excursion from Nagoya, Kyoto or Osaka. If you have time, we recommend that you stay overnight in Toba or Kashikojima.

3. Tokai District (Lower right)

The Tokai District has several notable cities/resorts: Shizuoka, Hamamatsu, Toyohashi and Lake Hamanako and Kanzanji Onsen. They, along with other Chubu Region cities, are described briefly.

4. Takayama (Middle center)

Takayama is located in a small valley at the western end of the Japan Alps. The city is famous for its historic streets and handicrafts. Located on the JR Takayama Honsen Line (which connects Nagoya and Toyama), a visit to Takayama can be an overnight excursion from Nagoya or a stop on the way on a trip from Nagoya to Japan Sea coast destinations such as Kanazawa or Unazuki. Gero, a hotspring resort, is between Nagoya and Takayama, and a favorite of Japanese travelers.

5. Hokuriku District (Upper center)

Kanazawa, a historic city that was ruled by the second most powerful lord of the Edo Era, is the most popular destination on the Japan Sea Coast. We tend to agree with those who think it is rather overrated and losing its traditional touch in a rush toward modernization and commercialization.

Toyama, a transportation hub, has a few attractions, if you have extra time.

Tateyama-Kurobe Alpine Route, a scenic cross-Alps sightseeing route, is described in this Chapter.

Unazuki, a hotspring resort at the northern end of the Japan Alps, is recommended as a base from which to explore the magnificent Kurobe Gorge. If natural attractions are your cup of tea, we definitely recommend Unazuki and Kurobe Gorge for the mountains and the hotsprings.

The Noto Peninsula is accessible for day-trips from Kanazawa. Wajima is famous for its lacquerware, and Wakura Onsen is one of Japan's most famous hotspring resorts (quite touristy).

Eiheiji Temple and Cape Tojimbo, both near Fukui, are introduced as an extra side-trip destination for those traveling between the Hokuriku District (Kanazawa/Toyama) and the Kansai Region (Kyoto/Osaka).

CHUBU REGION INTER-CITY TRANSPORTATION

Refer to Chubu Map 1. Transportation in each Chubu District is described in a separate section below. This introduction explains only the long distance train network of the Chubu Region.

Nagoya is on the JR Tokaido-Sanyo Shinkansen, easily accessible from major cities on Japan's Pacific Coast.

Nagiso, on the JR Chuo Saisen Line, is the gateway to Tsumago. Limited express trains (called "Shinano") run about once every hour between Nagoya and Nagano via Nakatsugawa, Nagiso and Matsumoto. All the limited express trains stop at Nakatsugawa, but not all of them stop at Nagiso. If the limited express train you are taking does not stop at Nagiso Station, you will have to transfer at Nakatsugawa Station to a local train to continue your trip to Nagiso. A limited express trip from Nagoya to Nagiso takes about 70 minutes, and the trip from Nagiso to Matsumoto takes another 70 minutes. Tsumago is only 10 minutes by bus from Nagiso Station.

There are four important train stations in **Ise-Shima National Park:** Iseshi and Uji-Yamada (see Chubu Map 8) provide access to Ise Jingu Shrine; Toba provides access to Mikimoto Pearl Island; and Kashikojima provides access to scenic Ago Bay. Kintetsu Railways operates deluxe limited express trains to the Ise-Shima area from Nagoya, Kyoto and Osaka. The Kintetsu deluxe trains run about once every hour from Kintetsu-Nagoya Station (adjacent to JR Nagoya Station) to Kashikojima via Uji-Yamada and Toba. The deluxe trains do not stop at Iseshi. The trip from Nagoya to Uji-Yamada takes about 80 minutes (an additional 12 minutes to Toba, and 45 minutes to Kashikojima). Similar deluxe trains run between Kyoto (leaving from JR Kyoto station) and Kashikojima via Iseshi, Uji-Yamada and Toba about once an hour. The trip to Iseshi takes about two hours (an additional 3 minutes to Uji-Yamada, 15 minutes to Toba, and 48 minutes to Kashikojima). Kintetsu also operates deluxe trains between Osaka (Kintetsu Namba Station in the Namba downtown area) and Kashikojima about once an hour. These trains do not stop at Iseshi. The trip from Osaka to Uji-Yamada takes about 1 hour and 45 minutes (an additional 12 minutes to Toba and 45 minutes to Kashikojima). The fares to Toba are 2,500 yen from Nagoya, 3,040 yen from Osaka, and 3,230 yen from Kyoto. If you have a Japan Rail Pass, consider JR service. The JR Kisei Honsen Line runs between Nagoya and Kii-Katsuura via Matsusaka and Taki. The JR Sangu Line connects Taki with Iseshi and Toba. There are several rapid service trains (called "Mie") a day running over these combined lines; they provide direct service between Nagoya and Iseshi (1 hour and 30 minutes) and Toba (an additional 15 minutes). Another option is taking a limited express (called "Nanki") on the JR Kisei Honsen Line to Taki (1 hour and 10 minutes), and transferring to a local train on the JR Sangu Line to continue to trip to Iseshi (20

minutes) or Toba (an additional 20 minutes). Toba is the last stop on the JR Sangu Line.

The JR Takayama Honsen Line connects the Pacific Coast (Nagoya) and the Japan Sea Coast (Toyama) via Gero and Takayama. Limited express trains (called "Hida") run about once every hour between Nagoya and Takayama. The trip takes about two hours. Service between Takayama and Toyama is less frequent (about five limited express trains per day). The Takayama to Toyama trip takes 90 minutes.

The JR Hokuriku Honsen Line runs between Osaka and Niigata, via Kyoto, Fukui, Kanazawa, Toyama and Naoetsu. Limited express trains (called "Raicho") run once every 30-60 minutes between Osaka and Toyama, via Kyoto, Fukui and Kanazawa. A few "Raicho" trains run beyond Toyama all the way to Niigata. There are additional limited express trains (called "Kagayaki") that operate several times a day between Kanazawa and Nagaoka to facilitate connections to the Joetsu Shinkansen (which stops at Nagaoka). In addition, commuter-type local trains supplement the limited expresses in particular areas, operating frequently, especially in the Fukui-Kanazawa-Toyama area. Travel times on the limited express between major Hokuriku Line cities are as follows: Osaka - (30 minutes) - Kyoto - (one hour and 30 minutes) - Fukui - (one hour) - Kanazawa - (30 minutes) - Toyama - (one hour) - Naoetsu - (one hour)- Nagaoka - (one hour) - Niigata.

Please note, too, that Toyama and Nagoya are directly connected by limited express trains (called "Shirasagi"). The Shirasagi trains run once every 60-90 minutes, stopping at Kanazawa, Fukui and Maibara. The trip from Nagoya to Kanazawa takes about three hours.

Nagoya and Vicinity

NAGOYA 名古屋

Nagoya is the center of Japan's third largest metropolitan area. Nagoya is becoming more cosmopolitan, and is increasingly the venue of international events. The city itself has several attractions, and it can be the starting point for day excursions to Inuyama (upper center, Chubu Map 2), Seto (Owari-Seto Station, middle right) and Toyota (lower right). An *i* Information Office is located in JR Nagoya Station.

In the civil war period (the 15th-16th centuries), the Nagoya vicinity was the scene of major battles of feudal lords such as Nobunaga Oda and Ieyasu Tokugawa. At the beginning of the 17th century, when the Tokugawa Shogunate gained control over the entire country and incorporated Nagoya into the area under its direct administration, the real development of the area began.

Nagoyajo Castle, a massive symbol of the power of the Tokugawa family, was completed in 1612. Most of the city, including the Castle, was destroyed during World War II. Ironically, the destruction during the war hastened the development of Nagoya as a modern city. Wide streets were laid out in the center of the city to accommodate heavy modern traffic. To keep a bit of green within the city, each of these streets was designed with a grassy median strip with trees. Nagoyajo Castle was reconstructed in 1959 as the spiritual symbol of the city. Nagoya is often called Chukyo (Central Capital) because it is located between the modern capital, Tokyo (Eastern Capital), and the ancient capital, Kyoto (Western Capital). Though the city has never been the official capital of Japan, it has always been the focal point for the Chubu Region.

Transportation in Nagoya

Nagoya has six subway lines as pictured on Chubu Map 3. They feature excellent signs in English and provide easy, efficient transportation for tourists as well as for local commuters. The Subway Higashiyama Line runs east to west, and connects Nagoya Station with Fushimi and Sakae, the major downtown area of Nagoya. The Subway Meijo Line runs north to south between its northern terminal of Ozone and Kanayama, passing Shiyakusho (the stop closest to Nagoyajo Castle). At Kanayama, the Meijo line branches into two lines: the Subway Yongo Line heads toward Nagoyako Port, while the other, which retains the Meijo name, passes Atsuta Jingu Shrine and heads for the terminus of Aratamabashi. The trains on this line alternate when they leave Ozone: i.e., if a train bound for Nagoyako Port comes first, the next will be bound for Aratamabashi. The Subway Tsurumai Line runs from northwest to southeast. At Akaike (middle center, Chubu Map 2) the Tsurumai Line cars run onto the Meitetsu Toyota Line, and operate all the way to its terminal, Toyotashi Station. The Subway Sakuradori Line, the newest subway, runs from east to west, providing an alternative to the Higashiyama line in the center-city area, between Nagoya Station and Imaike. Subway fares vary with the distance travelled (minimum 180 yen).

Outline of the City

Refer to Chubu Map 3. There are two major places of interest in Nagoya — Nagoyajo Castle (upper center) and Atsuta Jingu Shrine (lower center). If you have extra time, you can also visit the Noritake China Factory (upper left), the TV Tower (middle center) and the Tokugawa Museum (upper right). Nagoya's downtown area,

MAP 2 Outline of Nagoya and Vicinity

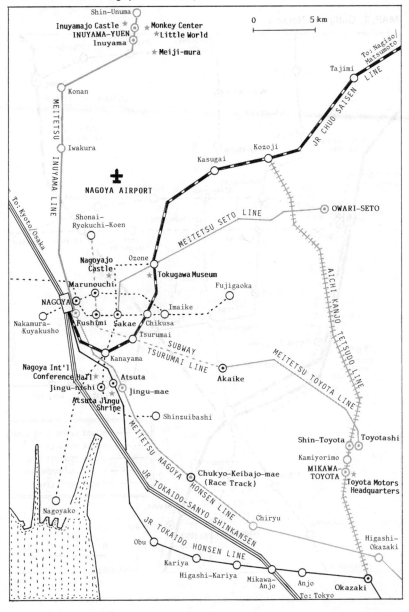

MAP 3 Outline of Nagoya

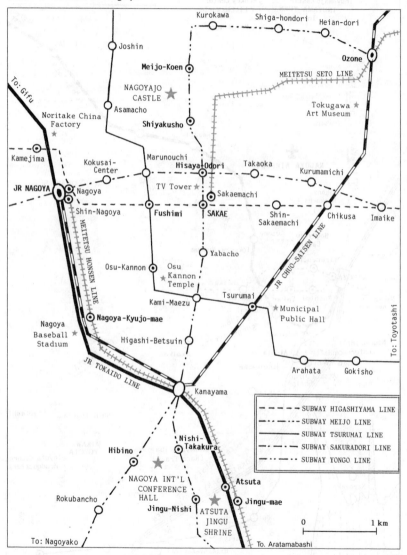

Sakae, is about 2.5 km (1.5 miles) from Nagoya Station, but the station district, and especially its underground shopping and restaurant malls, has itself become another city center. Many office buildings are located around the station. Governmental offices of both Nagoya City and Aichi Prefecture are southeast of Nagoyajo Castle. The *i* Information Office is located in JR Nagoya Station.

Places of Interest

Nagoyajo Castle 名古屋城 (Upper center, Chubu Map 3; also upper center, Chubu Map 4)

The Castle is a five-minute walk from Shiyakusho Station on the Subway Meijo Line. The original castle, a grand and impressive structure, was built by Ieyasu Tokugawa in 1612 and was famous for the twin gold dolphins atop the donjon. The present donjon was reconstructed in 1959, and two new gold dolphins were placed on its roof. The donjon's modern conveniences include elevators to the top of the building. The observatory affords an extensive view of the City of Nagoya and the Nobi Plain. The lower floors of the donjon house a museum that displays various artistic and historic objects rescued from the fire that

destroyed the original castle. Ninomaru Garden to the east of the donjon is typical of the refined castle gardens for which Japan is so famous. Hours: 9:30 AM to 4:30 PM. Admission: 400 yen.

Atsuta Jingu Shrine 熱田神宮 (Lower center, Chubu Map 3)

Take the Subway Meijo Line (Jingu-Nishi Station), the JR Tokaido Line (Atsuta Station) or the Meitetsu Honsen Line or Meitetsu Tokoname Line (Jingu-mae Station) to the Shrine.

Atsuta Jingu, set in densely wooded grounds, is one of the most important shrines in all of Japan. It was erected in the third century. The Shrine is especially famous as the repository of one of the emperor's three sacred symbols, the *Kusanagi-no-Tsurugi* (Grass Mowing Sword). The other two, the Mirror and the Jewel, are preserved at Ise Jingu Shrine and at the Imperial Palace respectively. Atsuta Jingu Shrine is still an object of deep respect among the people, and millions of worshippers visit here during the New Year's Holidays. Amateur groups often stage weekend performances in Noh Hall. The Shrine's Treasure House displays swords, mirrors and Shinto treasures. Hours: 9:00 AM to 4:30 PM. Closed the last Wednesdays and Thirsdays of each month. Admission: 300 yen.

Noritake China Factory ノリタケ・チャイナ (Upper left, Chubu Map 3; also upper left, Chubu Map 4) (optional)

The factory is a 15-minute walk from Nagoya Station and a five-minute walk from Kamejima Station on the Subway Higashiyama Line. Noritake is Japan's largest ceramics company, and its refined products are popular all over the world. The company welcomes foreign tourists to the factory to observe the manufacturing process. English speaking guides escort visitors and provide explanations. The tour takes about one and a half hours. Advance reservations should be made by calling the

MAP 4 Central Nagoya

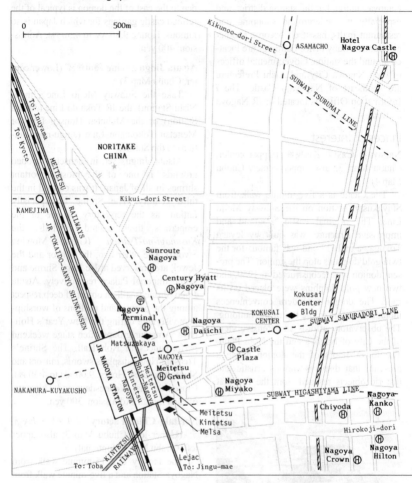

Welcome Center (052-562-5072). The factory is closed on Saturdays, Sundays, National Holidays, and from Dec. 29 through Jan. 6. There is no admission fee.

Tokugawa Art Museum 徳川美術館
(Upper right, Chubu Map 3) (optional)

Tokugawa Art Museum is a 10-minute walk from Ozone Station on the Subway Meijo Line, the JR Chuo Line, or the Meitetsu Seto Line. The Museum was built on the grounds of the former mansion of a high-ranking retainer of the Tokugawa family. Although the Museum owns 10,000 treasures (swords, suits of armor, paintings, pottery, lacquerware and other works of art), only a limited number of them can be displayed at any one time in the three small

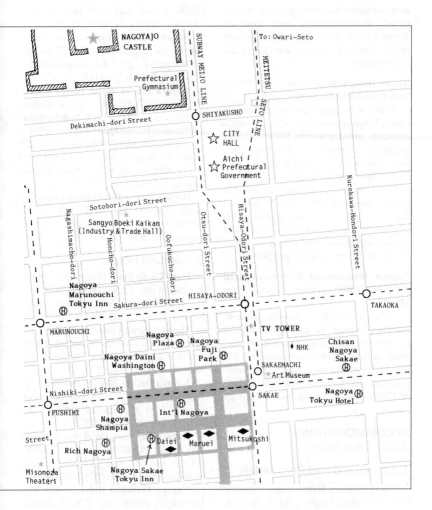

rooms. The world famous scroll of the story of Prince Genji *(Genji Monogatari)* is displayed only once a year. Unless you are lucky enough to be in Nagoya while this special exhibition is in progress, we cannot recommend that you allocate precious time to this Museum. Hours: 10:00 AM to 5:00 PM. Closed Mondays, and from Dec. 14 through Jan. 14. Admission: 1,000 yen.

Nagoya Station Vicinity
(Lower left, Chubu Map 4)

To the east of Nagoya Station there is a huge underground shopping center, the total length of which is 6 km (3.75 miles). It's so extensive that natives of the city as well as foreign visitors can easily get lost. Above the underground shopping center is one of Nagoya's principal business areas. This neighborhood is becoming a second "downtown," with department stores lined up across the street from the station. Although the area bustles during day, it is rather quiet in the evening.

Sakae Downtown (Lower right, Chubu Map 4; shaded on the map)

Sakae is Nagoya's version of Tokyo's Ginza. Shopping, eating and drinking establishments crowd this area. There's another extensive underground shopping area around Sakae subway station and the Meitetsu Seto Line's Sakae-machi Station (which is itself underground). Hisaya-dori Street is quite wide (100 m or 328 feet), and features a park at its center as well as the 180 m (590 foot) tall TV Tower. The tower has an observatory at an altitude of 100 m (328 feet). Hours: 10:00 AM to 5:50 PM.

Nagoya International Conference Hall 名古屋国際会議場 (Lower center, Chubu Map 3).

This new facility is often the venue of international meetings and conventions, and is a keystone of the city's movement toward sophistication and internationalization. It is only a several-minutes walk from Nishi-Takakura Station on the Subway Meijo Line or Hibino Station on the Subway Yongo Line.

ACCOMMODATIONS
(Refer to Chubu Map 4)

1. Deluxe and First Class Hotels

Hotel Century Hyatt Nagoya (middle left). 115 rooms. Singles (15,000 yen -) & Doubles (22,000 yen -). Add: 2-43-6, Meieki, Nakamura-ku, Nagoya. Tel: (052) 569-1717

International Hotel Nagoya (lower center). 172 singles (11,000 yen -) & 74 doubles (22,000 yen -). Add: 3-23-3, Nishiki, Naka-ku. Tel: (052) 961-3111.

Hotel Nagoya Castle (upper center). 86 singles (12,000 yen -) & 110 doubles (21,000 yen -). Add: 3-19, Hinokuchicho, Nishi-ku, Nagoya. Tel: (052) 521-2121.

Nagoya Hilton Hotel (lower center). 186 singles (25,000 yen -) & 237 doubles (26,000 yen -). Add: 1-3-3, Sakae, Naka-ku, Nagoya. Tel: (052) 212-1111.

Nagoya Kanko Hotel (lower center). 308 singles (12,000 yen -) & 169 doubles (24,000 yen -). Add: 1-19-30 Nishiki, Naka-ku, Nagoya. Tel: (052) 231-7711.

Nagoya Miyako Hotel (lower left). 226 singles (9,500 yen -) & 155 doubles (17,500 yen -). Add: 4-9-10, Meieki, Nakamura-ku, Nagoya. Tel: (052) 571-3211

Nagoya Tokyu Hotel (lower right). 311 singles (16,000 yen -) & 240 doubles (26,000 yen). Add: 4-6-8, Sakae, Naka-ku, Nagoya. Tel: (052) 251-2411.

2. Standard Hotels

Hotel Castle Plaza (lower left). 174 singles (8,300 yen -) & 82 doubles (16,500 yen -). Add: 4-3-25, Meieki, Nakamura-ku, Nagoya. Tel: (052) 582-2121.

Meitetsu Grand Hotel (lower left). 182 singles (10,000 yen -) & 58 doubles (20,000 yen -). Add: 1-2-4, Meieki, Nakamura-ku, Nagoya. Tel: (052) 582-2211.

Nagoya Daiichi Hotel (lower left). 217 singles (9,300 yen -) & 95 doubles (17,000 yen -). Add: 3-27-5, Meieki, Nakamura-ku, Nagoya. Tel: (052) 581-4411.

Nagoya Fuji Park Hotel (lower center). 186 singles (9,000 yen -) & 61 doubles (16,500 yen -). Add: 3-15-30, Nishiki, Naka-ku, Nagoya. Tel: (052) 962-2289.

Nagoya Terminal Hotel (middle left). 169 singles (9,000 yen -) & 85 doubles (16,500 yen -). Add: 1-1-2, Meieki, Nakamura-ku, Nagoya. Tel: (052) 561-3751.

3. Business Hotels

Chisan Hotel Nagoya Sakae (lower right). 126 singles (7,500 yen -) & 23 doubles (13,000 yen -). Add: 3-2, Sakaecho, Naka-ku, Nagoya. Tel: (052) 962-2411.

Hotel Chiyoda (lower center). 164 singles (6,200 yen -) & 30 doubles (13,000 yen -). Add: 1-16-10, Nishiki, Naka-ku, Nagoya. Tel: (052) 221-6711.

Nagoya Daini Washington Hotel (lower center). 298 singles (6,400 yen -) & 22 doubles (13,000 yen -). Add: 3-12-22, Nishiki, Naka-ku, Nagoya. Tel: (052) 962-7111.

Nagoya Marunouchi Tokyu Inn (middle center). 97 singles (8,500 yen -) & 89 doubles (14,500 yen -). Add: 2-17-18, Marunouchi, Naka-ku, Nagoya. Tel: (052) 202-0109.

Nagoya Plaza Hotel (lower center). 57 singles (5,000 yen -) & 116 doubles (9,500 yen -). Add: 3-8-21, Nishiki, Naka-ku, Nagoya. Tel: (052) 951-6311.

Nagoya Sakae Tokyu Inn (lower center). 120 singles (11,000 yen -) & 173 doubles (16,000 yen -). Add: 3-1-8, Sakae, Naka-ku, Nagoya. Tel: (052) 251-0109.

Hotel Rich Nagoya (lower center). 70 singles (7,500 yen -) & 30 doubles (11,000 yen -). Add: 2-3-9, Sakae, Naka-ku, Nagoya. Tel: (052) 231-5611.

Hotel Sunroute Nagoya (middle left). 213 singles (7,500 yen -) & 58 doubles (13,500 yen -). Add: 2-35-24, Meieki, Nakamura-ku, Nagoya. Tel: (052) 571-2221.

4. Welcome Inns

Nagoya Shampia Hotel (lower center). 145 singles & 52 doubles. Add: 2-20-5, Nishiki, Naka-ku, Nagoya. Tel: (052) 203-5858.

Nagoya Crown Hotel (lower center). 546 singles & 126 doubles. Add: 1-8-33. Sakae, Naka-ku, Nagoya. Tel: (052) 211-6633.

Hotel Lions Plaza Nagoya (5 minutes by taxi from JR Nagoya Station). 163 singles & 56 doubles. Add: 4-15-23, Sakae, Naka-ku, Nagoya. Tel: (052) 241-1500.

Hotel Kiyoshi Nagoya (10 minutes by taxi from JR Nagoya Station). 79 singles & 12 doubles. Add: 1-3-1, Heiwa, Naka-ku, Nagoya. Tel: (052) 321-5663.

Nagoya Crown Hotel (5 minutes by taxi from JR Nagoya Station). 672 rooms. Add: 1-8-33, Sakae, Naka-ku, Nagoya. Tel: (052) 211-6633.

TOYOTA 豊田

Toyota is known as the birthplace of the Matsudaira (Tokugawa) family, which, after a 150-year long civil war, unified the nation and established the Tokugawa Shogunate in 1603. There is a small district called "Matsudaira" in the southeastern corner of the city. The Matsudaira family, ancestors of Ieyasu Tokugawa, were the original leaders of this small area. By the time Ieyasu was born, they had expanded their territory to the south (Okazaki). Finally, under the leadership of Ieyasu, the family succeeded in uniting the nation. Kogetsuin Temple contains small monuments of the Matsudaira family in its precincts. The temple is about 35 minutes by car from Toyotashi Station (no bus service).

Today, Toyota is known as the headquarters of Toyota Motors. The city has a population of 325,000. About 50,000 are employed by Toyota Motors and many others work for smaller companies that produce auto parts for Toyota. It is no wonder that people often call Toyota the "Corporate Castle Town."

Transportation to Toyota

Toyota has several train stations. Toyotashi and Shin-Toyota Stations are in the downtown area. Mikawa-Toyota Station is the stop for the Toyota Company's headquarters and its main automobile factory (Refer to Chubu Map 2, lower right).

There are two options for a trip to Mikawa-Toyota Station. The first option uses Nagoya's subway system. The Subway Tsurumai Line runs between Shonai-Ryokuchi-Koen Station (in the northern part of the city; middle left) to Akaike Station (middle center). The Meitetsu Toyota Line provides rail service between Akaike Station and Toyotashi Station. The city subway continues beyond Akaike on the Meitetsu Railways track all the way to Toyotashi Station. The trip from Fushimi Station (in downtown Nagoya) to Toyotashi Station takes about 45 minutes. Shin-Toyota Station on the Aichi Kanjo Tetsudo Line is only a two-minute walk from Toyotashi Station and is connected by a fancy pedestrian deck. Mikawa-Toyota is the second stop from Shin-Toyota on the Aichi Kanjo Tetsudo Line; the ride takes a mere six minutes.

The second option involves JR trains. Take a local commuter train on the JR Tokaido Honsen Line from Nagoya to Okazaki (lower right). The trains run frequently and the ride takes about 45 minutes. At Okazaki Station, transfer to the Aichi Kanjo Tetsudo Line train for the 30-minute trip to Mikawa-Toyota Station. The Station even has a special underground passage leading to the gate of Toyota headquarters.

Incidentally, the city's downtown is around Toyotashi Station, with Sogo Department Store and a number of stores, restaurants and pubs.

Factory Visit

The city was once called Koromo. The rapid growth of Toyota Motors and its related auto industries has made the city one of Japan's manufacturing centers. As a matter of fact, the city Toyota is ranked No. 3 for industrial manufacturing, after only Tokyo and Osaka. The city was renamed "Toyota" in 1959. Its sister city relationship with Detroit reflects Toyota's current life.

Toyota Motors welcomes visitors to see its ultra-modern manufacturing factory. Visitors are required to make an appointment in advance. Call the Public Relations Department at (0565) 29-3355.

Hotels in Toyota

Hotel Toyota Castle (10 minutes by car from Toyotashi Station). Standard. 70 singles (7,000 yen -) & 19 doubles (15,500 yen

-). Add: 1-3-3, Shimobayashicho, Toyota. Tel: (0565) 31-2211.

Toyota Parkside Hotel (3 minute walk from Toyotashi Station). Business. 40 singles (5,000 yen -) & 3 doubles (9,500 yen -). Add: 1-7, Kosaka-Honcho, Toyota. Tel: (0565) 35-3003.

Toyota Station Hotel (5 minute walk from Toyotashi Station). Business. 30 singles (5,000 yen -) & 4 doubles (9,200 yen -). Add: 1-12-1, Kosaka-Honcho, Toyota. Tel: (0565) 35-3511.

SETO 瀬戸

In Japan, ceramics are popularly called "Seto-mono" (Seto objects). It is believed that pottery production began in Seto in the 8th century, and that Japan's first glazed pottery was produced here in the middle of the 9th century. The development of artistic pottery advanced when Chinese technology was introduced by Toshiro Kato in the 13th century, but the civil wars scattered the potters to remote areas, and Seto suffered a long stagnant period. Tamikichi Kato, who introduced advanced ceramic technology in the early 19th century, was responsible for Seto's revitalization. Today Seto prospers as Japan's largest producer of everyday ceramic products. Seto is the most typical of all Japanese pottery centers and has a long history of which it is quite proud.

Seto is described below in detail. In addition to Seto, there are two other famous pottery villages in the Nagoya vicinity:

Tajimi (middle center, Chubu Map 1). Tajimi is the home of Mino Pottery, which originated with Seto craftsmen who took refuge in the Tajimi area during the civil wars. The simple yet refined designs and color schemes used by this school of pottery have long been favored for tea ceremony.

Tokoname (lower center, Chubu Map 1). Tokoname pottery originated in the 12th century, and is noted for its natural finish.

The Tokoname School uses only simple, natural glazes or leaves its products unglazed. Tokoname vases are especially prized. The city now prospers as Japan's chief producer of industrial earthenware pipes.

Transportation to Seto

Seto is served by the Meitetsu Railways Seto Line. Trains for Seto leave from Sakae-machi Station (lower right, Chubu Map 4) in Nagoya's Sakae downtown area (two subway stops away from JR Nagoya Station). An underground passage connects the city subway's Sakae Station with the Meitetsu Sakae-machi Station. Owari-Seto Station (middle left, Chubu Map 5) is the last stop on the Meitetsu Seto Line. Commuter-type trains run frequently; the ride from Sakae-machi to Owari-Seto takes about 40 minutes (470 yen).

Places of Interest in Seto

Seto, a medium-sized city with a population of 124,000, is proud that it has the longest history of all of the many pottery villages scattered around Japan. The river that runs through the middle of the city is dark white from all the pottery clay, and the major streets of the area are crowded with

shops that display the products of the workrooms. Seto's Pottery Festival, which is held on the third Saturday and Sunday of September, is the largest open-air market of this kind and attracts hundreds of thousands of visitors to the city.

Ceramic Center 陶磁器センター (lower center, Chubu Map 5) is a Seto pottery museum. About 250 fine works, both old and new, are displayed on the second floor. The first floor is a souvenir shop and sells a variety of products at prices that range from about 300 yen to more than 1 million yen.

Hosenji Temple 宝泉寺 (lower right) has an impressive two-story pagoda.

Seto-Koen Park 瀬戸公園 (middle right) is elevated above the town. A hexagonal hall, itself made of pottery, contains a monument to Toshiro Kato, originator of Seto pottery. The 3.3 m (11 foot) tall hall, built in 1866, is the largest pottery product in Japan, and a very impressive structure.

Ceramic Dolls (Toningyo Juhachi-bankan) 陶人形十八番館 (middle center), is a pottery shop specializing in pottery dolls. This store is always up on new trends in pottery making and is a good place to look for small souvenir items.

Kamagami Jinja Shrine 窯神神社 (upper left) is located on a small hill atop a

MAP 5 Seto

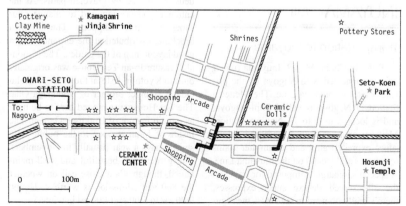

long flight of stone steps. The Shrine has several ceramic lion dogs (Guardians of the Shrine). A statue of Tamikichi Kato, who revitalized the city in the early 19th century, is located in the Shrine's precincts. There is a good view of the city from the shrine.

Pottery Clay Mine (upper left): This source of the clay used by the city's potters is to the west of Kamagami Jinja Shrine.

INUYAMA 犬山

Transportation to Inuyama

Refer to Chubu Map 2. Inuyama (upper left) is connected with Nagoya by the private Meitetsu Inuyama Line. The Meitetsu Station in Nagoya is called Shin-Nagoya, and is located next to JR Nagoya Station. Meitetsu operates both all-reserved deluxe super express trains and commuter trains (expresses and locals) on the Inuyama Line. A special surcharge is imposed for travel on the all-reserved deluxe super expresses; there's really no need to take it — the regu-

lar commuter line expresses will do fine — unless you feel the need to spend the extra money. Inuyama-Yuen (*not* Inuyama) is the station closest to Inuyama's major attractions; all trains stop at Inuyama-Yuen, as well as Inuyama. The trip from Nagoya takes about 30 minutes by express and 45 minutes by local (520 yen).

Places of Interest

Inuyama, a small city of 69,000, is laid out along the Kisogawa River. The city has been developed by the Meitetsu conglomerate into a recreation center for the people of Nagoya.

We describe in detail the area around Inuyamajo Castle. Other Inuyama attractions are explained briefly at the end of this section. They may be interesting for residents in Japan, but not too important for foreign visitors.

Inuyama-Yuen Station (middle right, Chubu Map 6) is close to the Kisogawa River. The promenade (shaded) along the river is very scenic, with Inuyamajo Castle standing high on a small hill. Cross the parking lot of the Meitetsu Inuyama Hotel and visit Uraku-en first.

Uraku-en Garden 有楽園 (middle center) is a complex of four tea houses. They are laid out in well-maintained Japanese gardens, connected by graveled paths. At the entrance you are required to change your shoes to straw slippers. The English brochure, distributed at the entrance, has a good layout map of the garden. The National Treasure Jo-an Tea House was originally built in Kyoto in 1618 at the order of Uraku Oda, a younger brother of Nobunaga Oda. The Tea House was moved here to be used as a main feature of Uraku-en Garden. The inside of Jo-an is open to the public only several days a year (usually in November). The gardens are beautiful and well-maintained, though it's a close call on whether the 800 yen admission is worth it. Hours: 9:00 AM to 5:00 PM (4:00 PM in winter).

Inuyamajo Castle 犬山城 (middle left). The approach to the castle grounds starts next to a vermilion shrine. You can also go through the shrine's *torii* gates, and join the approach behind the shrine. Stone steps curve along the stone walls and lead to the highest point of the hill. The donjon of the castle, Japan's oldest (built in 1537), looks like three stories from the outside but has four inside. In 1891, the donjon was severely damaged by earthquake. The government gave the castle to the Naruse family, whose successive generations had been the lords of this Castle since 1618, on the condition that they repair the damages. Since then, Inuyamajo has been the only privately owned castle in Japan. This is one of only four castles that are National Treasures — other three are Himejijo, Matsumotojo and Hikonejo. You can command a panoramic view from the top of the donjon — Nobi Plain to the south and the mountains across the Kisogawa River to the north. Hours: 9:00 AM to 5:00 PM. Closed Dec. 29-31. Admission: 300 yen.

Inuyama Artifacts Museum 犬山市文化資料館 (lower left) (optional) is in a modern building. Several Inuyama festival floats, as well as the area's historic objects, are displayed here. Inuyama Festival is held on the 1st or the 2nd weekend of April. Thirteen festival floats parade the city's main streets. Similar to those of the Takayama Festival, the floats feature acrobatic puppet shows. The festival is especially fantastic when the floats are decorated with 350 lanterns in the evening. Museum hours: 9:00 AM to 5:00 PM. Closed on Mondays and New Year's Holidays. Admission: 100 yen (including the addmission to the Annex across the street).

Cormorant Fishing 鵜飼. This 300-year old fishing method is still demonstrated in Inuyama (Kisogawa River) and in Gifu (Nagaragawa River) for tourists. At night

MAP 6 Inuyama

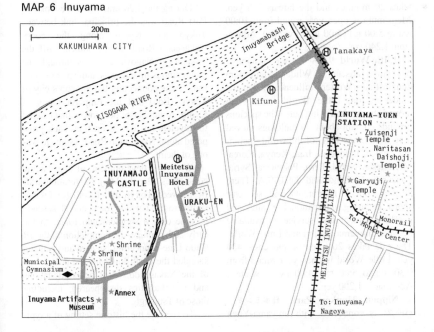

fishermen on small boats skillfully handle 12 cormorants each, making them catch fish. Spectators on separate boats watch the show while drinking and eating. Atmosphere is very touristy, but it can be a good entertainment on a hot summer night for those who happen to be staying at an area hotel. Reservations can be made at your hotel.

Other Places of Interest

Meiji-mura 明治村 is an open-air museum of Meiji-era buildings. After the Meiji Restoration in 1868, Japan enthusastically absorbed Western technologies, knowledge and fashion. Over 60 buildings were moved here from many parts of Japan, including the old Imperial Hotel designed by Frank Lloyd Wright. They are neatly laid out in the spacious grounds. Locomotives run around the grounds, providing transportation for nostalgic trips to the world of 100 years ago. A Meitetsu bus operates frequently between Inuyama Station and Meiji-mura. The ride takes 20 minutes and the fare is 360 yen. Meiji-mura is open year round from 10:00 AM to 5:00 PM (4:00 PM in winter). Admission: 1,240 yen.

Little World リトルワールド is another open-air museum. While Meiji-mura demonstrates Western influence on Japan's modernization, Little World features an around-the-world trip in hours. The spacious grounds contain about 30 buildings moved here from many parts of the world, including France, Indonesia, Iran, Kenya, Korea, Micronesia, Nepal, Peru, Polynesia, Syria, Tanzania, Thailand, and the U.S.A. There are, of course, restaurants and souvenir shops featuring international cuisine and goods. Frequent bus service is available between Inuyama Station and Little World. The ride takes 20 minutes and costs 420 yen. Little World is open year round from 9:30 AM to 5:00 PM (4:00 PM in winter). Admission: 1,200 yen.

Nippon Monkey Park 日本モンキーパーク is connected with Inuyama-Yuen Station via monorail (a 4-minute ride, 150 yen). The Park contains Monkey Center (zoo) and Playland. This is a good family destination. Hours: 9:30 AM to 5:00 PM (4:00 PM in winter). Admission: 880 yen.

Hotel in Inuyama

Meitetsu Inuyama Hotel (middle center, Chubu Map 6). First Class. 9 singles (13,000 yen -) & 74 doubles (17,500 yen -). Add: 107-1, Kitakoken, Inuyama. Tel: (0568) 61-2211.

TSUMAGO 妻籠

Tsumago can be visited easily in a one day excursion from Nagoya. Refer to Chubu Region Inter-City Transportation above for connections with Nagoya and other cities. Tsumago Bus Stop is pictured on Chubu Map 7 (middle center). You should skip Tsumago if you plan to visit Takayama.

During the Edo era, when the Tokaido Post Road was the principal link between Tokyo and Kyoto along the coast, Nakasendo Road, which branches off the Tokaido at Nagoya and runs through the mountainous inland, was another important trunk route connecting the Shogun's city of Tokyo (Edo) and the Emperor's city of Kyoto. A number of post towns that catered to travelers on foot or on horseback prospered along Nakasendo Road. Tsumago was one of them.

With the development of the Pacific coast cities after the Meiji Restoration, traffic between Tokyo and Kyoto (or Osaka) shifted to the Tokaido route, and Nakasendo became only a supplemental route. In the early 20th century, the completion of the JR Chuo Line connecting Nagoya and Nagano sounded the death knell for the post towns of the Nakasendo. Most accommodations and rest facilities disappeared, including those of Tsumago.

To recreate the historic setting of a typi-

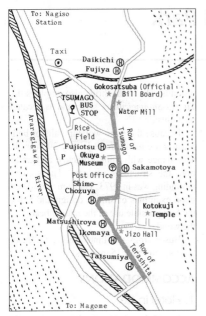

MAP 7 Tsumago

cal Edo era town, and to attract nostalgic tourists, the ruins in Tsumago were reconstructed in the 1960's. A half-mile stretch of the old Nakasendo Road in Tsumago is flanked by wooden houses restored and reconstructed in the style of the 19th century. English signs point you to "Row of Tsumago" (which consists mostly of restored buildings), and "Row of Terashita" (which is mostly reconstructions). This area is a camera buff's paradise. Several years ago this was a "boom" tourist attraction. The town was flooded with Japanese tourists and had more than 60 *minshuku* to lodge them. Today, with the tastes of Japanese travelers increasingly more exotic, Tsumago has lost some of its attraction; the number of *minshuku* has shrunk to about 30. But this is in your favor. Other than occasionally having to endure the onslaught from a Japanese tour

bus (and typical Tsumago stops for these tours are only about a half hour), you can enjoy Tsumago in peace. Many of the reconstructed buildings house restaurants, souvenir shops and small museums, of the "tourist-trap" type. We recommend staying overnight if you have time. Be forewarned that you cannot expect contemporary conveniences at lodgings in Tsumago, because the Tsumago people try to preserve history even in everyday modern life. That philosophy once attracted Japanese tourists, but today's spoiled tourists have tired of the town's lack of excitment and conveniences. They now tend to stay at *ryokan* in hotsprings or in hotels in Nagoya, and visit Tsumago as a daytime attraction.

Okuya Museum 奥谷郷土館 (middle center, Chubu Map 7) originally played an important role in accommodating traveling nobles and lords. The current building is an 1877 reconstruction and houses a small museum. Admission: 300 yen.

Gokosatsuba 御高札場 (upper right). This was an official billboard where the Tokugawa Shogunate posted orders to the people of Tsumago. The present board is a 1968 reconstruction.

Masugata 枡形. The original Nakasendo Road is shaded on the map. Between Row of Tsumago and Row of Terashita, the original path makes two sharp turns (middle center). This is a typical defensive design to prevent robbers and assasins from attacking the town easily. This part of the path preserves the original stone pavement, while other parts are paved with concrete.

Accommodations in Tsumago

There are about 30 *ryokan* and *minshuku* in the traditional houses. Many of them are marked on the map. You can request reservations for them at Tsumago Tourist Association. Address: Tsumago, Nagiso-machi, Nagano Prefecure. Tel: (0264) 57-3123.

Ise-Shima National Park
伊勢志摩国立公園

Ise-Shima National Park offers two major attractions — beautiful marine scenery along a rugged coast, and the solemn and impressive Ise Jingu Shrine. The area attracts several million travelers year round, tourists as well as pilgrims to Ise Jingu Shrine.

Refer to Chubu Region Inter-City Transportation section above for access from Nagoya (as well as from Kyoto and Osaka).

ISE   伊勢

Ise Jingu Shrine 伊勢神宮   (Middle left, Chubu Map 8)

Ise Jingu Shrine consists of two major shrines — Geku (Outer Shrine) and Naiku (Inner Shrine) and many minor buildings.

Geku, Outer Shrine 外宮, a seven-minute walk from Iseshi Station or Uji-Yamada Station, honors the Goddess of the Harvest. The wide main approach is lined with stately tall cedars, through which you can see Magatama-ike Pond. The main shrine is a complex of several buildings. The main hall, made of white Japanese cypress, uses a unique *Yuiitsu-Shinmeizukuri* design.

Naiku, Inner Shrine 内宮 is located 6 km (3.8 miles) to the southeast of the Outer Shrine. The Shrines are connected by a bus that runs every 15 minutes. The Inner Shrine is dedicated to the Goddess of the Sun, mythological ancestress of the imperial family. The Inner Shrine houses *Yata-no-Kagami*, the sacred Mirror that is one of the Three Sacred Treasures of the Japanese imperial family. Crossing the clear Isuzugawa River by bridge, the wide main approach leads to the main hall of the inner shrine. Huge cedar trees line both sides of the approach and enhance the sacred atmosphere of the grounds. The main shrine also employs the *Yuiitsu-Shinmeizukuri* style and is located on a hillside.

Because the main worship halls of both Shrines are reconstructed every 20 years in accordance with Shinto practice and tradition, the structures are new. The sixtieth rebuilding was in 1973. They are considered good examples of simple design and make the best possible use of the natural beauty of the wood.

Buses from the Inner Shrine to Iseshi Station run every 15 minutes.

ACCOMMODATIONS

1. Hotel in Ise

Ise Kokusai Hotel (10 minute walk from Iseshi Station). Business. 16 singles (6,000 yen -) & 35 doubles (10,000 yen -). Add: 2-9-11, Oseko, Ise, Mie Prefecure. Tel: (0596) 23-0101.

2. Welcome Inns in Ise

Ise City Hotel (3 minute walk from Iseshi Station or Uji-Yamada Station). 69 singles & 25 doubles. Add: 11-31, Fukiage, Ise, Mie Prefecture. Tel: (0596) 28-2111.

Hoshidekan (7 minute walk from Iseshi Station). 13 Japanese rooms. Add: 2-15-2, Kawasaki, Ise, Mie Prefecture. Tel: (0596) 28-2377.

TOBA   鳥羽

Toba (middle right, Chubu Map 8) is the center of Ise-Shima National Park, and most tourists to Ise-Shima spend a night or two in Toba. Many hotels and *ryokan* are located along scenic Toba Bay.

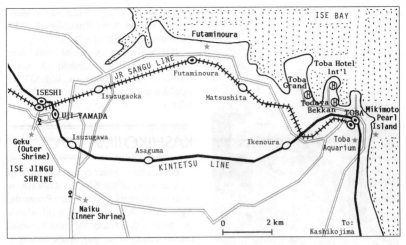

MAP 8 Ise-Shima

Mikimoto Pearl Island 御木本真珠島. Only a five-minute walk from Toba Station, this small island is connected to the mainland by a covered bridge. Kokichi Mikimoto started his experiments with cultured pearls here in the late 19th century. He succeeded in culturing pearl hemispheres in 1893 and round pearls in 1905. A variety of pearl products are on display in the museums. The women who dive for pearls here give demonstrations every 40-60 minutes. Hours: 8:30 AM to 5:00 PM. (9:00 AM to 4:30 PM in winter). Admission: 850 yen.

Toba Aquarium 鳥羽水族館 (optional) is just a few minutes on foot from Mikimoto Pearl Island. This large complex consists of several halls. In addition to the fish of the area, rare marine animals, such as Alaskan sea otters and Baikal seals, are on display here. The adjacent museum has an extensive collection of sea shells. Hours: 8:30 AM to 5:30 PM (9:00 AM to 5:00 PM in winter). Admission: 2,000 yen.

Sightseeing Boat in Toba Bay. A 50-minute sightseeing boat trip around Toba Bay operates frequently from the pier near Toba Station. The view of the rugged coast of Toba Bay is absolutely magnificent. You can get off the boat at Mikimoto Pearl Island, and reboard to return to the port. Fare: 1,350 yen. Admission to Mikimoto Pearl Island is not included.

ACCOMMODATIONS

1. Hotel in Toba

Toba Hotel International (2 minutes by taxi from Toba Station). First Class. 77 rooms. 28,000 yen and up per room. Add: 1-23-1, Toba, Mie Prefecture. Tel: (0599) 25-3121.

2. Ryokan in Toba

Todaya Bekkan (3 minute walk from Toba Station). First Class. 123 rooms. 18,000-25,000 per person. Add: 1-24-26, Toba, Mie Prefecture. Tel: (0599) 25-2500.

Toba Grand Hotel (5 minutes by taxi from Toba Station). First Class. 65 rooms. 15,000-18,000 yen per person. Add: 239-9, Obamacho, Toba, Mie Prefecture. Tel: (0599) 25-4141

FUTAMINOURA 二見ノ浦

Futaminoura (upper center, Chubu Map 8), several minutes walk from Futaminoura Station on the JR Sangu Line, is famous for two rocks the sea has eroded in a distinctive fashion. They are called the Husband-Wife rocks, and are joined by a thick straw rope. In the summer, the beach is crowded with swimmers and sun-bathers.

Ryokan in Futaminoura

Futamikan (10 minute walk from Futaminoura Station). First Class. 42 rooms. 15,000-20,000 yen per person. *Note: The*

Old Wing is a very traditional ryokan. Expensive. Add: 569-1, Futami-machi, Mie Prefecture. Tel: (05964) 3-2003.

Hamachiyokan (8 minute walk from Futaminoura Station). Standard. 33 rooms. 10,000-15,000 yen per person. Add: 537-26, Futami-machi, Mie Prefecture. Tel: (05964) 3-2050.

KASHIKOJIMA 賢島

Kashikojima (lower center, Chubu Map 1), a terminus of the Kintetsu Railways, is on the southern side of the Shima Peninsula. Ago Bay, with a number of small islands and pearl beds, features the most beautiful marine scenery of the area. A one-hour boat tour around peaceful and picturesque Ago Bay operates frequently from a pier near Kashikojima Station. Fare: 1,500 yen. Shima Marineland is an aquarium that is home to more than 2,500 fish.

ACCOMMODATIONS

1. Hotel in Kashikojima

Shima Kanko Hotel (5 minute walk from Kashikojima Station). First Class. 198 rooms. 22,500 yen and up per room. Add: Kashikojima, Agocho, Mie Prefecture. Tel: (05994) 3-1211.

2. Welcome Inn in Kashikojima

Ryokan Ishiyamaso (3 minute walk from Kashikojima Station to Kashikojima Port. The ryokan picks the guests up there in its own boat.) 10 Japanese rooms. Add: Kashikojima, Agocho, Mie Prefecture. Tel: (05995) 2-1527.

Tokai District 東海地方

Here we introduce briefly other major cities in the Tokai District, the area to the east of Nagoya facing the Pacific Ocean.

Toyohashi (lower left, Chubu Map 9) is a manufacturing city with a population of 335,000. Foreign auto makers, such as Benz, Volkswagen and Audi, have factories here.

Okazaki (lower left) is the birthplace of Ieyasu Tokugawa. Today, with a population of 305,000, Okazaki has become another manufacturing city. Mitsubishi Motors and Nisshin Textiles have large factories here.

Hamamatsu (lower center) has a population of 544,000. The city has two leading piano makers — Yamaha and Kawai, and enthusiastically promotes musical events. Two motorcycle manufacturers — Honda and Suzuki — also have large factories in Hamamatsu. Nearby Lake Hamanako (actually a lagoon) is famous for eel farming. Many *ryokan* are located in Kanzanji Onsen hotsprings on Lake Hamanako. Hamamatsu is also famous for its Kite Fly-

ing Festival on May 3-5.

Shizuoka (middle right), the capital of Shizuoka Prefecure, has a population of 471,000. Kunozan Toshogu Shrine can be reached by bus in 40 minutes from Shizuoka Station. The Shrine, one of the many Toshogu Shrines throughout Japan dedicated to Ieyasu Tokugawa, was built at the order of the second Tokugawa shogun and son of Ieyasu. It is a large compound on a hilltop reached by a long flight of stone steps from Kunozan-shita bus stop. A ropeway operates between Kunozan and Nihondaira Plateau (a 6-minute ride). Nihondaira is a popular observatory of Mt. Fuji to the north and the Pacific Ocean to the south. Shizuoka Festival, held in the city on April 1-5, features a daimyo procession.

Shimizu (middle right) is a port city and the base of a tuna fishing fleet. The city is also famous for its strawberries. Population: 242,000.

Fuji (upper right) is the pulp and paper manufacturing center. Population: 225,000.

MAP 9 Tokai District

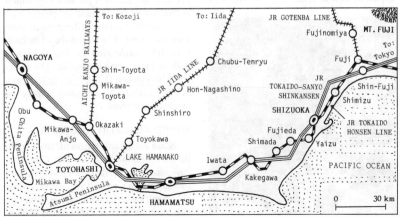

Takayama and Vicinity

TAKAYAMA 高山

Takayama Valley is located at the western foot of the Japan Alps. The Alps in this area consist of a number of 3,000 m (10,000 foot) tall mountains — they are referred to as the "Roof of Japan." When Hideyoshi Toyotomi unified Japan after almost 150 years of civil war, the feudal lord Nagachika Kanamori was assigned to govern the Takayama area in 1586. During the next 100 years, the Kanamori family successfully encouraged the development of agriculture and handicrafts and made Takayama one of the most prosperous local cities in Japan. In 1692, defeated in a political struggle with the Tokugawa Shogunate, the Kanamori family was exiled to northern area of Japan, and Takayama fell under the direct control of Tokugawa Shogunate. Because the Shogunate's principal interest in this prosperous area was in collecting taxes, economic activities were even further encouraged. Protected by the power of the Shogunate, Takayama merchants and craftsmen expanded their activities into the territories of other feudal lords, and underwrote cultural activities at home with the profits they made elsewhere. The elaborate floats still used in Takayama Festivals testify to the economic prosperity and high cultural standards achieved by the people of Takayama. One of Takayama's most charming features is its neighborhood of historic streets that preserve Edo architecture and atmosphere.

Approaching Takayama by train from either the direction of the Pacific Ocean or the Japan Sea, the tracks run along a narrow, beautiful river basin surrounded by mountains. The train ride is enjoyable in all seasons, but especially wonderful in winter, when the mountains are covered with snow. Even though snow and the severe winter cold of the area will restrict sightseeing activities, we recommend the winter train ride as a detour on a trip from Tokyo to Kyoto or back to Tokyo from Kyoto. It is amazing that a city as lovely as Takayama was built in such an isolated mountain valley. One of Takayama's most charming features is its neighborhood of historic streets that preserve Edo architecture and atmosphere. Takayama is a pleasant city with a population of 64,000, and its people welcome visitors; it is also well-organized, from a tourist's point of view, and shows its kindness and consideration for foreign visitors with its many signs in English. The excellent *i* Information Office in a kiosk in front of the Station has a good supply of brochures and maps.

Transportation in Takayama

Buses are the only means of "mass" public transportation in Takayama City. One day passes are available for 940 yen, and two day passes for 1,410 yen, but they probably won't make economic sense. Taxis are also plentiful. Because major places of inter-

est are located in a comparatively narrow area, tourists don't even have to use the buses except to visit Hida-no-Sato Village in Western Takayama. If you are a biker, rentals can be arranged at your hotel, and cycling is a good way to see Takayama.

Outline of Takayama

The main part of the city is to the east of the JR Takayama Line tracks. In addition to business and governmental offices, there are a number of places of historical interest in this part of the city. The area to the west of the railroad tracks is mountainous and less developed. Hida-no-Sato Village (an open-air museum) and Hida Minzokukan (Hida Folklore Museum) are here. They are perched on the mountainsides surrounded by thick forests.

Suggested Itinerary

One-and-a-half days are ideal for a visit to Takayama: a half day for Western Takayama, and a full day for Eastern Takayama. We have organized the itineraries that follow along those lines. If you can allocate only one day for Takayama, skip Western Takayama.

WESTERN TAKAYAMA

(Refer to Chubu Map 10.)

Takayama Station to Hida-no-Sato by Bus Buses for Hida-no-Sato leave from Platform No. 2 at Takayama Station Bus Terminal in front of JR station (upper right), about once every 30 minutes. The bus runs counter clockwise as pictured on the map (with arrows). The ride takes 10-15 minutes, and the fare is 200 yen. On the way to Hida-no-Sato, you will see a huge golden temple building (probably the biggest structure in Takayama). It is the headquarters of the Majikari religious group. It is quite incongruous in the quiet surroundings of the mountain village.

Hida-No-Sato Village 飛騨の里 (lower left) is Takayama's equivalent of Williamsburg, Virginia (on a smaller scale). Old farm houses, which were destined to be submerged with the construction of dams or which were in danger of being sold by their owners and demolished, have been moved here and preserved as living museums. They illustrate the life style of farmers and craftsmen of the Takayama area. More than 30 buildings are situated on a hillside around a small pond. Many of them are also used for demonstrations of handicraft techniques — lacquerware, carving, dyeing, woodenware and handmade paper. The village is located in a elevated area and provides visitors with a good view of the city, with the Japan Alps rising in the background. Hours: 8:30 AM to 5:00 PM. Admission: 520 yen. Your admission ticket also entitles you to entrance to Hida Minzokukan (Hold on to your ticket until you get there!).

Hida-no-Sato Village to Hida Minzokukan The walk from Hida-no-Sato Village to Hida Minzokukan is itself a trip through the living museum of the traditional Takayama area. The descending road is dotted with old houses, most of which are now souvenir shops or restaurants. Especially noteworthy are Gokura and Hida Goten. Gokura is an antique shop, in a big old converted warehouse. Hida Goten is the biggest wooden structure in Takayama. It was originally constructed as a rich farmer's house and was moved here for preservation. Its complicated roof and beautiful wall designs are quite impressive. Once you've passed Hida Goten, we recommend the alternative

to the walk along the main road — the "Walking Path" is marked in English.

Hida Minzokukan (Folklore Museum) 飛騨民族館 (middle center). The buildings of Hida Minozokukan are reconstructions set in a village, which also features traditional restaurants and souvenir shops specializing in craft items. Wakayama House was built in 1751 and transferred to this site in 1959. It is a good example of the *Gasshozukuri* architectural style — with a steep thatched roof shaped like hands joined in prayer. The interior features antique furniture and handicraft items. There is also a

preserved grain storehouse and an old one-story house (Nobuki House). The Mountain Museum exhibits materials collected in the Japan Alps by the Hida Mountaineering Club; unfortunately, the arrangement is rather unfocused.

The bus back to Takayama Station stops near Wakayama House. The walk back takes about 20-25 minutes.

EASTERN TAKAYAMA

(Refer to Chubu Map 11.)

The places of interest in Eastern Takaya-

MAP 10 Western Takayama

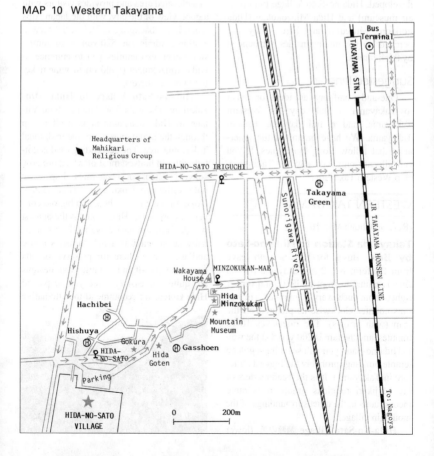

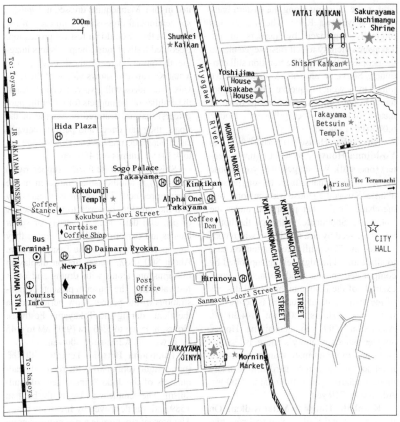

MAP 11 Eastern Takayama

ma are explained in the order we suggest for a walking tour.

Kokubunji Temple 国分寺 (middle left) was originally erected at the order or Emperor Shomu in 746 (Kokubunji Temples were built all over Japan at that time as subordinate branches of Nara's Todaiji Temple, or Temple of the Great Buddha). Today it is Takayama's oldest temple. The original buildings were burnt down during the civil wars. The present Main Hall was built in 1615 by the Kanamori family. The three-story pagoda, built in 1807, is the only one of this type in the Takayama area. A huge gingko tree in the precincts is 1,200 years old, and has been designated a Natural Monument.

Shunkei Kaikan 春慶会館 (upper center) (optional), a white warehouse-like building, exhibits exquisite lacquerware of the Shunkei School. The Shunkei School, established in Takayama at the beginning of the 17th century, is famous for its technique of making use of the natural beauty of the grains of the woods. Hours: 8:30 AM to 5:00 PM. Admission: 200 yen.

Morning Market 朝市 (middle center) (optional). An open-air morning market is held in the morning along the eastern bank of the Miyagawa River. The market was originally organized by farmers in the Takayama vicinity to sell fresh vegetables to the people of the city. The tradition still continues. Souvenir and snack vendors have joined in as well, to squeeze a few yen from tourists. The market is a treasure trove of local color and local flavors. Hours: 6:00 AM to 12 noon.

Kusakabe House 日下部民芸館 and **Yoshijima House** 吉島家住宅 (upper center) (optional). We suggest that you choose the one of these that is more to your personal taste. Kusakabe House was the home of a merchant family that prospered under the Tokugawa Shogunate. Although the house was destroyed by fire in 1875, it was reconstructed in 1879, with careful attention paid to all details. The high ceiling supported by complicated beams and pillars is good example of the unique architectural designs of the area. A small museum is behind the front rooms. Hours: 9:00 AM to 4:30 PM. Admission: 309 yen. Yoshijima House, another merchant family's house, is less finished and more intimate than its next-door neighbor. It has a nice garden, and many modest details. Hours: 9:00 AM to 5:00 PM. Admission: 250 yen.

Kusakabe House to Yatai Kaikan. On the way to Yatai Kaikan, you will pass two *torii* gates, as you approach the brilliant main hall of **Sakurayama Hachimangu Jinja Shrine** 桜山八幡宮神社 . The present structure is a 1976 reconstruction.

Yatai Kaikan 屋台会館 (upper right). This modern hall in the Shrine precincts displays floats used in the Takayama Festival. Takayama Festival is considered one of the three most spectacular of Japan's many festivals. It is held twice a year: in the spring, on April 14-15th and in the fall, on October 9-10th. The elaborate decorations and delicate, ornate carvings of the floats testify to the high artistic skill of Takayama craftsmen. Except at festival time, four floats are exhib-

ited in turn. Mannequins dressed in *kamishimo* ceremonial dress stand with each of the floats as they would in a festival procession. Recorded festival music helps visitors imagine the atmosphere of these celebrations. Yatai Kaikan also shows videos of the festivals. The videos will give you a good idea of the abilities of the puppets (or rather the puppeteers) that are featured on several of the floats: they can dance and perform complicated acrobatic maneuvers. Hours: 9:00 AM to 4:30 PM. Admission: 460 yen.

Shishi Kaikan 獅子会館 (upper right) (optional) is another small museum in the Shrine precincts. The *shishi* is a legendary lion-like creature believed to be a protector of peaceful daily life. A variety of *shishi* dances are performed all over Japan; they are especially popular in the Takayama area. About 800 *shishi* masks are on display in this museum along with drums and other festival items. The museum presents demonstrations of the puppet show performed on the floats during the Takayama Festivals. Hours: 8:05 AM to 5:45 PM (9:05 AM to 4:45 PM in winter). Admission: 500 yen.

Takayama Betsuin Temple 高山別院 (upper right) (optional) is the regional headquarters of the Jodo-Shinshu sect of Buddhism. The temple was originally built in 1589 and was destroyed by fire many times. The present structure is a recent reconstruction. Karamon Gate at the southern edge of the precincts is impressive.

Historic Streets 三町通り (Middle center, shaded)

This area of Takayama preserves the atmosphere of the old Edo era town. The three main streets are Kami-Ichinomachi-dori Street, Kami-Ninomachi-dori Street and Kami-Sannomachi-dori Street. The old buildings now house stores, restaurants, snack shops and galleries, but still maintain an 18th century ambiance. Several small museums are located in this area. All are optional; most of these establishments capitalize on their location in this picturesque area.

Kami-Ichinomachi-dori Street attractions: Oita Yachokan 老田野鳥館 (Wild Bird Museum) features displays of wild birds of the region and of the Japan Alps. Hours: 9:00 AM to 5:00 PM. Admission: 150 yen. **Takayama Kyodokan** 高山郷土館 (Museum of Local History) is housed in a former sake brewery. It displays items related to sake brewing, as well as firemen's equipment and various other local crafts and festival items. This museum is a center for the study of local history and is operated by Takayama City. Hours: 8:30 AM to 5:00 PM (9:00 AM to 4:30 PM in winter). Closed Mondays. Admission: 200 yen. **Kyodo Gangukan** 郷土玩具館 (Galley of Traditional Toys) features two floors displaying a large collection of toys. A toy shop is at the front of the establishment. Hours: 8:30 AM to 5:00 PM. Admission: 200 yen.

Kami-Ninomachi-dori Street attractions: Hirata Kinenkan 平田記念館 (Hirata Museum) features the collection of 10 generations of the Hirata family, which made candles and pomade. The collection focuses on lamps, and local porcelains and lacquerware. The house itself was built in 1897. Hours: 9:00 AM to 5:00 PM. Admission: 200 yen.

Kami-Sannomachi-dori Street attractions: This street preserves the most houses in their original style. **Hida Minzoku Kokokan** 飛騨民族考古館 (Hida Archeological Museum) is primarily of architectural interest; details of its construction suggest associations with *ninja*. Hours: 8:00 AM to 6:00 PM (9:00 AM to 5:00 PM in winter). Admission: 300 yen. **Fujii Bijutsu Mingeikan** 藤井美術民芸館 (Fujii Art and Folkcraft Museum) features a more sophisticated collection of porcelain, lacquerware, dolls, scrolls, combs and urns. The entrance gate was once the outer entrance gate of Takayama Castle (which was dismantled in the 17th century). Hours: 9:00 AM to 5:00 PM (8:00 PM in summer). Admission: 300 yen. **Hachiga Minzoku Bijutsukan** 八賀民俗美術館 (Hachiga Folk Art Gallery) features the private collection of folk art and antiques of the Hachiga family, including items related to Japanese Christianity. Hours: 9:00 AM to 5:00 PM (4:00 PM in winter). Closed Wednesdays from December to March. Admission: 200 yen.

Takayama Jinya 高山陣屋 (lower center) is a palace that was used as an administrator's office and residence from 1692 until the Tokugawa Shogunate was overthrown in 1868. It is the only building of its kind that is still standing. Civil and criminal proceedings were conducted in the Kitashirasu and Oshirasu, and official functions in the Hiroma. Takayama Jinya also features rice warehouses and other facilities related to tax collection. A visit here will give you a good idea of how the Shogunate conducted official business. It is a National Historic Site. Hours: 8:45 AM to 5:00 PM (4:30 PM in winter). Admission: 310 yen. A second Open-Air Morning Market operates near the Jinya.

Teramachi 寺町 (off the map, at the eastern end of Kokubunji-dori/Yasugawadori Street). This temple district features well-marked walking paths for the "Higashiyama Walking Course." We suggest that you follow only the first, northern part of the route unless you are a serious hiker. In addition to thirteen temples, five

shrines are also nestled in the hillsides. The area is a delight for photographers. While these shrines and temples are no match for the splendors of Kyoto, they are lovely, modest gems. You will probably agree that Takayama has a valid claim to status as a "Little Kyoto" based on this area. Eikyoin Temple, Kyushoji Temple, Unryuji Temple, Higashiyama-Hakusan-jinja Shrine, Daioji Temple, Toun-in Temple, Sogenji Temple, Tenshoji Temple, Higashiyama-Shimmei-Jinja Shrine, Zennoji Temple, Hokkeji Temple and Soyuji Temple are in the northern part of Teramachi.

Shopping

In addition to the many shops of the Historic Streets area, you might want to stroll along Kokubunji-dori Street (middle center), Takayama's principal shopping street. Many shops features handicraft items. They generally remain open until 8:00 PM.

ACCOMMODATIONS

1. Hotels in Takayama

Hida Hotel Plaza (upper left, Chubu Map 11). First Class. 7 singles (9,500 yen -) & 68 doubles (21,000 yen -). The hotel also has 62 Japanese rooms. Add: 2-60, Hanaokacho, Takayama. Tel: (0577) 33-4600.

Takayama Green Hotel (middle right, Chubu Map 10). First Class. 153 rooms. 17,000 yen and up per person with two meals. Add: 2-180, Nishino-Isshikicho, Takayama. Tel: (0577) 33-5500

New Alps Hotel (middle left, Chubu Map 11). Business. 34 singles (5,500 yen -) & 43 doubles (11,000 yen -). Add: 6, Hanasatocho, Takayama. Tel: (0577) 32-2888.

Hotel Alpha One Takayama (middle center, Chubu Map 11). Business. 117 singles (5,100 yen -) & 18 doubles (9,700 yen -). Add: 3-61, Honcho, Takayama. Tel: (0577) 32-2211.

2. Ryokan in Takayama

Kinkikan (middle center, Chubu Map 11). First Class. 15 rooms. 18,000 yen & up per person. Add: 48, Asahicho, Takayama. Tel: (0577) 32-3131.

Hishuya (lower left, Chubu Map 10). First Class. 16 rooms. 18,000 yen & up per person. Add: 2581, Kami-Okamotocho, Takayama. Tel: (0577) 33-4001.

Sogo Palace Takayama (middle center, Chubu Map 11). Standard. 33 rooms. 12,000 yen & up per person. Add: 54, Suehirocho, Takayama. Tel: (0577) 33-5000.

Hachibei (lower left, Chubu Map 10). Minshuku. 12 rooms. 8,000 yen & up per person. Add: 2561, Kami-Okamotocho, Takayama. Tel: (0577) 33-0573.

3. Welcome Inn in Takayama

Hotel Yamaichi (10 minutes by taxi from Takayama Station). 19 Japanese & 2 Western rooms. Add: 2777, Ishiuracho, Takayama. Tel: (0577) 34-6200.

GERO 下呂

Gero is a hotspring town, with a number of modern buildings nestled in a narrow valley along the Masudagawa River. There are more than 30 *ryokan* in Gero. Less than two hours by the JR Takayama Honsen Line from Nagoya, this hotspring is one of the most popular weekend destinations for residents of that metropolitan area. Its proximity to Takayama, which is only one hour away by train, has helped Gero also attract tourists from around the country who want to combine a visit to historic Takayama with a relaxing overnight stay at a hotspring.

As is the case with many hotspring resorts near huge cities (such as Atami Spa and Tokyo, and Arima Spa and Osaka), the town of Gero has a rather racy nightlife, and features quite a few strip joints, bars and cabarets. But the town is proud of its vigorous hotsprings, and its reputation as one of Japan's three best hotspring resorts. Vacationers from large Japanese cities find this a pleasant, relaxing atmosphere. If you like hotsprings, you should consider staying overnight in Gero, as most Japanese do, before or after your trip to Takayama.

ACCOMMODATIONS (Ryokan)

Hotel Suimeikan (3 minute walk from Gero Station). First Class. 244 rooms. 18,000 yen & up per person. Add: 1268, Koden, Gerocho, Gifu Prefecture. Tel: (05762) 5-2800.

Ogawaya (8 minute walk from Gero Station). First Class. 105 rooms. 17,000 yen & up per person. Add: 570, Yunoshima, Gerocho, Gifu Prefecture. Tel: (05762) 5-3121

Shirakaba Gyoen (5 minute walk from Gero Station). Standard. 12,000 yen & up per person. Add: 1089-1, Mori, Gerocho, Gifu Prefecture. Tel: (05762) 5-4411.

Okudaya Happoen (8 minute walk from Gero Station). Standard. 22 rooms. 12,000 yen and up per person. Add: 881, Yunoshima, Gerocho, Gifu Prefecture. Tel: (05762) 5-2838.

Hokuriku District 北陸地方

KANAZAWA 金沢

During the period of Japan's civil wars (15th-16th centuries), the Jodo-Shinshu sect of Buddhism established an autonomous government in Kanazawa. It was the only one of many such experiments to survive the onslaughts of neighboring feudal lords. The independent government stayed in power from 1488 to 1580, when the area was attacked by the forces of Nobunaga Oda, who by then had almost realized his great ambition of terminating the civil wars and uniting the nation.

During the Edo period, Kanazawa was the home of Japan's second most powerful feudal family, the Maedas (second, of course, only to the Tokugawas). To avoid confrontations with the Tokugawas, the Maedas stressed cultural activities rather than military affairs. Kutani pottery, Kaga Yuzen dyeing and other crafts were developed to high standards here; they still flourish today. Kanazawa is a modern city, but its many historical and cultural sites still testify to the area's unique historical background.

Outline of the City

Refer to Chubu Map 12. The area around JR Kanazawa Station (upper left) is relatively remote from both the city's downtown and major tourist attractions. It is primarily a center for many of Kanazawa's hotels. The most important tourist attraction of Kanazawa, Kenrokuen Garden (lower right), is located about 2.4 km (1.5 miles) southeast of JR Kanazawa Station. Major places of interest, such as Ishikawamon Gate, Seisonkaku Mansion, and the Museum for Traditional Products & Crafts, are located in the vicinity of Kenrokuen Garden. An *i* Information Office is located in Kanazawa Station, inside the reserved ticket office.

Samurai Houses (middle left) are preserved in the area to the west of Kanazawa's main street. Saihitsuan, located in the same area, is a small Kaga Yuzen dyeing factory. Oyama Jinja Shrine (middle center) is also within walking distance.

Kanazawa's downtown stretches north to south along the main street, between Musashigatsuji bus stop (upper center) and Katamachi bus stop (lower left). Most shops are between Musashigatsuji and Minamicho, while business offices are between

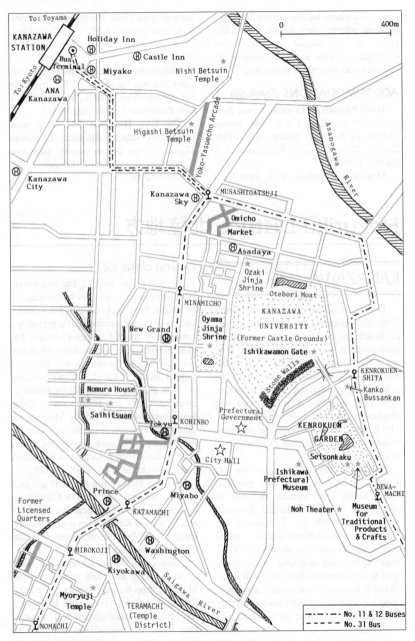

MAP 12 Kanazawa

Minamicho and Korimbo, and eating and drinking places between Korimbo and Katamachi. Government offices are to the east of Korimbo.

Kosenyo, the only Kutani pottery kiln in the city, is located to the south of the Saigawa River, near the Former Licensed Quarters (lower left). Myoryuji Temple (lower left), which is famous for its complicated interior structure, and which is nicknamed "Ninja Temple," is within walking distance of the pottery kiln, as are the former licensed quarters.

Transportation in Kanazawa

Using just three of the city's bus lines you can easily cover Kanazawa's major places of interest. As pictured on Chubu Map 12, the No. 31 bus runs south from Kanazawa Station along the main street. The No. 11 and No. 12 buses operate from Kanazawa Station to the southeast. You can use these buses to reach Kenrokuen Garden and the other major tourist destinations.

Suggested Itinerary

It is rather difficult to cover all the places introduced below. If you have only one full day in Kanazawa, skip the places marked optional.

Seisonkaku 成巽閣 (lower right) (optional). Take the No. 11 or No. 12 bus to Dewacho stop. Seisonkaku is a one-minute walk from this stop. Seisonkaku was constructed in 1863 by the 13th lord of the Maeda family as a residence for his mother. This two-story building is a monument of elegantly tasteful design. Seikoken Tea House and Hikakutei (Flying Crane Garden) are attached to the mansion. Hours: 8:30 AM to 4:30 PM. Closed on Wednesdays. Admission: 500 yen.

Museum for Traditional Products & Crafts 伝統産業工芸館 (lower right) (optional). All sorts of handicraft items, including pottery, Yuzen dyeing, lacquerware, gold, metal and wood items, hand-made toys and papers, are displayed here. The displays illustrate the glories of the high artistic standards the area developed during the feudal era. Hours: 9:00 AM to 4:30 PM. Closed on Thursdays and National Holidays. Admission: 250 yen.

Ishikawa Prefectural Museum 石川県立美術館 (lower right) (optional). This museum is famous for its display of Kutani ware. A large pheasant-shaped incense burner (National Treasure) by Ninsei Nonomura, the master Kutani potter, is the pride of the collection. Hours: 9:30 AM to 5:00 PM. Closed during changing of exhibits. Admission to the permanent collection: 350 yen.

Kenrokuen Garden 兼六園 (lower right). Kenrokuen literally means "a refined garden incorporating six different features." The famous features of the Garden are vastness, solemnity, precise arrangements, antiquity, elaborate use of water and scenic charm. Kenrokuen Garden was originally built in the 1670's by the fifth lord of the Maeda family. Succeeding generations expanded the garden and each added something of its own taste to it. The Garden as it

stands today was completed by the 12th lord in 1837. This Garden is popularly known as one of Japan's three best gardens, with the other two being Kairakuen in Mito and Korakuen in Okayama. These three were selected because they were owned by powerful feudal lords. Though they are charming, nobody would agree that they are "the best" three of Japan nowadays. From the highest points of the Garden, visitors can command a good view of the city, and can even see the Japan Sea in the distance. Hours: 7:00 AM to 5:00 PM (8:00 AM to 4:30 PM in winter). Admission: 300 yen.

If you don't want to visit Seisonkaku, the Museum for Traditional Products & Crafts and Ishikawa Prefectural Museum before proceeding to Kenrokuen Garden, you can get off No. 11 or No. 12 bus at Kenrokuenshita stop (middle right).

Ishikawamon Gate 石川門 (middle right) was the southern entrance to Kanazawajo Castle. The entire compound burned down in 1881; only a few structures, including the Gate, survived the fire. The magnificence of the Gate gives modern visitors some idea of the power of the Maeda family, and the beau-tifully arranged stone walls around the Gate testify to the high craft standards of the era. The castle grounds are now used by Kanazawa University, the Kanazawa local courts and other public offices. Visitors can enter the Ishikawamon Gate area, but the grounds themselves are not open to the public.

Kanko Bussankan 観光物産館 (middle right) (optional). The first and second floors of this building are large souvenir shops and restaurants. The third floor is the Ishikawa Prefectural Museum of Handicraft. Demonstrations of handicraft production, including Yuzen dyeing, gold foil, pottery, toys and lacquerware are held on the third floor. Hours: 9:00 AM to 5:00 PM. Closed on Thursdays in the winter. Admission to the third floor: 200 yen.

Kenrokuen to Samurai Houses. Enjoy a leisurely walk from Kenrokuen to the governmental district. There are a number of Kutani pottery shops along the street. Crossing downtown, you will soon be in the Nagamachi district, the former home of Kanazawa's samurai (middle left).

Samurai Houses 長町武家屋敷. The Nagamachi district was home to high ranking samurai during the Edo era. Several samurai houses and tile-roofed mud walls along the narrow street have been preserved. **Nomura House** 野村家 (optional), which was actually moved here from another part of the city, provides visitors a chance to see the interior of the house of a high-ranking samurai. A small but authentic Japanese-style garden is attached to the house, and armor and other samurai utensils are displayed in its various rooms. Hours: 8:30 AM to 5:30 PM (4:30 in winter). Admission: 400 yen. **Saihitsuan** 彩筆庵 (optional), one of the samurai houses, has been converted to a small Kaga Yuzen dye works. Kanazawa is proud of the high artistic standards of Kaga Yuzen dyeing, which is comparable to the fine work done in Kyoto. The delicate hand-painting process is demonstrated here. Visitors can listen to a lecture in Japanese or watch a video, and can observe the craftspeople at work. The staff also serves visitors tea and Japanese sweets. Hours: 9:00 AM to 12 noon and 1:00 PM to 4:30 PM. Closed Thursdays. Admission: 500 yen.

Other Places of Interest

Kosenyo Pottery Kiln 光仙窯 (optional) is the only kiln located in the city. Its sign includes the letters "K KP" at the top. This small factory, which looks like a regular house from the outside, carries out all the processes of pottery making, from designing and firing to painting. Demonstrations of the skillful craftsmanship involved are fascinating. Admission is free, but making a purchase at the souvenir shop is an almost necessary courtesy. Hours: 9:00 AM to 4:30 PM. Closed from Dec. 30 to Jan. 5.

Former Licensed Quarters 西郭 (lower left) (optional). Nishi-Kuruwa used to be one of Kanazawa's three licensed quarters. The establishments have been converted to drinking places. Several buildings have preserved their original appearance, and are good subjects for photographers. A gatehouse that was used as a checkpoint and as a means of keeping the women and girls who worked in the district from escaping has also been preserved.

Myoryuji Temple 妙立寺 (lower left) (optional). The most famous of the temples located on the southern side of the Saigawa River is Myoryuji Temple. Because of its complicated structure, with 29 staircases and 21 secret chambers, the Temple is popularly known as *Ninja-dera*, or Temple of Secret Agents. Guided tours are organized from time to time — on their own visitors would get lost in this tricky temple. Visitors also have to listen to a taped lecture in Japanese before the tour. Admission: 700 yen. Advance reservations need to be made to visit Myoryuji. The staff at your hotel can help by calling for reservations: (0762) 41-0888 (Japanese only). Due to the language barrier the Temple is rather reluctant to have foreign visitors.

Teramachi Temple District 寺町 (lower center) (optional). Like several other cities, Kanazawa has a temple district atop a hill overlooking the city. Many of the temples have lovely features and are quite proud of their history. Unfortunately, the busy street on which many of the temples of the district are now situated spoils its effect. You can spend as much as 4-5 hours to follow the 4.5 km (2.8 mile) walking tour laid out in the Teramachi District. In total, there are more than 50 temples and shrines in the area. Among the most notable are: Nekodera Temple, built in memory of a pet cat, and, formerly, a popular burial place for cats; Ryuenji Temple, which has a Zen garden behind the main building; Gannenji Temple, which Basho visited on his travels; Ryuzoji

Temple, which features a fancy new gate; and Daijoji, a branch of Eiheiji Temple (zen sect).

Oyama Jinja Shrine 尾山神社 (middle center) (optional) was built in 1873 to honor the memory of Toshiie Maeda, the first lord of the Maeda family. The Shrine's three-story Shimmon Gate is famous for its colorful stained glass windows on the third level; this is a very unusual structure for Japan. The Shrine's garden skillfully combines a pond, rocks, islets and bridges. Admission to the shrine grounds is free of charge.

Ozaki Jinja Shrine 尾崎神社 (middle center) (optional) is often described as Kanazawa's version of the famous Toshogu Shrine in Nikko. At the time Toshogu was built, local lords all over Japan, in demonstrations of their loyalty to the Tokugawa Shogunate, had Toshogu-type shrines built and dedicated to Ieyasu Tokugawa. Ozaki Jinja Shrine is one such shrine. The Shrine is in dire need of repair and does not retain much, if any, of its original magnificence.

Omicho Market 近江町市場 (middle center) (optional) will probably be the last place on a full-day sightseeing itinerary in Kanazawa. The Market is Kanazawa's kitchen. About 200 small shops, most of which sell food products, are concentrated in narrow, covered alleys. Visitors are amazed at the variety of seafood and the reasonable prices.

Yoko-Yasuecho Arcade 横安江町アーケード (upper center) (optional) is lined with many modern stores. Several shops dealing in Buddhist altars are scattered among them. The arcade can be an alternative destination, especially if you happen to get caught in the rain.

Edo-mura Village 江戸村 (41 minutes by bus from Kanazawa Station). If you are staying in Kanazawa for an extended period, you should consider a visit to Edo-mura Village, an open-air museum that features about 20 buildings of the Edo Era. Each building represents the typical dwelling of a different social class of the era. You can see the homes of farmers, merchants, craftsmen, priests and warriors. **Dampuen** 檀風苑, another open-air museum that displays the tools and products of various crafts, is connected to Edo-mura by frequent mini-bus service. Both facilities are open from 8:00 AM to 5:00 PM. Admission to both Edo-mura Village and Dampuen: 1,200 yen. To reach Edo-mura Village, take the No. 12 bus from Kanazawa Station or Kenrokuen-shita stop. The bus operates about once every 30 minutes. Edo-mura Village is a few minutes walk from Yuwaku-Onsen, the last stop of the bus.

ACCOMMODATIONS

(Refer to Chubu Map 12)

1. Hotels in Kanazawa

ANA Hotel Kanazawa (upper left). First Class. 114 singles (12,000 yen -) & 139 doubles (22,000 yen -). Add: 16-3, Showacho, Kanazawa. Tel: (0762) 24-6111.

Kanazawa Tokyu Hotel (middle center). First Class. 106 singles (12,000 yen -) & 142 doubles (20,000 yen -). Add: 2-1-1, Korimbo, Kanazawa. Tel: (0762) 31-2411.

Kanazawa New Grand Hotel (middle center). First Class. 25 singles (12,000 yen -) & 76 doubles (20,000 yen -). Add: 1-50,

Takaokacho, Kanazawa. Tel: (0762) 33-1311.

Kanazawa Miyako Hotel (upper left). First Class. 105 singles (12,000 yen -) & 95 doubles (20,000 yen). Add: 6-10, Konohanacho, Kanazawa. Tel: (0762) 31-2202.

Holiday Inn Kanazawa (upper left). Standard. 56 singles (11,000 yen -) & 109 doubles (16,500 yen -). Add: 1-10, Horikawacho, Kanazawa. Tel: (0762) 23-1111.

Kanazawa Sky Hotel (upper center). Standard. 56 singles (11,000 yen -) & 52 doubles (19,000 yen -). Add: 15-1, Musashimachi, Kanazawa. Tel: (0762) 33-2233.

Kanazawa Washington Hotel (lower center). Business. 165 singles (7,000 yen -) & 35 doubles (16,000 yen -). Add: 1-10-18, Katamachi, Kanazawa. Tel: (0762) 24-0111.

Kanazawa Prince Hotel (lower left). Business. 55 singles (6,000 yen -) & 102 doubles (12,000 yen -). Add: 2-23-7, Katamachi, Kanazawa. Tel: (0762) 23-2131.

Kanazawa City Hotel (upper left). Business. 81 singles (5,000 yen -) & 86 doubles (11,500 yen -). Add: 6-8, Showamachi, Kanazawa. Tel: (0762) 21-8888.

2. Ryokan in Kanazawa

Asadaya (middle center). Deluxe. 5 rooms. 50,000 yen & up per person. Add: 23, Jukkenmachi, Kanazawa. Tel: (0762) 31-2228.

Miyabo (lower center). First Class. 36 rooms. 16,000 yen & up per person. Add: 3, Shimo-Kakinokibata, Kanazawa. Tel: (0762) 31-4228.

Kiyokawa (lower left). First Class. 26 rooms. 20,000 yen & up per person. Add: 7-1, Kiyokawamachi, Kanazawa. Tel: (0762) 41-6123.

3. Welcome Inns in Kanazawa

Murataya Ryokan (12 minutes by taxi from Kanazawa Station). 11 Japanese rooms. Add: 1-5-2, Katamachi, Kanazawa. Tel: (0762) 63-0455.

Nogi Ryokan (3 minute walk from Kanazawa Station). 15 Japanese rooms. Add: 4-16, Konohanacho, Kanazawa. Tel: (0762) 21-8579.

Hinode Ryokan (1 minute walk from Kanazawa Station). 19 Japanese rooms. Add: 2-17-25, Honmachi, Kanazawa. Tel: (0762) 31-5224.

Kanazawa Castle Inn (upper left). Business. 16 singles & 92 doubles. Add: 10-16, Konohanacho, Kanazawa. Tel: (0762) 23-6300.

TOYAMA 富山

At the intersection of the JR Takayama and the JR Hokuriku train lines, Toyama (upper center, Chubu Map 1) is a pleasant modern city with a proud tradition. The Tateyama mountain range stands guard over the city. Tateyama (along with Mt. Fuji and Mt. Hakusan) is one of Japan's three Sacred Mountains. We include the information that follows for visits of a few hours. There's an *i* Information Office in JR Toyama Station.

Toyama Municipal Folkcraft Village 富山市民芸館. This museum sits at the foot of Kuresan-Koen Hill Park, which is also the home of **Chokeiji Temple** 長慶寺 and **Gohyaku Rakan** 五百羅漢. From Bus stop No. 14 in front of the Hokuriku Bank Building (across from JR Toyama Station), take the bus bound for Kurehayama Rojin Center. Get off at Anyobo stop (the stop for the return trip is across the street). Walk 250 m (775 feet) in the same direction the bus was going and follow the signs to the Folkcraft Village. The Village consists of eight separate museums, each housed in its own building. They are the Museum of Medicine Peddlars (this is a local industry and tradition); the Thatched Roof Folk Art Museum; the Folk Art Museum; Enzan-an Municipal Tea Ceremony House (260 yen extra for tea); the Museum of Ceramic Art; the Memorial Art Gallery of Gyujin Takamura;

and the Museum of Folklore. A ticket for admission to all of these museums is 620 yen. Admission to the separate museums is 100 yen each. Unless you have lots of time or a particular interest in pharmaceuticals or archaeology, we recommend the Thatched Roof Folk Art Museum, the Folk Art Museum and the Museum of Ceramic Art. Hours: 9:00 AM to 4:30 PM. Closed Mondays.

Climb up the hill past the Village's Administration Center to **Chokeiji Temple**. More than 500 stone Buddhas **Gohyaku Rakan (Five Hundred Disciples of Buddha)** are arrayed on the terraces adjacent to the temple.

Toyamajo Castle Grounds Park 富山城跡公園 is home to a replica of Toyamajo Castle, which houses the Museum of Local History, and Matsukawa Riverbank Sculpture Park — bronze sculptures are set among the cherry trees that line the river near the Castle Grounds. The Castle Grounds is open from 9:00 AM to 4:30 PM. Closed Mondays. Admission: 210 yen.

ACCOMMODATIONS (Hotels)

Toyama Daiichi Hotel (7 minute walk from Toyama Station). First Class. 45 singles (9,000 yen -) & 61 doubles (19,000 yen -). Add: 10-10, Sakuragicho, Toyama. Tel: (0764) 42-4411.

Meitetsu Toyama Hotel (5 minute walk from Toyama Station). Standard. 75 singles (9,000 yen -) & 36 doubles (18,000 yen -). Add: 2-28, Sakurabashidori, Toyama. Tel: (0764) 31-2211.

Daiichi Inn Toyama (in front of Toyama Station). Business. 105 singles (6,500 yen -) & 36 doubles (14,500 yen -). Add: 1-1-1, Sakuracho, Toyama. Tel: (0764) 42-6611.

Toyama Washington Hotel (7 minute walk from Toyama Station). Business. 210 singles (6,500 yen -) & 83 doubles (13,500 yen -). Add: 2-17, Honcho, Toyama. Tel: (0764) 41-7811.

TATEYAMA-KUROBE ALPINE ROUTE

立山黒部アルペンルート

The Tateyama-Kurobe Alpine Route traverses the northern part of the Japan Alps, from Toyama (middle left, Chubu Map 13) to Shinano-Omachi (lower right), utilizing various means of transportation. You can travel either direction. In this section we follow the east-bound travel itinerary.

The Alpine Route is open from the end of April through the beginning of November, depending on the snow conditions of the area. Advance reservations are required.

Toyama to Tateyama 立山. Take the Toyama Chiho Tetsudo Line train from Toyama Station to Tateyama Station. The ride takes about one hour and the fare is 1,010 yen.

Tateyama to Bijodaira 美女平. Tateyama Station is the real beginning of the Alpine Route. A cable car brings you from Tateyama up to Bijodaira in seven minutes (620 yen).

Bijodaira to Murodo 室堂. Buses run from Bijodaira to Murodo on spacious Midagahara Plateau. (A 55-minute ride; 1,630 yen). In May and June the plateau is still covered with thick snow. The huge Murodo bus terminal is a bit of a blot on the spectacular alpine scenery of the area. In this area you can usually see lingering snow until the end of July. Well-maintained pedestrian paths extend from the bus terminal to nearby scenic ponds and "Jigokudani" volcanic hells (a 20-minute walk).

Murodo to Daikanbo 大観峰. Take another bus from Murodo to Daikanbo (A 10-minute ride; 2,060 yen). The bus runs in a tunnel under the Tateyama mountains. The view of the Ushiro-Tateyama mountains from Daikanbo is breathtaking.

Daikanbo to Kurobedaira 黒部平.

Transfer to the steep ropeway from Daikanbo down to Kurobedaira. The ropeway descends 500 meters (1,640 feet) in just 7 minutes (1,240 yen).

Kurobedaira to Kurobeko 黒部湖. Next you take an underground cable car from Kurobedaira down to (Lake) Kurobeko. The 5-minute ride costs 820 yen. There is a 1 km (0.6 mile) long pedestrian path atop Kurobe Dam. The 186 m (610 foot) tall dam falls precipitously into Kurobe ravine on your left. It is amazing that such a huge dam was constructed in this steep ravine.

Kurobe Dam to Ogisawa 扇沢. A trolley bus runs (again, in the tunnel under the Ushiro-Tateyama mountains) from Kurobe Dam to Ogisawa. The ride takes 16 minutes and costs 1,240 yen.

Ogisawa to Shinano-Omachi 信濃大町. Finally, you will take a regular bus on a regular road, from Ogisawa to Shinano-Omachi Station on the JR Oito Line (A 40-minute ride; 1,250 yen). For transportation from Shinano-Omachi to your next destination, please see the Joetsu and Shin-etsu Chapter above.

UNAZUKI AND KUROBE GORGE 宇奈月・黒部峡谷

We recommend arriving in Unazuki late in the day, relaxing at one of the town's many hotspring hotels, and starting for Kurobe Gorge and Keyakidaira early the next morning.

Unazuki (middle center, Chubu Map 13) is the terminus of the Toyama Chiho Tetsudo Railroad. You can catch the Line at Toyama (middle left) or Uozu (upper left), on the JR Hokuriku Honsen Line. The ride takes 1 hour from Toyama and 30 minutes from Uozu (1,550 yen and 760 yen respectively). At Unazuki Station, vans from the *ryokan* of the town line up to meet the incoming trains.

MAP 13   Unazuki and Kurobe Gorge

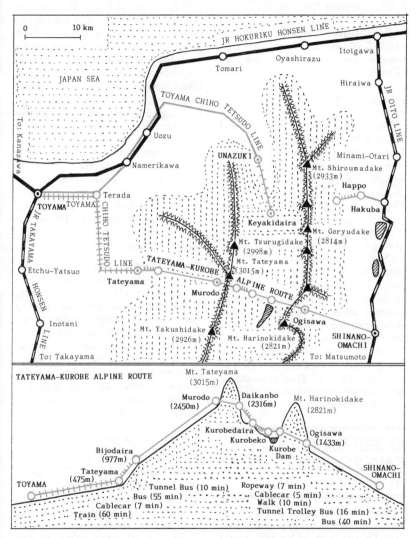

Ryokan in Unazuki

Unazuki Grand Hotel. First Class. 112 rooms. 18,000-25,000 yen per person. Add: 267, Momohara, Unazuki-machi, Toyama Prefecture. Tel: (0765) 62-1111.

Unazuki New Otani Hotel. First Class. 159 rooms. 18,000-25,000 yen per person. Add: 352-7, Unazuki-machi, Toyama Prefecture. Tel: (0765) 62-1041.

Enraku. First Class. 77 rooms. 18,000-

25,000 yen per person. Add: 347-1, Unazu-ki-machi, Toyama Prefecture. Tel: (0765) 62-1211.

Hotel Togen. First Class. 63 rooms. 18,000-22,000 yen per person. Add: 22-1, Unazuki-machi, Toyama Prefecture. Tel: (0765) 62-1131

KUROBE GORGE

The Kurobe Kyokoku Testudo Railroad Station is in a separate building from the Toyama Chiho Tetsudo Station, about 200 meters (656 feet) away. The Kurobe Kyokoku Tetsudo Railroad is a narrow-gauge line, more like a trolley than a train. When you buy your ticket, you'll have the option of an open or enclosed car. The trip along the Gorge to Keyakidaira takes approximately an hour-and-a-half. The route winds along the edge of both sides of the Gorge, slipping in and out of tunnels, over bridges and past huge dams. When you get off the train at Keyakidaira, walk through the station and go down two flights of steps to the hiking path to the Sarutobi Observation Platform, which will be to your left. The walk to Sarutobi takes about 15 minutes. If you don't want to walk, there's an observatory right on the roof of the station. No matter which way you choose to go, the views are breathtaking.

EIHEIJI TEMPLE & CAPE TOJIMBO

永平寺・東尋坊

Two important places of interest are located between Kanazawa and Kyoto. Cape Tojimbo is on the beautiful, rugged Japan Sea coast, and Eiheiji Temple, a bit inland, is still a prosperous training center for Zen priests (middle left, Chubu Map 1).

If you want to visit the Temple and the Cape on your way to Kanazawa from Kyoto/Osaka, take the Keifuku Echizen Line from Fukui to Eiheiji (The train runs about once every hour, and the ride takes 35 minutes. Fare: 710 yen). When you finish your visit to Eiheiji Temple, take a direct bus to Cape Tojimbo (Check the schedule of this bus service as soon as you arrive at Eiheiji Station because there are only four buses daily). The bus ride from Eiheiji Temple to Cape Tojimbo takes about 70 minutes (1,320 yen). After enjoying the view of the Japan Sea, take a bus (which runs frequently) to Awara-Onsen Station (680 yen) to catch a JR train to Kanazawa.

If you travel this route in reverse, from Kanazawa to Kyoto/Osaka, visit Cape Tojimbo first. Then take a bus to Eiheiji Temple. After the visit to the Temple take the Keifuku Echizen Line to Fukui Station and catch the train to Kyoto/Osaka.

Eiheiji Temple 永平寺 Eiheiji Temple, a 10-minute walk from the train station, was founded in 1244 as a Zen monastery. Two hundred monks live there, devoting themselves to Zen training. Visitors, including foreigners, are first guided to a reception hall for a 15-minute (rather tedious) explanation, in Japanese, of the temple's history and features. An English brochure is give to foreigners. Visiting this temple is the best way to understand how Zen training is conducted. The temple is open to the public from 5:00 AM to 4:00 PM. Admission: 400 yen (the tickets are sold in vending machines!).

Cape Tojimbo 東尋坊 The Cape is famous for its pillars of dark greyish andesite. Fifty meter (164 feet) tall cliffs supported by these pillars extend along the Japan Sea coast, creating a beautiful, rugged coastline. A 30-minute sightseeing boat operates frequently from the tip of the Cape. The view of the cliffs from the water is much more impressive than what you'll see staying on land. If your time is limited, take the elevator to the top of Tojimbo Tower.

The observatory is located 100 m (328 feet) above sea level, and commands a wide view of the Cape area. The area is filled with souvenir shops, vendors and restaurants, and is a bit noisy.

JR FARES BETWEEN MAJOR CITIES IN THE CHUBU REGION

1. JR FARES BETWEEN NAGOYA AND OTHER MAJOR CITIES ON THE JR TOKAIDO-SANYO SHINKANSEN

Refer to the JR Tokaido-Sanyo Shinkansen Fare Chart in the Transportation section of the Introduction Chapter above.

2. JR FARES BETWEEN NAGOYA AND MAJOR CITIES IN THE CHUBU REGION

To/From	Nagoya	Remarks
Okazaki	720 yen (40.1 km)	JR Tokaido Honsen Line local train
Iseshi	930 yen (57.5 km)	"Mie" rapid service train
Toba	1,260 yen (71.6 km)	"Mie" rapid service train
Nagiso	3,220 yen (98.9 km)	JR Chuo Saisen Line limited express
Matsumoto	5,750 yen (188.1 km)	JR Chuo Saisen Line limited express
Gero	4,410 yen (97.1 km)	JR Takayama Honsen Line limited express
Takayama	5,750 yen (150 km)	JR Takayama Honsen Line limited express
Toyama	7,300 yen (248.4 km)	JR Takayama Honsen Line limited express

3. JR FARES BETWEEN CITIES ON THE HOKURIKU HONSEN LINE
(Based on limited express trains)

To/From	Fukui	Kanazawa	Toyama	Niigata
Osaka	5,750 yen (190.9 km)	7,300 yen (267.6 km)	8,330 yen (327.1 km)	12,140 yen (581.2 km)
Kyoto	4,720 yen (148.1 km)	6,580 yen (224.8 km)	7,610 yen (284.3 km)	11,310 yen (538.4 km)
Fukui		2,890 yen (76.7 km)	4,410 yen (136.2 km)	9,150 yen (390.3 km)
Kanazawa	2,890 yen (76.7 km)		2,560 yen (59.5 km)	8,120 yen (313.6)
Toyama	4,410 yen (136.2 km)	2,560 yen (59.5 km)		6,990 yen (254.1 km)
Niigata	9,150 yen (390.3 km)	8,120 yen (313.6 km)	6,990 yen (254.1 km)	

KANSAI REGION

関西

The Kansai Region consists of six prefectures — Osaka (a population of 8.5 million), Hyogo (5.4 million), Kyoto (2.5 million), Nara (1.4 million), Shiga (1.2 million) and Wakayama (1.1 million). Kansai is Japan's second largest megalopolis.

It is generally agreed that at the dawn of Japanese history the first "nation" of Japan established its power base in Nara. The first permanent capital was built in Nara in 710, and then moved to Kyoto in 794. Kyoto remained Japan's political and cultural center for 1,100 years, until the Meiji Restoration in 1868. Even when the military governments of the shogun were established in Kamakura (in the 13th century) and in Edo or Tokyo (in the 17th-19th centuries), Kyoto, as the seat of the imperial family, was still considered the heart and soul of the country.

With the Meiji Restoration, the work of modernizing Japan fell to the powerful central government. All societal functions and powers were concentrated in Tokyo, which exercised phenomenal magnetic power, accumulating more and more people and wealth to the Tokyo area. Today that excessive concentration has created tremendous difficulties in the everyday life of Tokyoites, who pay the price for living at the center of Japanese society with smaller residences, long commuting times, overcrowded public transportation, lack of recreational facilities, etc. In addition, because the eyes of all of Japan are focused on Tokyo, universally acknowledging Tokyo culture as the most advanced and the most fashionable, many parts of Japan are losing their local cultures and colors.

The Kansai Region, to some extent, has refused to succumb to the influence of Tokyo. The area's glorious and heroic history has helped the Kansai people to go their own way. The Kansai people, with their strong pride in tradition, consider Tokyo to be a huge conglomeration of less sophisticated "rural" types. They are proud of their Kansai dialect, their way of business, their original arts and crafts, and their refined cuisine. The former imperial towns of Kyoto and Nara are determined to preserve their historic legacies (and the glorious memories attached to them). The former merchant town of Osaka is making efforts to develop as a more human and friendly 21st century city, in contrast to the impersonal efficiency of Tokyo. The port town of Kobe, with its own distinct culture and its own proud history, scoffs at its rival Yokohama, which, in the view of Kobe, has no role other than as a bedroom town for Tokyo.

Many foreign visitors have picked the Kansai Region as their No. 1 priority for their Japanese travel itineraries. We agree.

In this chapter we describe in detail the following eight cities and areas (Refer to Kansai Map 1):

1. **Osaka** (middle center). Japan's "Second City" and the industrial and commercial center of Western Japan. Foreign visitors, with the exception of business travelers, usually omit Osaka from sightseeing itineraries. Compared to the shogun's city of Tokyo (Edo) and the emperor's city of Kyoto, Osaka is known as the people's city. Osaka shows visitors another face of Japan. The Minami district of Osaka, near Namba Station, has extensive traffic-free shopping

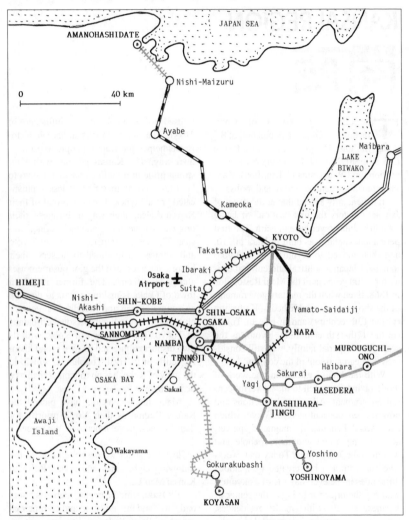

MAP 1 Outline of Kansai

arcades: compared to efficiency-minded Tokyo districts, it is kinder to pedestrians. In addition, many Kansai destinations, including Kyoto and Nara, can be visited easily from Osaka in day excursions. Some parts of Kyoto (Arashiyama) and many Southern Nara destinations are much more easily accessible from Osaka than from Kyoto. Koyasan is also within easy direct reach of Osaka. In short, if you are staying in Osaka, take advantage of the Kansai transportation network centered in Osaka, and explore the off-the-beaten track attractions of the Kansai Region.

2. **Kyoto** (middle right). The world famous historic city. Kyoto was the nation's capital for most of Japanese history. During World War II General MacArthur spared Kyoto from bombing. Though the central part of the city has been modernized, rather characterlessly, many outskirts of Kyoto preserve the city's historic legacies and retain a thoroughly charming atmosphere. We are sad to report that some of Kyoto's beautiful temples revel in the excessive commercialism and greed of a tourist trap town. Nevertheless, Kyoto is definitely Japan's No. 1 tourist city and a never-to-be-missed destination. For the purposes of our description, and to help you organize your time, we have divided Kyoto into six districts: Central, Eastern, Western, Arashiyama, Northern, and Southern. Each of these needs a full day to explore. **Amanohashidate** (upper left), located on the Japan Sea side of Kyoto Prefecture, is known for peaceful marine scenery on a long, pine-clad sandbar. We introduce Amanohashidate as a full-day excursion destination at the end of the Kyoto section.

3. **Nara** (middle right). Japan's oldest capital prospered from the 6th to the 8th centuries. The Nara-Koen Park area (Todaiji Temple and Kasuga Taisha Shrine) is a popular full-day trip destination from Kyoto and Osaka. The southern part of Nara City also has important historic treasures (Horyuji, Toshodaiji and Yakushiji Temples). Consider spending the night in Nara. The southern suburbs of Nara (lower right) are home to several interesting temples and shrines, including Murouji Temple, Hasedera Temple, Yoshinoyama and Kashihara Jingu Shrine. The Kintetsu Railways network makes this area easily accessible from Osaka and Kyoto.

4. **Koyasan** (lower center). Located in an isolated mountain region, Koyasan is a training center for Buddhist priests. Koyasan is also renowned for its *shukubo* (temple lodgings) and *shojin ryori* (vegetarian meals).

5. **Kobe** (middle center). This exotic international port city is a gourmet's paradise, especially famous for its beef. We recommend that you sample this particular tourist attraction, if your budget allows. Kobe is also gaining popularity as an international meeting venue. **Arima-Onsen Hotsprings**, a popular resort of the Kansai people, is described at the end of the Kobe section.

6. **Himeji** (middle left). The city is the proud home of what is generally agreed to be Japan's most elegant and magnificent castle. Himeji is easily visited in a day excursion from Kyoto, Osaka or Kobe. If you are planning a trip to the Inland Sea area (Sanyo Region below), you can easily incorporate a quick stop in Himeji.

7. **Lake Biwako** (upper right). There are several important historic buildings along the shores of Japan's largest lake.

8. **Kii Peninsula** (outside Kansai Map 1). Mountains fall precipitously into the Pacific Ocean at the end of the Kii Peninsula (the southern part of Kansai Region). Mercifully, there is no room for major industrial development in the Kii Peninsula. The area has several scenic hotspring resorts and offers fresh seafood.

Other Major Cities in Kansai

1. Osaka Prefecture

Sakai (middle center, Kansai Map 1). In the Muromachi Era (14th-16th centuries), Sakai was located on the border of three feudal "nations" — Settsu, Izumi and Kawachi. During the Ashikaga Shogunate, Sakai prospered as the nation's trading center under an autonomous government created by the town's merchants and craftsmen. The town, at that time, was also inhabited by foreign traders who sold guns and other Western products to the feudal lords. Sakai today is the heavy industry center and a bedroom town for Osaka, with a population of 800,000. Kansai International Airport is under construction on a man-made island off Sakai. With the completion of the new airport in 1994, Sakai will be a focal point of the new Kansai Region transportation network. It takes only 10 minutes from Osaka's Namba Station to Sakai via the Nankai Honsen Line.

Higashi-Osaka (around Fuse Station, lower center, Kansai Map 2). Adjacent to Osaka, this city has many machinery, metal and plastics factories, both large and small. Population: 498,000.

Toyonaka (middle right, Kansai Map 33). A Osaka bedroom town with a population of 403,000. Senri Life Science Center was completed here in 1992, and the city is promoting governmental and private research institutions related to life science. It takes 15 minutes from Osaka's Hankyu-Umeda Station to Toyonaka via the Hankyu Takarazuka Line.

Hirakata (middle center, Kansai Map 2). Hirakatashi Station on the Keihan Honsen Line is the city's transportation center. Hirakata prospered as a post town on the Tokaido Road in the feudal era. With the construction of numerous condominiums in recent years, the city's population has soared to 388,000. The city is now an education center, with several universities and colleges.

Takatsuki (middle center, Kansai Map 1). A bedroom city located halfway between Osaka and Kyoto. Matsushita Electronics and Sun Star have factories here. Population: 358,000.

Suita (middle center, Kansai Map 1). Just as Tokyo is expanding to the west, Osaka is growing to the north, with more and more rural areas surrendering to urban development. Suita is expected to grow into an Osaka secondary city center. This is where the World Exposition was held in 1970. The city has a population of 335,000. The city has two places of interest. **Hattori Ryokuchi Park** (upper center, Kansai Map 3) features Nihon Minka Shuuraku

Hakubutsukan 日本民家集落博物館 (Japan Folk House Museum), similar to Nihon Minkaen in Kawasaki (See the Kanto Chapter). Eleven traditional houses were moved here from many local areas. Hours: 9:30 AM to 5:00 PM (4:00 PM in winter). Closed on Mondays. Admission: 410 yen. Ryokuchi-Koen Station on the Kita-Osaka Kyuko Line is the stop for the museum. The Subway Midosuji Line operates beyond Esaka (the last stop of the subway) on to the Kita-Osaka Kyuko Line. You can reach Ryokuchi-Koen Station directly from Osaka's two major downtown areas (Umeda and Namba). The ride takes 14 minutes (310 yen) from Umeda, and 21 minutes (340 yen) from Namba. The Park is a 10-minute walk from Ryokuchi-Koen Station. **Banpaku Kinen Koen** 万博記念公園 (Expo Memorial Park, outside Kansai Map 3, to the north) is a spacious park built on the Expo 70 site. The Park contains the National Archeological Museum (10:00 AM to 5:00 PM, Closed on Wednesdays, Admission 360 yen); Expo Land, a playland featuring triple loop jetroller coasters; a Japanese garden laid out by the government for the Expo (9:00 AM to 5:00 PM, Closed on Wednesdays, Admission 210 yen); Cycling Land, a 2.8 km (1.75 mile) long cycling course (9:00 AM to 5:00 PM, Admission: 610 yen including 2 hour bike rental fee), plus Hobby Cycle Grounds featuring a variety of bikes (410 yen for 30 minutes). You can take the Subway Midosuji Line (and its extension onto the Kita-Osaka Kyuko Line) to Senri-Chuo Station, and then connect to Osaka Monorail to Banpaku-Kinen-Koen. It takes about 40 minutes from Osaka downtown.

Yao (lower center, Kansai Map 2). Another Osaka bedroom town with a population of 271,000. The city is promoting manufacturing factories to fill its industrial parks. Sharp Electric is the largest corporate resident of the city.

Neyagawa (middle center, Kansai Map 2). Many tumuli found in this city testify to the development of the area by powerful families at the dawn of Japanese history. With a population of 255,000, Neyagawa now is another Osaka bedroom town. Its train station is called Neyagawashi.

Ibaraki (middle center, Kansai Map 1) prospered as a castle town of the Katagiri clan in the feudal era. Today, Ibaraki is the manufacturing center of Matsushita and Toshiba, as well as an Osaka bedroom town. Yasunari Kawabata, a Nobel Prize novelist, was born here. Population: 250,000.

2. Hyogo Prefecture

Amagasaki (middle right, Kansai Map 33) is the manufacturing center of the Osaka-Kobe Industrial Zone. Mitsubishi Electric and Sumitomo Metal have large factories in the city. Population: 491,000.

Nishinomiya (middle center, Kansai Map 33). With 10 universities and colleges, Nishinomiya is trying to build a reputation as an education center. Many famous sake breweries are located in the city's Nada district. Nishinomiya Baseball Stadium is the home of the professional Hankyu Braves. Koshien Baseball Stadium is the mecca for high school baseball championships. Population: 414,000.

Akashi (outside Kansai Map 33 to the west). Japan's meridian is located in Akashi (plus 9 hours to Greenwich standard time). The eastern part of the city is its industrial zone, including large factories of Kawasaki Heavy Industries and Fujitsu. The city is developing its ocean front into a marine recreation center. Red snappers caught in Akashi Strait are generally considered Japan's best. Population: 272,000.

Kakogawa (outside Kansai Map 33 to the west). An industrial city with a huge Kobe Steel factory. Population: 241,000.

Takarazuka (upper center, Kansai Map 33). A hotspring resort and affluent residential city with a population of 201,000. **Takarazuka Grand Theater** features all female musical revues (daily except Wednesdays). The same type of female revues in Asakusa (Tokyo) are now only a memory, but the Takarazuka Revue is still a popular entertainment in Kansai. **Takarazuka Family Land** is a popular family destination, with a playland, hotspring baths, zoo, and botanical garden (9:00 AM to 5:00 PM, Closed on Wednesdays, Admission: 1,000 yen). The Hankyu Takarazuka Line connects the city with Osaka's Hankyu-Umeda Station. The ride takes 40 minutes.

Itami (middle center, Kansai Map 1). The home of Osaka International Airport. A variety of manufacturing industries are also located in Itami — from sake breweries to computer chip factories.

Ashiya (middle center, Kansai Map 33). Sandwiched between the Rokko mountains to the north and the Inland Sea to the south, Ashiya's beautiful setting has been known throughout history. Today, Ashiya is one of Japan's most luxurious residential cities. One out of every thousand citizens is a yen billionaire. Population: 86,000.

3. Shiga Prefecture

Shigaraki. A small pottery town with a population of 14,000. The town is filled with kilns and pottery shops. Fanciful pottery *tanuki* (raccoon dogs) are the specialty of Shigaraki. It takes 1 hour and 45 minutes by bus from Kyoto (Sanjo Ohashi Bus Terminal) to this pottery town.

KANSAI TRANSPORTATION

Osaka, Kyoto, Kobe and Nara are the major cities of the Kansai Region. These cities are conveniently connected by JR and many other private railways. The JR Tokaido-Sanyo Shinkansan serves Kyoto, Osaka (Shin-Osaka Station) and Kobe (Shin-Kobe Station), making all of these cities easily accessible for tourists. Those with JR Rail Passes can even use the Shinkansen for the short trips between these cities: the trip from Kyoto to Shin-Osaka takes only 16 minutes; the trip from Shin-Osaka to Shin-Kobe is another 15 minutes. Those who don't have Rail Passes and who have to pay train fares will find this entirely too expensive. We therefore are including information on local commuter train lines in this area.

1. Between Osaka and Kobe. Refer to Kansai Map 1 and Kansai Map 33. The JR Kobe Line provides commuter service between Osaka and Nishi-Akashi, via San-nomiya (in Kobe). There is frequent service: every five to ten minutes, and even more frequently in rush hour. The ride from Osaka to Sannomiya takes 36 minutes. The Hankyu Railways Kobe Honsen Line pro-vides parallel service, with trains running frequently (every 10-15 minutes) between Hankyu-Umeda Station in Osaka (near the JR Osaka Station) and Hankyu-Sannomiya Station in Kobe (adjacent to JR Sannomiya Station). Hankyu offers limited express, express and local service on this line. The trip from Osaka to Kobe takes 30-40 min-utes depending on the type of train, and the fare is 280 yen. In addition, the Hanshin Railways operates Osaka-Kobe commuter service. Kansai area residents might find this line convenient.

2. Between Osaka and Kyoto. See Kansai Map 2. Commuter trains run fre-quently on the JR Tokaido-Sanyo Honsen Line between Kyoto and Osaka. The ride from Kyoto takes 41 minutes to Shin-Osaka and an additional 6 minutes to Osaka. If you are headed for Osaka's downtown Namba area, it is easier to transfer to the Subway Midosuji Line at Shin-Osaka (The "Osaka" stop on the subway is Umeda Station, which is connected by underground passage to JR Osaka Station). The Hankyu Railways Kyoto Honsen Line provides service between Hankyu Umeda Station and Kawaramachi Station in downtown Kyoto. Again, Hankyu provides limited express, express and local train service every 5-10 minutes. The ride from Hankyu Umeda Sta-tion in Osaka to Kawaramachi in Kyoto takes 40-65 minutes, depending on the type of train and the fare is 350 yen. The Hankyu Arashiyama Line is a short spur off the Han-kyu Kyoto Honsen Line; it provides service to the Arashiyama area of Kyoto. Trains run about every ten minutes and the ride from Katsura to Hankyu Arashiyama takes 8 min-utes. The fare is 160 yen. The Keihan Hon-sen Line operates between Yodoyabashi in downtown Osaka and Demachiyanagi in eastern Kyoto. Again, there is limited express, express and local service. The ride from Yodoyabashi to Demachiyanagi via Keihan-Sanjo (Kyoto's main bus terminal and the stop for Kyoto's Gion downtown area) takes 50-90 minutes, depending on the type of train. The fare is 360 yen.

3. Between Osaka and Nara. See Kan-sai Map 2. The JR Kansai Honsen Line pro-vides service between these two cities, connecting Tennoji Station in Osaka with JR Nara Station. There is service about every 10 minutes, and the ride takes 40 min-utes. This line is especially convenient for visits to Horyuji Temple, one of Japan's great treasures. The Kintetsu Namba-Nara Line also provides Osaka-Nara service, con-necting Kintetsu Namba Station in Osaka with Kintetsu Nara Station. This line fea-tures special deluxe tourist trains as well as normal commuter trains. This deluxe train operates about once an hour. It travels between Osaka and Nara as a limited express, and the trip takes about 30 minutes. The fare is 480 yen, and there is a 440 yen surcharge for the privilege of riding in luxu-ry. All seats are reserved. The commuter trains on the Kintetsu Namba-Nara Line (express, rapid service and local) connect Osaka and Nara in 35-50 minutes, depend-ing on the type of train. The fare is the basic 480 yen.

4. Between Kyoto and Nara. See Kan-sai Map 2. The JR Nara Line connects Kyoto Station and Nara Station. Rapid ser-vice and local trains are available. The ride

MAP 2 Kyoto/Osaka/Nara Transportation Network

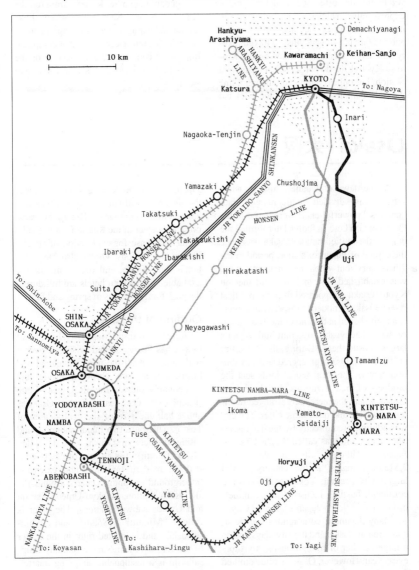

takes 45-60 minutes, depending on the type of train. The Kintetsu Kyoto Line connects Kyoto Station and Kintetsu-Nara Station. Again, this line offers special deluxe limited express trains, which operate about every 30 minutes. The ride takes about 30 minutes and the fare is 540 yen, plus a 440 yen luxury surcharge. Commuter trains on the Kintetsu Kyoto Line do not serve Kintetsu-Nara Station, but rather continue on the main line through Yamato-Saidaiji onto the Kintetsu

Kashihara Line, which provides service further to the south. If you use the Kintetsu commuter line, you have to transfer at Yamato-Saidaiji to another Kintetsu train (on the Kintetsu Namba-Nara Line, which links Osaka and Nara) for the short trip to Kintetsu-Nara Station. Because of this complication, we recommend the JR service or the Kintetsu deluxe service between Kyoto and Nara.

Osaka 大阪

At the dawn of Japanese history, when Japan was divided into many small "nations," powerful clans were based in the Osaka area. These fiefdoms later formed the core of the unified nation. Osaka was once the capital of Japan for a short period in the 7th century, but when a permanent capital was established first in Nara, and then in Kyoto, Osaka disappeared from the political scene. Osaka's modern prosperity as a merchant city began at the end of the 16th century, when Hideyoshi Toyotomi built Japan's largest castle here. During the Edo Era (1603-1868), Osaka prospered as a distribution center. The local feudal lords sent the products of their territories, mainly rice, to Osaka, where the merchants arranged distribution to Edo and other large cities. The city was administered directly by the Tokugawa Shogunate, and was called the "Kitchen of Japan." Although its population of 2,513,000, makes it the country's third largest city (trailing Yokohama), Osaka, a confident, bustling industrial and commercial center, is clearly Japan's "Second City."

Many Japanese corporations are headquartered in Osaka, and the city plays host to a large number of foreign business visitors every year. However, Osaka is often omitted from the itineraries of foreign tourists to

Japan. There is no denying that Osaka lacks the historical and cultural significance that appeals to foreign tourists. But, as the transportation center of the Kansai region, Osaka is an ideal base for exploration of several Kansai destinations. Osaka also has more hotels than Kyoto, and rooms are usually available when Kyoto hotels are full during the peak tourist seasons of spring and fall.

Outline of the City

Refer to Kansai Map 3. The city of Osaka has 26 wards and is spread over a wide area, but all the main municipal and business areas are clustered inside and immediately outside the JR Osaka Kanjo (Loop) Line. The area of Central Osaka is about half the size of the central area of Tokyo. There are two major shopping and eating districts in Osaka. One is called "**Kita**" (North): it is an area of newly constructed modern buildings and extensive underground shopping centers around the JR Osaka Station, Hankyu-Umeda Station and Umeda subway stations. The other is called "**Minami**" (South) and "Shinsaibashi," and is located right in the center of the JR loop (near Namba Station). Shinsaibashi is a fashionable shopping quarter, while Minami is famous for its eating and

MAP 3   Outline of Osaka

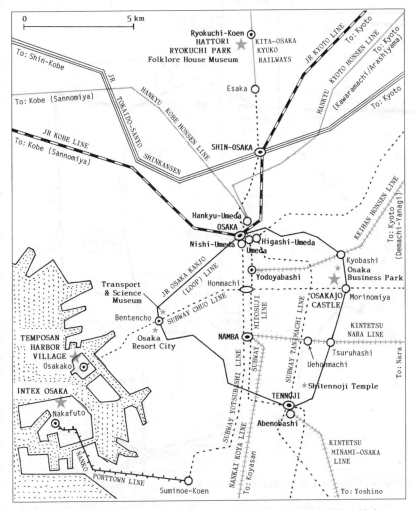

drinking facilities and theaters. Public institutions such as Osaka City Hall and Osaka Festival Hall are located on Nakanoshima island. Many business offices are located in the Osaka Station area, on Nakanoshima Island, and along the Midosuji main boulevard (running to the south from Osaka Sta-

tion). Osaka's two major historical sites are Osakajo Castle and Shitennoji Temple.

Intex Osaka (lower left), the large international trade show center, is located on a man-made island in a new waterfront development area, just outside the JR Loop Line. You can reach Intex via the Subway Yot-

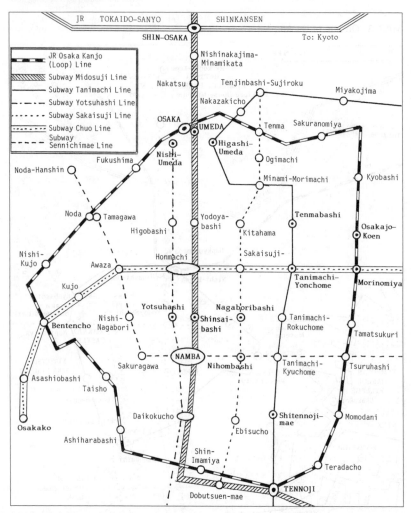

MAP 4 Osaka's Transportation Network

subashi Line. Transfer at Suminoe-Koen, the last stop on the line, to the Nanko Port-town Line, to the last stop, Nakafuto.

Temposan Harbor Village (lower left) is another waterfront development on a man-made island. Reminiscent of Baltimore's Harbor Place, it features a shopping and restaurant complex and an aquarium at the port facility. A 45-minute day cruise around the harbor leaves once an hour. Fare: 1,200 yen. A 2-hour dinner cruise leaves at 7:00 PM. Fare: 2,500 yen.

Hattori Ryokuchi Park (upper center) is a local excursion destination. Its park and preserved houses are described above in the Suita section.

The *i* Information Offices are located in JR Shin-Osaka and JR Osaka Stations.

Transportation in Osaka

Subways We have selected six of Osaka's lines, and indicated them on Kansai Map 4. You will probably use only the Subway Midosuji Line, which connects Shin-Osaka Station (upper center), Umeda Station (upper center, near JR's Osaka Station), Shinsaibashi (middle center), Namba (middle center) and Tennoji (lower right), Osaka's most important stations.

JR Osaka Kanjo (Loop) Line This loop line surrounds the central part of Osaka. Orange-colored trains run every 3-10 minutes and a trip around the whole loop takes about 40 minutes. All the stations on this loop line are pictured on Kansai Map 4.

NORTHERN OSAKA CITY

(Refer to Kansai Map 5)

KITA 北 (Upper left)

The northern part of the city, called "Kita," has tall office buildings and hotels rising into the sky, and complicated shopping malls spread underground. The area is centered around JR's Osaka Station, Hankyu Umeda Station, and Umeda subway station. This is the ultra-modern area of the contemporary city. It is not typical Osaka, and looks more like modern Tokyo.

Hankyu Conglomerate Area features several department stores, shopping malls and office buildings. Hankyu Grand Building, a 32-story modern building, is the main property of this area. It has a free observatory on the 31st floor that commands an extensive view of the city and Osaka Bay. Many restaurants and shops are located on 27th through 31st floors: these four floors are called "Hankyu Sanjunibangai" (Hankyu's 32nd Avenue).

Umeda Chika Center (Underground Shopping Mall) connects Osaka Station and the area's Umeda stations with the major buildings around them. The underground paths are lined with stores, restaurants and coffee shops that are very popular with the business people who work in the area. If you want to explore this labyrinth underground mall, you should leave yourself plenty of time because you're sure to get lost.

JR Osaka Station building itself is a high rise with 27 floors and four basements. The upper floors house department stores, restaurants and shopping arcades.

There are four new office buildings south of Osaka Station. They are numbered No. 1 through No. 4. The 32nd through the 34th floors of **No. 3 Building** house restaurants that command good views of the city.

Kita-Shinchi is Osaka's version of Tokyo's Ginza. It features expensive restaurants and hostess bars patronized by businessmen on fat expense accounts.

Sonezaki has several arcades with movie theaters and inexpensive restaurants, coffee and snack shops and bars.

NAKANOSHIMA 中之島

(middle left to middle center)

Nakanoshima is actually a small island between the Dojimagawa and Tosaborigawa Rivers. **Toyo Toji Museum** 東洋陶磁美術館 displays masterpieces of pottery and ceramics produced in China and Korea in ancient times and collected by the owner of the now bankrupt Ataka conglomerate. Hours: 9:30 AM to 4:30 PM. Closed Mondays. Admission: 400 yen. **Osaka Festival Hall** 大阪 フェスティバルホール is the most prestigious concert hall in Osaka. Many concerts by both Japanese and foreign artists are held here year round.

MAP 5 Downtown Osaka: Kita

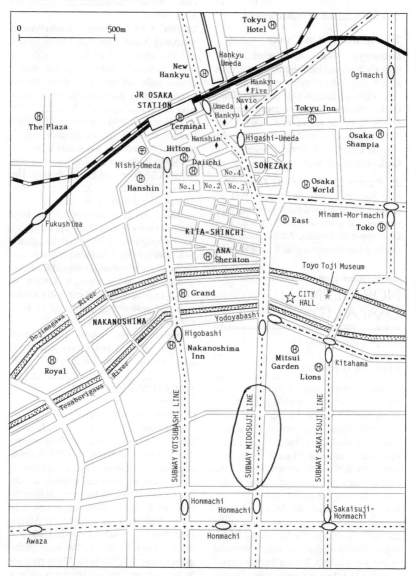

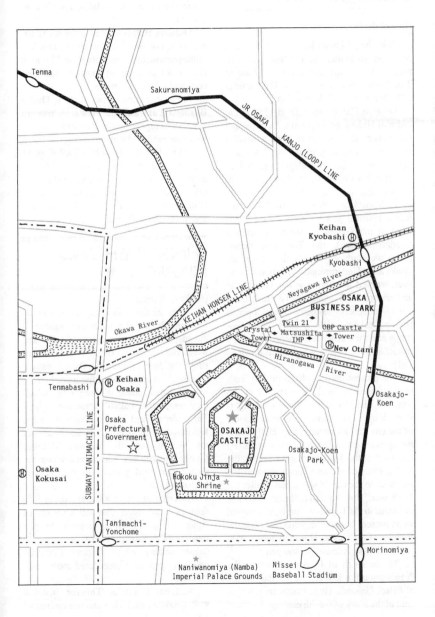

OSAKAJO CASTLE 大阪城

(Lower right)

Take the JR Osaka Kanjo (Loop) Line to Morinomiya Station, or the Subway Tanimachi Line or the Subway Chuo Line to Tanimachi-Yonchome Station. The Castle is a 10-15 minute walk from either.

Osakajo Castle was built in 1585 at the order of Hideyoshi Toyotomi. Even though the modern reconstruction is on a smaller scale than the grand original, the Castle still symbolizes the power Hideyoshi gained by means of his victories over the other feudal lords during the civil wars. After the death of Hideyoshi in 1598, Ieyasu Tokugawa seized political power. With the establishment of the Tokugawa Shogunate in Edo (modern Tokyo), the Toyotomi family realm was reduced to just the immediate Osaka area. Underground movements, however, worked to overthrow the Tokugawas and restore the Toyotomis. To crush these would-be rebels, Ieyasu's troops opened fire on Osakajo Castle in 1614. The Toyotomis and their allies were destroyed in the battle, and the Castle was burned down in 1615.

The present donjon (40 m or 130 feet), reconstructed in 1931, is a replica of the original. The top of the five-roofed eight-story donjon commands an extensive view of the city and its vicinity. Especially fascinating are the Castle's huge rock walls. At the order of the Tokugawa government, the feudal lords of western Japan donated the rocks when the Castle was repaired after the 1615 war. Hokoku Jinja Shrine, which is dedicated to the Toyotomi family, was moved to its present location in 1903 to honor the founder of the Castle. Hours (donjon): 9:00 AM to 4:30 PM. Admission: 400 yen.

To the south of Osakajo Castle is the **Naniwanomiya** 難波宮, the Namba Imperial Palace Grounds. Huge stones are reminiscent of the glory of the 7th century.

Nissei Baseball Stadium 日生球場 is the home of the Kintetsu Buffalos, a professional team.

Osakajo Hall is located at the northeastern corner of the Castle grounds. This is a multi-purpose hall that seats up to 15,000. It is used for a variety of sports events, concerts and large conventions.

Across the Hiranogawa River is **Osaka Business Park** (middle right). Its modern glass skyscrapers house electronic companies (including Matsushita, Fujitsu, Panasonic and KDD). Matsushita IMP displays and sells fashion goods of twelve different countries and features international restaurants. There is a sightseeing boat pier on the Hiranogawa River. The tour takes one hour and the fare is 1,600 yen.

SHINSAIBASHI AND MINAMI 心斎橋・南

(Refer to Kansai Map 6)

There are many shopping arcades in the Shinsaibashi and Minami district (shaded on the map). The arcades are traffic-free and wonderful on rainy days. These arcades show the face of the real Osaka; natives (*Naniwakko*) are proud of the more human, intimate atmosphere of their city, which they compare to Tokyo's impersonal gloss. Three department stores (Daimaru, Sogo and Parco) and modern shops and boutiques are located near the Subway Midosuji Line's Shinsaibashi Station and along the arcade that runs parallel to the Subway Midosuji Line.

America-mura アメリカ村 (upper left) features small stores that sell a variety of American goods, from clothing to pop music CD's. **Europa-mura** ヨーロッパ村 (upper center), which features European goods, is generally considered more fashionable.

National Bunraku Theater 国立文楽 劇場 (middle right). Bunraku is a traditional

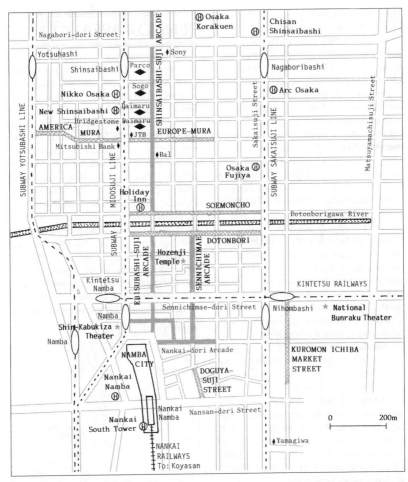

MAP 6   Downtown Osaka: Minami

puppet drama developed to new peaks of achievement in the Edo Era. Each puppet is manipulated by three puppeteers. The delicate movements of the eyes, mouths, fingers and arms of the puppets are sure to fascinate you even if you cannot follow the story exactly. The plays usually feature tragic stories of the feudal era. You can get information at (06) 212-1122, or at your hotel.

There are six runs a year at the National Theater; each lasts for about 20 days.

Streets on both sides of the Dotonbori-gawa River (middle center) — **Soemoncho** to the north, and **Dotonbori** to the south — are the entertainment center of the area. Many theaters as well as restaurants and bars are located here. Dotonbori Street features restaurants that display a gigantic mechanical crab sign, a huge shrimp sign, and a mechanical clown drummer. This area formerly had a reputation of being inexpensive (as compared to Kita-Shinshi), but it has gradually become rather expensive here too.

Shin-Kabukiza Theater 新歌舞伎座 (lower left) stages kabuki once a year in April (for about a 25-day run).

Hozenji Temple 法善寺 (middle center) has only a small hall and is surrounded by restaurants, bars and cabarets. Decorated with many paper lanterns and filled with the smell of incense, the temple is a symbol of traditional Osaka and the people of the city. Visiting the Temple is supposed to be helpful to those in pursuit of true love.

Namba City ナンバシティー (lower center) is a complex of stores and restaurants. Namba Station on the Nankai Koya Line is located in this building.

Doguyasuji Street 道具屋筋 (lower center). Osaka's version of Asakusa's Kappabashi Street, features shops dealing in restaurant utensils, plastic restaurant food samples, lacquerware, happi coats, *noren* curtains, lanterns, etc. It is a good place to find unusual souvenir items.

Kuromon Ichiba Market Street 黒門市場 (lower right) is Osaka's version of Tokyo's Ameya-Yokocho Shopping Street. This arcade houses hundreds of small food stores. It is Osaka's Kitchen.

Nihombashi 日本橋 (lower right, around the area marked Yamagiwa) is Osaka's version of Tokyo's Akihabara. Discount electronic goods shops are the main attraction of this neighborhood.

TENNOJI AREA   天王寺

(Refer to Kansai Map 7)

Shitenoji Temple 四天王寺 (middle right) is a five-minute walk from Shitennoji-mae Station on the Subway Tanimachi Line, and a 15-minute walk from the Tennoji Station of either the JR Osaka Kanjo (Loop) Line or the Subway Midosuji Line. Shitennoji Temple was originally erected in 593 at the order of Prince Shotoku, who later, in 607, had Horyuji Temple in Nara built. Shitennoji is known as the birthplace of Japanese Buddhism. The Temple was ravaged many times by fires and the original buildings were lost. The present concrete buildings were constructed in 1965 and have no historical value. They are, however, arranged according to the original design, and all the major buildings are positioned in a straight line. If you are interested in architecture, Shitennoji Temple is a good place to

MAP 7 Tennoji

study the development of Japanese Buddhist temple design. Hours: 9:00 AM to 5:00 PM. Admission: 200 yen. A flea market is held here on the 21st of every month.

Tennoji-Koen Park 天王寺公園 (middle left). You can visit Tennoji-Koen Park in conjunction with your visit to Shitennoji Temple. The Park is home to the Botanic Garden (Hours: 9:30 AM to 5:00 PM), Tennoji Zoo (Hours: 9:30 AM to 4:00 PM. Admission: 400 yen) and Keitakuen Garden (Hours: 9:30 AM to 5:00 PM. Admission: 500 yen). Keitakuen Garden was originally built by the owner of the Sumitomo conglomerate and later presented to the city of Osaka. The Garden, designed around a pond, is unexpectedly quiet amid the bustle of this great city.

Please note that the JR Tennoji, Subway Tennoji and Kintetsu Abenobashi Stations are connected by underground passages. Kintetsu Abenobashi Station is especially important for visits to destinations in southern Nara. The Tennoji area is developing into Osaka's third "downtown." There are extensive shopping arcades, department stores and other shopping and eating establishments here.

ACCOMMODATIONS

1. Deluxe Hotels in Osaka

ANA Sheraton Hotel (middle left, Kansai Map 5). 530 rooms. Single (18,000 yen -) & Double (30,000 yen -). Add: 1-3-1, Dojimahama, Kita-ku, Osaka. Tel: (06) 347-1112.

Miyako Hotel Osaka (lower right, Kansai Map 8). 608 rooms. Single (17,000 yen -) & Double (28,500 yen -). Add: 6-1-55, Uehonmachi, Tennoji-ku, Osaka. Tel: (06) 773-1111.

Nankai South Tower Hotel Osaka (lower center, Kansai Map 6). 548 rooms. Single (19,500 yen -) & Double (30,500 yen -). Add: 5-1-60, Namba, Chuo-ku, Osaka. Tel: (06) 646-1111.

Hotel New Otani Osaka (middle right, Kansai Map 5). 559 rooms. Single (29,500 yen -) & Double (34,000 yen -). Add: 1-4-1, Shiromi, Higashi-ku, Osaka. Tel: (06) 941-1111.

Osaka Hilton International (upper left, Kansai Map 5). 526 rooms. Single (31,500 yen -) & Double (37,000 yen -). Add: 1-8-8, Umeda, Kita-ku, Osaka. Tel: (06) 347-7111.

Osaka Nikko Hotel (upper left, Kansai Map 6). 640 rooms. Single (18,500 yen -) &

Double (30,000 yen -). Add: 1-3-3, Nishi-Shin-saibashi, Chuo-ku, Osaka. Tel: (06) 244-1111.

Hotel Plaza (upper left, Kansai Map 5). 532 rooms. Single (15,000 yen -) & Double (27,500 yen -). Add: 2-2-49, Oyodo-Mina-mi, Oyodo-ku, Osaka. Tel: (06) 453-1111.

Royal Hotel (middle left, Kansai Map 5). 1,200 rooms. Single (16,000 yen -) & Double (29,500 yen -). Add: 5-3-68, Nakano-shima, Kita-ku, Osaka. Tel: (06) 448-1121.

2. First Class and Standard Hotels in Osaka

Hotel Do Sports Plaza (middle center, Kansai Map 8). 113 singles (11,000 yen -) & 59 doubles (19,000 yen -). Add: 3-3-17, Minami-Senba, Chuo-ku, Osaka. Tel: (06) 245-3311.

Hotel Hanshin (upper left, Kansai Map 5). 177 singles (11,000 yen -) & 62 doubles (19,500 yen -). Add: 2-3-30, Umeda, Kita-ku, Osaka. Tel: (06) 344-1661.

Holiday Inn Nankai Osaka (middle left, Kansai Map 6). 80 singles (16,000 yen -) & 143 doubles (23,000 yen -). Add: 2-5-15, Shinsaibashisuji, Chuo-ku, Osaka. Tel: (06) 213-8281.

Hotel New Hankyu (upper left, Kansai Map 5). 543 singles (12,000 yen -) & 384 doubles (19,000 yen -). Add: 1-1-35, Shiba-ta, Kita-ku, Osaka. Tel: (06) 372-5101.

Osaka Daiichi Hotel (upper left, Kansai Map 5). 226 singles (11,000 yen -) & 247 doubles (21,000 yen -). Add: 1-9-20, Umeda, Kita-ku, Osaka. Tel: (06) 341-4411.

Osaka Grand Hotel (middle left, Kansai Map 5). 329 rooms. Single (12,500 yen -) & Double (23,000 yen -). Add: 2-3-18, Nakanoshima, Kita-ku, Osaka. Tel: (06) 202-1212.

Osaka Kokusai Hotel (lower center, Kansai Map 5). 389 rooms. 133 singles (9,500 yen -) & 256 doubles (18,000 yen -). Add: 2-33, Honchobashi, Chuo-ku, Osaka. Tel: (06) 941-2661.

Osaka Terminal Hotel (upper left, Osaka Map 5). 411 singles (14,000 yen -) &

231 doubles (25,000 yen -). Add: 3-1-1, Umeda, Kita-ku, Osaka. Tel: (06) 344-1235.

Osaka Tokyu Hotel (upper left, Osaka Map 5). 112 singles (15,000 yen -) & 225 doubles (24,000 yen -). Add: 7-20, Chaya-machi, Kita-ku, Osaka. Tel: (06) 373-2411.

Righa Royal Hotel Yotsuhashi (middle center, Kansai Map 8). 125 singles (10,000 yen -) & 16 doubles (19,500 yen -). Add: 1-10-12, Shinmachi, Nishi-ku, Osaka. Tel: (06) 534-1211.

Tennoji Miyako Hotel (lower center, Kansai Map 7). 54 singles (10,000 yen -) & 45 doubles (17,000 yen -). Add: 10-48, Hidenincho, Tennoji-ku, Osaka. Tel: (06) 779-1501.

Toyo Hotel (upper center, Kansai Map 8). 401 singles (16,500 yen -) & 177 doubles (23,000 yen -). Add: 3-16-19, Toyosaki, Oyodo-ku, Osaka. Tel: (06) 372-8181.

3. Business Hotels in Osaka

Arc Hotel Osaka (upper center, Kansai Map 6). 288 singles (7,000 yen -) & 94 doubles (12,000 yen -). Add: 1-19-18, Shi-manouchi, Chuo-ku, Osaka. Tel: (06) 252-5111.

Chisan Hotel Shin-Osaka (upper center, Kansai Map 8). 280 singles (7,000 yen -) & 105 doubles (11,500 yen -). Add: 6-2-19, Nishinakashima, Yodogawa-ku, Osaka. Tel: (06) 302-5571.

Chisan Hotel Shinsaibashi (upper center, Kansai Map 6). 252 singles (8,000 yen -) & 50 doubles (14,000 yen -). Add: 2-4-10, Minami-Senba, Chuo-ku, Osaka. Tel: (06) 263-1511.

East Hotel (middle center, Kansai Map 5). 97 singles (10,500 yen -) & 47 doubles (16,500 yen -). Add: 4-11-5, Nishi-Tenma, Kita-ku, Osaka, Tel: (06) 364-1151.

Hotel Keihan Kyobashi (middle right, Kansai Map 5). 190 singles (8,500 yen -) & 24 doubles (15,500 yen -). Add: 2-1-38, Higashi-Nodacho, Miyakojima-ku, Osaka. Tel: (06) 353-0321.

Hotel Keihan Osaka (middle center,

MAP 8 Hotels in Osaka

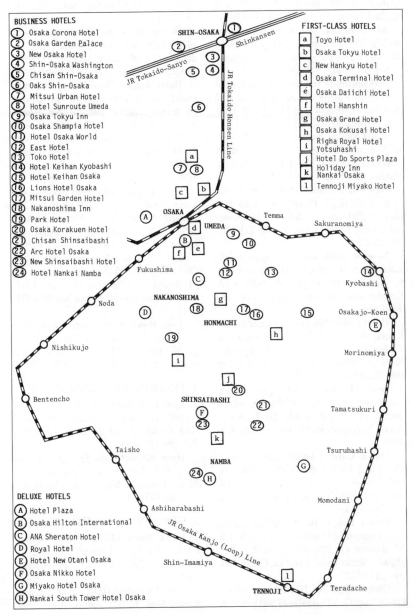

BUSINESS HOTELS
1. Osaka Corona Hotel
2. Osaka Garden Palace
3. New Osaka Hotel
4. Shin-Osaka Washington
5. Chisan Shin-Osaka
6. Oaks Shin-Osaka
7. Mitsui Urban Hotel
8. Hotel Sunroute Umeda
9. Osaka Tokyu Inn
10. Osaka Shampia Hotel
11. Hotel Osaka World
12. East Hotel
13. Toko Hotel
14. Hotel Keihan Kyobashi
15. Hotel Keihan Osaka
16. Lions Hotel Osaka
17. Mitsui Garden Hotel
18. Nakanoshima Inn
19. Park Hotel
20. Osaka Korakuen Hotel
21. Chisan Shinsaibashi
22. Arc Hotel Osaka
23. New Shinsaibashi Hotel
24. Hotel Nankai Namba

FIRST-CLASS HOTELS
a. Toyo Hotel
b. Osaka Tokyu Hotel
c. New Hankyu Hotel
d. Osaka Terminal Hotel
e. Osaka Daiichi Hotel
f. Hotel Hanshin
g. Osaka Grand Hotel
h. Osaka Kokusai Hotel
i. Righa Royal Hotel Yotsuhashi
j. Hotel Do Sports Plaza
k. Holiday Inn Nankai Osaka
l. Tennoji Miyako Hotel

DELUXE HOTELS
A. Hotel Plaza
B. Osaka Hilton International
C. ANA Sheraton Hotel
D. Royal Hotel
E. Hotel New Otani Osaka
F. Osaka Nikko Hotel
G. Miyako Hotel Osaka
H. Nankai South Tower Hotel Osaka

Kansai Map 5). 272 singles (7,000 yen -) & 62 doubles (12,000 yen -). Add: 1-2-10, Tanimachi, Chuo-ku, Osaka. Tel: (06) 945-0321.

Mitsui Urban Hotel (upper center, Kansai Map 8). 342 singles (8,500 yen -) & 66 doubles (17,000 yen -). Add: 3-18-8, Toyosaki, Kita-ku, Osaka. Tel: (06) 374-1111.

Nakanoshima Inn (middle left, Kansai Map 5). 225 singles (8,500 yen -) & 117 doubles (13,500 yen -). Add: 1-13-10, Edobori, Nishi-ku, Osaka. Tel: (06) 447-1122.

Hotel Nankai Namba (lower left, Kansai Map 6). 178 singles (7,000 yen -) & 36 doubles (12,000 yen -). Add: 1-17-11, Namba, Naniwa-ku, Osaka. Tel: (06) 649-1521.

New Osaka Hotel (upper center, Osaka Map 8). 229 singles (7,500 yen -) & 65 doubles (15,500 yen -). Add: 5-14-10, Nishinakashima, Yodogawa-ku, Osaka. Tel: (06) 305-2345.

New Shinsaibashi Hotel (upper left, Kansai Map 6). 228 singles (8,000 yen -) & 65 doubles (10,000 yen -). Add: 1-19, Sayamotocho, Nishi-ku, Osaka. Tel: (06) 444-0809.

Hotel Oaks Shin-Osaka (upper center, Kansai Map 8). 216 singles (7,000 yen -) & 48 doubles (12,000 yen -). Add: 1-11-34, Nishinakashima, Yodogawa-ku, Osaka. Tel: (06) 302-5141.

Osaka Corona Hotel (upper center, Osaka Map 8). 76 singles (6,500 yen -) & 50 doubles (12,000 yen -). Add: 1-3-21, Nishi-Awaji, Yodogawa-ku, Osaka. Tel: (06) 323-3151.

Osaka Garden Palace (upper center, Osaka Map 8). 191 singles (7,000 yen -) & 105 doubles (12,500 yen -). Add: 1-3-35, Nishi-Miyahara, Yodogawa-ku, Osaka. Tel: (06) 396-6211.

Osaka Fujiya Hotel (middle center, Osaka Map 6). 131 singles (7,000 yen -) & 48 doubles (13,500 yen -). Add: 2-2-2, Higashi-Shinsaibashi, Chuo-ku, Osaka. Tel: (06) 211-5522.

Osaka Korakuen Hotel (upper center, Osaka Map 6). 143 singles (9,500 yen -) &

49 doubles (16,500 yen -). Add: 2-12-22, Minami-Senba, Chuo-ku, Osaka. Tel: (06) 251-2111.

Osaka Tokyu Inn (upper center, Osaka Map 5). 250 singles (11,000 yen -) & 148 doubles (18,000 yen -). Add: 2-1, Doyamacho, Kita-ku, Osaka. Tel: (06) 315-0109.

Hotel Osaka World (upper center, Osaka Map 5). 138 singles (6,000 yen -) & 64 doubles (10,500 yen -). Add: 1-5-23, Sonezaki, Kita-ku, Osaka. Tel: (06) 361-1100.

Park Hotel (middle center, Osaka Map 8). 88 singles (6,000 yen -) & 65 doubles (10,000 yen -). Add: 1-19, Tsukamotocho, Nishi-ku, Osaka. Tel: (06) 444-0809.

Shin-Osaka Washington Hotel (upper center, Osaka Map 8). 370 singles (9,500 yen -) & 121 doubles (18,000 yen -). Add: 5-5-15, Nishinakashima, Yodogawa-ku, Osaka. Tel: (06) 303-8111.

Hotel Sunroute Umeda (upper center, Osaka Map 8). 165 singles (8,000 yen -) & 41 doubles (16,500 yen -). Add: 3-9-1, Toyosakicho, Kita-ku, Osaka. Tel: (06) 373-1111.

Toko Hotel (middle center, Osaka Map 5). 263 singles (7,000 yen -) & 38 doubles (13,500 yen -). Add: 1-3-19, Minamimorimachi, Kita-ku, Osaka. Tel: (06) 363-1201.

4. Hotels near Osaka Airport

Osaka Airport Hotel. 36 singles (11,000 yen -) & 67 doubles (18,000 yen -). Add: Osaka Airport Building, Toyonaka. Tel: (06) 855-4621

Hotel Airport Fuji. 55 singles (7,000 yen -) & 29 doubles (12,000 yen -). Add: 1-24-1, Hotaruike-Nishimachi, Toyonaka. Tel: (06) 843-8811.

5. Welcome Inns in Osaka

Lions Hotel Osaka (middle center, Kansai Map 5). 204 rooms. Add: 2-2-15, Koraibashi, Chuo-ku, Osaka. Tel: (06) 201-1511.

Mitsui Garden Hotel (middle center, Kansai Map 5). 371 rooms. Add: 2-5-7,

Koraibashi, Chuo-ku, Osaka. Tel: (06) 223-1131.

Osaka Shampia Hotel (upper center, Osaka Map 5). 299 rooms. Add: 6-23, Nansencho, Kita-ku, Osaka. Tel: (06) 312-5151.

Hotel Hokke Club (10 minute walk from JR Osaka Station). 149 Western & 98 Japanese rooms. Add: 12-19, Toganocho, Kita-ku, Osaka. Tel: (06) 313-3171.

Ebisuso Ryokan (4 minute walk from Ebisucho Station on the Subway Sakaisuji Line). 11 Japanese rooms. Add: 1-7-33. Nihombashi-Nishi, Naniwa-ku, Osaka. Tel: (06) 643-4861.

Kyoto 京都

The fertile land between the Kamogawa and Katsuragawa Rivers has been inhabited since the pre-historic era, and Emperor Kammu chose the area as his capital in 794. Kyoto, the "Seat of the Emperor," was laid out in a Chinese-style grid, with broad streets running east to west, and avenues north to south. During the civil wars of the 15th and 16th centuries, Kyoto was the scene of almost constant violence, and many of the city's cultural treasures were destroyed. When Hideyoshi Toyotomi finally succeeded in unifying the nation at the end of the 16th century, Kyoto was rebuilt. Modern Kyoto retains many of the structures and much of the charm of that era, and is today the home of more than 200 Shinto shrines, 1,500 Buddhist temples, and many other buildings of historical significance such as Nijojo Castle, Kiyomizudera Temple, Sanjusangendo Hall, Ryoanji Temple and the old Imperial Palace. It is also the home of several major museums, including the Kyoto National Museum. Today the city's population stands at 1,401,000.

Outline of the Area

Higashi-oji-dori Street on the east, Nishi-oji-dori Street on the west, Kujo-dori Street on the south and Kita-oji-dori Street on the north are the boundaries of central Kyoto (shaded on Kansai Map 9). Central Kyoto is only about half the size of central Tokyo.

Many of Kyoto's most interesting and important sites are located far beyond this core area. Careful advance planning is therefore essential if you want to make the best use of your valuable time and money.

Suggested Itineraries

The itineraries that follow allocate one day for Central Kyoto, two days for Eastern Kyoto, one day each for Western Kyoto, Arashiyama and Northern Kyoto (for a total of six days). Southern Kyoto also has several interesting destinations, and we have described several places of interest at the end of this chapter as supplemental destinations for an extra day.

Central Kyoto is outlined first, followed by Eastern Kyoto, Western Kyoto, Arashiyama and Northern Kyoto. This order is designed to promote easy understanding of the layout of the city for those who read this guide, but does not reflect destination priorities. We suggest that you spend your time in Kyoto as follows:

- If you have only one day: Visit Eastern Kyoto. Choose either one of the two-day itineraries.

- If you have two days: Add Western Kyoto.

- If you have three days: Add Central Kyoto.

- If you have four days: Add Arashiyama.

- If you have five days: Add Northern Kyoto

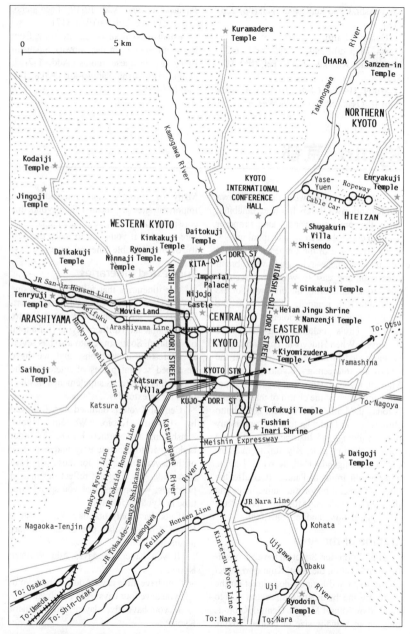

MAP 9 Outline of Kyoto

- If you have six days: Congratulations! Follow all itineraries as written.

- If you have more than six days: Add "Other Places of Interest."

Special Permissions

Katsura Detached Villa, Shugakuin Detached Villa, and Sento Gosho Imperial Palace all have excellent reputations, and visitors must apply at least a month in advance to the Imperial Household Agency for permission to visit them. Visitors must be over 20, and groups cannot be larger than four persons. Applications are accepted one to three months in advance. Application forms are available from the Imperial Household Agency itself, at the Tourist Information Centers in Tokyo, Kyoto and at Narita, as well as at the overseas offices of JNTO. They must be filled out and mailed to the Imperial Household Agency in Kyoto. If you persevere through this complicated process, and are lucky enough to be granted permission to visit these places, there is no admission charge. Tours, however, are only in Japanese. Tour times are set and you cannot change the admission time you are assigned. Tour times are as follows: Katsura Imperial Villa: 10:00 AM and 2:00 PM; Shugakuin Imperial Villa: 9:00 AM, 10:00 AM, 11:00 AM, 1:30 PM and 3:00 PM; Sento Imperial Palace: 11:00 AM and 1:30 PM. Personally, we feel that although these "special" places are worth visiting, they are not so special that you should make them a top priority. They are only some of the many impressive structures and lovely gardens of Kyoto.

Another temple in the southwestern portion of the city, Saihoji, has the same kind of reputation as Katsura Detached Villa and the others described above — and the same sort of requirements. Popularly called Kokedera, or Moss Temple, Saihoji Temple does have a lovely garden, but permission to visit can only be obtained by means of advance application to the Temple by mail (Saihoji Temple, 56 Matsuo Kamigaya-cho, Nishikyo-ku, Kyoto 615). If you are applying from abroad, you must state your full name, age, address, nationality and occupation as well as the date of your proposed visit. It is wise to include alternate dates, because the Temple is sometimes closed for religious ceremonies. You must also enclose international postal coupons to cover return postage. Tour times are at 10:00 AM and 1:00 PM. Once permission is obtained, you must make your visit at the time set by the Temple. All visitors to the Temple are required to listen to a one hour lecture — in Japanese only — before they are allowed to see the garden, and are expected to make a donation of 3,000 yen before they leave.

Nishi-Honganji Temple in Central Kyoto also has restricted entrance policies. Permission to enter the Temple's Daishoin Hall is difficult to obtain. Each of the many sections of Daishoin Hall has elegant paintings, carvings and other 16th century decorations. Potential visitors must send a postcard 7-10 days in advance to request permission to join a tour. Address: Nishi-Honganji Temple, Shimogyo-ku, Kyoto. Telephone: (075) 371-5181. Applications must be in Japanese.

Major Buses and the Subway in Kyoto

This section outlines the major bus networks and the subway. Refer to Kansai Map 10, but be aware that it is not drawn to scale: in relationship to its north-south axis, the east-west axis is about twice the size it should be.

Specific instructions on buses, the subway and trains to be used during your visit to Kyoto are included with the descriptions of each destination.

There is only one subway line in the city. It runs between Takeda Station, south of JR Kyoto Station, and Kitayama Station in the northern part of the city. In the central part

MAP 10 Kyoto's Transportation Network

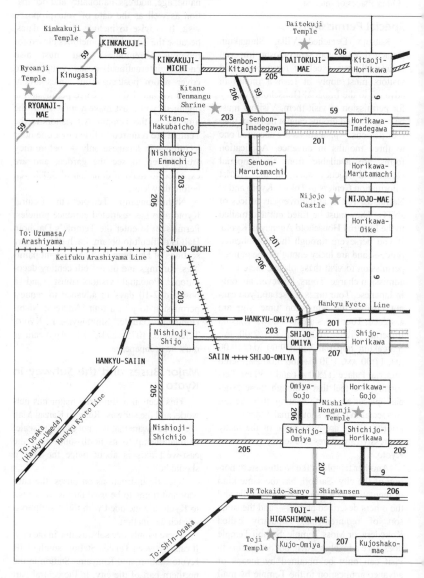

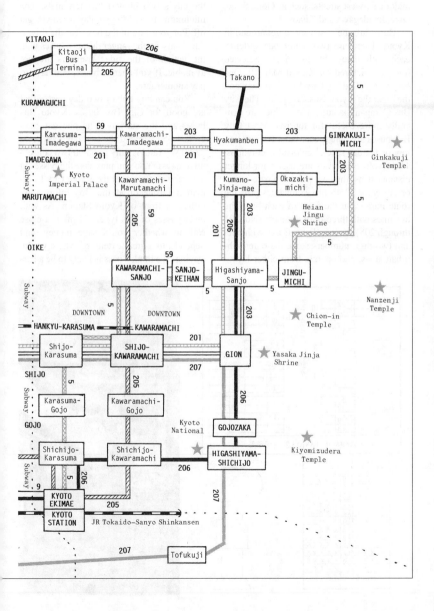

of Kyoto, the subway runs under Karasuma-dori Street, connecting Kyoto Station with major east-west streets, such as Gojo, Shijo, Oike, Imadegawa and Kitaoji.

Buses are the best way to get around in Kyoto. There are two major bus systems, each with many different lines. Selected lines are pictured on Kansai Map 10. One system is called the City Bus Company and the other the Kyoto Bus Company. The City Bus Company is large and its lines are generally more useful for tourists. Most City Bus buses are pale green, but a few are yellow or feature special colorful decorations. The Kyoto Bus buses are useful for longer distance trips: they are painted a pale brown or tan color. Both bus companies post the route number at the front of each bus. The bus lines with three-digit numbers (No. 201 through 208) are loop lines. Buses with one- and two-digit numbers serve the outer suburban areas, and operate from either Kyoto

Station (Kyoto-Ekimae, lower center, Kansai Map 10) or Sanjo-Keihan (middle right), the city's two biggest bus terminals. The minimum fare is 180 yen. Pay when you get off. Put your fare in the box near the driver. Fares vary on the longer distance buses with the length of the ride. Transfers are not available. If you change buses, you have to pay another fare.

You can buy one or two day passes that are good for City Bus buses, Kyoto Bus buses and the subway. The one day pass costs 1,050 yen and the two day pass costs 2,000 yen (and is only good on two consecutive days). You can purchase the passes at any subway station, at the Kyoto City Information Office or at the Bus Information Office in front of Kyoto Station. As with most passes of this type, it's often a close call on whether you'll save money, and depends, to a great extent, on where you're staying. We think a pass is likely to be a bar-

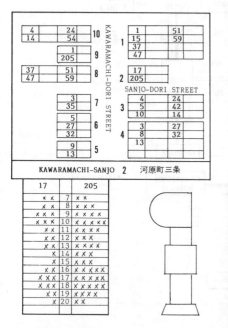

gain if you're following the complete Western Kyoto itinerary and hopping on and off buses all day, or if you're traveling great distances to the southwestern part of the city.

The Chart on the previous page is an exact copy of the chart at Kawaramachi-Sanjo, the busiest bus stop in Kyoto. Other bus stops are much simpler. The signs for City Bus buses are now often posted on four-sided columns by the bus stops, but used to be on flag-shaped signs (you'll still find a few of these), contrasting with the

MAP 11 Outline of Kyoto's Core

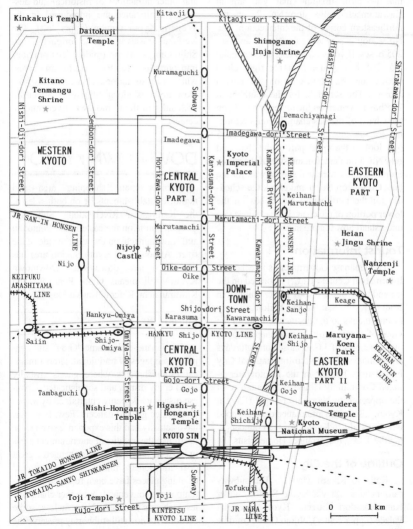

Kyoto Bus signs, which have round tops. As shown on the Chart, the name of the stop is written in both Japanese and English. The upper part of each bus stop chart ("A" on the Chart) shows your present location and the location of the other bus stops with the same name (there are 10 stops named Kawaramachi-Sanjo). Imagine that you are at Kawaramachi-Sanjo stop No. 2, on the northeastern corner of the intersection. The No. 2 stop is served by the No. 17 and No. 205 buses. If you want to take a southbound No. 205 bus, you are in the right place (Remember that traffic is on the left in Japan!). The schedule for the southbound 205 bus is written on the lower part ("B" on the Chart) of the bus chart. If you are looking for the stop for the northbound No. 5 bus, look at the upper part of the chart and find No. 5 on the left-hand side of the street. Stop No. 6 is where you should wait for the bus. Go to stop No. 6 and check the schedule for the northbound No. 5 bus on the lower portion of the chart. It's easy once you understand how it's organized.

Tourist Information

The Japanese Government's free Tourist Information Center (T.I.C.) is located on the ground floor of the Kyoto Tower building in front of Kyoto Station. The building is easy to find thanks to the distinctive (and, in the view of many, ugly) candle-shaped tower that sits atop it. T.I.C. is closed on Saturdays and Sundays. The Kyoto International City Foundation, housed in the Kyoto International Community House at the entrance of the approach to Nanzenji Temple (Eastern Kyoto), also has an information desk and good free materials. In Kyoto, it is the Foundation, not the T.I.C., that arranges Home Visits.

Outline of the City

Refer to Kansai Map 11. The subway runs north/south via Kyoto Station, under Karasuma-dori Street. Kyoto Imperial Palace (upper center), Nijojo Castle (middle center), Nishi-Honganji Temple and Higashi-Honganji Temple (lower center) will be introduced in the Central Kyoto section below. Major temples and shrines as well as several museums are introduced in the Eastern Kyoto section below (middle right). Daitokuji Temple, Kinkakuji Temple and other attractions of historical and aesthetic significance are introduced in the Western Kyoto section (upper left). The Keifuku-Arashiyama Line originating at Shijo-Omiya Station (middle left) provides transportation to the Arashiyama area, which is also introduced below. Kyoto's Downtown is along Shijo-dori Street on both sides of the Kamogawa River (middle center).

DOWNTOWN KYOTO

Kyoto's main shopping area and nightlife establishments lie on both sides of the Kamogawa River along Shijo-dori Street. Gion is on the eastern and Pontocho and Kawaramachi on the western side of the river. Although the Kyoto Station area has become a new downtown, "Downtown Kyoto" still means Gion, Pontocho and Kawaramachi. Refer to Kansai Map 12.

GION　祇園

For Japanese, the name "Gion" still conjures up images of traditional, almost magical establishments where guests (usually men) enjoy drinks and sophisticated Japanese dishes while being entertained by *maiko* (apprentice geisha) dancers. Few, however, have actually had this experience. And Gion itself, like the traditional entertainment areas in most Japanese cities, has changed a great deal in modern times: many traditional drinking places have been replaced by contemporary, convenient, but rather characterless cabarets and bars. Nevertheless, some sections of Gion still stubbornly preserve the atmosphere of the ancient capital, and the area still features many good restaurants, which are slightly more expensive than those on the other side of the Kamogawa River. Gion is a great place for a leisurely evening stroll and a good dinner.

Strolling in Gion

The southern part of Hanamikoji-dori Street (lower right) between Shijo-dori Street and Gion Corner is lined with traditional buildings with wooden lattice windows and lanterns at their entrances. Walking here will give you a taste of what the old entertainment quarters were like. **Shin-Monzen-dori Street** 新門前通り, between Nawate-dori Street and Hanamikoji-dori Street (middle right), is a street of crowded wooden houses, most of which house art and antique shops. English is spoken at many of these shops. They are generally open from 9-10 AM to 5-6 PM. This street is a must for anyone interested in good antiques or authentic backstreet atmosphere. Don't expect any amazing bargains here. **Kasagen** (lower right, on Shijo-dori Street), another good place to look for souvenirs, specializes in traditional paper umbrellas. **Kyoto Craft Center** (lower right) is another good source of handcrafted souvenirs.

Theaters

Minamiza Theater 南座 (lower center, just east of the Kamogawa River) is the oldest theater in Japan. During the feudal era, entertainers, whose social status was very low, performed in public on the dry bed of the Kamogawa River. When kabuki was created, in the early part of the Edo era, it was first performed there as well. The new drama became so popular with the general public in Kyoto that Japan's first permanent theater was established where Minamiza Theater stands today. There are three or four kabuki programs at Minamiza Theater each year (each run lasts 20-25 days).

Gion Kaburenjo Theater 祇園歌舞練場

(lower right) is a training center for the *maiko* of the Gion area. For more than a century, a public dance performance has been given each April.

Gion Corner ギオンコーナー is a small theater (250 seats) attached to Gion Kaburenjo Theater. It was specially designed to introduce foreign tourists to a variety of traditional Japanese arts. Gion Corner is not the place to go if you expect high artistic standards, but it does allow you to sample a bit of everything, including Japanese dance, *bunraku* puppet theater, *gagaku* court dance and music, tea ceremony, etc. The theater is open from March 1 through November 29 daily, except for August 16. Two performances are presented each evening: the first at 7:40 and the second at 8:40. Admission: 2,500 yen.

Restaurants

Kikusui (lower right) is a Western restaurant in a four-story building. The restaurant grill on the first floor is reasonable. The dining room on the second floor is elegant and more expensive. Au Bec Fin Opera (lower right) is a very expensive French restaurant. Izutsu and Mikaku (middle right) are both steak restaurants. The former is rather Westernized, while the latter is a Japanese-style steak restaurant that also serves *sukiyaki* and *shabu-shabu*. Both expensive. Nawate Toriyasu (middle right) is a moderate Japanese restaurant that features *yakitori, sukiyaki* and *shabu-shabu*. Torishige (middle right) specializes in chicken dishes (moderate). Belle Epoche (middle right) is an expensive Japanized French restaurant. Maharaja Gion (middle right) and Maharaja (lower right) are discos. Shanao (middle right) is a moderate Chinese restaurant. Mitoko and Junidanya (lower right) are authentic Japanese restaurants (expensive). Tengiku (lower right) is an expensive counter-style tempura restaurant. Arco Iris (lower right) is a moderate Spanish restaurant.

MAP 12 Downtown Kyoto

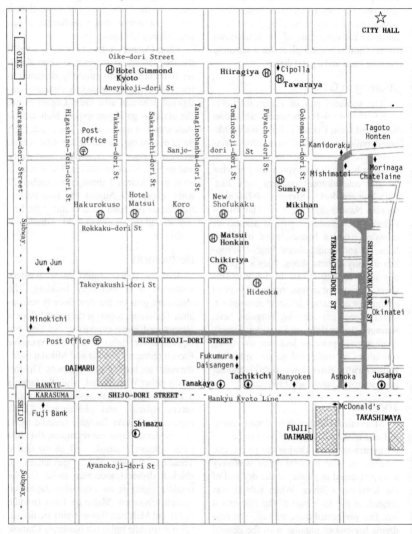

☆
CITY HALL

OIKE

Oike-dori Street

⊕ Hotel Gimmond
Kyoto
Aneyakoji-dori St

Hiiragiya ⊕

♦Cipolla
⊕ Tawaraya

Karasuma-dori-Street

Higashino-Toin-dori St

Post
Office
⊕

Takakura-dori St

Sakaimachi-dori St

Sanjo-

Yanaginobanba-dori St

Tominokoji-dori St

dori   St

Fuyacho-dori St

Gokomachi-dori St

Kanidoraku ♦

Tagoto
Honten
♦

Subway

Hakurokuso
⊕

Hotel
Matsui
⊕

Koro
⊕

New
Shofukaku
⊕

⊕
Sumiya

Mishimatei ♦

Mikihan
⊕

Morinaga
Chatelaine

Rokkaku-dori St

⊕ Matsui
Honkan

Jun Jun
♦

Chikiriya
⊕

TERAMACHI-DORI ST

SHINKYOGOKU-DORI ST

Takoyakushi-dori St

♦
Hideoka ⊕

Minokichi
♦

Okinatei
♦

Post Office ⊕

NISHIKIKOJI-DORI STREET

⊠
DAIMARU ⊠

Fukumura ♦
Daisangen ♦

Tanakaya ⊙

Tachikichi
⊙

Manyoken
♦

Ashoka
♦

Jusanya
⊙

HANKYU-
KARASUMA

-   - SHIJO-DORI STREET - - Hankyu Kyoto Line - - - - -

SHIJO

Fuji Bank

Shimazu
⊙

FUJII-
DAIMARU

♦ McDonald's
TAKASHIMAYA
⊠

Subway

Ayanokoji-dori St

KAWARAMACHI　河原町

Strolling in Kawaramachi

The intersection of Kawaramachi-dori and Shijo-dori streets (lower center) is Kyoto's version of the Ginza. Three large department stores, **Hankyu**, **Takashimaya** and **Fujii Daimaru**, and modern as well as traditional specialty shops line Shijo-dori Street. **Jusanya** (lower center, near the entrance to Shinkyogoku) deals in all sorts

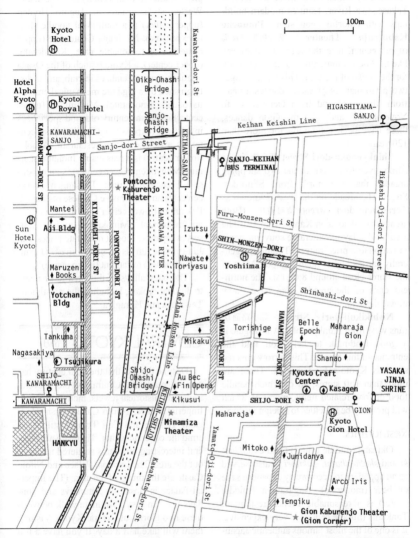

of exotic combs and hair ornaments. **Tachikichi** (lower center) is the main store of a famous Kiyomizu-yaki pottery chain. **Tanakaya** (lower center) specializes in clay Kyoto dolls. **Shimazu** (lower left) is another doll store. **Tsujikura** (lower center) deals in traditional umbrellas and lanterns. Northeast of the main intersection are Pontocho-dori Street and Kiyamachi-dori Street, two more of Kyoto's typical nightlife areas. **Pontocho-dori Street** 先斗町通り has more old buildings, while **Kiyamachi-dori Street**

木屋町通り, which runs along the narrow Takasegawa River, features modern buildings with colorful neon signs. **Pontocho Kaburenjo Theater** 先斗町歌舞練場 (upper center, near the Kamogawa River), like the Gion Kaburenjo, is a training center for the *maiko* of the area. This theater stages two performances of *maiko* dances a year, from May 1-24 and from October 15 to November 7, and, like the Gion dances, these have been a tradition for more than 120 years.

Shinkyogoku-dori Street 新京極 is the name given to eastern of the two shopping arcades that run north from Shijo-dori Street. The arcade on the west is known as **Teramachi-dori Street** 寺町通り (Both arcades are shaded on Kansai Map 12). The arcades display innumerable souvenir items in reasonable price ranges. Teramachi generally carries higher quality goods. Most of the stores close around 8:00 PM. The northern ends of the arcades also have many movie theaters.

Nishikikoji-dori Street 錦小路通り runs west from Shinkyogoku. A *torii* gate is a good landmark to help you find the entrance to this arcade. This narrow covered street is Kyoto's food market. There are more than 150 stores, all of which handle food or food-related items, many of which will probably be novelties to foreign visitors.

Restaurants

Okinatei (middle center) features *sukiyaki* and *shabu-shabu*. *Yakitori* is also served as an appetizer to accompany Japanese sake or beer (moderate). Nagasakiya (middle center) is a reasonable French restaurant. Tankuma (middle center) is very expensive. It is one of the most famous authentic Japanese restaurants in Kyoto. Yotchan Building (middle center) is a restaurant building housing coffee shops, a spaghetti shop, a French restaurant and a Chinese restaurant. Aji Building (literally "Taste Building") (middle center) is another restaurant complex. Mantei (middle center) is a reasonable Western-style restaurant. Tagoto Honten (upper center) is a traditional noodle shop (inexpensive). Morinaga Chatelaine (upper center) is a reasonable cafe. Kanidoraku (upper center), a Kyoto branch of the Osaka establishment, specializes in crab, and is distinguished by a gigantic mechanical crab on its outside (moderate). Mishimatei (upper center) is over a century old, and specializes in *sukiyaki* (expensive). Cipolla (upper center) is a deluxe Italian restaurant. Ashoka (lower center) is a reasonable Indian restaurant. Manyoken (lower center) is an expensive French restaurant. Daisangen (lower center) is an inexpensive Chinese restaurant. Fukumura (lower center) is a moderate Italian restaurant. Minokichi (middle left) serves Japanese food at moderate prices. Jun Jun (middle left) is an *okonomiyaki* (Japanese omelettes) restaurant (inexpensive).

The back alleys of this area have many traditional ryokan, including the prestigious Tawaraya and Hiiragiya.

CENTRAL KYOTO 洛中

Despite the fact that the 20th century has put its mark on Central Kyoto, several important historical jewels, including Kyoto Imperial Palace, Nijojo Castle, Nishi-Honganji Temple and Toji Temple still stand amid the concrete welter. There are also several interesting museums scattered throughout the area. The Imperial Palace and Nijojo Castle are the musts of the area. (The Imperial Palace is closed on Saturdays and Sundays.) It's an easy 15-minute walk between these two glories of Central Kyoto. Visiting them will take half a day. If you have a full day for Central Kyoto, select one or two of the other destinations introduced below.

Kyoto Imperial Palace 京都御所 (Upper right, Kansai Map 13)

Even though Japanese must apply in

advance for permission to visit the Imperial Palace, foreign visitors are accorded special privileges (if the party does not exceed 10 persons). However, there are rules: foreign visitors are only admitted if they arrive at the office of the Imperial Household Agency in the Palace grounds by 9:40 AM and have passports to prove nationality.

Take the subway to Imadegawa Station or a bus to Karasuma-Imadegawa stop. The 50-minute guided tour starts at 10:00 AM at Seishomon Gate. An afternoon English guided tour starts at 2:00 PM. To join the afternoon tour, you have to arrive at the Household Agency's Office by 1:40 PM. Closed Saturdays, Sundays, December 25-January 5, May 14-17 and on irregular special occasions when the Palace is used for official Agency functions. No admission charge. Telephone: (075) 211-1215. If you are visiting Kyoto Imperial Palace, you can take advantage of being there to ask the Imperial Household Agency officials for permission to visit the other special facilities the Agency manages, i.e, Katsura Villa, Shugakuin Villa and Sento Palace. If you are lucky, there might be some openings and you might be able to get immediate or short-term permission to visit these restricted locations. Please note that all visitors to these other facilities must be at least 20 years of age. More details on visiting these special places appear above.

Kyoto Imperial Palace has been destroyed by fire many times, and the present buildings date from 1855. The original palace, built in 794 when the capital was moved to Kyoto, was located to the west of the present building, and was twice its size. The covered corridor that surrounds the spacious, white-gravel courtyard has three gates. The guided tour will take you to the courtyard, and give you a chance to take a close look at **Shishinden Hall**, the symbolic palace building at the northern end of the courtyard. Many important ceremonies of the imperial family were held here. Visitors are then led to the **Oikeniwa** (Pond Garden), a lovely Japanese-style garden. On the left-hand side of the garden are **Kogosho** (Minor Palace for Small Receptions) and **Gogakumonjo** (Study Hall). Turning to the left, the guide leads visitors back to Seishomon Gate, the entrance to the Palace.

Nishijin Textile Center 西陣織会館 (Upper left, Kansai Map 13) (optional)

Nishijin Textile Center is about 0.7 km (0.4 miles) from the Palace. If you skip the Center, walk to Nijojo Castle from the Imperial Palace.

The history of Nishijin textiles began in 794 when the newly organized imperial court established a special new agency for textiles. It produced refined and elegant textiles for the imperial family and the aristocracy for centuries. During the "Onin-no-Ran" civil war of the 15th century, the central part of Kyoto was reduced to ashes. The textile craftsmen scattered to various parts of Japan, where they learned new patterns and skills. After the war, when the craftsmen returned to Kyoto, they gravitated to the area called Nishijin and established a guild. Since then, the name Nishijin has been synonymous with fine textile products.

The Nishijin Textile Center was constructed in 1976 to display contemporary products and to demonstrate weaving techniques. Its dark, seven-story building is quite distinctive. A special feature of the Center is its live kimono fashion show, with lovely models wearing extremely expensive and elaborate kimono in a variety of patterns and colors. The show is presented at regular intervals between 10:00 AM and 4:00 PM (quite touristy). Hours: 9:00 AM to 5:00 PM. Closed on Sundays and Holidays. Admission to the kimono show: 400 yen.

Nijojo Castle 二条城 (Lower left, Kansai Map 13)

Nijojo Castle was built in 1603 as a residence for Ieyasu Tokugawa, the first Toku-

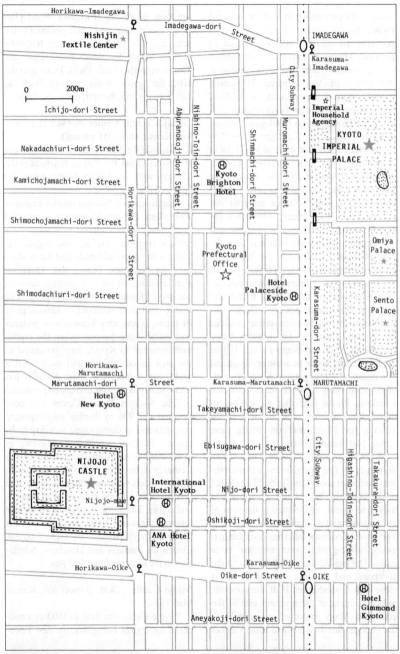

MAP 13 Central Kyoto Part I

gawa Shogun. Nijojo served as the Shogun's temporary residence when he traveled to Kyoto from his base in Edo. In 1868, when the 15th Tokugawa Shogun, Yoshinobu, relinquished power to the imperial court (the Meiji Restoration), the Castle became the temporary seat of the Emperor's new government. Despite the stern appearance of the moats and stone walls that surround the Castle grounds, the buildings inside are clearly those of a gracious noblemen's estate. The Castle has two major complexes — Honmaru Palace located inside the inner moats, and Ninomaru Palace in the eastern grounds. The major attractions of the Castle are in the Ninomaru Palace section — the original Honmaru Palace and its donjon were destroyed by fire in the 18th century. The present Honmaru Palace was built as the residence of Prince Katsura and was moved from Kyoto Imperial Palace to its present site in 1893. Several Western elements are incorporated in its design. The interior is closed to the public except for short periods in spring and fall.

The original architectural beauty and lavish interior decorations of Ninomaru Palace (National Treasure) are still intact. Entrance to Ninomaru Palace is through the brilliantly designed Karamon Gate. The six buildings of the Palace are each divided into many chambers, all of which are decorated with exceptional paintings, carvings and metalwork. The corridor of the first building is designed to squeak like a nightingale when it is walked upon. It is said that this was an alarm device designed to prevent assassins from penetrating to the inner halls. Especially noteworthy are the paintings on the sliding screens in Ohiroma Hall. The Hall was used for the meetings of shogun and feudal lords. It's easy to recognize this hall because a number of mannequins in formal costumes are arranged here to represent the scene when the 15th shogun announced his decision to return the power of government to the Emperor. Ninomaru Garden, designed by Enshu, is, in its own right, as famous as the Castle. Nijojo is open daily from 8:45 AM to 4:00 PM. Admission (covering both Ninomaru Palace and the Garden): 500 yen.

Kodai Yuzen-en Yuzen Gallery 友禅美術館 (Upper left, Kansai Map 14) (optional)

Kodai Yuzen-en (Yuzen Textile and Dye Museum) is recommended only for those interested in traditional textiles. Like Nishijin Textiles, Yuzen Dyeing, which dates from 794, got its start with imperial patronage. The first floor of the museum is used for displays of Yuzen masterpieces, and the second and third floors are devoted to demonstrations of the traditional technique. Yuzen kimono are extremely expensive, but smaller items such as ties, folding fans and scarves

are affordable. Hours: 9:00 AM to 5:00 PM. Closed for the New Year Holiday. Admission: 500 yen (tea an additional 300 yen).

Nishi-Honganji Temple 西本願寺 (Middle left, Kansai Map 14)

Take a south-bound No. 9 bus from the stop on the eastern side of Horikawa-dori Street, in front of Nijojo Castle. This is the only bus that goes directly to Nishi-Honganji stop.

As pictured on Kansai Map 14, there are two Honganji Temples, Nishi (West) and Higashi (East), side by side. Honganji Temple was the headquarters of the Jodo-shin-shu or Ikkoshu sect of Buddhism, the only feudal era sect that reached the farmers and the poor. The sect's religious teachings had definite political overtones, and for that reason, Jodo-shinsu was constantly oppressed by the rulers and its headquarters moved from place to place. Nevertheless, it remained tremendously influential. In the 15th century, in the central Japan Sea Coast area of Kanazawa, adherents of the sect managed to defeat the local feudal lord and establish an autonomous government that ruled for as long as 100 years. In Osaka, the sect accumulated enough military might to wage an 11-year battle against Nobunaga Oda. When Hideyoshi Toyotomi finally succeeded in unifying the nation, he realized that it would be necessary to make concessions to this powerful group: he sponsored construction of the headquarters for the sect in Kyoto in 1591. But when Ieyasu Tokugawa came to power, he plotted against Jodo-shinshu. He threw his support behind Kyojo, a priest who had failed in his own political maneuvering within the sect, and had another temple constructed for Kyojo to the east of the original headquarters. He then split the subordinate temples of the sect all over Japan into two groups. Since then, the original temple has been called Nishi-Honganji, and the new one Higashi-Honganji. The main building of the east (Higashi) temple is much larger (as a matter of fact, this 1895 structure is the largest wooden structure in Kyoto), but many objects of historical and artistic significance are found in the west (Nishi) temple.

Entrance to the Nishi-Honganji Temple precincts is free of charge. Upon entering at either Goeidomon Gate (northern side) or Hondomon Gate, visitors encounter huge, impressive 300-year old wooden structures. Among the temple's many buildings, the most important are Daishoin Hall, which runs from east to west, and Karamon Gate, which is located along the southern walls. Daishoin Hall was moved to Nishi-Honganji from Fushimijo Castle. As explained at the beginning of the Kyoto section, admission to Daishoin Hall is restricted. Karamon Gate was originally located at Fushimijo Castle, which was constructed by Hideyoshi Toyotomi and is said to have been magnificently lavish. Unfortunately, Ieyasu Tokugawa had Fushimijo Castle destroyed when he defeated the dictatorial Toyotomi family and founded the Tokugawa Shogunate. The elaborate carvings and decorations on Karamon Gate give us some idea of the lost splendors of the castle. Two noh stages and a small garden are attached to the Hall. Even if you don't obtain permission to enter Daishoin Hall, it is still worthwhile visiting the Temple to see the grandeur of the most influential Buddhist sect.

The Costume Museum 風俗博物館 (Middle center, Kansai Map 14, near Nishi-Honganji Temple) (optional)

The Costume Museum is a small establishment on the fifth floor of an office building. An English sign is posted at the entrance. The museum displays Japanese costumes from pre-historic times to the Meiji Era. Unexpectedly beautiful. Hours: 9:00 AM to 5:00 PM. Closed on Sundays. Admission: 400 yen.

Toji Temple 東寺 (Lower left, Kansai Map 11) (optional)

If you are continuing on to Toji Temple,

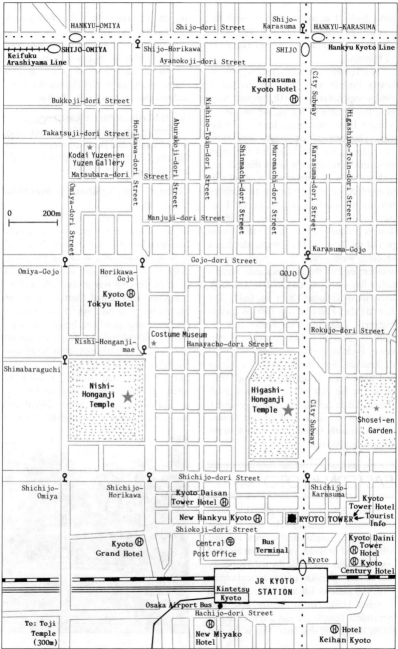

MAP 14 Central Kyoto Part II

leave Nishi-Honganji Temple through the southern gate and go to Omiya-dori Street. You can walk all the way to Toji Temple in 15 minutes.

Toji Temple, officially called Kyo-o-go-kokuji Temple, was originally erected in 796 by imperial edict. In 818, Emperor Saga gave the Temple to Kukai, the founder of Shingon Buddhism, as headquarters for his sect. The original buildings were burnt down during the civil wars, but the major structures were rebuilt between the 15th and 17th centuries. A number of important religious objects from the 8th and 9th centuries have survived and are preserved in the Temple. The ticket office is located inside the Temple grounds, at the entrance to the main part of the Temple. The Temple also has a spacious garden with three ponds. At the southern end of the garden stands Japan's tallest five-story pagoda (56 m or 184 feet), a National Treasure, built in 1644. The Kondo (Main Hall), built in 1606, is another National Treasure. The Kodo (Lecture Hall), constructed in 1491, contains 21 statues of Buddha, gods and guardians; fifteen of these date from the 8th and 9th centuries and have been designated National Treasures. On the 21st of each month a small flea market is held in the Temple precincts, and an antique fair is held the first Sunday of every month. Hours: 9:00 AM to 4:30 PM. Admission: 500 yen.

EASTERN KYOTO 東山

Eastern Kyoto nestles against Higashiyama (Eastern Mountain). The area contains innumerable temples and shrines in quiet settings, and provides visitors with an ideal opportunity to appreciate the natural beauty and cultural splendors of this ancient capital city. The famous Silver Pavilion, Nanzenji Temple, Heian Jingu Shrine and Kiyomizudera Temple are just a few examples of the delights of this area. This is the area

we give top priority, and Eastern Kyoto is introduced in two one-day itineraries.

If your time is limited, we recommend choosing either the Northern or the Southern part of Eastern Kyoto. It's a difficult choice: one of us prefers the Southern part and the other prefers the Northern part.

Day 1: Northern Part of Eastern Kyoto

Refer to Kansai Map 15. Find your way to Ginkakuji-michi Bus Stop (upper center). Ginkakuji Temple is a five-minute walk from the stop.

Ginkakuji Temple (Silver Pavilion) 銀閣寺 (Upper right)

Silver Pavilion, popularly called Ginkakuji Temple in Japanese and formally known as Jishoji Temple, was built in 1482 by Shogun Yoshimasa Ashikaga. The power of the Ashikaga Shogunate was eclipsed as a result of the civil war of the 15th century, and Yoshimasa retired from the world of politics to spend his days in this exquisite country retreat indulging himself in wine, women and cultural activities. He intended that his villa be a counterpart to the famous Gold Pavilion that his grandfather, Yoshimitsu, had built, and planned to have the entire structure covered with silver foil. But he died before this was accomplished, and his grand residence was converted into a

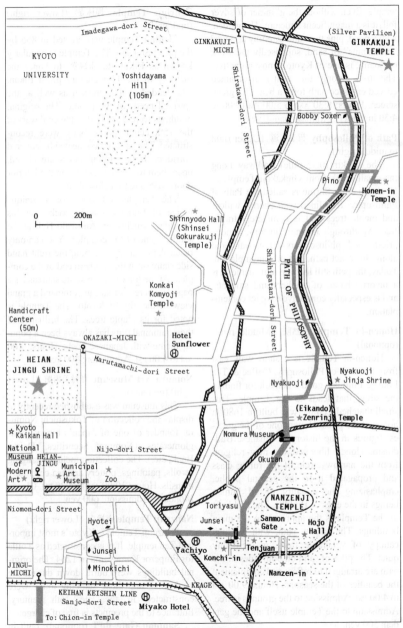

MAP 15 Eastern Kyoto Part I

temple. Even without the glimmer of silver foil, it is a magnificent structure. The garden, with a pond, pine trees and carefully arranged "mountains" of sand, supposedly the work of Soami, is one of Kyoto's most attractive. The trees along the neatly maintained curved entrance path form a beautiful green screen. Hours: 8:30 AM to 5:00 PM (9:00 to 4:30 in winter). Admission: 400 yen.

Path of Philosophy 哲学の道 (Upper right to middle right)

The 1.2 km (0.75 mile) walkway along the small creek from Ginkakuji Temple to Nyakuoji Jinja Shrine is called the Path of Philosophy. It is lined with cherry, willow and maple trees and is completely traffic free. All through Japanese history, famous priests and philosophers have wandered along this quiet path, lost in contemplation. Today, the path still lives up to its name: it is a favorite haunt of teachers and students, and is especially conducive to quiet contemplation.

Honen-in Temple 法然院 (Middle right) (optional)

Honen-in Temple is a short walk east from the Path of Philosophy. Coffee & Tea Lounge **Pino** is a good landmark for finding the street that leads to the Temple. This small thatched Temple was built in 1680 in honor of the priest Honen, one of the greatest figures in the history of Japanese Buddhism. Honen liberated the new religion from the narrow circle of the ruling class and propagated it to the general public, emphasizing the equality of all human beings in the eyes of Buddha. The highlight of the Temple is the approach to the main buildings. The narrow path, with its thick canopy of venerable trees, is incredibly quiet. The piles of sand on both sides of the path are arranged to reflect and complement the beauties of the seasons. Hours: 9:00 AM to 4:00 PM. Admission to the grounds is free. Admission to the Temple itself and the garden: 500 yen.

Zenrinji Temple 禅林寺 (Lower right) (optional)

Zenrinji Temple was erected in 856 by the priest Shinsho. The Temple is popularly known as **Eikan-do** 永観堂 to honor the memory of the 11th century priest Eikan, who tended to the physical as well as the spiritual needs of the people. The original buildings were destroyed in the civil wars of the 15th century, but many were reconstructed. The halls are connected by covered corridors. If the sliding doors are closed, open them to see the screens on the interior doors. (Be sure to reclose them.)

The Temple is famous for its unique image of Buddha looking back over his shoulder, which is in Amidado Hall at the southern end of the complex. You can only reach Amidado by climbing the right hand side staircase at the southern end of the complex. At the top of the opposite staircase is a pagoda where visitors can command a grand view of the city of Kyoto. The Temple is noted for its maple trees. The brilliance of their autumnal tints has always been a popular theme with Japanese poets. Hours: 9:00 AM to 4:00 PM. Admission: 400 yen.

Nomura Art Museum 野村美術館 (Lower right) (optional)

This museum was established recently to display the collection of Tokushichi Nomura, founder of one of Japan's biggest conglomerates (Nomura Securities, Daiwa Bank, etc.). The collection includes hanging scrolls, paintings, pottery and tea ceremony utensils. Hours: 10:00 AM to 4:30 PM. Closed Mondays. Admission: 600 yen.

Nanzenji Temple 南禅寺 (Lower right)

Nanzenji Temple is Kyoto's most important Zen temple. It was constructed as a villa for Emperor Kameyama in 1264. The original buildings were burnt down during the civil wars, and those standing today were constructed in the late 16th century. Entrance to the precincts is free of charge.

Sanmon Gate 山門 (optional), built in

1628, is famous for the splendid view of Kyoto from its top floor, which is reached by a steep, narrow stairway. Unless you really enjoy climbing, we recommend spending your time and money on other facilities in the precincts. Admission to Sanmon Gate: 250 yen. Hours: 9:00 AM to 5:00 PM.

Hojo Hall 方丈 (National Treasure) was moved here from Kyoto Imperial Palace in the early 17th century. Its chambers are divided by sliding doors covered with brilliant paintings of the Kano school, the most famous of which is the "Tiger Drinking Water." The garden attached to the hall is in typical Zen style, with stones, elaborately-shaped trees and sand. The stones and trees clustered in one area of the spacious garden are said to represent tigers crossing a stream. Admission to Hojo Hall: 350 yen. Hours: 8:30 AM to 4:30 PM.

There are three more minor temples here; each has a beautiful garden. **Nanzen-in Temple** 南禅寺 (optional) is located at the southern end of the precincts. A small creek (runoff from Lake Biwako) flows on an elevated brick waterway — a very unusual structure in feudal Japan. The path to Nanzen-in Temple goes under this "Roman" novelty. The garden is designed around a pond surrounded by wild trees from Higashiyama Mountain. Reflecting its beginnings as an imperial villa, the garden features many elegant maple trees and beautiful mosses. Admission to Nanzen-in: 150 yen. Hours: 8:30 AM to 5:00 PM (4:30 PM in winter). **Tenjuan Temple** 天授庵 (optional) also has an attractive garden, and is often the least crowded of the temples in the Nanzenji complex. Admission to Tenjuan: 300 yen. Hours: 8:30 AM to 5:00 PM (4:30 PM in winter). **Konchi-in Temple** 金地院 (optional), just outside the main precincts, is famous for its elaborate garden, which dates from 1627. The *bonsai* trees, rocks and sand of the garden represent deep mountains and an ocean with two islands. This typically Japanese use of limited space is considered one of the best works of Enshu. Admission to Konchi-in: 400 yen. Hours: 8:30 AM to 5:00 PM (4:30 PM in winter).

Restaurants in the area. There are a lot of restaurants in the Nanzenji Temple area. The specialty of the area is *yudofu*, boiled tofu dishes. This temple cuisine is surprisingly varied and sophisticated. Okutan and Junsei are among the most famous restaurants here. Hyotei (lower left; literally "gourd") has a reputation virtually unparalleled in Japan. Eating here is quite an event, not one you should expect to experience unless you are someone's guest or you are willing to invest at least 15,000 yen for lunch yourself.

Heian Jingu Shrine 平安神宮 (Middle left)

It's about a 15-minute walk from Nanzenji Temple to Heian Jingu Shrine.

Heian Jingu Shrine was built in 1895 to commemorate the 1,100th anniversary of the city of Kyoto, and dedicated to two famous emperors — Kammu, the founder of Kyoto, and Komei, the last emperor to live in the city. The Shrine consists of the East and West Honden (Main Halls), the Daigokuden (Great Hall of State), two pagodas, the Otemon Gate (Main Gate), a spacious white-gravel front yard, and a garden. A huge *torii* gate stands to the south of the Shrine at the entrance to the broad main approach. The brightly colored vermilion-red buildings are reduced scale replicas of the first Imperial Palace (two-thirds the size of the original). The Garden at the rear of the Shrine is famous for its weeping cherries, maples, azaleas, irises and water lilies. The Garden is a living relic of the brilliant days of the imperial and aristocratic families at the dawn of Japanese history. Hours: 8:30 AM to 5:30 PM (4:30 PM in winter). Admission to the precincts is free. Admission to the Garden: 500 yen.

Several of Kyoto's cultural institutions are located to the south of the Shrine. They include: the National Museum of Modern

Art, the Municipal Art Museum and the Kyoto Zoo.

Day 2: Southern Part of Eastern Kyoto

Refer to Kansai Map 16.

Shorein-in Temple 青蓮院 (Upper right) (optional)

Find your way to Jingu-michi Bus Stop. If you decide to skip Shoren-in and Chion-in and start your day at Maruyama-Koen Park, you should find your way to Gion Bus Stop and walk to Maruyama-Koen.

Shoren-in Temple, popularly called Awata Palace, is famous as the residence of the head abbot of the Tendai sect of Buddhism. In the past, this position was so highly regarded that it was always reserved for a member of the imperial family. The present buildings were erected in 1895. Especially notable are the sliding screens of the Main Hall, survivors of an earlier time, graced with paintings by Mitsunobu Kano, Motonobu Kano, and other leading artists of the late 16th and early 17th centuries. The garden, which is considered one of the best in Kyoto, was designed in part by Soami, and in part by Enshu, two of Japan's greatest landscape artists. Hours: 9:00 AM to 5:00 PM. Admission: 400 yen.

Chion-in Temple 知恩院 (Upper right) (optional)

Chion-in Temple, erected in 1234, is the grand headquarters of the Jodo sect of Buddhism, and is one of the largest and most famous temples in all of Japan. The oldest of the buildings that have survived the repeated fires that ravaged the temple are the Main Hall and the Abbot's Quarters, which date from 1633 and 1639. Chion-in's two-story Sanmon Gate, at a height of 24 m (79 feet), is considered the most imposing of all the temple gates in Japan. The corridor connecting the Main Hall with the Daihojo Hall is constructed so that at every step the floor emits a sound resembling the song of the nightingale. This wonderful quirk of construction is thought to be the work of Jingoro Hidari, the master sculptor famous for the Sleeping Cat of the Toshogu Shrine in Nikko. The sliding screens of the Daihojo Hall are decorated with beautiful paintings of the Kano school. The garden attached to the abbot's apartments is the work of Enshu. The belfry houses the largest temple bell in Japan, which was cast in 1633. Seventeen people are needed to ring it! Entrance to the precincts is free of charge. The entrance to the inside of the buildings is located at the northern side of the Main Hall. Hours: 9:00 AM to 4:30 PM (4:00 PM in winter). Admission: 300 yen.

Maruyama-Koen Park 円山公園 (Upper right)

Maruyama-Koen Park, Kyoto's main public park, is a beautiful landscaped garden laid out at the foot of Higashiyama Mountain at the eastern end of Shijo-dori Street. The Park is really a series of gardens designed around ponds. There are many vendors, restaurants and souvenir shops, and the Park always has a festival atmosphere. The Park features a statue of Ryoma Sakamoto and Shintaro Nakaoka, reformists who contributed the most to the demise of Japan's feudal era by welding together a coalition of anti-Tokugawa clans. These heros of modern Japan were assassinated in Kyoto, probably by agents of conservative forces, and did not live to see the fulfillment of their dream. All the new government structures of Meiji Japan were based on Sakamoto's thinking. Modern Japanese society is thus modeled on the ideas of this pioneer who voluntarily made himself a masterless samurai to devote his full energies to the anti-Tokugawa movement.

Yasaka Jinja Shrine 八坂神社 (upper center), a vermilion shrine on the way from Gion Bus Stop, is famous as the host of Gion Matsuri Festival, Kyoto's biggest festival (held every July).

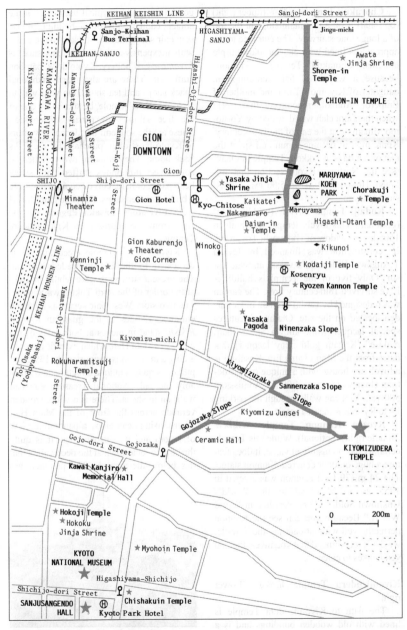

MAP 16 Eastern Kyoto Part II

Chorakuji Temple 長楽寺 (upper right) (optional) is on a mountain slope at the top of a long stone stairway. The entrance to the approach is lined with elegant, dark-purple lanterns. Chorakuji Temple is famous because it was here that Kenreimon-in, daughter of Kiyomori Taira and mother of Emperor Antoku, renounced the world when the Taira clan was defeated by Yoritomo Minamoto at the end of the 12th century. Kenreimon-in became a nun and spent the rest of her days at Jakkoin Temple in Ohara (see the Northern Kyoto section that follows). Hours: 9:00 AM to 5:00 PM. Admission: 500 yen.

Kodaiji Temple 高台寺 (middle right) (optional). This lovely temple was built in 1605 by the widow of Hideyoshi Toyotomi. Its construction was financed by Ieyasu Tokugawa, Hideyoshi's vassal and successor. Only five of the Temple's buildings have survived 18th century fires. The garden was redesigned by Enshu from an older garden located on the site. Otama-ya features special lacquer work known as "Kodaiji maki-e" (Kodaiji gold inlay lacquer) that dates from the Momoyama Era. Kasai-tei is a lovely tea house, with a unique roof structure. Hours: 9:00 AM to 4:00 PM. Admission: 500 yen. You can walk through the parking lot to Ryozen Kannon Temple.

Ryozen Kannon Temple 霊山観音 (middle right) (optional). While this Temple certainly has no historical value, it does feature a huge outdoor concrete Kannon statue. The 24 m (79 feet) Kannon was erected in 1955 as a "Memorial to the World's Unknown Soldiers Who Perished in World War II." Because you can see the Kannon perfectly well without entering the Temple, we don't recommend that you invest the 200 yen it takes to enter.

Kiyomizudera Temple 清水寺 (Lower right)

The path to Kiyomizudera Temple is lined with old wooden buildings and is a good example of a typical backstreet of the ancient capital. Most of the buildings house souvenir shops that are stocked to the eaves with inexpensive traditional items such as *Kiyomizu-yaki* pottery, Kyoto dolls, bamboo crafts, etc. There are also many traditional snack shops and tea shops. On your way to Kiyomizudera Temple, be sure to try one of the free samples of *yatsuhashi* cookies. These are the souvenir that Japanese visitors to Kyoto most often purchase for the folks back home. They come in two varieties — soft, sweet dumplings stuffed with sweet bean paste, or hard, curved cookies that taste a bit like ginger snaps. Only the latter travel well. **Five-story Yasaka Pagoda** can be seen from the approach to Kiyomizudera Temple.

Kiyomizudera Temple, erected in 798, is dedicated to the Eleven-headed Kannon. The present structures were rebuilt in 1633 at the order of the third Tokugawa Shogun. The two-story West Gate serves as the main entrance. Statues of the guardian *Kongo-Rikishi* stand in niches at both sides of the gate. The Main Hall, which extends out over a cliff and which is supported by 139 giant pillars, is quite a unique structure, and probably the only National Treasure you can walk on in shoes. There is a wide, wooden veranda across the front of the Main Hall where visitors can enjoy a panoramic view of Kyoto and its surroundings. It is quite thrilling to look down at the deep valley that lies below the veranda. The precincts are

open from dawn to dusk (6:00 AM to 6:00 PM). Admission to veranda: 300 yen.

Chishakuin Temple 智積院 (Lower center) (optional)

Chishakuin Temple is famous for its brilliant paintings of the Hasegawa School (a rival of the Kano School), and its garden. The colorful paintings, which feature the beauties of the four seasons, are displayed in a special exhibition hall. Because they are arranged at the height they would normally be in a Japanese-style room, you have to sit down to really appreciate them. The garden, laid out about 400 years ago, centers around a large pond that extends under a veranda. Because most people hurry directly to San-jusangengo Hall from Kiyomizudera Temple, you can spend a quiet, relaxed time at this garden. Hours: 9:00 AM to 4:30 PM. Admission: 350 yen.

Sanjusangendo Hall 三十三間堂 (Lower left)

Sanjusangendo Hall is the popular name given to Rengeoin Temple. It was so named because of the 33 ("sanjusan") spaces between the pillars in the long, narrow hall. Although the hall is only 10 m. (33 feet) wide, it is 120 m (394 feet) long. The original Temple, erected in 1164 at the order of the retired but still powerful Emperor Goshi-rakawa, was destroyed by fire in 1249 and rebuilt in 1266. It chief image is a wooden, thousand-handed Kannon in a seated position. This National Treasure was carved in 1254 by Tankei, a master sculptor of the Kamakura Era. The Kannon is surrounded by statues of 28 faithful followers (National Treasures), and an additional one thousand and one smaller statues of the Kannon fill the remainder of the gallery. Hours: 8:00 AM to 5:00 PM (4:00 in winter). Admission: 400 yen.

Kyoto National Museum 京都国立博物館 (Lower left)

Kyoto National Museum was built in 1879 by the Imperial Household Agency as a repository for precious art objects and other treasures. It is divided into three sections — history, fine arts and handicrafts. Its 17 exhibit rooms house some 2,000 pieces of rare and valuable art, and historical and religious objects. Set aside as much time as possible for this museum. The Museum is especially recommended for a rainy day. Hours: 9:00 AM to 4:30 PM (no admission after 4:00 PM). Closed Mondays. Admission: 400 yen.

Other Places of Interest

Kawai Memorial Hall 河井寛次郎記念館 (lower left) displays representative art works of Kanjiro Kawai, the most distinguished potter of the *Kiyomizu-yaki* school. Hours: 10:00 AM to 5:00 PM (4:30 PM in winter). Closed Mondays. Admission: 700 yen.

Hokoji Temple 方広寺 (lower left) was built at the order of Hideyoshi to house Japan's biggest image of Buddha. Larger even than that of Nara's Todaiji Temple (which is now Japan's largest statue), the huge Buddha was recast three times before finally falling victim to fires and earthquakes. Only the old stone walls along the western side of the precincts remain to give us an idea of Hideyoshi's grand scheme for the Temple complex. A large temple bell, cast at the order of Hideyori Toyotomi, Hideyoshi's successor, also stands in the Temple grounds. The inscriptions on the bell say, "Peace for the Nation, and Prosperity for the People." Two of the Chinese characters used in the inscription are characters used in Ieyasu Tokugawa's name as well. On the inscription these two characters were split — unluckily — and another character interspersed. Ieyasu took this as an insult and claimed that the unlucky inscription illustrated the Toyotomi clan's desire to destroy his influence. For Ieyasu this constituted an excuse to commence hostilities, and the resulting battle at Osakajo Castle led to the ascendancy of the Tokugawas and the collapse of the Toyotomi family. **Hokoku**

Jinja Shrine 豊国神社, in the Hokoji Temple precincts, was built to honor Hideyoshi Toyotomi.

WESTERN KYOTO   洛西

Western Kyoto, adjacent to the central part of the city, is home to famous temples such as the Gold Pavilion and Ryoanji.

Refer to Kansai Map 17. The Western Kyoto itinerary starts at Daitokuji Temple (upper right). Find your way to Daitokuji-mae Bus Stop. After visiting Daitokuji, take a bus to Gold Pavilion, and then to Ryoanji Temple. After enjoying the Rock Garden at Ryoanji, continue by bus to Ninnaji Temple, or visit lovely Tojiin Temple. If you still have time, visit Myoshinji Temple or Kitano-Tenmangu Shrine.

Daitokuji Temple 大徳寺 (Upper right)

Daitokuji is a large temple located in the northwestern corner of the city. The entrance to the Temple precincts is near Daitokuji-mae Bus Stop.

The original Temple was founded in 1319, but was lost to fire during the 1467 civil war. The Temple was revitalized by Hideyoshi Toyotomi in the 16th century, and many smaller buildings in the precincts were constructed by local feudal lords, to express their loyalty to Hideyoshi. Sanmon Gate, Buddha Hall, Lecture Hall and the Main Hall are located in a straight line from south to north, surrounded by about 20 subordinate temples. Several of them are open to the public. Among them are:

Ryugen-in Temple 龍源院 is a Zen temple. Its Hojo Hall, gate and porch are National Treasures, and the temple is sur-

MAP 17 Western Kyoto

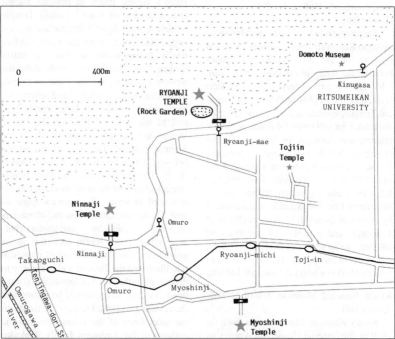

rounded by five small Zen gardens. Hours: 9:00 AM to 5:00 PM. Admission: 300 yen.

Daisen-in Temple 大仙院 (National Treasure) is the most famous of the small temples. This temple has one of Japan's most famous Zen gardens: with rocks and sand, it represents a grand view of mountains, ravines and the ocean. Sliding screens

feature brilliant paintings of the Kano School. Hours: 9:00 AM to 5:00 PM (4:30 PM in winter). Admission: 400 yen.

Hoshun-in Temple 芳春院 features a lovely pavilion and garden designed around a pond. Hours: 8:30 AM to 4:30 PM. Admission: 300 yen.

Kotoin Temple 高桐院 is famous for its

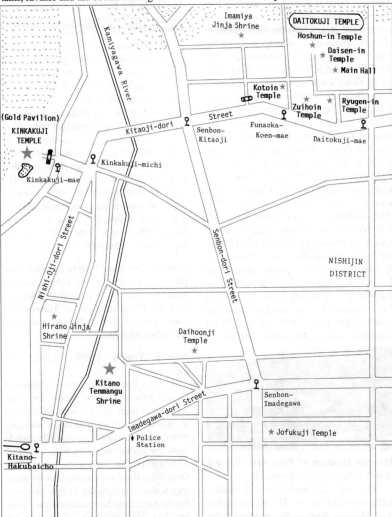

tea house and maple trees. Hours: 9:00 AM to 4:30 PM. Admission: 300 yen.

Kinkakuji Temple (Gold Pavilion) 金閣寺 (Upper center)

Take the No. 205 bus from Daitokuji-mae Bus Stop to Kinkakuji-michi Bus Stop.

The Gold Pavilion, whose popular Japanese name is Kinkakuji, and which is formally known as Rokuonji Temple, was constructed in 1397 by the third Ashikaga shogun, Yoshimitsu, who spent the latter part of his life here in retirement. His son, Yoshimochi, in accordance with the dictates of his father's will, had the villa converted to a Buddhist temple. The garden still reflects the beauty of the refined contemplative life of the Ashikagas, but most of the original buildings have been destroyed by repeated fires, including the tragic loss, by arson, in July 1950, of the precious Gold Pavilion itself. A new Gold Pavilion — an exact reproduction of the original — was erected on the same spot in October 1955. After walking through Chumon Gate, you will see two shimmering gold pavilions. One is the three-story golden building with the bronze phoenix on its roof. The other is its reflection in the calm, beautiful pond that lies in front of the Pavilion. The walls of the Pavilion are completely covered with gold foil. A recent restoration has left it gleaming and glowing. Hours: 9:00 AM to 5:30 PM (5:00 PM in winter). Admission: 300 yen.

Domoto Museum of Fine Arts 堂本印象 美術館 (Middle center) (optional)

You can walk easily from Kinkakuji Temple to this museum. This Kyoto Prefectural Museum displays the works of Insho Domoto, the modern Japanese artist, and his disciples. The collection features paintings, pottery and sculpture. Hours: 10:00 AM to 5:00 PM. Closed Mondays. Admission: 500 yen.

Ryoanji Temple 龍安寺 (Middle left)

If you don't visit the Museum, you should take the No. 59 bus to Ryoanji-mae stop. Ryoanji Temple belongs to the Rinzai sect of zen Buddhism, and was founded in 1473 by Katsumoto Hosokawa, a powerful Kyoto feudal lord, whose grave is in the Temple grounds. It is famous for its rock garden, which is thought to be the work of Soami. Dating from the late 15th century and consisting of only rocks and pebbles, it is regarded as the quintessential zen garden. Some say that the 15 rocks arranged on the surface of white pebbles look like islands on a huge ocean, while other think that they look like tigers crossing a big river. The rocks are so arranged that visitors can only see 14 of them at once, no matter what the angle from which they view the garden. Hours: 8:00 AM to 5:00 PM (8:30 AM to 4:30 PM in winter). Admission: 350 yen.

Options after Your Visit to Ryoanji Temple

After visiting Ryoanji Temple, take the same bus (No. 59) to Ninanji Bus Stop, or walk the 10-minute distance. Alternatively, you can walk to Toji-in Temple, which features a beautiful garden.

Ninnaji Temple 仁和寺 (Lower left) (optional)

Ninnaji Temple was formerly known as Omuro Palace. Emperor Koko, the Temple's first patron, ordered work on it begun in 886, but passed away before it was completed. His successor, Emperor Uda, had the work completed two years later, and when he retired became the Temple's first abbot. Originally, there were more than 60 buildings scattered around the Temple precincts, but frequent fires have reduced their number. The oldest buildings still standing date from the first half of the 17th century. The five-story pagoda, about 33 m (108 feet) tall, was built in 1637. The Main Hall (National Treasure) at the northernmost end of the precincts was formerly the Main Ceremonial Hall of the Imperial Palace and was moved here in the early 17th century. The Main Hall contains a wooden image of Amitabha (National Treasure) as its chief object of worship. Admission to the grounds: 350 yen. General hours for Ninan-ji: 9:00 AM to 5:00 PM.

Admission to **Goten Hall**, the palace the abbots used as their residence, costs an additional 350 yen. Goten features a lovely garden.

Admission to the **Treasure House** costs an additional 400 yen. Treasure House hours: 9:00 AM to 4:00 PM. Open only April 1–May 24. The Treasure House features Muromachi screens and sculpture from the Heian, Kamakura and Edo eras.

If Ninnaji Temple is your last stop for the day, take the No. 59 bus back to the city, or take the Keifuku Kitano Line train from Omuro Station to Kitano-Hakubaicho Station, where you can connect to the Loop buses. If you have more time, we recommend that you visit Myoshinji Temple.

Myoshinji Temple 妙心寺 (Lower center) (optional)

You can easily walk the 800 m (0.5 mile) from Ninnaji to Myoshinji, and frequent bus service is also available. Take the No. 8, No. 10 or No. 26 bus from the stop right in front of the South Gate of Ninnaji Temple (make sure to take one going east, from the northern side of the road).

Upon entering the precincts of Myoshinji Temple at the North Gate, you'll feel that you're walking along a stone path running between temple after temple. Myoshinji, like Daitokuji Temple, is one of the few temples that has enough of its original buildings intact to give you some idea of the magnificent scale of Japan's traditional temple architecture. It was founded in 1337 on the site of Emperor Hanazono's imperial villa. There are more than 40 minor buildings, and each has its own refined garden. Japan's oldest bell (National Treasure), cast in 698, hangs in a belfry near South Gate. Four of Myoshinji's buildings are open to the public:

Main Hall 本堂: You will see the entrance on your left just after passing under the elevated corridor between the main buildings. The most noted feature of the Main Hall is the picture of a dragon painted on the ceiling of Hatto (Ceremonial) Hall. The painting is often described as "A Dragon Glaring in Eight Directions" because his eyes seem to stare at you no matter where you stop to look up at him. Hours: 9:00 AM to 4:00 PM. Admission: 400 yen.

Taizoin Temple 退蔵院, erected in 1404, is renowned for its landscaped garden, which represents a stream coursing down a mountain and forming a river. The grounds are quiet and quite beautiful. Hours: 9:00 AM to 5:00 PM. Admission: 400 yen.

There are a great many other small temples in the Myoshinji precincts. A stroll through the northern part of the Temple precincts is quite pleasant.

Toji-in Temple 等持院 (Middle center)

This family temple of the Ashikagas is off the beaten tourist path. It has a lovely garden and is the perfect place for a peaceful retreat. The garden features Fuyoike Pond and Seirentei Teahouse. Hours: 8:00 AM to 5:00 PM. Admission: 400 yen.

After visiting Toji-in Temple, you can take the Keifuku Kitano Line train from Toji-in Station to Kitano-Hakubaicho Station, where you can connect to the Loop buses. If you still have time, you may wish to visit Kitano-Tenmangu Shrine.

Kitano-Tenmangu Shrine 北野天満宮 (Lower center) (optional)

This Shrine is dedicated to Michizane Sugawara, a famous 10th century scholar and courtier who lost out in palace intrigue but who still has a reputation as one of the great geniuses of Japanese history. Students preparing for crucial exams often ask his blessing at this Shrine. The present building dates from the 16th century, is an excellent example of lavish Momoyama architecture, and is a National Treasure. On the 25th of every month, a flea market is held on the grounds of this Shrine. No admission charge to the grounds. This flea market, and that at Toji Temple, are Kyoto's largest. The Treasure House is open from 10:00 AM to 4:00 PM. Admission: 200 yen.

ARASHIYAMA　嵐山

The peaceful surroundings, gentle mountains and the clear waters of the Katsuragawa River made the Arashiyama district a favorite of emperors and nobles throughout Japanese history. Arashiyama preserves peaceful natural settings as they were in the feudal era. Because of its historical importance, we give top priority to Eastern Kyoto, but we personally love the western-most part of Kyoto most. Walking along the narrow paths here and visiting the area's many historic sites, are, in our opinion, the best ways to experience the beauty that is Kyoto.

Refer to Kansai Map 18. Keifuku-Arashiyama Station (lower center) is 7.2 km (4.5 miles) from Shijo-Omiya. The Keifuku Arashiyama trains that connect the two operate every 10-15 minutes. The ride takes 20 minutes. Along this line, at Uzumasa Station, there are two places of interest:

Koryuji Temple　広隆寺　(Lower right) (optional)

Koryuji Temple is just a few minutes from Uzumasa Station on foot. A huge wooden gate marks the entrance to the precincts of Koryuji Temple, which was founded in 622 by Kawakatsu Hata, one of Kyoto's most powerful aristocrats. It was designed as a memorial for Regent Shotoku,

who promulgated Japan's first "Seventeen-Article" Constitution. The Reihoden Treasure House is home to more than 50 masterpieces of Asuka, Nara and Heian sculpture. The exquisite statues, all of which were originally objects of worship, reflect the artistic splendor of those ancient eras, and many of them are National Treasures. Perhaps the most famous of all is the Miroku-Bosatsu, which was selected as Japan's first National Treasure and well deserves this honor. Strong yet gentle, serene and compassionate, the enigmatic beauty of the face of this Buddha casts its spell over every visitor to the Treasure House. The Treasure House is open from 9:00 AM to 5:00 PM (4:30 PM in winter). Admission: 500 yen. The Keiguin Hall (National Treasure) is an elegant octagonal structure located in the northwestern part of the Temple precincts.

Toei Uzumasa Movieland　東映太秦映画村 (Lower right) (optional)

The Movieland is just a 10-minute walk from Koryuji Temple. If you are more interested in history and culture, we recommend that you skip Movieland and go directly to Arashiyama. However, if you're tired of shrines and temples, this will be a good change-of-pace.

Toei Uzumasa Movieland, owned by the Toei Movie Company, has large open-air sets that recreate the buildings, bridges and streets of feudal and modern Japan. There are also indoor studios and museums. You can watch as the cameras roll on famous

movie stars dressed in period costumes. It takes one hour just to tour the facilities, and a thorough visit to the world through the looking glass will probably take two or three hours. Hours: 9:00 AM to 5:00 PM (9:30 AM to 4:00 PM in winter). Closed December 21-January 1. Admission: 1,800 yen.

Arashiyama 嵐山

If you are staying at a hotel near Kyoto Station and skipping Koryuji Temple and the Movieland, you can take the JR San-in Honsen Line commuter train to Saga Station (middle center). The ride takes 19 minutes.

Arashiyama is also easily visited from Osaka via the Hankyu Railways. See Kansai Transportation above.

There are several bicycle rental shops near Arashiyama Station and Togetsukyo Bridge for cycling fans, but we recommend that you enjoy walking through the area.

Togetsukyo Bridge 渡月橋 (Lower center)

Arashiyama stretches along the Katsura-gawa River (the river is also called Oigawa). The view from the northern bank of the river of Togetsukyo Bridge with the beautiful Arashiyama foothills in the background is especially lovely. It is no wonder that throughout Japanese history, emperors, aristocrats and shogun loved the area. Modern Japanese, too, are particularly fond of this area.

Tenryuji Temple 天竜寺 (Middle left)

Tenryuji Temple was founded in 1339 by Takauji, the first Ashikaga Shogun, in memory of Emperor Godaigo. The noted priest and landscape artist, Muso-Kokushi, was its first abbot. The Temple was repeatedly ravaged by fire, and the present buildings date only from 1900, but the famous garden preserves the style of the 14th century original. Complementing its natural surroundings, the Tenryuji garden testifies to the great creative abilities of Muso Soseki, who designed it in 1340. Hours: 8:30 AM to 5:30 PM (5:00 PM in winter). Admission: 600 yen (the interior of the main building and the garden); 500 yen (garden only.)

Okochi Sanso Villa 大河内山荘 (Middle left) (optional)

When you leave Tenryuji from the north exit of its garden (if you see a small pond with an image of Buddha and a statue of a frog, you'll know you're going in the right direction for the north exit), you'll pass through a narrow street with thousands of beautiful bamboos. The westernmost part of Kyoto is famous for its bamboo forests, and this one is considered the best. Enjoy the green serenity of the bamboos — and be thankful you're on foot — this is something you'd never see from a tour bus.

Okochi Sanso villa, the lavish home of the late Denjiro Okochi, a famous star of samurai films, is of no interest itself, but the garden is beautiful, and the view of Arashiyama and the city of Kyoto from the upper part of the grounds is splendid. Hours: 9:00 AM to 5:00 PM. Admission: 800 yen. The price of admission entitles you to powdered tea and a cake as well as the view.

Jojakkoji Temple 常寂光寺 (Middle left)

The approach to the main buildings of Jojakkoji temple passes through two gates and up old stone steps. The view of the thatched roofs of the gates from the top of the steps is especially lovely: don't forget to look back. A two-story pagoda stands at the highest point of the grounds, and is surrounded by many trees. The temple is also famous for its colorful maple leaves in November. Hours: 9:00 AM to 5:00 PM. Admission: 200 yen.

Nison-in Temple 二尊院 (Middle left)

Nison-in Temple was erected in 841 at the order of Emperor Saga. The approach to the main grounds is up a wide, stone-paved slope lined on both sides with cherry, maple and other trees whose beauty varies with the seasons. The main hall houses two images of Buddha. Visitors can ring the temple's

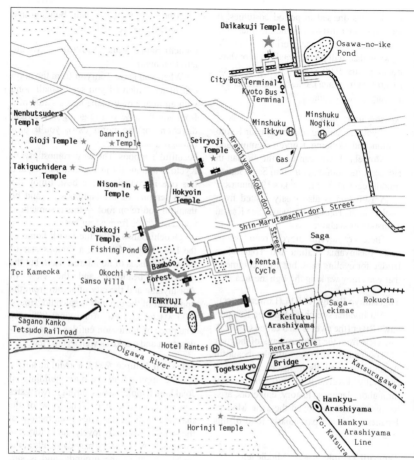

MAP 18 Arashiyama

"Bell of Happiness." Hours: 9:00 AM to 4:30 PM. Admission: 300 yen.

Detour (optional)

After you visit Nison-in Temple, the suggested itinerary calls for you to head east to Hokyoin and Seiryoji Temples. If, however, you are a good walker and have enough time to make a detour, we suggest that you visit three temples to the north (upper left).

Gioji Temple 祇王寺 and **Takiguchi-dera Temple** 滝口寺 were the scenes of sentimental love stories of olden times. Although they have little historic value, these two small temples standing in beautiful bamboo forests are quite impressive. Admission: 300 yen each.

Nenbutsudera Temple 念仏寺 is in an area called Adashino. Adashino was the extreme end of Kyoto, and the bodies of the poor and the unknown were discarded here.

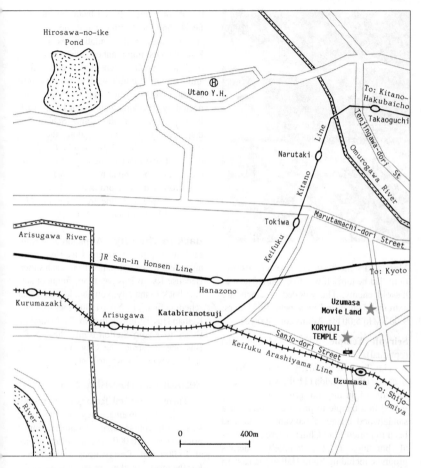

After the Meiji Restoration, the scattered bones were collected and buried in the grounds of Nenbutsudera Temple. Thousands of stone images of Buddha, dedicated to the dead, sit in the precincts — a very unusual scene. Admission: 400 yen.

Hokyoin Temple 宝筐院 (Middle left) (optional)

Even few Japanese know about this temple. The tombs of two men, Yoshiakira Ashikaga and Masatsura Kusunoki, who were fierce rivals during Japan's medieval era, are located side by side in the precincts of Hokyoin Temple. Masatsura helped Emperor Godaigo regain power from the Kamakura Shogunate. Even though the Emperor triumphed in 1333, he was again soon supplanted, this time by the Ashikagas. Yoshiakira had great respect for his enemy Masatsura, and when he died in battle, Yoshiakira had this temple built to honor

Masatsura's memory. He also left instructions that he himself was to be buried next to his old enemy. The wooded precincts are extremely quiet and very peaceful. Hours: 9:00 AM to 5:00 PM. Admission: 400 yen.

Seiryoji Temple 清涼寺 (Middle left) (optional)

This Temple, popularly known as Saga-Shakado (Saga Buddha Hall), was originally the villa of an imperial prince. It was converted to a temple to provide a home for a sandalwood image of Sakyamuni that had been imported from China. There are several buildings in the temple's spacious grounds, including Sutra Hall at the eastern end of the grounds, repository of thousands and thousands of sutras arranged on revolving shelves. Supposedly, if you spin the shelves, it has the same effect as reading the innumerable volumes of sutras contained on them! Admission to the precincts is free of charge. Hours: 9:30 AM to 4:30 PM. Admission to the Main Hall and the garden: 300 yen.

Daikakuji Temple 大覚寺 (Upper center)

Daikakuji Temple was originally built as a villa for Emperor Saga in the early 9th century. After its conversion to a Temple,

the abbots were selected from the imperial family and the Temple maintained its high social status and reputation as one of Kyoto's most important establishments. The original structures were destroyed by fires and the present buildings date from the 16th century. Many of these buildings are connected by corridors (watch your head). Brilliant paintings of the Kano School are displayed in the chambers along the corridors. The Temple's Osawa-no-ike Pond was designed so Emperor Saga could enjoy the pleasures of boating at his country retreat. It is surrounded by a promenade lined with cherry, maple and pine trees. Hours: 9:00 AM to 4:30 PM. Admission: 500 yen.

Back to The City As pictured on Kansai Map 18, the Kyoto and City Bus terminals are a bit of a distance from each other. Because Kyoto Bus has more frequent service back to the city, you should check that schedule first. The No. 61 Bus goes to Sanjo Keihan Bus Terminal; the No. 71, 80 and 81 Buses to Kyoto Station. Only the No. 28 Bus operates from the City Bus terminal, and it goes back to Kyoto Station.

Restaurants in Arashiyama

There are several famous name restaurants in Arashiyama; they specialize in *kaiseki* full course Japanese dinners. Lunch prices start at 10,000 yen, and dinners start at 15,000 yen. Reservations are required. For the most part, these restaurants are in the vicinity of Hotel Rantei (lower left, near Togetsukyo Bridge). The hotel itself is quite famous for *kaiseki* cuisine. Kitcho is the most famous restaurant in all of Japan. Lunch at Kitcho starts at 50,000 yen, and dinner at 60,000 yen. Hyakuraku is more reasonable, with set course meals starting at 8,000 yen. In addition, there are many inexpensive restaurants in the vicinity of Arashiyama and Saga Stations.

NORTHERN KYOTO
洛北

Refer to Kansai Map 9 (upper right). Enryakuji Temple is located on top of Mt. Hieizan, which separates the city of Kyoto and Lake Biwako. Ohara is located further to the north in a rural district. The suggested itinerary for Northern Kyoto involves visits to Ohara in the morning and Enryakuji Temple in the afternoon. Because the visit to Enryakuji Temple requires at least a 1-km (0.6 mile) walk on a mountain path (one that is *not* steep), those who don't want to walk too much should spend more time in Ohara and return to the city directly. If you skip Ohara and visit Enryakuji Temple in the morning, you can take a ropeway down Mt. Hieizan to Lake Biwako. From the ropeway, you can take the Keihan Ishizaka Line train to Hama-Otsu, or directly to Ishiyamadera. See details in the Lake Biwako section below.

Transportation to Ohara from the City

You can take either the No. 17 or No. 18 bus from Kyoto Station to Ohara. If it is easier for you to start from Sanjo Keihan bus terminal, take either the No. 16 or No. 17 bus. The trip from Kyoto Station takes about one hour, and the trip from Sanjo Keihan to Ohara takes about 40 minutes.

OHARA   大原

Refer to Kansai Map 19. Ohara Bus Stop is pictured in the lower center of the map.

Ohara, located in the quiet northern suburbs of Kyoto, is surrounded by mountains. Though the area is slowly modernizing, it still preserves much of the atmosphere of the ancient capital. Several destinations in this area are real gems. If you plan to visit Enryakuji Temple (and we recommend that

you do), visit the temples on the eastern side of Ohara, skipping Jakkoin Temple, which is located on the western side. If you decide to skip Enryakuji Temple, you should be sure to include a visit to Jakkoin.

Sanzen-in Temple 三千院 (Lower right)

The approach to Sanzen-in Temple is a gentle paved slope that runs alongside a small creek. Many souvenir shops and restaurants are, unfortunately, located here as well, cluttering and commercializing this lovely natural setting. Sanzen-in Temple was originally located on Mt. Hieizan and was a branch of Enryakuji Temple. The Temple was moved to its present site in the 15th century. There are three buildings and beautiful gardens in the spacious precincts. The main hall houses an Amitabha trinity: the two disciples that flank Buddha are seated, which is quite unusual — it makes these goddesses seem very relaxed and merciful. The Temple grounds and the approach have a reputation as one of Kyoto's best maple viewing locations in November. Hours: 8:30 AM to 5:00 PM (4:30 PM in winter). Admission: 500 yen.

Other Temples in Eastern Ohara

Jikko-in Temple 実光院 (middle right) (optional) is only 250 meters (750 feet) north of Sanzen-in Temple, but because group tours only visit Sanzen-in and then rush off to Jakkoin Temple on the other side of Ohara, Jikko-in Temple and the other temples located north of Sanzen-in are never very crowded. Unlike most temples, Jikko-in does not have a ticket office at its entrance. Upon entering the gate, you should ring the gong. The 500 yen admission should be paid to attendant who will lead you to a chamber overlooking a small garden. Powdered tea and a cake are served. Because the tea is served in a very casual manner, you can just relax and enjoy the delicate flavor of the tea and the view of the beautifully manicured garden, even if you

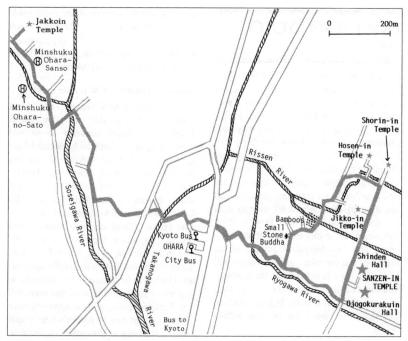

MAP 19 Ohara

don't know anything about the etiquette of tea ceremony. This Temple also has a collection of tiny bells in one corner of the visitors' chamber, each of which has a distinctive but delicate tone. When the Temple was a training center for new monks, the bells were used to help the novices learn their prayers. Hours: 9:00 AM to 5:00 PM.

Shorin-in Temple 勝林院 (middle right) (optional). The grounds of this Temple are quite extensive. Even from the outside, visitors can see a building that dates from 1013. Shorin-in Temple is famous as the place where the priest Honen (remember Honen-in Temple in Eastern Kyoto?) debated and refuted the high ranking priests of other sects. Hours: 9:30 AM to 5:00 PM. Admission: 200 yen.

Hosen-in Temple 宝泉院 (middle right) (optional) is famous for its 500-year old pine tree shaped like Mt. Fuji; this marvelous example of the gardener's art is just inside the entrance. As with Jikkoin Temple, there is no ticket window. This time you have to hit a wooden gong to inform the staff of your arrival. Again, you pay a 500 yen admission and are led to a chamber where tea and a cake are served in a casual manner. The room faces a bamboo forest and the pillars on that side of the room frame the beautiful garden. Hours: 9:00 AM to 5:00 PM.

To Go or Not to Go to Enryakuji If you have decided to visit Enryakuji Temple, take a Kyoto Bus back to Yase-Yuenchi (Yase Playland), which you passed on your way to Ohara in the morning. You can take any of the Kyoto buses headed back to the city.

If you are not going to visit Enryakuji Temple, visit Jakkoin Temple in Ohara, and then take a bus back to the city. The No. 16 and No. 17 Kyoto Buses go to Sanjo Keihan terminal, and the No. 17 and No. 18 Kyoto Buses go to Kyoto Station.

Jakkoin Temple 寂光院 (Upper left)

Jakkoin Temple, erected in 594, is famous as the scene of a Taira clan tragedy. After ascending the ladder of power at the imperial court, the Taira clan was destroyed by the Minamotos. Empress Kenreimonin, a daughter of Kiyomori Taira and mother of Emperor Antoku, renounced the world at Chorakuji Temple, and lived the rest of her life at Jakkoin praying for the repose of the souls of her son and other members of the Taira family. The Temple is located at the top of a long stone stairway, and is surrounded by thick woods. If you are lucky enough to be at Jakkoin at a quiet time, its solemn atmosphere will remind you of this heroine's tragic life. Hours: 9:00 AM to 5:00 PM (4:30 in winter). Admission: 500 yen.

MT. HIEIZAN 比叡山

To Mt. Shimeidake Refer to Kansai Map 20. Yase cable car station is a few minutes walk from Yase-Yuenchi bus stop (Expanded area map is in the upper left corner of Kansai Map 20). The cable car operates every 30 minutes. The ride takes nine minutes and the fare is 520 yen. Transfer to the ropeway at Hiei for the trip to Sancho stop. The ropeway operates every 30 minutes. The ride takes 3 minutes. Fare: 300 yen

A revolving observatory with restaurant is located on the top of Mt. Shimeidake. If the weather permits, you have a panoramic view of Lake Biwako to the east, Osaka Bay to the west and the surrounding mountains.

Enryakuji Temple 延暦寺 (Upper right half of Kansai Map 20)

Find the path to Hieizan ski grounds, which feature traditional snow skiing in winter and "lawn" skiing the rest of the year. The narrow mountain path zigzags down amid huge cedar trees toward the ski grounds. Turn to the right before you reach the ski grounds. As pictured on Kansai Map 20, several sign posts (with signs written in Japanese) lead you to the Temple. Once you come to the large stone monument with a carving of the Amitabha trinity, the Temple precincts are not far at all. The path crosses over a road just before the Temple.

If you are a good walker, we recommend that you visit the West Precincts (upper center) first. They are to the north, and further down the slope. The return walk is pretty tough even though the approach is paved. If you decide to visit the West Precincts, use the bridge to cross the road. The major structures in the West Precincts are Jodoin Temple, Ninaido Hall and Shakado Hall, the main hall at the northern end of the grounds. All the buildings are surrounded by huge cedar trees, and since the number of visitors is relatively small, the precincts are filled with an atmosphere of esoteric Buddhism. There is now a shuttle bus between the West Precincts and the East Precincts (and the Yokawa Precincts, which we do not describe) during tourist seasons.

The East Precincts (middle right) are what most visitors see at Enryakuji Temple. Enryakuji was founded by the priest Saicho in 788. Enryakuji and Koyasan are the two giants of Japanese Buddhism and have played leading roles throughout their 1,200-year long histories. Many new religious sects were established by priests who studied at Enryakuji Temple. At the peak of its prosperity, Enryakuji Temple contained 3,000 buildings in three major precincts and in the surrounding valleys. The Temple even organized a private military force as big as that of a feudal lord. Because of this force, and because of the Temple's influence in political matters, Nobunaga Oda attacked Enryakuji in 1571. Most of the buildings were burned to the ground and thousands of

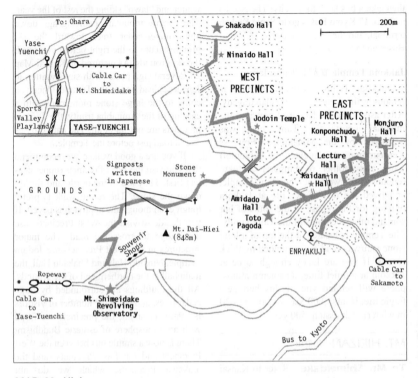

MAP 20 Hieizan

soldiers, priests and other residents of the Temple grounds were killed in the battle. Most of the present structures were constructed in the middle of the 17th century. Konponchudo Hall is the main hall of the Temple. Toto Pagoda is a recently completed gigantic two-story brilliant red structure.

Back to the City Take a bus back to the city. The No. 6 (going to Sanjo Keihan terminal), the No. 7 (to Kyoto Station via Sanjo Keihan) and the No. 51 (to Kyoto Station) buses all stop at the Enryakuji stop (lower right, Kansai Map 20). Because each bus operates only every 2-3 hours, take whichever one comes first (there is at least one bus every hour). The ride to Kyoto Sta-

tion takes about one hour. Enryakuji is not the first stop for these buses, so make sure that the bus you get on is headed for Kyoto.

As indicated on Kansai Map 20, there is another way to go back to Kyoto via Lake Biwako: a cable car to Sakamoto (lower right), and then a 15-minute walk to Sakamoto train station. Take the Keihan Ishizaka Line to Hama-Otsu, and then the Keihan Kyoshin Line to Keihan Sanjo in Kyoto (or the JR Tokaido Honsen Line commuter train from Otsu to Kyoto). Though the view of Lake Biwako from the cable car is fantastic, the rest of the connections are time consuming and the train rides boring, and we do not recommend this route for tourists unless you allocate one full day for Hieizan and Lake Biwako, and plan to stop at Hama-otsu to enjoy a boat ride on Lake Biwako.

SOUTHERN KYOTO
洛南

Although we have not "officially" organized a Southern Kyoto itinerary, or suggested that this area is a must for visitors to Kyoto, we do recommend that you visit some or all of the destinations described here. Some of Kyoto's true gems are located in the southern suburbs. Due to the fact that they are so spread out (and that public transportation is therefore rather inefficient), they are usually omitted from itineraries. If you have time, we suggest that you visit Southern Kyoto.

Byodoin Temple 平等院 (Lower right, Kansai Map 9)

Byodoin Temple is located in Uji City to the south of Kyoto (actually half way to Nara). The Temple is a 15-minute walk from Uji Station on the JR Nara Line (a 20-minute ride from Kyoto Station).

Byodoin Temple, popularly known as Phoenix Temple, was originally built as a villa for Michinaga Fujiwara, the most powerful aristocrat of the Heian Era. His son, Yorimichi, converted the villa to a Temple, and intended to create a Heaven on earth by adding many more magnificent structures and gardens. Even though most of the buildings were lost in the war at the middle of the 14th century, Phoenix Hall still stands in a garden designed around a large pond. Hours: 8:30 AM to 5:00 PM. Admission: 400 yen.

Fushimi Inari Shrine 伏見稲荷 (Middle center, Kansai Map 9)

Fushimi Inari Shrine is a few minutes walk from Inari Station on the JR Nara Line. Inari is the second stop from Kyoto Station, and the ride takes only 5 minutes.

Fushimi Inari Shrine is the headquarters of about 40,000 Inari shrines all over Japan. The origin of the Shrine is not clear. The Shrine was moved to the present site in 1438. Through a huge *torii* gate, a number of vermilion structures stand in the spacious grounds. Beyond the main precincts, a number of small shrines are scattered along the mountainous paths of Mt. Inariyama. Most parts of the path are beneath hundreds of thousands of vermilion *torii* gates contributed by people from all around Japan. No admission charge.

Tofukuji Temple 東福寺 (Middle center, Kansai Map 9)

Tofukuji Temple is a 15-minute walk from Tofukuji Station on the JR Nara Line. Tofukuji is the first stop from Kyoto Station. Erected in 1255, Tofukuji Temple is one of the five most important Zen temples in Kyoto. The huge Sanmon Gate and the Main Hall were constructed in this century. However, there are about 25 subordinate temples in the wide precincts, and each one has its own garden. Especially noteworthy is Hojo, which has a rock garden and a moss garden. No admission to the grounds. Hojo Hours: 9:00 AM to 4:00 PM. Admission to Hojo: 300 yen.

Daigoji Temple 醍醐寺 (Lower right, Kansai Map 9)

To visit Daigoji Temple, you can take the "Higashi-9" City Bus from Keihan-Sanjo Bus Terminal to Sanpoin-mae bus stop (about 40 minutes).

Mt. Daigosan rises in the southwestern corner of Kyoto City. The whole mountain is part of the precincts of Daigoji Temple, and more than 70 buildings are scattered over the mountain. The temple precincts are divided into two parts: Shimo-Daigo (lower Daigo) and Kami-Daigo (upper Daigo).

The main approach to Shimo-Daigo is lined on both sides with cherry trees. **Sanpoin Temple** 三宝院, a subordinate temple on the grounds, is famous for its paintings of the Kano School and its landscaped garden. Hours: 9:00 AM to 5:00 PM. Admission: 500 yen. **Hojuin** 宝聚院 (Treasure House) exhibits Buddha images, paintings, and other temple treasures. The Treasure House is open to the public only twice a year (early April to early May, and mid-October to mid-November). An elegant five-story pagoda is the only structure that has survived from the time of the founding of the Temple in 951.

Kami-Daigo was a training center for Buddhist priests. A 3.5 km (2 mile) steep path runs in the woods from Shimo-Daigo to Kami-Daigo. In the grounds of Kami-Daigo are several historic structures built in the 12th through the 15th centuries. If you like hiking, you should visit Kami-Daigo (a roundtrip hike from Shimo-Daigo takes about 3 hours).

OTHER PLACES OF INTEREST IN KYOTO

Katsura Detached Villa 桂離宮 (Middle left, Kansai Map 9)

The Villa is a 5-minute walk from Katsura-rikyu-mae Bus Stop. You can take the No. 33 or No. 60 bus from Kyoto Station.

Katsura Detached Villa is located in a bamboo forest on the western side of the Katsuragawa River. To visit the Villa, you must apply for permission to the Imperial Household Agency in Kyoto in advance. The tours are conducted in Japanese only.

See the beginning part of the text on Kyoto above for additional details.

The Villa was constructed over a period of 50 years, starting in 1620. The garden was built around a large pond with five small islets. The main villa and several small tea houses face the pond.

Shugakuin Detached Villa 修学院離宮 (Middle right, Kansai Map 9)

You can take the No. 5 City Bus from Kyoto Station to Shugakuin-rikyu-michi. The bus passes Sanjo Keihan Bus Terminal and Ginkakuji-michi. The entrance of the Detached Villa is about a 10-minute walk from the bus stop.

The application process for a special permission is the same as for Katsura Detached Villa. Tours are conducted in Japanese only.

This villa was constructed by the Tokugawa Shogunate in 1655 to entertain the emperor of the time. Three large gardens are located in a broad hilly area and pedestrian paths connect the gardens. The upper garden, designed around a large pond, is most impressive. The upper garden also commands a good view of the area.

Shisendo 詩仙堂 (Middle right, Kansai Map 9)

Shisendo is a 5-minute walk from Ichijoji-Sagarimatsu Bus Stop, which is also served by the No. 5 City Bus.

Shisendo was built in 1641 by Jozan Ishikawa, a famous poet of the Edo Era. He lived here in isolation from the worldly life. The garden is considered one of the best in Kyoto. You should not forget Shisendo if you are in the area for a visit to Shugakuin Detached Villa. Hours: 9:00 AM to 5:00 PM. Admission: 400 yen.

MAJOR FESTIVALS IN KYOTO

April 8: Hanamatsuri Festival to celebrate the birthday of Shaka. Held at many temples, such as Chion-in (Eastern Kyoto),

Nishi-Honganji (Central Kyoto) and Seiryo-ji Temple (Arashiyama).

May 3: Kankosai Festival of Fushimi Inari Shrine. Miniature shrines are carried on main streets, such as Gojo-dori and Kawara-machi-dori Streets.

May 15: Aoi Matsuri Festival features a colorful imperial procession on the main streets of the city from the Imperial Palace to Kamigamo Jinja Shrine.

Third Sunday of May: Mifune Matsuri Festival reproduces the scene of boating by nobles (near Togetsukyo Bridge in Arashiyama).

June 1-2: Takigi Noh (open-air noh performance) at Heian Jingu Shrine.

July 17: Gion Matsuri Festival. A 1,000 year old festival featuring a gorgeous procession of festival floats on main streets in the city.

August 16: Gozan Okuribi Festival or Bonfires on Five Mountains. Spectacular bonfires are lighted on the city's five mountains. The fires can be seen from downtown.

August 16: Manto Nagashi Festival. A number of paper lanterns with candles are floated on the river to send the spirits of ancestors back to Heaven (during the middle of August, they are supposed to visit earth). The festival is held in the Arashiyama area.

Second Sunday of October: Jinkosai Festival features a procession of miniature shrines and festival floats on Nishi-oji-dori Street.

October 22: Jidai Matsuri Festival is a living reproduction of Japanese history. A huge procession featuring various costumes from olden times to the Meiji Restoration is held on main streets in the city.

Second Sunday of November: Momiji Matsuri or Maple Viewing Festival. Tradi-

tional music and many dances and dramas are performed on boats in the Arashiyama area.

ACCOMMODATIONS IN KYOTO

1. Hotels in Kyoto

(1) Deluxe Hotels

Takaragaike Prince Hotel (Near the Kyoto International Conference Hall — upper center, Kansai Map 9). 322 rooms. Single (32,000 yen -) & Double (35,000 yen -). Add: Takaragaike, Sakyo-ku, Kyoto. Tel: (075) 712-1111.

Miyako Hotel (lower center, Kansai Map 15). Deluxe. 528 rooms. Single (17,000 yen -) & Double (24,000 yen -). Add: Keage, Higashiyama-ku, Kyoto. Tel: (075) 771-7111.

Kyoto Brighton Hotel (upper center, Kansai Map 13). 183 rooms. Single (24,000 yen -) & Double (29,500 yen). Add: Nakadachiuri, Shinmachidori, Nakagyo-ku, Kyoto. Tel: (075) 441-4411.

(2) First Class Hotels

ANA Hotel Kyoto (lower center, Kansai

Map 13). 303 rooms. Single (12,500 yen -) & Double (21,500 yen -). Add: Nijojo-mae, Horikawa-dori, Nakagyo-ku, Kyoto. Tel: (075) 231-1155.

Hotel Fujita Kyoto (upper center, Kansai Map 21). 189 rooms. Single (15,500 yen -) & Double (21,500 yen). Add: Nijo-Ohashi, Nakagyo-ku, Kyoto. Tel: (075) 222-1511.

International Hotel Kyoto (lower center, Kansai Map 13). 283 rooms. Single (13,000 yen -) & Double (20,500 yen -). Add: Nijo, Horikawadori, Nakagyo-ku, Kyoto. Tel: (075) 222-1111.

Kyoto Hotel (upper center, Kansai Map 12). Under construction. Add: Kawaramachi-Oike, Nakagyo-ku, Kyoto. Tel: (075) 211-5111.

Kyoto Grand Hotel (lower left, Kansai Map 14). First Class. 506 rooms. Single (14,000 yen -) & Double (20,500 yen -). Add: Horikawa-Shiokoji, Shimogyo-ku, Kyoto. Tel: (075) 341-2311.

Kyoto Royal Hotel (upper center, Kansai Map 12). First Class. 331 rooms. Single (11,500 yen -) & Double (23,000 yen -). Add: Kawaramachi, Sanjo, Nakagyo-ku, Kyoto. Tel: (075) 223-1234.

New Miyako Hotel (lower center, Kansai Map 14). First Class. 714 rooms. Single (11,500 yen -) & Double (20,500 yen -). Add: Kyotoeki-Hachijoguchi, Minami-ku, Kyoto. Tel: (075) 661-7111.

(3) Standard and Business Hotels

Holiday Inn Kyoto (30 minutes by taxi from Kyoto Station). Standard. 270 rooms. Single (8,500 yen -) & Double (18,000 yen -). Add: 36, Nishi-Hirakicho, Takano, Sakyo-ku, Kyoto. Tel: (075) 721-3131.

Karasuma Kyoto Hotel (upper right, Kansai Map 14). Business. 84 singles (10,000 yen -) & 168 doubles (16,500 yen -). Add: Karasuma-Shijo-sagaru, Shimogyo-ku, Kyoto. Tel: (075) 371-0111.

Hotel Keihan Kyoto (lower right, Kansai Map 14). Standard. 118 singles (8,000 yen -) & 190 doubles (15,500 yen -). Add:

Higashi-Kujo, Minami-ku, Kyoto. Tel: (075) 661-0321.

Kyoto Century Hotel (lower right, Kansai Map 14). Standard. 48 singles (11,000 yen -) & 189 doubles (21,500 yen -). Add: Shiokoji-sagaru, Higashino-Toindori, Shimogyo-ku, Kyoto. Tel: (075) 351-0111.

Kyoto Daini Tower Hotel (lower right, Kansai Map 14). Standard. 70 singles (7,500 yen -) & 220 doubles (11,500 yen -). Add: Shichijo-sagaru, Higashino-Toindori, Shimogyo-ku, Kyoto. Tel: (075) 361-3261.

Kyoto Park Hotel (lower left, Kansai Map 16). Standard. 268 rooms. Single (10,500 yen -) & Double (20,500 yen -). Add: 644-2, Sanjusangendo-Mawarimachi, Higashiyama-ku, Kyoto. Tel: (075) 523-3111.

Kyoto Tokyu Inn (10 minutes by taxi from Kyoto Station). Standard. 390 rooms. Single (8,500 yen -) & Double (13,000 yen -). Add: 35-1, Hananookacho, Kami-Kazan, Yamashina-ku, Kyoto. Tel: (075) 593-0109.

Kyoto Tower Hotel (lower right, Kansai Map 14). Standard. 38 singles (7,500 yen -) & 118 doubles (14,000 yen -). Add: Shichijo-sagaru, Karasumadori, Shimogyo-ku, Kyoto. Tel: (075) 361-3211.

Hotel New Hankyu Kyoto (lower center, Kansai Map 14). Standard. 56 singles (10,500 yen -) & 258 doubles (18,500 yen -). Add: Shiokojidori, Shimogyo-ku, Kyoto. Tel: (075) 343-5300.

Hotel New Kyoto (middle left, Kansai Map 13). Standard. 27 singles (9,500 yen -) & 274 doubles (16,000 yen -). Add: Horikawa-Marutamachi, Kamigyo-ku, Kyoto. Tel: (075) 801-2111.

Hotel Rich Kyoto (middle center, Kansai Map 21). Standard. 24 singles (8,000 yen -) & 83 doubles (13,000 yen -). Add: Gojo-agaru, Kawaramachidori, Shimogyo-ku, Kyoto. Tel: (075) 341-1131.

Sun Hotel Kyoto (middle center, Kansai Map 12). Business. 98 singles (7,000 yen -) & 56 doubles (11,500 yen -). Add: Sanjo, Kawaramachi, Nakagyo-ku, Kyoto. Tel: (075) 241-3351.

Hotel Sunflower Kyoto (middle center, Kansai Map 15). Business. 2 singles (10,500 yen -) & 52 doubles (16,500 yen -). Add: 51, Higashi-Tennocho, Okazaki, Sakyo-ku, Kyoto. Tel: (075) 761-9111.

2. Ryokan in Kyoto

(1) Deluxe Ryokan

Tawaraya Ryokan (upper center, Kansai Map 12). 19 rooms. 40,000 yen & up per person. Add: Fuyacho-Anekoji-agaru, Nakagyo-ku, Kyoto. Tel: (075) 211-5566.

Hiiragiya Ryokan (upper center, Kansai Map 12). 33 rooms. 35,000 yen & up per person. Add: Fuyacho-Anekoji-agaru, Nakagyo-ku, Kyoto. Tel: (075) 221-1136.

Sumiya Ryokan (upper center, Kansai Map 12). 26 rooms. 35,000 yen & up per person. Add: Fuyachodori-Sanjo-sagaru, Nakagyo-ku, Kyoto. Tel: (075) 221-2188.

Seikoro (middle center, Kansai Map 21). 24 rooms. 26,000 yen & up per person. Add: Tonyachodori-Gojo-sagaru, Higashiyama-ku, Kyoto. Tel: (075) 561-0771.

Yachiyo (lower center, Kansai Map 15). 26 rooms. 22,000 yen & up per person. Add: 34, Nanzenji-Fukuchicho, Sakyo-ku, Kyoto. Tel: (075) 771-4148.

(2) First-class Ryokan

Chikiriya (middle left, Kansai Map 12). 49 rooms. 20,000 yen & up per person. Add: Tominokoji-nishiiru, Takoyakushi-dori, Nakagyo-ku, Kyoto. Tel: (075) 221-1281.

Kyo-Chitose (upper center, Kansai Map 16). 11 rooms. 20,000 yen & up per person. Add: 545, Gionmachi-Minamigawa, Higashiyama-ku, Kyoto. Tel: (075) 531-0157.

Yoshiima Ryokan (middle right, Kansai Map 12). 19 rooms. 20,000 yen & up per person. Add: Yamatooji-Higashiiru, Shinmonzen, Higashiyama-ku, Kyoto. Tel: (075) 561-2620.

Mikihan Ryokan (middle center, Kansai Map 12). 43 rooms. 18,000 yen & up per person. Add: Fuyacho-kado, Rokkaku-

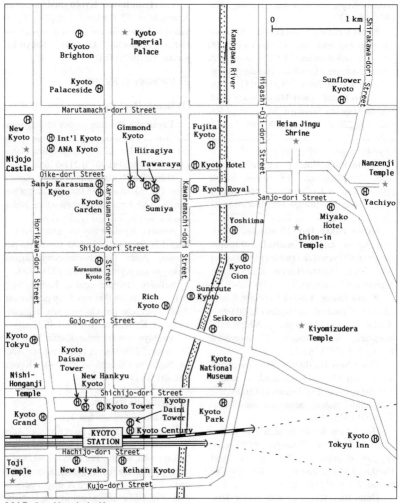

MAP 21 Hotels in Kyoto

dori, Nakagyo-ku, Kyoto. Tel: (075) 221-0428.

(3) Standard Ryokan

Ryokan Hakurokuso (middle left, Kansai Map 12). 61 rooms. 12,000 yen & up per person. Add: Higashino-Toin-Higashiiru,

Rokkaku-dori, Nakagyo-ku, Kyoto. Tel: (075) 221-7846.

Ryokan Hideoka (middle center, Kansai Map 12). 21 rooms. 12,000 yen & up per person. Add: Tominokoji-Higashiiru, Takoyakushi-dori, Nakagyo-ku, Kyoto. Tel: (075) 221-2667.

3. Welcome Inns in Kyoto

Kyoto Daisan Tower Hotel (lower center, Kansai Map 14). 118 Western rooms. Add: Shinmachidori-Shichijo-sagaru, Shimogyo-ku, Kyoto. Tel: (075) 343-3111.

Hotel Gimmond Kyoto (upper left, Kansai Map 12). 140 Western rooms. Add: Takakura, Oike-dori, Nakagyo-ku, Kyoto. Tel: (075) 221-4111.

Kyoto Gion Hotel (lower right, Kansai Map 12). 131 Western rooms. Add: 555, Gionmachi-Minamigawa, Higashiyama-ku, Kyoto. Tel: (075) 551-2111.

Hotel Hokke Club Kyoto (3 minute walk from Kyoto Sation). 26 Japanese & 108 Western rooms. Add: Karasuma-Chuo-guchi, Shimogyo-ku, Kyoto. Tel: (075) 361-1251.

Kyoto Palaceside Hotel (middle right, Kansai Map 13). 119 Western rooms. Add: Shimodachiuri, Karasumadori, Kamigyo-ku, Kyoto. Tel: (075) 431-8171.

Kyoya Ryokan (8 minute walk from Kyoto Station). 10 Japanese rooms. Add: Higashino-Toin-Higashiiru, Shimo-Juzuyamachidori, Shimogyo-ku, Kyoto. Tel: (075) 371-2709.

Matsubaya Ryokan (8 minute walk from Kyoto Station). 11 Japanese rooms. Add: Higashino-Toin-Nishi, Kami-Juzuyamachidori, Shimogyo-ku, Kyoto. Tel: (075) 351-3727.

Hotel Matsui (middle left, Kansai Map 12). 40 Japanese rooms. Add: Takakura-Higashiiru, Rokkakudori, Nakagyo-ku, Kyoto. Tel: (075) 221-6688.

Matsui Inn (10 minutes by taxi from Kyoto Station). 35 Japanese rooms. Add: Rokkaku-sagaru, Yanaginobanba, Nakagyo-ku, Kyoto. Tel: (075) 221-3535.

Hotel Oaks Kyoto Shijo (10 minutes by taxi from Kyoto Station). 138 Western rooms. Add: Nishino-Toin, Shijo, Shimogyo-ku, Kyoto. Tel: (075) 371-0941.

Ohtomo Bekkan Inn (5 minute walk from Kyoto Sation). 17 Japanese rooms. Add: Shichijo-agaru, Akezudori, Shimogyo-ku, Kyoto. Tel: (075) 341-6344.

Pension Higashiyama (10 minutes by taxi from Kyoto Station). 2 Japanese & 11 Western rooms. Add: Shirakawaguchi, Sanjo-sagaru, Higashiyama-ku, Kyoto. Tel: (075) 882-1181.

Pension Station Kyoto (5 minute walk from Kyoto Station). 4 Japanese & 9 Western rooms. Add: Shichijo-agaru, Shinmachidori, Shimogyo-ku, Kyoto. Tel: (075) 882-6200.

Ryokan Hiraiwa (5 minutes by taxi from Kyoto Station). 21 Japanese rooms. Add: 314, Hayaocho, Kaminoguchi-agaru, Shimogyo-ku, Kyoto. Tel: (075) 351-6748.

Ryokan Ohto (7 minutes by taxi from Kyoto Station). 12 Japanese rooms. Add: Kamogawa-Higashi, Shichijo, Higashiyama-ku, Kyoto. Tel: (075) 541-7803.

Sanjo Karasuma Kyoto Hotel (middle left, Kansai Map 21). 147 Western rooms. Add: Karasuma, Sanjodori, Nakagyo-ku, Kyoto. Tel: (075) 256-3331.

Hotel Sunroute Kyoto (middle center, Kansai Map 21). 144 Western rooms. Add: Matsubara, Kawaramachidori, Shimogyo-ku, Kyoto. Tel: (075) 371-3711.

AMANOHASHIDATE
天の橋立

Amanohashidate, the "Bridge of Heaven," is the name of the place where, as the story goes, two figures of Japanese mythology, the god *Izanagi-no-Mikoto* and the goddess *Izanami-no-Mikoto,* conceived the islands of Japan, to which Izanami later gave birth. The "Bridge of Heaven" is actually a 3.6 km (2.2 mile) long pine-clad sandbar that separates Miyatsu Bay from Asoumi Lagoon. Geography and mythology aside, Amanohashidate is indisputably a beautiful place, as evidenced by its popularity as summer resort for the upper classes of

the Osaka-Kyoto-Kobe area and its official designation as a place of scenic beauty. (It's part of the traditional "Scenic Trio" that all Japanese try to visit at one point in their lives — the other two places being Matsushima near Sendai and Miyajima in the Inland Sea near Hiroshima.) Because of its popularity, it's best to visit Amanohashidate before or after the summer season.

Transportation to Amanohashidate

Amanohashidate is connected with Kyoto by direct train service. There are two limited express trains in the morning and two in the afternoon in each direction between the two cities. If you take one of the morning trains (which leave Kyoto at 9:30 AM and 10:00 AM), you will arrive in Amanohashidate around noon. After spending 4-5 hours sightseeing there, you can easily return to Kyoto the same day. (The return trains leave late in the afternoon.) These trains run over three lines: two JR and one of another company. From Kyoto to Ayabe, the trains run on the JR San-in Honsen Line; from Ayabe to Nishi-Maizuru, the trains run on the JR Maizuru Line; from Nishi-Maizuru to Amanohashidate, the trains run on Kita-Kinki Tango Railways track. If you are using a JR Rail Pass, you have to pay for this third section of the trip.

Viewing Amanohashidate (Ichinomiya District)

Refer to Kansai Map 22.

When you get off the train from Kyoto, walk through Chionji Temple to the boat pier. The fifteen minute trip across the lagoon to the town of Ichinomiya gives you a view of the Amanohashidate sandbar on your right. A combination ticket costs 1,120 yen one way and is good for the boat as well as the lift and bus described below.

When you get off the boat at Ichinomiya, walk through the large yellow *torii* gates. When you reach the main Shrine building, follow the path and you'll come to a street crammed full of souvenir shops; the entrance to the cable car and the chair lift is on your right. The ropeway and lift run about once every 15 minutes. The four-minute ropeway ride takes you to Kasamatsu Park, which provides the most celebrated view of Amanohashidate.

When you get off the ropeway, go up the steps to the observatory. (There's another observatory as you get off the ropeway, but it is completely ruined by tacky restaurants and souvenir shops and loudspeakers blaring sentimental music.) The observatory up the steps is *the* one. Japanese believe that one's view of Amanohashidate is enhanced if you stand with your back to it, lean down and look at it upside down, through your legs. From this perspective, the Bridge of Heaven is supposed to look like it's suspended in mid-air! Give it a try — it can't hurt! Even straight on, the view is quite nice.

You can next take the bus from Kasamatsu to Nariaiji Temple. The six-minute ride provides great glimpses of Asoumi Lagoon and the mountains. The Temple dates back to the beginning of the 8th century and belongs to the Koyasan-Shingon sect of Buddhism. It is the 28th stop on the pilgrimage tour of 33 Western Japan Kannon temples. The red entrance gate to the Temple has many colorful carvings of animals. The Main Hall also features

MAP 22 Amanohashidate

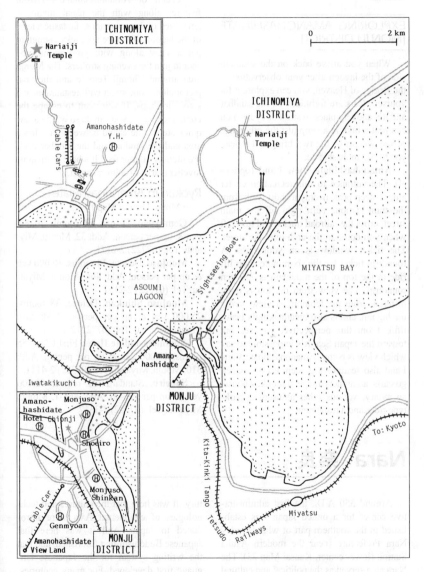

lavishly detailed carvings. There's a snack shop and garden adjacent to the Temple grounds.

EXPLORING AMANOHASHIDATE (MONJU DISTRICT)

When you arrive back on the southern side of the lagoon after your observation of the Bridge of Heaven, you can explore it for yourself. Cars are forbidden on the sandbar and it's a lovely place to stroll or cycle. You can rent a bike at a shop just the other side of the second of the two bridges that lead you to Amanohashidate.

Amanohashidate View Land (optional). The entrance to this recreation center atop a steep peak is only a short walk from the train station. Turn right off the main street, cross the railroad tracks, and turn left when you come to the arch over the street. The ticket window is on your right. A roundtrip ticket for the six-minute chair lift ride to the top of the mountain is 750 yen roundtrip. The view from the top is quite different from the Ichinomiya view across the lagoon, and is also breathtakingly beautiful. From this perspective, you see out toward the Japan Sea. It's impossible to say which view is better. Amanohashidate View Land also features a garden, lawn croquet, go carts, an archery range, a monkey house, an aviary, various other amusement-park-type rides and a restaurant.

EVENING STROLLS

Several of Amanohashidate's *ryokan* feature, along with the usual luxurious amenities of Japanese inns, fantastic views of the lagoon. If you're not lucky enough to get a view along with your room, you should join the evening strollers. The Monju area around Chionji Temple and the boat pier includes one street with restaurants and souvenir shops. If you want to escape the commercial area, you can do so within a few quick steps. The island between the Monju area and the sandbar and the sandbar itself are literally at your feet. It's hard to imagine lovelier places to enjoy a sunset.

Ryokan in Amanohashidate
(See Monju District Map.)

Genmyoan. Deluxe. 31 rooms. 30,000 yen & up per person. Add: 32, Monju, Miyatsu. Tel: (07722) 2-2171.

Monjuso. Deluxe. 14 rooms. 30,000 yen & up per person. Add: 466, Monju, Miyatsu. Tel: (07722) 2-2151.

Monjuso Shinkan. Deluxe. 38 rooms. 25,000 yen & up per person. Add: 510, Monju, Miyatsu. Tel: (07722) 2-7111.

Amanohashidate Hotel. First Class. 55 rooms. 18,000 yen & up per person. Add: 310, Monju, Miyatsu. Tel: (07722) 2-4111.

Shoeiro. Standard. 21 rooms. 12,000 yen & up per person. Add: 468-1, Monju, Miyatsu. Tel: (07722) 2-3317.

Nara 奈良

Around 350 A.D., the first administrative center for a united Japan was established in the southern part of what is today Nara Prefecture (near the modern Asuka Station (lower center, Kansai Map 23). The Nara area served as the political and cultural center of Japan until the end of the 8th century. It was here that the cultures and technologies of continental Asia were introduced to Japan. And it was here that Japanese Buddhism first flourished, and that the writing system for the Japanese language first developed. For many centuries, however, the actual capital was moved to a new location each time a new emperor ascended the throne. Japan's first permanent capital was founded in Nara in 710 by Emperor Kammu. Today's visitors to the city will find many portions of this ancient capital dating from the 6th-8th centuries still intact. As of 794, when the capital was moved to Kyoto, Nara lost its political significance, and was thus spared the damage other areas suffered during the civil wars. Modern industrialization has also passed Nara by. With great foresight, modern Nara's inhabitants decided to construct the spacious garden park that now surrounds the area containing Nara's venerable structures. Today the city's population stands at 350,000.

MAP 23 Outline of Nara

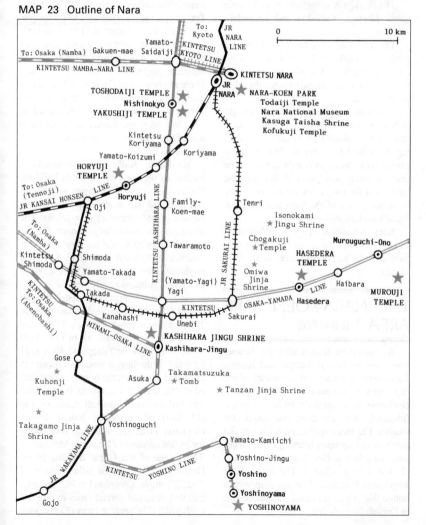

We have divided Nara into three parts. One is the Nara-Koen Park area; the second is the Ikaruga area; and the third is a remote area of Nara Prefecture far south of the city.

The Nara-Koen Park area includes: Todaiji Temple (the Great Buddha Temple); Kasuga Taisha Shrine; and other historic legacies laid out around the Park.

The Ikaruga area includes three historic gems: Horyuji, Yakushiji and Toshodaiji Temples.

The remote area is actually reached more easily from Osaka, and is recommended for those staying there. It is also recommended for those who have already visited the other areas of Nara.

Individual travelers who stay overnight in Nara have the extra treat of being able to stroll in Nara-Koen Park in the early morning or in the late afternoon. This beautiful garden park, home to Nara's famous tame deer, is completely peaceful during these hours, and the only other visitors are likely to be the ghosts of the lords and ladies of Japan's ancient aristocracy.

Nara Municipal Tourist Information Center is located on Sanjo-dori Street near Sarusawa-no-Ike Pond (middle center, Kansai Map 24).

THE NARA-KOEN PARK AREA 奈良公園周辺

As shown on Kansai Map 24, famous sites such as Todaiji Temple and Kasuga Taisha Shrine are located to the east of the city center. Circle bus lines — running both clockwise and counter-clockwise — operate frequently and are quite convenient for tourists. The buses operate on a 150 yen flat fare system (pay upon boarding). The clockwise loop bus is No. 2, and the counter-clockwise loop is No. 1. The route of the loop buses is indicated on the map with a dotted line. There are taped announcements in English for each stop.

Todaiji Temple 東大寺 (Upper right)

Todaiji Temple was originally constructed at the order of Emperor Shomu in 752. Though most tourists see only the statue of the Great Buddha in the main building (Daibutsuden), the wide temple precincts contain a number of buildings and sculptures of great historical and cultural significance. **Nandaimon Gate** 南大門 (National Treasure) is the main entrance to the temple. The Gate, reconstructed in 1199, is supported by 19 pillars, and is a good example of the Chinese architectural technology the Japanese imported in the 12th century. There are two 8.1 m (26 foot) tall statues of guardians in niches on both sides of the gate. These two National Treasures, carved in 1203 by Unkei and Kaikei, are representative of the high artistic achievements of the Kamakura Era.

Kaidan-in Hall 戒壇院 (optional) is located to the west of the main building. Kaidan-in was the most important ceremonial Buddhist hall in all of Japan, and was the site of ordinations of new priests. The small hall is particularly famous for the exquisite clay images of the Four Heavenly Guardians (National Treasures) that were produced in the 7th century. Hours: 8:00 AM to 4:30 PM. Admission: 400 yen.

The present huge **Daibutsuden Hall** 大仏殿 (Hall of the Great Buddha, National Treasure) was constructed in 1708 after repeated fires. The hall, 57 m (187 feet) wide, 50 m (164 feet) deep and 48 m (157 feet) tall, is the largest wooden structure in the world. However, the original, constructed in 752, was 1.5 times larger than the present hall. In front of the hall stands a 4.5 m (15 foot) tall octagonal bronze lantern (National Treasure), which is noteworthy for its fine carvings of Heavenly Maidens.

The Image of the Great Buddha in the Daibutsuden Hall is the holiest object of Todaiji Temple. Completed in 752, the original was damaged several times by fire and earthquake. The present 16 m (53 foot) tall

statue was repaired quite extensively in 1692. Hours: 7:30 AM to 5:30 PM (8:30 AM to 4:30 PM in winter). Admission: 400 yen.

To the east of the main buildings, atop a flight of stone steps, there are several structures including the old Bath House and Belfry (National Treasure). Further to the east, in an elevated location, are Nigatsudo Hall (February Hall), Sangatsudo Hall (March Hall), and Shigatsudo Hall (April Hall).

Nigatsudo Hall 二月堂. The view of the city of Nara from the corridor of Nigatsudo Hall is not to be missed. Nigatsudo is also famous as the home of an elaborate fire festival held in early March. The interior is not open to the public.

Sangatsudo Hall 三月堂, built in the middle of the 8th century, is the oldest building in the Todaiji complex. It contains more than a dozen spectacular statues produced in the 8th century. Hours: 8:00 AM to 5:30 PM. Admission: 400 yen.

Kasuga Taisha Shrine 春日大社
(Middle right)

Passing Tamukeyama Hachimangu Shrine, walk to the south skirting the western foot of Mt. Wakakusayama (342 m or 1,115 feet). The right side of the street is lined with souvenir shops and restaurants. As the paved street curves toward the left, you will see a flight of stone steps on your right. Take this short cut down to the small stream at the bottom, and walk across

Kasuga Taisha Shrine's wide parking lot. **The Treasure House** 春日大社宝物館 (optional) of the Shrine, located at the southern end of the parking lot, is housed in a modern two-story concrete building. It displays the Shrine's treasures, which include noh masks and equipment for Shinto ceremonies. Hours: 8:30 AM to 4:30 PM (9:00 AM to 4:00 PM in winter). Admission: 350 yen.

To the south of the Treasure House stands a *torii* gate, the formal entrance to Kasuga Taisha Shrine. (As a matter of fact, this is the second of the Shrine's *torii* gates. The first is located far to west, near the National Museum.) Both sides of the approach to the Shrine are lined with stone lanterns of various sizes and shapes. Altogether there are about 3,000 lanterns along the approach. Twice a year, in early February and in the middle of August, all of them are lighted, creating a solemn, dream-like atmosphere. Through the *torii* gate, you come first to Tochakuden (Arrival Hall), then to Minamimon Gate (South Gate) 南門, entrance to the main buildings of Kasuga Taisha Shrine. Covered red and green corridors extend in two different directions from the gate, and surround the major buildings of the Shrine. The Shrine was originally erected in 710, and its buildings were reconstructed periodically according to Shinto tradition, which requires that places of worship be pulled down and then completely rebuilt at regular intervals (usually every 20 years). The spacious grounds of the Shrine are inside Minamimon Gate. Several of the natural wood buildings, including **Haiden Hall** (Offering Hall) 拝殿 and **Naoraiden** (Entertainment Hall) 直会殿, are used for various Shinto ceremonies. Behind Chumon Gate (Middle Gate) are four **Honden Halls** (Main Shrines) 本殿, each in the same architectural style and each a National Treasure. They were last rebuilt in 1893, supposedly for the 56th time. Hours: 9:00 AM to 4:00 PM. Admission: 350 yen.

MAP 24 Nara-Koen Park

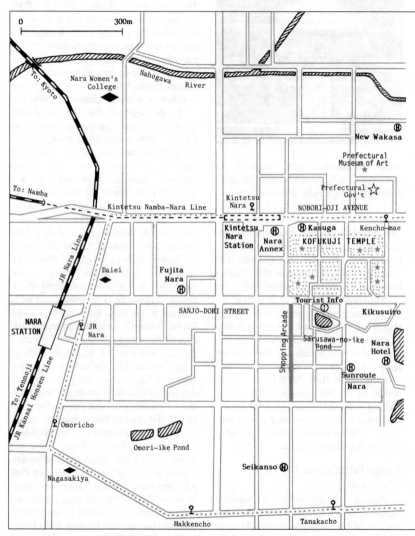

Shin-Yakushiji Temple 新薬師寺
(Lower right) (optional)

After passing Wakamiya Jinja Shrine, the narrow path enters a thick, refreshing and romantic forest. Crossing a wider street, you'll come to a T-shaped intersections, where you should turn right. The traffic mirror and small store are good landmarks to help you find the street that leads to Shin-Yakushiji Temple.

Shin-Yakushiji Temple was originally erected in the middle of the 8th century at

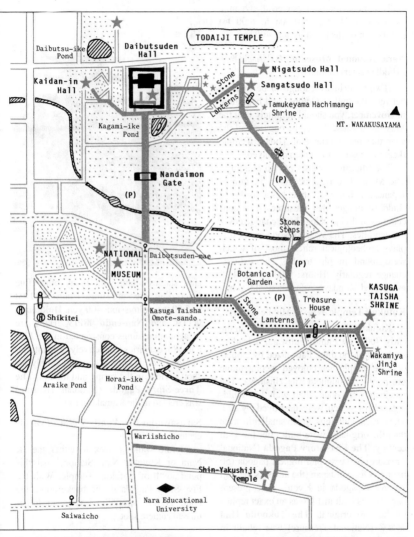

the order of Empress Komyo, in thanksgiving for the recovery of Emperor Shomu from a serious illness. Only the original Dining Hall (the present Main Hall, National Treasure) has survived; the other buildings were destroyed by fire and typhoon and were reconstructed after the 13th century. At the center of the dark Main Hall sits the image of Yakushi-Nyorai (God of Medicine, National Treasure), which is surrounded by clay images of Twelve Divine Generals. Eleven of the 12 originals remain, and are National Treasures. They are especially famous for their powerful, dynamic expressions. Hours: 8:30 AM to 6:00 PM (5:00 PM in winter). Admission: 400 yen.

Nara National Museum 奈良国立博物館
(Middle center) (optional)

If you are lucky enough to be in Nara between the end of October and beginning of November, you should definitely visit the Museum because that is the one time of the year that the treasures of Todaiji Temple (kept in Shosoin House) are displayed.

The Museum consists of two buildings. The Main Hall, patterned on a traditional Japanese architectural style, has a display of Buddhist images that illustrates how conceptions of divine beings have changed over the centuries. The Western-style annex displays archeological relics, most of which were found in old tombs. The exhibits change regularly. Hours: 9:00 AM to 4:30 PM. Closed Mondays. Admission: 400 yen.

Kofukuji Temple 興福寺 (Middle center)

Kofukuji Temple was constructed in the early 700's by Fuhito Fujiwara, a leading aristocrat of the time. Patronized by emperors, the temple has enjoyed incomparable prosperity throughout its history. The precincts were once filled with 175 buildings, all of which were destroyed by fire. The present buildings, much smaller in scale than the originals, were built after the 13th century. **The Five-Story Pagoda** (National Treasure) is the second highest pagoda (50 m or 164 feet) in Japan (the tallest is the Toji Temple's pagoda in Kyoto). The present pagoda was built in 1426 as an exact replica of the 730 original. **The Tokondo Hall** 東金堂 (National Treasure) was rebuilt in 1415 from the plans of the 726 original. It houses several National Treasure statues from the 8th century. Tokondo Hours: 9:00 AM to 5:00 PM. Admission: 200 yen. **The Treasure House** 宝物堂 is a concrete building that houses more than 20 National Trea-

sure statues along with many other fine objets d'art. Treasure House Hours: 9:00 AM to 5:00 PM. Admission: 400 yen. **Hokuendo** 北円堂 and **Nan-endo** 南円堂 Halls are octagonal buildings constructed in the 13th and 18th centuries respectively. The interior of Hokuendo is open to the public only for short periods in the spring and the fall. **The Three-Story Pagoda** (National Treasure) was erected in the Kamakura Era.

Sarusawa-no-Ike Pond 猿沢池 (Middle center)

Before walking back to either the JR Nara or Kintetsu Nara Station, visit this pond south of Kofukuji Temple. With the Five-Story Pagoda in the background, the pond is an especially lovely not-to-be-missed camera shot.

ACCOMMODATIONS
(Refer to Kansai Map 24)

1. Hotels in Nara

Nara Hotel (middle center). First Class. 123 rooms. Single (13,000 yen -) & Double

(24,000 yen -). Add: Nara-Koen-nai, Nara. Tel: (0742) 26-3300.

Hotel Fujita Nara (middle left). First Class. 118 rooms. Single (11,000 yen -) & Double (17,000 yen -). Add: 47-1, Sanjo-machi, Nara. Tel: (0742) 23-8111.

Hotel Sunroute Nara (middle center). Standard. 95 rooms. Single (8,500 yen -) & Double (15,500 yen -). Add: 1110, Taka-batakecho, Nara. Tel: (0742) 22-5151.

2. Ryokan in Nara

Shikitei (middle center). Deluxe. 10 rooms. 45,000 yen & up per person. Add: 1163, Takabatakecho, Nara. Tel: (0742) 22-5531.

Kikusuiro (middle center). Deluxe. 17 rooms. 45,000 yen & up per person. Add: 1130, Takabatake-Bodaicho, Nara. Tel: (0742) 23-2001.

Kasuga Hotel (middle center). Deluxe. 42 rooms. 20,000 yen & up per person. Add: 40, Noboriojicho, Nara. Tel: (0742) 22-4031.

3. Welcome Inns in Nara

Ryokan Seikanso (lower center). 13 Japanese rooms. Add: 29, Higashi-Kitsuji-cho, Nara. Tel: (0742) 22-2670.

Matsumae Ryokan (7 minute walk from Nara Station). 13 Japanese rooms. Add: 28, Higashi-Terabayashicho, Nara. Tel: (0742) 22-3686.

Tsubame Ryokan (5 minutes by taxi from JR Nara Station). 5 Japanese rooms. Add: 243, Jogonji, Nishi-Kitsujicho, Nara. Tel: (0742) 26-0177.

Pension Nara Club (10 minutes by taxi from JR Nara Station). 10 Western rooms. Add: 21, Kita-Mikadocho, Nara. Tel: (0742) 22-3450.

THE IKARUGA AREA
斑鳩・西の京

Horyuji Temple, the world's oldest wooden building, is located in the Ikaruga area of Nara Prefecture. Two more important historic legacies, Toshodaiji Temple and Yakushiji Temple, are located in the nearby Nishinokyo area. Visiting these three places is an ideal one-day excursion from Kyoto or Osaka (or Nara City, if you have stayed overnight there).

Transportation and Suggested Itineraries

From Kyoto

Refer to Kansai Maps 2 and 23. Take an express train on the Kintetsu Nara Line from Kyoto to Yamato-Saidaiji Station. Express trains operate about once every hour and the ride takes about 40 minutes. Transfer at Yamato-Saidaiji to a local train on the Kintetsu Kashihara Line. Your destination, Nishinokyo, is the second stop (a 4-minute ride). Please note that Nishinokyo Station (Kansai Map 25) is served by only local trains (expresses do not stop there). The ride costs 540 yen from Kyoto.

Yakushiji Temple is just a 5-minute walk from Nishinokyo Station, and Toshodaiji Temple is a 10-minute walk from Yakushiji Temple. After your visit to these two temples, take a bus from Toshodaiji-mae Bus Stop (Kansai Map 25) to Horyuji Stop. Be sure to use the Toshodaiji-mae Bus Stop across the creek, not the one right in front of the Temple. The buses run about once every 30 minutes, and the ride takes 35 minutes (510 yen).

After Horyuji, walk about 10 minutes to JR Horyuji Station. Take the JR Kansai Honsen Line commuter train from Horyuji to Nara (frequent service, an 11-minute ride), and then transfer at Nara to the JR Nara Line back to Kyoto (a 45-60 minue ride).

From Osaka (Tennoji Station)

Refer to Kansai Maps 3 and 23. Tennoji Station is on the JR Osaka Kanjo (Loop) Line. Tennoji is also served by Subway Midosuji Line. Take the JR Kansai Honsen

Line commuter train from Tennoji Station to Horyuji Station (frequent service, a 31-minute ride). Visit Horyuji Temple first. Then take a bus from Horyuji Stop to Yakushiji-mae Stop. The buses run about once every 30 minutes and the ride takes 35 minutes (510 yen). Visit Yakushiji and Toshodaiji Temples. Take the same bus (which you took from Horyuji to Yakushiji) in the same direction from Toshodaiji-mae to JR Nara Station (a 30-minute ride, 210 yen). You can catch the JR Kansai Honsen Line commuter train from Nara back to Osaka's Tennoji Station.

From Nara City

The No. 52 bus serves both Kintetsu Nara Station and JR Nara Station. Take this bus to Toshodaiji-mae Stop (a 30-minute ride, 210 yen). After visiting Toshodaiji and Yakushiji Temples, continue on the same bus from Yakushiji-mae stop to Horyuji. After Horyuji, you can take the JR Kansai Honsen Line train (to Nara or to Osaka's Tennoji Station, depending on your destination). Refer to Kansai Map 23.

Toshodaiji Temple 唐招提寺 (Upper center, Kansai Map 25)

Toshodaiji Temple was erected in 759 by the Chinese priest Ganjin, who visited Japan at the invitation of Emperor Shomu. Ganjin was 66 when he finally arrived in Japan, twelve years after the invitation was issued. His attempts to reach Japan from the continent were thwarted by political interference by Chinese officials, five shipwrecks, and various diseases, one of which left him blind. Despite these difficulties, Ganjin fulfilled the imperial commission and supervised the construction of this magnificent temple.

Toshodaiji Temple, unlike most other temples, has suffered no fires or other accidents; its original buildings still stand. **Kondo Hall** 金堂 (Main Hall, National Treasure) contains a 4.7 m (10 foot) image of Sakya as its main object of worship. The eight pillars at the front of Kondo Hall are entastic (i.e., the balloon almost imperceptibly). This borrowing from Greek architecture testifies to the fact that cultural exchange via the "Silk Road" had an impact even in Nara as early as the 8th century. Behind Kondo Hall is **Kodo Hall** 講堂 (Lecture Hall, National Treasure), which was moved from Nara Imperial Palace in celebration of Ganjin's completion of the temple. Nara Imperial Palace was completely destroyed in a later era, and this Kodo Hall is the only relic we have today of palace architecture of the Nara Era. A graceful atmosphere pervades the precincts. Hours: 8:30 AM to 4:30 PM. Admission: 300 yen. **The Treasure House** 新宝蔵 is open to the public from March 20 to May 19 in the

MAP 25 Path of History

spring, and from September 15 to November 5 in the fall.

Yakushiji Temple 薬師寺 (Lower center, Kansai Map 25)

The street connecting Toshodaiji and Yakushiji Temples is popularly called the "Path of History" because emperors and nobles used this path when they visited these two important temples.

Yakushiji Temple was originally erected in the Asuka district (further to the south) by Emperor Temmu in 680, and was moved to its present location in 718. The gorgeous buildings of Yakushiji were called "Heavenly Palace," and the temple enjoyed the patronage of successive emperors. Unfortunately, all of the buildings except East Tower, a three-story pagoda constructed in 730, were destroyed by fires and earthquakes. The 34 m (112 foot) tall **East Tower Pagoda** appears to have six stories because three decorative roofs are interspersed between the real ones. The balanced beauty of East Tower has been described as "frozen music." **Toindo Hall** 東院堂 was built in the Kamakura Era (the 13th century) and houses a Kannon statue created in the 7th century (National Treasure). **Kondo Hall** 金堂 was rebuilt in 1976, and a reconstruction of **West Tower Pagoda** was completed in 1981, as part of a very controversial project. These two replicas of the originals are painted vermilion and seem glaringly out of place, set as they are against the subdued elegance of the other buildings, but those who planned these new buildings took the long view — because they knew it would eventually settle, they had the new West Tower built to stand slightly taller than East Tower. Thus, the original balance of the two towers will be restored in the future, albeit the distant future. Hours: 8:30 AM to 5:00 PM. Admission: 400 yen.

Horyuji Temple 法隆寺 (Kansai Map 26)

Because of its isolation from Nara City,

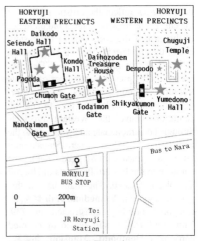

MAP 26 Horyuji Temple

foreign tourists often skip Horyuji. This is a mistake. In light of its historical significance and the number of treasures exhibited there, Horyuji Temple should be given great, if not top, priority for Nara area destinations, especially for those staying in Osaka.

Pine trees flank the main approach to the temple, which was originally erected in 607 by Prince Shotoku, the promulgator of the first Japanese constitution. The original structures were destroyed by fire in 670, but the present buildings of the Western Precincts were reconstructed immediately, at the end of the 7th century. They are possibly the oldest wooden structures in the world. The buildings in the Eastern Precincts were built sometime later, around 739. All the buildings of Horyuji are National Treasures. On both sides of **Chumon Gate** 中門 are images of Deva Kings that were sculpted in 711. Inside the Gate is the main part of Horyuji Temple. At the right is **Kondo Hall** 金堂 (Main Hall). To the left is a **Five-Story Pagoda** (34 m or 112 feet), with roofs that decrease in size toward the top; the pagoda projects an ethereal yet stable image. Inside the pagoda are 95 images clustered in four groups. The varied faces of these images reflect the artistic realism of the era. There are several other old buildings to the east of the corridors. At the eastern end of the Western Precincts is **Daihozoden** 大宝蔵殿 (Great Treasure House). This concrete building preserves hundreds of temple treasures, including images, statues, carvings and metal work from the 7th and 8th centuries. Leave the Western Precincts through Todaimon Gate and walk east to the end of the wide lane, where Shiyakumon Gate (a typical four-legged gate), the entrance to the Eastern Precincts of Horyuji Temple, is located. The main hall of this part of Horyuji is **Yumedono Hall** 夢殿, an octagonal building constructed in 739. Yumedono Hall is surrounded by covered corridors. **Dempodo Mansion** 伝法堂, located to the north of the corridors, is representative of mansion architecture for the nobles of the 8th century. Horyuji Temple is open to the public from 8:00 AM to 5:00 PM (3:00 PM in winter). Admission: 700 yen.

Chuguji Temple 中宮寺 (upper right) is adjacent to the northeastern corner of the Eastern Precincts of Horyuji Temple. It is a quiet, neat nunnery, and is especially

famous for its wooden statue of Miroku Bosatsu (National Treasure), whose soft and tender features have been pronounced the consummate expression of mercy. It is also said that her face changes delicately with changes in temperature and humidity. Hours: 9:00 AM to 4:15 PM (3:45 PM in winter). Admission: 300 yen.

REMOTE SOUTHERN NARA PREFECTURE
奈良南郊

The southern part of Nara Prefecture is quite mountainous. Several important temples and shrines are located in the area's quiet thickly wooded forests. Some of these places, especially Murouji Temple, are given top priority by Japanese, but seldom visited by foreign tourists, due to the area's rather inconvenient access from Kyoto. We have selected four destinations in the area, and describe them in two full-day itineraries: (1) Murouji and Hasedera Temples; and (2) Yoshinoyama and Kashihara Jingu

MAP 27 Southern Nara Transportation

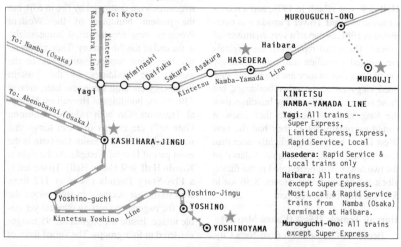

Shrine. You can visit this area from either Osaka or Kyoto, but travel from Osaka is easier.

MUROUJI AND HASEDERA TEMPLES

Transportation from Osaka

The Kintetsu Railways operates a variety of commuter trains on the Osaka-Yamada Line from Osaka's Namba Station as pictured on Kansai Map 2. We recommend that you visit Murouji Temple first and then Hasedera Temple. Most express trains run between Namba Station and Haibara Station (one stop before Murouguchi-Ono), while some run beyound Haibara. When you take a Kintetsu train from Namba, make sure that it is one that goes all the way to Murouguchi-Ono Station. The ride takes 55-80 minutes (760 yen). Murouguchi-Ono Station is located on a small hill. Buses to Murouji Temple originate from a plaza below the train station. The bus schedule is coordinated with arriving trains. The ride to Morouji Temple takes 15 minutes (340 yen). If your group includes 2-3 persons, a taxi is not a bad idea. After your visit to Murouji Temple, take the same bus back to Murouguchi-Ono Station. Take any westbound train from Murouguchi-Ono to Haibara (one stop), most of the trains are expresses. At Haibara you have to transfer to a rapid service or a local train to reach Hasedera (one stop). This transfer is annoying but necessary, because Hasedera Station is not served by express trains. After visiting Hasedera, take a Kintetsu train to Sakurai, and then catch an express at Sakurai back to Osaka's Namba Station.

Transportation from Kyoto

Refer to Kansai Maps 2 and 27. Take an express train on the Kintetsu Kashihara Line from Kyoto to Yagi (sometimes called "Yamato-Yagi"). The ride takes one hour. At Yagi, transfer to the Kintetsu Osaka-Yamada Line for the trip to Murouguchi-Ono (an additional 20-30 minute ride; the fare from Kyoto is 870 yen). Follow the same arrangements described above (From Osaka). After visiting Hasedera Temple, take a train back to Yagi, and transfer there to the Kashihara Line express train back to Kyoto.

Murouji Temple 室生寺 (Upper right, Kansai Map 28)

When you get off the bus, you'll see two bridges: a black one right in front of you and a red one a bit beyond. The red bridge is the main entrance to the Temple.

Murouji Temple is located in a quiet valley of the Murougawa River. Established in the seventh century by Kobo Daishi, who also founded Koyasan, Murouji is popularly called "Women's Koya," because it allowed

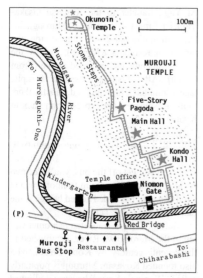

MAP 28 Murouji Temple

not-to-be-missed shot for camera buffs. It dates from the 7th century. There is a long steep stone stairway up the mountain to the Okunoin (Inner Temple), where the novices were trained. Hours: 8:00 AM to 4:30 PM. Admission: 400 yen.

There are several inexpensive restaurants and snack shops near the Murouji Bus Stop.

Hasedera Temple 長谷寺 (Kansai Map 29)

Hasedera Station is a small station used almost exclusively by visitors to Hasedera Temple. The Station is located on a small hill. When you come out of the Station, walk under the "Welcome Arch" and follow the stone steps down the hill. Cross the Hatsusegawa River and you'll be on the main approach to the Temple. It's about a 20-minute walk from the Station to the Temple.

women to visit throughout its history, while Koyasan did not accept women visitors until modern times.

Magnificent buildings are scattered on the hillside, and stone steps connecting these historic structures run through beautiful forests. The first building you'll come to is **Mirokudo Hall** 弥勤堂, which houses a magnificent Miroku Bosatsu statue. This statue, a National Treasure, dates from the seventh century. The next building is **Kondo** 金堂, the Main Hall, which is also a National Treasure. Kondo houses an impressive collection of wooden sculptures from the early 9th century. **Hondo Hall** 本堂, the Main Temple of the compound, is the next building you'll come to. It is a National Treasure that dates from the Kamakura Era, and is noted primarily for its architecture. The most impressive of Morouji's buildings is the 16 m (53 foot) **Five-Story Pagoda** (National Treasure). The Pagoda, viewed from the bottom of the stone steps that lead to it, is featured in many posters and picture books, and is a

MAP 29 Hasedera Temple

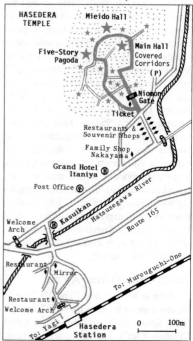

Hasedera Temple was founded in 686. It is often called the "Temple of Flowers," because a variety of flowers bloom in the grounds from spring through fall. Hasedera is especially famous for its peonies, which bloom from the end of April to the middle of May. A number of buildings stand in densely wooded precincts on the mountain side. Three hundred and ninety-nine covered stone steps lead visitors to **Hondo** 本堂, the Main Hall. These long corridors are quite impressive; there are beautiful flowers and trees alongside the corridors. An 8 m (27 feet) statue of an eleven-faced Kannon is the main object of worship in Hondo Hall. **Mieido Hall** 御影堂 is dedicated to Kobo Daishi. **The Five-Story Pagoda**, which dates from 1954, stands on the top of the hillside, at the highest point of Hasedera's precincts. Hours: 9:00 AM to 4:30 PM. Admission: 400 yen.

YOSHINOYAMA AND KASHIHARA JINGU SHRINE

Yoshinoyama is the home of Kinpusenji Temple, which was founded in the 7th century as a training center of Buddhist priests. In 1336, the Ashikaga Shogunate, Japan's second military government, overthrew Emperor Godaigo and established a government in Kyoto headed by a puppet Emperor. Emperor Godaigo fled to Yoshinoyama and established a rival imperial court there. This southern imperial court was eventually reconciled with the Ashikaga government and two courts merged after 57 years.

While Yoshinoyama has lost the solemn atmosphere of the Buddhist training center, it still has several important historic buildings. The area is also known as Japan's absolutely best place for cherry blossom viewing.

Kashihara Jingu Shrine is dedicated to Emperor Jimmu. Though its historic value is low, its grand buildings and thickly-wooded wide grounds are quite impressive. Because Kashihara Jingu Shrine is easily visited in conjuction with a visit to Yoshinoyama, we have included the Shrine in this section.

Transportation from Osaka

The Kintetsu Railways operates direct trains on the Yoshino Line from Osaka's Abenobashi Station (connected with Tenno-ji Station by underground passages) (Kansai Map 2) to Yoshino via Kashihara-Jingu (Kansai Map 27). The ride on an express train takes 1 hour and 30 minutes (850 yen). Deluxe super express trains run on the same line about once every 30 minutes. The ride takes about 1 hour and 15 minutes and the fare is 1,570 yen. A 5-minute ropeway ride takes you up to Yoshinoyama (460 yen roundtrip). After visiting Yoshinoyama, take the Kintetsu train back to Kashihara-Jingu Station. After visiting the Shrine, take the same Kintetsu Yoshino Line train back to Abenobashi.

Transportation from Kyoto

Refer to Kansai Maps 23 and 27. Take the Kintetsu Kashihara Line express train to Kashihara-Jingu Station, the last stop on the line. The ride takes about 70 minutes (760 yen). Deluxe super express trains run on the same line about once every hour. The deluxe super express ride takes 50 minutes and the fare is 1,480 yen. Transfer at Kashihara-Jingu Station to the other Kintetsu express train (the Kintetsu Yoshino Line, which comes from Osaka's Abenobashi) to Yoshino, the last stop on the line. Follow the itinerary described above (From Osaka), returning after your visit to Yoshinoyama to Kashihara-Jingu. After your visit to Kashihara-Jingu Shrine, take the Kintetsu Kashihara Line back to Kyoto.

Yoshinoyama 吉野山 (Kansai Map 30)

Kinpusenji Temple was originally erected in Mt. Yoshinoyama as a training center for Buddhist priests. The temple grounds cover a hillside, which is dotted by a number of buildings. The area is divided into

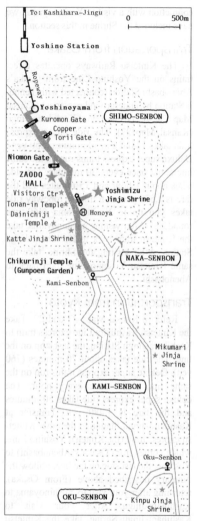

MAP 30 Yoshinoyama

buildings and tourist facilities are located between Shimo-Senbon and Naka-Senbon (Lower and Middle Thousand Cherries).

When you get off the ropeway, Kuromon Gate marks the beginning of the Yoshinoyama complex. You will soon pass a copper *torii* gate. **Zaodo Hall** 蔵王堂 is next. It is the current Main Hall of Kinpusenji Temple, and was built in 1591 under the sponsorship of Hideyoshi Toyotomi. It is Japan's second largest wooden structure (after Todaiji Temple in Nara). Admission to the grounds is free. Admission to the interior of Zaodo Hall: 300 yen. Hours for Zaodo Hall: 9:00 AM to 5:00 PM.

Yoshimizu Jinja Shrine 吉水神社, located below the main street (shaded on the map), was the site of Emperor Godaigo's court. Within the Shrine is the room he used as his throne room. There is also a display of historic objects from that era, and the Shrine has a beautiful garden as well. It is quite sobering to realize that the vast imperial powers were once centered in such a modest location. Yoshimizu Jinja Shrine Hours: 8:00 AM to 5:00 PM. Admission: 400 yen.

Chikurinji Temple 竹林寺 is famous for its garden. Chikurinji Temple Hours: 8:00 AM to 5:00 PM. Admission: 300 yen. The main street, lined with many *ryokan*, restaurants and souvenir shops, is disappointingly touristy. Watch for cars, which are unfortunately allowed in this historic area.

At noted above, Yoshinoyama is especially famous for its cherry blossoms in April. The cherry trees start blooming at the foot of the mountain in early April, and then gradually ascend the mountain, with the trees on the summit blooming at the end of the month.

There is a shuttle bus between Kami-Senbon and Oku-Senbon (middle center, lower right, Kansai Map 30). If you want to go all the way to Oku-Senbon (the Inner Shrine), you'll use this bus. If you are visiting in cherry blossom season, we recommend that you take the bus up and walk

four sections: Shimo-Senbon; Naka-Senbon; Kami-Senbon; and Oku-Senbon. These names (literally "Thousands of Cherries") refer to the cherry trees for which the area is noted. These reflect the topographical divisions of the area: Lower; Middle; Upper and Topmost (Inner Shrine). Most of the historic back down from Oku-Senbon (It's a one-and-a-half hour walk).

Kashihara Jingu Shrine 橿原神宮 (Left, Kansai Map 31)

Japan's first history book, *Nihonshoki*, reports that the court of the nation's first emperor, Jimmu, was at the site of what is now Kashihara Jingu Shrine. As a general matter, however, the veracity of the *Nihonshoki* must be doubted because it was compiled with the aim of glorifying the imperial court rather than accurately recording the events that led to the establishment of Japan's first central government. It should be viewed as a collection of myths rather than facts. It is, nevertheless, true that the first imperial court was established in this area.

Kashiharu Jingu Shrine was constructed in 1889 and dedicated to Emperor Jimmu. On the occasion of the mythological 2,600th anniversary of the foundation of Japan in 1940, 1.5 million trees were planted here by volunteers from all over the country. Today, the grand shrine buildings stand in spacious grounds surrounded by thick woods.

Kashihara Jingu Shrine is only a ten-minute walk from Kashihara Jingu Station. There is no admission to the Shrine grounds, which are open from dawn to dusk.

Kashihara Archeological Museum 橿原考古博物館 is located in the Shrine grounds. The museum displays archeological objects unearthed in the area. Clay images and other items found in old tombs are also exhibited in the Museum. Hours: 9:00 AM to 5:00 PM Admission: 300 yen.

MAJOR FESTIVALS IN NARA

January 15: Grass Burning Festival at Mt. Wakakusayama in Nara-Koen Park. Fires are set at 6:00 PM. Todaiji and Kofukuji Temples, silhouetted against the fire, create a spectacular image.

February 2 or 3 (on the day of Setsubun, the Bean Scattering Festival): Mantoro Festival at Kasuga Taisha Shrine. About 3,000 lanterns are lit and create a magical, solemn atmosphere.

March 1-14: Omizutori Festival at Nigatsu-do Hall of Todaiji Temple. A fire festival every night, with the biggest one on the 12th.

May 1: Shomu-Tenno-sai at Todaiji Temple. The festival is designed to honor the founder of the Temple of the Great Buddha. A colorful parade in traditional costumes is held.

May 11-12: Takigi Noh at Kofukuji Temple.

MAP 31 Kashihara Jingu Shrine

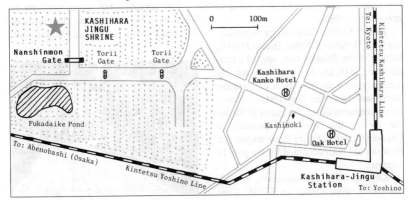

Firelight noh performances by masters of the four major noh schools in Japan (from 4:00 PM).

August 14-15: Mantoro Festival at Kasuga Taisha Shrine (see above).

August 15: Daimonji-Okuribi Festival. A spectacular bonfire in the shape of the character for "big" is lighted at 8:00 PM on Mt. Koenzan, not far from the city.

September 15: Shiba Noh. A firelight noh performance on the grass meadow of Nara-Koen Park (from 5:30 PM).

December 17: Kasuga-Wakamiya-Omatsuri. A large procession with all participants dressed in traditional costumes.

KOYASAN 高野山

Koyasan is a 5.6 km (3.5 mile) long and 2.2 km (1.4 mile) wide tableland hid amid 900 m (3,000 foot) tall mountains. It is inhabited by 6,000 people, and the area has the usual facilities of a modern town including schools, banks and amusement places, but as a temple town it also has its own character and atmosphere. All accommodations available here are in temples, and they serve only special vegetarian foods, the traditional diet of the priests. There are about 120 temples scattered throughout the area, set amid magnificent forests.

To visit Koyasan is to enter a mysterious world of Buddhism. Kukai (Kobo Daishi), founder of the Shingon sect, opened a temple here in 816, and Koyasan has since that time prospered as the capital of Japanese Buddhism. The more than 100,000 monuments commemorating the giants of Japanese history that line the approach to Okunoin Cemetery testify to the respect that Koyasan has been accorded for the past 12 centuries.

Koyasan is an ideal one-night, two-day destination from Osaka or Kyoto. Even though it is possible to make a one-day excursion here from Osaka, it is more enjoyable to stay overnight and experience staying in a temple.

Transportation to Koyasan

Refer to Kansai Map 2. The Nankai Koya Line operates direct trains between Osaka's Namba Station and Gokurakubashi. There are four deluxe express trains in each direction every day. The ride takes one hour and fifteen minutes and the fare is 1,540 yen. In addition to the deluxe trains, there are also many commuter trains on the Nankai Koya Line. They operate about once every 30 minutes, and the ride takes one hour and forty minutes and the fare is 790 yen. Transfer at Gokurakubashi to a cable car, which will take you up the mountain to Koyasan. The fare is 360 yen.

Refer to Kansai Maps 2, 3 and 4. If you travel to Koyasan from Kyoto, take the JR Tokaido Honsen Line commuter train to Shin-Osaka (or take the Shinkansen if you have a JR Rail Pass). Transfer there to the Subway Midosuji Line to Namba Station. Nankai Railways Namba Station is connected with the Subway Station by an underground passage. Follow the route explained above to Koyasan.

Transportation in Koyasan

Two important bus routes originate at Koyasan cable car station. One operates between Koyasan Station and Okunoin-mae

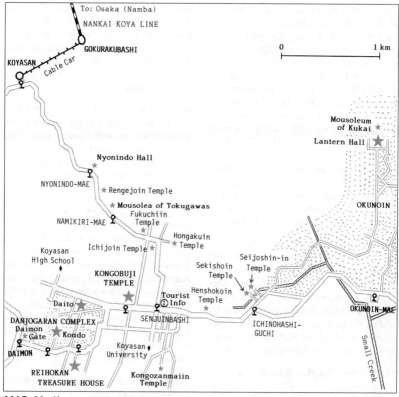

MAP 32 Koyasan

(lower right, Kansai Map 32) via Senjuin-bashi (lower center). The other bus operates between Koyasan Station and Daimon Gate (lower left), again via Senjuinbashi. The buses operate every 10-20 minutes, connecting with the arriving cable cars. Taxis are also plentiful in Koyasan.

Places of Interest

Koyasan can be divided into two sections: the western part contains the temple precincts where many grand structures and the Reihokan Treasure House are located; the eastern part is a cemetery where more than 100,000 tombs of historic figures and the mausoleum of Kukai are located. The cemetery area is shaded with cedar trees hundreds of years old. Visit one part of the city the afternoon of the day you arrive and the other half the following day. If your time is limited, skip the places marked optional.

Okunoin 奥の院 (Upper right)

The stone-paved main approach to Okunoin begins at Ichinohashi, but there is a shortcut to Okunoin from Okunoin-mae bus stop that bypasses some of the approach. You can start your walking tour at either Ichinohashi-guchi or Okunoin-mae. The 2 km (1.3 mile) long main approach is lined on both sides with a variety of monuments, statues and gravestones. It is very difficult to think of a historical figure for whom there isn't a monument along this path. You'll probably see a number of pilgrims dressed in white and carrying wooden staffs as you walk along the path. At the end of the path is Lantern Hall. There are 11,000 lanterns all through the Hall. There are also two fires in the Hall — one has been burning since 1016 and the other since 1088. The mausoleum of Kukai is behind Lantern Hall. The entire area is densely wooded; the huge trees prevent any sunshine from breaking through. The mysterious atmosphere is enhanced by the pervasive smell of incense. A visit here will help you understand why Koyasan has been so important to Japanese Buddhism.

Kongobuji Temple 金剛峯寺 (Lower left)

Kongobuji Temple was erected in 1592 at the order of Hideyoshi Toyotomi as a family temple for his mother, and later became Koyasan's main temple. The chambers of the main building are separated by sliding doors decorated with brilliant pictures by artists of the Kano school. Hours: 8:00 AM to 5:00 PM. Admission: 350 yen.

Danjogaran Complex 壇上伽藍
(Lower left)

The Danjogaran Complex consists of more than 15 halls, and the sight of these magnificent buildings never fails to impress visitors. The complex has suffered repeated fires, but the oldest building dates from 1198. The two most important buildings are Kondo and Daito. **Kondo** 金堂 is the main hall of the complex, and **Daito** 大塔 is a gigantic pagoda. Even though Daito dates only from 1937, it is a very impressive two-story vermilion structure. The entrance to the complex is free of charge. Admission to the interiors of Kondo and Daito is 100 yen each.

Reihokan Treasure House 霊宝館
(Lower left)

Reihokan preserves about 5,000 trea-

sures of Koyasan, 180 of which have been designated National Treasures and Important Cultural Properties. Koyasan's proud artistic achievements are displayed here. The exhibits are changed periodically. Hours: 9:00 AM to 4:00 PM (5:00 PM in summer). Admission: 500 yen.

Daimon Gate 大門 (Lower left) (optional)

In olden times, the main entrance to Koyasan was through Daimon Gate. This huge structure is located in the western-most part of the tableland and commands a fine view of the surrounding mountains and valleys.

Kongozanmaiin Temple 金剛三昧院
(Lower center) (optional)

Kongozanmaiin Temple dates from 1211 and was erected in commemoration of Yoritomo Minamoto, the founder of the Kamakura Shogunate, Japan's first military government, which was established in 1192. The two-story pagoda, built in 1223, is a National Treasure. Kyakuden Hall (Guest Hall) is famous for the gorgeous paintings on its sliding screens. Open from dawn to dusk. Admission free.

Mausolea of the Tokugawas 徳川家霊台
(Middle left) (optional)

Mausolea of the first and the second Tokugawa Shoguns are located here. As is the case with many of the shrines, monuments and mausolea related to the Tokugawas, the buildings in Koyasan feature brilliant gold and silver ornamentation. Hours: 8:00 AM to 5:00 PM. Admission: 100 yen.

Accommodations in Koyasan

The only accommodations available in Koyasan are in temples. Fifty-three out the 120 temples in the area offer lodgings. The facilities are basically the same as a regular Japanese-style inn. The greatest differences are that the kitchens prepare the same vegetarian dishes for guests that are served to the priests and that the accommodations are imbued with the solemn atmosphere of the temple precincts. The rates are 8,000-12,000 yen per person, including dinner and breakfast. We list some of these lodgings below if you want to make advance reservations, which we do recommend for spring and fall weekend visits to Koyasan. If you arrive in Koyasan without reservations, the Tourist Information Office near Senjuinbashi Bus Stop (lower center) will make lodging arrangements for you.

Sekishoin Temple (lower center). Tel: (0736) 56-2734

Henshokoin Temple (lower center). Tel: (0736) 56-2124

Ichijoin Temple (middle left). Tel: (0736) 56-2214

Hongakuin Temple (middle center). Tel: (0736) 56-2711

Fukuchiin Temple (middle left). Tel: (0736) 56-2021

Rengejoin Temple (middle left). Tel: (0736) 56-2231

KOBE 神戸

Because the early development of Japan took place in the western part of the archipelago where the calm Inland Sea was the main transportation route, Kobe has been a prosperous port town since the pre-historic period. The early port was called Muko-no-Minato. The area was opened to foreign traders in 1868, at the end of the nation's long period of isolation. Because Kobe has had a large foreign population for more than one hundred years, it has the cosmopolitan atmosphere of an international city. Kobe beef is a famous specialty of the city, and Kobe's sophisticated restaurants feature all sorts of international dishes, making the city a gourmets' paradise. The city's population is 1,448,000.

Outline of the Area

Kobe, sandwiched between the sea on the south and Mt. Rokkosan on the north, is quite long from northeast to southwest. The area around Sannomiya Station (lower left,

MAP 33 Outline of Kobe

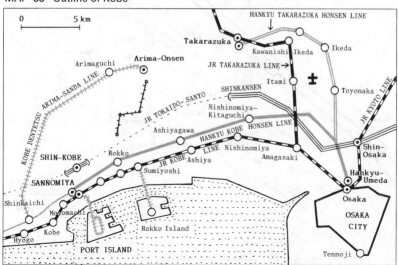

Kansai Map 33) is the center of the city. Port Island (lower left), a large man-made island, was constructed several years ago to expand port facilities, especially container facilities, and to provide convenient residential and recreational areas for the people of Kobe. Port Island is now also the city's prime convention and exhibition venue. An *i* Information Office is located in JR Sannomiya Station. Please note that Shin-Kobe Station (the Shinkansen Station) is to the north of Sannomiya Station. They are connected by the city's subway.

Places of Interest in Downtown Kobe

The main areas of Kobe explained below can be covered on foot. If you get tired, Kobe has plenty of taxis.

The wide boulevard stretching south from Sannomiya Station is called **Flower Road** (middle right, Kansai Map 34) and is decorated with flowers of the season. On the eastern side of the road are exotic restaurants and pubs. Old western-style buildings reminiscent of the adventurous early foreign traders dot the area. Along the western side

MAP 34 Downtown Kobe (Sannomiya)

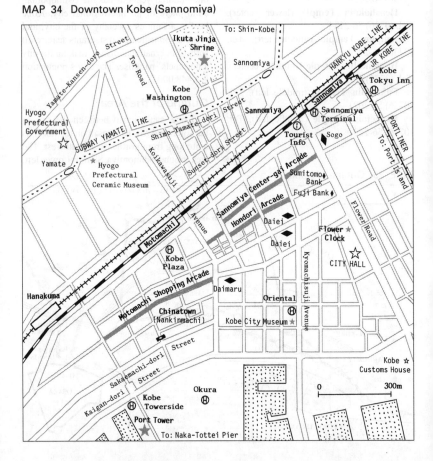

of the boulevard there are many sculptures by contemporary artists. City Hall and many businesses, both Japanese and foreign, are located to the west of Flower Road.

The main shopping district of Kobe stretches along the southern side of the JR and the Hankyu lines. Shopping arcades are shaded on Kansai Map 34. The arcades between Sannomiya and Motomachi Stations (Sannomiya Center-gai Arcade and Hondori Arcade) contain modern buildings, while the arcade to the south of Motomachi Station (Motomachi Shopping Arcade) features traditional specialty shops.

A small **Chinatown** (called "Nankin-machi" 南京町) is located to the south of the Motomachi Shopping Arcade. It's not as large or as grand as Yokohama's Chinatown, but it has a good reputation for excellent food.

There is an extensive **underground shopping mall**, with fashion boutiques, souvenir shops, restaurants and coffee shops located under the northern part of Flower Road, around JR's Sannomiya Station.

Tor Road (upper left to middle center) runs from north to south, crossing under the elevated railroad tracks. The street, which slopes up gently as it goes north, is lined with horse chestnuts, and is always peaceful and quiet. This favorite promenade of the people of Kobe is dotted with specialty shops and good restaurants.

The northern side of Sannomiya Station is called Ikuta. With clusters of eating and drinking facilities, it is Kobe's busiest nightlife area. In the middle of the glittering neon signs of the night spots is **Ikuta Jinja Shrine** 生田神社 (upper center). The woods behind the vermilion shrine were once quite extensive and were the subject of a famous poem in olden times.

Port Tower ポートタワー (lower left) provides an excellent bird's-eye view of the port and the city. The 108 m (354 foot) tower is located in the middle of Naka-Tottei Pier. Elevators take you from the second floor to the observatory at the top. Hours: 9:00 AM to 8:30 PM. Admission: 500 yen. The third and fourth floors of the tower are a museum that displays objects related to the history of Kobe Port and ocean transportation. Admission to the museum is part of admission to the observatory.

Port Island

Refer to Kansai Map 35. Port Island is connected with JR Sannomiya Station by automatic monorails called Portliners. The monorail makes a counterclockwise loop and stops at eight stations. The island features large container terminals for international ocean freight, a number of condominiums, International Conference Center Kobe, International Exhibition Hall and recreational facilities such as a planetarium and sports fields. You are most likely to visit this area if you are attending an international conference or exhibition. If you are just sightseeing and want to take a stroll in the area, get off the monorail at Shimin-Hiroba Station

MAP 35 Port Island

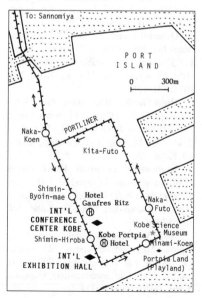

and walk to Minami-Koen Station. Even if you don't get off and take a walk, it is fun to take the monorail to see the port and the new development. The full loop trip takes 27 minutes. Portliner platforms are located on the second floor at the eastern corner of the JR Sannomiya Station. The fare for the entire loop is 220 yen.

ACCOMMODATIONS

1. Hotels in Kobe

Hotel Okura Kobe (lower center, Kansai Map 34). Deluxe. 489 rooms. Single (19,500 yen -) & Double (27,000 yen -). Add: 2-1, Hatobacho, Chuo-ku, Kobe. Tel: (078) 333-0111.

Kobe Portpia Hotel (lower center, Kansai Map 35). Deluxe. 778 rooms. Single (15,000 yen -) & Double (27,000 yen -). Add: 6-10-1, Minatojima-Nakamachi, Chuo-ku, Kobe. Tel: (078) 302-1111.

Shin-Kobe Oriental Hotel (adjacent to JR Shin-Kobe Station). First Class. 582 rooms. Single (14,000 yen -) & Double (25,000 yen -). Add: 1-chome, Kitanocho, Chuo-ku, Kobe. Tel: (078) 291-1121.

Oriental Hotel (middle center, Kansai Map 34). First Class. 190 rooms. Single (11,500 yen -) & Double (26,000 yen -). Add: 25, Kyo-machi, Chuo-ku, Kobe. Tel: (078) 331-8111.

Hotel Gaufres Ritz (lower center, Kansai Map 35). First Class. 114 rooms. Single (10,500 yen -) & Double (21,500 yen -). Add: 6-1, Minatojima-Nakamachi, Chuo-ku, Kobe. Tel: (078) 303-5555.

Sannomiya Terminal Hotel (upper right, Kansai Map 34). Standard. 130 singles (9,500 yen -) & 60 doubles (18,000 yen -). Add: 8, Kumoi-dori, Chuo-ku, Kobe. Tel: (078) 291-0001.

Kobe Washington Hotel (upper center, Kansai Map 34). Business. 125 singles (9,500 yen -) & 93 doubles (17,000 yen -). Add: 2-11-5, Shimoyamate-dori, Chuo-ku, Kobe. Tel: (078) 331-6111.

Kobe Tokyu Inn (upper right, Kansai Map 34). Business. 127 singles (9,500 yen -) & 109 doubles (16,500 yen -). Add: 6-1-5, Kumoi-dori, Chuo-ku, Kobe. Tel: (078) 291-0109.

Kobe Plaza Hotel (middle center, Kansai Map 34). Business. 95 singles (7,500 yen -) & 49 doubles (13,500 yen -). Add: 1-13-12, Motomachi-dori, Chuo-ku, Kobe. Tel: (078) 332-1141.

Quality Inn Kobe (10 minute walk from Sannomiya Station). Business. 62 singles (7,500 yen -) & 48 doubles (12,500 yen -). Add: 4-1-12, Isogami-dori, Chuo-ku, Kobe. Tel: (078) 241-2233.

Kobe Towerside Hotel (lower left, Kansai Map 34). Business. 70 singles (5,000 yen -) & 63 doubles (10,000 yen -). Add: 6-1, Hatoba-cho, Chuo-ku, Kobe. Tel: (078) 351-2151.

2. Welcome Inn in Kobe

Kobe Gajoen Hotel (3 minute walk from Hanakuma Station). 64 Western rooms. Add: 8-4-23, Shimoyamate-dori, Chuo-ku, Kobe. Tel: (078) 341-0301.

ARIMA ONSEN HOTSPRINGS
有馬温泉

Located close to Kobe and Osaka, Arima Onsen Hotspring (upper center, Kansai Map 33) is a popular weekend resort for area residents, and may be of interest if you enjoy hotsprings.

Transportation to Arima Onsen

The Hankyu Kobe Honsen Line provides transportation to Shinkaichi (lower left, Kansai Map 33), where you can catch the Kobe Dentetsu Arima-Sanda Line to Arima Onsen, the last stop. The ride from Shinkaichi to Arima Onsen takes about 40 minutes. The fare is 470 yen.

There is also bus service to Arima Onsen from Sannomiya Station and Shin-Kobe Station. The ride takes 35 minutes from

Shin-Kobe and 40 minutes from San-nomiya, and the fare is 630 yen from each.

If you are traveling from Osaka, there is frequent bus service from Osaka and Shin-Osaka Stations to Arima Onsen. The ride takes about one hour from Shin-Osaka and 70 minutes from Osaka. Fare: 1,100 and 1,230 yen, respectively.

Ryokan in Arima Onsen

Nakanobo Zuien. Deluxe. 54 rooms. 28,000 yen & up per person. Add: 808, Arimacho, Kita-ku, Kobe. Tel: (078) 904-0781.

Arima Grand Hotel. Deluxe. 151 rooms. 25,000 yen & up per person. Add: 1304, Arimacho, Kita-ku, Kobe. Tel: (078) 904-0181.

Arima Gyoen. First Class. 80 rooms. 18,000 yen & up per person. Add: 1296, Arimacho, Kita-ku, Kobe. Tel: (078) 904-3737.

Arima Royal Hotel. Standard. 50 rooms. 16,000 yen & up per person. Add: 987, Arimacho, Kita-ku, Kobe. Tel: (078) 904-0541.

Ryokan Ichimonji. Standard. 19 rooms. 16,000 yen & up per person. Add: 797, Arimacho, Kita-ku, Kobe. Tel: (078) 904-0565.

HIMEJI 姫路

Himeji was a prosperous castle city in the feudal era. Himejijo Castle is a National Treasure and is generally considered Japan's most elegant, beautiful castle. You can easily visit Himeji from Kansai cities (Kyoto, Osaka and Kobe) or you can include Himeji in an Inland Sea area itinerary. There is an *i* Information Office in the train station.

Transportation to Himeji

Himeji is served by the JR Tokaido-Sanyo Shinkansen (several "Hikari" each day, and all "Kodama" trains). The Shinkansen ride takes 55 minutes from Kyoto, 37 minutes from Shin-Osaka and 22 minutes from Shin-Kobe. The ride on the JR

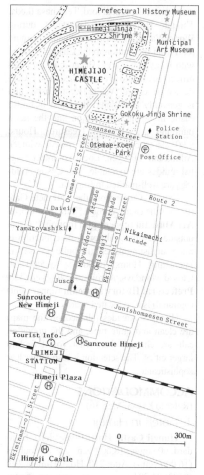

MAP 36 Himeji

Sanyo Honsen Line, the local commuter line, takes 2 hours and 10 minutes from Kyoto, one hour and 30 minutes from JR Osaka Station and 65 minutes from JR San-nomiya Station in Kobe.

Places of Interest

Himejijo Castle 姫路城 (upper center, Kansai Map 36), in an extensive compound of about 80 buildings, was built in 1601 at the order of the feudal lord, Terumasa Ikeda. Though Himeji was devastated during World War II, the Castle survived. The main road from the Station to the Castle is graced with many sculptures. Because of its magnificent scale and gracious design, the Castle is often called "White Heron Castle" and is generally considered the most beautiful castle in Japan. The donjon and the main buildings are National Treasures. Hours: 9:00 AM to 5:00 PM (4:00 PM in winter). Admission: 500 yen. Local volunteer English guides are available. The Castle buildings are well-marked in English.

Exit the Castle from the Karamete Gate (the northeastern corner). **The Municipal Art Museum** (upper right) (optional) is just outside this gate. Although its collection is rather undistinguished, the building itself is interesting. Hours: 10:00 AM to 5:00 PM. Closed Mondays. Admission. 200 yen. **The Prefectural History Museum** (upper right) (optional) is also located nearby.

Himeji's Arcades (shaded on the map) are clean and quite nice, and the goods on sale are cheaper than what you'll find in larger cities. The selection is also rather less sophisticated.

ACCOMMODATIONS
(Refer to Kansai Map 36)

1. Hotels in Himeji

Himeji Castle Hotel (lower left). Standard. 90 singles (8,000 yen -) & 76 doubles (16,000 yen -). Add: 210, Hojo, Himeji. Tel: (0792) 84-3311.

Hotel Sunroute New Himeji (middle left). Business. 18 singles (7,000 yen -) & 11 doubles (14,500 yen -). Add: 241, Ekimaecho, Himeji. Tel: (0792) 23-1111.

Hotel Himeji Plaza (lower left). Business. 176 singles (6,500 yen -) & 34 doubles (10,000 yen -). Add: 158, Toyosawacho, Himeji. Tel: (0792) 81-9000.

2. Welcome Inn in Himeji

Hotel Sunroute Himeji (middle center).

79 rooms. Add: 195-9, Ekimaecho, Himeji. Tel: (0792) 85-0811.

LAKE BIWAKO 琵琶湖

Lake Biwako is Japan's largest lake with an area of 674 square kilometers (263 square miles). The Lake is larger than Tokyo City (the total of the 23 urban wards). The deepest part of the lake is 103 m (339 feet). The lake is located in Shiga Prefecture. There are *i* Information Offices in JR Otsu Station and JR Hikone Station.

OTSU 大津
(Lower left, Kansai Map 37)

Otsu, capital of Shiga Prefecture with a population of 260,000, is the center of the area. Otsu Station is on the JR Tokaido Honsen Line, and is connected with Kyoto by frequent commuter train service. The ride from Kyoto to Otsu takes only 10 minutes. If you are staying in the central or eastern part of Kyoto, you can take a streetcar-type train (Keihan Keishin Line) from Kyoto's Keihan Sanjo Station to Hama-Otsu Station (a 25-minute ride). Thus, Lake Biwako is easily visited from Kyoto in a day, or even a half day excursion. Biwako Kisen's sightseeing boat pier is a one-minute walk from Hama-Otsu Station, and a 20-minute walk from JR Otsu Station (through downtown). A one-and-a-half hour sightseeing boat (called Michigan) operates about once every 2 hours (2,600-5,000 yen depending on the class).

Onjoji Temple 園城寺, popularly called Miidera Temple, is located in the northwestern part of Otsu. The temple is a 15-minute walk from Hama-Otsu Station. There is bus service between JR Otsu Station and Miidera (a 10-minute ride). Onjoji Temple once belonged to Enryakuji Temple on Mt. Hieizan. Later, the temple was separated from Enryakuji and became the headquar-

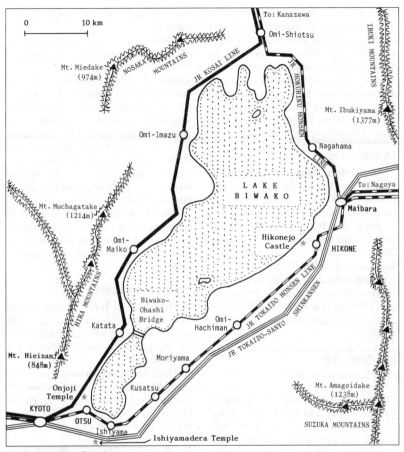

MAP 37 Lake Biwako

ters of its own sect. The precincts spread along a slope of Mt. Nagarasan, and contain about 20 buildings. Daimon Gate is the main entrance and features two *Nio* guardian statues made by Unkei, the 13th century sculptor, in side niches. Kondo is a huge main hall built in the 16th century. A three-story pagoda has elegant curves on its roofs. On the northern side of Onjoji Temple is **Enman-in Temple** 円満院, which has an impressive garden. Omi Folklore Museum is housed in one of the temple buildings.

Ishiyamadera Temple 石山寺 has several National Treasure buildings from the 8th century. To reach Ishiyamadera you can take the Keihan Ishizaka Line train from Hama-Otsu Station to Ishiyamadera, the last stop on the line (a 16-minute ride). There is also bus service between JR Otsu Station and Ishiyamadera-Sanmon-mae (a 20-minute ride). Todaimon Gate is a huge structure with two *Nio* guardian statues; it is the main entrance to the temple. The approach is lined with azalea bushes. The

National Treasure Main Hall was originally built in the Heian Era and partially rebuilt in the Kamakura Era. It is said that a small chamber of the Main Hall was used by Murasaki Shikibu when she wrote *Genji Monogatari*, Japan's first novel. A National Treasure two-story pagoda was built at the order of Yoritomo Minamoto. Hojoden is the treasure house. Temple treasures are displayed here in the spring and the fall.

Hotels in Otsu

Otsu Prince Hotel (5 minutes by taxi from JR Otsu Station). Deluxe. 510 rooms. Double (27,500 yen -). Add: 4-7-7, Nionohama, Otsu. Tel: (0775) 21-1111.

Royal Oak Hotel (10 minutes by taxi from JR Otsu Station). Deluxe. 198 rooms. Double (27,500 yen -). Add: 23-1, Kayanoura, Otsu. Tel: (0775) 43-0111.

Biwako Hotel (7 minutes by taxi from JR Otsu Station). Standard. 91 rooms. Single (7,000 yen -) & Double (17,000 yen -). Add: 5-35, Yanagigasaki, Otsu. Tel: (0775) 24-1511.

HIKONE 彦根
(Middle right, Kansai Map 37)

This area was the site of major battles throughout the feudal era. When the Tokugawa Clan unified the nation in 1603, Hikone was given to the Ii family, Tokugawa kinsmen. The town prospered under the reign of this powerful family. When Commodore Perry visited Japan in 1854, Naosuke Ii, the lord of Hikone, was prime minister of the Tokugawa Shogunate. He agreed to open several ports for foreign trade. At the same time he executed many revolutionaries and reformists. His cruel execution rather inspired the alliance of the anti-Tokugawa forces that led to the Meiji Restoration four years later. Naosuke Ii still enjoys the respect of the Hikone people, even though he has been generally regarded a leader of the conservative feudal establishment. Naosuke himself was assassinated by reformists.

Today, Hikone is the second largest city of Shiga Prefecture, with a population of 99,000. The Japan Center of the State Universities of Michigan is located in Hikone. **Hikonejo Castle** 彦根城 was built in early 17th century, and its original buildings still stand intact. Hikonejo is one of Japan's four National Treasure castles. The approach to the donjon is lined with impressive stone walls. The top floor of the donjon commands a great view of Lake Biwako. **Genkyuen** 玄宮園, in the northern part of the castle grounds, is a large landscaped garden. Hikone Station is on the JR Tokaido Honsen Line. You can reach Hikone from Kyoto in one hour by commuter train. The Castle is a 10-minute walk from the station.

Hotels in Hikone

Hikone Prince Hotel (7 minutes by taxi from JR Hikone Station). First Class. 102 rooms. Double (18,500 yen -). Add: 1435-91, Ajiroguchi, Matsubaracho, Hikone. Tel: (0749) 26-1111.

Hotel Sunroute Hikone (1 minute walk from JR Hikone Station). Business. 72 rooms. Single (6,500 yen -) & Double (12,500 yen -). Add: 9-14, Asahicho, Hikone. Tel: (0749) 26-0123.

KII PENINSULA 紀伊半島

The Kii Peninsula extends along the eastern half of Osaka Bay. With densely wooded mountains located in the middle of the peninsula, the area was left behind during the industrial development along the other parts of the Pacific Ocean coast. The Kii Peninsula has several popular hotspring resorts and historic remains. If you are staying in Osaka or Nagoya, and looking for an overnight hotspring destination, you should consider the Kii Peninsula. The area is

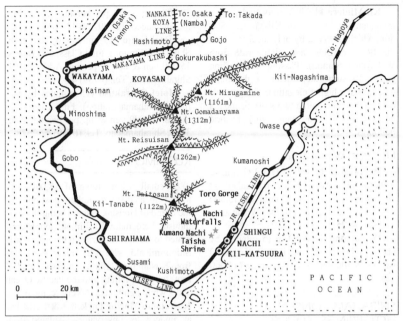

MAP 38 Kii Peninsula

strongly recommended to fresh seafood lovers and hotspring fans.

Transportation

The JR Kisei Line skirts the edge of the Kii Peninsula, connecting Osaka (Tennoji Station) and Nagoya. No train runs the entire length of the 442 km (276 miles) between Tennoji and Nagoya.

JR limited express trains (called "Kuroshio") run between Tennoji and Shingu (lower center, Kansai Map 38). Kuroshio trains operate about once every 30 minutes. The ride from Tennoji takes 40 minutes to Wakayama (upper left), 2 hours to Shirahama (lower left), 2 hours and 50 minutes to Kushimoto (lower center), 3 hours and 30 minutes to Kii-Katsuura (lower center), and 3 hours and 45 minutes to Shingu, the last stop.

JR limited express trains (called "Nanki") run between Nagoya and Kii-Katsuura about every 1-2 hours. The ride from Nagoya takes 3 hours and 20 minutes to Shingu, and 3 hours and 40 minutes to Kii-Katsuura.

WAKAYAMA 和歌山

Wakayama is the capital of Wakayama Prefecture with a population of 401,000. In the Edo era the Tokugawa family governed the Wakayama area directly, to keep control over the feudal lords of Western Japan. In addition to its Edo headquarters, the Tokugawas governed three strategic cities directory — Mito, to the north of Tokyo (to control Northern Japan); Nagoya (to keep an eye on the lords of Central Japan); and Wakayama (to control Western Japan). The reconstructed **Wakayamajo Castle** 和歌山城 stands on a small hill in the city center. A small local museum is housed in the castle. The top floor of the donjon commands a panoramic view of the city.

Kii-Miidera 紀三井寺 is located along a mountainside in front of Kii-Miidera Station, which is served by only local trains on the JR Kisei Line (a 6-minute ride from Wakayama Station). Passing a vermilion gate, 230 stone steps lead to the main precincts at a higher elevation. The grounds contain the main hall, a two-story pagoda, a hexagonal hall and many other historic buildings.

Hotels in Wakayama

Wakayama Terminal Hotel (1 minute walk from Wakayama Station). Standard. 82 singles (8,000 yen -) & 57 doubles (15,500 yen -). Add: 5-18, Tomodacho, Wakayama. Tel: (0734) 25-3333.

Wakayama Tokyu Inn (5 minutes by taxi from Wakayama Station). Business. 70 singles (8,500 yen -) & 95 doubles (14,000 yen -).

SHIRAHAMA ONSEN HOTSPRINGS 白浜温泉

Shirahama is the most popular hotspring resort of the Kii Peninsula. Many deluxe *ryokan*, whose atmosphere is generally a little noisy, thanks to tour groups, are located along the sea coast. The area has beautiful marine scenery and many sports facilities, including golf courses and tennis courts. Fishing and swimming are also popular here. **Senjojiki** 千畳敷 has the most scenic coast line. Nearby **Sandanbeki** 三段壁 has 50 m (164 foot) tall wide cliffs, similar to Cape Tojimbo in the Chubu Region. A pedestrian path along the cliffs can be reached by elevator. **World Safari** is a zoo, where animals are kept in open spaces; visitors observe from a safari bus (called Kenya). The *i* Information Office is located in JR Shirahama Station.

Ryokan in Shirahama Onsen

Hotel Kawakyu (10 minutes by taxi from Shirahama Station). Deluxe. 71 rooms.

30,000 yen & up per person. Add: 3745, Shirahamacho. Tel: (0739) 42-2661.

Hotel Senjo (15 minutes by taxi from Shirahama Station). First Class. 103 rooms. 15,000 yen & up per person. Add: 1680-1, Shirahamacho. Tel: (0739) 42-3470.

Hotel Sanrakuso (15 minutes by taxi from Shirahama Station). First Class. 116 rooms. 15,000 yen & up per person. Add: 3008, Shirahamacho. Tel: (0739) 42-2678.

KUSHIMOTO 串本

A small fishing town of 18,000. The town is located at the southernmost point of the island of Honshu. Fishing being the only industry here, many Kushimoto people emigrated to foreign countries in the past. **Cape Shionomisaki** 潮岬 (20 minutes by bus from Kushimoto Station) features 60 m (197 foot) tall cliffs falling into the Pacific Ocean and a white lighthouse. A very scenic place. **Kushimoto Marine Park** 串本海中公園 has an underwater observatory. Isolated from the areas of heavy industrial development, the sea around Kushimoto has clear waters, and you can see a variety of fish in a natural setting. The park also contains an aquarium called Marine Pavilion. Glass boats operate frequently from the Park. The Park is 15 minutes by bus from Kushimoto Station. **Hashiguiiwa** 橋杭岩, a progression of about forty grotesquely-shaped rocks that form a sort of stepping stone bridge are a famous local work of natural art (a 5 minute bus ride from Kushimoto Station).

Ryokan in Kushimoto

Kushimoto Hotel Urashima (10 minute walk from Kushimoto Station). First Class. 120 rooms. 15,000 yen & up per person. Add: 2300 Kushimoto, Kushimotocho. Tel: (07356) 2-1011.

Ryokan Kaigetsu (5 minute walk from Kushimoto Station). Standard. 33 rooms. 12,000 yen & up per person. Add: 1758, Kushimoto, Kushimotocho. Tel: (07356) 2-0011.

KATSUURA ONSEN HOTSPRINGS 紀伊勝浦温泉

Katsuura is known for its complicated rocky coast line. Hotsprings gush forth all over this seaside town. *Ryokan* are located on the area's small islands and on the rocky peninsulas. Many of them have no road connections with Kii-Katsuura Station. These *ryokan* shuttle their guests by boats between the train station and their properties.

Most tourists use Katsuura as a base from which to explore Nachi Waterfalls, Kumano Nachi Taisha Shrine, and Torokyo Gorge (explained below). A 40-minute sightseeing boat operates from the pier near Kii-Katsuura Station about every 1-2 hours (920 yen). The boat cruises around small islets called "Kino-Matsushima."

Ryokan in Katsuura

Nakanoshima (reachable only by boat). First Class. 158 rooms. 15,000 yen & up per person. Add: 1179-9, Nachi-Katsuuracho. Tel: (07355) 2-1111.

Hotel Urashima (reachable only by boat). First Class. 504 rooms. 15,000 yen & up per person. Add: 116502, Nachi-Katsuuracho. Tel: (07355) 2-1011.

Ichinotaki (4 minutes by taxi from Kii-Katsuura Station). Standard. 37 rooms. 12,000 yen & up per person. Add: 752, Nachi-Katsuuracho. Tel: (07355) 2-0080.

The Kumano mountains are steep and densely wooded. The area was originally used as a training center for Shinto and Buddhist priests. Three shrines of the area have been especially popular among pilgrims since the Heian era. Even imperial family members often visited these shrines, traveling the distance of about 300 km (188 miles) from Kyoto on mountainous roads.

Kumano Nachi Taisha Shrine 熊野那智大社 is one of the three sacred shrines of the Kumano mountains. The Shrine and **Nachi Waterfall** 那智滝 are only about 500 m (1,640 feet) away each other. Most visitors go the shrine first and then the waterfall. You can take a bus from Kii-Katsuura Station to Nachisan (about 25 minute ride). The main approach to the Kumano Nachi Taisha Shrine is up 500 stone steps. The main hall consists of five buildings dedicated to five Shinto gods. The precincts also include the Shrine's Treasure House, Seiganji Temple, and a three-story pagoda. Nachi Waterfall is only a five-minute walk from the pagoda. The 133 m (436 foot) waterfall is narrower but much taller than Nikko's Kegon Waterfalls. It is worshipped as the main object of Hiryu Jinja Shrine. You can take a bus from Nachino-Taki-mae bus stop back to Kii-Katsuura. If you don't want to climb up the 500 stone steps of Kumano Nachi Taisha Shrine, you can visit the waterfall first, and then visit the shrine, using the stone steps to descend to Nachisan bus stop.

Torokyo Gorge 瀞峡. The Kitayama-gawa River, running through the Kumano mountains, eroded deep gorges on its way to the Pacific Ocean. The most scenic part of the gorges is called Torokyo. You can explore the gorge's precipitous cliffs and emerald green waters by waterjet.

Bus and waterjet operations are coordinated in "tours" from Shingu Station. There are 8 tours daily. First you take the bus for 35 minutes from Shingu Station to Shiko, the pier for the waterjet. The boat explores the scenic parts of Torokyo Gorge in two hours. Take the bus back to Shingu Station. The entire "tour" costs 5,000 yen, including the roundtrip bus ride from Shingu and the waterjet.

JR FARES BETWEEN MAJOR STATIONS IN THE KANSAI REGION

1. JR FARES BETWEEN THE STATIONS ON THE TOKAIDO-SANYO SHINKANSEN

Refer to the Tokaido-Sanyo Shinkansen fare chart in the Transportation section of the Introduction Chapter

2. JR FARES BETWEEN MAJOR STATIONS IN THE KANSAI REGION

(Fares are based on commuter trains)

To/From	Osaka	Tennoji	Kyoto	Nara	Sannomiya
Osaka		190 yen (10.7 km)	610 yen (39 km)		530 yen (30.6 km)
Tennoji	190 yen (10.7 km)			610 yen (37.5 km)	
Kyoto	610 yen (39 km)			720 yen (41.7 km)	1,030 yen (69.6 km)
Nara		610 yen (37.5 km)	720 yen (41.7 km)		
Sannomiya	530 yen (30.6 km)		1,030 yen (69.6 km)		

3. JR FARES BETWEEN MAJOR STATIONS ON THE KISEI LINE

(Based on limited express trains)

To/From	Tennoji	Nagoya
Wakayama	2,250 yen (61.3 km)	
Shirahama	5,030 yen (166.8 km)	
Kushimoto	6,160 yen (220.4 km)	
Kii-Katsuura	6,570 yen (247.1 km)	7,270 yen (240.1 km)
Shingu	6,880 yen (262 km)	6,960 yen (225.2 km)

SANYO REGION

山陽

The western part of Japan's main island is sometimes called "Chugoku" after the mountains that run east-west down the spine of the island. The mountains divide this area into two parts: the southern part, facing the Inland Sea, is known as the Sanyo Region (the "sunny" region) and enjoys mild weather throughout the year. The northern part, facing the Japan Sea, is known as the San-in Region (the "shady" region); it has severe snowy winters and cooler summers. We introduce the Sanyo Region in this Chapter, while the San-in Region is described separately in the next Chapter.

The Sanyo Region is convenient for tourists, and the beautiful Inland Sea area has much to offer. All major cities of this region, which lie along the Inland Sea coast, are on the JR Tokaido-Sanyo Shinkansen line. It is thus very easy to travel quickly and efficiently to the Sanyo Region from the major urban areas of Tokyo, Nagoya, Kyoto and Osaka. A visit to this Region can also be easily combined with travel to Kyushu Island, too. See more details on the Tokaido-Sanyo Shinkansen in the Transportation Chapter above.

Refer to Sanyo Map 1. The Sanyo Region itself can be divided into two parts — the Eastern Inland Sea District (right half) and the Western Inland Sea District (left half). The eastern area includes Okayama, Kurashiki and Inbe, while the western area includes Hiroshima, Miyajima and Onomichi.

While there is a great deal of local boat service connecting islands of the Inland Sea

with major cities of the Sanyo Region or Shikoku Island, there are few pure pleasure cruises, which is a shame considering the beauty of the Inland Sea. We do describe several sightseeing boats that operate in the Hiroshima area. There is also boat service between Hiroshima and Matsuyama (on Shikoku Island), which you will use if you travel in both the Shikoku and Sanyo Regions.

The preeminent Sanyo destinations are Miyajima and Kurashiki. Both have charming historic artifacts. Personally, we prefer Miyajima. The two major Sanyo cities, Hiroshima and Okayama, while both perfectly pleasant places, are not "must-sees" for tourists. They should be considered supplemental destinations in connection with visits to Miyajima or Kurashiki. Onomichi has a number of small lovely temples as well as a good view of the Inland Sea, and is the number three tourist priority for Sanyo. Inbe, famous for its Bizen potteries, is recommended only for those particularly interested in that craft. Please remember, too, that Himeji (upper right), which is included in the Kansai Chapter, is also situated on the JR Tokaido-Sanyo Shinkansen, and can easily be incorporated into a Sanyo itinerary (requiring an additional 3-4 hours).

We suggest that you plan an itinerary from Kyoto/Osaka as outlined below. The same itinerary will also work from Tokyo or Nagoya if you get a very early start the first day.

1. If you have only one night (two days):

You have two alternatives to choose from as follows:

(1) Visit Kurashiki first. A full afternoon in Kurashiki should be enough to stroll the historic district and visit several of the museums. Overnight in Kurashiki; visit Okayama, Inbe or Himeji the second day, and proceed to your next destination.

(2) Visit Hiroshima first and spend the afternoon there. Overnight in Hiroshima, or in Miyajima if you want to stay in a ryokan (which will be more costly). Visit Miyajima the second day, and then proceed to your next destination.

2. If you have two nights (three days):

You can cover both the eastern and western parts of the Region as follows:

Day 1. Arrive in Kurashiki; afternoon sightseeing and overnight accommodations there.

Day 2. Kurashiki to Hiroshima by train (via Okayama). Afternoon sightseeing in Hiroshima.

Day 3. Visit Miyajima, and proceed to your next destination.

3. If you have one more night:

We suggest that you add Onomichi after your visit to Miyajima, or between Kurashiki and Hiroshima.

Other major cities in the westernmost part of the Sanyo Region are described at the end of this Chapter. Refer to Sanyo Map 9.

SANYO REGION TRANSPORTATION NETWORK

Refer to Sanyo Map 1. The JR Tokaido-Sanyo Shinkansen runs along the Inland Sea. All major cities are served by the

MAP 1 Outline of Sanyo

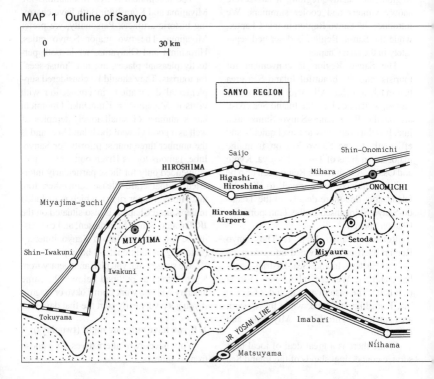

Shinkansen, including Okayama, Shin-Kurashiki, Shin-Onomichi, Mihara and Hiroshima. However, Shin-Kurashiki and Shin-Onomichi Stations are at a distance from the downtown areas of those cities. When you visit Kurashiki, it is better to get off the Shinkansen at Okayama and transfer to a JR local train to Kurashiki Station. JR Kurashiki Station is right in downtown Kurashiki. If you visit Onomichi either from Kurashiki or Hiroshima, it is also better to take a JR local train to Onomichi Station. Onomichi Station is within walking distance of the major attractions of the city. However, if you are visiting Onomichi after a visit to the Kansai Region or the Kyushu Region, you can take the JR Tokaido-Sanyo Shinkansen to Shin-Onomichi Station, and then a bus to Onomichi Station.

Local trains run frequently on the JR Sanyo Honsen Line between Okayama and Iwakuni, parallel to the JR Tokaido-Sanyo Shinkansen, to meet the needs of the local people. These trains serve such key stations as Kurashiki and Onomichi (close to the downtown areas) and Miyajima-guchi (the gateway to Miyajima island).

The JR Hakubi Line provides one gateway to the San-in Region, connecting Okayama and Izumoshi, via Matsue. Please note that you can also catch the Hakubi Line train at Kurashiki Station. The other gateway to the San-in Region is the JR Yamaguchi Line, which links Ogori with Masuda, via Tsuwano.

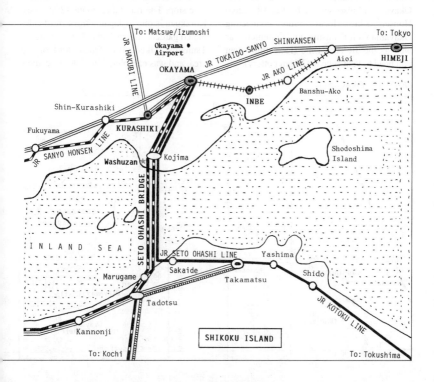

Eastern Inland Sea District

We describe (1) Okayama, (2) Bizen (Inbe), and (3) Kurashiki in detail. Washuzan, an observatory of the Inland Sea, is also briefly introduced in this section.

OKAYAMA 岡山

Okayama, a city of 587,000, is the capital of Okayama Prefecture and the transportation center of the area. Okayama is served by both "Hikari" and "Kodama" Shinkansens. Long distance trains on the JR Hakubi Line (for Matsue and Izumoshi) originate at Okayama Station. Many long distance trains to Shikoku (Takamatsu, Kochi and Matsuyama) also originate here. Okayama is also served by the JR Sanyo Honsen Line (local trains connecting Okayama with Kurashiki and Onomichi), as well as the JR Ako Line (local trains that you need to visit Inbe for Bizen pottery).

JR Okayama Station (middle left, Sanyo Map 2) features a statute of Momotaro, the "Peach Boy" of Japanese mythology. An *i* Information Office is located in the station building. Two streetcars operate from the terminal in front of JR station. There are department stores, shops and restaurants along Momotaro-dori Street, the city's main street.

Places of Interest

Refer to Sanyo Map 2.

Korakuen Garden 後楽園 (middle right). Take the Okayama Denkitsudo (the "Okaden") bus from Platform 9 in front of JR Okayama Station. Get off at Korakuen-mae stop. The ride takes about 12 minutes. Korakuen is one of Japan's three most celebrated gardens. It was laid out at the order of Tsunamasa Ikeda, the feudal lord of the area, and was completed in 1700. It features

MAP 2   Okayama

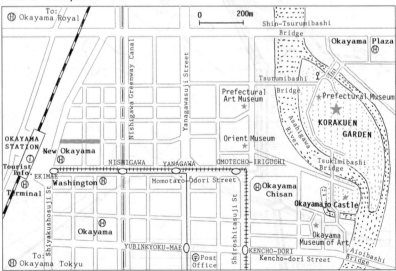

several fields, ponds, waterfalls and tea pavilions, including one that even has a stream flowing through it. The Garden is famous for its vistas: its wide open spaces are a special treat in Japan. Korakuen Garden's reputation is well deserved. Hours: 7:30 AM to 5:20 PM (8:00 AM to 4:20 PM in winter). The 300 yen admission tickets you need for the park are sold in vending machines.

Okayamajo Castle 岡山城 (lower right)(optional). When you leave Korakuen Garden to the south (main exit), follow the path to the river, enjoying the short walk to Tsukimibashi Bridge. Follow the path and enter the Castle grounds through Rokamon Gate. The distinctive black castle, nicknamed Crow Castle, was built in 1573. Only the turrets are originals. The donjon and gates are 1966 reconstructions. Armor, swords, clothing and lacquer items are on display in the donjon. Hours: 9:00 AM to 5:00 PM. Admission: 700 yen. Closed Dec. 29 through Jan. 02.

Okayama Museum of Art 岡山美術館 (optional), near the castle, has a good collection of paintings, ceramics, lacquerware and armor. It displays treasures of the Ikeda family. The building is modeled after a traditional samurai residence and houses a collection of 4,000 items, only a portion of which can be displayed at any given time. Hours: 9:00 AM to 5:30 PM. Admission: 300 yen.

Okayama Orient Museum (Museum of Near Eastern Art) 岡山オリエント 美術館 (middle center) (optional) displays more than 3,000 archeological finds and art treasures from ancient Persia and Mesopotamia. Hours: 8:00 AM to 5:00 PM. Closed Mondays. Admission: 300 yen.

Okayama Prefectural Art Museum 岡山県立美術館 (middle center) (optional) traces the history and culture of the Okayama area with archeological, arts and crafts displays. Hours: 9:00 AM to 6:00 PM (9:30 AM to 5:00 PM in winter). Closed Mondays. Admission: 180 yen.

Back Downtown. Take a streetcar from the Omotecho-Iriguchi stop for the five-minute trip back to the station, or walk back along Momotaro-Odori, the street on which the streetcar runs.

ACCOMMODATIONS
(Refer to Sanyo Map 2)

1. Hotels in Okayama

Okayama Tokyu Hotel (5 minutes by taxi from Okayama Station). First Class. 94 singles (10,000 yen -) & 140 doubles (20,500 yen -). Add: 3-2-18, Otomo, Okayama. Tel: (0862) 33-2411.

Okayama Kokusai Hotel (15 minutes by taxi from Okayama Station). First Class. 69 singles (10,000 yen -) & 120 doubles (19,500 yen -). Add: 4-1-16, Kadota-Honcho, Okayama. Tel: (0862) 73-7311.

Hotel New Okayama (middle left). First Class. 17 singles (12,000 yen -) & 61 doubles (19,000 yen -). Add: 1-1-25, Ekimaecho, Okayama. Tel: (0862) 23-8211.

Okayama Royal Hotel (5 minutes by taxi from Okayama Station). First Class. 70 singles (10,000 yen -) & 81 doubles (17,500 yen -). Add: 2-4, Ezucho, Okayama. Tel: (0862) 54-1155.

Okayama Plaza Hotel (upper right). Standard. 36 singles (8,000 yen -) & 47 doubles (15,000 yen -). Add: 2-3-12, Hama, Okayama. Tel: (0862) 72-1201.

Okayama Terminal Hotel (middle left). Business. 161 singles (7,500 yen -) & 36 doubles (13,000 yen -). Add: 1-5, Ekimotocho, Okayama. Tel: (0862) 33-3131.

Okayama Washington Hotel (middle left). Business. 167 singles (7,200 yen -) & 43 doubles (14,000 yen -). Add: 3-6-201, Honcho, Okayama. Tel: (0862) 31-9111.

Chisan Hotel Okayama (middle center). Business. 148 singles (6,500 yen -) & 64 doubles (10,500 yen -). Add: 1-1-13, Marunouchi, Okayama. Tel: (0862) 25-1212.

2. Welcome Inn in Okayama

Matsunoki Ryokan (3 minute walk from Okayama Station). Add: 19-1, Ekimotocho, Okayama. Tel: (0862) 53-4111.

BIZEN (INBE) 備前（伊部）

The JR Ako Line (local trains only) takes about 40 minutes from Okayama to Inbe. This tiny town is the traditional home of Bizen pottery, which is distinguished by its warm earthen tones and its lack of a glaze. It takes only a few minutes to explore the whole town, but it is easy to lose yourself for hours in its many pottery shops. If the owners aren't busy, you're likely to be invited into the workrooms and kilns that adjoin most of the shops. Watch the traffic on the busy road that parallels the train tracks and on the curving street on which most of town's kilns are located. Refer to Sanyo Map 3.

Bizen Pottery Traditional and Contemporary Art Museum 備前焼会館 (middle right) is the large building to the right as you emerge from the station. It displays outstanding examples of modern Bizen pottery as well as pieces from the Edo, Momoyama and Muromachi Eras. Hours: 9:30 AM to 4:30 PM. Admission: 300 yen.

Tenshin Jinja Shrine 天津神社 and **Inbe Jinja Shrine** 忌部神社 (both upper right) (optional). These are small local shrines. Tenshin Jinja Shrine features a large number of Bizen pottery items. Inbe Jinja Shrine is a long climb up the hill on which it is situated.

KURASHIKI 倉敷

Refer to Sanyo Map 4. With industrial development in its Mizushima District, Kurashiki has become a major Sanyo city with a population of 418,000. At the same time, the city has carefully preserved its historic district in the canal area. The historic district is an arts center and a living museum, and is easily visited on foot from JR

MAP 3 Inbe

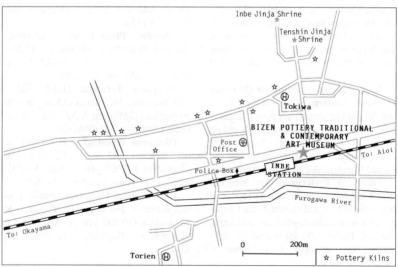

Kurashiki Station. While it is immensely popular and widely admired, it is, to our taste, a bit too contrived.

During the feudal era Kurashiki was a rice and cotton shipping and distribution center. The distinctive white walls that flank the city's picturesque canal are the trademark of modern Kurashiki. There are two shopping arcades near JR Kurashiki Station

(shaded on Sanyo Map 4), and the central tourist and museum area (lower center, shaded) is only a 10-minute walk from the station. Kurashiki is considerate of its many foreign tourists, and has generally good signs in English. "Bikan area" (beautiful scenery area) signs indicate the way to the tourist area. Most of Kurashiki's attractions are closed on Mondays, and open other days

MAP 4 Kurashiki

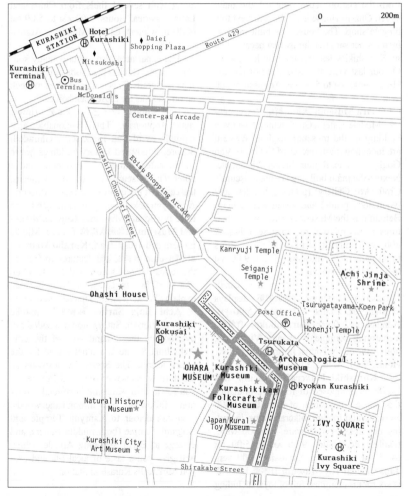

of the week. The *i* Information Office is located in JR Kurashiki Station.

Places of Interest

Ohashi House 大橋家 (middle left) (optional). Kurashiki's main thoroughfare (Kurashiki Chuodori Street) is pleasantly westernized, and features several shops that specialize in *Bizen-yaki*, the local pottery. Ohashi House is about a 5-minute walk from the station. Turn right off the main street. Ohashi House is on the left, next to a bicycle shop. The house was built in 1796 by a former samurai family that became one of Kurashiki's leading mercantile powers. On our last visit, it was in need of repairs. Hours: 9:00 AM to 5:00 PM. Admission: 300 yen.

Ohara Museum 大原美術館 (lower center). Modeled after a Greek temple, the main building of the museum displays Western art, including masterpieces of El Greco, Van Gogh, Cezanne, Renoir, Monet, Manet, etc. Next to the main building are the museum's Craft Art Gallery (pottery, textiles and woodblock prints) and Asian Art Gallery. Behind it is the Museum Annex, which features works of modern Japanese artists. A 800 yen combination ticket admits visitors to all parts of the museum. Hours: 9:00 AM to 5:00 PM (4:30 in winter).

Other attractions along the canal: **Kurashiki Museum** 倉敷美術館 displays Western art. Hours: 9:00 AM to 5:00 PM. Admission: 200 yen. **Kurashikikan** 倉敷館, a charming example of Japanese Victoriana, houses the city's Tourist Information Office. Hours: 9:00 AM to 5:30 PM (5:00 PM in winter). **Kurashiki Folkcraft Museum** 倉敷民芸館 is composed of four rice granaries that house a collection of more than 4,000 Japanese and foreign folkcraft items, including ceramics, woodenware, bamboo ware, textiles, etc. Hours: 9:00 AM to 5:00 PM (4:15 PM in winter). Admission: 500 yen. **Japan Rural Toy Museum** 日本郷土玩具館 is six rooms crammed full of toys, including the dolls used for *hinamatsuri*, Girls' Festival, and the flying fish standards used for Boys' Day, as well as animal figures (from the Japanese zodiac) and the roly-poly *daruma* Buddha dolls that bring good luck. The Museum has a lovely little garden. Hours: 8:00 AM to 5:00 PM. Open year round. Admission: 310 yen. **Archaeological Museum** 倉敷考古館 displays artifacts unearthed in Japan, including large *haniwa*, along with several finds from China and Latin America. Hours: 9:00 AM to 5:00 PM (4:30 in winter). Closed Mondays. Admission: 400 yen.

The canal area also features many souvenir shops, which sell all sorts of traditional Japanese crafts. This is a good place to stock up on presents for those back home.

Ivy Square アイビースクエア (lower right) (optional). This fashionable area reminds us of San Francisco's Ghiradelli Square. Renovated factory buildings house shops, cafes, museums, restaurants and a hotel. The museums are not, by any means, the equal of the impressive Ohara Museum. A 500 yen ticket gains you admission to the three Ivy Square Museums: **Kojima Memorial Museum** 児島虎次郎館 features Middle Eastern and Western art; **Kurabo Memorial Museum** 倉紡記念館 features artifacts of the industrial revolution; and **Ivy Gakken** アイビー学館, an educational display that explains Western art for Japanese students.

Achi Jinja Shrine 阿智神社 (middle right) (optional). Sitting atop a wooded hill overlooking the cultural area of the city, Achi Jinja Shrine is a quiet retreat for the weary tourist. The Shrine has festivals on the third weekends of May and October. If you're tired of Kurashiki's official attractions, follow the path through the woods. You can detour to Kanryuji Temple and Seiganji Temple (both middle center), and emerge at Ebisu Shopping Arcade, which will give you a taste of local life and lead you back to JR Kurashiki Station.

ACCOMMODATIONS
(Refer to Sanyo Map 4)

1. Hotels in Kurashiki

Kurashiki Kokusai Hotel (middle center). Standard. 15 singles (10,500 yen -) & 58 doubles (16,500 yen -). Add: 1-1-44, Chuo, Kurashiki. Tel: (0864) 22-5141.

Hotel Kurashiki (upper left). Business. 59 singles (8,500 yen -) & 71 doubles (16,000 yen -). Add: 1-1-1, Achi, Kurashiki. Tel: (0864) 26-6111.

Kurashiki Plaza Hotel (5 minutes by taxi from Kurashiki Station). Business. 108 singles (7,000 yen -) & 40 doubles (14,000 yen -). Add: 2-510, Oimatsucho, Kurashiki. Tel: (0864) 27-0001.

Kurashiki Ivy Square (lower right). Business. 180 singles (7,000 yen -) & 102 doubles (12,000 yen -). Communal baths. Add: 7-2, Honcho, Kurashiki. Tel: (0864) 22-0011.

2. Ryokan in Kurashiki

Ryokan Kurashiki (lower right). Deluxe. 20 rooms. 25,000 yen & up per person. Add: 4-1, Honcho, Kurashiki. Tel: (0864) 22-0730.

Ryokan Tsurukata (middle center). Deluxe. 13 rooms. 25,000 yen & up per person. Add: 1-3-15, Chuo, Kurashiki. Tel: (0864) 24-1635.

Kurashiki Ishiyama Kadan (10 minutes by taxi from Kurashiki Station). Standard. 77 rooms. 15,000 yen & up per person. Add: 1-25-23 Chuo, Kurashiki. Tel: (0864) 22-2222.

Misono Ryokan (10 minutes by car from Kurashiki Station). Standard. 22 rooms. 15,000 yen & up per person. Add: 3-4-1, Oimatsucho, Kurashiki. Tel: (0864) 22-3618.

3. Welcome Inns in Kurashiki

Kurashiki Terminal Hotel (upper left). Business. 144 singles & 68 doubles. Add: 1-7-2, Achi, Kurashiki. Tel: (0864) 26-1111.

Young Inn Kurashiki (2 minute walk from Kurashiki Station). 39 Western rooms. Add: 1-14-8, Achi, Kurashiki. Tel: (0864) 25-3411.

Kokumin Ryokan Ohguma (2 minute walk from Kurashiki Station). 13 Japanese rooms. Add: 3-1-2, Achi, Kurashiki. Tel: (0864) 22-0250.

WASHUZAN 鷲羽山

Washuzan Hill is located on the southern tip of Kojima Peninsula (middle center, Sanyo Map 1). There is an observatory (with the inevitable restaurants and souvenir shops) atop the hill, which has long been famous as one of the best places for a grand view of the "Shimmering Inland Sea." A number of small islands dot the peaceful waters, which are highlighted beautifully by the play of the sunshine. The coastline of Shikoku Island is visible in the distance. The view from Washuzan is reproduced over and over again in paintings, scenic photos and travel brochures. The Seto Ohashi Bridge starts near Washuzan and connects Honshu to Shikoku, linking many small Inland Sea islands along the way. The view from Washuzan encompasses this example of super modern technology. Frequent bus service connects Washuzan with both Okayama and Kurashiki Stations. The rides take 40 and 70 minutes respectively. From Okayama, take the Shimoden bus from Platform No. 1 behind the Terminal Hotel. From Kurashiki, take the bus from Platform No. 5 or 6 from the bus center in front of JR Kurashiki Station.

Seto Ohashi Bridge. The Bridge, opened in 1988 after nine and a half years of construction, actually consists of six bridges that hopscotch across several islands between Honshu and Shikoku. The double-decker bridges carry both automobile and train traffic. The first of the bridges, Shimotsui Bridge (1,447 m, 4,747 feet), links Honshu and Hitsuishi Island. Next are

Hitsuishi-jima Bridge (792 m, 2,598 feet) and Iwakura-jima Bridge (792 m, 2,598 feet), two matching cable-strayed bridges, passing over Iwakuro Island and Wasashima Island. The Yoshima Bridge (877 m, 2,877 feet), a very large scale truss bridge, provides the link to Yoshima Island. The last stage of the Seto Ohashi Bridege is two suspension bridges: the Kita Bisan Bridge and the Minami Bisan Bridge. They are very large suspension bridges; the Kita (north) portion is 1,611 m (5,285 feet) long, and the Minami (south) portion is 1,723 m (5,652 feet). They complete the link to Sakaide on Shikoku.

Seto Ohashi Memorial Bridge Museum 架橋記念館 is located near Kojima Station on the JR Seto Ohashi Line. The museum building itself is shaped like an ancient Japanese *taikobashi* bridge. The museum features a scale-model of the Seto Ohashi Bridge, and displays models of many of the world's other great bridges. Hours: 9:00 AM to 5:20 PM. Closed Mondays. Dec. 27 through Jan. 5. Admission: 510 yen. East of JR Kojima Station is Kojima Port Sightseeing Pier. One hour boat tours that feature the bridge leave regularly. Fare: 1,500 yen.

Western Inland Sea District

We describe (1) Onomichi, (2) Hiroshima (including sightseeing boat service), and (3) Miyajima in this section.

ONOMICHI 尾道

This Inland Sea shipping center is a famous attraction for Japanese tourists because of its lovely temples, three of which are National Treasures. The problem for foreigners is that the walking tour that most serious Japanese visitors follow is marked only by granite sign posts with the names of the temples carved in characters. Because it is impossible to reproduce on a map or describe in words the complicated twists and turns of the streets and alleys of this ancient town, we have selected the best of Onomichi's temples and described them for a half-day walking tour.

Transportation in Onomichi

Onomichi has a good bus system, and several routes cater to tourists. There is frequent bus service between Shin-Onomichi Station (on the JR Tokaido-Sanyo Shinkansen) and Onomichi Station (on the JR Sanyo Honsen Line). The ride takes 13 minutes and the fare is 160 yen. Except for the chair lift trip, the itinerary we describe below can also be accomplished on foot by good walkers.

Suggested Itinerary

Refer to Sanyo Map 5. **Senkoji Temple** 千光寺 (middle center, Sanyo Map 5). From JR Onomichi Station (lower left) walk along Onomichi's main road, which runs parallel to the JR tracks. It's not pretty, but things will improve! There's an entrance to the Senkoji-Koen Park chair lift to your left just as you come to the first pedestrian bridge. When you get off the chair lift (a 3-minute ride, 270 yen), follow the path to Senkoji Temple. On the way, you'll pass gnarled pines and rocks on which generations of poets have carved their odes to the beauty of the Inland Sea. The Temple was founded in 806, and extends out over a platform with another great view of the Inland Sea. You can follow the path down from the Temple

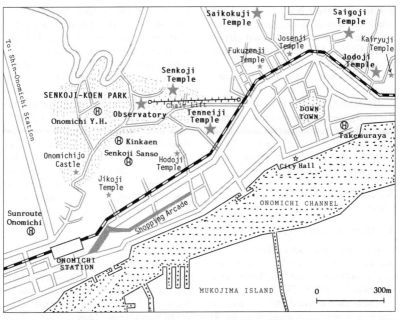

MAP 5 Onomichi

to Onomichi's main street, or return via the ropeway and continue along the main road again. The walk down takes about 20 minutes and you'll pass several monuments and temples tucked in among the residential area. Once you reach the main road, turn left and follow it until you've passed under the second pedestrian bridge, and then turn left for Saikokuji Temple.

Saikokuji Temple 西国寺 (upper center). This temple has a long approach and is a bit of a climb from the main road. It features a giant straw sandal (the kind pilgrims wear) on Niomon Gate, its biggest gate. The first of the temple buildings that you'll come to is Kondo Hall, with red trim. Go to the right of Kondo Hall and up the stairs. On the next level there are several buildings, including one that houses the sanctuary. Walk behind the buildings, passing under the veranda, and up another flight of stairs through the cemetery to get a good look at

the impressive three story pagoda, which also has red trim, and which makes it clear why Saikokuji is a National Treasure.

On the way back, just before you reach the main road, you'll come to **Josenji Temple** 浄泉寺, a lovely old gem, marked by pale blue iron gates (there's another entrance on the main road).

Jodoji Temple 浄土寺 (upper right). Continue along the main road again. After you pass another pedestrian bridge, you'll come to a three way intersection. You'll be able to see the harbor on your right. Go up the stone steps under the railroad tracks. Jodoji Temple was founded in 616. It too is a National Treasure and features a pagoda. The Temple has a beautiful garden (Admission: 300 yen) and a Treasure House, which exhibits many Buddhist statues and paintings (Admission: 200 yen).

When you finish at Jodoji Temple, turn left just outside the gate and follow the path to **Kairyuji Temple** 海竜寺, a small, lovely temple that houses an image of a thousand-handed and thousand-eyed Kannon who can see sounds! Go back out to the main street through the entrance to Jodoji Temple, and catch the bus back to the station across the street.

If you have extra time to wander about in this lovely town, any path up from the main road will lead you to temples. Among the most famous are Saigoji Temple, Josenji Temple, Fukuzenji Temple, Tenneiji Temple, Hodoji Temple and Jikoji Temple.

ACCOMMODATIONS
(Refer to Sanyo Map 5)

1. Hotels in Onomichi

Hotel Sunroute Onomichi (lower left). Standard. 52 singles (6,500 yen -) & 15 doubles (15,000 yen -). Add: 5-3, Temmancho, Onomichi. Tel: (0848) 25-3161.

Onomichi Kokusai Hotel (7 minutes by taxi from Onomichi Station). Business. 46 singles (5,500 yen -) & 21 doubles (12,000 yen -). Add: 1-9-335, Niihama, Onomichi. Tel: (0848) 25-5931.

2. Ryokan in Onomichi

Nishiyama Bekkan (10 minutes by taxi from Onomichi Station). Deluxe. 16 rooms. 30,000 yen & up per person. Add: 678-1, Sanbacho, Onomichi. Tel: (0848) 23-3145.

Senkoji Sanso (middle left). Standard. 34 rooms. 17,000 yen & up per person. Add: 15-20, Nishi-Dodocho, Onomichi. Tel: (0848) 22-7168.

Hotel Kinkaen (middle center). Standard. 36 rooms. 14,000 yen & up per person. Add: 17-53, Nishi-Dodocho, Onomichi. Tel: (0848) 22-7151.

HIROSHIMA   広島

This city got its name when the feudal lord Terumoto Mori built a castle here at the end of the 16th century and named it "Hiroshima"-jo (Broad Island Castle). The Mori family was followed by the Fukushima family, and then the Asanos, who, by encouraging industry, laid the foundation for the development of the castle town. On August 6, 1945, at 8:15 AM, Hiroshima was atom-bombed. The city was completely flattened in an instant, and more than 200,000 lives lost. Two years later the citizens of Hiroshima held their first Peace Festival. Its theme was "No more Hiroshimas." It has since become an annual event to promote world peace. Now the city, with a population of 1,062,000, serves as a major Sanyo administrative, educational and communications center.

Outline of the Hiroshima Area

Refer to Sanyo Map 6. Hiroshima Station (upper right) is served by both "Hikari" and "Kodama" trains on the JR Tokaido-Sanyo Shinkansen, as well as local trains on the JR Sanyo Honsen Line.

Miyajima-guchi Station (middle left) is only 25 minutes by JR local train from Hiroshima. A streetcar also runs between

MAP 6
Outline of Hiroshima and Miyajima

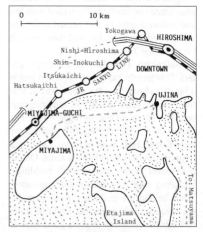

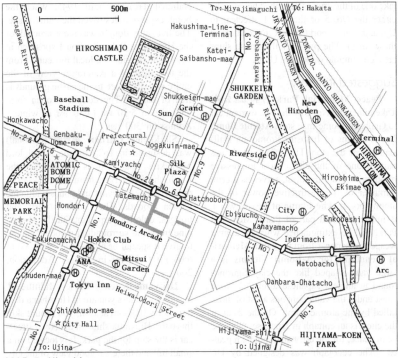

MAP 7 Hiroshima

Hiroshima Station and Miyajima-guchi Station. The Miyajima-guchi boat pier is only a 3-minute walk from JR Miyajima-guchi Station. JR and a second company operate frequent boat service between Miyajima-guchi and Miyajima. If you have a Japan Rail Pass, be sure to take a JR boat.

Ferries and hydrofoils operate from Hiroshima's Ujina Port (middle right) to Matsuyama on Shikoku Island. Sightseeing boats in the Hiroshima area also operate from Ujina. Ujina is connected with JR Hiroshima Station by streetcars.

Outline of the City

Refer to Sanyo Map 7. There are four major places of interest in Hiroshima — Peace Memorial Park (middle left); Hiroshimajo Castle (upper center); Shukkeien Garden (upper center); and Hijiyama-Koen Park (lower right). The downtown section of the city is on the southern side of the east-west main street (Shopping arcades are shaded on the map). Many drinking spots and obscure cabarets are located around the eastern end of the shopping arcades (Shinkawa district). Hiroshima Prefectural Government and other governmental offices are located on the northern side of the main street. These places and JR Hiroshima Station are conveniently connected by several streetcars as explained next. The *i* Information Office is located in Peace Memorial Park.

Transportation in Hiroshima

Hiroshima has eight streetcar lines. The five pictured on the map are most convenient and useful for tourists. If you plan to take one of the cruises described below, take either the No. 5 or the No. 1 streetcar to Ujina, the city's port (the last stop on both of these lines). The piers for the cruise ships are a one-minute walk from Ujina.

Suggested Itinerary

Peace Memorial Park 平和記念公園. Take either the No. 2 or the No. 6 street car to Genbaku-Dome-mae stop. **Atomic Bomb Dome** (Ruins of Industry Promotion Hall) stands near the stop. The dome, which was part of one of the city's most impressive building's before the blast, serves as a grim reminder of the destructive power of the atomic bomb. **The Flame of Peace,** which is in the northern part of Peace Memorial Park, will be extinguished when all atomic weapons disappear from the earth. **Memorial Cenotaph for A-Bomb Victims** is a large vault shaped like the clay figurines found in ancient Japanese tombs. A stone chest under the vault contains a list of those killed by the atomic bomb. On the front of the chest is an epitaph in Japanese: "Repose ye in peace, for the error shall not be repeated." The cenotaph was designed by Dr. Kenzo Tange, a world-renowned Japanese architect, so that those standing in front of it can see the Flame of Peace and the Atomic Bomb Dome beyond it. **Peace Memorial Museum** displays objects and photographs that illustrate the devastation caused by the atomic bomb (9:00 AM to 6:30 PM; 5:30 PM in winter; 50 yen). Even though viewing the displays is an uncomfortable experience, it is one that should not be avoided. On the second floor of the adjacent Peace Memorial Hall, documentary films on the A-bomb are shown from time to time, one in English and another in Japanese.

Hiroshimajo Castle 広島城 (optional) is about 0.8 km (0.5 miles) from Peace Memorial Park; your feet are the best means of transportation there. Hiroshimajo Castle was originally constructed in 1589 by Terumoto Mori. The donjon was registered as a National Treasure until 1945, when the bomb explosion destroyed the entire castle. The five-story donjon was reconstructed for the Hiroshima Rehabilitation Exposition in 1958. The interior is a local museum. From the top, there is a panoramic view of the entire city. Entrance to the castle grounds is free of charge. The donjon is open from 9:00 AM to 5:30 PM (4:30 PM in winter). Admission: 300 yen.

Shukkeien Garden 縮景園 (optional) was designed in 1620 by the feudal lord Nagaakira Asano. It is situated on the Kyobashigawa River, from which water is drawn to make streams and ponds within the garden grounds. The Garden's islets and bridges, colorful carp, fantastically shaped pine trees and surrounding woods combine to give it special beauty. Hours: 9:00 AM to 6:00 PM (5:00 PM in winter). Admission: 200 yen.

Hijiyama-Koen Park 比治山公園 (optional). Unless you are in Hiroshima during cherry blossom season, you should skip this park. Hijiyama-shita on the No. 5 streetcar is the stop for the park. It is located on a small hill and there's a good view of the city from its summit.

Hiroshima Municipal Baseball Stadium (middle left) is the home of the professional Hiroshima Carps.

ACCOMMODATIONS
(Refer to Sanyo Map 7)

1. Hotels in Hiroshima

ANA Hotel Hiroshima (lower left). First Class. 136 singles (11,500 yen -) & 187 doubles (20,500 yen -). Add: 7-20, Nakamachi, Naka-ku, Hiroshima. Tel: (082) 241-1111.

Hiroshima Grand Hotel (upper center). First Class. 179 singles (10,500 yen -) & 183 doubles (18,500 yen -). Add: 4-4, Hatchobori, Naka-ku, Hiroshima. Tel: (082) 227-1313.

Hiroshima Terminal Hotel (middle right). Standard. 218 singles (10,000 yen -) & 216 doubles (19,000 yen -). Add: 1-5, Matsubaracho, Minami-ku, Hiroshima. Tel: (082) 262-1111.

Mitsui Garden Hotel (lower left). Standard. 188 singles (7,500 yen -) & 86 doubles (14,000 yen -). Add: 9-12, Nakacho, Naka-ku, Hiroshima. Tel: (082) 240-1131.

Hiroshima City Hotel (middle right). Standard. 88 singles (7,000 yen -) & 76 doubles (13,000 yen -). Add: 1-4, Kyobashicho, Minami-ku, Hiroshima. Tel: (082) 263-5111.

Hiroshima Riverside Hotel (middle center). Standard. 57 singles (6,500 yen -) & 26 doubles (13,000 yen -). Add: 7-14, Kamioricho, Naka-ku, Hiroshima. Tel: (082) 227-1111.

Arc Hotel Hiroshima (lower right). Business. 166 singles (7,000 yen -) & 59 doubles (13,500 yen -). Add: 1-45, Nishi-Kojincho, Minami-ku, Hiroshima. Tel: (082) 263-6363.

Hiroshima Tokyu Inn (lower left). Business. 229 singles (7,500 yen -) & 55 doubles (13,000 yen -). Add: 3-17, Komachi, Naka-ku, Hiroshima. Tel: (082) 244-0109.

Hotel Silk Plaza (middle center). Business. 186 singles (6,500 yen -) & 46 doubles (12,500 yen -). Add: 14-1, Hatchobori, Naka-ku, Hiroshima. Tel: (082) 227-8111.

Sun Hotel Hiroshima (upper center). Business. 127 singles (6,500 yen -) & 44 doubles (10,500 yen -). Add: 7-25, Kami-Hatchobori, Naka-ku, Hiroshima. Tel: (082) 228-3351.

2. Welcome Inns in Hiroshima

Hotel New Hiroden (upper right). 260 singles & 82 doubles. Add: 14-9, Osugacho, Minami-ku, Hiroshima. Tel: (082) 263-3456.

Hokke Club Hiroshima (lower left). 265 singles & 145 doubles. Add: 7-7, Nakamachi, Naka-ku, Hiroshima. Tel: (082) 248-3371.

Hotel Sun Palace (3 minute walk from Hiroshima Station). 59 singles & 16 doubles. Add: 10-12, Matsubaracho, Minami-ku, Hiroshima. Tel: (082) 264-6111.

Hiroshima Central Hotel (5 minutes by taxi from Hiroshima Station). 107 singles & 16 doubles. Add: 1-8, Kanayamacho, Naka-ku, Hiroshima. Tel: (082) 243-2222.

Hotel New Ginkaku (7 minute walk from Hiroshima Station). 17 Japanese & 8 Western rooms. Add: 8-19, Kyobashicho, Minami-ku, Hiroshima. Tel: (082) 261-8628.

New Matsuo (3 minute walk from Hiroshima Station). 12 Japanese & 12 Western rooms. Add: 14-9, Kami-Osugacho, Higashi-ku, Hiroshima. Tel: (082) 262-3141.

Mikawa Ryokan (5 minute walk from Hiroshima Station). 13 Japanese rooms. Add: 9-6, Kyobashicho, Minami-ku, Hiroshima. Tel: (082) 261-2719.

INLAND SEA CRUISES
瀬戸内海クルーズ

Setonaikai Kisen Cruises

Setonaikai Kisen Company 瀬戸内海汽船 operates several cruises from March 1 through November 30 as listed below. All cruises require advance reservations.

Round One-day Cruise 瀬戸内海高速クルーズ1日往復 starts at Miyajima Island (8:35 AM) and stops at Ujina Pier of Hiroshima (9:00 AM). In addition to the cruising in the Inland Sea, you will visit Omishima and Setoda for sightseeing. The main attraction of Omishima is **Oyamazumi Jinja Shrine** 大山祇神社. The present buildings are 1427 reconstructions. Because several feudal lords dedicated treasures to the Shrine every time they won a battle in the Inland Sea area, the Treasure House of the Shrine has Japan's best collection of samurai armor and swords. The stop at Setoda features **Kosanji Temple** 耕三寺. This temple was built by a successful businessman born in Setoda. All the buildings are modeled on famous structures all over Japan, and the temple itself is a museum of replicas of National Treasures. The replicas include copies of Yomeimon Gate of Toshogu Shrine; the Silver Pavilion of Kyoto; and Yumedono Hall of Horyuji Temple in Nara. The cruise arrives back at Ujina (Hiroshima) at 5:20 PM and then at Miyajima at 5:42 PM. The fare is 12,000 yen, including lunch.

One Way Cruise B 瀬戸内海高速クルーズ片道B starts at Miyajima Island (8:35 AM) and stops at Ujina (9:00 AM). You will also visit Omishima and Setoda for sightseeing (see above). The cruise finishes at Onomichi at 2:54 PM. The fare is 9,000 yen without lunch, or 11,000 yen with lunch.

One Way Cruise A 瀬戸内海高速クルーズ片道A is the reverse route of Cruise B above. The boat leaves Onomichi at 11:40 AM and arrives at Ujina at 5:20 PM and at Miyajiama at 5:42 PM. The fare is the same as Cruise B.

Ginga Lunch Cruise 銀河ランチクルーズ. This boat service is handy for transportation from Hiroshima to Miyajima, or vice versa. The boat leaves Ujina at 11:45 AM and arrives at Miyajima at 12:55 PM. The return trip leaves Miyajima at 1:00 PM and arrives at Ujina at 1:55 PM. The one-way fare is 6,000 yen or 8,000 yen depending on the lunch menu.

Ginga Dinner Cruise 銀河ディナークルーズ. This two-and-a-half hour cruise is especially popular in summer time. The boat leaves Ujina at 6:45 PM and cruises around Miyajima Island, while serving dinner on board. The marine scenery is especially beautiful in the glow of the sunset. The cruise can be a little noisy if you happen to be on board with Japanese groups. The boat returns to Ujina at 9:10 PM. The fare is 10,000 yen to 20,000 yen depending on the dinner menu.

MIYAJIMA 宮島

Miyajima, also called Itsukushima, is an island about 30 km (19 miles) in circumference. It is famous for its shrine built on supports that extend into the sea. Tame deer wander about the island.

Suggested Itinerary in Miyajima

Refer to Sanyo Map 8. The boat piers on Miyajima Island (upper center) are located about 0.8 km (0.5 miles) north of Itsukushima Jinja Shrine (lower left). The approach to the Shrine is a pleasant promenade along the Inland Sea, the southern half of which is lined with stone lanterns.

Itsukushima Jinja Shrine 厳島神社 is dedicated to the three daughters of *Susano-o-no-Mikoto,* a Shinto god. The buildings, which have been rebuilt several times, consist of a Main Shrine and several minor shrines and halls — all connected by wide corridors or galleries, which are built above the sea on both sides of the Shrine. When the tide comes in, the entire edifice seems to be floating. The major buildings of the Shrine have been designated National Treasures. A vermilion *torii* gate rises out of the sea about 160 m (525 feet) from the shore. This 16 m (53 foot) tall *torii* gate, the largest in Japan, was erected in 1875, and is a symbol of the island. Itsukushima Jinja Shrine is open to the public from 6:30 AM to 6:00 PM (5:00 PM in winter). Admission: 300 yen.

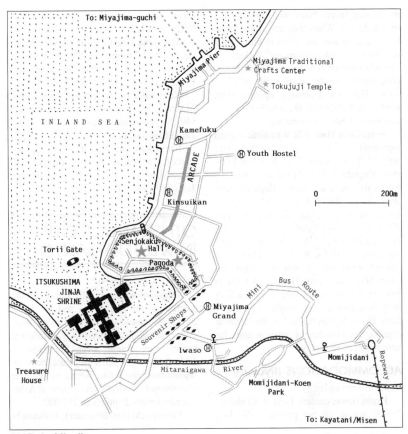

MAP 8 Miyajima

Treasure House 厳島神社宝物館 is just across the street from the exit of the Shrine. This modern structure contains nearly 4,000 objects, more than 130 of which have been designated National Treasures or Important Cultural Properties. Hours: 6:30 AM to 6:00 PM (5:00 PM in winter). Admission: 300 yen.

Momijidani-Koen Park 紅葉谷公園 (lower center) and **Mt. Misen** 弥山 (outside the map). Momijidani-Koen Park (Maple Valley Park) is a quiet retreat on a hillside amid groves of maple trees. A free mini-bus operates between the two stops as pictured on the map every 20 minutes, but because it's so lovely, we suggest that you consider walking through the Park to the ropeway station (lower right). The ropeways take visitors almost to the top of Mt. Misen. The first ropeway, a small six-passenger car, connects Momijidani Station with Kayatani Station. The cars operate every 30 seconds. A larger gondola, with a capacity of 26, operates every 15 minutes from Kayatani to Shishiiwa. The real summit of Mt. Misen (530 m or 1,730 feet) is a 15-20 minute walk from Shishiiwa Station. From the gondola, and, of course, from Shishiiwa, visitors have a splendid view of Inland Sea National Park and its many islets. Many wild monkeys live on Mt. Misen. When they are playing near Shishiiwa, visitors are asked to check their handbags in complimentary lockers in Shishiiwa Station. There is no danger to visitors, but the monkeys are rather mischievous. The two ropeways operate from 8:00 AM to 6:20 PM (9:00 AM to 5:00 in winter). Fares: 1,500 yen round trip.

Senjokaku Hall 千畳閣 (middle center) (optional). When you return to the shrine area, visit Senjokaku Hall and the **Five-story Pagoda** 五重塔. These two structures are located on a hill, atop a flight of steep steps. Senjokaku Hall, or the Hall of One Thousand Mats, is an old building that Hideyoshi Toyotomi dedicated to Itsukushima Jinja Shrine in 1587. Though the original plans called for Senjokaku Hall to be painted vermilion, it was left unpainted when Hideyoshi died. Hours: 9:00 AM to 5:00 PM. Admission 350 yen. Nearby, a five-story pagoda soars to a height of 27 m (90 feet). Thatched with the bark of the Japanese cypress, it is a mixture of Japanese and Chinese architectural styles.

ACCOMMODATIONS (Ryokan)

(Refer to Sanyo Map 8)

Iwaso (lower center). Deluxe. 45 rooms. 25,000 yen & up per person. Add: 345, Miyajimacho, Hiroshima Prefecture. Tel: (0829) 44-2233.

Miyajima Grand Hotel (lower center). First Class. 67 rooms. 18,000 yen & up per person. Add: 362, Miyajimacho, Hiroshima Prefecture. Tel: (0829) 44-2411.

Kamefuku (upper center). First Class. 71 rooms. 18,000 yen & up per person. Add: 849, Miyajimacho, Hiroshima Prefecture. Tel: (0829) 44-2111.

Kinsuikan (middle center). First class. 39 rooms. 18,000 yen & up per person. Add: 1133, Miyajimacho, Hiroshima Prefecture. Tel: (0829) 44-2131.

OTHER MAJOR CITIES IN WESTERN SANYO

(Refer to Sanyo Map 9)

Shimonoseki (lower left). Located at the junction of the Inland Sea and the Japan Sea, Shimonoseki was a key transportation center throughout history. Many historic sea battles were fought near Shimonoseki. Today, overnight ferries operate between Shimonoseki and Pusan, Korea, and provide international travelers with an unusual Asian itinerary option. Population: 257,000.

Yamaguchi (middle center). Yamaguchi

MAP 9 Other Sanyo Cities

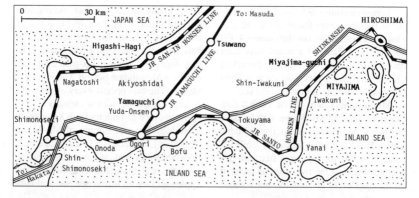

is the most historic city in Western Sanyo. The original city was laid out in the 14th century by the Ouchi family, and was modeled on Kyoto. Yamaguchi was the headquarters of the Choshu Clan during their battles against the Tokugawa forces in the middle of the 19th century. The city features several important historic legacies, including the five-story pagoda of Rurikoji Temple. Population: 126,000. Most tourists to Yamaguchi stay overnight at a ryokan in nearby Yuda-Onsen Hotsprings.

Bofu (lower center). In the 7th century the imperial government in Nara established an administrative base here. The city was the site of the battles between the forces of the Tokugawa Shogunate and the Choshu Clan, a leader of the anti-Tokugawa alliance of the middle of the 19th century. Today, Bofu is an industrial city with a large Mazda Motors factory. Populaton: 118,000.

Iwakuni (middle right). A former castle town of the Iwakini Clan. The city has a U.S. military base. The Kintaikyo Bridges, elegantly shaped wooden bridges, are one of the most popular tourist spots in Western Sanyo. The city is served by the JR Tokaido-Sanyo Shinkansen (Shin-Iwakuni Station), and by local trains on the JR Sanyo Honsen Line (Iwakuni Station). Population: 111,000.

Tokuyama (middle center). In the feudal era Tokuyama prospered as the area's sea transportation center. The petroleum industry has developed here after World War II. Population: 110,000.

Akiyoshidai (middle left) is a limestone plateau. Shuhodo Cave is Japan's largest cavern and a popular tourist spot of the area. Buses run about once an hour between Yamaguchi Station and Shuhodo (about a one-hour ride).

JR FARES BETWEEN MAJOR CITIES IN THE SANYO REGION
(Based on local trains).
For Shinkansen fares, Refer to the Tokaido-Sanyo Shinkansen fare chart in the Transportation section of the Introduction Chapter above.

To/From	Okayama	Kurashiki	Hiroshima
Okayama		310 yen (15.9 km)	2,880 yen (171.3 km)
Inbe	560 yen (30.2 km)	1,090 yen (62.5 km)	
Kurashiki	310 yen (15.9 km)		2,470 yen (145.4 km)
Onomichi	1,260 yen (78.4 km)		1,420 yen (82.9 km)
Hiroshima	2,880 yen (171.3 km)	2,470 yen (145.4 km)	
Miyajima-guchi	3,190 yen (183. 1 km)	2,880 yen (167.2 km)	390 yen (21.8 km)

SAN-IN REGION

山陰

In our opinion, this is the best of the off-the-beaten-track areas of Japan. The San-in Region is blessed with a relatively gentle climate, a rich history and lovely coastal and mountain scenery. Due to comparatively inconvenient (no Shinkansen) transportation to this area, foreign tourists often pass it by. We urge that you give serious consideration to the San-in District if you have extra days in Japan. It has much to offer.

Refer to San-in Map 1. We describe four major destinations in this area:

(1) Matsue (upper right), a castle town noted for its beautiful lakefront scenery;

(2) Izumo (upper right; Izumoshi is its JR station name), site of the famous Izumo Taisha Shrine;

(3) Hagi (middle left; JR Higashi-Hagi is the city's main train station), an unspoiled historic city and home of subtly gorgeous pottery; and

(4) Tsuwano (middle left), another castle town famous for its variety of handicrafts.

The following is a standard San-in itinerary, starting from Kyoto or Osaka.

Day 1. Arrive Matsue

Arrive in Matsue about noon. Afternoon city sightseeing.

Day 2. Matsue/Izumo/Hagi

Visit Izumo in the morning. Afternoon train to Hagi.

MAP 1 Outline of San-in

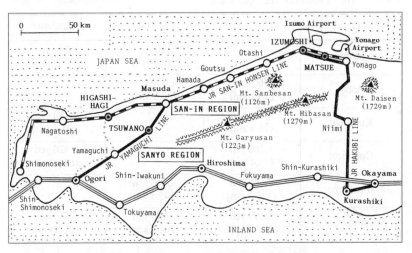

Day 3. Hagi

Full day sightseeing of Hagi.

Day 4. Hagi/Ogori

Bus from Hagi to Ogori, or combine two JR trains (Hagi to Masuda, and Masuda to Ogori).

Tsuwano and the southern suburbs of Matsue are also introduced in this chapter. They are optional destinations for those with extra time. You need two additional days to include all of these destinations as follows:

Day 1. Arrive Matsue.

Afternoon sightseeing.

Day 2. Matsue. Southern suburbs.

Day 3. Matsue/Izumo/Hagi

Day 4. Hagi

Day 5. Hagi/Tsuwano

Day 6. Tsuwano/Ogori

Other Major Cities in the San-in District

Tottori (outside San-in Map 1 to the east). Tottori, a former castle town, is now the capital of Tottori Prefecture, with a population of 141,000. The city has Japan's largest sand dunes along the Japan Sea. Tottori is reached by JR limited express trains (called "Sakyu") in 2 hours and 45 minutes from Okayama.

Yonago (upper right). Yonago is traditionally called the "Osaka of San-in." Sandwiched between two large castle towns, Tottori and Matsue, Yonago functioned as the commercial and distribution center of the area. Adachi Museum of Art is in the city's suburbs. JR "Yakumo" limited expresses take 2 hours from Okayama to Yonago.

SAN-IN REGION TRANSPORTATION NETWORK

Refer to San-in Map 1. The JR Hakubi Line connects the Sanyo and San-in Regions. Limited express trains (called "Yakumo") run about once every hour between Okayama (lower right) and Izumoshi (upper right), via Kurashiki, Niimi, Yonago and Matsue. The ride from Okayama to Matsue takes two and a half hours, and it is an additional 30 minutes to Izumoshi.

The JR San-in Honsen Line runs along the Japan Sea coast. There are frequent trains between Matsue and Izumoshi — a 30 minute trip by limited express and a 45 minute trip by local train. Two trains run daily from Matsue to Hagi (Higashi-Hagi Station) via Izumoshi and Masuda — the "Sanbe" express train in the morning and the "Isokaze" limited express train in the afternoon. The ride to Higashi-Hagi takes about 4 hours from Matsue and three and a half hours from Izumoshi. Local trains run about once every two hours between Higashi-Hagi and Masuda on the JR San-in Line.

The JR Yamaguchi Line connects the Inland Sea (Ogori) and the Japan Sea (Masuda) via Tsuwano. Several limited express trains (called "Oki") run on this line every day. "Oki" limited express trains actually originate at Yonago Station and run on the JR San-in Honsen Line tracks to Masuda, and then branch off on to the JR Yamaguchi Line to Ogori. Several additional local trains also operate between Masuda and Ogori. The ride from Masuda to Tsuwano takes about 30 minutes by limited express and 40 minutes by local train. The ride from Masuda to Ogori takes about one-and-a-half hours by limited express and two-and-a-half hours by local.

There is also bus service between Higashi-Hagi and Ogori about once every hour. JR and Bocho Kotsu alternate operating buses on this route. If you have a Japan Rail Pass, make sure that you take a JR bus. The ride from Higashi-Hagi to Ogori takes about 1 hour and 30 minutes, and the fare is 1,900 yen.

Izumo Airport, to the northwest of Matsue, is served by flights from Tokyo, Osaka and Fukuoka. Buses run between Izumo

Airport and Matsue Onsen Station (lower left, San-in Map 2) via JR Matsue Station (lower right). The ride takes 40 minutes.

MATSUE 松江

Matsue is the capital of Shimane Prefecture, site of an ancient province called Izumo. Many local sites proudly retain that ancient name. Matsue is very much a water-oriented city. Located near, but not on, the Japan Sea, it is situated at the conjunction of Nakaumi Lagoon and Lake Shinjiko. Matsue is probably most familiar to non-Japanese as the first Japanese home of Lafcadio Hearn (Yakumo Koizumi), the 19th century's foremost interpreter of Japan to the West. This small, graceful city is also a rich repository of archeological treasures.

Refer to San-in Map 2. An *i* Information Office is located in JR Matsue Station (lower right).

The city's main shopping streets, not far from JR Matsue Station, are shaded on the map.

Transportation in Matsue

The best way to get around Matsue is on the city's excellent bus system. The main bus terminal is located at JR Matsue Station. Stops 1 and 2 are right in front of the station, and Stops 3, 4 and 5 are on the adjacent traffic island.

Places of Interest In Downtown-Matsue

Matsuejo Castle 松江城 (middle left). Take any bus from Stop No. 1, 2, 4 or 5 at Matsue Station. The ride to Kencho-mae stop (middle center) takes about 10 minutes. When you get off the bus, walk to the north, past the modern municipal buildings, to the entrance to the Castle compound. The Castle grounds feature Matsue Cultural Museum, Matsue Jinja Shrine, Gokoku Jinja Shrine and Shiroyama Inari Shrine as well as the

Castle itself. The Castle was built in 1611 by Yoshiharu Horio. The donjon (reconstructed in 1642), and a few of the other old structures still stand. According to Hearn, it is "fantastically grim" and "grotesquely complex." The donjon is 30 m (98 feet) tall, and the view from its top floor encompasses Lake Shinjiko and the city, with the mountains in the distance. The lower floors have interesting displays of helmets, armor, swords, screens and scrolls. Hours: 8:30 AM to 5:00 PM. Admission: 400 yen.

Matsue Cultural Museum 松江郷土館 (optional) is housed in **Kounkaku**, a distinctive Western-style building constructed in 1903 as an accommodation for Emperor Meiji (who unfortunately never made it to Matsue). It has served as a museum since 1973 and exhibits documents, implements and arts and crafts items. Hours: 8:30 AM to 5:00 PM. Admission: 200 yen. **Matsue Jinja Shrine** 松江神社 (optional) is between Kounkaku and Matsuejo Castle.

Hearn (Koizumi Yakumo) Memorial Museum 小泉八雲記念館 (upper left). After leaving the Castle, follow the curves of the moat. Turn right at the traffic signal. The Museum is on the left. It is the first in a long line of traditional buildings — the remnants of the Shiominawate Quarter where the high-ranking samurai once lived. Lafcadio Hearn arrived in Matsue in 1890 to teach English, and fell seriously ill early in 1891. A local woman, Setsu Koizumi, nursed him back to health and later became his wife. Hearn remained in Matsue for only 15 months, but loved this city and recorded his impressions of it in several of his essays. Hearn had a long and distinguished career in Japan as an editor and teacher, and his works helped to introduce Japan to the West. He became a Japanese citizen and took the name Yakumo Koizumi. The Memorial Museum houses an extensive collection of Hearn memorabilia. Hours: 8:30 AM to 5:00 PM. Admission: 250 yen.

Hearn House (The Koizumi Residence) 小泉八雲旧居 (optional) is next to the Memorial Museum. Hearn lived in this house for five months in 1891. The few rooms open to visitors look out on the garden he described in "In a Japanese Garden," one of the essays in his *Glimpses of Unfamiliar Japan*. Hours: 9:00 AM to 4:30 PM (4:00 PM in winter). Admission: 200 yen.

Tanabe Art Museum 田部美術館 (upper left) (optional). This lovely small museum displays the treasures of the Tan-

MAP 2 Matsue

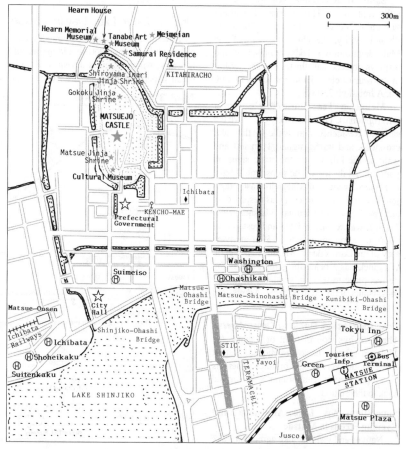

abe family, Izumo aristocrats for five generations. It was established by Choemon Tanabe, a former governor of Shimane Prefecture, in 1979. Exhibits change regularly. Tea bowls and other tea ceremony utensils are the strong suit of the Tanabe collection. The building was designed by Kiyonori Kikutake, and is intended to capture the spirit of a tea house in a modern structure. If you are interested in tea ceremony or a general museum aficionado, this is a must. Hours: 9:00 AM to 5:00 PM. Closed Mondays. Admission: 500 yen.

Samurai Residence 武家屋敷 (upper left) (optional). This typical feudal-era samurai residence was built in 1730 by the Shiomi family, the chief retainers of the Matsudaira daimyo. Today it preserves and displays objects that illustrate everyday life in the warrior class. Hours: 8:30 AM to 5:00 PM. Admission: 250 yen.

Meimeian Tea House 明々庵 (upper left) (optional). Turn left when you leave the samurai Residence and walk to the next crosswalk and traffic signal. Turn left and walk up the hill. Go up the stone steps on your left. At the top of the steps, you'll have a spectacular view of Matsuejo Castle donjon. The original Meimeian was designed by and built for Lord Fumai Matsudaira in 1779. It was rebuilt in 1928 and restored in 1966, to commemorate the 150th anniversary of the Lord's death. Meimeian is a gem. It's quiet, has a beautiful garden and is the perfect place to relax in soothing surroundings. Hours: 9:00 AM to 5:00 PM. Admission: 200 yen (350 yen extra for tea).

Transportation Back to Downtown. There's a bus stop in front of Tanabe Art Museum. Buses back to Matsue Station leave about every 15-20 minutes. There is also a bus stop at Kitahoricho, with service back to the Station.

Suggestions for Late Afternoon and Evening Strolls in Matsue

Natives and visitors alike agree that Lake Shinjiko at sunset is Matsue's most spectacular natural asset; local tourist offices publish detailed information on sunset times. Be sure to stop at **Matsue Ohashi Bridge** 松江大橋 (middle center), which is locally considered the best place from which to view the beauties of Lake Shinjiko at sunset.

There is a group of more than 10 temples in the **Teramachi** area 寺町 (lower center). Although the neighborhood itself is not particularly attractive, these small temples are modest gems. They are all neat and clean, and have not been exploited or spoiled as "tourist attractions."

Itinerary for an Extra Day in Matsue

Refer to San-in Map 3. If you stay only one night in Matsue, you should ignore this itinerary, which includes a visit to a traditional paper-making village, an excavation

MAP 3 Matsue Suburbs

site and archeological museum and two of Matsue's most famous shrines. The distances covered are great, and the bus service relatively infrequent. It's important to check return schedules when you get off the bus. Note that the visits to the Shrines involve a fair amount of walking.

Note: Infrequent bus service to Bessho makes it difficult to visit all of these destinations in one day. Consider skipping Bessho. If you are especially interested in handmade paper, you might consider a visit just to Bessho. If you decide to visit all these destinations, you'll have to take a very early bus to Bessho and take a taxi from Bessho to Fudokino-oka Center (which should cost about 1,500 yen).

Abe Eishiro Memorial Museum 阿部栄四郎記念館 (lower right) in Washi-no-Sato Paper Making Village. The bus trip from Matsue Station (Platform No. 3) to Bessho (the terminus of the bus route) takes 36 minutes. The only buses from Matsue that will get you to Bessho while the Abe Eishiro Memorial Museum is open leave at 8:14 AM, 9:54 AM and 12:29 PM. Fare: 520 yen.

When you get off the bus, walk straight along the town's main road. Walk past the first street on your left and turn left at the next intersecting road, walking down the

Lake Shinjiko

slope to the Memorial Museum, the large white building with dark gray tiles.

The Memorial Museum has exhibits on Abe's life, and displays paper-making implements as well as samples of the master's craft. The Memorial Museum also has Japanese language videos on Eishiro Abe's life that are relatively easy to follow.

Eishiro Abe used paper making methods first introduced into Japan 1,200 years ago, refining them to a high level of sophistication. Abe, who was named a Living National Treasure in 1968, elevated this craft to an art. Hours: 9:00 AM to 4:30 PM. Closed Tuesdays. Admission: 500 yen.

On your way back to the bus stop, you can stop in at the Abe workshop (owned by his son) to see the paper being made. A sign that says "Izumo handmade paper" in English marks the venerable wooden building. The craftsmen and women are very gracious about letting visitors watch them work.

Fudokino-oka Center 風土記の丘センター (Middle center)

If you have visited Bessho, take a taxi to Fudokino-oka Center. If you are not going to Bessho, the buses from Matsue Station to Fudokino-oka-iriguchi leave from Platform 3 about once every 30 minutes.

An ancient state called Izumo was centered in what are now the southern suburbs of Matsue. Many tumuli of 4th-7th century *kofun* (burial mounds) are scattered throughout the area. The Shimane Prefectural government has established Fudokino-oka Center to preserve and protect the area's precious cultural artifacts. The Fudokino-oka Center building, itself modeled on the ancient tumuli of Izumo, displays various ancient implements and large *haniwa* clay figures excavated from tumuli in the area. The observatory on the roof top gives you an excellent opportunity to observe tumuli in the Center's grounds. The grounds also encompass a restored 6th century dwelling and the foundations of a medieval samurai house. Hours: 9:00 AM to 5:00 PM. Closed Mondays. Admission: 150 yen.

Kamosu Jinja Shrine 神魂神社 (Middle center)

When you leave the Fudokino-oka Center, turn left to the National Treasure Kamosu Jinja Shrine. The Shrine is constructed in the *Taisha-zukuri* style, one of the oldest known architectural styles of Japan. Izumo Taisha Shrine is also of this style. The walls and ceilings of the Shrine are ornamented with beautiful paintings. Hours: from dawn to dusk. Admission free.

If you want to return to Matsue from Kamosu Jinja Shrine, go back to Fudokino-oka-iriguchi bus stop.

Yaegaki Jinja Shrine 八重垣神社 (Middle left)

Yaegaki Jinja Shrine is a 30-minute walk from Kamosu Jinja Shrine. Follow the shaded route on the map. This Shrine was the subject of one of Lafcadio Hearn's essays. The gods enshrined here are believed to have special influence in matters of romance. Behind the Shrine is a mysterious wood with miniature shrines and a quiet pond. If you visit here, you'll understand why Hearn was so enchanted by Japan. Admission to the grounds is free. Admission to the interior: 200 yen.

Buses back downtown from Yaegaki-Jinja-mae stop are relatively infrequent. There is more frequent service from Yaegaki-danchi-iriguchi stop.

ACCOMMODATIONS
(Refer to San-in Map 2)

1. Hotels in Matsue

Hotel Ichibata (lower left). First Class. 42 singles (7,500 yen -), 46 doubles (16,500 yen -) & 50 Japanese rooms (21,000 yen -). Add: 30, Chidoricho, Matsue. Tel: (0852) 22-0188.

Matsue Tokyu Inn (lower right). Standard. 102 singles (7,500 yen -) & 73 doubles (15,500 yen -). Add: 590, Asahicho, Matsue. Tel: (0852) 27-0109.

Matsue Washington Hotel (middle center). Business. 100 singles (7,100 yen -) & 56 doubles (14,000 yen -). Add: 2-22, Higashi-Honcho, Matsue. Tel: (0852) 22-4111.

Green Hotel Matsue (lower right). Business. 120 singles (5,700 yen -) & 40 doubles (10,500 yen -). Add: 493-1, Asahicho, Matsue. Tel: (0852) 27-3000.

Matsue Plaza Hotel (lower right). Business. 161 singles (3,500 yen -) & 17 doubles (7,500 yen -). Add: 469-1, Asahicho, Matsue. Tel: (0852) 26-6650.

2. Ryokan in Matsue

Suimeiso (middle left). First Class. 47 rooms. 18,000 yen & up per person. Add: 26, Nishichamachi, Matsue. Tel: (0852) 26-3311.

Ohashikan (middle center). Standard. 29 rooms. 18,000 yen & up per person. Add: 40, Suetsugi-Honcho, Matsue. Tel: (0852) 21-5168.

Suitenkaku (lower left). Standard. 66 rooms. 15,000 yen & up per person. Add: 39, Chidoricho, Matsue. Tel: (0852) 21-4910.

Shoheikaku (lower left). Standard. 14 rooms. 15,000 yen & up per person. Add: 38, Chidoricho, Matsue. Tel: (0852) 23-8000.

3. Ryokan in Tamatsukuri Onsen

Only for hotspring fans. Tamatsukuri Onsen hotsprings is located to the southwest of Matsue. Frequent bus service is available from Matsue Station (30-minute ride, 460 yen).

Chorakuen. Deluxe. 102 rooms. 22,000 yen & up per person. Add: Tamatsukuri-Onsen, Tamayucho. Tel: (0852) 62-0111.

Choseikaku. Deluxe. 82 rooms. 18,000 yen & up per person. Add: Tamatsukuri-Onsen, Tamayucho. Tel: (0852) 62-0711.

Minami Bekkan. First Class. 18,000 yen & up per person. 54 rooms. Add: 1218-8, Tamatsukuri, Tamayucho. Tel: (0852) 62-0711.

Tamai Bekkan. Standard. 15,000 yen &

up per person. 52 rooms. Add: 1247, Tamat-sukuri, Tamayucho. Tel: (0852) 62-0524.

IZUMO 出雲

You can visit Izumo from Matsue in a half-day excursion, or you can stop here on your way from Matsue to Hagi. Izumo Taisha is the oldest shrine location in Japan. Legend has it that this is the place to which the Shinto god *Okuninushi-no-Mikoto* retired after introducing medicine and agri-culture to Japan. Nearby Cape Hinomisaki provides scenic views of the Japan Sea. However, we recommend it only for seascape enthusiasts. You will see coasts just as beautiful from the train windows on your trip from Izumoshi to Higashi-Hagi.

If you follow our suggested itinerary, you should take a JR train from Matsue (around 8:00 AM) to Izumoshi (a 30-minute ride by limited express, and a 45-minute ride by local). At Izumoshi, take the bus for

MAP 4 Izumo

Izumo Taisha Shrine from Bus Stop No. 1 in front of the train station (in front of the department store to the right as you exit the station). The trip to the Shrine (the terminus of the bus) takes 26 minutes, and the fare is 450 yen. The bus terminates at Ichibata Bus Terminal (upper left, San-in Map 4) next to Izumo Taisha Shrine. Buses leave about every half hour, as do buses back to Izu-moshi from Izumo Taisha (Platform No. 2). There is also a private rail connection, on the Ichibata Railway, between Matsue Onsen and Izumo-Taisha, via Kawato. Ser-vice is less frequent than the bus service.

After spending 1-2 hours at the Shrine, take a bus back to Izumoshi, and catch the JR "Isokaze" limited express train for Higashi-Hagi. The train leaves Izumoshi around 1:00 PM.

Izumo Taisha Shrine 出雲大社 (Upper half, San-in Map 4)

You can walk from the bus terminal to a side entrance to Shrine precincts, but even if you do so, it's worth it to walk back to the entrance to the Shrine, which is marked by a giant *torii*. The approach to the Main build-ing is impressive: the path has a lovely wooded garden on both sides, with a large number of magnificent pines. **The Treasure House** 宝物館 has an impressive collection of swords and other items of historical inter-est. Hours: 8:00 AM to 4:30 PM. Admission: 150 yen.

There are several noodle shops along the

town's main street. They feature homemade *wari-go-soba*, the buckwheat specialty noodles of the area. Buses back to Izumoshi Station, originating at the Ichibata bus terminal, make stops on Taisha's main street on their way back to Izumoshi.

Cape Hinomisaki 日御碕

The bus to Cape Hinomisaki also leaves from the Ichibata bus terminal next to the Shrine. Buses to the Cape leave about once an hour. The trip takes 25 minutes. Most of the ride is along a coast road with beautiful views of the Japan Sea. As the bus turns onto the coast road, you'll see a rock, pine-clad islet with its own small *torii*.

The Cape Hinomisaki bus terminal is next to Hinomisaki Jinja Shrine. After you explore the Shrine, exit from the gate to the left of its main building and walk toward the water and the pier for "glass boat" tours (available April 29-September 30; half-hour tour). To continue on foot to the Cape, turn right and follow the path up the hill. The walk to the Cape's famous Lighthouse takes about 10 minutes. The first part is up a wooded hill with lovely views of the Sea. When you reach the commercial street with souvenir and snack shops, bear to your left (whenever there's a choice on this walk, bear left).

Cape Hinomisaki Lighthouse 日御碕 燈台, opened in 1961, has 460,000 candle power, and is Asia's tallest. The view of the Japan Sea is spectacular. Admission: 100 yen. Hours: 8:30 AM (9:00 AM in winter) to 4:00 PM. You can also stroll around the walkways laid out along the Cape.

Ryokan in the Izumo Taisha Area
(Refer to San-in Map 4)

Takenoya Ryokan (middle center). Standard. 44 rooms. 18,000 yen & up per person. Add: 857, Kizuki-Minami, Taisha-machi. Tel: (0853) 53-3131.

Inabaya Ryokan (middle left). Standard. 30 rooms. 12,000 yen & up per person.

Add: 721, Kizuki-Higashi, Taishamachi. Tel: (0853) 53-3180.

Fujiwara Ryokan (lower center). Standard. 19 rooms. 11,000 yen & up per person. Add: 858-1, Kizuki-Minami, Taisha-machi. Tel: (0853) 53-2009.

HAGI 萩

Refer to San-in Map 5. Located on the Japan Sea side of Yamaguchi Prefecture near the southern tip of the main island of Honshu, Hagi is a lovely traditional castle town and port. It is surrounded by hills on the east, west and south. Most of Hagi's tourist attractions are situated on an island surrounded by the Hashimotogawa River, the Matsumotogawa River and the Japan Sea (middle center). The Mori family ruled Hagi for thirteen generations, and eventually sparked a revolt against the Tokugawas. The late 19th century Meiji Restoration and modernization of Japan were initiated by young Mori samurai, who organized the nation's first farmers' militia, and who worked to break down caste distinctions, activities that were extremely revolutionary even at the end of the feudal era. Hagi is also famous for its almost 400-year tradition of pottery making. *Hagi-yaki* ware is distinguished by its subtle pastel colors and sophisticated glazes. Tea ceremony masters rank *Hagi-yaki* second only to the austere *Raku-yaki* of Kyoto. There are scores of pottery shops throughout the city.

You can follow the itinerary outlined below in a busy one-and-a-half days or in two leisurely days. If you have only one day in Hagi, you should be able to visit the town's Jokamachi (Central Hagi), Horiuchi and Castle areas (Western Hagi), and, if you are lucky, Teramachi (Central Hagi) and/or Tokoji Temple (Eastern Hagi) as well. The city's tourist information office (which does not specialize in information for foreign visitors) is in the governmental area, at the rear

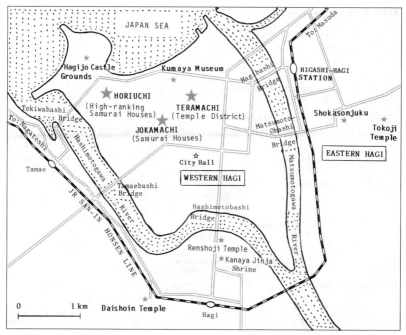

MAP 5 Outline of Hagi

of building in which it is located (lower center, San-in Map 6).

Transportation in Hagi

Higashi-Hagi (upper right, San-in Map 5) is the city's main train station. JR express and limited express trains stop at Higashi-Hagi Station, not Hagi Station (lower center).

The best way to get around this compact city is by bicycle. Hotels have supplies of bikes and there are rental shops throughout the city.

CENTRAL HAGI

(Refer to San-in Map 6)
Jokamachi 城下町

Kumaya Museum 熊谷美術館 (middle center). The Museum has no sign in English, but its entrance is marked by a big black gate that looks something like an elongated *torii*. The museum's impressive collection of scrolls, screens and pottery is housed in traditional Hagi warehouses. You can also walk around and observe the former residence of the Kumayas, who handled all the commercial transactions of the Mori family. The Kumayas were proponents of Western technology and sponsors of the Hagi-based revolutionary movement. Hours: 9:00 AM to 5:00 PM. Admission: 500 yen.

Kikuya House 菊屋家住宅 (lower center). Built in 1604, this was the residence of wealthy merchant family. Walking through this house will give you a good idea of family life in the Edo period. The garden is beautiful. There is a museum behind the residence, with old maps of the Hagi area, scrolls, screens, kimono and *Hagi-yaki* pottery. Hours 9:00 AM to 5:00 PM. Admission: 370 yen.

After a visit to the Kikuya House, you

MAP 6 Western Hagi

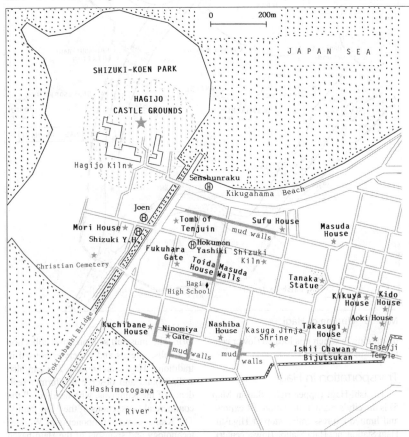

can stroll or cycle through Jokamachi (optional). The traditional whitewash and lattice architecture adds to the charm of the neighborhood. The camellias and *natsumikan* (Japanese "mandarin" oranges) for which Hagi is famous grace many of the gardens in this area, often hanging over the whitewashed walls. Other (optional) points of interest in this area include: **Takasugi House** 高杉晋作旧宅 (lower center). Shinsaku Takasugi learned the philosophy of Shoin Yoshida at his local school (See the Eastern Hagi section below). After Shoin's

execution, Takasugi took over his work. He founded the *Kiheitai,* a military group, and overthrew the Choshu conservatives, moving the state toward modernization. He died shortly before the Meiji Restoration. **Ishii Chawan Bijutsukan (Tea Bowl Museum)** 石井茶碗美術館 (lower center). This collection of tea bowls is a good example of why the restrained beauty of *Hagi-yaki* is so cherished by devotees of the tea ceremony. Hours: 9:00 AM to 5:00 PM. Closed Tuesdays and from January 1 through January 30. Admission: 350 yen. **Enseiji Temple** 円政寺

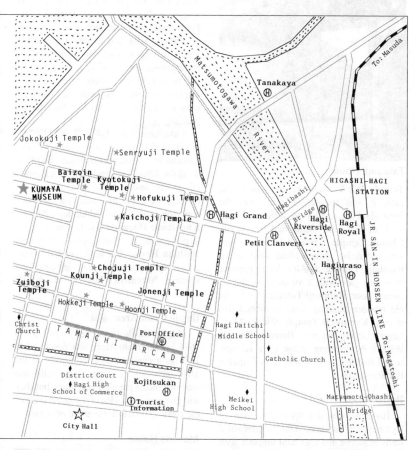

(lower center). Lovely small garden and temple. **Kido House** 木戸孝允旧宅 (lower center). Koin Kido worked for modernization of Japan through diplomatic channels, meeting with leaders of other states. His family was of samurai rank, and traditionally served as physicians for the feudal lords. No admission charge. Hours: 7:00 AM to 6:00 PM (8:00 AM to 5:00 PM in winter). Next to Kido House is **Aoki House** 青木周弼旧宅. Aoki worked to introduce Western medical knowledge to Japan, teaching himself Dutch to achieve his goals. (At the time the only contact with the West was with Dutch traders who were allowed ashore only at Dejima, an island off Nagasaki.)

If you have an extra hour or two:

We suggest that you explore the many lovely temples in Hagi's **Teramachi** 寺町 (middle center). Most Japanese tourists pass these peaceful places by, but they are full of unexpected surprises and delights. We suggest an early morning or sunset stroll. **Kounji Temple** 広雲寺: Wooden trimmed temple, *jizo*, stone memorials. **Jonenji**

Takasugi House

Temple 常念寺: Note the carvings on the gate. It was transferred here from the Jurakudai Palace of Kyoto, which was built by Hideyoshi and dismantled by Ieyasu. **Chojuji Temple** 長寿寺: A large cemetery surrounded by whitewashed mud walls. **Kaichoji Temple** 海潮寺: An impressive two-story gate with a veranda around its second floor. **Hofukuji Temple** 保福寺: An old wooden building. Lots of bibbed jizo statues. **Kyotokuji Temple** 亨徳寺: Much larger. Lovely garden. **Baizoin Temple** 梅蔵院: A charming statue of a relaxed, seated Buddha, and a collection of smaller Buddha statues.

Horiuchi 堀内

Horiuchi was the residential area of high-ranking samurai. Old whitewashed walls of stones and tiles held together with mud still stand in front of most houses in this area.

Masuda House 益田家物見矢倉 (middle center). Surrounded by a high wall, this was the site of the residence of the Prime Minister of the State Government.

Sufu House 周布家 (middle center) is an old wooden samurai residence. You can enter and look around. The beach is only one block away here, and you may not be able to resist the temptation to wander there for a few minutes.

Toida Masuda House Walls 問田益田
家旧宅土塀 (middle left). These are the longest mud walls in Hagi. Typical of the Horiuchi samurai residence area.

Shizuki Kiln 指月窯 (middle center). If you have time to visit only one *Hagi-yaki* pottery shop, this should be it. For most, this will be just a place to browse: the pieces on display are lovely, but many of them are quite expensive. The kiln is in the adjacent building.

Fukuhara Gate 福原家門 (middle left) is a beautiful wooden gate — again all that remains of a samurai residence. **Tomb of Tenjuin** 天樹院墓所 (middle left), a memorial to Terumoto Mori, founder of the Choshu Clan, and his wife, is a quiet and very romantic place. Admission: 20 yen. **Kuchibane House** 口羽家 (lower left), the largest samurai house gate remaining. **Nashiba House** 梨羽家 (lower left), comparatively larger house of a middle-ranking samurai. **Ninomiya Gate** 二の宮家長屋門 (lower left).

Hagijo Castle Area 萩城

Hagijo Castle (upper left) was built in 1604 by Terumoto Mori, and destroyed in 1874 as a demonstration of loyalty to the Meiji government. Huge stonewalls and spacious moats are all that remain, but they will give you some idea of the grand scale of the castle. The castle ruins are now part of

Masuda House

Shizuki-Koen Park. We suggest a picnic lunch on the Castle grounds.

Mori House 厚狭毛利家長屋 (middle left). This row house type structure was home to samurai foot soldiers. It is 5 m (16.5 feet) wide and 51.5 m (170 feet) long. Hours 8:00 AM to 6:30 PM (8:30 AM to 4:30 PM in winter). Admission: 200 yen. The ticket you purchase here will also gain you admission to the Castle ruins.

Inside the Castle grounds: **Hagijo Kiln** 萩城窯. This is a good place to observe the potters at work. The shop has a large selection. **Shizukiyama Jinja Shrine** 指月山神社. Nestled against the mountain, this Shrine was built in 1879. Its fine, mellowed wood makes it seem less austere than many other shrines. **Fukuhara House** 福原家書院. This was the residence of the Fukuhara family, the Mori Clan's administrative officers. **Hananoe Tea House** 花江茶亭. A beautiful garden and lovely tea house. No admission charge. The attendants will make tea for you in the thatched roof building for 300 yen. When you leave the Tea House, climb the steps to the top of the Castle walls. At the top, the moat is at your feet, and mountains and water all around. There is also a path that leads up to the top of the

mountain, for an even better view. It's a hard 20-minute climb.

Christian Cemetery キリシタン殉教者墓地 (middle left). A forgotten corner of the castle area with lots of atmosphere.

If you have time:

On the other side of the Hashimotogawa River, **Daishoin Temple** 大照院 (lower center, San-in Map 5) is about a 15-minute bicycle trip from the Hagijo Castle area. Cross the river over either the Tokiwabashi Bridge or the Hashimotobashi Bridge. Be careful on the busy road. The Temple foliage is spectacular in the fall, as is the garden in the spring. Hours: 9:00 AM to 4:30 PM. Admission: 100 yen. You can also take the train from Higashi-Hagi to Hagi and walk to Daishoin Temple from there. The local train between these two stations runs at most once an hour. There is also bus service between Hagi and Higashi-Hagi Stations.

EASTERN HAGI

(Refer to San-in Map 7)

We recommend Tokoji Temple (middle right) and suggest that you cycle along the canal to it. You can add Shoin Jinja Shrine

MAP 7   Eastern Hagi

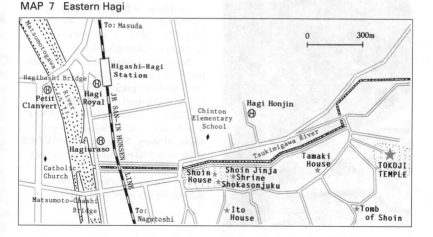

(lower center) either before or after a visit to Tokoji Temple. If you have extra time and are interested in Japanese history, we suggest that rather than retracing the path along the canal from Tokoji, you leave the temple from its western gate and go up the hill to the Tomb of Shoin Yoshida (lower right), and from there downhill to Tamaki House, from there to Ito House (lower center) and then back to the Shoin Jinja compound. Shoin Yoshida's Tomb is at the top of a hill and commands a grand view of the Japan Sea. You'll have to walk your bike up the hill, but it's easier in this direction than going uphill from Tamaki House (We tried it both ways!).

Tokoji Temple　東光寺

Tokoji Temple, the Mori family temple, is about a 15-minute bicycle ride from downtown Hagi. It was founded in 1691 by Yoshinari, the third Mori lord. Some of the Temple structures date from the 17th century. Sanmon is the Temple's impressive, three story gate. Behind the Main Building are the lanterns for which Tokoji Temple is so famous. Row upon row of lanterns, the

Tokoji Temple

smell of the pine trees, the deep, quiet peace of a natural setting: a thoroughly Japanese atmosphere. At the end of the lantern area are ten large stone monuments commemorating five Mori lords and their ladies. Hours: 8:30 AM to 5:30 PM Admission: 100 yen.

Shoin Yoshida Memorials

All the attractions in this area other than Tokoji Temple relate in one way or another to Shoin Yoshida. Yoshida, a pre-Meiji Era philosopher, educator and revolutionary, was born in 1830. Although he was executed by the Tokugawa Shogunate at the age of 29, his influence lived on and shaped the Meiji Era. His execution fired the revolutionary movement in the Hagi area, and spurred Takasugi and the rebel faction to overthrow the conservative officials of the Mori family.

Tomb of Shoin Yoshida 吉田松陰の墓 is located at the site of his birthplace. There's a statue of Yoshida and his favorite student as well as the foundations of the house where the great teacher was born. There's also a spectacular view of the Japan Sea.

Tamaki House 玉木文之進旧宅, a thatched house, was the home of Shoin's uncle and teacher.

Ito House 伊藤博文旧宅. Hirobumi Ito, another of Shoin's students, was the first Meiji Prime Minister. A statue of Ito stands next to his small thatched house.

Shoin Jinja Shrine 松陰神社. In addition to the Shrine itself, the precincts feature the **Shokasonjuku** 松下村塾, Shoin's school, a **Memorial Hall** 松陰遺墨展示館 exhibiting his writings (9:00 AM to 5:00 PM, 4:30 PM in winter, Admission 100 yen), and **Shoin History Museum** 吉田松陰歴史館 (9:00 AM to 5:00 PM, Admission 550 yen), as well as Shoin's House. No English. In the History Museum, dioramas tell the dramatic story of Shoin's arrest and execution.

ACCOMMODATIONS

1. Hotel in Hagi

Hagi Grand Hotel (middle right, San-in Map 6). Standard. 13 singles (9,500 yen -), 14 doubles (17,500 yen -) & 163 Japanese rooms (16,500 yen -). Add: 25, Kohagicho, Hagi. Tel: (08382) 5-1211.

2. Ryokan in Hagi

Hokumon Yashiki (middle left, San-in Map 6). First Class. 48 rooms. 30,000 yen & up per person. Add: 210 Horiuchi, Hagi. Tel: (08382) 2-7521.

Hagi Honjin (middle center, San-in Map 7). First Class. 116 rooms. 15,000 yen & up per person. Add: 385-8, Chinto, Hagi. Tel: (08382) 2-5252.

Senshunraku (middle left, San-in Map 6). Standard. 93 rooms. 12,000 yen & up per person. Add: Kikugahama, Horiuchi, Hagi. Tel: (08382) 2-0326.

Hagi Royal Hotel (middle right, San-in Map 6). Standard. 52 rooms. 12,000 yen & up per person. Add: 3000-5, Chinto, Hagi. Tel: (08382) 5-9595.

Hotel Tanakaya (upper right, San-in Map 6). Standard. 20 rooms. 10,000 yen & up per person. Add: 3083-2, Shinkawacho, Hagi. Tel: (08382) 2-7538.

Kojitsukan (lower center, San-in Map 6). Standard. 30 rooms. 10,000 yen & up per person. Add: 78, Tohicho, Hagi. Tel: (08382) 2-0868.

Kasayama Kanko Hotel (10 minutes by taxi from Higashi-Hagi Station). Standard. 54 rooms. 12,000 yen & up per person. Add: 4-1, Koshigahama, Hagi. Tel: (08382) 5-0311.

TSUWANO   津和野

Perched in the mountains, the 700-year-old castle town of Tsuwano is often referred to as the Kyoto of San-in. A great many traditional samurai homes are preserved in Tsuwano. Tsuwano is also famous for the colorful carp that swim in the streams that line the town's streets. Spring and early summer are lovely in this tiny mountain town, and irises bloom all along the streams.

Transportation in Tsuwano

Without a doubt, the best ways to get around in Tsuwano are on foot or by bicycle. Many bike rental shops are scattered throughout the town.

Tsuwano Walking Tour Itinerary

Refer to San-in Map 8. Start sightseeing at **Catholic Church** 津和野カソリック教会 (middle right), evidence of what was once a strong Christian influence in Tsuwano. In an effort to completely obliterate Christianity, which had gained many adherents in various parts of Kyushu, the Tokugawa Shogunate dispersed Japan's Christians around the country, trying to force them to renounce their religion by isolating and torturing them in unfamiliar and hostile environments. A group of Nagasaki Christians was exiled to Tsuwano. This tatami-matted church, built in 1931, is modeled on Nagasaki's Oura Tenshudo Church. Hours: 8:00 AM to 6:00 PM. Admission: 100 yen.

Once you leave the church, you'll be in the heart of Tsuwano's most famous and most scenic area: the distinctive whitewashed and lattice-patterned buildings are the town's signature.

Bear to your right, cross the JR tracks, and go through the large *torii* gate. Miei Jinja Shrine, which is located on the Tsuwanogawa River, will be in front of you. **Taikodani Inari Jinja Shrine** 太鼓谷稲成神社 (middle center) is nearby. Enter the approach to the Shrine through the first of the 1,174 closely ranked red *torii* gates that make a tunnel up the steep mountain slope. Climbing, for the 10 minutes it takes to reach the Shrine, through *torii* after *torii* is an amazing experience. The Shrine itself is a relatively large complex, trimmed in the same bright red as the *torii* gates. Open from dawn to dusk. Admission free.

Walk through the Shrine compound, and down the slope on the other side, which will lead you to a chair lift ropeway that will take you, in 5 minutes, to the mountaintop **Tsuwanojo Castle Grounds** 津和野城跡 127 m (483 feet) above the town. When you get off the lift, follow the path to the south through the woods for about 10 minutes, to the Eastern Gate entrance to the Castle ruins. The view from the summit is fantastic: the river and town below and terraced rice paddies and mountains in the distance. From this marvelous vantage point you can easily understand why the *daimyo* would choose this as the site of his castle; you'll also understand how sitting at the top of one's world like this could reinforce an opinion of self-importance and superiority. The view from the lift on the way down is also quite spectacular. Hours: 9:00 AM to 5:20 PM (5:00 PM in winter). Admission: 410 yen.

MAP 8 Tsuwano

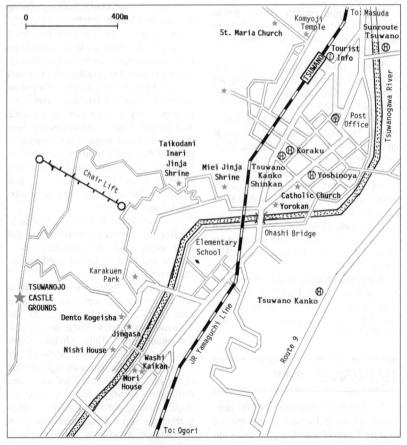

Dento Kogeisha 津和野伝統工芸舎 (lower center). The workers here, who make paper according to methods more than 1,000 years old, are quite nice about letting visitors observe. The Center has a large shop. Hours: 8:30 AM to 4:30 PM. Closed Fridays December through February. There is no admission charge.

The entrance of **Jingasa** 陣笠 (lower center) is back off the street. This two story museum displays many historical artifacts, such as armor, guns, lacquerware, household goods and antique coins and paper money. It also displays models wearing the costumes of Tsuwano's *Sagi-Mai* Heron Dance Festival, an annual event every July 20th and 27th. Hours: 8:30 AM to 5:00 PM. Admission: 300 yen.

Nishi House 西周旧宅 (lower center) is on a quiet residential street. There is no admission charge. Amane Nishi, 1829-1897, was the first Japanese of his era to become interested in and try to promulgate western philosophies, and was an active politician in the exciting Meiji Era of Japan. Hours: 8:30 AM to 5:00 PM. Admission free.

Mori House 森鷗外旧宅 (lower center). Ogai Mori (1862-1922), another famous figure of the Meiji Era, was an army doctor, a writer and a translator whose life was an unending quest to reconcile western and Japanese traditions. Hours: 8:30 AM to 5:00 PM. Admission free.

Continue to **Washi Kaikan** 石州和紙会館 (lower center) on the corner. There is no admission charge. The first floor of this building is devoted to demonstrations of the paper maker's craft. The second floor houses a small museum that displays samples of handmade paper from all parts of Japan, and a huge souvenir shop. Hours: 8:00 AM to 5:00 PM. Admission free.

If you still have time, you should explore the area behind Tsuwano Station (upper right). The hard climb up the hill to Otometoge Pass and **St. Maria Church** 聖マリア教会 takes about 8 minutes. There's a small waterfall to your left as you climb. There is no admission charge. The tiny chapel, which was built in 1951, is a memorial to the Christian exiles who were tortured and martyred at this site. Its stained glass windows depict the sufferings of the martyrs. Otometoge, the Pass of the Virgin, is named for the daughter of a local lord who wandered up this lonely pass and disappeared after being rejected by the prince to whom she was betrothed.

ACCOMMODATIONS
(Refer to San-in Map 8)

1. Hotel in Tsuwano

Hotel Sunroute Tsuwano (upper right). 9 singles (7,500 yen -), 19 doubles (12,000 yen -) & 22 triples (22,000 yen -). Add: 845-1, Terada, Tsuwanocho, Shimane Prefecture. Tel: (08567) 2-3232.

2. Ryokan in Tsuwano

Tsuwano Kanko Hotel Shinkan (middle right). First Class. 30 rooms. 16,000 yen & up per person. Add: Ushiroda, Tsuwanocho, Shimane Prefecture. Tel: (08567) 2-0332.

Ryokan Yoshinoya (middle right). Standard. 36 rooms. 12,000 yen & up per person. Add: Ushiroda, Tsuwanocho, Shimane Prefecture. Tel: (08567) 2-0531.

Ryokan Koraku (middle right). Standard. 25 rooms. 12,000 yen & up per person. Add: Ushiroda, Tsuwanocho, Shimane Prefecture. Tel: (08567) 2-0501.

JR FARES BETWEEN MAJOR CITIES IN THE SAN-IN REGION
(Based on limited express trains)

To/From	Okayama	Matsue	Izumoshi	Masuda
Okayama		5,750 yen (188 km)	6,580 yen (220. 7 km)	
Kurashiki		5,440 yen (172.1 km)	6,270 yen (204.8 km)	
Matsue	5,750 yen (188 km)		1,780 yen (32.7 km)	5440 yen (162.6 km)
Izumoshi	6,580 yen (220.7 km)	1,780 yen (32.7 km)		4,410 yen (129.9 km)
Masuda		5,440 yen (162.6 km)	4,410 yen (129.9 km)	
Higashi-Hagi		6,580 yen (220.1 km)	5,750 yen (187.4 km)	2,560 yen (57.5km)
Tsuwano				1,780 yen (34.1 km)
Ogori				3,390 yen (103.3 km)

SHIKOKU REGION

The smallest of Japan's four main islands, Shikoku, lies across the Inland Sea from the main island of Honshu. Mountains range from east to west across the center of Shikoku, where life seems quieter and gentler amid the green of the island's mountains and the blue of the surrounding waters. Shikoku is famous as a center of Buddhism, and every year thousands of pilgrims (usually newly retired couples) make a walking tour of the island's eighty-eight temples associated with the great priest Kobo Daishi.

A visit to Shikoku clearly falls into the off-the-beaten-track category. Traditionally, only Takamatsu has been included on the itineraries of foreign visitors to Japan,

thanks to what used to be relatively inconvenient transportation links to Shikoku from other major Japanese cities. The completion of the Seto Ohashi Bridge in 1989 changed Shikoku forever, making it accessible, both physically and psychologically, to the main island of Honshu in ways never imaginable before. See the Sanyo Chapter for more details on the Seto Ohashi Bridge. The opening of the Bridge greatly improved access to Shikoku, and major Shikoku cities are now connected by direct train service with Okayama, which is on the Tokaido-Sanyo Shinkansen (details below).

Refer to Shikoku Map 1. We describe four destinations in Shikoku: Takamatsu (upper right), Kochi (lower center) and Mat-

MAP 1 Outline of Shikoku

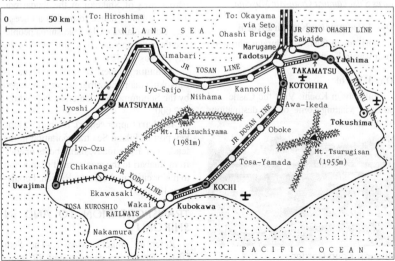

suyama (middle left) all prospered as castle towns in the feudal era and are still the capitals of Kagawa, Kochi and Ehime Prefectures respectively. Kotohira (upper right, near Takamatsu) is famous for its Kotohiragu Shrine.

If your time is limited, you can easily visit Takamatsu in two days (one night) as a detour from a Sanyo (Inland Sea) itinerary. You can even visit Takamatsu in a rather hectic day excursion from Okayama.

We believe the entire island of Shikoku is well worth the investment of time (five days) needed to travel around it, visiting all four of the destinations described in this Chapter. Our suggested itinerary is as follows:

Day 1. Arrive Takamatsu

Starting from Osaka, Kyoto or Nagoya, you can easily arrive in Takamatsu around noon. Visit Ritsurin-Koen Garden in the afternoon. If you get a very early start (around 7:00 AM), you can even follow this itinerary from Tokyo.

Note: Add an extra day to the itinerary if you also visit suburban Yashima, which features Shikokumura Open-Air Museum.

Day 2. Takamatsu/Kotohira/Kochi

Visit magnificent Kotohiragu Shrine on your way to Kochi.

Day 3. Kochi

Full day in Kochi. Visit the Castle, and consider visiting some of the destinations along the coast.

Ritsurin-Koen Garden

Day 4. Kochi/Matsuyama

The Japan Railways (JR) bus is the most popular way to travel between these two cities. You will have time for afternoon sightseeing in Matsuyama. If you are a railroad buff, you can combine three JR trains from Kochi to Matsuyama (details below). If you choose to travel this way, most of your day will be spent on trains. You can stay at a downtown hotel in Matsuyama, or at a *ryokan* at Dogo-Onsen hotsprings in the eastern part of the city. (The hotspring area is a little pricier.)

Day 5. Matsuyama/Hiroshima (or Okayama)

Morning sightseeing in Matsuyama. Cross the Inland Sea to Hiroshima by ferry or hydrofoil, or take a direct train back to Okayama.

Other Major Cities in Shikoku
(Refer to Shikoku Map 1)

Tokushima (middle right). Capital of Tokushima Prefecture with a population of 260,000. Under the Hachisuka Clan, Tokushima was the most powerful and prosperous area of Shikoku in the feudal era. The Awa-Odori dance festival is a once-a-year extravaganza of the Tokushima people, and the most popular tourist attraction of the city (August 12-15).

Niihama (upper center). Niihama is Shikoku's main industrial center, developed by the Sumitomo conglomerate. Population: 132,000.

Imabari (upper center). Imabari was the key port of Inland Sea transportation in the feudal era. Even today, many boats operate from Imabari to the area's small islands and to major cities in the Sanyo Region. Population: 123,000.

TRANSPORTATION TO AND IN SHIKOKU

Refer to Shikoku Map 1. The Seto Ohashi Bridge has changed how JR trains operate to and in Shikoku. Access from Okayama is now much easier, and Takamatsu's importance as Shikoku's transportation center has declined.

Okayama on the main island of Honshu is the starting point for the three JR lines to Shikoku. The JR Seto Ohashi Line runs between Okayama and Takamatsu via Kojima and Sakaide. Rapid service trains (called "Marine Liners") operate once every 30 minutes. The ride takes one hour.

JR's limited express trains (called "Nanpu") run between Okayama and Kochi via Tadotsu and Kotohira, combining the JR Seto Ohashi Line (Okayama-Tadotsu) and the JR Dosan Line (Tadotsu-Kochi). There are five limited express trains operating daily. The ride from Okayama to Kochi takes about 2 hours and 30 minutes. A few trains operate beyond Kochi to Nakamura via Kubokawa. The portion between Kochi and Kubokawa is still the JR Dosan Line, but the portion between Kubokawa and Nakamura is owned by the Tosa Kuroshio Railways.

JR's limited express trains (called "Shiokaze") run between Okayama and Matsuyama via Tadotsu, Kannonji and Imabari, combining the JR Seto Ohashi Line (Okayama-Tadotsu) and the JR Yosan Line (Tadotsu-Matsuyama). The "Shiokaze" trains run once every 1-2 hours. The ride from Okayama to Matsuyama takes about 2 hours and 40 minutes. A few of the trains run beyond Matsuyama to Uwajima.

Takamatsu is still the terminal of three JR lines in Shikoku:

(1) The JR Dosan Line runs between Takamatsu and Nakamura via Tadotsu, Kotohira, Kochi and Kubokawa. Five limited express trains (called "Shimanto") operate on this line each way daily. Three of them run only between Takamatsu and Kochi. The ride from Takamatsu to Kotohira takes 40 minutes, and Kotohira to Kochi an additional 1 hour and 40 minutes. In addition to the "Shimanto" limited expresses, local trains run on the JR Dosan Line

between Takamatsu and Kotohira about once every hour to facilitate travel to Kotohira Shrine. The ride on the local train from Takamatsu to Kotohira takes about 70 minutes. Please note that the Tadotsu-Kotohira-Kochi section of the JR Dosan Line is served by two types of limited express trains — "Nanpu" trains to/from Okayama and "Shimanto" trains to/from Takamatsu. Accordingly, you can expect hourly JR limited express train service between Kotohira and Kochi.

(2) The JR Yosan Line runs between Takamatsu and Uwajima via Tadotsu, Kannonji, Imabari and Matsuyama. There are seven limited express trains (called "Ishizuchi") operating on this line each way daily. Most of them run only between Takamatsu and Matsuyama. The ride from Takamatsu to Matsuyama takes about 2 hours and 50 minutes. Please also note that the Tadotsu-Matsuyama section of the JR Yosan Line is served by two types of JR limited expresses — "Shiokaze" to/from Okayama and "Ishizuchi" to/from Takamatsu.

(3) The JR Kotoku Line runs between Takamatsu and Tokushima via Yashima. Both limited express trains (called "Uzushio") and local trains run on this line about once every hour. You may use this line to visit to Yashima. The ride from Takamatsu to Yashima takes 10 minutes by limited express and 15 minutes by local.

JR bus service (called "Nangoku") is the most popular method of transportation between Kochi and Matsuyama. The buses operate about once every hour and the ride takes about 3 hours and 20 minutes.

You can travel by train (from Kochi to Matsuyama) around the circumference of Shikoku if you combine three JR trains as follows: Take a morning limited express train (called "Ashizuri") on the JR Dosan Line from Kochi to Kubokawa. The ride takes about 1 hour and 15 minutes. Change at Kubokawa to the JR Yodo Line to Uwajima. Only local trains run on this line.

Strangely, the Kubokawa-Wakai (4.4 km or 2.75 miles) portion of this line is owned by the Tosa Kuroshio Railways. If you are travelling on a Japan Rail Pass, you must pay a small charge to this tiny local railroad company even if you take a through JR local train from Kubokawa to Uwajima. The ride takes about 2 hours. More frequent train service is available between Uwajima and Matsuyama (the JR Yosan Line). Limited express trains (called "Ishizuchi," "Shiokaze" or "Uwakai") runs about once every 90 minutes. The ride takes 1 hour and 45 minutes. You may wish to enjoy a little sightseeing in the charming city of Uwajima, which prospered as a castle city of the Date family, a minor branch of the famous Date family of Sendai. Shikoku's four major cities — Takamatsu, Kochi, Matsuyama and Tokushima — have airports. Several daily flights connect them with other major cities, such as Tokyo (Haneda Airport), Osaka, Nagoya, Fukuoka and Sapporo.

TAKAMATSU　高松

Founded as a castle town in 1588, Takamatsu was the headquarters of the Matsudaira family during the Tokugawa period. It's modern population is 329,000. The home of Ritsurin-Koen Garden, renowned as one of Japan's most beautiful gardens, Takamatsu today is the capital and cultural center of Kagawa Prefecture. There are two major tourist destinations in Takamatsu: Ritsurin-Koen Garden, and Yashima to the east of the city.

Transportation in Takamatsu

Refer to Shikoku Map 2. Takamatsu has excellent bus service, and a commuter train line, the Takamatsu Kotohira Railways, popularly called the "Kotoden," that terminates at Takamatsu Chikko Station just across the street from JR Takamatsu Station (both upper center).

Outline of the City

The area between the Kotoden Line on the east and Chuo-dori, the city's main street, on the west, is Takamatsu's downtown. Two arcades run north to south and east to west (shaded on the map). Department stores, souvenir shops, restaurants and coffee shops crowd the narrow streets that intersect the arcades. The *i* Information Office is located in a small round white building in front of the JR Takamatsu Station.

Places of Interest in the City

Castle Grounds 玉藻城跡 (Upper center) (optional)

The entrance to this park is across the street from JR Takamatsu Station. Tamamojo Castle was built in 1588 by Chikamasa Ikoma, and later became the home of the ruling Matsudaira family. Only a few turrets of the castle, and remnants of the moats and the wall remain. The park, however, is lovely — a charming place for strolling and relaxing. Hours: 8:30 AM to 6:00 PM. Admission: 100 yen.

Hidari Jingoro Museum 左甚五郎美術館 (upper center) (optional). If you leave the park through the eastern gate, Hidari Jingoro Museum is a few minutes walk away. The museum is housed in a

Tamamojo Castle Grounds

MAP 2 Takamatsu

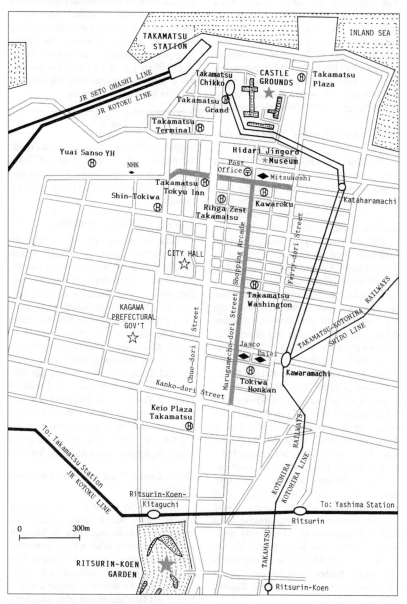

three-story tan stucco building with two white balconies. This small museum has a fine collection of the works of Hidari Jingoro, who is most famous as the sculptor of the sleeping cat at Nikko's Toshogu Shrine and the designer of the nightingale corridor of Kyoto's Chion-in Temple. Recommended for art history majors only. Hours: 10:00 AM to 5:30 PM. Open year round. Admission: 500 yen.

Ritsurin-Koen Garden 栗林公園 (Lower center)

The bus for Ritsurin-Koen Garden leaves from Stop No. 2 in front of the Takamatsu Grand Hotel, across the street from JR Takamatsu Station. The trip to the Garden takes about 20 minutes. You can also reach the Garden on the Kotoden Line train — Ritsurin-Koen stop, or on a JR Kotoku Line train from JR Takamatsu Station — Ritsurin-Koen Kitaguchi stop is closest to the Garden (only local trains stop here).

If you take the bus, when you get off use the underpass to cross the street and reach the East Gate of Ritsurin-Koen Garden. Admission to the Garden is 310 yen. The 590 yen combination ticket, in addition to the garden itself, gains you admission to the **Sanuki Folkcraft Museum** 讃岐民芸館 and the **Kikugetsutei Tea House** 掬月亭. Enjoying tea ceremony at Kikugetsutei will cost you another 340 yen. Recommended only for those especially interested in tea ceremony. The room where the tea is served has a lovely view of the tea garden, but a walk around the pond is also quite satisfying.

Sanuki Folkcraft Museum is on your right after you enter the Garden. It displays impressive pieces of local pottery, lovely wooden furniture and some antique items such as lacquerware, etc. Hours: 8:45 AM to 4:00 PM (3:00 PM on Wednesdays). Next to Sanuki Folkcraft Museum is another building, which houses a prefectural tourism office and a shop featuring local Kagawa Prefecture products.

A leisurely stroll around the clearly marked paths of Ritsurin-Koen Garden is a treat in any season. It is dotted with ponds, a variety of lovely bridges and one surprising vista after another. In season, the cherry blossoms, azaleas and irises are magnificent. The northern part of the Garden is less dramatic and much quieter than the southern part, but it has its own rewards.

YASHIMA 屋島

Refer to Shikoku Map 3. Yashima (middle right), in the eastern suburbs of Takamatsu, is famous as a historic battle site, and home of an innovative tradition-conserving museum.

Transportation to Yashima

Take the Kotoden train from either the Ritsurin-Koen Station or the Takamatsu Chikko Station to Yashima. (If you take the train from the Kotoden Ritsurin-Koen Station you'll have to change at Kawaramachi — where the Yashima-bound trains leave from Platform No. 3). The Kotoden trains run about once every 15-30 minutes. There is also JR service to Yashima, although it operates less frequently. The JR trains start from JR Takamatsu Station. You can take either a limited express or a local train. If you visit Yashima after Ritsurin-Koen Garden, you can also catch a JR train at Ritsurin-Koen Kitaguchi, the stop closest to the Garden (the North Exit). Only local trains stop at the Ritsurin-Koen Kitaguchi Station.

Shikokumura Open Air Museum 四国村 (Middle right)

As you walk up the hill from the train station, you'll see a shrine ahead. The entrance to Shikokumura Open Air Museum is next to the shrine. It has a brown signboard with a waterwheel. Hours: 8:30 AM to 5:00 PM (4:30 PM in winter). Admission: 500 yen.

The Open Air Museum features a collection of old farmhouses and other traditional

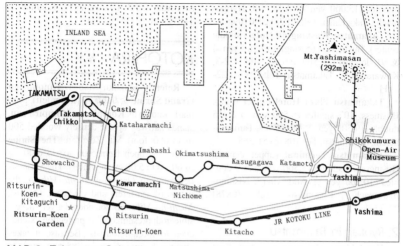

MAP 3 Takamatsu Suburbs

Shikoku structures of the type that have grown rarer and rarer with the years. It is a surprisingly pleasant and educational place. It is attractively laid out, and occasional English signs help you get your bearings. The buildings that have been relocated here include a mill, a paper-making workshop, a stone carving shop, and several traditional farm houses. The museum within the grounds is not worth it — it only exhibits implements and crafts that you can see displayed in the other buildings for free! The Open Air Museum is a thoroughly enjoyable experience if you have extra time in the Takamatsu area.

Mt. Yashimasan 屋島山 (Upper right)

Mt. Yashimasan can be reached by cable car in just five minutes. The cable car runs from approximately 7:00 AM to 7:00 PM. It costs 1,010 yen roundtrip. The flat, wide mountain top is covered by pine trees, and commands a grand view of the Inland Sea.
Yashimaji Temple 屋島寺 has, in its Treasure House, artifacts gathered from the battlefield of the 1185 clash between the Minamoto and the Taira Clans that led to

the establishment of Japan's first Shogunate in Kamakura by Yoritomo Minamoto. Hours: 9:00 AM to 5:00 PM. Admission: 260 yen.

ACCOMMODATIONS
(Refer to Shikoku Map 2)

1. Hotels in Takamatsu

Takamatsu Kokusai Hotel (10 minutes by taxi from Takamatsu Station). First Class. 35 singles (9,000 yen -) & 49 doubles (16,000 yen -). Add: 2191-1 Kitamachi, Takamatsu. Tel: (0878) 31-1511.

Rihga Zest Takamatsu (middle center). Standard. 71 singles (8,000 yen -) & 52 doubles (21,500 yen -). Add: 9-1, Furushin-machi, Takamatsu. Tel: (0878) 22-3555.

Keio Plaza Hotel Takamatsu (lower center). Standard. 94 singles (8,000 yen -) & 62 doubles (16,000 yen -). Add: 11-5, Chuomachi, Takamatsu. Tel: (0878) 34-5511.

Takamatsu Grand Hotel (upper center). Standard. 65 singles (8,000 yen -) & 71 doubles (14,500 yen -). Add: 1-5-10, Kotobuki-machi, Takamatsu. Tel: (0878) 51-5757.

Takamatsu Tokyu Inn (upper center). Business. 101 singles (7,000 yen -) & 86 doubles (15,000 yen -). Add: 9-9, Hyogo-machi, Takamatsu. Tel: (0878) 21-0109.

Takamatsu Washington Hotel (middle center). Business. 165 singles (7,700 yen -) & 91 doubles (14,800 yen -). Add: 1-2-3, Kawaramachi, Takamatsu. Tel: (0878) 22-7111.

Takamatsu Plaza Hotel (upper right). Business. 107 singles (5,500 yen -) & 15 doubles (9,500 yen -). Add: 7-15, Tamamo-machi, Takamatsu. Tel: (0878) 51-3655.

Takamatsu Terminal (upper center). Business. 35 singles (5,500 yen -) & 9 doubles (10,500 yen -). Add: 10-17, Nishino-marumachi, Takamatsu. Tel: (0878) 22-3731.

2. Ryokan in Takamatsu

Hotel Kawaroku (upper center). First Class. 70 rooms. 18,000 & up per person. Add: 1-2, Hyakkenmachi, Takamatsu. Tel: (0878) 21-5666.

Tokiwa Honkan (middle center). First Class. 23 rooms. 18,000 yen & up per per-son. Add: 1-8-2, Tokiwamachi, Takamatsu. Tel: (0878) 61-5577.

KOTOHIRA 琴平

Refer to Shikoku Map 4. **Kotohiragu Grand Shrine** 金刀比羅宮 (lower left), pop-ularly known as **Kompira** or **Kompira-san**, stands halfway up the densely wooded 500 m (1,650 foot) Mt. Zozusan. The Shrine grounds is open from 5:00 AM to 6:00 PM (6:00 AM to 5:00 PM in winter). The Shrine is dedicated to *Omono-Nushi-no-Mikoto*, the patron of sea-farers and voyagers. *Omono-Nushi-no-Mikoto* is considered a very acces-sible god; presumably his protection extends even to foreign tourists. Because it takes about an hour to climb the 785 stone steps to the main shrine buildings, we suggest that you get an early morning start, especially in warm weather, so you won't be hiking up Mt. Zozusan in the midday sun.

Turn left when you emerge from the JR

MAP 4 Kotohira

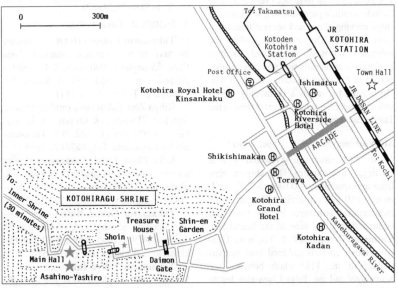

Kotohira Station (upper right), and walk until you come to a cross street with an arcade, where you should turn right. Walk through the arcade, cross the bridge, and go straight until you come to the steps to the Shrine. It's about a 15-minute walk to this point from the station — this is the beginning of the approach to Kompira-san. Souvenir shops line the ascent to Daimon, the Main Gate of the Shrine, another 10-minute climb.

Like most Shinto shrines, Kompira-san, which claims its origins in antiquity, has been rebuilt again and again throughout its history. **Daimon Gate** 大門 is an impressive two-story structure, with huge wooden statues standing in its niches. Past Daimon Gate, the path is lined with stone lanterns and memorial tablets. The Shrine's **Treasure House** 宝物館 is the smaller of the two white buildings on your right just before the second torii gate after Daimon. Hours: 9:00 AM to 4:00 PM. Admission: 200 yen. The Treasure House museum, which most Japanese tourists neglect, displays large vases and other ceramic items, beautiful pieces of sculpture, lovely scrolls and *noh* masks, and an impressive collection of swords, helmets and armor.

At the next landing, **Shoin** 書院, which was built in 1659, is on your right. The carvings on the outside of the "parlor" building are well worth the detour off the main path. Its interior features sliding doors decorated by Okyo Maruyama, the famous 18th century landscape artist.

The climb to the next landing is a rather difficult one, but you're rewarded at the landing with the lovely double-roofed, early 19th century **Asahino Yashiro (Rising Sun Hall)** 旭社, famous for its beautiful, intricate carvings of animals, flowers, etc.

The main buildings of the Shrine are on the next landing, which also has a spectacular view of Takamatsu and the mountains and water that surround it. **The Main Hall** 本殿, which is constructed on stilts like Kyoto's Kiyomizudera Temple, was rebuilt

about 100 years ago. Walk to the **Votive Picture Hall** 絵馬殿, the last of the buildings in the main shrine compound, for another grand view, and be sure to take a walk around the Votive Hall's open air display of its surprisingly eclectic collection of pictures.

The ascent up the additional 583 steps to **Okusha (Inner Shrine)** 奥社 is a climb of another 30 minutes. The Inner Shrine is usually visited by only the most religious of the thousands of pilgrims who come to Kompira-san every year.

The path down from the main shrine compound gives you a good opportunity to observe the carvings tucked under the roof of Asahino Yashiro Rising Sun Hall.

At the foot of the steps to the Shrine, there are seemingly endless variety of souvenir shops and restaurants where you can stop to have a snack of fresh, handmade *Sanuki* udon noodles.

ACCOMMODATIONS
(Refer to Shikoku Map 4)

1. Ryokan in Kotohira

Kotohira Royal Hotel Kinsankaku (middle center). First Class. 222 rooms. 21,000 yen & up per person. Add: 685-11, Kotohiracho. Tel: (0877) 75-0500.

Kotohira Grand Hotel (middle center). First Class. 90 rooms. 21,000 yen & up per person. Add: 977-1, Kotohiracho. Tel: (0877) 75-3218.

Kotohira Kadan (lower right). First Class. class: 57 rooms. 20,000 yen & up per person. Add: 1241, Kotohiracho. Tel: (0877) 75-3232.

Kotohira Riverside Hotel (middle right). First Class. 30 rooms. 15,000 yen & up per person. Add: 246-1, Kotohiracho. Tel: (0877) 75-1880.

Shikishimakan (middle center). Standard. 48 rooms. 13,000 yen & up per person. Add: 713, Kotohiracho. Tel: (0877) 75-5111.

Toraya Ryokan (middle center). Standard. 50 rooms. 12,000 yen & up per person. Add: 814, Kotohiracho. Tel: (0877) 75-3131.

Ishimatsu Ryokan (middle right). Standard. 34 rooms. 12,000 yen & up per person. Add: 302, Kotohiracho. Tel: (0877) 75-2236.

2. Welcome Inn in Kotohira

Kotobuki Ryokan. 6 Japanese & 1 Western rooms. Add: 245-5, Shinmachi, Kotohiracho. Tel: (0877) 73-3872.

KOCHI 高知

Kochi, with a population of 314,000, is the administrative center of Kochi Prefecture. In a lovely natural setting, the city is surrounded by hills to the north and the east. The Kumagawa and Kagamigawa Rivers flow through the city into Urado Bay, which in turn opens into the much large Tosa Bay.

The names Kochi and Tosa (the name of the feudal era province in this area) are linked in the minds of most Japanese with Ryoma Sakamoto, a brilliant politician who played a key role in overturning the Tokugawa feudal system. Sakamoto was born in 1835 to a low class, half-samurai, half-farmer family. He broke away from the rigid class system that was designed to control lives like his, taking himself to Nagasaki, where he organized a trading company. While he was building his commercial empire, he was also building an alliance of anti-Tokugawa samurai, establishing the military base necessary to promote the restoration of the imperial government (which, at the time was synonymous with modernization and democratization) and the ruin of the Tokugawa Shogunate. He was assassinated in Kyoto in 1867 at the age of 33, and died without seeing the triumph of his alliance and his ideas.

Outline of the City

Refer to Shikoku Map 5. JR Kochi Station (upper right) is in the northern part of the city. Kochi's downtown area is centered at Harimayabashi intersection (middle right). The train station and the Castle are located within the urban core, but several of the area's beautiful attractions, such as Godaisan-Koen Park and Katsurahama Beach, are at a bit of a distance, closer to the water. The *i* Information Office is located in JR Kochi Station.

Transportation in Kochi

Kochi has a streetcar system with two principal lines that cross at Harimayabashi. They run frequently and charge a flat rate fare of 170 yen.

Kochi is also served by several different bus companies, including the Toden Bus Company and the Kochi Ken Kotsu Bus Company. Fares on these buses vary with the distance travelled. These buses provide transportation for visits to Godaisan-Koen Park and Katsurahama Beach, as described below.

Places of Interest in Kochi

Kochijo Castle and Park 高知城 (middle left). This was the site of a fortress as early as the 14th century. Construction of the present castle began in 1601 at the order of Lord Kazutoyo Yamanouchi, and was completed in 1611. The Castle was destroyed by fire in 1727, and reconstruction was completed in 1753. The Castle was again repaired after World War II. The Castle is about a 20-minute walk from Kochi Station or from the Harimayabashi downtown area. If you're in Kochi on Sunday, you'll find the walk particularly interesting because Kochi's famous Phoenix Boulevard Sunday Open Air Market will be in full swing, and you'll be able to sample all sorts of local specialty foods.

As Phoenix Boulevard deadends, you'll see Otemon Gate. Enter the Castle grounds and climb the steps to the Castle itself. Hours: 9:00 AM to 5:00 PM. Admission: 350 yen.

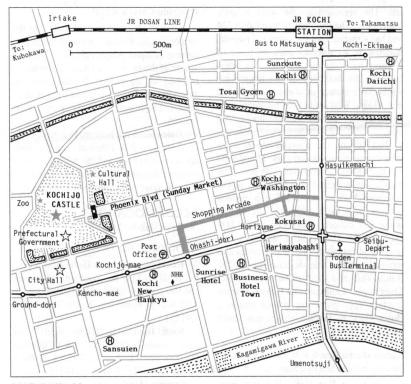

MAP 5 Kochi

The compact, whitewashed donjon is quite elegant. Follow the arrows to the museum area, which displays armor and other items of historical interest, and then into the donjon. The top floor of the donjon has a wonderful view of the city and the mountains. When you've descended from the donjon, follow the signs to the right, through various tatami rooms, to Kaitokukan, the lord's drawing room, situated on a lovely garden.

Godaisan-Koen Park 五台山 and **Chikurinji Temple** 竹林寺 (Southeastern part of the city; outside Shikoku Map 5)

The terminal for the Toden buses to Godaisan-Koen Park and Chikurinji Temple is next to Seibu Department Store at Harimayabashi (middle right). Buses leave about once an hour. The fare to Godaisan is 300 yen. You can buy your ticket at the window before you board the bus. We suggest using Conversation Card 5 to make sure you catch the right bus. The ride to Godaisan-Koen Park's Chikurinji stop takes about 20 minutes. When you get off the bus, the path to your right leads to an observatory building. There's a fantastic view from its roof of the mountains and the bays. A lovely park and garden extend below the observatory.

If you return to the road and follow it downhill for about 5 minutes, you will come to a small cluster of souvenir shops. The entrance to Chikurinji Temple is on your left. The approach up the steps is quite impressive. The temple was founded in 724 and has a magnificent five-story red pagoda, matched in its splendor only by some of Kyoto's most famous temples. The areas between the buildings of the temple are dotted with statues of *daruma* and bibbed *jizo*. Hours: 8:00 AM to 6:00 PM. Admission to the garden and the treasure house: 200 yen.

Just beyond the souvenir shops are a greenhouse, museum and park. Hours 9:00 AM to 5:00 PM. Admission: 350 yen. This complex is dedicated to the memory of Dr. Tomitaro Makino (1862-1957), a famous botanist from the Kochi area. The Greenhouse has collection of more than 1,000 exotic plants. The beautiful park has broad lawns and rolling fields, rock gardens and terraced gardens that descend toward the water. This is a great place for a picnic. There is also a museum that features science displays appropriate for school children. Buses back to Harimayabashi run about once an hour.

Katsurahama Beach 桂浜 (Southern end of the city; outside Shikoku Map 5).

The Kochi Ken Kotsu Bus trip from Harimayabashi to Katsurahama Beach, and its view of Tosa Bay, takes about 35 minutes and costs 530 yen. The bus stop is at platform No. 1 in front of Kochi's Chuo-Koen Park next to the Kokusai Hotel (middle right). The bus runs about once every 30 minutes. Katsurahama Beach features a recreation and amusement area that is probably of interest only for local people. The beach is gravelly rather than sandy — and a cooling dip on a hot day is recommended. On clear days, the view out to sea is incomparable — beautiful blue upon blue. There's a path up to an observatory that shares the top of a rocky cliff with a red *torii* gate. There's also a hiking path through the woods. The buses back to Harimayabashi run about once every 30 minutes.

Ryugado Cavern 竜河洞

Located about 25 km (15 miles) to the east of Kochi, Ryugado is one of the largest caverns in Japan. About a quarter of the total length of the caves — 4 km, or 2.5 miles — is open to the public. Guided tours (in Japanese only) are conducted from time to time, and highlight the secrets of this natural treasure.

Toden buses run between Harimaya-bashi (Toden-Seibu Bus Terminal) and Ryugado about once an hour, and the ride takes about an hour (960 yen). We recommend the Cavern only for those with time to spare in Kochi.

ACCOMMODATIONS
(Refer to Shikoku Map 5)

1. Hotels in Kochi

Kochi New Hankyu Hotel (lower center, Shikoku Map 5). Standard. 94 singles (10,500 yen -) & 104 doubles (20,000 yen -). Add: 4-2-50, Honmachi, Kochi. Tel: (0888) 73-1111.

Kochi Daiichi Hotel (upper right). Standard. 50 singles (8,000 yen -) & 69 doubles (16,000 yen -). Add: 2-2-12, Kita-Honmachi, Kochi. Tel: (0888) 83-1441.

Sunrise Hotel (lower center). Business. 57 singles (7,500 yen -) & 24 doubles (15,500 yen -). Add: 2-2-31, Honmachi, Kochi. Tel: (0888) 22-1281.

Kochi Washington Hotel (middle center). Business. 138 singles (7,500 yen -) &

34 doubles (15,500 yen -). Add: 1-8-25, Ottesuji, Kochi. Tel: (0888) 23-6111.

Kochi Kokusai Hotel (middle right). Business. 54 singles (7,500 yen -) & 31 doubles (14,000 yen -). Add: 1-1-2, Harimayamachi, Kochi. Tel: (0888) 22-4111.

Hotel Sunroute Kochi (upper right). Business. 110 singles (7,000 yen -) & 12 doubles (14,500 yen -). Add: 1-1-28, Kita-Honmachi, Kochi. Tel: (0888) 23-1311.

Business Hotel Town (lower center). Business. 70 singles (5,500 yen -) & 28 doubles (8,000 yen -). Add: 1-5-26, Honmachi, Kochi. Tel: (0888) 25-0055.

2. Ryokan in Kochi

Sansuien Hotel (lower left). First Class. 153 rooms. 19,000 yen & up per person. Add: 1-3-35, Takashomachi, Kochi. Tel: (0888) 22-0131.

Tosa Gyoen (upper center). First Class. 113 rooms. 19,000 yen & up per person. Add: 1-4-8, Okawasuji, Kochi. Tel: (0888) 22-4491.

MATSUYAMA 松山

Matsuyama, with a population of 445,000, is Shikoku's largest city. It is the capital of Ehime Prefecture, and its educational, cultural and commercial center. Dogo Onsen Spa, located in the eastern part of the city, is one of Japan's oldest hotsprings. In the 14th century the area prospered as a castle town. The present city developed when Matsuyamajo Castle was built at the order of Yoshiakira Kato in 1602.

Soseki Natsume, the famous Meiji-era novelist (whose portrait graces Japan's 1,000 yen bills), taught English at a high school at Matsuyama when he was young. His novel "Botchan" was based on his experiences here.

Outline of the City

Refer to Shikoku Map 6. Matsuyama's downtown area is at the southern foot of the Castle park area (middle center), on the northern side of Iyo Railways Matsuyamashi Station (lower center). The area around JR Matsuyama Station is much less developed. The downtown area features several arcades crammed full of department stores, shops and restaurants (shaded on the map). The *i* Information Office is located in JR Matsuyama Station.

Transportation in Matsuyama

Matsuyama has two main train stations. The first, JR Matsuyama Station is the terminal for JR long distance trains. JR buses to/from Kochi operate from the stop in front of JR Matsuyama Station. Matsuyamashi Station (lower center) is the terminal of the local commuter lines operated by the Iyo Railways. Both city streetcars and buses serve these two main stations as well.

Buses run frequently between Dogo Onsen (upper right) and Matsuyama Kankoko Port (western edge of the city), where ferries and hydrofoils to Hiroshima (Ujina Port) originate. You can catch these buses at the stop in front of JR Matsuyama Station. The ride from JR station to the Port takes 25 minutes and the fare is 410 yen. If you stay at a *ryokan* in Dogo Onsen hotsprings, the ride from Dogo to the Port takes 43 minutes (560 yen).

Places of Interest in Matsuyama

Matsuyamajo Castle 松山城 (Middle center)

Construction of the castle was begun in 1602 at the order of Yoshiakira Kato, and continued until 1627. In 1635, the Castle became the home of the Matsudaira family, which ruled the Matsuyama area during the Tokugawa period. The donjon was reconstructed in the 19th century, after it was struck by lightning, and again in the 20th century, after it was damaged during the war. Since the mid-60's, Matsuyama has worked hard at restoring this municipal symbol, and has succeeded splendidly. A visit to the Castle, which sits high above the city, will give you an excellent idea of life in feudal Shikoku. Hours: 9:00 AM to 5:00 PM (4:00 PM in winter). Admission: 260 yen.

A ropeway operates on the eastern side of the hill (middle center) on which the Castle stands. A three-minute ride takes you to the Castle (it operates about once every 10 minutes, 160 yen). A walk around the many gates and turrets of the Castle will give you a good idea of the scale of many feudal castle compounds. The donjon has a fantastic view of the mountains and the water that frame Matsuyama, and houses a museum that displays a good collection of armor and swords, as well as lacquer items, scrolls, screens and kimono.

If you have some extra time, we suggest that you walk back down from the Castle

rather than taking the ropeway, stopping at **Shinonome Jinja Shrine** 東雲神社. The path is to the right of the ropeway as you return from the Castle. It's a lovely wooded downslope that parallels and eventually passes under the cable and lift lines. The path will lead you to the back of the Shrine, which features beautiful dark wood and shining gold trim. From the Shrine, it's another 5-minute walk down the steps back to the street.

Shikido Hall 子規堂 (Lower center) (optional).

Near Matsuyamashi Station, next to Shojuji Temple, this building is a replica of the residence of Shiki Masaoka (1867-1902), a famous Meiji-era *haiku* poet. The house is a good sample of middle class Meiji life. The temple cemetery is behind and to the left of

MAP 6 Matsuyama

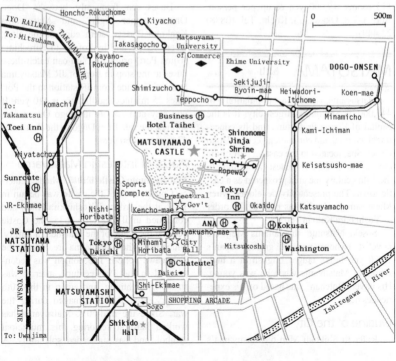

the residence, and there's an antique street-car in front of the residence that Japanese tourists find a real delight. Hours: 8:30 AM to 5:00 PM. Admission: 50 yen.

Kasuri Kaikan Iyo Textile Hall 民芸伊予カスリ会館 (Northwestern part of the city; outside the map) (optional)

A twenty-minute Iyo Tetsu Bus ride from Matsuyamashi Station (10 minutes from JR Matsuyama Station — platform No. 1). Get off the bus at Kumanodai Stop, and walk back about 200 m (220 yards) to the entrance to Kasuri Kaikan Iyo Textile Hall. The entrance is back off the street, to your left as you walk through the bus parking lot. A clearly marked path leads you through the factory and an explanation of the dyeing and spinning process for this local craft. Iyo Kasuri "splashed-pattern" textiles are a specialty of the Matsuyama area, and have been made here for almost 200 years. Many of the beautiful items on sale in the souvenir shop are rather expensive, but after viewing the backbreaking work that goes into their creation, you'll probably understand why. Hours: 8:00 AM to 4:50 PM. Admission: 50 yen. The buses back to Matsuyama run about once every fifteen minutes.

Dogo Onsen 道後温泉 (Upper right) (optional)

Dogo Onsen Spa can be reached by streetcar from either JR Matsuyama Station or the Iyo Railway's Matsuyamashi Station in 15 minutes (150 yen). Many Japanese tourists who visit Matsuyama stay at a *ryokan* in Dogo Onsen hotsprings, instead of a downtown hotel. **Dogo Onsen Honkan** 道後温泉本館 was the original communal hotspring bath house used by all visitors to Dogo in the days before each *ryokan* had its own baths. The traditional building has been

preserved as a symbol of Dogo Onsen. **Dogo Onsen Park** 道後公園 is located at the site of the 14th century Yuchikujo Castle, and is a lovely place for a stroll.

Further to the east, at higher elevation, is located Oku-Dogo Onsen hotsprings. The city's most deluxe resort hotel is located here.

ACCOMMODATIONS
(Refer to Shikoku Map 6)

1. Hotels in Matsuyama

ANA Matsuyama (middle center). First Class. 195 singles (9,000 yen -) & 133 doubles (19,500 yen -). Add: 3-2-1, Ichibancho, Matsuyama. Tel: (0899) 33-5511.

Kokusai Hotel Matsuyama (middle right). Standard. 28 singles (7,500 yen -) & 42 doubles (11,500 yen -). Add: 1-13, Ichibancho, Matsuyama. Tel: (0899) 32-5111.

Matsuyama Tokyu Inn (middle center). Business. 177 singles (7,500 yen -) & 65 doubles (15,000 yen -). Add: 3-3, Ichibancho, Matsuyama. Tel: (0899) 41-0109.

Hotel Sunroute Matsuyama (middle left). Business. 91 singles (7,500 yen -) & 19 doubles (15,500 yen -). Add: 391-8, Miyatacho, Matsuyama. Tel: (0899) 33-2811.

Matsuyama Washington Hotel (middle right). 155 singles (7,000 yen -) & 35 doubles (14,000 yen -). Add: 1-7-1, Nibancho, Matsuyama. Tel: (0899) 45-8111.

Toei Inn Matsuyama (middle left). Business. 126 singles (7,000 yen -) & 30 doubles (12,500 yen -). Add: 1-34-1, Miyanishi, Matsuyama. Tel: (0899) 24-2121.

Chateautel Matsuyama (lower center). Business. 122 singles (6,500 yen -) & 33 doubles (11,000 yen -). Add: 4-9-6, Sanbancho, Matsuyama. Tel: (0899) 46-2111.

Tokyo Daiichi Hotel Matsuyama (lower left). 100 singles (6,000 yen -) & 28 doubles (14,000 yen -). Add: 6-16, Minami-Horibatacho, Matsuyama. Tel: (0899) 47-4411.

2. Welcome Inn Matsuyama

Business Hotel Taihei (upper center). Business. 124 Western rooms. Add: 3-1-15, Heiwadori, Matsuyama. Tel: (0899) 43-3560.

3. Ryokan in Dogo Onsen

Kowakuen. Deluxe. 76 rooms. 19,000 yen & up per person. Add: 1-1, Dogo-Sagitanicho, Matsuyama. Tel: (0899) 45-5911.

Yamatoya. First Class. 97 rooms. 18,000 yen & up per person. Add: 20-8, Dogo-Yunomachi, Matsuyama. Tel: (0899) 41-1137.

Juen. First Class. 76 rooms. 15,000 yen & up per person. Add: 4-4, Dogo-Sagitanicho, Matsuyama. Tel: (0499) 41-0161.

4. Accommodations in Oku-Dogo Onsen

Hotel Oku-Dogo. Deluxe. 223 Western rooms & 80 Japanese rooms. 18,000 yen & up per person. Add: 267, Suemachi, Matsuyama. Tel: (0899) 77-1111.

Dogo Onsen

JR FARES BETWEEN MAJOR STATIONS IN THE SHIKOKU REGION

1. Okayama-Takamatsu: based on rapid service trains.
2. Other segments: based on limited express trains.

To/From	Okayama	Takamatsu	Kochi	Matsuyama
Okayama		1,260 yen (72.1 km)	5,440 yen (179.3 km)	6,270 yen (214.4 km)
Takamatsu	1,260 yen (72.1 km)		5,030 yen (159.6 km)	5,750 yen (194.7 km)
Tokushima		2,390 yen (74.8 km)		
Kotohira	2,720 yen (64.0 km)	1,940 yen (44.3 km)	4,100 yen (115.3 km)	
Kochi	5,440 yen (179.3 km)	5,030 yen (159.6 km)		
Matsuyama	6,270 yen (214.4 km)	5,750 yen (194.7 km)		
Uwajima	8,120 yen (311.3 km)	7,610 yen (291.6 km)	2,650 yen (161.9 km)	3,220 yen (96.9 km)

KYUSHU REGION

九州

Kyushu, the third largest of Japan's islands, is at the southwestern end of the archipelago. The JR Tokaido-Sanyo Shinkansen runs from Tokyo all the way to Kokura, and then to Hakata (Fukuoka) via the Kanmon Undersea Tunnel. Kyushu is divided into two districts: North Central Kyushu and Southern Kyushu.

NORTH CENTRAL KYUSHU

Refer to Kyushu Map 1. The highlight of a visit to North Central Kyushu is the trans-island trip from Nagasaki (middle left) to Beppu (middle right) via Shimabara, Kumamoto and Mt. Asozan.

Fukuoka (upper center), the largest city of Kyushu, is becoming Western Japan's international hub. Fukuoka Airport is served by many international flights, and the city is enthusiastically promoting international conventions and events. Many foreigners will have chance to visit the city for such an event. Fukuoka does not have much to offer to sightseers and is usually skipped in typical tourist itineraries.

Karatsu (upper left) is famous for its pottery and ceramics and is recommended for pottery enthusiasts.

Huis Ten Bosch (middle left), also called Nagasaki Holland Village, is not particularly interesting for foreign tourists, but we describe it briefly because this large theme park is an epoch-making project in the history of Japanese resort development.

The 1991 eruptions of Mt. Fugendake in Unzen, the largest in recent history, forced hundreds to abandon their houses.

Destinations introduced in this Chapter were not damaged in the eruptions.

We recommend a five day itinerary for North Central Kyushu:

Day 1. Arrive Nagasaki

JR limited express trains take a little over 2 hours from Hakata (Fukuoka) to Nagasaki. It is ideal to visit Nagasaki after a trip in the Inland Sea area (Sanyo Region). It is not difficult to travel to Nagasaki from Okasa or Kyoto. From Tokyo, it is a tough one day trip (about an 8-9 hour train trip on two JR lines).

Day 2. Nagasaki

A full day sightseeing in Nagasaki.

Day 3. Nagasaki/Shimabara/Kumamoto

Travel by trains and boat, with a stop at Shimabarajo Castle.

Day 4. Kumamoto/Mt. Asozan/Beppu

Travel by train and bus to Mt. Asozan. After a visit to this active volcano, continue your train ride to Beppu. You can also join a sightseeing bus (Japanese language only) from Kumamoto to Beppu via Mt. Asozan.

Day 5. Leave Beppu for your next destination

SOUTHERN KYUSHU

Refer to Kyushu Map 1. Southern Kyushu features several interesting destinations. We suggest a three day (two nights) itinerary as an extension of the North Central Kyushu itinerary above.

Day 5. Beppu/Miyazaki

Arrive in Miyazaki (lower right) around

MAP 1 Outline of Kyushu

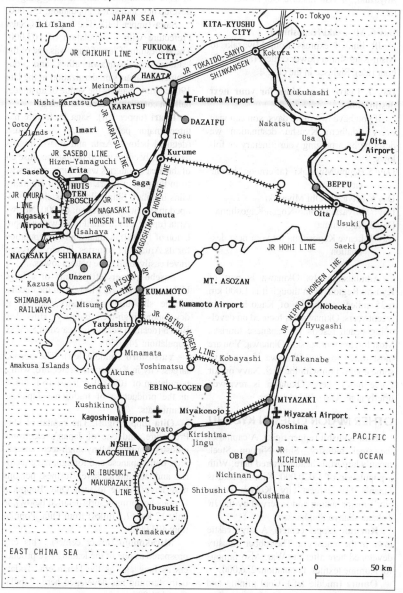

noon. You can spend the afternoon in Miyazaki, or visit historic Obi (lower center).

Day 6. Miyazaki/Kagoshima

JR limited express from Miyazaki to Nishi-Kagoshima (lower center) (about a 2-hour ride). Sightsee in the city.

Day 7. Leave Kagoshima for your next destination

If you have two more days, you can visit every Southern Kyushu destination we describe by arranging your itinerary as follows:

Day 5. Beppu/Miyazaki (afternoon in the city)
Day 6. Miyazaki/Obi/Miyazaki
Day 7. Miyazaki/Ebino-Kogen/Kagoshima
Day 8. Kagoshima
Day 9. Leave Kagoshima for your next destination

Administratively, Okinawa is part of Kyushu Region, even though it is 1,000 km (625 miles) southwest of Kagoshima. In recent years, Okinawa has focused on developing beach resorts for Japanese tourists. Most foreign tourists skip Okinawa. You are most likely to visit Okinawa if you have some connection with the U.S. Navy or Air Force bases there. Okinawa is reviewed briefly at the end of this Chapter.

OTHER MAJOR CITIES IN KYUSHU

Kita-Kyushu (upper right). A capital of the steel industry. Shin Nippon Steel, Japan's largest, is headquartered here. With a population of 1,020,000, Kita-Kyushu is Japan's 11th largest city. Kokura is the city's major station and is served by the JR Tokaido-Sanyo Shinkansen.

Kurume (upper center). A large castle town in the feudal era. The rubber industry developed here after the War. Also famous for Kurume textiles. Population: 226,000.

Omuta (middle left). Coal mining and related industries once made Omuta a key industrial city in Kyushu. With the decline of coal mining, the city is struggling to develop new industries. Population: 152,000.

Saga (upper left). The capital of Saga Prefecture with a population of 167,000. The Nabeshima Clan of Saga was one of the leading anti-Tokugawa allies and contributed to Japan's modernization in the late 19th century. Saga is the venue of an annual balloon competition each November.

Imari (upper left). Saga Prefecture has three major pottery centers — Karatsu (detailed below), Arita and Imari. Imari's name has become world famous because all of the area's potteries were shipped overseas from the port in Imari. There still are many kilns in Imari. Shipbuilding has also developed in the city. Population: 62,000. Nearby Arita (upper left) (a small town with a population of 14,000) maintains a high reputation for its Arita-yaki potteries. Pottery fans can travel easily to all three pottery towns.

Sasebo (upper left). Home of a large U.S. base for the 7th Fleet. With the decline of the shipbuilding industry, Sasebo is developing high-tech industry. Huis Ten Bosch (detailed below) is located in Sasebo. Population: 246,000.

Yatsushiro (middle left). The second largest city in Kumamoto Prefecture, with a population of 109,000. Yatsushiro is No. 1 in the production of traditional Japanese tatami mats.

Oita (upper right). The capital of Oita Prefecture, and one of Japan's electronic industry centers. Many high-tech companies, both Japanese and foreign, have factories and laboratories here. Business persons may have chance to visit Oita. Beppu, a famous hotspring resort (detailed below), is only 12 km (7.5 miles) from Oita. Population: 404,000.

Miyakonojo (lower center). This city prospered as one of the leading rice producers as long ago as the Heian era. Today, dairy farming has developed here. Population: 131,000.

Nobeoka (middle right). A former castle town and, today a leading manufacturing center. Asahi Chemical has a huge factory here. Population: 132,000.

TRANSPORTATION NETWORK IN KYUSHU

Refer to Kyushu Map 1. Kyushu's two "gateway" cities, Kokura (Kita-Kyushu City) and Hakata (Fukuoka City) are served by the JR Tokaido-Sanyo Shinkansen.

The JR Nippo Honsen Line runs along the eastern coast of Kyushu, connecting Kokura with the tourist attractions of Beppu, Miyazaki and Kagoshima (Nishi-Kagoshima Station). Limited express trains (called "Nichirin") run once every 30-60 minutes between Kokura and Oita via Beppu. About once every 90 minutes one of the "Nichirin" trains runs beyond Oita to Miyazaki. Four "Nichirin" trains a day run the entire distance between Kokura and Nishi-Kagoshima. The ride between major stations takes: Kokura (1 hour and 35 minutes) Beppu (11 minutes) Oita (3 hours 25 minutes) Miyazaki (50 minutes) Miyakonojo (30 minutes) Kirishima-Jingu (45 minutes) Nishi-Kagoshima.

Hakata is the terminus of the Tokaido-Sanyo Shinkansen and of several intra-Kyushu JR lines.

The JR Kagoshima Honsen Line runs between Hakata and Nishi-Kagoshima via Kumamoto. Two types of limited express trains (the "Ariake" and the "Tsubame") run on this line. The "Ariake" trains run only between Hakata and Kumamoto (about once an hour). The "Tsubame" trains run the full distance of the JR Kagoshima Line between Hakata and Nishi-Kagoshima, about once an hour. The ride between major stations takes: Hakata (1 hour and 30 minutes) Kumamoto (20 minutes) Yatsushiro (2 hours 10 minutes) Nishi-Kagoshima.

The JR Nagasaki Honsen Line connects Hakata with Nagasaki. Limited express trains (called "Kamome") run about once every hour, and the ride from Hakata to Nagasaki takes a little over 2 hours.

The JR Sasebo Line connects Hakata with Sasebo. "Midori" limited express trains run about once every hour, and the ride takes 1 hour and 50 minutes. The opening of Huis Ten Bosch near Sasebo has resulted in a large number of extra seasonal JR limited express trains (called "Huis Ten Bosch") on the Sasebo Line directly from Hakata to Haus Ten Bosch Station (1 hour and 50 minutes).

Huis Ten Bosch can be reached from Nagasaki in one and a half hours by rapid service train (called "Seaside Liner") on the JR Omura Line.

Karatsu, a famous pottery and castle city, is also connected by train with Hakata. Fukuoka's city subway (Line No. 1) runs between Hakata and Meinohama. The JR Chikuhi Line runs between Meinohama and Karatsu (commuter trains). The city subway runs onto the JR Chikuhi Line all the way to Karatsu. The ride takes 1 hour and 20 minutes and operates frequently.

The JR Hohi Line runs across the central part of Kyushu between Beppu and Kumamoto via Oita and Aso, skirting scenic Mt. Asozan. Three limited express trains (called "Aso") a day run on this line. The ride from Beppu takes 15 minutes to Oita, 2 hours to Aso and 3 hours to Kumamoto.

The JR Misumi Line runs the short distance between Kumamoto and Misumi. Only local trains operate on this line, and the trip takes one hour.

The JR Hisatsu-Kitto Line (popularly called the Ebino-Kogen Line) runs between Miyazaki and Kumamoto, via Kobayashi. "Ebino" express trains run three times a day on this line. The ride from Miyazaki takes 1 hour to Miyakonojo, one-and-a-half hours to Kobayashi, and four-and-a-half hours to Kumamoto. There is also bus service from Miyazaki to Kobayashi.

The JR Nichinan Line extends from Miyazaki to Shibushi, via the historic town of Obi. Only local trains run on this line —

about once every hour. The trip from Miyazaki takes 30 minutes to Aoshima, and two-and-a-half hours to Obi.

The JR Ibusuki-Makurazaki Line runs from Nishi-Kagoshima to Yamakawa via Ibusuki, a popular hotspring resort. Rapid service and local trains run between Nishi-Kagoshima and Ibusuki about once every 30-60 minutes. The trip takes 50 minutes by rapid service train, and 1 hour and 20 minutes by local.

All major cities in Kyushu — Fukuoka, Nagasaki, Kumamoto, Kagoshima, Miyazaki and Oita — have airports. Convenient air service is available from Tokyo (Haneda Airport), Osaka and other major cities. In Japan, domestic air transportation is expensive. If you are able to use a Japan Rail Pass, we recommend travel by rail rather than by air. If you live in Japan or are not otherwise eligible for a Rail Pass and can afford air travel, it will save you a great deal of time.

North Central Kyushu

FUKUOKA 福岡

Fukuoka, with a population of 1,193,000, is the largest city on Kyushu Island, and the cultural, political, education and transportation center of Southern Japan. Because it is so close to the Asian Continent, advanced continental culture was imported to Japan through the Fukuoka area at the dawn of the nation's history. The Mongolians who conquered China and established the Yuan Dynasty there attempted invasions of Japan twice, both times in vain — in 1274 and in 1281 — in this area.

The area got its name in 1600 when Nagamasa Kuroda, a feudal lord, was assigned here and named his new castle "Fukuoka"-jo. From then on the area to the west of the Nakagawa River, where the samurai lived, was called Fukuoka, while the area east of the river, where the merchants and craftsmen resided, was called Hakata. Fukuoka natives still proudly call themselves *Hakata-kko*, even after the politicians chose "Fukuoka" as the name for the whole city. The Japan Railways station is named Hakata instead of Fukuoka.

The *i* Information Office is located in JR

Hakata Station, as well as in the IMS Building in Tenjin (downtown).

Transportation to Fukuoka

Hakata Station (middle center, Kyushu Map 2) is the terminus of the 1,177 km (735 mile) long Tokaido-Sanyo Shinkansen that originates in Tokyo.

Fukuoka Airport offers flights to all major airports in Japan, as well as many foreign cities. Fukuoka Airport is located close to the city center, and is connected by city subway with JR Hakata Station (10 minutes) and other major parts of the city.

Transportation in Fukuoka

There are two city subways in Fukuoka. Subway No. 1 runs between Fukuoka Airport and Meinohama, via JR Hakata Station, Nakasu-Kawabata (nightlife area), Tenjin (downtown) and Ohori-Koen (recreational area). Subway No. 2 (not important for tourists) runs to the northeast from Nakasu-Kawabata.

EASTERN FUKUOKA

Refer to Kyushu Map 3. Most Fukuoka hotels are located around JR Hakata Station (lower right).

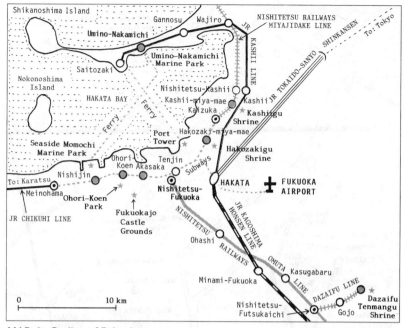

MAP 2 Outline of Fukuoka

Kushida Jinja Shrine 櫛田神社 (middle center) is Fukuoka's most important shrine and is dedicated to the *Shinto* god *Susano-o-no-Mikoto*. The floats used for the Hakata Yamagasa Festival (July 1-15) are on display in the museum attached to the Shrine. They feature feudal era costumes and objects, and are quite colorful and elaborate. Hours: 9:00 AM to 5:00 PM. Admission: 200 yen.

Nakasu 中洲 (middle center). In the center of the city there is an islet surrounded by the Nakagawa and Hakatagawa Rivers called Nakasu (this literally means central sand bar); it is one of Japan's most famous nightlife districts. In this tiny area (250 m from east to west and 1,500 m from north to south), there are over 2,500 restaurants, bars and other nightspots.

The nearby **Tenjin** 天神 (middle left, around subway Tenjin Station and Nishitetsu Fukuoka Station) area is Fukuoka's main shopping district. Extensive underground arcades are located here.

New ocean front development (upper left) is underway, targeting at making the area Fukuoka's international convention, meeting and exhibition center. Fukuoka Kokusai Center is the venue of large conventions and sports meetings, including the Fukuuoka Sumo Tournament in November every year. Port Tower Hakata is an observatory. The view from Port Tower is not as good as the one from Fukuoka Tower below.

WESTERN FUKUOKA

Refer to Kyushu Map 4.

Fukuokajo Castle Grounds 福岡城址 (lower right). Only a few gates and one turret still remain, but the castle is located on a 48 m (157 foot) high hill and commands a bird's-eye view of the city.

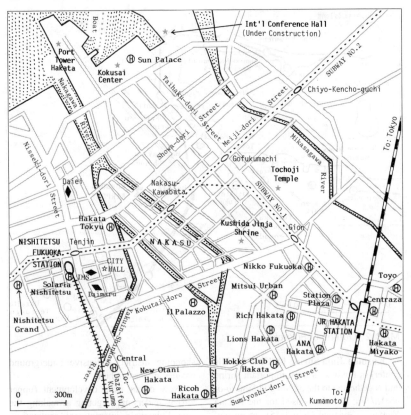

MAP 3 Eastern Fukuoka

Ohori-Koen Park 大濠公園 (lower center). The Park is laid out around a large pond 2 km (1.25 miles) in circumference. Several bridges provide access to the islet in the center of the pond.

Seaside Momochi Marine Park シーサイドももち海浜公園 (upper left) is a large ocean front development, the pride of Fukuoka. The Park features a 1.4 km beach and other recreational facilities. **Fukuoka Tower** 福岡タワー is a 234 m (780 foot) tall glass building. You can reach the observatory by elevators. Hours: 9:30 AM to 11:00 PM (10:00 AM to 9:00 PM in winter). Admission:

800 yen. **Saibu Gas Museum** 西部ガスミュージアム is a good place to learn about energy generation. Hours: 10:00 AM to 5:00 PM. Closed on Mondays. Admission free. **Fukuoka City Museum** 福岡市博物館 displays historic objects of the area, including a National Treasure golden seal presented by China to the King of Wa, a small "nation" in the prehistoric era. **Marizon** マリゾン is a shopping and restaurant pavilion built over the water. Twin Dome is an indoor sports complex. One of the domes has been completed and is the home of the professional Fukuoka Daiei Hawks baseball team.

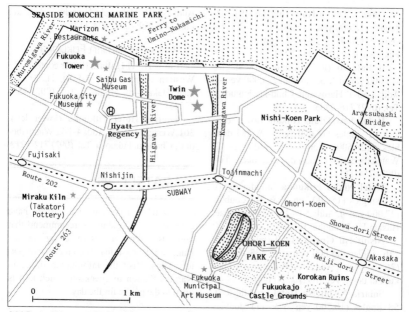

MAP 4 Western Fukuoka

OTHER PLACES OF INTEREST

Umino-Nakamichi Marine Park 海の中
道海浜公園 (upper center, Kyushu Map 2) is
spacious recreation area for the people of
Fukuoka. Ferry boats operate from the piers
near Port Tower and in the Seaside
Momochi Marine Park.

Dazaifu Tenmangu Shrine 太宰府
天満宮 (lower right, Kyushu Map 2) can be
reached by the Nishitetsu Railways from
Nishitetsu-Fukuoka Station. Only several
commuter trains run to Dazaifu Station
directly. You need to combine two trains —
one on the Omuta Line from Nishitetsu-
Fukuoka to Nishitetsu-Futsukaichi, and the
other from Nishitetsu-Futsukaichi to Daizaifu. The ride takes 40-50 minutes for the
entire trip (310 yen). In the Nara and Heian
Eras, a branch of Kyoto's imperial court was
established in Daizaifu to conduct trade and
diplomatic contacts with China and other

Asian countries. Dazaifu Tenmangu Shrine,
dedicated to Michizane Sugawara (Refer to
Kyoto's Kitano-Tenmangu Shrine for
details), is the most important historic monument in northern Kyushu, and welcomes
hundreds of thousands of visitors every
year.

ACCOMMODATIONS
(Refer to Kyushu Map 3)

1. Deluxe and First Class Hotels in Fukuoka

ANA Hotel Hakata (lower right). 175
singles (12,500 yen -) & 153 doubles
(24,000 yen -). Add: 3-3-3, Hakataekimae,
Hakata-ku, Fukuoka. Tel: (092) 471-7111.

Hakata Miyako Hotel (lower right).
164 singles (10,000 yen -) & 99 doubles
(17,000 yen -). Add: 2-1-2, Hakataeki-
Higashi, Hakata-ku, Fukuoka. Tel: (092)
441-3111.

Hakata Tokyu Hotel (middle left). 169 singles (16,000 yen -) & 88 doubles (25,000 yen -). Add: 1-16-1, Tenjin, Chuo-ku, Fukuoka. Tel: (092) 781-7111.

Il Palazzo (lower center). 18 singles (15,000 yen -) & 33 doubles (24,000 yen -). Add: 3-13-1, Haruyoshi, Chuo-ku, Fukuoka. Tel: (092) 716-3333.

Hotel New Otani Hakata (lower center). 22 singles (18,000 yen -) & 353 doubles (28,500 yen -). Add: 1-1-2, Watanabedori, Chuo-ku, Fukuoka. Tel: (092) 714-1111.

Hotel Nikko Fukuoka (middle right). 141 singles (15,500 yen -) & 211 doubles (27,000 yen -). Add: 2-18-15, Hakataekimae, Hakata-ku, Fukuoka. Tel: (092) 482-1111.

Nishitetsu Grand Hotel (middle left). 136 singles (15,000 yen -) & 133 doubles (26,000 yen -). Add: 2-6-60, Daimyo, Chuo-ku, Fukuoka. Tel: (092) 771-7171.

Solaria Nishitetsu Hotel (middle left). 58 singles (10,500 yen -) & 111 doubles (19,500 yen -). Add: 2-2-43, Tenjin, Chuo-ku, Fukuoka. Tel: (092) 761-1155.

2. Standard and Business Hotels in Fukuoka

Hotel Station Plaza (lower right). 161 singles (10,000 yen -) & 76 doubles (17,500 yen -). Add: 2-1-1, Hakataekimae, Hakata-ku, Fukuoka. Tel: (092) 431-1211.

Hotel Centraza Hakata (lower right). 83 singles (9,500 yen -) & 109 doubles (16,000yen -). Add: 4-23, Chuogai, Hakata-ku, Fukuoka. Tel: (092) 461-0111.

Hotel Rich Hakata (lower right). 105 singles (7,500 yen -) & 67 doubles (14,000 yen -). Add: 3-27-15, Hakataekimae, Hakata-ku, Fukuoka. Tel: (092) 451-7811.

Mitsui Urban Hotel Fukuoka (lower right). 258 singles (7,000 yen -) & 51 doubles (13,500 yen -). Add: 2-8-15, Hakataekimae, Hakata-ku, Fukuoka. Tel: (092) 451-5111.

Toyo Hotel (lower right). 224 singles (6,500 yen -) & 50 doubles (10,000 yen -). Add: 1-9-36, Hakataeki-Higashi, Hakata-ku, Fukuoka. Tel: (092) 474-1121.

3. Welcome Inns in Fukuoka

Lions Hotel Hakata (lower center). 313 Western rooms. Add: 3-5-10, Hakataeki-mae, Hakata-ku, Fukuoka. Tel: (092) 451-7711.

Central Hotel Fukuoka (lower left). 361 Western rooms. Add: 4-1-2, Watanabe-dori, Chuo-ku, Fukuoka. Tel: (092) 712-1212.

KARATSU 唐津

If you are a pottery enthusiast, or have extra time in Kyushu, we recommend that you visit Karatsu before going on the Nagasaki. Karatsu features a number of pottery kilns. Visit the information office in Karatsu Station to check on which kiln is open to the public for the day.

Suggested Itinerary

Refer to Kyushu Map 5.

Kinshoji Temple 近松寺 (middle left) (optional). This is the family temple of the Ogasawaras, feudal lords who governed the area during the Edo Era. The temple is famous as the burial place of Monzaemon Chikamatsu. Chikamatsu wrote *joruri*, the chanted dramatic stories from which the modern *bunraku* puppet plays evolved. He was extremely prolific and wrote more than 50 plays. He has been called the father of Japanese drama. The temple also has a small museum that displays the family treasures of the Ogasawaras.

Hikiyama Tenjijo Hall 曳山展示場 (upper left). Karatsu Kunchi Festival (November 2-4) is famous for its colorful festival floats. Fifteen districts of the city have their own floats, each designed in a distinctive shape, such as a samurai helmet, a dragon, a fish, etc. These impressive floats are displayed in Hikiyama Tenjijo Hall. Magnificently finished with gold and silver

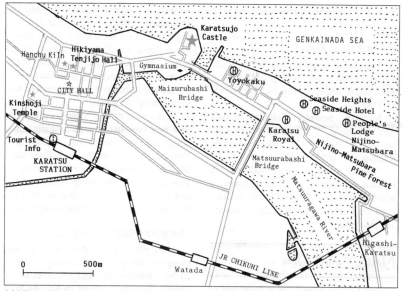

MAP 5 Karatsu

foil and lacquer, they testify to the high artistic standards of the area. Hours: 9:00 AM to 5:00 PM. Admission: 200 yen.

Karatsujo Castle 唐津城 (upper center). Karatsujo Castle stands on a small hill facing the Genkainada Sea. Because of its white walls and its ideal location right on the water, the castle is popularly known as Maizurujo or Flying Crane Castle. The present building is a 1966 reconstruction. The view from the castle grounds of the sea, the city and Rainbow Pine Beach to the east is well worth the effort of climbing the long stone stairway.

Nijo-no-Matsubara (Rainbow Pine Beach) 虹ノ松原 (middle right) (optional). You can walk to Niji-no-Matsubara in 15 minutes from Karatsujo Castle, or take a taxi at the exit of Karatsujo Castle (there are usually many waiting there). This pine forest is 0.6 km (0.4 miles) wide and 5 km (3 miles) long. Most of the pine trees are over 350 years old. This is the most beautiful forest of its kind in all of Japan.

Pottery Kilns in Karatsu. Karatsu pottery is characterized by its plain dark brown glaze. Simple, and austerely beautiful, it is often used for tea ceremony. If you are unfamiliar with the process of pottery making, you will be impressed with the skillful handiwork of the potters. Among the leading kilns of the city are **Hanchu Kiln, Kyozan Kiln, Kojiro Kiln** and **Ochanomizu Kiln.** There are a number of pottery shops along the city's main street and shopping arcade (shaded on the map), which run between JR Karatsu Station (middle left) and City Hall.

ACCOMMODATIONS
(Refer to Kyushu Map 5)

1. Hotels in Karatsu

Karatsu Royal Hotel (middle right). First Class. 200 rooms. Double (23,000 yen -). Add: 4-9-20, Higashi-Karatsu, Karatsu. Tel: (0955) 72-0111.

Karatsu Seaside Hotel (middle right). Standard. 63 rooms. Double (19,000 yen -).

Add: 4-182, Higashi-Karatsu, Karatsu. Tel: (0955) 73-5185.

2. Ryokan in Karatsu

Yoyokaku (upper center). Standard. 22 rooms. 12,000 yen & up per person. Add: 2-4-40, Higashi-Karatsu, Karatsu. Tel: (0955) 72-7181.

Karatsu Seaside Heights (middle right). Standard. 59 rooms. 12,000 yen & up per person. Add: 4-182, Higashi-Karatsu, Karatsu. Tel: (0955) 73-5185.

Note: All major accommodations in Karatsu are located along the picturesque Niji-no-Matsubara Beach. Fresh seafood from the Genkainada Sea is their specialty and their pride.

NAGASAKI 長崎

See Kyusyu Map 6 for an overview of the area. Nagasaki was a small fishing village until the middle of the 16th century, when the Portuguese started trading there. Christianity, which was introduced by the Jesuits, soon took root in the area, but it was prohibited at the end of the century by Hideyoshi Toyotomi, the military leader who completed the unification of Japan after a long period of civil war. He forced those who had converted to renounce their religion. Twenty-six faithful Christians refused to do so, and were executed in 1597 at what is now Nishizaka-Koen Park. All of these martyrs were named saints by the Pope in 1862.

In 1639, the Tokugawa Shogunate adopted isolationism as a national policy and closed all Japanese ports except Nagasaki to foreign traders. The Tokugawas wanted to shut out the Christian influence of the European traders, and, at the same time, wanted to monopolize foreign trade, keeping all the profits for the Shogunate. Only Dutch and Chinese traders with no connections with Christian missionaries were allowed to continue trading at Nagasaki. Thus, during the nation's long period of isolation, Nagasaki became the eyes through which Japan watched the changes of the world. Until isolationism was finally abandoned in the 19th century, all modern ideas, science and technology were introduced into Japan through Nagasaki.

In the modern era, Nagasaki prospered as a port city and became a shipbuilding center. An atomic bomb was exploded over Nagasaki on August 9, 1945, three days after the H-bomb explosion at Hiroshima. The city rebuilt and rehabilitated rapidly, and today, with a population of 442,000, Nagasaki is the center of Western Kyushu.

Transportation in Nagasaki

Most places of interest, nightlife and shopping centers are conveniently connected by streetcars. The city's four different streetcar lines are pictured on Kyushu Map 7. A one-day pass, which allows unlimited rides on the four lines, can be purchased at major hotels; the passes cannot be purchased on the streetcars themselves.

Outline of the City

Refer to Kyushu Map 7. Even though there are many shopping, eating and drinking establishments in its vicinity, JR's Nagasaki Station (middle center) is rather isolated from the city's downtown (lower right). The majority of the city's night spots and shopping centers are in the southern part of the city. Local government offices and business properties are located between

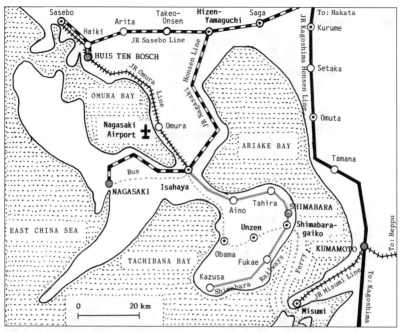

MAP 6 Outline of Nagasaki District

downtown and Nagasaki Station. Most of Nagasaki's cultural and historical attractions are also located in the southern part of the city. The northern part of the city contains A-bomb-related sites and monuments. Mt. Inasayama, the best place to view the whole city, is located to the west of Nagasaki Station. The *i* Information Office is located in front of JR Nagasaki Station.

Places of Interest

The suggested itinerary that follows can be adapted for only one full day of sightseeing in Nagasaki. However, because two one-day itineraries are ideal for Nagasaki (one full day for the southern historic area, and one more full day for the northern and central areas), we have described Nagasaki that way, and have, of course, suggested how you can select major attractions to adapt for a one-day itinerary.

Day 1 Itinerary

Oura Tenshudo Church 大浦天主堂 (lower left). Take the No. 5 streetcar to Oura-Tenshudo-shita stop, and walk past the Nagasaki Tokyu Hotel to the church. Oura Tenshudo Church is a wooden Gothic-style building constructed in 1864 to honor the 26 martyrs of Nagasaki. The Church features impressive stained glass windows, and has been designated a National Treasure. Hours: 8:00 AM to 6:00 PM. Admission: 200 yen.

Glover Mansion グラバー邸 (lower left). Glover Mansion is the oldest Western style building in Japan. The mansion is famous as the setting of Chio-Chio-san's house in Puccini's "Madama Butterfly." On the grounds of the Glover Mansion is a living museum consisting of several Western style buildings that were moved here from their original locations around Nagasaki. They are on a hillside equipped with escala-

MAP 7 Nagasaki

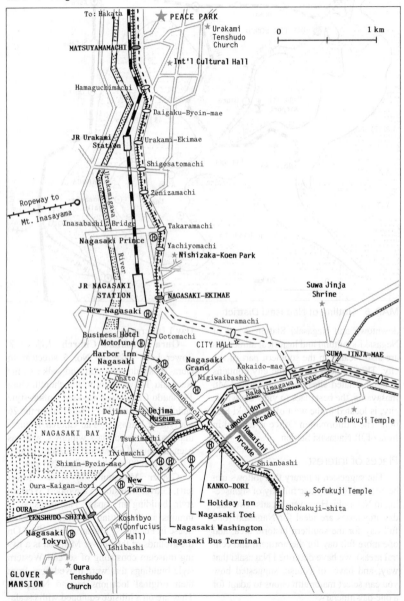

tors that ease your trip to the top. Probably the best way to appreciate the museum is to take the escalators to the top, and then walk down, visiting the various houses located on the hillside. You can have a good view of the port of Nagasaki from the grounds. Hours: 8:30 AM to 5:00 PM. Admission: 600 yen.

Jurokubankan Mansion 十六番館 (optional). Jurokubankan, another Western style building located right outside the exit of the Glover Mansion grounds, is a museum that contains historical and cultural objects that illustrate the early Western and Christian influence in Japan. Hours: 8:30 AM to 5:00 PM.

To Ishibashi Streetcar Stop. A narrow street that runs east from Jurokubankan Mansion leads to the square in front of Oura Tenshudo Church. Instead of returning along the same street that you took on your way to the Church, take the narrow path stretching to the southeast. The path travels down a hillside on which a number of small, typical Nagasaki houses are perched.

Note: If you are spending only one day in Nagasaki, take the No. 5 streetcar from Ishibashi to Tsukimachi (lower center), and then transfer to the No. 1 streetcar, getting off at Matsuyamamachi (upper left) for a visit to Peace Park.

Koshibyo (Confucius Hall) 孔子廟 and **Hollander Slope** オランダ坂 (lower left) (optional). Koshibyo Hall was built in 1893

by the Chinese residents of Nagasaki and was dedicated to Confucius. The present building was reconstructed after World War II. The Hall contains Chinese arts and crafts, as well as a restaurant and many souvenir shops. Hours: 8:30 AM to 5:00 PM. Admission: 515 yen. Hollander Slope runs up the hillside. The path was so named because the Dutch traders often took walks here. After your walk up the slope, take the No. 5 streetcar from Shimin-Byoin-mae stop (lower left) to Tsukimachi (lower center), or you can continue to walk to Dejima Museum (0.6 km or 0.4 miles).

Dejima Museum 出島資料館 (middle center). The site of Dejima Museum was the only place foreigners were allowed to live and trade for more than 200 years. The original Dutch traders' residence still stands here. There are also miniature replicas of the secluded trading houses. Hours: 9:00 AM to 5:00 PM. Closed on Mondays. Admission: free.

Suwa Jinja Shrine 諏訪神社 (middle right) (optional). Returning to the Tsukimachi stop, take the east-bound No. 5 streetcar to Suwa-Jinja-mae. Suwa Jinja Shrine was constructed at the order of the feudal government to promote Shintoism and to help wipe out Christian influence in the area. Slowly, it became very popular with the people of Nagasaki. A 277-step stone stairway leads to the wooded precincts and the magnificent shrine buildings. The Shrine is famous as the home of Okunchi Festival, which is held each year from October 7-9. The precincts are open year round to worshippers and visitors. No admission charge.

Downtown Nagasaki

When you finish at Suwa Jinja Shrine, it may be late in the afternoon. Take the west-bound No. 4 or No. 5 streetcar to Nigiwaibashi stop (or walk the distance of about 0.4 miles or 0.6 km). Then enjoy a stroll across Meganebashi Bridge (Eyeglasses Bridge) and around the downtown area.

The street that runs northeast from Kanko-dori streetcar stop is Kanko-dori Arcade. Hamaichi Arcade intersects it. Modern stores and specialty shops crowd both of these streets. Many restaurants are also located in the area. The southern part of the wide street where the streetcars run is crowded with many drinking places and pachinko pinball parlors. Chinatown is further to the southwest (around Nagasaki Washington Hotel).

Day 2 Itinerary

Peace Park 平和公園(upper center). You should begin your second day with a visit to Peace Park. Take either the No. 1 or No. 3 streetcar to Matsuyamamachi stop.

Note: If you are spending just one day in Nagasaki, you should visit Peach Park after Glover Mansion. See Day 1 Itinerary.

Peace Park was built on a small hill near the spot over which the A-bomb exploded on August 9, 1945. The Park's 10 m (32 feet) bronze statue embodies the wishes of the people of Nagasaki for peace. It is the work of Seibo Kitamura. The Park also features many statues and sculptures presented by foreign countries. It is open year round.

Urakami Tenshudo Church 浦上天主堂 (upper center) (optional). Urakami Tenshudo Church was built by faithful Christians who secretly adhered to their religion throughout the 200 years that it was banned by the Tokugawa shoguns. When freedom of religion was guaranteed with the

Meiji Restoration, these believers built the largest Catholic Church in East Asia with their own hands. The present building was reconstructed in 1959 to replace the original, which was destroyed by the A-bomb.

International Cultural Hall 長崎国際文化会館 (upper center). International Cultural Hall is located in a quiet park. It displays objects that illustrate the devastation caused by the atomic bomb. Looking at the panel displays and the twisted remains of objects destroyed by the A-bomb is by no means a pleasant experience, but it is an important one. The Hall is open from 9:00 AM to 5:00 PM. Admission: 50 yen.

Nishizaka-Koen Park 西坂公園 (middle center). Take the southbound No. 1 or No. 3 streetcar from Matsuyamamachi stop to Nagasaki-ekimae. Nishizaka-Koen is on a small hill northeast of Nagasaki Station. The twenty-six faithful Christians who defied the government mandate to renounce their religion were executed here in 1597. A bronze monument honoring the martyrs was completed in 1962. The Park's museum features objects related to Christianity in Japan. Museum Hours: 9:00 AM to 5:00 PM. Admission: 200 yen.

Mt. Inasayama 稲佐山 (middle left) (optional). The bus to Inasayama Ropeway Station uses a bus stop located under the huge pedestrian bridge in front of Nagasaki Station. Take the north-bound No. 3 bus. Ropeway-mae stop is your destination. The ride takes about five minutes. The ropeway station is on a hillside. You can take two ropeways to a high elevation of Mt. Inasayama. They operate every 20 minutes from 9:00 AM to 10:00 PM (5:00 PM in winter). The combined ticket is 1,280 yen roundtrip. The top of Mt. Insayama (1,089 feet, or 332 m, a five-minute walk from the ropeway station) has a fantastic view of the city of Nagasaki. The summit also commands a beautiful view of Saikai National Park. For the return trip from Ropeway-mae stop to Nagasaki Station, you have to take a different bus because most buses in Nagasaki operate as one-way loops. You should take the southbound No. 30 or No. 40 bus to Nagasaki Station.

Nagasaki Harbor Sightseeing Boat. If you are interested in a boat ride in Nagasaki Harbor, take the southbound No. 1 streetcar to Ohato Stop (middle center) and then walk west for three minutes to the boat pier. A 60-minute sightseeing tour boat leaves three times a day, at 10:15 AM, 11:40 AM and 3:15 PM. Fare: 900 yen.

ACCOMMODATIONS

(Refer to Kyushu Map 7)

1. Hotels in Nagasaki

Nagasaki Prince Hotel (middle center). First Class. 174 rooms. Double (24,000 yen -). Add: 2-26, Takaramachi, Nagasaki. Tel: (0958) 21-1111.

Nagasaki Tokyu Hotel (lower left). First Class. 30 singles (14,000 yen -) & 192 doubles (24,000 yen -). Add: 1-18, Minami-Yamatemachi, Nagasaki. Tel: (0958) 25-1501.

Hotel New Nagasaki (middle center). First Class. 146 rooms. Double (23,000 yen -). Add: 14-5, Daikokumachi, Nagasaki. Tel: (0958) 26-8000.

Nagasaki Grand Hotel (middle center). First Class. 47 singles (10,000 yen -) & 72 doubles (17,000 yen -). Add: 5-3, Manzaimachi, Nagasaki. Tel: (0958) 23-1234.

Hotel New Tanda (lower left). Standard. 60 singles (8,500 yen -) & 99 doubles (17,500 yen -). Add: 2-24, Tokiwamachi, Nagasaki. Tel: (0958) 27-6121.

Nagasaki Washington Hotel (lower center). Business. 114 singles (6,500 yen -) & 62 doubles (15,500 yen -). Add: 9-1, Shinchimachi, Nagasaki. Tel: (0958) 28-1211.

Nagasaki Bus Terminal Hotel (lower center). Business. 142 singles (5,000 yen -) & 19 doubles (8,500 yen -). Add: 1-14, Shinchimachi, Nagasaki. Tel: (0958) 21-4111.

Nagasaki Toei Hotel (lower center). Business. 111 singles (8,000 yen -) & 60 doubles (14,500 yen -). Add: 7-24, Dozamachi, Nagasaki. Tel: (0958) 22-2121.

Harbor Inn Nagasaki (middle center). Business. 142 singles (6,000 yen -) & 32 doubles (10,500 yen -). Add: 8-17, Kabashimamachi, Nagasaki. Tel: (0958) 27-1111.

Business Hotel Motofuna (middle center). Business. 94 singles (5,500 yen -) & 23 doubles (9,500 yen -). Add: 5-4, Motofunamachi, Nagasaki. Tel: (0958) 21-2400.

2. Welcome Inns in Nagasaki

Nishi Kyushu Daiichi Hotel (1 minute walk from Nagasaki Station). 83 Western rooms. Add: 2-1, Daikokumachi, Nagasaki. Tel: (0958) 21-1711.

Ryokan Sansuiso (5 minute walk from Nagasaki Station). 22 Japanese & 6 Western rooms. Add: 2-25, Ebisumachi, Nagasaki. Tel: (0958) 24-0070.

Minshuku Ryokan Tanpopo (10 minute walk from Nagasaki Station). 12 Japanese rooms. Add: 21-7, Hoeicho, Nagasaki. Tel: (0958) 61-6230.

HUIS TEN BOSCH (NAGASAKI HOLLAND VILLAGE)
ハウステンボス

As described above, Holland was the only Western country permitted access to Japan during the isolationist period (the 17th-19th centuries). Since then, Nagasaki has maintained and nurtured its relationaship with all things Dutch. In commemoration of this relationship, Huis Ten Bosch, a new theme park, has been developed. It was completed and opened to the public in 1992. This large scale resort development has attracted a great deal of attention and is often compared to Tokyo Disneyland. The Village is divided into eight theme parks, and also includes expensive residential developments. The entrance to the Village is only a 5-minute walk from JR Huis Ten

Bosch Station (upper right). Each of the eight theme parks is described below:

1. Breukelen features a Dutch castle. A small museum in the Castle displays swords and armor of medieval Europe.

2. Kinderdijk is modeled on a 17th century Dutch farmhouse and features windmills, a cheese factory and 300,000 tulips.

3. Nieuwstad boasts of several theaters and restaurants laid out around a plaza.

4. Utrecht features a 105 m (344 foot) Tower modeled after Holland's oldest church. There is an observatory at 80 m (262 feet). Eighteen restuarnats feature various international cuisines.

5. Museumstad is home to several museums, galleries and theaters.

6. Binnenstad is Huis Ten Bosch's central plaza, which is used for outdoor events. This area also features a large number of souvenir shops. The Hotel Amsterdam is a replica of the original. Rooms at this 203-room property start at 32,000 yen for doubles.

7. Spakenburg is another event plaza designed around seafood markets and restaurants. Harbor cruises leave from here. Hotel Europe is at the northern end of this area. Again, it is a replica of the original in Amsterdam. Rooms at this 329-room property start from 34,000 yen for doubles.

MAP 8   Huis Ten Bosch

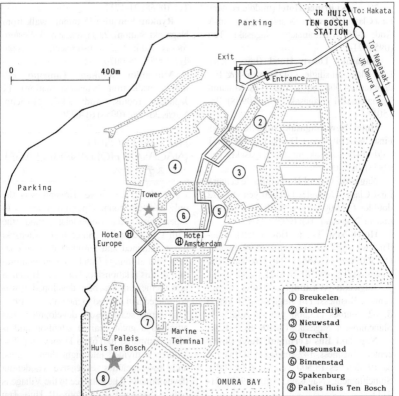

8. Paleis Huis Ten Bosch is a replica of a Dutch palace and houses a museum that displays masterpiece paintings by both Dutch and Japanese artists.

Huis Ten Bosch Hours: 9:00 AM to 9:00 PM (7:00 PM in winter). Basic admission "Passports" cost 3,900 yen. Admission to most of the eight areas requires additional payments. You'll have to purchase a 5,600 yen magnetized card to be able to pay for these additional admissions as well as for all taxis, shuttle boats, etc. that operate in the Village.

SHIMABARA AND UNZEN 島原・雲仙

Refer to Kyushu Map 6. There are two ways to travel from Nagasaki (middle left) to Kumamoto (lower right).

The easiest route involves taking a through bus that originates in Nagasaki at the Bus Terminal in front of JR Nagasaki Station. The bus runs along the scenic southern shore of the peninsula to Obama, and then climbs to Unzen. After visiting the volcanic "hells" in Unzen, the bus continues to Shimabara-gaiko and crosses Ariake Bay by ferry to Misumi. The bus makes a short detour to visit the scenic Amakusa-Gokyo (Five Bridges of Amakusa), and then proceeds to Kumamoto. It stops at JR Kumamoto Station, and terminates at Kotsu Center Bus Terminal in downtown Kumamoto. Kyushu Kokusai Kanko Bus operates four buses daily each way (with Japanese language only guides). The bus route is indicated with a dotted line on the map. The ride takes about 7 hours. The fare is 7,540-9,970 yen, depending on the time of departure (three morning buses include lunch; one afternoon bus does not).

The other route requires you to travel on your own. Take the JR Nagasaki Honsen Line from Nagasaki to Isahaya, and then transfer there to the Shimabara Railways. We recommend that you stop at Shimabara to visit Shimabarajo Castle and the samurai houses. Then continue on the Shimabara Railways to Shimabara-gaiko. After enjoying a one-hour cruise across Ariake Bay, take the JR Misumi Line from Misumi to Kumamoto. This full-day trip is an enjoyable sightseeing event in itself.

SHIMABARA 島原

Shimabara, with Ariake Bay to its east and Mt. Mayuyama (2,687 feet, or 819 m) rising to its west, is a bright, scenic city. Christian missionaries were very successful in this area. In 1638, the teaching of this new faith, and the severity of the taxes levied by the military government spurred the local farmers to revolt. The Tokugawa Shogunate dispatched a huge force to suppress the rebellion, and, after three months of intense battles, 37,000 rebels were massacred. Amid the peaceful atmosphere of the city today, it is difficult to imagine the bloody tragedy of the Christians and farmers 350 years ago.

Shimabarajo Castle 島原城 (lower center, Kyushu Map 9). Shimabarajo Castle is located at the end of the main street that begins at the train station. It was originally built in 1625, and the donjon was reconstructed in 1964. The entrance to the castle grounds is on the western side. The grounds are open from 8:00 AM to 6:00 PM (5:00 PM in winter). Admission to the grounds: 20 yen. Admission to the donjon: 300 yen.

There is a great view of Ariake Bay from the top of the donjon. The six-story donjon is also a museum that displays Christian objects on the second floor, samurai weapons and armor on the third and pottery on the fourth. Especially noteworthy is the collection of Christian objects. They are classified according to the eras when Christianity was introduced in Japan and when it was prohibited by the military government. Admission to the donjon includes admission to the Seibo Memorial Museum. The eastern

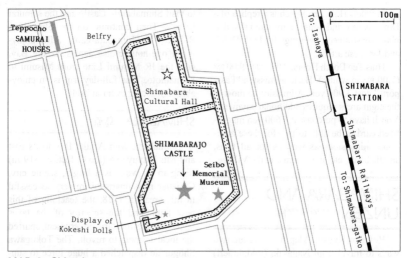

MAP 9 Shimabara

turret houses this Museum, which displays the works of Seibo Kitamura, a famous sculptor born in the area. The Peace Statue in Nagasaki's Peace Park is the work of Seibo. The western turret is used for display of a collection of *kokeshi* wooden dolls that includes samples of this popular folkcraft item from all parts of Japan.

Samurai Houses 武家屋敷跡 (upper left). Samurai houses still stand in Teppocho, northwest of the Castle. A clear creek, which was used for drinking water, still runs between the mud walls that surround the wooden houses. Two houses, which were residences of lower-class samurai, are open to the public. Teppocho preserves the atmosphere of the feudal city and is one of the best of several places like this in various parts of the country. Hours: 9:00 AM TO 5:00 PM. No admission.

KUMAMOTO 熊本

Kumamoto's prosperity began when Kiyomasa Kato, one of the most influential of Hideyoshi Toyotomi's generals, had a magnificent castle built here in 1601. The city was later granted by the Tokugawa Shogunate to the feudal lord Tadatoshi Hosokawa. Throughout the Edo Era, Kumamoto prospered under the rule of successive generations of the Hosokawa family. After the Meiji Restoration, when Japan moved toward modernization and democratization, samurai warriors who resisted the new order fought their last battle in Kumamoto.

Kumamoto is often called the "forested city." The many trees in every neighborhood of this lovely city help create and maintain its fresh and pleasant atmosphere.

Transportation in Kumamoto

Refer to Kyushu Map 10. Streetcars are the most convenient public transportation. There are two streetcar lines — No. 2 and No. 3. The route number is posted on the front of the car. Only the No. 2 line is pictured on the map. The No. 3 line is not useful for tourists. The No. 2 line operates every 5-6 minutes.

Outline of the City

JR Kumamoto Station (lower left) is

rather isolated from the city's downtown, but thanks to the No. 2 streetcar, it is quite easy to reach the downtown area from the Station. The downtown area is located to the south of Kumamotojo Castle (upper right). Kumamotojo Castle is the major attraction in Kumamoto, and is easily accessible by streetcar (Kumamotojo-mae stop). The *i* Information Office is located at JR Kumamoto Station.

Places of Interest

Kumamotojo Castle. 熊本城 Kumamotojo Castle is especially famous for its delicately curved stone walls in the *musha gaeshi* style. The curve served a defensive purpose, and prevented attackers from climbing them. The defensive capabilities of the Castle were tested a few years after the Meiji Restoration when the imperial forces barricaded themselves against samurai who had been deprived of the privileges and social status they enjoyed during the feudal era. The imperial army survived for 55 days against the fierce attacks by rebels and eventually won the battle. The major buildings were burnt down in this battle. The present castle was reconstructed in 1960. There are two major entrances to the Castle. To better see the magnificent stone walls, we recom-

MAP 10 Kumamoto

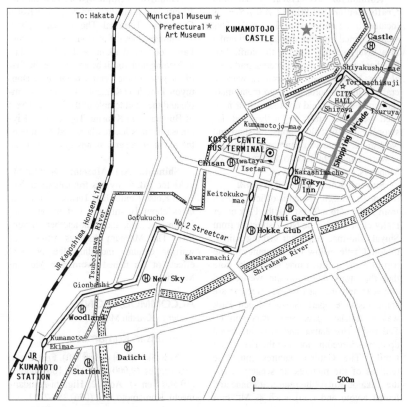

mend that you get off the street car at Kumamotojo-mae stop and use the southwestern entrance. The approach leading to the donjon, which is located on the highest point of the grounds, may help you imagine what it was like for the 17th century samurai who ascended these stone steps on their way to pledge allegiance to their feudal lord. The interior of the six-story donjon is a museum that houses historical objects related to the feudal lords who governed the Kumamoto area. The castle grounds are open from 8:30 AM to 5:30 PM (4:30 PM in winter). Admission to the grounds: 200 yen. Admission to the donjon: 300 yen. Combination ticket (500 yen) available.

Kumamoto Prefectural Traditional Crafts Center 熊本県伝統工芸センター is located to the northeast of the Castle. This well-designed museum displays local crafts in a lovely setting. Among the crafts featured are ceramics, paper lanterns, traditional toys, bamboo bath accessories, wooden crafts, knives, swords and *higo* metal inlay (gold and silver inlaid on steel, a four hundred year old craft originally used for swords). The first floor houses a shop and workshops where you can observe artisans at work. Hours: 9:00 AM to 5:00 PM. Closed Mondays. Admission: 190 yen.

Suizenji-Koen Park 水前寺公園 (optional). Suizenji-Koen is officially open from 7:00 AM to 6:00 PM, but the Park never really closes. Take the No. 2 streetcar from Shiyakusho-mae stop after visiting Kumamotojo Castle. Allow 15-20 minutes for the trip to Suizenji-Koen-mae stop. Take note that the stops there for the west-bound streetcar and the east-bound streetcar are some distance apart. Suizenji-Koen Park was established over 300 years ago by Tadatoshi Hosokawa and was improved upon by succeeding lords of the Hosokawa family. The Garden features miniature replicas of the picturesque scenery along the Tokaido Road (the road that connected feudal Kyoto and Edo), such as Mt. Fuji

and Lake Biwako. Itsumi Jinja Shrine, located in the Park, is a former Hosokawa tea house.

Downtown Kumamoto

Kumamoto has extensive shopping arcades. Two department stores — Shiroya and Tsuruya — are located in the arcades, and one more department store — Iwataya-Isetan — is located near Kotsu Center Bus Terminal. Most drinking and eating establishments are located to the northwest of these arcades.

Some Optional Attractions If You have Time:

Honmyoji Temple 本妙寺. Take the No. 12 city bus from Platform No. 36 at Kotsu Center Bus Terminal. The ride takes about 10 minutes. Get off at Honmyoji-mae stop. Fare: 160 yen. Walk in the direction the bus was going and you'll be able to see the first of the gates of the Temple compound. Honmyoji Temple is Kumamoto's grandest temple and the head temple of the Nichiren Sect of Buddhism in Kyushu. The tomb of Kiyomasa Kato is located here and a statue of the samurai general stands guard over the city.

Shimada Art Museum 島田美術館. Take the No. 6 city bus from Platform No. 36 at Kotsu Center Bus Terminal. The ride takes about 10 minutes. Get off at Jikei-Byoin-mae stop, and walk another 10 minutes. The Museum dispalys artifacts of warrior culture, including the personal effects of the famed swordsman Musashi Miyamoto.

ACCOMMODATIONS

(Refer to Kyushu Map 10)

1. Hotels in Kumamoto

New Sky Hotel (lower left). First Class. 130 singles (9,000 yen -) & 166 doubles (19,500 yen -). Add: 2, Higashi-Amidaji-machi, Kumamoto. Tel: (096) 354-2111.

Kumamoto Hotel Castle (upper right). Standard. 90 singles (10,000 yen -) & 112 doubles (17,000 yen -). Add: 4-2, Jotomachi, Kumamoto. Tel: (096) 326-3311.

Mitsui Garden Hotel Kumamoto (middle right). Business. 189 singles (7,000 yen -) & 34 doubles (13,000 yen -). Add: 1-37, Konya-Imamachi, Kumamoto. Tel: (096) 352-1131.

Chisan Hotel Kumamoto (middle center). Business. 153 singles (7,000 yen -) & 48 doubles (12,500 yen -). Add: 4-39, Karashimacho, Kumamoto. Tel: (096) 322-3911.

Kumamoto Tokyu Inn (middle right). Business. 92 singles (7,500 yen -) & 46 doubles (10,500 yen -). Add: 7-25, Shin-Shigai, Kumamoto. Tel: (096) 322-0109.

Woodland Hotel (lower left). Business. 118 singles (5,500 yen -) & 40 doubles (9,000 yen -). Add: 1-14-19, Kasuga, Kumamoto. Tel: (096) 325-6511.

2. Welcome Inn in Kumamoto

Hokke Club Kumamoto (middle center). 140 Western & 4 Japanese rooms. Add: 20-1, Toricho, Kumamoto. Tel: (096) 322-5001.

MT. ASOZAN 阿蘇山

Refer to Kyushu Map 11. Geologically, Mr. Asozan is a typical volcano chain. A 128 km (80 mile) rim of outer mountains surrounds a wide caldera valley. It is in this valley that the JR Hohi Line runs, and where approximately 100,000 people live. In the center of the valley rise the main mountains of Mt. Asozan. There are five main peaks — 1,300-1,600 m (4,300-5,200 feet) above sea level. The crater of one of them — Mt. Naka-dake — still emits steam and demonstrates the wild and mysterious powers of nature.

We suggest that you visit Mt. Asozan on

MAP 11 Mt. Asozan

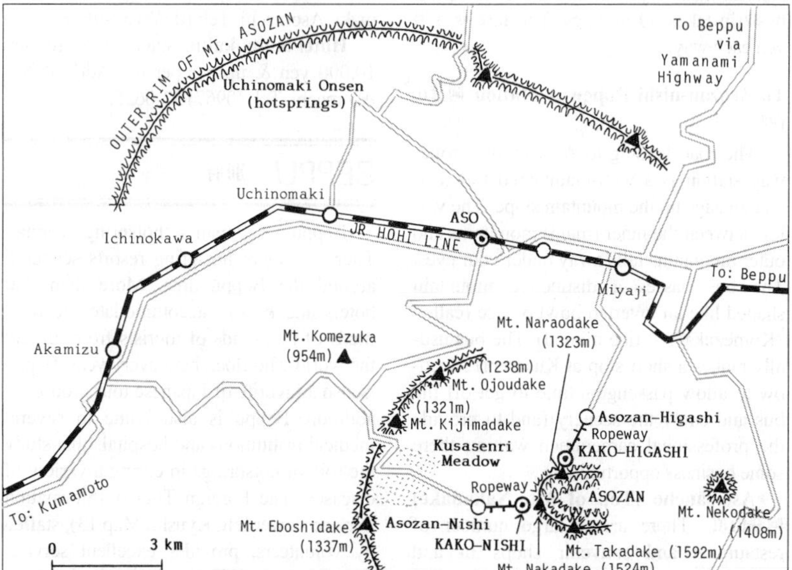

your way to Beppu from Kumamoto. If you don't follow this trans-Kyushu route, you can still visit Mt. Asozan in one day from Kumamoto (allow 7-8 hours).

One way to traverse the island is by bus operated by the Kyushu Kokusai Kanko Bus Company. The bus originates at JR Kumamoto Station, and stops at Kotsu Center Bus Terminal in downtown Kumamoto. The bus trip includes a visit to Mt. Asozan, and a drive through the scenic Yamanami mountain highway to Beppu. The ride takes about 7 hours. There are four buses daily each way. The fare is 8,280-10,180 yen (with lunch). Three additional buses are operated by the same company, but they do not visit Mt. Asozan.

The other route is by train. You follow the entire route of the JR Hohi Line, with a stop at Aso Station. A roundtrip bus trip takes you from Aso Station to Mt. Asozan. The Sanko bus (marked "Aso Sanjo-sen") runs about once every hour, and the trip takes 40 minutes from the JR Aso Station to Asozan-nishi ropeway station. The return bus trip takes 30 minutes. The fare is 570 yen each way.

To Asozan-nishi Ropeway Station 阿蘇山西駅

The road leading to Asozan-nishi ropeway station is a well-maintained toll road that zigzags up the mountain slope. The valley between the inner (main) mountains and outer mountains falls away under your eyes. The bus passes a distinctive mountain shaped like an inverted bowl of rice (called "Komezuka" — rice mound). The bus usually makes a short stop at Kusasenri Meadow to allow passengers time to get off the bus and enjoy the scenery (and to provide the professional cameramen waiting there some business opportunities).

Aso-sancho (Top of Mt. Nakadake) 阿蘇山頂. There are a large number of restaurants and souvenir shops in and around the ropeway station. The 0.9 km (0.6 mile) long ropeway operates every 8 minutes and takes visitors to the top of Mr. Nakadake in only 4 minutes (Fare: 410 yen each way). From the ropeway you can see a pleasant walking path on the lava slope. If the weather permits, and if you are a good walker, it is enjoyable to take the path on your way back to Asozan-nishi bus terminal.

The crater of Mt. Nakadake is 1.1 km (0.7 miles) wide from north to south, 0.4 km (0.25 miles) long from east to west and about 100 m (330 feet) deep. Steam billows forth from the bottom of the crater, and the pedestrian paths along its edge are dotted with shelters.

Ryokan in Uchinomaki Onsen

Note: Uchinomaki Onsen Hotsprings (upper center) is a 13-minute bus ride from Aso Station.

Hotel Kadoman. First Class. 92 rooms. 16,000 yen & up per person. Add: Uchinomaki, Asomachi. Tel: (0967) 32-0615.

Hotel Soyokaku. Standard. 83 rooms. 12,000 yen & up per person. Add: Uchinomaki, Asomachi. Tel: (0967) 32-0621.

Hotel Sannokaku. Standard. 57 rooms. 10,000 yen & up per person. Add: 482-2, Asomachi. Tel: (0967) 32-0625.

BEPPU 別府

Beppu is Japan's hotspring capital. There are eight hotspring resorts scattered around the Beppu area. More than 200 hotels and *ryokan* accommodate the hundreds of thousands of tourists from around the world who flock here every year. Beppu is also a favorite of Japanese tour groups. In addition, Beppu is also home to several medical institutions and hospitals that study the role of hotsprings in curing a variety of diseases. The Foreign Tourist Information Service (lower left, Kyushu Map 13), staffed by volunteers, provides excellent service. We recommend that you skip the information kiosk in the train station and walk to the Foreign Tourist Information Service.

Transportation to Beppu

The airport for Beppu is Oita Airport, to the northeast of Beppu. Several flights arrive daily from Tokyo, Osaka, Nagoya and Matsuyama. Airport buses connect the airport and Beppu Station (70 minutes). Hovercrafts also operate between the airport and Beppu Kokusai Kankoko Pier (45 minutes).

You can also travel to Beppu by steamship. The Kansai Steamship Company operates three daily trips each way between Osaka and Beppu via Kobe (boarding in Kobe is easier). Unfortunately, all of them are overnight trips, and pass through the beautiful scenery of the Inland Sea in the dark.

Transportation in Beppu

With some care and effort, you can get around Beppu on the local buses, the Kamenoi buses (blue). Oita buses (red) also operate in the area. The local bus platform is to your left as you exit the station. The bus platform straight ahead is for the Japanese tour buses. At Beppu Station Tourist Information kiosk you can buy a one day pass for the Kamenoi buses (a "My Beppu Free" pass) for 800 yen. The Kamenoi buses will take you to most Beppu destinations. Only Oita buses go to Takasakiyama Monkey Park. The loop bus route is pictured on Kyushu Map 12 (shaded).

BEPPU HOTSPRING BY HOTSPRING

Beppu has eight hotspring resorts — Beppu, Kankaiji, Kannawa, Hamawaki, Myoban, Kamegawa, Shibaseki and Horita. The first three have significant tourist facilities and attractions.

The main attractions in Beppu are the large hotspring baths attached to most of the area's accommodations. Most of the baths have separate facilities for men and women, but some do not. If its an issue for you, check before you go. Even though Japan is much more sophisticated about foreigners than it used to be, be aware that you might be the object of some curiosity at the baths. Most modern accommodations have private hotspring baths in each guest room, a boon for those who aren't ready for Japanese communal baths.

Beppu Hotspring

Refer to Kyushu Map 13. Located conveniently close to JR Beppu Station (middle left), Beppu Hotspring is the town's most

MAP 12   Outline of Beppu

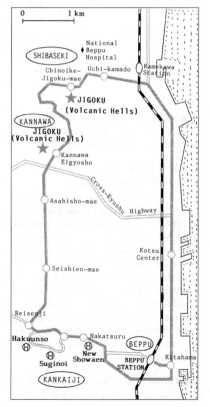

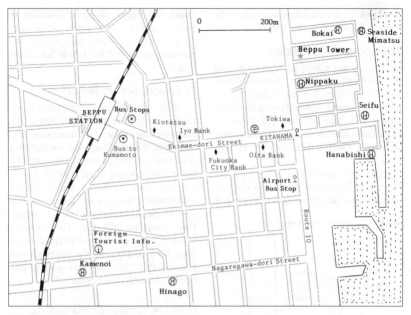

MAP 13 Downtown Beppu

developed area: its major streets are lined with souvenir shops, bars, cabarets and other night life/entertainment facilities. It is interesting to see the thousands of tourists strolling in the evening, each wearing a *yukata* robe bearing the name of his or her hotel/*ryokan*. The most popular facility in this area is **Takegawara Onsen,** where visitors can enjoy "sand baths" — attendants bury you in warm, black volcanic sand for a unique sauna experience. Hours: 9:00 AM to 6:00 PM. Admission: 600 yen. (6:00 AM to 1:00 AM for the regular hotspring baths, which cost 60 yen).

Beppu Tower (upper right) located to the east of Beppu Station, is the a 100 m (330 foot) tall TV tower. Its observatory is 55 m (180 feet) above sea level.

Cable Rakutenchi ケーブル楽天地 is a recreation complex at the western end of Beppu Hotspring (outside the map). Located in the middle of Mt Funabarayama, this hill-side amusement park contains a zoological garden, a playland, a small museum for hotspring science, and a planetarium.

Kankaiji Hotspring
(Lower left, Kyushu Map 12)

Two of the most deluxe accommodations in Beppu — New Showaen and Suginoi Hotel — are in a quiet, hilly area that overlooks the city. Kankaiji Hotspring is very popular among couples and foreign visitors, as well as deluxe group tours. Suginoi Palace, attached to Suginoi Hotel (but nevertheless open to visitors), is a huge complex of several hotspring baths, including the famous jungle bath, swimming pools, bowling alleys, theater restaurants, etc. Many Japanese tourists spend a full day at leisure here.

Kannawa and Shibaseki Hotsprings

Kannawa Hotspring (upper left, Kyushu

Map 12) is famous for its "Jigoku" volcanic "hells." Take the No. 16 Kamenoi bus from the Station to Kannawa Eigyosho stop (middle center, Kyushu Map 14) to visit most of the "hells," and from there get back on the No. 16 bus to go to the Chinoike and Tatsumaki hells. Get off at the Chinoike-Jigoku-mae stop.

Kannawa (and adjacent Shibaseki) has more than 10 hells, representing different volcanic activities, and is laid out with an eye to the tourist trade. The nine most famous are indicated on Kyushu Map 14 with stars. They are: Chinoike Jigoku (Blood Pool Hell—a bright red pool, thanks to iron oxide); Tatsumaki Jigoku (Tornado Hell—a geyser); Yama Jigoku (Mountain Hell—a mudspring); Kamado Jigoku (Oven Hell—steam emerging from rocks); Umi Jigoku (Sea Hell—clear green, bubbling water); Shiraike Jigoku (White Pool Hell—

white mud beneath steaming waters); Oniyama Jigoku (Devil's Mountain Hell—home to hundreds of crocodiles); Kinryu Jigoku (Golden Dragon Hell—spouting steam); and Bozu Jigoku (Monk's Hell—bubbling mud ponds). Admission to the hells is 300 yen each. A 1,500 yen combination ticket will gain you admission to all but the last. Hours: 8:00 AM to 5:00 PM. The area also has ten public baths and charming shops and *ryokan* along its narrow winding streets. Take the No. 16 bus back to the Station. If you want to make this trip in reverse, start out from the Station on the No. 26 bus.

Takasakiyama Monkey Park 高崎山自然公園

Mt. Takasakiyama, a 628 m (2,090 foot) tall peak located between Beppu and Oita Stations, is home to approximately 1,600 wild monkeys. Ten minutes by Oita bus from Beppu Station.

Originally, the monkeys conducted frequent raids on area farms. To keep them away from their crops, the farmers began feeding the monkeys. The Monkey Park, which is now quite a tourist attraction, was the eventual result. The monkeys are divided into three groups: each has its own leader and jealously protects its territory. The Monkey Park has a central feeding area, and during the morning, each of the groups makes a separate visit there. The visits are the highlight for tourists, and offer great photo opportunities.

ACCMMODATIONS
(Refer to Kyushu Map 13)

1. Beppu Hotspring

Hotel Shiragiku (5 minute walk to the west from Beppu Station). First Class. 140 rooms. 15,000 yen & up per person. Add: 16-36, Uedanoyu-machi, Beppu. Tel: (0977) 21-2111.

Kamenoi Hotel (lower left). First Class.

MAP 14 Jigoku—Volcanic Hells

31 Western & 57 Japanese rooms. 15,000 yen & up per person. Add: 5-17, Chuo-cho, Beppu. Tel: (0977) 22-3301.

Hanabishi Hotel (middle right). First Class. 119 rooms. 15,000 yen & up per person. Add: 2-14-29, Kitahama, Beppu. Tel: (0977) 22-1211.

Hotel Seifu (middle right). First Class. 193 rooms. 15,000 yen & up per person. Add: 2-12-21, Kitahama, Beppu. Tel: (0977) 24-3939.

Hotel Bokai (upper right). Standard. 65 rooms. 13,000 yen & up per person. Add: 3-8-7, Kitahama, Beppu. Tel: (0977) 22-1241.

Hinago Hotel (lower center). Standard. 124 rooms. 13,000 yen & up per person.

Add: 7-24, Akibacho, Beppu. Tel: (0977) 22-1111.

Seaside Hotel Mimatsu (upper right). Standard. 46 rooms. 12,000 yen & up per person. Add: 3-14-17, Kitahama, Beppu. Tel: (0977) 23-4301.

2. Kankaiji Hotspring

New Showaen (lower center, Kyushu Map 12). Deluxe. 33 rooms. 25,000 yen & up per person. Add: 2178, Minami-Tateishi, Beppu. Tel: (0977) 22-3211.

Suginoi Hotel (lower left, Kyushu Map 12). First Class. 88 Western, 28 Japanese & 467 combination rooms. 20,000 yen & up per person. Add: 2272, Minami-Tateishi, Beppu. Tel: (0977) 24-1141.

Southern Kyushu

MIYAZAKI 宮崎

The development of Miyazaki followed the Meiji Restoration, when the city was chosen as the capital of Miyazaki Prefecture. Miyazaki now has a population of 287,000. Palm trees line the city's major streets, and Miyazaki has a pleasant subtropical atmosphere. Miyazaki is a good base of operations for exploring Aoshima, Obi and other destinations south of the city.

Downtown Miyazaki

Refer to Kyushu Map 15. Downtown Miyazaki is to the west of JR Miyazaki Station. *Transportation Note: Miyako City Bus Terminal near JR Minami-Miyazaki (off the map, south of the Oyodogawa River) is the central point of the city's bus transportation system. You can take a direct express bus to Ebino-Kogen Plateau from this station. See Kirishima section below.*

Places of Interest

Miyazaki Jingu Shrine 宮崎神宮 (upper center). Miyazaki Jingu Shrine is just a 15-minute walk from JR Miyazaki Jingu Station. The Shrine was dedicated to Emperor Jimmu, a rather mythological figure who established the Yamato imperial court. Miyazaki Prefectural Museum is located in the clear, wide grounds of the Shrine. The Museum displays historic and archeological objects of the area. Hours: 9:00 AM to 5:00 PM. Closed on Mondays. Admission: 200 yen.

Heiwadai-Koen Park 平和台公園 (north of the map). A 15- minute walk from Miyazaki Jingu Shrine. This spacious garden was constructed in 1940 to celebrate the 2,600th anniversary of the mythological foundation of the nation of Japan. The neatly maintained gardens feature ancient clay images (*haniwa*).

ACCOMMODATIONS
(Refer to Kyushu Map 15)

1. Hotels in Miyazaki

Sun Hotel Phoenix (15 minutes by taxi from Miyazaki Station). First Class. 263 rooms. Double (24,000 yen -). Add: 3083, Hamayama, Miyazaki. Tel: (0985) 39-3131.

Seaside Hotel Phoenix (15 minutes by taxi from Miyazaki Station). Standard. 173

MAP 15 Miyazaki

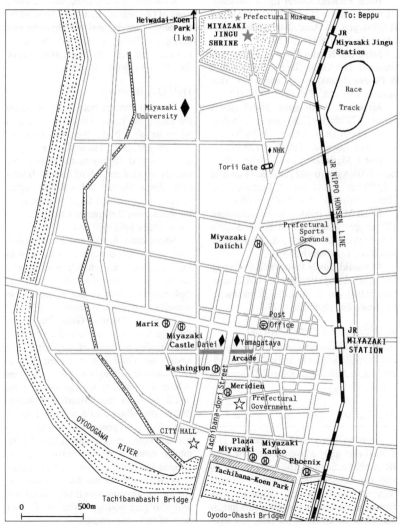

rooms. Single (11,500 yen -) & Double (20,000 yen -). Add: 3083, Hamayama, Miyazaki. Tel: ;(0985) 39-1111.

Hotel Plaza Miyazaki (lower center). First Class. 164 rooms. Double (18,500 yen -). Add: 1-1, Kawaharacho, Miyazaki. Tel: (0985) 27-1111.

Hotel Phoenix (lower right). Standard. 92 rooms. Single (11,500 yen -) & Double (19,000 yen -). Add: 2-1-1, Matsuyama, Miyazaki. Tel: (0985) 23-6111.

Miyazaki Kanko Hotel (lower center). Standard. 180 rooms. Single (10,000 yen -) & Double (14,000 yen -). Add: 1-1-1, Matsuyama, Miyazaki. Tel: (0985) 27-1212.

Miyazaki Washington Hotel (lower center). 173 singles (7,500 yen -) & 35 doubles (13,000 yen -). Add: 3-1-1, Tachibanadori-Nishi, Miyazaki. Tel: (0985) 28-9111.

Hotel Meridien (lower center). Business. 100 singles (6,600 yen -) & 74 doubles (12,000 yen -). Add: 3-1-11, Tachibanadori-Higashi, Miyazaki. Tel: (0985) 26-6666.

Hotel Marix (middle center). Business. 183 singles (5,000 yen -) & 44 doubles (8,500 yen -). Add: 15-8, Chigusacho, Miyazaki. Tel: (0985) 28-6161.

Miyazaki Castle Hotel (middle center). Business. 92 singles (4,500 yen -) & 23 doubles (9,000 yen -). Add: 5-7, Chigusacho, Miyazaki. Tel: (0985) 28-8123.

2. Welcome Inn in Miyazaki

Miyazaki Leman Hotel (10 minutes by taxi from JR Miyazaki Station). 218 Western rooms. Add: 1-5-2, Kyozuka, Miyazaki. Tel: (0985) 53-1131.

AOSHIMA 青島

Aoshima (lower right, Kyushu Map 1) is a small islet, only a five-minute walk from JR Aoshima Station. The islet, connected with the mainland by a bridge, is covered with subtropical plants. Aoshima Jinja Shrine, an impressive vermilion structure, is located in the center of the islet. The shallow, rocky shore surrounding the islet has eroded into a unique formation called the "Devil's Washboard."

OBI 飫肥

Kyushu's "Little Kyoto," the old castle town of Obi, was the traditional home of the Ito family, which ruled the Miyazaki area during the Tokugawa Era. Obi is a small town and the best way to get around is on foot. Refer to Kyushu Map 16.

Half Day Itinerary

Turn left from the train station and cross the Shuyagawa River, and at the intersection where there's a Post Office, turn right and walk straight ahead. The road will run uphill a bit and lead directly to the steps of the heavily wooded grounds of **Tanoue Hachiman Jinja Shrine** 田上八幡神社 (upper center). After the first flight of steps up to the Shrine, you'll encounter a huge tree with a mini-shrine built right into it.

Shintokudo 振徳道 was established in 1801 as the official school for the sons of local samurai. The school's most famous graduate was Jutaro Komura, a Meiji Era diplomat. The entrance gate to Shintokudo is itself an impressive structure.

Proceed to **Otemon Gate.** The size of the huge two-story gate will give you some idea of what the scale of the Castle must have been. Once you've passed through Otemon Gate, turn right and go up the steps behind the wall. At the top of the steps you'll come to the **Historical Museum** 歴史資料館. Obijo Castle was home to the Ito family for 14 generations, and this well-laid-out Museum is a sort of attic for Ito family items. It displays swords, armor, kimono and castle utensils, such as lacquer trays. When you pay the 300 yen admission fee for the Museum you'll get a ticket that will also gain you admission to all other parts of the Castle grounds.

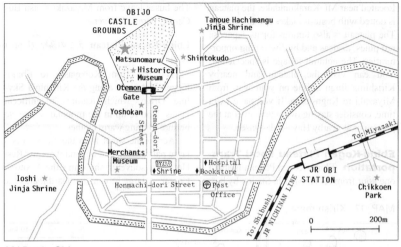

MAP 16   Obi

Up the stairway to the left is **Matsuno-maru**松尾ノ丸, an exact reproduction of the residence of the Ito family. You can walk all through this graceful building, and the bilingual brochure distributed at the Castle Grounds explains the function of each of its rooms.

When you leave Matsunomaru, walk in the opposite direction from the Historical Museum, and climb the steps to the top of the **Castle Ruins** 飫肥城址. The trees here are majestic and the view of the mountains in the distance quite spectacular.

As you leave the Castle Grounds through Otemon Gate, **Yoshokan** 予章館 will be on your right. The ticket from the Castle Grounds will gain you admission here as well. You can walk all around this typical Obi scholarly samurai residence. Before you leave, be sure to explore the garden, which is particularly lush in spring and summer.

Walk along Otemon-dori Street until you get back to the main street. This is the **Honmachi** 本町 section of Obi, traditional home of the merchants of the area. The old neighborhood was destroyed when the road was widened in 1980, but several of the modern

merchants had their homes reconstructed in the original style. One of the finest old buildings has become the **Merchants Museum** 商家資料館 . This large, two-story white building has a wooden first floor exterior. It was built by Gohei Yamamoto, a lumber merchant, in 1866. The Museum displays utensils, equipment and furniture of the old Honmachi merchant families.

If you have time:

Ioshi Jinja Shrine 五百羅神社 (lower left) has a lovely garden and a peaceful pond. Behind the Shrine is a cemetery with Ito family graves.

Chikkoen Park 竹香園 (lower right). The entrance to this park is on the east side of the train station. Follow the path up the hill. It's an extremely peaceful place — the only sound you can hear here is the creaking of the bamboo trees.

KIRISHIMA   霧島

Ebino-Kogen Plateau is located on the border between Miyazaki and Kagoshima Prefectures. Refer to Kyushu Map 17.

Located near Mt. Karakunidake, the plateau is dotted with beautiful lakes and hotsprings. The plateau is also famous for its Japanese red pines, azaleas and bird watching opportunities. The autumn foliage is spectacular. You can visit the plateau and nearby Kirishima Jingu Shrine on your way from Miyazaki to Kagoshima. If you have extra time, consider staying overnight either at the plateau or at nearby Hayashida-Onsen.

Ebino-Kogen Plateau Local Transportation Ebino-Kogen Plateau is about one hour from JR Kobayashi Station by bus.

The buses leave from Miyazaki Kotsu Bus Center. Fare: 1,200 yen.

Ebino-Kogen Plateau えびの高原 (Upper center)

The trip from Kobayashi to Ebino-Kogen Plateau is along the Kirishima Skyline Drive, which features magnificent vistas. You're up in the mountains here, so be sure to bring warm clothes.

Across the street from the bus stop is a large parking lot, and beyond it are the Rest House, a souvenir shop and the Visitors' Center. A large brown signboard marks the

MAP 17 Kirishima

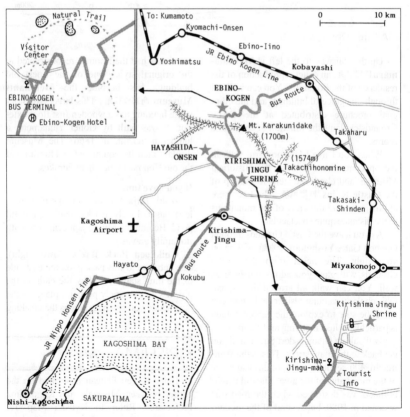

entrance to **Ebino-Kogen Natural Trail** えびの高原散策路. A leisurely hike along this circular path will take less than 2 hours. You'll see three beautiful crater lakes on this walk, and the path is dotted with observatory platforms. When the path goes uphill, there are steps to ease the way. The first of the three ponds is Byakushi-Ike. The second, Rokkannon-miike, the largest of the three, is famous for its magnificent cobalt blue color. The third pond, a twenty-minute hike from Rokkannon-miike, is Fudoike. On your way back to the Visitors' Center and Bus Center, you'll pass sulphurous hotsprings that are a constant reminder of the volcanic origins of the topography of this plateau. You'll also pass a field of *susuki* pampas grass that, thanks to the mineral content of the groundwater, takes on an orange-red tint in the fall.

In summer months, ambitious hikers can climb to the top of Mt. Karakunidake in about one hour.

Ryokan in Ebino-Kogen

Ebino-Kogen Hotel (lower left, upper insert map). Standard. 18 Western & 27 Japanese rooms. 15,000 yen & up per person. Add: 1495, Suenaga, Ebino. Tel: (0984) 33-1155

To Kirishima Jingu Shrine

If you travel to Kagoshima on a Hayashida Bus from Ebino-Kogen Plateau, you should make a stop on the way at Kirishima Jingu Shrine. The trip between Ebino-Kogen Plateau and Kirishima Jingu Shrine is via Hayashida-Onsen, and the ride takes about 60 minutes. As the bus descends from the Plateau, there are great views of the mountain peaks above and of Sakurajima and Kagoshima Bay below. You can also catch occasional glimpses of plumes of steam escaping from the hotsprings that dot the region.

Hayashida-Onsen 林田温泉

Hayashida-Onsen is the largest hotspring resort in Kirishima, and is located between Ebino-Kogen Plateau and Kirishima Jingu Shrine. If you are a hotspring enthusiast and have an extra day, you may wish to overnight here.

Hotel in Hayashida Onsen

Hotel Hayashida Onsen. First class. 448 rooms. 15,000 yen & up per person. Add: 3958, Takachiho, Kagoshima Prefecture. Tel: (0995) 78-2911

Kirishima Jingu Shrine 霧島神宮 (Middle center)

When you get off the bus at Kirishima-Jingu-mae, recross the bridge the bus crosses just before the stop, and climb the steps to the Shrine. Set among Japanese cedars, this lavish shrine is dedicated to *Ninigi-no-Mikoto*, grandson of the Japanese sun goddess *Amaterasu-Omikami*. In addition to the fantastic carvings of flowers and animals on the main building, the Shrine also features a magnificent view of Sakurajima. The maple leaves in the fall are absolutely breathtaking.

KAGOSHIMA 鹿児島

Kyushu's southernmost city, Kagoshima, is situated on a lovely bay. The city's most famous feature is Sakurajima, the active volcano located on the bay. Southern Kyushu is an area rich in tourist attractions, and Kagoshima is its administrative, commercial and cultural center. The people of this area are as warm and sunny as the climate. Kagoshima, the capital of Kagoshima Prefecture, has a population of 529,000.

Outline of the City

Refer to Kyushu Map 18. Kagoshima's downtown area is centered around the Tenmonkan streetcar stop. The arcades (shaded on the map) are crowded with shops and restaurants. This a pleasant place to take an evening stroll. The backstreets off the arcades feature a seamier sort of establishment. Nishi-Kagoshima (rather than Kagoshima) is the main JR station, and the terminus of long distance trains (lower left). The *i* Information Office is located in front of JR Nishi-Kagoshima Station.

Transportation in Kagoshima

Kagoshima is served by the streetcar line shown on the map. During rush hour, the streetcars run as frequently as once every 4 minutes; at other times, they run about once every 15 minutes. You can also get around to many of the city's sightseeing attractions on foot. Several bus companies operate lines in the city and to outlying areas.

Places of Interest

St. Francis Xavier Church ザビエル教会 (middle center) (optional). St. Francis Xavier was among the first European visitors to Kagoshima. He arrived in August 1549 and stayed for ten months, after Takahisa Shimazu, the Lord of Satsuma, granted him permission to preach in the area.

Terukuni Jinja Shrine 照国神社 (upper center) (optional). A 6-8 minute walk from Xavier Memorial and Church. This Shrine is dedicated to the memory of Nariakira Shi-

MAP 18 Kagoshima

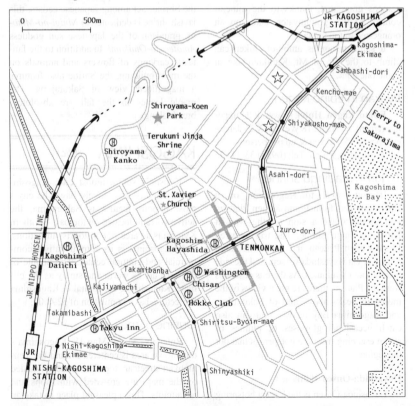

mazu (1809-1858), the Satsuma Lord who introduced Western technology to southern Kyushu before the Meiji Restoration made such pioneering fashionable.

Shiroyama-Koen Park 城山公園 (upper center) (optional). When you leave the Shrine, turn right. Follow the waterway to the corner, and turn right again. Follow the street back to the foot of the mountain, where you'll find a path on your right that will take you up to the Shiroyama-Koen Park Observatory. It's a relatively hard 15-minute climb. The Observatory is at the site of a 14th century castle, and has a fantastic view of Sakurajima, Kagoshima Bay, and, on clear day, Mt. Kaimondake, Kyushu's "Little Mt. Fuji." If you plan to visit the Isoyama Recreation Ground Observatory above Iso-Teien Garden (described next), a trip to Shiroyama-Koen Park will probably be redundant.

Iso-Teien Garden 磯庭園
(Upper left, Kyushu Map 19)

About a ten-minute ride from the Kagoshima Station stop (25 minutes from Nishi-Kagoshima) on the Hayashida Bus line, Iso-Teien Garden was laid out in 1660 by Mitsuhisa Shimazu, the 19th Lord of Satsuma, whose family ruled this area for 700 years. Hours: 8:30 AM to 5:30 PM Admission: 500 yen.

Just past the entrance to the Garden is a complex that contains a restaurant, a snack shop and a Rest House. Keep going, and you'll reach the Main Villa, the Shimazu family home, which has a lovely view of Kagoshima Bay. You can walk around the villa but can't enter. Wander through the rest of the garden: there's a lovely pond, a miniature waterfall, a plum grove, a bamboo grove, a small shrine, and *Kyokusui-no-Niwa*, the site of noble poetry-composing parties. Between the Rest House and the Shimazu Villa there's a ropeway that will take you to the top of the mountain behind the Garden in just 3 minutes.

The view from **Isoyama Recreation Ground** 磯山リクリエーショングランド (optional) at the summit is unparalleled, with spectacular vistas of Sakurajima and Kagoshima Bay. There's an amusement park-type playland, with go-carts and other rides, but there's also a lovely formal garden and a natural area where you can stroll (after crossing the Kurenaibashi Suspension Bridge).

Shoko Shuseikan Historical Museum 尚古集成館 (optional). Your ticket from Iso-Teien Garden will gain you free admission here, where the hours are the same as at the Garden. The 28th Lord of Satsuma, Nariakira Shimazu, became fascinated with the technology of the West, and built an industrial complex here in the middle of the 19th century, where 1,200 employees manufactured guns, swords, farm implements and Western-style glassware and ceramics. The Museum tells the story of this enterprise and displays some of its products, along with items of historical interest related to the history of the Shimazu family. The Museum has few signs in English, but does give visitors a good idea of the fervor with which the Japanese adopted Western technology and made it their own.

Sakurajima 桜島 (Kyushu Map 19)

If you have extra time, you can take the ferry to Sakurajima, rent a bike and cycle around this volcanic island. If your time is limited, the best way to see Sakurajima is on one of the regularly scheduled Japanese sightseeing buses. The 3-hour "B Course" tour operates twice a day, at 9:30 AM and 1:30 PM, and costs 1,700 yen. The tour bus makes stops at an observation platform and Satsuma-yaki pottery kiln. The tour features great views of the volcano, the bay and the island's eerie lava fields.

We recommend that you get an early start and take the morning tour. Take the No. 1 or the No. 2 streetcar to Sanbashi-dori stop (upper right, Kyushu Map 18), and

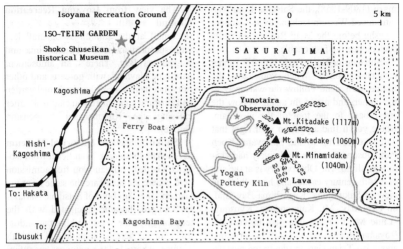

MAP 19 Kagoshima Suburbs

walk toward the water. The block between the street where the streetcars run and the port is a wholesale food distribution center, and, in the morning hours, an open-air market. You'll walk through stands selling all sorts of fish, pickles, nuts, beans, flowers and packaged foods. With an early start, you'll have time to linger here and enjoy yourself.

If you plan to take the 9:30 AM "B Course" tour, you should be on the ferry by 9:00 AM. The ferry entrance is at the end of the street — just walk directly on. The ferry ride takes about 15 minutes, and the 100 yen fare is collected at the Sakurajima terminal at the end of the ride. At Sakurajima, go down the stair to the platform for the regularly scheduled sightseeing buses. The clerk at the ticket window will direct you to the "B Course" tour bus.

Before the 1990 eruption of Mt. Fugendake of Unzen, Sakurajima was considered the most active of Japan's major live volcanos. Sakurajima used to be an island, but its great 1914 eruption created a peninsula that now links it to the mainland on the eastern side of Kagoshima Bay. The Sakurajima

volcano actually has three cones — Mt. Kitadake (1,117 m or 3,689 feet), Mt. Nakadake (1,060 m or 3,533 feet) and Mt. Minamidake (1,040 m or 3,466 feet), of which only the last is still active. Sakurajima is also famous for its tiny natsu-mikan (Japanese mandarin oranges) and its giant daikon (white radishes). Daikon as large as 1.5 m (5 feet) in diameter have reputedly grown here!

The view from the observation platform where the bus makes its first stop is a great one — on clear days you can see Mt. Kaimondake, a graceful cone-shaped extinct volcano, to the south, and Mt. Kirishimayama to the north. The next stop, at the *Satsuma-yaki* kiln, is a rather long one. You'll have a chance to wander through the workshop and observe the potters at work. *Satsuma-yaki* comes in two varieties: one has a plain dark brown glaze, and the other a white glaze decorated with colorful floral patterns. After the stop at the kiln, the bus drives through the vast lava field created by the 1914 explosion of the volcano, which sent three billion tons of debris cascading down from the peaks. The rocks, of all sizes and shapes, create a sort of lunar landscape. The bus returns you to the ferry pier at the end of the tour.

ACCOMMODATIONS
(Refer to Kyushu Map 18)

1. Hotels in Kagoshima

Shiroyama Kanko Hotel (upper left). First Class. 144 singles (10,500 yen -) & 249 doubles (18,500 yen -). Add: 41-1, Shin-Shoincho, Kagoshima. Tel: (0992) 24-2211.

Kagoshima Tokyu Hotel (10 minutes by taxi from Nishi-Kagoshima Station). First Class. 64 singles (11,000 yen -) & 124 doubles (18,500 yen -). Add: 22-1, Kamoike-Shinmachi. Kagoshima. Tel: (0992) 57-2411.

Kagoshima Hayashida Hotel (middle center). Standard. 119 singles (8,000 yen -) & 62 doubles (14,000 yen -). Add: 12-22, Higashi-Sengokucho, Kagoshima. Tel: (0992) 24-4111.

Kagoshima Washington Hotel (middle center). Business. 172 singles (7,500 yen -) & 58 doubles (14,500 yen -). Add: 12-1, Yamanokuchicho, Kagoshima. Tel: (0992) 25-6111.

JR FARES BETWEEN MAJOR STATIONS IN THE KYUSHU REGION
1. When only local trains run between certain cities, the fares are based on local trains.
2. Other city pairs are based on limited express trains.

To/From	Hakata	Kumamoto	Nishi-Kagoshima	Kokura	Beppu	Miyazaki
Hakata		3,690 yen (118.4 km)	7,710 yen (317.1 km)		5,650 yen (189.3 km)	
Isahaya	4,000 yen (129 km)					
Nagasaki	4,620 yen (153.9 km)					
Misumi		640 yen (36.5 km)				
Beppu	5,650 yen (189.3 km)	5,030 yen (160.1 km)	8,230 yen (345 km)	4,000 yen (120. 8 km)		5,850 yen (219.1 km)
Nishi-Kagoshima	7,710 yen (317.1 km)	5,340 yen (198. 7 km)		10,080 yen (465.8 km)	8,230 yen (345 km)	4,000 yen (125.9 km)
Ibusuki			930 yen (50. 3 km)			
Miyazaki			4,000 yen (125.9 km)	7,920 yen (339.9 km)	5,850 yen (219.1 km)	
Obi						720 yen (42.4 km)
Aso		2,030 yen (49.9 km)			3,690 yen (110.2 km)	

Kagoshima Chisan Hotel (middle center). Business. 168 singles (7,500 yen -) & 28 doubles (14,500 yen -). Add: 2-7, Yamanokuchicho, Kagoshima. Tel: (0992) 24-3211.

Kagoshima Tokyu Inn (lower left). Business. 112 singles (7,500 yen -) & 76 doubles (12,500 yen -). Add: 5-1, Chuocho, Kagoshima. Tel: (0992) 56-0109.

2. Welcome Inns in Kagoshima

Hokke Club Kagoshima (lower center). Business. 108 Western rooms. Add: 3-22, Yamanokuchicho, Kagoshima. Tel: (0992) 26-0011.

Nakazono Ryokan (3 minutes by taxi from Kagoshima Station). 15 Japanese rooms. Add: 1-18, Yauicho, Kagoshima. Tel: (0992) 26-5125.

Amami Ryokan (7 minute walk from Nishi-Kagoshima Station). 14 Japanese rooms. Add: 12-19, Uenosonocho, Kagoshima. Tel: (0992) 57-7397.

OKINAWA 沖縄

Isolated in the South China Sea, away from the main Japanese islands, Okinawa

MAP 20 Outline of Okinawa

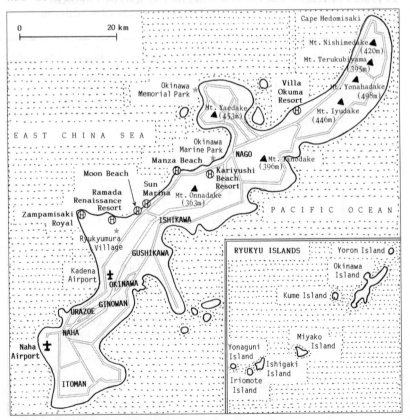

was long an independent kingdom. It was not officially incorporated into Japan until after the Meiji Restoration. When the American occupation after World War II came to an end in the rest of Japan, Okinawa remained under U.S. control, and was used as a U.S. Far East strategic military base, especially during the Korean and Vietnamese wars. Returned to Japanese control in 1972, Okinawa embarked on an ambitious development plan. In 1975, Okinawa was host to the World Ocean Exposition. Since then, capitalizing on its wonderful subtropical weather, Okinawa has developed many ocean resorts.

Okinawa is popular among Japanese, but is still seldom incorporated in the itineraries of foreign visitors to Japan, except for U.S. military personnel and their families.

The *i* Information Office is located in Naha Airport.

Places of Interest

Naha 那覇 (lower left, Kyushu Map 20; also refer to Kyushu Map 21), with a population of 308,000, is Okinawa's capital and largest city. Kokusai-dori (International Street) Boulevard is the main street of Naha. Tsuboya pottery, which was developed during the time of the Ryukyu Kingdom, is the area's representative handicraft, and about 10 kilns preserve this tradition.

Shuri 首里, in the northeastern corner of Naha, was once the capital of the Ryukyu Kingdom, and is now the cultural center of Okinawa. Shurei-no-Mon Gate is from the former Shurijo Castle, the symbol of Okinawa. Okinawa Prefectural Museum displays historical and cultural objects of the Ryukyu Kingdom. Shurijo Castle is a 1992 reconstruction of the power base of the former Ryukyu Kingdom.

Okinawa 沖縄 (middle left, Kyushu Map 20), the second largest city, was developed by U.S. military forces, and still has a large population of American and other foreign residents. Very different from other Japanese cities.

Moon Beach and **Manza Beach** are two typical modern Okinawa ocean resorts. **Ryukyumura Village** 琉球村 is an amusement park, and displays 5,000 *habu* (poisonous snakes). **Okinawa Marine Park** 沖縄海洋公園 has ocean sports facilities and a submarine observatory. You can see beautiful tropical fish and corals.

Ocean Expo Memorial Park 海洋博記念公園 (upper center, Kyushu Map 20) was

MAP 21　Naha and Shari

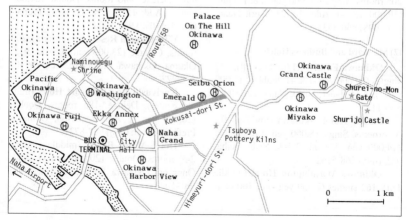

built on the 1975 World Expo site. The park contains an aquarium, a marine museum, an ocean sports complex, a playland, etc.

ACCOMMODATIONS

1. Hotels in Naha (Refer to Kyushu Map 21)

(1) Deluxe and First Class

Palace on The Hill Okinawa (upper center). 145 rooms. Double (26,000 yen -). Add: 165, Uenoya, Naha. Tel: (098) 864-1111.

Naha Tokyu Hotel (15 minutes by taxi from Naha Airport). 208 rooms. Single (18,000 yen -) & Double (24,500 yen -). Add: 1002, Ameku, Naha. Tel: (098) 868-2151.

Okinawa Harbor View Hotel (lower left). 334 rooms. Single (16,000 yen -) & Double (23,000 yen -). Add: 2-46, Senzaki, Naha. Tel: (098) 853-2111.

Okinawa Grand Castle (middle right). 340 rooms. Single (16,000 yen -) & Double (22,500 yen -). Add: Yamakawacho, Shuri, Naha. Tel: (098) 886-5454.

Okinawa Miyako Hotel (middle right). First Class. 295 rooms. Single (11,000 yen -) & Double (18,000 yen -). Add: 40, Matsukawa, Naha. Tel: (098) 887-1111.

Hotel Seibu Orion (middle center). 205 rooms. Single (10,000 yen -) & Double (19,000 yen -). Add: 1-2-21, Anri, Naha. Tel: (098) 866-5533.

(2) Standard and Business Hotels

Okinawa Fuji Hotel (middle left). 137 singles (10,000 yen -) & 41 doubles (15,000 yen -). Add: 1-6-1, Nishi, Naha. Tel: (098) 868-1118.

Pacific Hotel Okinawa (middle left). 373 rooms. Single (8,000 yen -) & Double (14,000 yen -). Add: 3-5-1, Nishi, Naha. Tel: (098) 868-5162.

Okinawa Washington Hotel (middle left). 162 singles (7,500 yen -) & 100 doubles (15,000 yen -). Add: 2-32-1, Kume, Naha. Tel: (098) 869-2511.

Naha Grand Hotel (middle center). 55 singles (6,500 yen -) & 75 doubles (10,500 yen -). Add: 1-5-7, Matsuo, Naha. Tel: (098) 862-6161.

Hotel Emerald (middle center). 64 singles (5,500 yen -) & 20 doubles (10,500 yen -). Add: 1-2-25, Anri, Naha. Tel: (098) 862-8001.

Hotel Ekka Annex (middle left). 42 singles (6,500 yen -) & 86 doubles (9,000 yen -). Add: 1-3-11, Kumochi, Naha. Tel: (098) 861-1181.

2. Hotels in Other Okinawa Destinations (Refer to Kyushu Map 20)

Ramada Renaissance Resort (middle left). Deluxe. 362 rooms. Double (34,000 yen -). Add: Onnason, Okinawa Prefecture. Tel: (098) 965-0707.

Sun Marina Hotel (middle center). 196 rooms. Double (28,000 yen -). Add: Onnason, Okinawa Prefecture. Tel: (098) 965-2222.

Manza Beach Hotel (middle center). 401 rooms. Double (27,000 yen -). Add: Onnason, Okinawa Prefecture. Tel: (098) 965-1211.

Zampamisaki Royal Hotel (middle left). Deluxe. 486 rooms. Double (24,000 yen -). Add: 1575, Uza, Okinawa Prefecture. Tel:(098) 958-5000.

Villa Okuma Resort (upper right). 200 rooms. Cottage (23,000 yen -). Add: 913, Okuma, Okinawa Prefecture. Tel: (0980) 41-2222.

Kariyushi Beach Resort Hotel (middle center). Deluxe. 185 rooms. Double (20,000 yen -). Add: Onnason, Okinawa Prefecture. Tel: (098) 967-8731.

Hotel Moon Beach (middle center). 249 rooms. Double (20,000 yen -). Add: Onnason, Okinawa Prefecture. Tel: (098) 965-1020.

HOKKAIDO REGION

北海道

Hokkaido is Japan's northernmost island. Its cold weather, which, at least early on, made it unsuitable for Japanese agriculture, also protected it from influence of the central government. Traditionally, it was the province of the Ainu, aborigines with many cultural similarities to Native Americans. Sadly, their historic destiny has also been similar to that of Native Americans.

When the Matsumae Clan asserted the authority of the central government (at that time, the Shogunate) here in the 16th century, its influence only extended to a small southern part of the island. The balance of the vast undeveloped areas of the island remained the home of the Ainu, who lived in small autonomous hunter and gatherer family groups.

The development or colonization of Hokkaido got started in earnest under the auspices of the new imperial government after the Meiji Restoration of 1868. A Hokkaido government was established first in Hakodate in 1869, and then, in 1871, in Sapporo, which at the time was newly developed.

Since then, Hokkaido has been Japan's "new frontier." The island accounts for 22% of the total land of the Japanese archipelago, but is home to only 5% of the nation's total population. Hokkaido offers magnificent natural wonders, including mysterious caldera lakes, wild forests, volcanic mountains, and hotsprings, along with a vigorous frontier atmosphere. If your primary interests are Japanese culture and history, Hokkaido does not have much to offer in the traditional sense. Hokkaido's historical buildings are Western-style and date from the 19th century; they are not likely to prove particularly exotic for foreign visitors. We recommend Hokkaido for nature lovers. Our description is divided into two areas — Southwestern and Central Eastern. Refer to Hokkaido Map 1.

SOUTHWESTERN HOKKAIDO

Southwestern Hokkaido features two major cities — Sapporo and Hakodate — and the hotspring resorts of Noboribetsu and Lake Toyako. This area provides a living history demonstration of the development of Hokkaido, and displays its natural beauty in Shinkotsu-Toya National Park. Thanks to easy access from the main island of Honshu, this area attracts the majority of Japanese tourists who visit Hokkaido. We suggest the following five day (four night) itinerary for this region:

Day 1. Arrive in Sapporo

You can easily fly from Tokyo or Osaka to Sapporo (middle left, Hokkaido Map 1). If you travel by rail from Tokyo to Sapporo, it will take more than 12 hours — the JR Tohoku Shinkansen to Morioka (three and a half hours), a limited express train on the JR Tohoku Honsen Line to Aomori (two and a half hours), a rapid service train on the JR Kaikyo Line to Hakodate (two and a half hours) via the Seikan Undersea Tunnel (lower left), and then a limited express train to Sapporo (three and a half hours). It might well be too tiring to do all of this in one day. We suggest that you visit other Tohoku destinations (such as Sendai or Hiraizumi) on

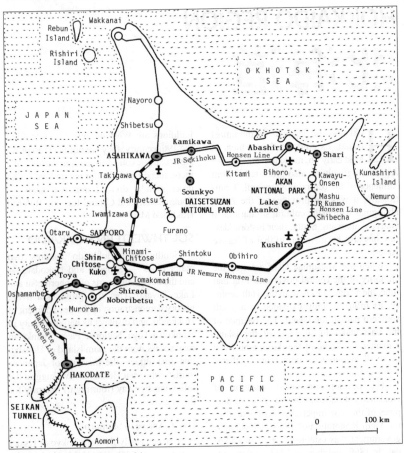

MAP 1 Outline of Hokkaido

the way to Sapporo, and spread the train trips out over two days.

Day 2. Sapporo
Day 3. Sapporo/Shiraoi/Lake Toyako
(Toya Station; middle left)
Day 4. Lake Toyako/Hakodate (lower left)
Day 5. Leave Hakodate for your next destination.

If your time is limited, you can skip sightseeing in Hakodate and continue your train ride to Honshu.

If you have one more day, you can include Noboribetsu as suggested below. The itinerary that follows is recommended only for those who enjoy *onsen* (hotsprings).

Day 1. Arrive Sapporo
Day 2. Sapporo
Day 3. Sapporo/Shiraoi/Noboribetsu
Day 4. Noboribetsu/Lake Toyako
Day 5. Lake Toyako/Hakodate, or continue train travel to Honshu.

OTHER MAJOR CITIES IN SOUTH-WESTERN HOKKAIDO

Otaru (middle left) once prospered, along with Hakodate, as a major trading port. With the development of Sapporo, Otaru's importance diminished. Today its population is 163,000.

Muroran (middle left) is an industrial city with a population of 118,000. It was formerly an iron ore refinery and shipbuilding center. With the decline of those industries, the city has focused on developing hi-tech expertise.

Tomakomai (middle left) has a population of 161,000 and is the center of Japan's paper pulp industry. Recently, Tomakomai has focused on the biotech, aerospace and automobile industries.

CENTRAL EASTERN HOKKAIDO

Central Eastern Hokkaido is less developed. Akan National Park (middle right), which features many caldera lakes surrounded by wild forests, is one of the most beautiful in Japan. Daisetsuzan National Park (middle center) is the "roof of Hokkaido," and justifiably proud of its splendid gorges and mountain scenery. Most accommodations in the area are in hotspring resorts. Starting from Sapporo, you need five days (four nights) to visit the area:

Day 1. Sapporo/Kushiro/Lake Akanko
Day 2. Lake Akanko
Day 3. Akanko/Bihoro/Sounkyo
Day 4. Sounkyo
Day 5. Sounkyo/Sapporo

If you have an extra day or two, we suggest that you visit Abashiri and Asahikawa. If you don't, however, you won't be missing much.

TRANSPORTATION NETWORK IN HOKKAIDO

With the completion of the Seikan Undersea Tunnel, Hokkaido is connected with the main island of Honshu. Access to Hokkaido has improved — both physically and psychologically. At 54 km (34 miles), the **Seikan Undersea Tunnel** is the world's longest undersea tunnel. It took more than 40 years to complete. The portion under the sea is 23 km (14.4 miles). At its deepest, the tunnel is 240 m (787 feet) below sea level. The Tunnel was opened in 1989.

According to JR, it runs limited express trains from Hakodate to Sapporo on three different lines. However, because they all operate as if they were one line, we call the Hakodate-Sapporo line the JR Hakodate Honsen Line. Limited express trains, (called "Hokuto") run between Hakodate and Sapporo via Toya, Noboribetsu, Tomakomai, and Minami-Chitose, once every one or two hours. The "Hokuto" trains do not stop at Shiraoi. In addition to the "Hokuto" limited expresses, "Suzuran" limited expresses run between Higashi-Muroran and Sapporo five times a day. The "Suzuran" trains do stop at Shiraoi, as well as at Noboribetsu, Tomakomai and Minami-Chitose. If you plan to visit Shiraoi, you must take a "Suzuran." The distances between the major stations on the "Suzuran" is as follows: Hakodate (1 hour) Toya (25 minutes) Higashi-Muroran (12 minutes) Noboribetsu (12 minutes) Shiraoi (13 minutes) Tomakomai (16 minutes) Minami-Chitose (30 minutes) Sapporo.

From Sapporo, the JR Hakodate Honsen Line extends to Asahikawa. Limited express trains run once every 30 minutes between Sapporo and Asahikawa. The trains are named the "Lilac" and the "White Arrow." The ride takes one-and-a-half hours.

Beyond Asahikawa, the JR Sekihoku Honsen Line runs all the way east to Abashiri on the Okhotsk Sea, via Kamikawa and Bihoro. Five limited express trains (which are named "Okhotsk") run daily between Sapporo and Abashiri, operating on the JR Hakodate Honsen Line and the JR Sekihoku Honsen Line. The ride between the major stations is as follows: Sapporo (1 hour and 30 minutes) Asahikawa (45 minutes) Kamikawa (1 hour and 40 minutes) Bihoro (25 minutes) Abashiri.

Again, traveling over several different "lines," limited express trains named "Ozora" connect Sapporo and Kushiro. We have decided to call this "line" the JR Nemuro Honsen Line. The "Ozora" trains run about once every two hours. The ride from Sapporo to Kushiro takes about five hours.

The JR Kunmo Honsen Line connects Abashiri with Kushiro via Shari, Kawayu-Onsen and Mashu. Only local trains run on this line, providing for the everyday needs of the local people. You are likely to use this line only if you visit Gensei-Kaen or Shari from Abashiri. Local trains run between Abashiri and Shari via Gensei-Kaen about once every two hours.

Buses are especially important in Hokkaido. They are described as relevant below.

Southwestern Hokkaido

SAPPORO 札幌

With a population of 1,664,000, Sapporo, the capital of Hokkaido, is the fifth largest city in Japan, and the largest city north of Tokyo. When Japan was unified by the modern imperial government in 1868, and the development of Hokkaido started under the auspices of the new government, the area of Sapporo was wilderness, with a small Ainu population and a few Japanese families. In just a little over 100 years, Sapporo has developed into a modern city. Sapporo has two *i* Information Offices. One is in the Odori subway station concourse (called "Aurora Town," middle center, Hokkaido Map 3) and the other is in the City Hall complex (middle right).

Transportation to Sapporo

By Air: Sapporo Airport (locally called Chitose Airport) is about 28 miles to the southeast of Sapporo (middle left, Hokkaido Map 1). Three major Japanese airlines (Japan Air Lines, All Nippon Airways, and Japan Air System) maintain daily flights between Sapporo and the following major cities in Japan: Tokyo (frequent flights from Haneda Airport, and a few flights a day from Narita Airport), Osaka, Fukuoka,

Hiroshima, Nagoya, Kanazawa, Niigata, Sendai, Oita, Nagasaki, Kumamoto, Miyazaki, Kagoshima, Matsuyama, Takamatsu, Akita, Yamagata, Toyama, Okayama, Aomori, Misawa and Hakodate. Sapporo Airport is connected with JR Shin-Chitose-Kuko Station, and trains operate to Sapporo Station about once every 10 to 30 minutes (the ride takes about 50 minutes). Buses also operate between the Airport and major downtown hotels (Keio Plaza, Sapporo Prince and ANA Hotel Sapporo: a 60-minute ride — fare: 750 yen).

By Train: See Introduction to Hokkaido section.

Outline of the City

Refer to Hokkaido Map 2. Sapporo's downtown spreads south of JR Sapporo Station.

Sapporo has three subways — the Nanboku and Toho Lines run north to south and the Tozai Line, which runs east to west, intersects them at Odori Station. These subway lines provide tourists with handy intracity transportation. A streetcar that circles the southern part of the city is another convenient way to take an easy tour of Sapporo (middle center). The streetcar is especially useful for visits to Mt. Moiwayama.

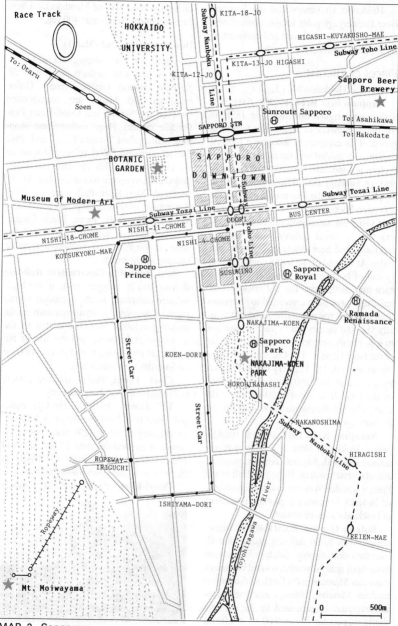

MAP 2 Sapporo

Hokkaido University and the Sapporo Beer Brewery, popular tourist destinations, are located to the northwest and northeast of JR Sapporo Station, respectively.

Places of Interest

Refer to Hokkaido Map 2.

Sapporo Beer Brewery サッポロビール公園 (upper right), established in 1876, is the oldest brewery in Japan. The factory is proud of its completely automated modern facilities. A guided tour (in Japanese) of the factory is conducted several times each day (except Sunday) from 9:00 AM to 3:30 PM. Applications for the tour are accepted at the reception booth near the entrance gate. The tour visits the automated production facilities and a small gallery exhibiting old machines and beer labels in chronological order. At the end of the tour a complimentary can of beer (or soft drink) is offered to each tour participant. The old brick factory buildings have been converted to "Sapporo Beer Garden" restaurants. Most people actually visit the factory not to join the tour but to enjoy fresh beer and Mongolian barbecue at the Beer Garden. The Garden is open for dinner as well. The Brewery can be reached by taxi for about 1,200 yen from the center of the city. It is about a 20-minute walk from Higashi-Kuyakusho-mae Station on the Subway Toho Line.

Nakajima-Koen Park 中島公園 (middle center, Hokkaido Map 2) is a huge recreational area with a sports complex, playland and elaborate gardens. Hoheikan Hall in the Park, a wooden Western building constructed in 1880, is another important monument of Hokkaido's development.

Botanic Garden 北大付属植物園 (upper center), with 5,000 different plants from all over the world, displays flowers of the season from April until November (closed in winter). Batchelor Museum in the Garden, also known as Ainu Museum, displays costumes, arms and everyday objects used by the northern aboriginal peoples. Hours: 9:00 AM to 4:00 PM (3:30 in winter). Closed Mondays (and Sundays in winter). Admission: 400 yen.

Downtown (Hokkaido Map 3)

There are three department stores — Sogo, Tokyu and Sanbankan — near JR Sapporo Station (upper center). Office buildings and hotels are concentrated between the Station and Odori-Koen Park (middle center). Huge underground shopping malls, called "Aurora Town" and "Pole Town" surround Odori subway stations so the city's bustling life can continue unimpeded even in severe winter weather. To the south of Odori-Koen Park there are many department stores and shops, such as Marui, Marusa, Mitsukoshi, Parco, Daiei, Cosmo, etc. Susukino, a huge restaurant and bar zone, is the center of Sapporo's nightlife (shaded on the map).

Old Hokkaido Government Building 北海道庁旧庁舎 (upper left), a red-brick western structure, is the symbolic monument of Sapporo. A small museum in the building exhibits paintings related to the developmental history and the life of the people. Hours: 9:00 AM to 5:00 PM (1:00 PM on Saturday). No admission.

Clock Tower 時計台 (middle center) (optional) is the symbol of the city.

TV Tower テレビ塔 (middle right) (optional) is 142 m (469 feet) tall. It has an observatory at 90 m (294 feet) that commands a panoramic view of the city and Ishikari Plain. Hours: 9:00 AM to 8:30 PM (6:30 PM in winter). Admission: 600 yen.

Odori-Koen Park 大通公園 (middle

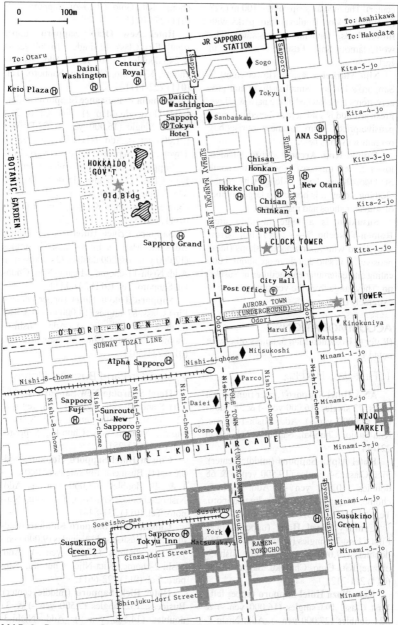

MAP 3   Downtown Sapporo

center). The median strips of the 100 m (328 foot) wide Odori Boulevard are parks with flower beds, fountains and statues. The world-famous Snow Festival is held here in early February.

Nijo Market 二条市場 (lower right) is Sapporo's kitchen. Small seafood and grocery stores are crowded along narrow alleys. Fresh seafood is sold here at incredibly inexpensive prices. Many Japanese tourists buy bargain souvenirs here.

Tanuki-Koji Arcade 狸小路 (shaded: lower center) runs east to west to the south of Odori-Koen Park. Along with many clothing stores, it is home to a large number of souvenir shops and restaurants.

Susukino is a huge nightlife area. **Ramen Yokocho** ラーメン横丁 is a narrow alley lined with *ramen* noodle shops (inexpensive). It is said that there are about 5,000 eating and entertainment facilities in Susukino. They range from the very inexpensive to extremely expensive.

ACCOMMODATIONS

(Refer to Hokkaido Map 3, unless otherwise noted.)

1. First-class Hotels

ANA Hotel Sapporo (upper right). First Class. 73 singles (16,000 yen -) & 387 doubles (25,000 yen -). Add: Nishi-1-chome, Kita-Sanjo, Chuo-ku, Sapporo. Tel: (011) 221-4411

Hotel Alpha Sapporo (middle center). First Class. 54 singles (19,500 yen -) & 68 doubles (30,500 yen -). Add: Nishi-5-chome, Minami-Ichijo, Chuo-ku, Sapporo. Tel: (011) 221-2333.

Century Royal Hotel (upper center). First Class. 75 singles (17,000 yen -) & 240 doubles (27,000 yen -). Add: Nishi-5-chome, Kita-Gojo, Chuo-ku, Sapporo. Tel: (011) 211-2121

Keio Plaza Hotel Sapporo (upper left). First Class. 193 singles (16,000 yen -) & 324 doubles (27,000 yen -). Add: Nishi-7-

chome, Kita-Gojo, Chuo-ku, Sapporo. Tel: (011) 271-0111.

Hotel New Otani Sapporo (upper right). First Class. 40 singles (16,000 yen -) & 243 doubles (27,500 yen -). Add: Nishi-1-chome, Kita-Nijo, Chuo-ku, Sapporo. Tel: (011) 222-1111

Ramada Renaissance Sapporo (middle right, Hokkaido Map 2). First Class. 323 rooms. Single (16,000 yen -) & Double (21,000 yen -). Add: 1-1-1, Toyohira-Shijo, Toyohira-ku, Sapporo. Tel: (011) 821-1111.

Sapporo Grand Hotel (middle center). First Class. 234 singles (14,000 yen -) & 335 doubles (22,000 yen -). Add: Nishi-4-chome, Kita-Ichijo, Kita-ku, Sapporo. Tel: (011) 261-3311

Sapporo Prince Hotel (middle center, Hokkaido Map 2). First Class. 98 singles (12,000 yen -) & 200 doubles (24,000 yen -). Add: Nishi-11-chome, Minami-Nijo, Chuo-ku, Sapporo. Tel: (011) 241-1111.

Sapporo Tokyu Hotel (upper center). First Class. 87 singles (14,000 yen -) & 167 doubles (25,000 yen -). Add: Nishi-4-chome, Kita-Shijo, Chuo-ku, Sapporo. Tel: (011) 231-5611.

2. Standard and Business Hotels

Hotel Sunroute New Sapporo (middle left). Standard. 190 singles (11,500 yen -) & 121 doubles (19,500 yen -). Add: Nishi-6-chome, Minami-Nijo, Chuo-ku, Sapporo. Tel: (011) 251-2511.

Chisan Hotel Sapporo Honkan (middle right). Business. 149 singles (7,000 yen -) & 49 doubles (13,000 yen -). Add: Nishi-2-chome, Kita-Nijo, Chuo-ku, Sapporo. Tel: (011) 231-8441.

Chisan Hotel Sapporo Shinkan (middle right). Business. 114 singles (9,000 yen -) & 48 doubles (17,000 yen -). Add: Nishi-2-chome, Kita-Nijo, Chuo-ku, Sapporo. Tel: (011) 222-6611.

Hotel Rich Sapporo (middle center). Business. 132 singles (7,500 yen -) & 31 doubles (14,500 yen -). Add: Nichi-3-

chome, Kita-Ichijo, Chuo-ku, Sapporo. Tel: (011) 231-7891.

Sapporo Daiichi Washington Hotel (upper center). Business. 94 singles (9,000 yen -) & 107 doubles (16,500 yen -). Add: Nishi-6-chome, Kita-Gojo, Chuo-ku, Sapporo. Tel: (011) 222-3311.

Sapporo Daini Washington Hotel (upper left). Business. 94 singles (9,000 yen -) & 107 doubles (16,500 yen -). Add: Nishi-4-chome, Kita-Shijo, Chuo-ku, Sapporo. Tel: (011) 222-3211.

Sapporo Fuji Hotel (middle left). Standard. 76 singles (10,000 yen -) & 85 doubles (19,000 yen -). Add: Nishi-7-chome, Minami-Nijo, Chuo-ku, Sapporo. Tel: (011) 281-5081.

Sapporo Tokyu Inn (lower center). Business. 248 singles (9,500 yen -) & 321 rooms (18,000 yen -). Add: Nishi-5-chome, Minami-Shijo, Chuo-ku, Sapporo. Tel: (011) 531-0109.

Susukino Green Hotel 1 (lower right). Business. 126 singles (8,000 yen -) & 135 doubles (14,500 yen-). Add: Nishi-2-chome, Minami-Shijo, Chuo-ku, Sapporo. Tel: (011) 511-4111.

Susukino Green Hotel 2 (lower left). Business. 66 singles (7,500 yen -) & 157 doubles (13,000 yen -). Add: Nishi-7-chome, Minami-Shijo, Chuo-ku, Sapporo. Tel: (011) 511-9111.

3. Welcome Inns in Sapporo

Hokke Club Sapporo (middle center). 109 rooms. Add: Nichi-3-chome, Kita-Nijo, Chuo-ku, Sapporo. Tel: (011) 221-2141.

Hotel Sunroute Sapporo (upper center, Hokkaido Map 2). 78 rooms. Add: Nishi-1-chome, Kita-Shichijo, Kita-ku, Sapporo. Tel: (011) 737-8111.

Nakamuraya Ryokan (7 minute walk from JR Sapporo Station). 27 Japanese rooms. Add: Nishi-7-chome, Kita-Sanjo, Chuo-ku, Sapporo. Tel: (011) 241-2111.

Hotel Daitokan (5 minutes by taxi from JR Sapporo Station). 30 Western and 15

Japanese rooms. Add: Nishi-8-chome, Kita-Ichijo, Chuo-ku, Sapporo. Tel: (011) 231-0385.

SHIKOTSU-TOYA NATIONAL PARK
支笏洞爺国立公園

Refer to Hokkaido Map 4. Shikotsu-Toya National Park features two volcanic lakes, Lake Shikotsuko (upper center) and Lake Toyako (middle left). A number of hotspring resorts are also located in this area, including the famous Noboribetsu-Onsen (middle center). Shiraoi (middle center) is the home of the Ainu Folklore Museum. Our suggested itinerary is as follows: from Sapporo, take the "Suzuran" limited express on the JR Hakodate Honsen Line to Shiraoi. After visiting the Museum, continue on the train to Toya. The bus ride from JR Toya Station to Toyako Bus Terminal takes only 15 minutes (Fare: 280 yen). Overnight in the hotspring resort on the Lake. After sightseeing in Toyako, continue to Hakodate. If you have time after Shiraoi, you may wish to stay overnight in Noboribetsu-Onsen before continuing to Lake Toyako. For additional details, see Transportation Network in Hokkaido section above.

Lake Shikotsuko 支笏湖 is about 40 minutes by bus from JR Minami-Chitose Station, or about 55 minutes by bus from JR Shin-Chitose-Kuko Station. The fares are 660 yen and 700 yen, respectively. The main feature of this lake is the sightseeing boat that leaves frequently: it circles the lovely clear lake. The tour takes 30 minutes and the fare is 930 yen. A longer tour takes one and a half hours. It operates four times a day and the fare is 1,700 yen.

SHIRAOI 白老

Refer to Hokkaido Map 5. Shiraoi is a tiny local town with a population of 23,000.

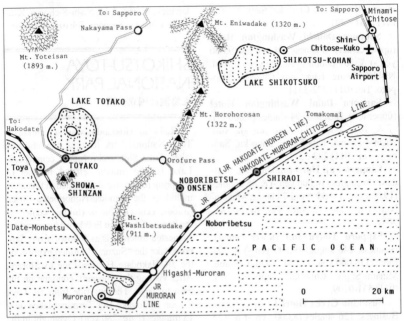

MAP 4 Shikotsu-Toya National Park

It is famous as the site of the **Ainu Folklore Museum** アイヌ民族資料館 (upper right). Due to its location near the Pacific Ocean and its comparatively mild weather, a fairly large number of Ainu settled here long before the development of Hokkaido by Japanese. In 1965, the Ainu village in Shiraoi was moved to the shores of Lake Porotoko (a 10-minute walk from Shiraoi Station), and since then has served as the Ainu Museum. Several original Ainu houses are preserved here to give visitors an idea of

MAP 5 Shiraoi

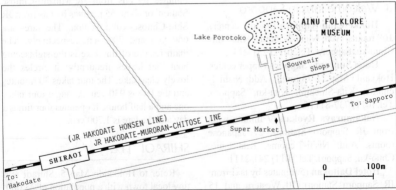

the traditional lifestyle. An 18 m (60 feet) statue of *Korobokkuru* (chief of the village) stands at the entrance, and brown bears (believed by Ainu to be messengers of God) are displayed in the village. A huge building contains a number of souvenir shops. The most popular souvenir item is a carved brown bear holding a salmon in its mouth, a traditional Ainu handicraft. The area is quite touristy, but provides some idea of Ainu culture and history. The Ainu Folklore Museum, the first one of its kind, not only displays daily life utensils of the Ainu but also gives the visitor a scientific explanation of the history of the Ainu, and other northern minorities. The panel displays are bilingual (Japanese-English). Among the many so-called "Ainu Museums" in Hokkaido, this is far and away the best. There are rental row boats on Lake Porotoko. The Lake becomes a natural ice skating rink in winter.

NOBORIBETSU-ONSEN 登別温泉

Refer to Hokkaido Map 6. Noboribetsu Onsen Bus Terminal (lower center) is a 15-minute bus ride from JR Noboribetsu Station (Fare: 290 yen). Noboribetsu Onsen is one of Japan's most famous hotspring spas. Major *ryokan* are within a few minutes walk of the Bus Terminal. To meet the needs of the large number of tourists who visit here throughout the four seasons, most accommodations have built modern concrete buildings with 100-400 rooms, which is very large for Japanese *ryokan*. Fortunately the interiors of the guest rooms remain traditionally Japanese. As is the case with many large hotspring resorts, there are a number of adult entertainment facilities along the main street (shaded on the map). Daiichi Takimotokan has about 30 large baths and can accommodate 1,000 bathers at a time. Its baths are open not only to its guests

MAP 6 Noboribetsu

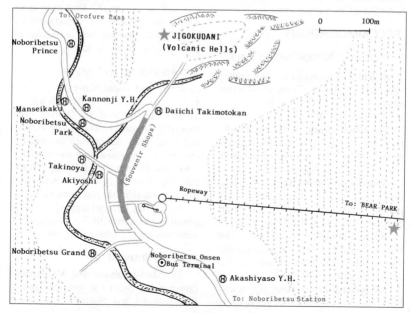

but also to visitors. If you are a hotspring enthusiast, you may want to visit what is described as Japan's largest hotspring facility.

Jigokudani 地獄谷 (upper center), a volcanic "hell" valley, is at the northern end of the main street and is the source of hotspring waters. Sulphur and steam escape from the valley, demonstrating the wondrous power of nature.

Mt. Shihoreizan 四方嶺山, (549 m or 1,650 feet) is another attraction of Noboribetsu. The mountain top can be reached easily by double track ropeways. (A chair lift operates between Noboribetsu Spa and the bottom station of the ropeway (middle center). You can also easily walk up to the ropeway station in only five minutes. About 130 bears live in the brown bear sanctuary (Bear Park) on top of the mountain. A reproduction of an Ainu Village, called *Yukara-no-Sato*, is also located here (quite touristy). The summit commands a panoramic view of the area, including the Pacific Ocean to the south, Lake Kuttarako to the east and Noboribetsu Onsen to the west.

ACCOMMODATIONS

1. Ryokan in Noboribetsu Onsen

Daiichi Takimotokan (middle center). First Class. 336 rooms. 20,000 yen & up per person. Add: 55, Noboribetsu-Onsen, Noboribetsu. Tel: (0143) 84-2111.

Noboribetsu Park Hotel (middle left). First Class. 185 rooms. 18,000 yen & up per person. Add: 100 Noboribetsu-Onsen, Noboribetsu. Tel: (0143) 84-2335.

Noboribetsu Grand Hotel (lower left). First Class. 261 rooms. 18,000 yen & up per person. Add: 154, Noboribetsu-Onsen, Noboribetsu. Tel: (0143) 84-2101.

Hotel Takinoya (middle left). First Class. 72 rooms. 18,000 yen & up per person. Add: 162, Noboribetsu-Onsen, Noboribetsu. Tel: (0143) 84-2222.

Noboribetsu Prince Hotel (upper left). First Class. 299 rooms. 15,000 yen & up per person. Add: 203, Noboribetsu-Onsen, Noboribetsu. Tel: (0143) 84-2255.

2. Welcome Inns in Noboribetsu Onsen

Ryokan Hanaya (Hanaya-mae bus stop between JR Noboribetsu Station and Noboribetsu-Onsen Bus Terminal). 18 Japanese rooms. Add: 134, Noboribetsu-Onsen, Noboribetsu. Tel: (0143) 84-2521.

Ryokan Kiyomizu (3 minute walk from Noboribetsu-Onsen Bus Terminal). 17 Japanese rooms. Add: 60, Noboribetsu-Onsen, Noboribetsu. Tel: (0143) 84-2145.

LAKE TOYAKO 洞爺湖

Refer to Hokkaido Map 7. Lake Toyako is the crown jewel of Southern Hokkaido. Almost perfectly round in shape, the Lake is especially beautiful when reflecting the cobalt blue of the clear sky. Nakanoshima Island sits at its center. Lake Toyako measures about 48 km (30 miles) in circumference and is 19.2 m (63 feet) deep at its deepest point. Modern accommodations are located on the southern shore of the lake; all of them feature hotspring baths.

Transportation to Toyako

If you have visited Noboribetsu Onsen, you can take a bus from there directly to Toyako Bus Terminal via Orofure Toge Pass (middle center, Hokkaido Map 4). Several buses make the trip each day and the ride takes one hour and thirty minutes. Fare: 1,400 yen. The bus stops at the top of Orofure Toge Pass for 10-15 minutes to allow passengers to enjoy the panoramic view.

Toyako Bus Terminal (upper left) is also served by buses from JR Toya Station (frequent service; a 15-minute ride; 280 yen).

Places of Interest

Mt. Showa-Shinzan and Mt. Usuzan (lower right). Buses run between Toyako Bus Terminal and Showa-Shinzan once

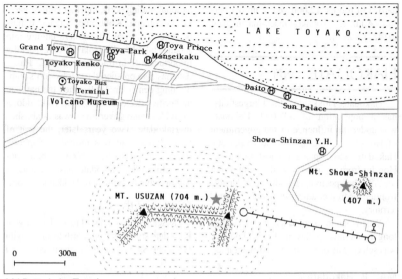

MAP 7 Lake Toyako

every 30-60 minutes. The ride takes 15 minutes. Fare: 290 yen. Mt. Showa-Shinzan 昭和新山 (literally "A New Mountain in the Showa Era") was formed when volcanic Mt. Usuzan erupted in 1943-45, creating a 407 m (1,346 feet) mountain in the middle of a flat farm field. Steam still escapes from the crevices on the mountain side. The summit of Mt. Usuzan 有珠山 (704 m or 2,310 feet above sea level) can be reached by ropeway. Roundtrip ropeway fare: 1,350 yen. The view of Lake Toyako from the gondola is breath-taking, with graceful Mt. Yoteisan (often called Ezo-Fuji or Mt. Fuji of Hokkaido) rising behind the lake. The observatory on the top of the mountain commands a good view of the Pacific Ocean to the south.

Sightseeing boat: (optional) A 90-minute sightseeing boat operates frequently from the piers near Toyako Bus Terminal. The boat makes a stop at Nakanoshima Island and passengers can visit its Prefectural Forest Museum. The fare for the boat tour is 970 yen. Admission to the Museum is an additional 200 yen.

Volcano Museum 火山博物館 (optional) is housed on the second floor of Toyako Bus Terminal. The history of Mt. Showa-Shinzan is explained with photographs and models. Hours: 8:30 AM to 5:30 PM (9:00 AM to 4:00 PM in winter). Admission: 400 yen.

Ryokan in Toyako

Toyako Park Sun Palace (middle right). First Class. 459 rooms. 18,000 yen & up per person. Add: Sobetsu-Onsen, Sobetsu-machi. Tel: (01427) 5-4126.

Toya Prince Hotel (upper center). First Class. 248 rooms. 15,000 yen & up per person. Add: 7, Toyako-Onsen-machi. Tel: (01427) 5-2211.

Toya Park Hotel (upper left). First Class. 167 room. 14,000 yen & up per person. Add: 38, Toyako-Onsen-machi. Tel: (01427) 5-2445.

Toyako Manseikaku (upper center). First Class. 246 rooms. 12,000 yen & up per person. Add: 21, Toyako-Onsen-machi. Tel: (01427) 5-2171.

Toyako Kanko Hotel (upper left). Standard. 134 rooms. 12,000 yen & up per person. Add: 33, Toyako-Onsen-machi. Tel: (01427) 5-2111.

HAKODATE   函館

Hakodate, Hokkaido's third largest city, has a population of 307,000. Hakodate was under the influence of the government of Honshu as long ago as the feudal era. Hakodate was Japan's outpost to protect Honshu from incursions by the Ainu. From the Ainu perspective, Hakodate was Japan's frontier for further advances into their sacred territory.

When Japan abandoned its 250-year-long isolationist policy in 1855, Hakodate was selected as one of the five official international trading ports, together with Nagasaki, Yokohama, Kobe and Niigata. It thus became a gateway of Western culture into Japan. Hakodate Port played an especially important role in trade with Russia. Hakodate has also prospered as Hokkaido's shipbuilding center. In 1869, when the national authorities decided to develop Hokkaido, a local Hokkaido government was established in Hakodate. Two years later, the seat of local government was moved to Sapporo. While Sapporo is the symbol of contemporary Hokkaido, Hakodate has remained a sort of living monument of Hokkaido history.

Outline of the City

Refer to Hokkaido Map 8. The city of Hakodate stretches from north to south, with Hakodate Station located in the middle. An *i*

MAP 8 Hakodate

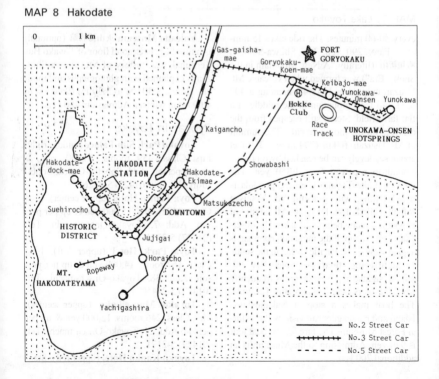

Information Office is just outside JR Hakodate Station. Downtown Hakodate is to the east of Hakodate Station. The southern part of the city is the historic district with several monumental buildings. Mt. Hakodateyama (lower left) rises at the southern end of the peninsula. The northern part of the city has been developed into a new downtown. Goryokaku (upper right), the first Western-style fort built in Japan, is another historical monument reminiscent of the historic role of Hakodate.

Many *ryokan* are located in the Yunokawa-Onsen Hotspring area (upper right), while Western style hotels are grouped downtown.

Transportation in the City

Hakodate has three streetcar lines (No. 2, No. 3 and No. 5, as pictured on the map) that serve the entire city, providing handy transportation to tourists as well as the people of Hakodate.

Tourist Attractions

Fort Goryokaku 五稜郭 (optional) is the only tourist attraction in northern Hakodate. This fort was built in 1857 by the Tokugawa Shogunate to protect against feared Russian aggression against Japan. Instead of being used to protect Japan

against the Russians, the fort became the scene of the last battle between supporters of the feudal Tokugawa Shogunate and the Imperial Army of the new Meiji government. The fort is now used as a park and is open to the public. The Park itself is free. Nearby Goryokaku Tower has an observatory at its top. Hours: 8:00 AM to 8:00 PM (9:00 AM to 6:00 PM in winter). Admission: 520 yen.

The southern part of the city is the "must-see" area of Hakodate. Refer to Hokkaido Map 9.

Old Public Hall 旧函館区民会堂 (middle left) (optional), a 5-minute walk from Suehirocho streetcar stop, is a wooden Western-style building constructed in 1910. It is a symbol of Japanese enthusiasm of that time for Western culture. Hours: 9:00 AM to 7:00 PM (5:00 PM in winter). Admission to the interior: 300 yen.

Japan Orthodox Hakodate Resurrection Church ハリストス正教会 (lower left) (optional) was originally built in 1862 and was replaced by the present building in 1916. This impressive wooden Byzantine-style structure enhances the exotic atmosphere of Hakodate (illuminated at night). Hours: 10:00 AM to noon and 1:00 PM to 5:00 PM (3:00 PM in winter). Worshippers welcome free of charge.

Mt. Hakodateyama 函館山 (lower left) (335 m or 1,100 feet) can be reached by

MAP 9 Downtown Hakodate

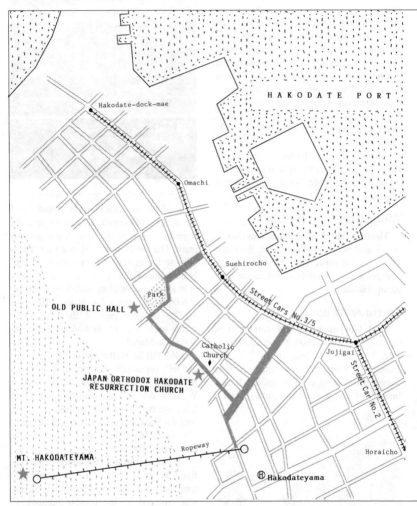

ropeway. There are TV towers and restaurants on the flat mountain top. The summit commands a panoramic view of the city, the Pacific Ocean and the surrounding mountains. The night view of the city from the summit is especially gorgeous. Japanese (or at least the city fathers of Hakodate) believe this is one of the three best night views in the world, ranking with Naples and Hong Kong. The ropeway operates frequently from 9:00 AM to 10:00 PM in the summer (April 21 through October 20), and 10:00 AM to 6:00 PM the rest of the year. Roundtrip fare: 1,130 yen.

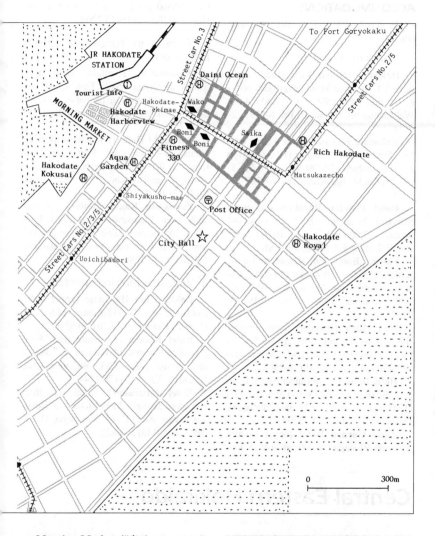

Morning Market 朝市 (upper center). This group of small shops is located near JR Hakodate Station. The shops sell all sorts of food products, and specialize in fresh seafood such as crabs, salmon, cod roe and squid. It is quite a tourist attraction.

Downtown Hakodate (shaded on the map) stretches to the east of Hakodate Station. Several department stores are located along the main street (Wako, Boni and Saika) where the streetcars run, and many restaurants and night spots are clustered on the narrow alleys on both sides of the main street.

ACCOMMODATIONS

(Refer to Hokkaido Map 9, unless otherwise noted.)

1. Hotels in Hakodate

Hakodate Harbor View Hotel (upper center). First Class. 94 singles (10,000 yen -) & 172 doubles (19,500 yen -). Add: 14-10, Wakamatsucho, Hakodate. Tel: (0138) 22-0111.

Hakodate Kokusai Hotel (upper center). First Class. 53 singles (10,000 yen -) & 172 doubles (19,500 yen -). Add: 5-10, Otemachi, Hakodate. Tel: (0138) 23-8751.

Hotel Hakodate Royal (middle right). Standard. 30 singles (9,000 yen -) & 104 doubles (17,000 yen -). Add: 16-9, Omoricho, Hakodate. Tel: (0138) 26-8181.

Fitness Hotel 330 Hakodate (upper center). Business. 69 singles (10,000 yen -) & 42 doubles (16,000 yen -). Add: 6-3, Wakamatsucho, Hakodate. Tel: (0138) 23-0330.

Hotel Rich Hakodate (upper right). Business. 34 singles (7,500 yen -) & 52 doubles (13,000 yen -). Add: 16-18, Matsukazecho, Hakodate. Tel: (0138) 26-2561.

Hotel Daini Ocean (upper right). Business. 97 singles (6,000 yen -) & 51 doubles (12,000 yen -). Add: 20-11, Wakamatsucho, Hakodate. Tel: (0138) 27-2700.

Aqua Garden Hotel (upper center). Business. 91 singles (6,000 yen -) & 28 doubles (10,500 yen). Add: 19-13, Otemachi, Hakodate. Tel: (0138) 23-2200.

2. Ryokan in Yunokawa Onsen Hotsprings

Wakamatsu (1 minute walk from Yunokawa-Onsen stop). First Class. 18 rooms. 24,000 yen & up per person. Add: 1-2-27, Yunokawacho, Hakodate. Tel: (0138) 59-2171.

Hanabishi Hotel (1 minute walk from Yunokawa-Onsen stop). First Class. 133 rooms. 21,000 yen & up per person. Add: 1-16-18, Yunokawacho, Hakodate. Tel: (0138) 57-0131.

Yunokawa Kanko Hotel (2 minute walk from Yunokawa-Onsen stop). First Class. 205 rooms. 17,000 yen & up per person. Add: 2-4-20, Yunokawacho, Hakodate. Tel: (0138) 57-1188.

3. Welcome Inns in Hakodate

Hokke Club Hakodate (upper right, Hokkaido Map 8). 112 rooms. Add: 27-1, Honcho, Hakodate. Tel: (0138) 52-3121.

Hotel Kikuya (3 minute walk from Hakodate Station). 14 Western & 7 Japanese rooms. Add: 8-23, Wakamatsucho, Hakodate. Tel: (0138) 26-1144.

Hotel Maruyasu (13 minute walk from Hakodate Station). 30 Western & 5 Japanese rooms. Add: 17-19, Omoricho, Hakodate. Tel: (0138) 26-4822.

Central Eastern Hokkaido

AKAN NATIONAL PARK
阿寒国立公園

Refer to Hokkaido Map 10. If you start your trip to Central Eastern Hokkaido from Sapporo, the JR Nemuro Honsen Line provides the most convenient and enjoyable transportation to Kushiro (lower center). The trip takes four hours. If you start your Hokkaido trip at Kushiro, you can fly there from major cities on Honshu.. If your time is limited, we suggest you immediately con-

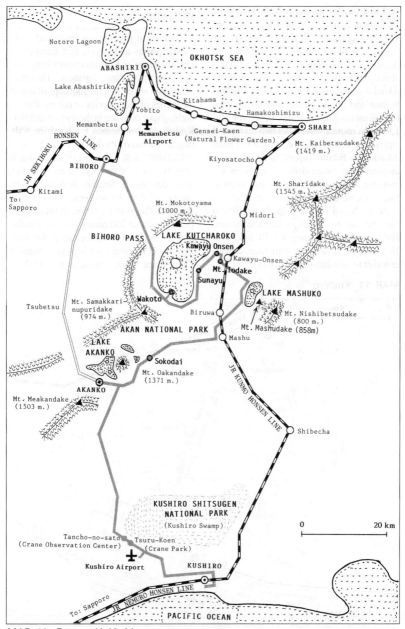

MAP 10 Eastern Hokkaido

nect to a bus to Akanko (middle left) from JR Kushiro Station or from Kushiro Airport. The bus originates at JR Kushiro Station and stops at Kushiro Airport on the way to Akanko Bus Terminal. The bus operates about once every 2 hours. The ride to Akanko takes about 2 hours from Kushiro Station and about 1 hour and 40 minutes from Kushiro Airport. Fares: 2,440 yen and 1,940 yen respectively. After two nights and sightseeing at Lake Akanko, take a bus from Akanko to Bihoro (upper left). This bus operates only twice daily — early in the morning and late morning — and stops at major scenic sites on the route. The bus route is shaded on the map. From Bihoro continue on to Sounkyo (middle center, Hokkaido Map 1), using the JR Sekihoku Honsen Line. If you have extra time, consider a visit to Abashiri (upper center).

KUSHIRO 釧路

Thanks to popular, romantic and sentimental poems and novels that feature this city, the name of Kushiro evokes images of the exotic for most Japanese. However, unless you are tracing the footsteps of one of the heroes of these stories or poems, there is nothing special to see in this city of 205,000. Kushiro is also famous for **Kushiro Shitsugen National Park** (Kushiro Swamp) 釧路湿原国立公園 (lower center, Hokkaido Map 10) north of the city. Japanese cranes, now designated Special Natural Monuments, inhabit the swamps. They retreat deep into the swamps during warm seasons. In winter, about 200 cranes visit the Tanchono-Sato crane observation center for feeding. About 20 cranes are kept year round in Tsuru-Koen Park. Because the Park is

MAP 11 Kushiro

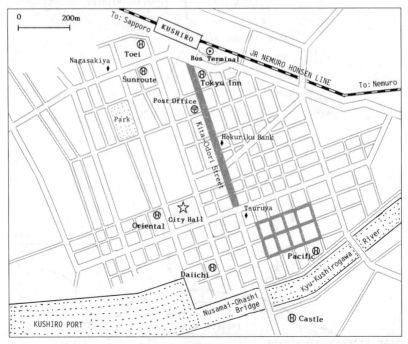

designed to protect this endangered species rather than exhibit the birds to visitors, you may be able to see only a few on the other side of the fence.

If you arrive in Kushiro by train in late afternoon, you'll have to stay overnight. Refer to Hokkaido Map 11. The city's main boulevard, Kita-Odori Street (shaded) stretches to the south from the Station. Nusamai-Ohashi Bridge, with a harbor view to the west, is especially romantic in cold winter weather. Kushiro's nightlife zone is also shaded on the map (lower right).

Hotels in Kushiro
(Refer to Hokkaido Map 11)

Kushiro Castle Hotel (lower right). Standard. 16 singles (8,000 yen -) & 41 doubles (14,000 yen -). Add: 2-5, Okawacho, Kushiro. Tel: (0154) 43-2111.

Kushiro Pacific Hotel (lower right). Standard. 46 singles (7,500 yen -) & 19 doubles (11,000 yen -). Add: 3-5, Suehirocho, Kushiro. Tel: (0154) 25-8811.

Kushiro Tokyu Inn (upper center). Business. 64 singles (7,000 yen -) & 86 doubles (13,000 yen -). Add: 13-1-14, Kita-Odori, Kushiro. Tel: (0154) 22-0109.

Hotel Sunroute Kushiro (upper center). Business. 121 singles (6,500 yen -) & 15 doubles (13,000 yen -). Add: 13-26, Kuroganecho, Kushiro. Tel: (0154) 24-2171.

Kushiro Toei Hotel (upper center). 122 singles (7,000 yen -) & 25 doubles (12,000 yen -). Add: 14-9-2, Kuroganecho, Kushiro. Tel: (0154) 23-2121.

Kushiro Daiichi Hotel (lower center). Business. 54 singles (6,500 yen -) & 26 doubles (12,000 yen -). Add: 3-2, Nishikicho, Kushiro. Tel: (0154) 23-7481.

LAKE AKANKO 阿寒湖

Lake Akanko lies surrounded by wild forests and between two graceful mountains — Mt. Oakandake (1,371m, 4,498 feet) and Mt. Meakandake (1,503m, 4,931 feet). About ten modern *ryokan* have been built in the hotspring resort along the southern shore of the lake. All the *ryokan* are within walking distance of the Akanko Bus Terminal (lower right, Hokkaido Map 12).

Lake Akanko is especially famous for *marimo*, green weeds shaped like balls. *Marimo* are found only in a few lakes in Japan, Switzerland and North America, and the ones in Lake Akanko are considered the most beautiful for their large size and balanced shape.

A sightseeing boat operates frequently and visits picturesque parts of the lake. The boat also stops at Nakanoshima Island. The tour takes about 85 minutes and the fare is 820 yen. You can see displays of a number of *marimo* in tanks at the small museum on the island. Admission to the museum: an additional 200 yen.

The Akanko Visitor Center 阿寒湖 ビジターセンター (upper right) displays flora and fauna of the area as well as several *marimo*. Hours: 9:00 AM to 8:00 PM (5:00 PM in winter).

Bokke ボッケ (upper right) is a hotspring near the lake. Steam from underground constantly creates bubbles on the surface of small muddy ponds, a very unusual natural phenomenon.

Ainu Cotan アイヌコタン (lower left) is a cluster of souvenir shops featuring Ainu handicrafts. Forty-five Ainu families (a total of 250 inhabitants) live in this area. Ainu dances are performed six times per day in a small hut at the end of the street. Each performance lasts about 30 minutes (quite touristy) (optional). Admission to the dance: 1,000 yen. A number of souvenir shops also line the main street (shaded on the map). Most tourists, after enjoying hotspring baths in their *ryokan*, take a walk along the main street dressed in *yukata*.

Ryokan in Akanko
(Refer to Hokkaido Map 12)

The address for all of these ryokan is: Akankohan, Akan-machi.

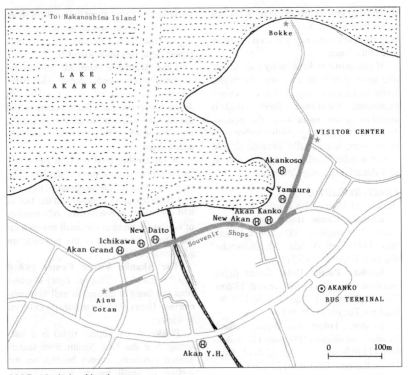

MAP 12 Lake Akanko

New Akan Hotel (middle center). First Class. 280 rooms. 18,000 yen & up per person. Tel: (0154) 67-2121.

Hotel Akankoso (middle center). First Class. 94 rooms. 18,000 yen & up per person. Tel: (0154) 67-2231.

Akan Grand Hotel (middle left). First Class. 193 rooms. 15,000 yen & up per person. Tel: (0154) 67-2531.

Hotel Yamaura (middle center). Standard. 93 rooms. 15,000 yen & up per person. Tel: (0154) 67-2311.

Hotel Ichikawa (middle left). Standard. 89 rooms. 15,000 yen & up per person. Tel: (0154) 67-2011.

Akan Kanko Hotel (middle center). Standard. 70 rooms. 12,000 yen & up per person. Tel: (0154) 67-2611.

FROM AKANKO TO BIHORO
阿寒—美幌パノラマコース・バス

Refer to Hokkaido Map 10. The bus trip from Akanko to Bihoro covers the highlights of Akan National Park. The scheduled bus stops for 10-20 minutes at several scenic points along the route to allow passengers to enjoy the variety of natural beauties and wonders. The bus route is shaded on Hokkaido Map 10. Fare: 5, 490 yen.

Sokodai 双湖台 is an observatory overlooking two small lakes — Panketo and Penketo Lakes. The area is still covered by extensive wild forests and is a paradise for wild animals, especially bears.

Lake Mashuko 摩周湖 is the gem of Akan National Park. Surrounded by 200 m

(656 foot) precipitous cliffs, this quiet mysterious caldera lake is filled with dark blue water (212 m or 696 feet in depth). There is a small island in the center of the Lake. Both No. 1 and No. 3 Observatories are located on the western side of the Lake. Mt. Mashudake and Mt. Nishibetsudake beyond it rise on the other side of the Lake. The area is foggy, especially in May through July, and the Lake seldom shows its entire shape to visitors. However, some consider the Lake is much more attractive when it is half hidden by mist.

Mt. Iodake 硫黄岳 is an active volcano. Sulphur fumes escape from a number of crevices on the mountainside and the area is filled with the smell of sulphur.

Kawayu Onsen 川湯温泉 is another famous hotspring resort in the beautiful forest.

Sunayu 砂湯 is a scenic hotspring resort on the eastern shore of Lake Kutcharoko. Hotsprings well up even on the beach.

Wakoto 和琴半島 is another small hotspring resort. Wind surfing is popular on the Lake in this area.

Bihoro Pass 美幌峠. Leaving Lake Kutcharoko the bus zigzags up to Bihoro Pass. The view from the Pass, especially that of Lake Kutcharoko, is truly breathtaking. Before descending to the north to Bihoro city, you bid farewell to Akan National Park here.

The bus stops in front of JR Bihoro Station, and then continues to Memanbetsu Airport, the last stop. You can fly back to Tokyo from Memanbetsu Airport if your time is limited. We suggest that you take a train on the JR Sekihoku Honsen Line to Kamikawa to proceed to Sounkyo. If you have one or two extra nights, we recommend that you visit Abashiri on the Okhotsk Sea. In the pages that follow, we explain the Abashiri area first, and then the Sounkyo/Asahikawa area.

ABASHIRI   網走

Abashiri has long been called "The Town of Outlaws" because Abashiri Prison used to be reserved for brutal criminals and political offenders serving life sentences. Abashiri has a population of 43,000 and is located in beautiful natural surroundings — Lake Abashiriko to the southwest, Notoroko Lagoon to the northwest, the Okhotsk Sea to the north, and Lake Tofutsuko to the east. The city is also famous as a place where one can see icebergs floating by its shore (February and March).

Transportation to Abashiri

The JR Sekihoku Honsen Line connects Abashiri and Sapporo via Asahikawa. Several limited express trains run daily between the two cities. Supplemental local trains run on the same line for short distances to meet local needs. The JR Kunmo Line runs between Abashiri and Kushiro. Because major tourist attractions between them are more conveniently reached by bus, this line is not popular with tourists. Memanbetsu Airport is about 16 km (10 miles) to the south of the city. Several daily flights are available to and from Tokyo. An airport bus runs between Memanbetsu Airport and Abashiri Station (a 30-minute ride; fare 670 yen).

Modern *ryokan* are located in the hotspring area on the eastern shore of Lake Abashiriko (10 minutes by taxi from Abashiri Station), while business hotels are concentrated downtown.

Places of Interest

Abashiri Prison Museum 博物館網走監獄 (lower left, Hokkaido Map 13) (optional). Abashiri Prison has often been featured in *yakuza* (Japanese mafia) movies. The original Abashiri Prison buildings and gates were moved to this location to be preserved. In Hokkaido's early frontier period prisoners were important resources of labor in the

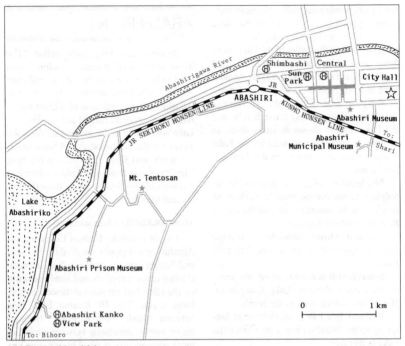

MAP 13 Abashiri

area. The primitive, simple cells tell the story of the cruel life of the prisoners in this cold northern exile. Thousands of Japanese tourists visit here to satisfy the curiosity created by the films. Several buses run between Abashiri Station and the Museum, but you may end up using a taxi. Hours: 8:00 AM to 6:00 PM (9:00 AM to 5:00 PM in winter). Admission: 1,030 yen.

Abashiri Municipal Museum 網走市立

美術館 (upper right) (optional), located in the primitive Ainu fort, has several rooms exhibiting historic objects and daily utensils of the Ainu and other northern aborigines. Hours: 9:00 AM to 5:00 PM. Closed Mondays and holidays in winter only. Admission: 100 yen.

Abashiri Museum 網走郷土博物館 (upper right), popularly called Hokkaido Museum of Northern Peoples, displays many paintings featuring the lifestyles of northern aboriginal peoples. Hours: 9:30 AM to 4:30 PM. Closed Mondays and holidays. Admission: 250 yen.

Natural Flower Garden 原生花園 (upper center, Hokkaido Map 10). If you visit Abashiri in June or July, we suggest that you visit the Natural Flower Garden to the east of the city. The JR Kunmo Honsen Line runs along Okhotsk Sea here. Take the

MAP 14 Shari

train beyond Gensei-Kaen Station to Hamakoshimizu Station, and enjoy a leisurely walk along Lake Tofutsuko to the Natural Flower Gardens, and then return to Abashiri from Gensei-Kaen Station by train. Rental cycles are also available near Hamakoshimizu Station. In other months, we suggest that you enjoy the natural scenery from the train window, especially graceful Mt. Sharidake (1,545 m, 5,069 feet), and stay on the train until Shari Station (upper right). **Shari** 斜里 (Hokkaido Map 14) is a small town (population of 15,000) that functions as a shipping center for the area's logging industry. It is the northeastern-most point in Hokkaido that can be reached by train. If you have a wait for a return train to Abashiri, you should visit the **Shiretoko Museum** 知床博物館, a 15-minute walk from Shari Station. The unexpectedly modern museum displays flora and fauna of the Shiretoko Peninsula (National Park) as well as daily utensils of northern aboriginal tribes excavated in the area. Hours: 9:00 AM to 5:00 PM. Closed Mondays, holidays and the last day of each month. Admission: 200 yen.

ACCOMMODATIONS
(Refer to Hokkaido Map 13)

1. Hotels in Abashiri

Abashiri Central Hotel (upper right). Business. 48 singles (6,000 yen -) & 53 doubles (10,500 yen -). Add: Nishi-3-chome,

Minami-Nijo, Abashiri. Tel: (0152) 44-5151.

Hotel Sun Park (upper right). Business. 71 singles (6,500 yen -) & 19 doubles (11,500 yen -). Add: Nishi-4-chome, Minami-Nijo, Abashiri. Tel: (0152) 44-3131.

2. Ryokan in Abashiri

Hotel View Park (lower left). Standard. 221 rooms. 12,000 yen & up per person. Add: 23, Yobito, Abashiri. Tel: (0152) 48-2211.

Abashiri Kanko Hotel (lower left). Standard. 109 rooms. 12,000 yen & up per person. Add: 23, Yobito, Abashiri. Tel: (0152) 48-2121.

ASAHIKAWA AND SOUNKYO
大雪山国立公園

Refer to Hokkaido Map 15. Sounkyo Gorge (lower right) is in Daisetsuzan National Park. Combined with the area's hotsprings, it attracts thousands of visitors each year to enjoy the natural beauties and pleasures of the area.

Transportation to Sounkyo and Asahikawa

Kamikawa Station (upper center) on the JR Sekihoku Honsen Line is the gateway to Sounkyo. Buses operate from Kamikawa to Sounkyo about once every hour, meeting all

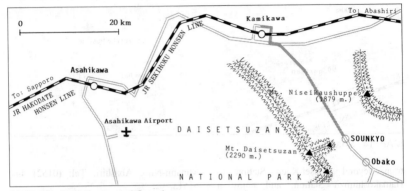

MAP 15 Asahikawa and Sounkyo

trains. If you follow our suggested itinerary you will catch a bus to Sounkyo here. Some of these buses run to and from Asahikawa beyond Kamikawa. The bus stop in Asahikawa is in front of JR Asahikawa Station. The ride to Sounkyo from Kamikawa takes about 30 minutes; and about 50 minutes from Asahikawa. The fares are 750 yen and 1,800 yen respectively.

There are several daily flights between Tokyo's Haneda Airport and Asahikawa Airport (middle left, Hokkaido Map 15) and one flight daily each to Osaka and Nagoya. Airport buses run between the airport and JR Asahikawa Station. The trip takes 40 minutes and the fare is 540 yen. If your time is limited, air travel is a convenient way to finish your Hokkaido trip and return to Tokyo.

SOUNKYO 層雲峡

Refer to Hokkaido Map 16. Sounkyo, or Gorges Reaching to the Clouds, is in the

MAP 16 Sounkyo

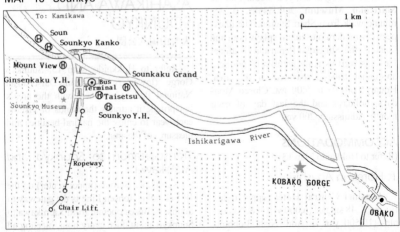

heart of Daisetsuzan National Park. The 8 km (5 mile) long narrow valley between Sounkyo and Obako is flanked by precipitous cliffs that create gorgeous palisades scenery. All the accommodations in Sounkyo have hotspring baths.

Sounkyo Valley (Hokkaido Map 16)

To enjoy the Sounkyo Valley, between Sounkyo Bus Terminal (upper left) and Obako (lower right), you have to either walk or cycle (rental bicycles are available), because the automobile road passes through a tunnel under Kobako Gorge, the most scenic part of the valley. If you walk, we suggest that you take a taxi from your hotel to Obako first (infrequent bus service is also available from Sounkyo Bus Terminal to Obako), and then walk back on the cycling path to your hotel. The cycling path sometimes runs separately from the automobile road, but for the most part is alongside the road. Watch for buses and cars. A small tunnel near the souvenir shops in Obako marks the beginning of your exploration. A number of small waterfalls tumbling down precipitous cliffs create picturesque scenery. The walk is refreshing and invigorating.

Sounkyo Ropeway. A 1.6 km (1 mile) ropeway trip takes you from Sounkyo terminal to the 5th grade of Mt. Kurodake (part of the Daisetsuzan mountains). Ropeway roundtrip fare: 1,390 yen. You can then go by chair lift to the 7th grade. Roundtrip chair lift fare: 500 yen. The observatory there commands a panoramic view of the Daisetsuzan mountains. The balanced shape of Mt. Niseikaushupe rising over Sounkyo valley is especially impressive.

ACCOMMODATIONS
(Refer to Hokkaido Map 16)

1. Ryokan in Sounkyo

Note: the address for each of these ryokans is: Sounkyo, Kamikawa-machi.

Hotel Taisetsu (upper left). First Class.
244 rooms. 14,000 yen & up per person. Tel: (01658) 5-3211.

Sounkaku Grand Hotel (upper left). First Class. First Class. 201 rooms. 14,000 yen & up per person. Tel: (01658) 5-3111.

Hotel Soun (upper left). First Class. 234 rooms. 14,000 yen & up per person. Tel: (01658) 5-3311.

Mount View Hotel (upper left). First Class. 103 rooms. 14,000 yen & up per person. Tel: (01658) 5-3011.

Sounkyo Kanko Hotel (upper left). Standard. 325 rooms. 12,000 yen & up per person. Tel: (01658) 5-3101.

2. Welcome Inn in Sounkyo

Pension Yukara (several minutes walk from Sounkyo Bus Terminal). 8 Western & 3 Japanese rooms. Tel: (01658) 5-3216.

ASAHIKAWA 旭川

Asahikawa, with a population of 360,000, is the second largest city in Hokkaido. The city is modern and clean, but is rather characterless. After your visit to Sounkyo, you can take a train from Kamikawa to Sapporo, skipping Asahikawa. If you have already visited Sapporo and Southern Hokkaido, you can fly back to Tokyo from Asahikawa Airport.

Places of Interest

Refer to Hokkaido Map 17.

Shopping Park Street (lower center). A traffic-free pedestrian mall lined with department stores, shops and restaurants.

Yukara Textiles 優佳良織工芸館分館 (middle left): Yukara Textiles originated in Asahikawa. They use the natural beauties of Hokkaido for their design motifs. Stubbornly clinging to manual processes, the textile makers have won a number of awards at major international exhibitions. A small store/exhibition hall in the downtown area is just a 10-minute walk from Asahikawa Station. A free shuttle bus operates from here to

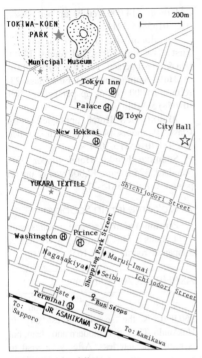

MAP 17 Asahikawa

the Main Workshop/Museum located to the west of the city (about a 15-minute ride).

Tokiwa-Koen Park 常盤公園 (upper left) contains several public halls and gardens, as well as the Municipal Museum and statues commemorating the centennial of Hokkaido's development.

Hotels in Asahikawa

Asahikawa Palace Hotel (upper center, Hokkaido Map 17). First Class. 153 singles (10,500 yen -) & 105 doubles (20,000 yen -).

Add: 6-chome, Shichijo-dori, Asahikwa. Tel: (0166) 25-8888.

New Hokkai Hotel (middle center). Standard. 82 singles (10,000 yen -) & 106 doubles (17,000 yen -). Add: 6-chome, Gojo-dori, Asahikawa. Tel: (0166) 24-3111.

Asahikawa Terminal Hotel (lower center). Standard. 112 singles (7,500 yen -) & 45 doubles (14,500 yen -). Add: 7-chome, Miyashita-dori, Asahikawa. Tel: (0166) 24-0111.

Asahikawa Tokyu Inn (upper center). Standard. 40 singles (7,500 yen -) & 66 doubles (13,500 yen). Add: 6-chome, Hachijo-dori, Asahikawa. Tel: (0166) 26-0109.

Toyo Hotel (upper center). Standard. 55 singles (7,500 yen -) & 44 doubles (12,500 yen -). Add: 7-chome, Shichijo-dori, Asahikawa. Tel: (0166) 22-7575.

Asahikawa Washington Hotel (lower center). Business. 213 singles (6,000 yen -) & 42 doubles (10,500 yen -). Add: 6-chome, Ichijo-dori, Asahikawa. Tel: (0166) 25-3311.

Asahikawa Prince Hotel (lower center). Business. 172 singles (5,500 yen -) & 67 doubles (10,000 yen -). Add: 7-chome, Ichijo-dori, Asahikawa. Tel: (0166) 22-5155.

JR FARES BETWEEN MAJOR STATIONS IN SOUTHWESTERN HOKKAIDO

1. Fares from Aomori: based on a rapid service train (Aomori-Hakodate) plus a limited express train (in Hokkaido).

2. Other fares: based on limited express trains.

To/From	Aomori	Hakodate	Toya	Sapporo
Hakodate	2,880 yen (160.4 km)		5,030 yen (153.8 km)	7,610 yen (318.7 km)
Toya	7,710 yen (314.2 km)	5,030 yen (153.8 km)		5,440 yen (164.9 km)
Noboribetsu	8,740 yen (367.4 km)	6,270 yen (207 km)	2,560 yen (53.2 km)	4,100 yen (111.7 km)
Shiraoi	8,950 yen (386.3 km)	6,580 yen (225.9 km)	2,890 yen (72.1 km)	3,220 yen (92.8 km)
Sapporo	10,180 yen (479.1 km)	7,610 yen (318.7 km)	5,440 yen (164.9 km)	
Asahikawa	12,760 yen (615.9 km)	10,280 yen (455.5 km)	8,120 yen (301.7 km)	4,410 yen (136.8 km)

JR FARES BETWEEN MAJOR CITIES IN EASTERN CENTRAL HOKKAIDO

1. When only local trains run between certain cities, the fares are based on local trains.

2. Other city pairs are based on limited express trains.

To/From	Kushiro	Bihoro	Abashiri	Asahikawa
Sapporo	8,640 yen (348.5 km)	8,940 yen (367.6 km)	9,150 yen (398.3 km)	4,410 yen (136.8 km)
Bihoro			1,780 yen (30.7 km)	6,580 yen (230.8 km)
Hamakoshimizu			390 yen (22.1 km)	
Shari			720 yen (41 km)	
Kamikawa		5,440 yen (177.3 km)	6,270 yen (208 km)	2,150 yen (53.5 km)
Asahikawa		6,580 yen (230.8 km)	7,300 yen (261. 5 km)	

TOHOKU REGION

東北

Tohoku, the northeastern part of Japan's main island, has always (along with Hokkaido) been the nation's least developed area, both economically and culturally. Its severe winter weather and mountainous topography have caused industrial development here to lag far behind Central Japan, where the famous Japanese "economic miracle" has been in full flower for years. But nature is unspoiled here, and the region has beautiful mountains and sea coasts. The region's natural beauties and the simple, warm hospitality of the people have long fascinated visitors. The region has also clung to its traditional crafts; they provide extra interest for those traveling in Tohoku.

1. Along the JR Tohoku Shin-kansen

The JR Tohoku Shinkansen provides convenient links between Tokyo and major Tohoku cities, such as Fukushima, Sendai and Morioka. Many important Tohoku destinations are easily accessible thanks to the Tohoku Shinkansen. Four districts are explained in detail in this Chapter. Sendai and its vicinity should be your first choice for a Tohoku destination. Transportation in each district is explained in the each section of the Chapter.

(1) Sendai and vicinity, including Matsushima, Shiogama, Hiraizumi, Yamadera, and Narugo (sometimes pronounced Naruko) (middle center and middle right, Tohoku Map 1).

(2) Fukushima and Bandai Kogen, including Aizu-Wakamatsu (lower center).

(3) Morioka and Rikuchu Kaigan National Park (middle right).

2. Northern Tohoku

Limited express trains run between Morioka and Aomori. Aomori is the gateway to Hokkaido via the Seikan Undersea Tunnel, the world's longest. Aomori is also the jumping off point for visits to nearby Hirosaki, a famous castle town, and beautiful Lake Towadako. These destinations are explained in the pages that follow:

(1) Aomori (upper center, Tohoku Map 1)
(2) Hirosaki (upper center)
(3) Lake Towadako (upper center)

3. Along the JR Yamagata Shin-kansen

The newly-inaugurated JR Yamagata Shinkansen (which runs between Tokyo and Yamagata) is not particularly helpful for most international tourists. Although it has greatly improved access from Tokyo to the famous Zao ski (and hotspring) resort, there are few destinations of historic or cultural interest along this line. In our estimation, this should be the last choice for a Tohoku destination. We describe two major cities along this line:

(1) Yonezawa (lower center, Tohoku Map 1)
(2) Yamagata (middle center)

4. Japan Sea Coast of Tohoku

We recommend one special destination on the Japan Sea Coast of Tohoku. Hagurosan is famous as a pilgrimage destination and features several important his-

MAP 1 Outline of Tohoku

toric sites. Travel to this area from Tokyo is easiest on the JR Joetsu Shinkansen to Niigata (lower left), and then a limited express train on the JR Uetsu Honsen Line to Tsuruoka, the gateway to Hagurosan. It is not impossible to travel to Tsuruoka from other major Tohoku cities, but the train connections are very inconvenient and the trip takes much longer. We also introduce Akita, the principal city of the Japan Sea Coast of Tohoku, as well as the castle town of Kakunodate.

    (1)Tsuruoka and Hagurosan (middle left, Tohoku Map 1)
    (2)Akita (middle left)
    (3)Kakunodate (middle center)

5. Other Major Tohoku Cities

Although we do not provide detailed information, the following are short introductions to other major Tohoku cities:

Iwaki (lower right): Five cities and eight towns merged to make Iwaki City in 1961. It is Tohoku's second largest city (after Sendai), with a population of 360,000. Physically, Iwaki is the largest city in Japan — its land area far exceeds that of even Tokyo and Osaka.

Koriyama (lower center): An industrial city on the Tohoku Shinkansen with a population of 311,000. The JR Bandai-Saisen Line, which provides a link to Aizu-Wakamatsu, originates here.

Hachinohe (upper right): A commercial city between Morioka and Aomori on the JR Tohoku Honsen Line) with a population of 243,000. Hachinohe is the center of the area's agricultural industry and is especially famous for its apples.

Ishinomaki (middle right): A port city near Sendai with a population of 123,000. It is the terminus of the JR Senseki Line.

Sakata (middle left): A commercial city near Tsuruoka (on the JR Uetsu Honsen Line) with a population of 102,000. In the feudal era, Sakata developed as the area's commercial center, while Tsuruoka pros-

pered as the political and military base of the Shonai Clan. Devastated by a fire in 1976, Sakata lost many of its buildings of historic interest.

Misawa (upper right), with a large U.S. military base, is promoting international exchanges. The city's goal is to become the area's education center. Population: 42,000.

TRANSPORTATION IN TOHOKU
(Tohoku Map 1)

The JR Tohoku Shinkansen runs between Tokyo and Morioka. The "Yamabiko" Shinkansen runs the full distance at once an hour intervals. Several "Yamabiko" trains stop only at Sendai, but most of them stop at Omiya, Utsunomiya, Koriyama, Fukushima, Sendai, and all the stations north of Sendai. The "Aoba" Shinkansen runs between only Tokyo and Sendai once an hour, stopping at all stations. The trip between major stations takes: Tokyo (5 minutes) Ueno (20 minutes) Omiya (30 minutes) Utsunomiya (35-50 minutes); Koriyama (15 minutes) Fukushima (25-30 minutes) Sendai (15 minutes) Furukawa (20 minutes) Ichinoseki (45 minutes) Morioka. The fastest "Yamabiko" train takes only one hour and 45 minutes between Tokyo and Sendai, and 2 hours and 40 minutes between Tokyo and Morioka, while the slowest "Aoba" takes two and a half hours between Tokyo and Sendai.

Local JR trains on the Senseki Line (to Matsushima), the Senzan Line (to Yamadera) and the Rikuu-Tosen Line (to Narugo) are explained in the respective sections below.

Most Yamagata Shinkansens (called "Tsubasa") run from Tokyo to Fukushima attached to the JR Tohoku Shinkansen. At Fukushima, the silver-colored Yamagata Shinkansen cars are uncoupled and continue their journey on newly-renovated track to Yamagata. The "Tsubasa" Shinkansen operates about once an hour. The ride from Tokyo takes about 2 hours and 15 minutes to Yonezawa and about 3 hours to Yama-gata.

Limited express trains (called "Hat-sukari") run between Morioka and Aomori on the Tohoku Honsen Line about once every hour. The ride from Morioka takes about 40 minutes to Hachinohe, and about 2 hours and 15 minutes to Aomori.

Aomori and Hirosaki are connected by the JR Ou Line. Several limited express trains and many local trains run between these two cities once every 30-60 minutes. The ride takes 30 minutes by limited express and 60 minutes on the local trains. The limited express trains run from Hirosaki to Akita (and beyond). The ride from Aomori to Akita takes one-and-a-half hours to two hours.

The JR Uetsu Honsen Line runs along the Japan Sea Coast between Niigata and Akita. Limited express trains (called "Inaho") run once every 1-2 hours. The ride from Nii-gata takes 1 hour and 45 minutes to Tsuruoka, and three and a half hours to Akita. As explained above, if you combine the Jo-etsu Shinkansen from Tokyo to Niigata (about 2 hours) and the "Inaho" limited express from Niigata to Tsuruoka, you can reach Tsuruoka from Tokyo in about four hours.

Sendai and Vicinity

OUTLINE OF THE AREA

Refer to Tohoku Map 2. Thanks to easy access from Tokyo via the Tohoku Shinkansen (only a 2-hour ride), the Sendai area is Tohoku's most popular tourist desti-nation. The area includes Tohoku's largest city — Sendai (lower center), the historic city of Hiraizumi (upper right) and scenic Matsushima (lower right). We suggest using Sendai as a base to explore the city itself and: (1) Hiraizumi (upper right); (2) Mat-sushima and Shiogama (lower right); (3) Yamadera (lower left); and (4) Narugo (upper center; if you are interested in hot-springs). The typical three-day itinerary from Tokyo (or from other Tohoku destina-tions, such as Lake Towadako or Rikuchu Kaigan) is as follows:

Day 1. Tokyo/Hiraizumi/Sendai

Take the Tohoku Shinkansen from Tokyo to Ichinoseki, and then visit Chusonji and Motsuji Temples in Hiraizumi. Take the Tohoku Shinkansen from Ichinoseki back to Sendai, and stay overnight in Sendai.

Day 2. Sendai/Shiogama/Matsushima/Sendai

Take the JR Senseki Line from Sendai to Hon-Shiogama to visit Shiogama Jinja Shrine. Then take a sightseeing boat from Hon-Shiogama to Matsushima-Kaigan across the scenic Matsushima Bay. After visiting Zuiganji Temple and other historic places in Matsushima-Kaigan, return to Sendai by the JR Senseki Line.

Day 3. Sendai/Tokyo

After sightseeing in Sendai, return to Tokyo on the Tohoku Shinkansen. You can visit Bandai Kogen or Nikko on your way back to Tokyo from Sendai.

SENDAI 仙台

Sendai is the capital of Miyagi Prefec-ture, and Tohoku's economic and cultural capital as well. It was established in the 17th century by a *daimyo* named Masamune Date, whose shadow still looms large for the modern inhabitants of this provincial capital. Today Sendai's population is 898,000.

Toward the end of the civil war period (the end of the 16th century), the military genius Masamune Date unified the smaller feudal lords of the Tohoku district and established a power base in Sendai. Because the capital at Kyoto was so far away, Masamune did not participate in the struggles or the bloody battles then being waged by those seeking central political power. He remained an influential feudal lord under the Tokugawa Shogunate. The people of Tohoku still say that Masamune would have been the person to complete the unification of Japan if he had been born 20 years earlier and somewhere closer to Kyoto. The belief, regardless of its validity, reflects the respect the people of the area still have for this one-eyed hero. Throughout the Edo era, Sendai prospered as the largest castle city in Tohoku under successive generations of the Date family. After World War II, Sendai

MAP 2 Outline of Sendai District

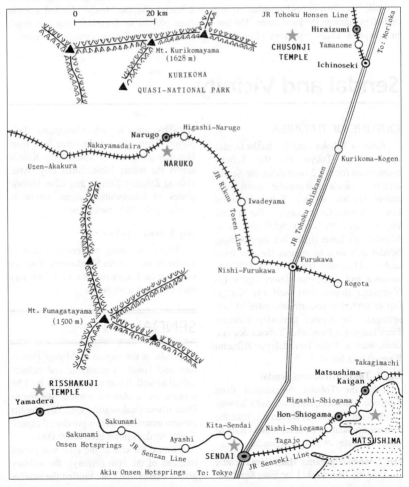

was redeveloped as a modern city, but its quiet air of a feudal town, surrounded by thick green woods, has been preserved successfully. Even though Sendai lacks buildings of historical interest because of the devastation of the war, it is one of Japan's most livable cities. With its clean shopping arcades and generally pleasant atmosphere, it is also one of the most comfortable cities in Japan for an evening stroll.

Outline of the City

Refer to Tohoku Map 3. Sendai Station (middle right) is a four-story building. An *i* Information Office is located on the second floor of the Station. Sendai also operates an English language "Hot-Line" telephone service to help foreign visitors with special problems: 224-1919. The Tohoku Shinkansen platforms are located on the fourth floor. Exits are located on the second floor and the ground floor. The taxi stand is outside the ground floor exit. If you are walking to your hotel, use the second floor exit. You will be surprised at the extensive maze of pedestrian bridges outside the station.

Sendai has two shopping arcades (shaded on the map). The arcade running east to west is called Chuo-dori Street and the one that runs north to south is called Higashi-Ichibancho-dori Street. Both of them are lined with department stores (such as Daiei, Fujisaki and Mitsukoshi), souvenir shops, restaurants and small stores specializing in local crafts, such as wooden *kokeshi* dolls and iron wind chimes. Many drinking spots and obscure cabarets are located on Kokubunji-dori Street (middle center). The area is completely safe; don't be afraid to explore this colorful nightlife zone and its jovial people. Women alone after about 8 PM, however, might discover that alcohol can inspire even shy country people to make proposals not likely to be sanctioned by Miss Manners. Government offices are located on the northern side of Jozenji-dori Avenue (upper center), and business offices are located along Hirose-dori, Aoba-dori and Higashi-Nibancho-dori Avenues.

Transportation in Sendai

Buses are the major means of mass public transportation in Sendai. The central part of the city is easily accessible on foot from all major hotels. A subway, running north to south and passing JR Sendai Station, is not useful for tourists. Sendai's bus system is perhaps the most complicated one in all of Japan. There are more than 60 bus stops on the western side of the station. Even if you can read the destination names in Japanese, you really can't use the buses unless you also have a thorough knowledge of local geography. Because you will probably visit only one or two places of interest in Sendai (there really are no more than one or two), it is better to use taxis.

Places of Interest

Zuihoden Hall 瑞鳳殿 (lower center), the mausoleum of Masamune Date, is located on a small hill and surrounded by thick cedar trees. The original hall, a National Treasure, was a splendid structure with elaborate carvings and decorations but was lost to fire during the war. The present building

MAP 3 Sendai

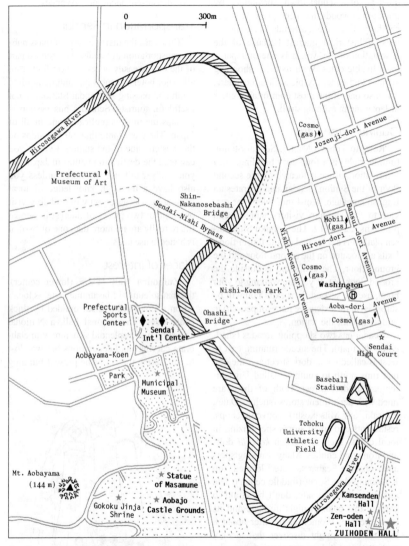

is an exact replica of the original. **Kansenden Hall** 感仙殿 and **Zen-oden Hall** 善応殿, the mausolea of the second and third lords of the Date family, are also located near Zuihoden. Hours: 9:00 AM to 4:00

PM. Admission: 515 yen (covers all three monuments).

Aobayama-Koen Park 青葉山公園 (middle and lower left) was built on the former Aobajo Castle grounds. The grounds

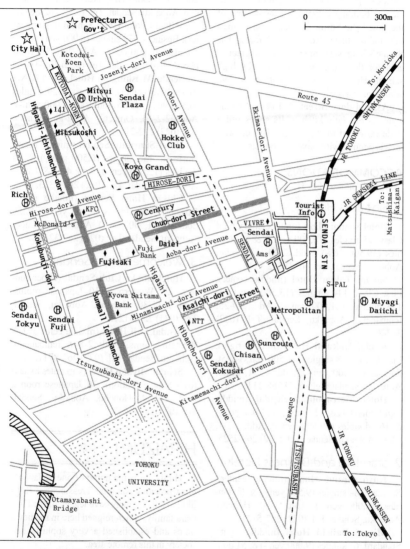

are covered with thick woods, and remains of the castle and the statue of Masamune Date are located there. The Sendai Municipal Museum, Sendai International Center, and Prefectural Sports Center are also in the Park.

Osaki Hachimangu Shrine 大崎八幡宮 (outside map; about 2 miles northwest from Sendai Station; optional). This National Treasure Shrine was built in 1607 at the order of Masamune Date to offer thanks for the area's prosperity. This magnificent black lacquer building is typical of the designs of the time. The Shrine is located on a small hill, and is surrounded by a thick forest. The Shrine's long, steep approach is the practice area for the track team of a nearby high school. Hours: 9:00 AM to 4:00 PM. No admission charge.

Asaichi-dori Street 朝市通り (middle right) is Sendai's kitchen. Its shops sell a wide variety of food products. This colorful area is popular with Japanese tourists.

ACCOMMODATIONS

(Refer to Tohoku Map 3)

1. First-class Hotels

Hotel Sendai Plaza (upper center). First Class. 95 singles (10,000 yen -) & 83 doubles (19,500 yen-). Add: 2-20-1, Honcho, Aoba-ku, Sendai. Tel: (022) 262-7111.

Sendai Tokyu Hotel (middle center). First Class. 144 singles (13,500 yen -) & 155 doubles (21,000 yen -). Add: 2-9-25, Ichibancho, Aoba-ku, Sendai. Tel: (022) 262-2411.

Sendai Kokusai Hotel (middle right). First Class. 178 singles (11,500 yen -) & 56 doubles (19,500 yen -). Add: 4-6-1, Chuo, Aoba-ku, Sendai. Tel: (022) 268-1111.

Hotel Metropolitan Sendai (middle right). First Class. 132 singles (11,000 yen -) & 161 doubles (19,500 yen -). Add: 1-1-1, Chuo, Aoba-ku, Sendai. Tel: (022) 268-2525.

2. Standard and Business Hotels

Koyo Grand Hotel (middle center). Standard. 84 singles (9,500 yen -) & 48 doubles (18,000 yen -). Add: 2-3-1, Honcho, Aoba-ku, Sendai. Tel: (022) 267-5111.

Miyagi Daiichi Hotel (middle right). Standard. 67 singles (9,000 yen -) & 51 doubles (15,000 yen -). Add: 1-2-45, Tsutsujigaoka, Miyagino-ku, Sendai. Tel: (022) 297-4411.

Hotel Rich Sendai (middle center). Standard. 181 singles (8,000 yen -) & 43 doubles (16,000 yen -). Add: 2-2-2, Kokubucho, Aoba-ku, Sendai. Tel: (022) 262-8811.

Mitsui Urban Hotel Sendai (upper center). Business. 173 singles (8,000 yen -) & 39 doubles (16,000 yen -). Add: 2-18-11, Honcho, Aoba-ku, Sendai. Tel: (022) 265-3131.

Sendai Washington Hotel (No. 1 & No. 2) (middle center). Business. 529 singles (6,500 yen -) & 85 doubles (14,000 yen -). Add: 2-2-10, Omachi, Aoba-ku, Sendai. Tel: (022) 222-2111.

Hotel Sunroute Sendai (middle right). Business. 138 singles (6,500 yen -) & 24 doubles (12,500 yen -). Add: 4-10-8, Chuo, Aoba-ku, Sendai. Tel: (022) 262-2323.

Chisan Hotel Sendai (middle right). Business. 200 singles (6,500 yen -) & 50 doubles (11,500 yen -). Add: 4-8-7, Chuo, Aoba-ku, Sendai. Tel: (022) 262-3211.

3. Welcome Inns in Sendai

Hotel Hokke Club Sendai (upper center). 128 Western & 10 Japanese rooms. Add: 2-11-30, Honcho. Aoba-ku, Sendai. Tel: (022) 224-3121.

Sendai Fuji Hotel (middle center). 179 Western rooms. Add: 2-8-9, Ichibancho, Aoba-ku, Sendai. Tel: (022) 262-8711.

Sendai Miyako Hotel (4 minutes by taxi from Sendai Station). 36 Japanese rooms. Add: 2-9-14, Honcho, Aoba-ku, Sendai. Tel: (022) 222-4647.

HIRAIZUMI 平泉

Hiraizumi is the home of one of Japan's most precious National Treasures — Konjikido Hall, an impressive legacy of the Fujiwara family, which reigned here in medieval times and established a very sophisticated society in this remote area.

The Fujiwara family operated a strong local government in Hiraizumi from 1089 to 1189. An efficient economy and political stability enabled three generations of Fujiwaras to nurture a level of culture comparable to that of Kyoto, and unequalled by any other local area. Chusonji Temple and Motsuji Temple are symbols of Tohoku culture in the medieval era. Yoritomo Minamoto, the founder of the first military government in Japan, defeated the fourth leader of the Fujiwaras in 1189, and the 100-year long prosperity of the north disappeared, never to return. Today, the city's population is only 17,000.

The area is also famous for its lacquerware and ironware, such as wind chimes and kettles. Many souvenir shops are located near the Chusonji bus stop and along the approach to the Temple.

Transportation to Chusonji Temple

Refer to Tohoku Map 4. A visit to Chusonji Temple requires a long walk on a hilly path. You can leave your bags in a coin locker at Ichinoseki Station (JR Tohoku Shinkansen). The bus going to Chusonji operates every 20-30 minutes from early morning until early evening. The ride from Ichinoseki to Chusonji (via JR Hiraizumi Station) takes 26 minutes. Fare: 330 yen.

The JR Tohoku Line operates between Ichinoseki and Hiraizumi almost every hour. However, because Chusonji Temple is not really close to Hiraizumi Station, you'll end up on the same bus, for the Hiraizumi to Chusonji portion of the trip. Traveling this way just takes too much time. Even if you have a Japan Rail Pass, we recommend that you take the bus from Ichinoseki.

Chusonji Temple 中尊寺 (Upper center, Tohoku Map 4)

Allow at least two hours for this visit.

MAP 4 Hiraizumi

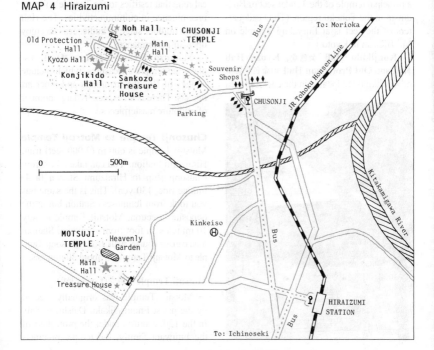

The entrance to the main approach to Chusonji Temple is a stone bridge, which leads to a steep slope.

Chusonji Temple was erected in the 9th century. It prospered under the reign of the Fujiwara family in the 11th and 12th centuries. At its peak there were more than 40 buildings in the precincts (which actually cover all of one small mountain). Chusonji Temple lost most of its buildings to fire in 1337. Only Konjikido Hall (Golden Hall) and Kyozo Hall (Sutra Hall) survived the fire. Most of the other buildings were reconstructed in the Edo Era. The 1 km (0.6 mile) approach to Konjikido Hall is shaded by tall cedar trees; the many small halls along this path add to the solemn atmosphere of the grounds.

The Main Hall of Chusonji Temple 中尊寺本堂 is located about halfway up the approach. Chusonji Temple is still active as a principal temple of the Tendai sect of Buddhism in the Tohoku region. (The headquarters of the sect is at Enryakuji Temple on Mt. Hieizan in Kyoto.)

Konjikido Hall 金色堂, **Kyozo Hall** 経蔵 and **Old Protection Hall** 旧金色堂履堂 of Konjikido are located in the enclosed area

at the end of the approach. The ticket office is at the entrance to the enclosure. Hours: 8:00 AM to 5:00 PM (8:30 AM to 4:30 PM in winter). The 500 yen admission also covers admission to Sankozo Treasure House below. Konjikido Hall, a small golden hall built in 1124, is coated with black lacquer and covered entirely with gold foil. It is especially famous for the delicate decorative art works of its interior; they testify to the high artistic achievements of the area in the 12th century. Konjikido Hall, which has been designated a National Treasure, is contained within a large concrete structure completed in 1968. The Old Protection Hall, which used to house Konjikido, has been moved to the north. Kyozo Hall, originally constructed in 1108 as a two-story building, lost its second floor to fire in 1337. The first floor was repaired and preserved.

Noh Hall 能楽堂 is an important historical relic that testifies to the Temple's former preeminence in cultural activities. The Hall has an outdoor stage so audiences can enjoy open air performances.

Sankozo Treasure House 讃衡蔵 displays the temple's treasures, which include images of Buddha, paintings and other art objects. There is an especially large number of sculpture masterpieces.

Chusonji Temple to Motsuji Temple

Motsuji Temple is 600 m (2,000 feet) from Hiraizumi Station. You can take a bus from Chusonji stop to Hiraizumi Station (a 4-minute ride; 130 yen). This is the same bus you took from Ichinoseki Station but in the opposite direction. Motsuji Temple is only 10 minutes on foot from Hiraizumi Station. You can, of course, walk from Chusonji Temple to Motsuji Temple in about 30 minutes.

Motsuji Temple 毛越寺 (Lower left)

Motsuji Temple was originally erected by the priest Ennin (Jikaku Daishi) in 850. In the 12th century, under the protection of the Fujiwara family, the temple precincts contained 40 minor temples and as many as 500 lodgings, and was probably one of the nation's biggest religious establishments. All the structures were lost in repeated fires and only a few were reconstructed later. However, the original garden, which features an imaginary heaven (Jodo) and is considered among the best of those designed in the Heian Era, is still intact. This spacious garden is the best place possible to get an idea of what the medieval aristocrats and priests expected their heaven to be like. The grounds are open from 8:00 AM to 5:00 PM (8:00 AM to 4:30 PM in winter). The 500 yen admission also covers the Treasure House in the precincts.

After visiting Motsuji Temple, walk back to Hiraizumi Station and take a bus (or the JR train) back to Ichinoseki, and then the JR Tohoku Shinkansen to Sendai.

1. Ryokan in Hiraizumi

Kinkeiso (middle center, Tohoku Map 4). First Class. 71 rooms. 15,000 yen & up per person. Add: 15, Osawa, Hiraizumi. Tel: (0191) 46-2241.

2. Hotel in Ichinoseki

Hotel Sunroute Ichinoseki (1 minute walk from Ichinoseki Station). Business. 78 singles (7,000 yen -) & 11 doubles (14,000 yen -). Add: 53, Kami-Otsukigai, Ichinoseki. Tel: (0191) 26-4311.

SHIOGAMA AND MATSUSHIMA
塩釜・松島

Matsushima (literally Pine Island) is one of three places in Japan acclaimed as the nation's most beautiful sites. Matsushima Bay, dotted with more than 200 small and uniquely shaped pine-tree clad islets, is famous for its peaceful and picturesque scenery. Matsushima is also famous for

Zuiganji Temple, Tohoku's most important Zen temple. The one-day excursion from Sendai outlined below also incorporates a visit to Shiogama, a leading fishing town and site of the fabulous Shiogama Jinja Shrine, and includes a boat ride in Matsushima Bay as well. This area is very popular with Japanese tourists, and unfortunately has succumbed to the "typical" Japanese sightseeing atmosphere — groups on large buses, noisy announcements and a surfeit of souvenir shops.

Transportation

The JR Senseki Line runs northeast from Sendai, stopping at Hon-Shiogama (Main Shiogama) and Matsushima-Kaigan (Matsushima Coast) Stations. The commuter trains on this line operate every 30 minutes from early in the morning until late at night. The Senseki Line leaves Sendai from either Platform No. 1 or No. 2, located in the northeastern corner of the station. Walk to the north on the ground floor of Sendai Station building until you find the "Senseki Line" signs in English. The signs will lead you to the underground passage that connects with the Senseki Line platforms. There are both local and rapid service trains. Both stop at Hon-Shiogama and Matsushima-Kaigan. The ride to Hon-Shiogama takes about 25 minutes, and the ride to Matsushima-Kaigan about 35 minutes.

A sightseeing boat runs between Hon-Shiogama and Matsushima-Kaigan across Matsushima Bay, one of the highlights of this itinerary.

HON-SHIOGAMA 本塩釜

(Tohoku Map 5)

Shiogama is one of Japan's leading fishing ports. The city is filled with the lively spirit of the fishermen as well as a fishy smell!

Shiogama Jinja Shrine 塩釜神社 (upper left) is located to the west of Hon-Shiogama Station in a hilly forest. The Shrine was erected at the end of the 8th century. Throughout history, it was always well respected by the leading lords of the area. The present buildings were constructed in 1704 at the order of the fourth lord of the Date family. The main approach, up 200 steep stone steps, is on the western side of the Shrine. While the ancient tree-shaded stone steps are very impressive, the approach is a long distance from the train station, and you have to walk on a street with heavy traffic. We therefore recommend a southern approach (shaded on the map). After passing the first large *torii* gate, the path is a quiet, stone-paved, traffic-free gentle slope up. There are two shrines, Shiogama Jinja Shrine and Shibahiko Jinja Shrine, on a small hill. The former is the main structure of the precincts. Both of them are magnificent vermilion buildings. Entrance to the Shrine grounds is free of charge and the grounds remain open from dawn to dusk. A small museum in a modern two-story building displays miniature festival shrines, swords, hanging scrolls, paintings and armor on its first floor. The second floor features exhibits on whaling and fishery. There is a good view of the city and Matsushima Bay from the museum's roof. Hours: 8:00 AM to 4:30 PM (9:00 AM to 3:30 PM in winter). Admission: 200 yen. The Shrine's Harbor Festival, held in early August, is famous for its colorful parade of fishing boats.

To Matsushima-Kaigan by Boat

The pier, where you can catch the boat to Matsushima-Kaigan, is to the east of the train station (lower right). Sightseeing boats between Shiogama and Matsushima-Kaigan operate every 30 to 60 minutes (less frequently in winter). Some of the boats are very fanciful, shaped like a dragon and a peacock. There are two classes of seats on the boat — first and second. The ride takes one hour, and the second class cabin is quite comfortable. Fares: 2800 yen (first class); 1400 yen (second class).

The boat cruises Matsushima Bay, skirting numerous small islands, all of which have been formed into grotesque shapes by the waves. Oddly shaped pine trees that look like *bonsai* grow on each island. A modern power station ruins the marine scenery at the beginning of the cruise, but for most of the trip you will have an uninterrupted view of the artistry of nature. This is the scenery that thoroughly fascinated the brilliant *haiku* poet Basho, more than 300 years ago. The bamboo sticks you will see in the water are

MAP 5 Shiogama

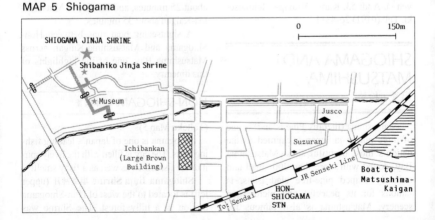

frames for cultivating seaweed, and the logs that float on the surface of the water are used by oyster farmers.

If you arrive in Matsushima other than by boat, you might be interested in the 45-minute harbor cruise, which leaves from a pier to the east of Godaido Hall (lower right, Tohoku Map 6). Boats leave approximately once every hour and the fare for the cruise is 1,400 yen.

MATSUSHIMA 松島

(Tohoku Map 6)

All of Matsushima's places of interest are located within walking distance of both Matsushima-Kaigan Pier (lower center) and the JR train station (lower left). You need about three hours to cover the area.

Godaido Hall 五大堂 (lower right) is located on a tiny island connected to the coast by a small bridge. It was originally built in 807 by Tamuramaro Sakanoue, a military leader who invaded the area at the order of the emperor. Masamune Date had the present hall built in 1600. The traditional architecture of the small temple complements the picturesque marine scenery. The inside of the Hall is not open to the public.

Fukuurajima Island 福浦島 (lower right) (optional) is connected with the coast by a vermilion pedestrian bridge. The island itself is a botanical garden. Hours: 8:00 AM to 4:30 PM. Admission: 150 yen.

Zuiganji Temple 瑞厳寺 (upper center) is the most important Zen temple in northern Japan, and dates from 827. The present buildings were constructed in 1609 at the order of Masamune. Sanmon Gate is the entrance to the main approach, which leads straight to the main temple precincts. You should turn to the right to see the numerous images of Buddha carved on the cliffs. In the olden days novices at the Temple were set the arduous task of carving these images as part of their training. The ticket office is at the entrance to the main precincts. Hours: 7:30 AM to 5:00 PM (8:00 AM to 4:00 PM in winter). Admission: 500 yen. The Main Hall, a gigantic wooden structure, houses masterpieces of carving and painting that reflect the brilliant artistic trends of the early 17th century. The Treasure House displays impressive Buddhist images and historical objects related to the Date family.

Entsuin Temple 円通院 (upper left) (optional) is also called Rose Temple because of the large number of rose bushes on its grounds. The mausoleum of Mitsumune Date, a grandson of Masamune, and the landscaped garden are worthy of special attention. Hours: 8:30 AM to 5:00 PM (4:00 PM in winter). Admission: 300 yen.

Kanrantei 観瀾亭 (lower center) (optional) was used by the lords of each generation of the Date family for moon viewing parties on summer nights. The house was originally a tea house at Fushimijo Castle in Kyoto, and was later presented to Masamune by Hideyoshi Toyotomi. Hours: 8:00 AM to 5:00 PM. Admission: 200 yen.

Ryokan in Matsushima-Kaigan

Matsushima Century Hotel (middle

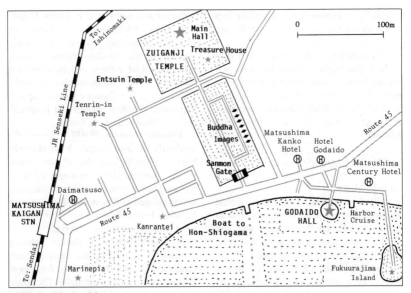

MAP 6 Matsushima

right). First Class. 54 Western & 66 Japanese rooms. 20,000 yen & up per person. Tel: (022) 354-4111.

Hotel Taikanso (3 minutes by taxi from Matsushima-Kaigan Station). First Class. 215 rooms. 20,000 yen & up per person. Tel: (022) 354-2161.

Matsushima Kanko Hotel (middle center, Tohoku Map 6). Standard. 28 rooms. 15,000 yen & up per person. Tel: (022) 354-2121.

Hotel Godaido (middle right). Standard. 78 rooms. 15,000 yen & up per person. Tel: (022) 354-3171.

YAMADERA 山寺

Risshakuji Temple is popularly known as Yamadera, which literally means Mountain Temple. The Temple was built in 860 as a Buddhist training center, and is most famous as one of the favorite Temples of Basho, the famous itinerant poet of the Edo Era.

Transportation

Yamadera Station is served by the JR Senzan Line, which connects Sendai and Yamagata. Local and rapid service trains operate to Yamadera about once every 30-60 minutes. The ride from Sendai takes about 50 minutes; the ride from Yamagata takes only about 15 minutes. Yamadera's small train station exists only to serve pilgrims and tourists on their way to the Temple.

Risshakuji (Yamadera) Temple 立石寺 (Tohoku Map 7)

The path from the train station leads inevitably to the Temple precincts. The Temple's main building is **Konponchudo Hall, 根本中堂** (optional) which is the first building one comes to after entering. Yamadera Temple is a branch temple of the Tendai sect of Buddhism, which is headquartered at Enryakuji Temple on Kyoto's Mt. Hieizan. The lantern in Konponchudo Hall has supposedly been burning steadily with fire originally brought from Enryakuji

Temple more than 1,100 years ago. Admission to Konponchudo Hall: 200 yen. **Hihokan** 秘宝館 is the Temple's Treasure Hall (optional). It exhibits Buddhist statues. Admission to Hihokan: 200 yen. **Sanmon Gate** marks the entrance to the training portion of the Temple grounds, and is at the foot of the path to Okunoin. The path to Okunoin at the very top of the mountain is up one thousand stone steps. The ticket office is next to Sanmon Gate. Admission: 500 yen. On the path up the thickly wooded mountain, you will see a stone monument to the poet Basho on your left, with an engraving of one of his most famous poems:

MAP 7 Yamadera

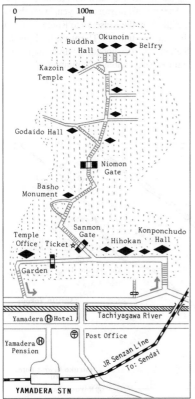

Shizukesaya, Iwa ni, Shimiiru Semi no Koe. (The silence is so complete that even the song of the cicadas is absorbed into the rocks.) The impressive **Niomon Gate** is about half-way to the top. Detour to **Godai-do Hall,** a simple wooden structure, to rest and to enjoy the magnificent view. Minor temples along the path also serve as rest stations (and souvenir shops). Next to **Kazoin Temple** is a gigantic rock. A unique hut built onto the rock houses a miniature three-story vermilion pagoda that is one of the Temple's most revered historical relics. At the top of the mountain there are three buildings: the **Belfry, Okunoin,** and **Buddha Hall** (which features a glittering golden Buddha). Once you've made it to the top of this mountain, you'll have a better idea of how this Temple has instilled a sense of discipline in generations of religious recruits. Hours: 9:00 AM to 4:30 PM.

When you descend to Sanmon Gate, turn right and exit the Temple through its lovely Garden.

NARUKO 鳴子

Naruko, a small hotspring town northwest of Sendai, is famous for *kokeshi* dolls — a traditional hand-made wooden craft, for its abundance of hotspring water and for Narukokyo Gorge, a scenic natural wonder. Fans of hotsprings or nature lovers should consider an overnight visit to Naruko.

Transportation

From Sendai, take the JR Tohoku Shinkansen to Furukawa, the first stop to the north (15 minutes). Transfer to the JR Rikuu Tosen Line to Narugo. Local and rapid service trains run about once an hour. The ride from Furukawa to Narugo takes about 40 minutes on the rapid service train and about 60 minutes on the local. Incidentally, the official name of the town is Naruko, but JR insists on calling the train station Narugo, which echoes the sound of a typical Tohoku accent.

Places of Interest

Refer to Tohoku Map 8. Most of the hot-spring resort hotels are located south of the Station (an easy 5-10 minute walk). The main street parallels the train tracks (shaded on the map), and features a number of souvenir shops as well as workshops of *kokeshi* doll makers. For a small village, Naruko boasts an impressive number of modern, deluxe *ryokan*.

Naruko's secondary attraction is **Narukokyo Gorge** 鳴子峡 (lower left). It is especially beautiful in the spring, with the new growth, and in the fall, with its spectacular foliage. If you have a half day to spare, we recommend a hike in the Gorge. You can walk from the Station or the hotspring area (about 15 minutes) to Otanihashi Bridge (middle center). There is a big signboard with a map (as well as an English sign: "Kurikoma Quasi-National Park") at the entrance to the hiking trail, which runs along the river. The one-hour hike through the tall peaks and past the waterfalls and cascades of the Gorge is a delight. The safe and well-paved path crosses and recrosses the Gorge on bridges and features a few rest stations along the way. At the end, climb the stone steps to the parking lot, which leads to Route 47, a wide national road, on which you can walk back to the Station or the hotspring area. Before the tunnel, take the road that veers off to the right (an upslope at the beginning) and walk in the woods to the **Nihon Kokeshikan Museum** 日本こけし館. The Museum has a spacious garden and displays over 5,000 *kokeshi* dolls collected from all over Japan. It is the biggest museum of its kind. Hours: 8:30 AM to 5:00 PM. Admission: 300 yen. Walk down the hill from the Museum to Route 47 again (beyond the tunnel). The walk back to the Station or the hotspring area will take approximately another 25 minutes.

MAP 8 Naruko

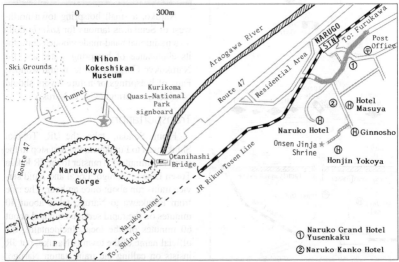

ACCOMMODATIONS
(Refer to Tohoku Map 8)

1. Ryokan in Naruko

Hotel Masuya (middle right). First Class. 54 rooms. 20,000 yen & up per person. Add: 82, Yumoto, Naruko. Tel: (0229) 83-2212.

Naruko Hotel (middle right). First Class. 137 rooms. 15,000 yen & up per person. Add: 36, Yumoto, Naruko. Tel: (0229) 83-2001.

Honjin Yokoya (middle right). First Class. 76 rooms. 15,000 yen & up per person. Add: 58-10, Yumoto, Naruko. Tel: (0229) 83-3155.

2. Welcome Inn in Naruko

Ryokan Bentenkaku (3 minutes by taxi from Narugo Station). 21 Japanese rooms. Add: 87, Kurumayu, Naruko. Tel: (0229) 83-2461.

Bandai-Asahi National Park
磐梯朝日国立公園

Bandai-Kogen Heights, surrounded by the magnificent Mt. Bandaisan and a number of beautiful lakes and ponds, is the highlight of Bandai-Asahi National Park. Thanks to the completion of the JR Tohoku Shinkansen and the development of picturesque mountain roads, Bandai-Kogen can easily be visited from Tokyo.

Aizu-Wakamatsu is a historic city. It prospered as the largest Edo Era castle town in Southern Tohoku. The loyalty of the Aizu Clan to the Tokugawa Shogunate ultimately

MAP 9 Outline of Bandai-Asahi National Park

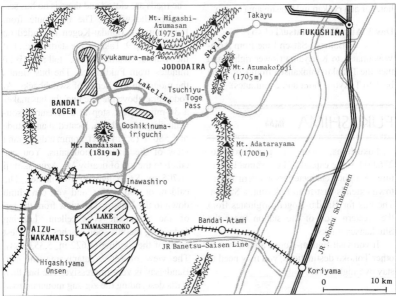

led to Aizu resistance against the imperial forces in 1868. Higashiyama Onsen, located in a narrow valley in the southeastern corner of the city, is a popular hotspring. Most visitors to Aizu-Wakamatsu spend a night there.

We introduce this area as a three-day itinerary from Tokyo. You can easily combine a trip here with other Tohoku destinations. Refer to Tohoku Map 9.

Day 1. Tokyo/Fukushima/Bandai-Kogen

Take the Tohoku Shinkansen from Tokyo to Fukushima (1 hour and 40 minutes) (upper right), and then take a bus from Fukushima to Bandai-Kogen (middle left), via the scenic "Bandai-Asahi Skyline" and "Bandai-Asahi Lakeline" toll roads (an enjoyable 3 hour ride). Overnight in Bandai-Kogen.

Day 2. Bandai-Kogen/Aizu-Wakamatsu

Take a bus from Bandai-Kogen to Aizu Wakamatsu (1 hour and 20 minutes) (lower left). The bus first runs on a pleasant mountain road skirting Mt. Bandaisan, and then along the northern shore of Lake Inawashiroko. Overnight at a downtown hotel or at a ryokan in Higashiyama Onsen.

Day 3. Aizu-Wakamatsu/Tokyo

The JR Banetsu-Saisen Line from Aizu-Wakamatsu to Koriyama (lower right), and then the Tohoku Shinkansen from Koriyama back to Tokyo (1 hour and 20 minutes).

FUKUSHIMA 福島

Fukushima, with a population of 276,000, is the capital of Fukushima Prefecture. A rather characterless modern downtown extends east from Fukushima Station. The bus for Bandai-Kogen originates from the western side of the station (near the Shinkansen tracks).

If you visit Bandai-Kogen after a visit to other Tohoku destinations, you may need to stay overnight here.

Hotels in Fukushima

Fukushima View Hotel (1 minute walk from Fukushima Station). Standard. 79 singles (8,000 yen -) & 36 doubles (14,000 yen -). Add: 13-73, Otacho, Fukushima. Tel: (0245) 31-1111.

Fukushima Washington Hotel (2 minute walk from Fukushima Station). Business. 141 singles (7,000 yen -) & 22 doubles (14,000 yen -). Add: 2-36, Sakaecho, Fukushima. Tel: (0245) 21-1711.

Fukushima Tokyu Inn (1 minute walk from Fukushima Station). Business. 79 singles (7,000 yen -) & 62 doubles (12,000 yen -). Add: 11-25, Sakaecho, Fukushima. Tel: (0245) 23-0109.

Fukushima to Bandai-Kogen

The bus for Bandai-Kogen leaves from the western (less developed) side of JR Fukushima Station. There are only three buses a day: 8:00 AM, 10:40 AM and 1:30 PM. The fare to Bandai-Kogen is 2,620 yen, and the entire trip takes a little over three hours. The roads are closed and there is no bus service in the winter. The bus route from Fukushima to Bandai-Kogen is shaded on Tohoku Map 9. Takayu, the starting point of the "Bandai-Azuma Skyline" toll road, is 30 minutes from Fukushima. The bus climbs the mountain in a series of switchbacks. At Jododaira, above the tree line, the bus makes a 30-minute rest stop at a restaurant/souvenir shop. **Jododaira,** located at an altitude of 1,580 m (5,214 feet), commands a grand view of the Azuma mountains. You can climb to the top of nearby Mt. Azumakofuji (1,705 m, 5,626 feet) in 10 minutes. The caldera on top is dry, and you can climb down to the bottom. The view from the top of the mountain is excellent. Leaving Jododaira, the bus soon reaches the highest point of the Skyline (1,622 m, 5,353 feet). The view of Mt. Adatarayama and Mt. Bandaisan is very impressive. The bus then starts descending the zig-zag mountain road into the woods leading to Tsuchiyu Toge Pass (1,230 m, 4,059 feet).

Turning west at Tsuchiyu Pass, the bus follows the "Bandai-Azuma Lakeline" toll road, through beautiful forests. You can see the lovely trio of Bandai-Kogen: Lake Hibarako, Lake Onogawako and Lake Akimotoko, from time to time through the woods. The blue lakes are a striking contrast to the deep green of the woods. The bus usually proceeds first to Goshikinuma-iriguchi, then to Kyukamura-mae, and finally to Bandai-Kogen, the last stop.

BANDAI-KOGEN
磐梯高原

Refer to Tohoku Map 10. The Bandai-Kogen Bus Terminal (lower left), near Lake Hibarako, is at the center of the plateau. There are many restaurants and souvenir shops in this area.

Goshikinuma 五色沼 (Five Colored Ponds) is the name given to the many small ponds located between Lake Hibarako and Lake Akimotoko. Varied in size and shape, each one of the ponds has water of a different color. **Goshikinuma Natural Trail** 五色沼自然探勝路 is a sylvan promenade that passes most of the Goshikinuma Ponds. Rental row boats are available on Bishamonnuma Pond, the largest one — near Goshikinuma-iriguchi bus stop.

Lake Hibarako 檜原湖 is the largest lake in Bandai-Kogen. A 30-minute sightseeing boat operates frequently from the pier near Bandai-Kogen Bus Terminal. Boats leave frequently and the fare is 820 yen. Pleasant walking paths run along the eastern shore of the lake.

Ryokan in Bandai-Kogen
(Refer to Tohoku Map 10)

Note: The address for each of these is the same: Hibara, Kita-Shiobara-mura.

Hotel Banso (lower right, Tohoku Map 10). First Class. 20 rooms. 20,000 yen & up per person. Tel: (0241) 32-2111.

Urabandai Royal Hotel (lower right).

MAP 10   Bandai-Kogen Heights

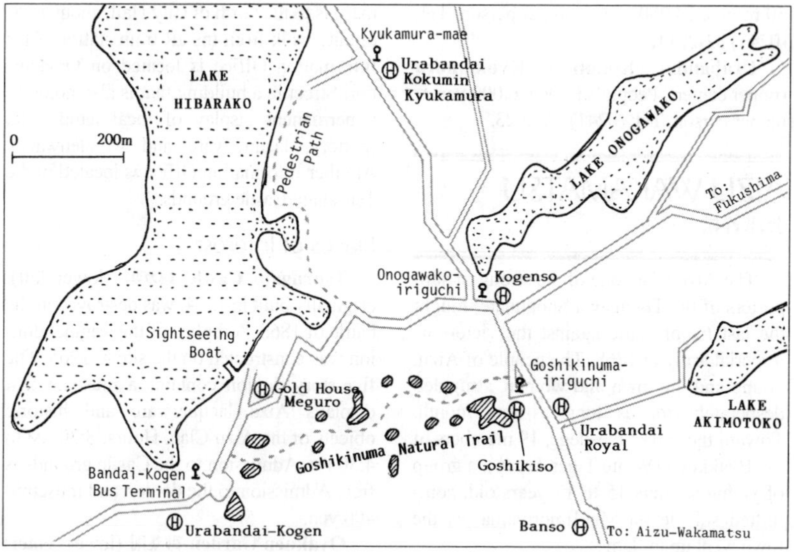

First Class. 235 rooms. 20,000 yen & up per person. Tel: (0241) 32-3111.

Urabandai-Kogen Hotel (lower left). First Class. 47 rooms. 20,000 yen & up per person. Tel: (0241) 32-2211.

Hotel Kogenso (middle center). Standard. 58 rooms. 14,000 yen & up per person. Tel: (0241) 32-2531.

Hotel Goshikiso (lower right). Standard. 50 rooms. 14,000 yen & up per person. Tel: (0241) 32-2011.

Urabandai Kokumin Kyukamura (upper center). People's Lodge. 6,000 yen & up per person. Tel: (0241) 32-2923.

AIZU-WAKAMATSU
会津若松

The Aizu Clan, one of the strongest supporters of the Tokugawa Shogunate, fought the last major battle against the victorious imperial army in 1868. The people of Aizu, young and old, men and women, struggled desperately for as long as one month. Toward the end of the siege, 19 members of the Byakkotai (White Tiger Troop), a group of young soldiers 15 to 17 years old, committed suicide on Mt. Iimoriyama, as the town went up in flames.

Bandai-Kogen to Aizu-Wakamatsu

The bus to Aizu-Wakamatsu originates at Urabandai Kokumin Kyukamura and stops at Bandai-Kogen Bus Terminal and Goshikinuma-iriguchi. Approximately 6 buses make the trip to Aizu-Wakamatsu each day. The ride to JR Aizu-Wakamatsu Station takes about 1 hour and 30 minutes and the fare is 1,500 yen.

Transportation in Aizu-Wakamatsu

Refer to Tohoku Map 11. There are two loop bus lines around the city (clockwise and counter-clockwise), starting from Aizu-Wakamatsu Station (upper left, Tohoku Map 11). Tsurugajo-Minamiguchi (lower left), the stop for the castle, is on the loop lines. There is also bus service between Aizu-Wakamatsu Station and Higashiyama Onsen (to the southeast of the city, outside of the map). Oyakuen-iriguchi (middle center) and Bukeyashiki-mae (lower right) stops are on this line.

Downtown Aizu-Wakamatsu

The city's downtown (shaded area on the map) is to the north of City Hall, about a 15-minute walk from the JR train station. An *i* Information Office is located on Omachi-dori Street in a building that is also home to a permanent display of local handicrafts (pottery, lacquerware and woodenware). Another Information Office is located in the Tsurugajo Castle grounds.

Places of Interest

Tsurugajo Castle 鶴ガ城 (lower left), originally built in 1384, was destroyed in the battle of 1868. A replica of the original donjon was constructed on the site in 1965. The five-story donjon contains a museum that displays Aizu lacquerware and historic objects of the Aizu Clan. Hours: 8:30 AM to 4:30 PM. Admission to the Castle grounds is free. Admission to the donjon and museum: 400 yen.

Oyakuen Garden 御薬園 (lower center)

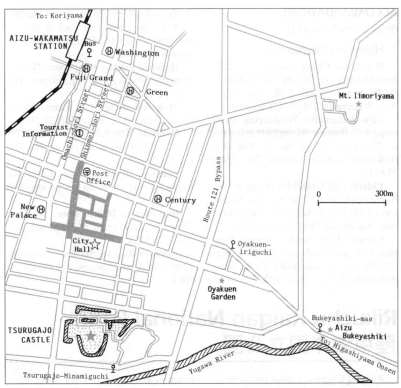

MAP 11 Aizu-Wakamatsu

(optional) is a beautiful landscaped garden laid out around a large pond. At the order of the Aizu lord it was originally constructed as an herb garden. Hours: 8:30 AM to 5:00 PM. Admission: 300 yen.

Aizu Bukeyashiki 会津武家屋敷 (lower right) (optional) features the Aizu samurai. Many replicas of Aizu samurai houses are displayed here. The main building is the mansion of Tanomo Saigo, Aizu's Prime Minister. Hours: 8:30 AM to 5:00 PM. Admission: 800 yen.

Mt. Iimoriyama 飯盛山 (upper right) (optional). This is the site of the famous suicide of the young soldiers. The small mountain has a number of monuments, including several from foreign countries. It is rather difficult to reach Mt. Iimoriyama by public transportation; it is therefore recommended only for aficionados of Meiji Restoration history.

ACCOMMODATIONS

(Refer to Tohoku Map 11)

1. Hotels in Downtown

Hotel New Palace (middle left). Standard. 53 singles (5,500 yen -) & 20 doubles (9,000 yen -). Add: 2-78, Nakamachi, Aizu-Wakamatsu. Tel: (0242) 28-2804.

Aizu-Wakamatsu Washington Hotel (upper left). Business. 94 singles (6,500 yen -) & 52 doubles (12,500 yen -). Add: 201, Byakkocho, Aizu-Wakamatsu. Tel: (0242) 22-6111.

Ekimae Fuji Grand Hotel (upper left). Business. 69 singles (5,000 yen -) & 13 doubles (9,000 yen -). Add: 5-25, Ekimaecho, Aizu-Wakamatsu. Tel: (0242) 24-1111.

Century Hotel (middle center). Business. 87 singles (7,000 yen -) & 24 doubles (12,500 yen -). Add: 8-30, Ueno, Aizu-Wakamatsu. Tel: (0242) 24-1900.

2. Ryokan in Higashiyama Onsen

Note: The address for each of these is the same: Yumoto, Higashiyama-machi, Aizu-Wakamatsu.

Harataki Bekkan Konjakutei. Deluxe. 25 rooms. 30,000 yen & up per person. Tel: (0242) 27-6048.

Mukotaki. Deluxe. 32 rooms. 20,000 yen & up per person. Tel: (0242) 27-7501.

Harataki Shinkan. First Class. 36 rooms. 15,000 yen & up per person. Tel: (0242) 27-6048.

Fudotaki Ryokan. First Class. 42 rooms. 15,000 yen & up per person. Tel: (0242) 26-5050.

Higashiyama Daiichi Hotel. Standard. 27 rooms. 12,000 yen & up per person. Tel: (0242) 26-8585.

Arimaya Ryokan. Standard. 18 rooms. 12,000 yen & up per person. Tel: (0242) 26-2001.

Rikuchu Kaigan National Park
陸中海岸国立公園

Rikuchu Kaigan is famous for the beautiful marine scenery of its rugged rocky coast. Until the completion of the Sanriku Railways Kita-Rias Line, infrequent bus service was the only transportation available along the narrow coastal roads, and the area was popularly called the "Tibet of Japan." Even though the train service is not as frequent as that of other areas, Rikuchu Kaigan is now an accessible destination. We suggest the following 3-day itinerary from Tokyo. Refer to Tohoku Map 12.

Day 1. Arrive Kuji

If you start your trip from Morioka (upon arrival from Tokyo on the JR Tohoku Shinkansen or after a trip to Lake Towadako or the Sendai area), take a JR bus from Morioka (lower left) to Kuji (upper center). The bus operates seven times a day in each direction and the ride takes about three hours. The bus passes scenic Hiraniwa Kogen Heights. If you come from the north (upon arrival at Misawa Airport, or on your way back to Tokyo from Hokkaido), take the JR Hachinohe Line from Hachinohe (upper left) to Kuji. The train operates approximately every 60-90 minutes and the ride takes about 2 hours. Overnight in Kuji.

Day 2. Kuji/Shimanokoshi/Miyako/Morioka

Take a train on the Kita-Rias Line from Kuji to Shimanokoshi (middle right). The trains operate about once an hour. The ride takes 50 minutes. Most of the trip is through tunnels, but you can catch occasional views of lovely small fishing villages along the coast. Enjoy a 45-minute boat ride at Shimanokoshi (available about once every 90 minutes; fare 1,200 yen). The boat visits the

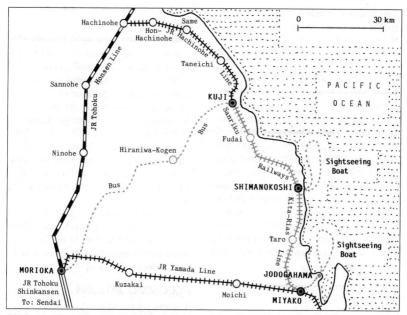

MAP 12 Rikuchu Kaigan National Park

"Alps of the Sea" of Kitayamazaki, a stretch of 200 m (656 foot) precipitous cliffs rising from the sea. After the boat ride, continue by train to Miyako (lower right). If you start from Kuji around 8:00 AM you will be in Miyako around noon. (The ride from Shimanokoshi to Miyako takes about 40 minutes.) Take a bus from Miyako Station to Jodogahama (lower right) (about a 15-minute ride, frequent service; fare 150 yen). Jodogahama (Heavenly Beach) is a sunken beach. Its white rocks and green pine trees are a typical Japanese seascape. A 40-minute sightseeing boat trip operates about once every hour from Jodogahama. Fare: 1,000 yen. Stay overnight in Miyako, or you can proceed to Morioka by late afternoon train. The JR Yamada Line operates between Miyako and Morioka about once every 2 hours. The ride to Morioka takes about 2 hours and 30 minutes.

Day 3. Travel Onward

Travel back to Tokyo or on to other Tohoku destinations.

KUJI 久慈

Kuji, which once prospered as a castle town of the Kuji family, is now a small city with a population of 40,000. The JR Kuji Station and Kuji Station on the Kita-Rias Line are located side by side. The city is famous for the traditional Kokuji-yaki pottery of the area.

Accommodations in Kuji

Kuji Grand Hotel (2 minute walk from Kuji Station). Business hotel. 46 singles (5,600 yen -) & 10 doubles (11,000 yen -). Add: 10-15, Kawasakicho, Kuji. Tel: (0194) 52-2222.

Hotel Fukunoya (5 minute walk from

Kuji Station). Standard ryokan. 25 rooms. 10,000 yen & up per person. Add: 1-3-5, Nakanohashi, Kuji. Tel: (0194) 53-5111.

SHIMANOKOSHI　島ノ越

Shimanokoshi is a tiny fishing village. The Shimanokoshi Station is a colorful fairy tale building. There is literally nothing in the station area. The pier for the sightseeing boat is about 200 m (656 feet) from the station. A 45-minute sightseeing boat operates about once every 60-90 minutes. The small boat cruises along the precipitous cliffs of Rikuchu Kaigan National Park. Kitayamazaki, popularly called the "Alps of the Sea," features sunken rocks washed by rough Pacific waves and is the highlight of the boat trip.

MIYAKO　宮古

Miyako, with a population of 62,000, is the largest city in the Rikuchu Kaigan area. The small downtown stretching to the north from the station is typical of local cities. The highlight of Miyako is Jodogahama Beach. Buses operate once every 20-30 minutes from the station. The beautiful rock formations there are natural works of art. In the summer the beach is crowded with bathers. The sightseeing boat around the rock formations starts from near Jodogahama Bus Stop.

Ryokan in Miyako

Jodogahama Park Hotel. First Class. 75 rooms. 15,000 yen & up per person. Add: Jodogahama, Miyako. Tel: (0193) 62-2321.

Sawadaya Shinsenkaku. Standard. 29 rooms. 12,000 yen & up per person. Add: 7-2, Kurodacho, Miyako. Tel: (0193) 62-3753.

Kumayasu Ryokan. Standard. 26 rooms. 8,000 yen & up per person. Add: 2-5, Shinmachi, Miyako. Tel: (0193) 62-3545.

MORIOKA　盛岡

Refer to Tohoku Map 13. The terminal station of the JR Tohoku Shinkansen (middle left). The city is the capital of Iwate Prefecture and has a population of 232,000. A number of modern hotels are located near the station to provide overnight accommodations for those who start their Tohoku trips here. JR buses to Towadako and Kuji (Rikuchu Kaigan) originate at the bus terminal on the eastern side of Morioka Station. An *i* Information Office is located in the Station.

Morioka's downtown (shaded on the map) is across the Kitakamigawa River from JR Morioka Station. Iwate-Koen Park (lower right) was built on the grounds of the former Moriokajo Castle.

ACCOMMODATIONS

(Refer to Tohoku Map 13)

1. Hotels in Morioka

Hotel Higashi-Nihon (upper center). Standard. 129 singles (8,000 yen -) & 76 doubles (16,000 yen -). Add: 3-3-18, Odori, Morioka. Tel: (0196) 25-2131.

Hotel Royal Morioka (middle center). Standard. 52 singles (8,000 yen -) & 45 doubles (15,500 yen -). Add: 1-11,11, Saien, Morioka. Tel: (0196) 53-1331.

Morioka Grand Hotel Annex (upper center). Business. 18 singles (7,500 yen -) & 90 doubles (15,000 yen -). Add: 1-9-16, Chuo-dori, Morioka. Tel: (0196) 25-5111.

Hotel Rich Morioka (middle left). Business. 155 singles (7,000 yen -) & 43 doubles (12,500 yen -). Add: 7-15, Ekimae-dori, Morioka. Tel: (0196) 25-2611.

Hotel Sunroute Morioka (upper left). Business. 150 singles (6,500 yen -) & 32 doubles (12,500 yen -). Add: 3-7-19, Odori, Morioka. Tel: (0196) 25-3311.

Morioka New City Hotel (upper left). Business. 96 singles (6,000 yen -) & 22 dou-

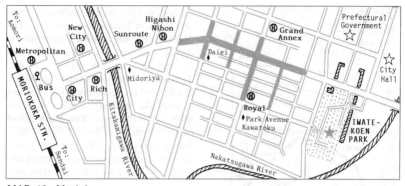

MAP 13   Morioka

bles (9,500 yen -). Add: 13-10, Ekimae-dori, Morioka. Tel: (0196) 54-5161

2. Welcome Inns in Morioka

Hotel Metropolitan Morioka (middle left, Tohoku Map 13). 180 Western rooms.

Add: 1-44, Ekimae-dori, Morioka. Tel: (0196) 25-1211.

Kumagai Ryokan (8 minute walk from Morioka Station). 11 Japanese rooms. Add: 3-2-5, Osawakawara, Morioka. Tel: (0196) 51-3020.

Northern Tohoku 東北北部

Refer Tohoku Map 14. Aomori (upper center) is the main gateway to Lake Towadako (middle center). Hirosaki (middle left) is a castle town, an ideal half-day excursion destination from Aomori.

Transportation to Aomori

The bus terminal is adjacent to Aomori Station. You can reach Aomori by the JR Tsugaru Kaikyo Line from Hakodate, Hokkaido (through the Seikan Undersea Tunnel). From Tokyo you can use the JR Tohoku Shinkansen to Morioka (lower right) and then the JR Tohoku Honsen Line to Aomori. The combined train ride takes about 6 hours. You can also fly from Tokyo (Haneda Airport) to Aomori Airport. An airport bus runs between Aomori Station and the Airport in 40 minutes. The bus schedule is designed around the flight schedules. The

fare from the Station to the Airport is 550 yen.

Suggested Itinerary

The following is a typical itinerary in the area:

Day 1. Arrive in Aomori

If you have a full afternoon in Aomori, we suggest that you visit Hirosaki instead of staying in Aomori. Hirosaki is more interesting from the tourist's point of view.

Day 2. Aomori/Lake Towadako

In the morning, take the JR bus to Lake Towadako. Visit Oirase Valley and enjoy a boat ride across the Lake. Overnight on the Lake.

Day 3. Lake Towadako/Morioka

Take an early afternoon JR bus to

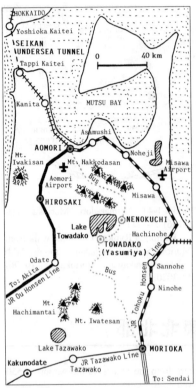

MAP 14 Outline of Northern Tohoku

Morioka, and then return to Tokyo via the JR Tohoku Shinkansen, or proceed to other Tohoku destinations.

AOMORI 青森

Refer to Tohoku Map 15. Aomori, with a population of 292,000, is the capital of Aomori Prefecture. The city is especially famous for its Nebuta Festival (August 3-7), a colorful event featuring processions of Nebuta floats. **Munakata Shiko Memerial Museum of Art** 棟方志功記念館 (lower right) displays works of Shiko Munakata (1903-1975), one of the world's outstanding woodblock print artists. The museum build-

ing is shaped like the famous Shosoin Treasure House of Todaiji Temple in Nara. **The Market near the Station** (upper left) is Aomori's kitchen. A number of small shops are crowded in the narrow arcades. **Tourism & Products Center** 青森県観光物産館アスパム (upper center) is a modern pyramid-like building housing souvenir shops and restaurants. **The Main Street** (shaded) stretches to the east from Aomori Station and is lined with department stores, souvenir shops and restaurants. **Aomori Bay Bridge** provides a beautiful view of the city.

ACCOMMODATIONS
(Refer to Tohoku Map 15)

1. Hotels in Aomori

Hotel Aomori (middle right). Standard. 61 singles (11,500 yen -) & 84 doubles (17,000 yen -). Add: 1-1-23, Tsutsumicho, Aomori. Tel: (0177) 75-4141.

Hotel Sunroute Aomori (middle left). Standard. 88 singles (7,000 yen -) & 35 doubles (12,500 yen -). Add: 1-9-10, Shinmachi, Aomori. Tel: (0177) 75-2321.

Aomori Grand Hotel (middle left). Standard. 91 singles (6,500 yen -) & 44 doubles (11,500 yen -). Add: 1-1-23, Shinmachi, Aomori. Tel: (0177) 23-1011.

Hotel New Aomorikan (middle left). Business. 70 singles (6,500 yen -) & 20 doubles (11,500 yen -). Add: 1-3-2, Shinmachi, Aomori. Tel: (0177) 22-2865.

2. Welcome Inn in Aomori

Aomori Kokusai Hotel (middle left). 69 Western rooms. Add: 1-6-18, Shinmachi, Aomori. Tel: (0177) 22-4321.

HIROSAKI 弘前

You can reach Hirosaki from Aomori on the JR Ou Line. Several limited express trains and many local trains run between these two cities once every 30-60 minutes.

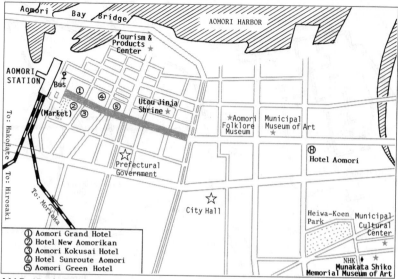

MAP 15 Aomori

① Aomori Grand Hotel
② Hotel New Aomorikan
③ Aomori Kokusai Hotel
④ Hotel Sunroute Aomori
⑤ Aomori Green Hotel

The ride takes 30 minutes by limited express, and 60 minutes on the local trains. The limited express trains run from Hirosaki to Akita (and beyond). Hirosaki prospered as a castle town in the feudal era. Hirosaki is also famous for its Neputa Festival (August 1-7), which is similar to Aomori's Festival.

Refer to Tohoku Map 16. Hirosaki's downtown is centered around Chuo Hirosaki Station (lower center), which is served by the local Konan Railways (commuter trains). The area around JR Hirosaki Station (lower right) is comparatively less developed, though there are a few department stores and restaurants.

Hirosakijo Castle 弘前城 (left) is a 15-minute walk from JR Hirosaki Station. The Castle was built in 1611. The three-story donjon is located in the center of neatly maintained grounds. The Castle is especially popular at the end of April, when 3,000 cherry trees display their beautiful flowers. Hours: dawn to dusk. Admission is usually free, but during the cherry blossom season there is a 300 yen admission charge.

Tsugaru Neputa-mura 津軽ねぷた村 (upper left) is an exhibition hall of festival floats and accoutrements. With festival music in the background, you can feel the atmosphere of the colorful, gay summer event. Attached to the exhibition hall is one of Tohoku's most famous landscaped gardens, Yokien Garden. The garden features pine trees, rocks and ponds. Hours: 9:00 AM to 5:00 PM (4:00 PM in winter). Admission: 500 yen.

Samurai Houses 武家屋敷 : To the north of the Castle is the old residential district. Even though most of the old houses have been replaced, the hedges and streets preserve the atmosphere of the samurai era. Iwata House 岩田家 (upper center) is the most famous one in the area.

ACCOMMODATIONS
(Refer to Tohoku Map 16)

1. Hotels in Hirosaki

City Hirosaki Hotel (lower right). Standard. 59 singles (7,500 yen -) & 80 doubles

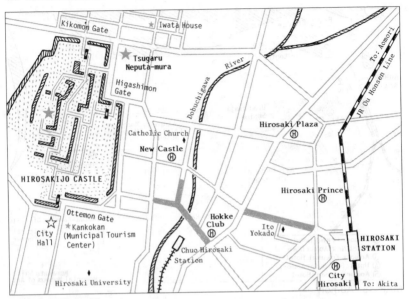

MAP 16 Hirosaki

(14,000 yen -). Add: 1-1-2, Omachi, Hirosaki. Tel: (0172) 37-0109.

Hotel New Castle (middle center). Standard. 22 singles (7,000 yen -) & 33 doubles (12,500 yen -). Add: 24-1, Kamisayashimachi, Hirosaki. Tel: (0172) 36-1211.

Hirosaki Prince Hotel (middle right). Business. 78 singles (5,500 yen -) & 16 doubles (10,500 yen -). Add: 1-3-4, Ekimae, Hirosaki. Tel: (0172) 33-5000.

2. Welcome Inn in Hirosaki

Hokke Club Hirosaki (lower center). 116 Western & 6 Japanese rooms. Add: 126, Dotemachi, Hirosaki. Tel: (0172) 34-3811.

LAKE TOWADAKO
十和田

Refer to Tohoku Map 17. Yasumiya (also called Towadako) (lower center) is the last stop of the JR bus from Aomori. But you should get off the bus at Nenokuchi (middle right) so you can enjoy a boat ride across the Lake from Nenokuchi to Yasumiya. Leaving the city of Aomori, the bus runs along a refreshing mountain road, skirting the Hakkoda mountains. Hakkoda is a heavy snow zone and a mecca for spring skiing. On the way, the bus makes short stops at scenic points so passengers can enjoy the views. Because of the heavy snow, the road to Towadako is closed from the middle of November until the middle of April. There are two major attractions in the Towadako area — the lake itself and Oirase Valley.

Oirase Valley 奥入瀬渓谷 (Middle right)

The JR bus from Aomori runs along the Oirasegawa River and you can enjoy the scenic beauty of the river, falls, trees and rocks even from the windows of the bus. The bus operates about once an hour. If you want to walk Oirase Valley (as most people do), use a baggage delivery service. At

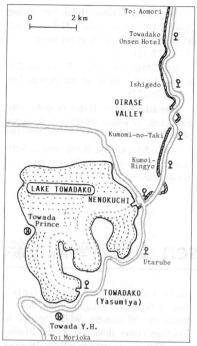

MAP 17 Lake Towadako

Towadako Onsen Hotel stop (upper right), attendants ask all passengers if they are interested in baggage service. You can send your bag to Nenokuchi stop (middle right) via this special service and free yourself for a walk in Oirase Valley. Continue on the bus to Ishigedo or Kumoi-no-Taki, and then start your walking tour along Oirasegawa River to Nenokuchi. The walk takes about 3 hours and 30 minutes from Ishigedo, and 2 hours and 30 minutes from Kumoi-no-Taki. You can pick up your bag at the small hut in front of the Nenokuchi Bus Stop. You can take a boat from Nenokuchi to Yasumiya (Towadako), as explained above.

The ride from Aomori Station to Towadako Onsen Hotel takes about 2 hours; Nenokuchi is an additional 40 minutes; and it is a further 25 minutes to Towadako Terminal (Yasumiya).

Lake Towadako 十和田湖

Lake Towadako is a caldera lake 46 km (29 miles) in circumference and 327 m (1,073 feet) deep. Sightseeing boats connect Nenokuchi and Yasumiya (Towadako). The view from the boat of Ogura Peninsula is especially impressive. Most accommodations are located in the Yasumiya area (See Tohoku Map 18). Enjoy a leisurely walk along the lake. The "Statue of Girls" (upper left, Tohoku Map 18) is the final work of Kotaro Takamura, and a symbol of Lake Towadako. Towada Jinja Shrine (upper left) is a few minutes walk from the statue.

ACCOMMODATIONS
(Refer to Tohoku Map 17)

1. Hotel in Towadako

Towada Prince Hotel (middle left, Tohoku Map 17). First Class. 66 rooms. Double (18,500 yen -). Add: Towadako, Kosakamachi. Tel: (0176) 75-3111.

Note: This is the only decent western-

MAP 18 Yasumiya

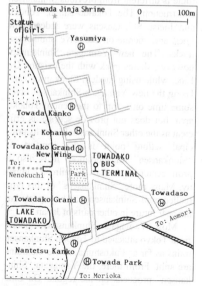

style resort hotel in this area. A hotel courtesy bus operates between Towadako Bus Terminal and the hotel.

2. Ryokan in Towadako

Note: The address for each of these is the same: Yasumiya, Towadako-machi.

Yasumiya Hotel (upper center). First Class. 76 rooms. 18,000 yen & up per person. Tel: (0176) 75-2321.

Kohanso (middle left). First Class. 38 rooms. 18,000 yen & up per person. Tel: (0176) 75-2021.

Towadako Grand Hotel New Wing (middle left, Tohoku Map 18). First Class. 45 rooms. 15,000 yen & up per person. Tel: (0176) 75-1111.

Towadaso (lower right). First Class. 216 rooms. 14,000 yen & up per person. Tel: (0176) 75-2221.

Towada Kanko Hotel (middle left). First class. 72 rooms. 18,000 yen & up per person. Tel: (0176) 75-2111.

Towadako Grand Hotel (middle left). Standard. 118 rooms. 10,000 yen & up per person. Tel: (0176) 75-1111.

Along the JR Yamagata Shinkansen 山形新幹線沿線

The JR Yamagata Shinkansen started service in July 1992. Construction of the new Shinkansen Line was designed to stimulate travel to the Yamagata area, but this route is different from previous Shinkansen construction. The Tokaido-Sanyo, Tohoku and Joetsu Shinkansens were indeed new lines, and operate on exclusive Shinkansen tracks. The new Yamagata Shinkansen, however, shares track with the existing Ou Line, while using modern Shinkansen cars. Using the new Yamagata Shinkansen saves some time on a trip to the central Tohoku area, but does not provide service as efficient as the other Shinkansen Lines. Its principal selling point is the comfort of "Shinkansen" transportation. It is also a profit center for the East JR railroad company. Many more "Shinkansens" of this type (called mini-Shinkansen) can be expected in the near future in other parts of Japan.

Most Yamagata Shinkansens operate from Tokyo attached to Tohoku Shinkansen trains as far as Fukushima, where the trains are split. From there, the Yamagata "Shinkansen" proceeds on the regular Ou Line tracks to its terminus at Yamagata. The ride from Tokyo to Yamagata takes about 2 hours and 50 minutes, while the ride to Yonezawa takes about 2 hours and 10 minutes. This line is most useful for Japanese travelers on their way to the area's famous ski and hotspring resorts, such as Mt. Zaosan.

The area has few sites of interest to tourists, but we describe two castle cities along this new Shinkansen route: Yamagata and Yonezawa. They are recommended as destinations for repeat travelers to the Tohoku region.

YAMAGATA 山形

Refer to Tohoku Map 19. This castle town of 244,000 is the capital of Yamagata Prefecture. The downtown of the city is centered at the JR Station (lower left). An *i* Information Office is located in the Station. Nanokamachi-dori Street (shaded on the map), which leads to Yamagata's governmental center, is the city's principal shopping street and home to several department stores, such as Matsuzakaya, Onuma and Senzokuya.

Yamagata is especially famous for its summer festival — Hanagasa Odori Dance Parade — in early August. The three-day Festival features ten thousand dancers dressed in *yukata* and carrying flower-decorated straw hats parading on the city's main street. As many as 900,000 visitors jam the city to witness this spectacle.

The city's major tourist attraction is Kajo-Koen Park, site of the former Castle (upper left). Only reconstructed Higashi Otemon Gate (Main Eastern entrance to the Castle) and the moats remain. The Park also features a statue of Yoshiaki Mogami, the prominent feudal lord responsible for the development of the city. The local government has devoted the Castle grounds to municipal sports facilities — a swimming pool, baseball diamonds, tennis courts and a gymnasium. The Park is open dawn to dusk and there is no admission charge.

Two museums are adjacent to the Castle grounds: **The History Museum** 最上義光歴史館 (Upper center) (optional) is dedicated to Yoshiaki Mogami and features items of local interest. Hours: 9:00 AM to 4:30 PM. Closed on Mondays. Admission: 300 yen. **The Yamagata Museum of Art** 山形美術館 (optional) displays Western art and some Japanese works. It specializes in Picasso, Chagall and Rodin. Hours: 10:00 AM to 5:00

MAP 19 Yamagata

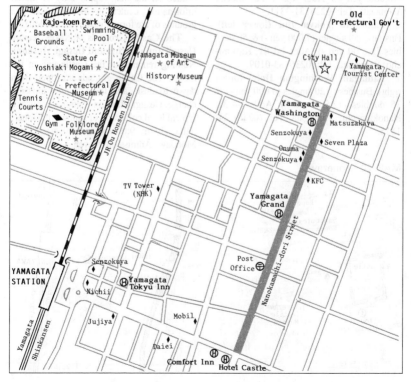

PM. Closed Mondays. Admission: 500 yen.

The Old Prefectural Government Building 旧山形県庁 (upper right) (optional) is a neo-Baroque style building erected in 1916. It has been renovated and serves as a museum and a symbol of the influence of Western culture in early modern Japan.

ACCOMMODATIONS

(Refer to Tohoku Map 19)

1. Hotels in Yamagata

Yamagata Grand Hotel (middle center). Standard. 48 singles (8,500 yen -) & 61 doubles (16,500 yen -). Add: 1-7-42, Honcho, Yamagata. Tel: (0236) 41-2611.

Hotel Castle (lower center). Standard. 106 singles (8,500 yen -) & 12 doubles (16,000 yen -). Add: 4-2-7, Tokamachi, Yamagata. Tel: (0236) 31-3311.

Yamagata Tokyu Inn (lower left). Business. 50 singles (7,000 yen -) & 50 doubles (11,500 yen -). Add: 1-10-1, Kasumi-cho, Yamagata. Tel: (0236) 33-0109.

Yamagata Washington Hotel (upper right). Business. 120 singles (6,000 yen -) & 35 doubles (12,500 yen -). Add: 1-4-31, Nanokamachi, Yamagata. Tel: (0236) 24-1515.

YONEZAWA 米沢

Refer to Tohoku Map 20. The Uesugi of Niigata were one of Japan's leading families during the civil war period of the 16th century. They were generally considered to be one of the few clans capable of achieving central power. After the establishment of the Tokugawa Shogunate, the Uesugis were moved from Niigata to the even more remote area of Yonezawa. Yonezawa prospered throughout the Edo Era under the twelve-generation rule of the Uesugis.

Yonezawa today has a population of 93,000. The downtown is to the west of the JR Station (middle right), across the Matsukawa River. The main shopping street is shaded on the map (upper left). A tourist information center is located near the grounds of the former castle (middle left).

The Castle Grounds 米沢城跡 feature **Uesugi Jinja Shrine and Uesugi Museum.** Nothing remains of the Castle except the moats. The Castle grounds are open from dawn to dusk, and there is no admission charge. Uesugi Museum (optional) houses a typical local collection of military paraphernalia. Hours: 9:00 AM to 4:30 PM. Closed Mondays. Admission: 50 yen.

MAP 20 Yonezawa

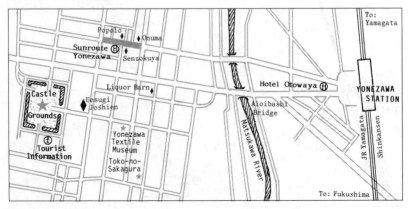

In the neighborhood of the Castle there are two sites of interest to tourists. **Yonezawa Textile Museum** 米沢織物歴史資料館 (optional). Hours: 10:00 AM to 4:00 PM. Closed in winter. Admission: 300 yen. **Toko-no-Sakagura**東光の酒蔵(optional)is a sake factory and museum owned by one of the leading sake brewers of Tohoku. The displays explain the traditional brewing techniques and the specialized tools of the trade. Hours: 9:00 AM to 4:30 PM. Admission: 300 yen.

Mausoleum of the Uesugi Family 上杉家廟所 (off the map; 2 km to the west of the Station) (optional). Twelve small shrines commemorate each generation of the Uesugis. Hours: 9:00 AM to 5:00 PM. Admission: 200 yen. Buses from the Station run only about once every 60-90 minutes.

Yonezawa is also famous for the local beef. We suggest you try it. There are several restaurants in the Castle area. Uesugi Joshien (middle left) is a huge, brand new restaurant and souvenir shopping center, constructed in traditional style.

Accommodations in Yonezawa

Most tourists visiting Yonezawa stay in Yamagata or at nearby Zao and Tengendai hotspring resorts.

Tokyo Daiichi Hotel Yonezawa (5 minutes by taxi from Yonezawa Station). Business. 55 singles (7,500 yen -) & 8 doubles (16,000 yen -). Add: 1-13-3, Chuo, Yonezawa. Tel: (0238) 24-0411.

Hotel Sunroute Yonezwa (upper left). Business. 76 singles (6,000 yen -) & 14 doubles (11,500 yen -). Add: 3-3-1, Montocho, Yonezawa. Tel: (0238) 21-3211.

Japan Sea Coast of Tohoku
日本海沿岸

As elsewhere in Japan, industrial and transportation development in Tohoku is lopsided and heavily weighted to the Pacific Ocean side (those cities along the JR Tohoku Shinkansen). The area along the Japan Sea coast is a chief producer of rice, and the access from other Tohoku cities is very inconvenient. Though Tsuruoka and Hagurosan are in Yamagata Prefecture, it is not easy to incorporate these destinations in itineraries to other major Tohoku cities, as described below. You should consider planning a separate trip from Tokyo to this area (possibly combined with a trip to Joetsu destinations, such as Sado Island and Niigata).

Transportation to Tsuruoka

The fastest train travel to Tsuruoka from Tokyo is the combination of the JR Joetsu Shinkansen (Tokyo-Niigata, about 2 hours) and the JR Uetsu Honsen Line (the Niigata-Tsuruoka trip, on the "Inaho" limited express, takes about 2 hours — it only operates about once every 2 hours).

There is one flight daily from Tokyo (Haneda Airport) to Shonai Airport. A 40-minute bus ride connects the Airport with JR Sakata Station.

If you want to cross Tohoku from west to east, from Tsuruoka to Sendai, you need to make the following (rather complicated) train connections (see Tohoku Map 1): From Tsuruoka to Amarume, take the local train on the JR Uetsu Honsen Line (20 minutes); from Amarume to Shinjo, take the JR Rikuu-Saisen Line (1 hour on the local); from Shinjo to Yamagata, take the JR Ou Line (about 1 hour on the limited express, or 1 hour and 30 minutes on the local); and from Yamagata to Sendai, take the JR Senzan Line (about 1 hour and 30 minutes on the local).

TSURUOKA 鶴岡

Tsuruoka prospered as a feudal castle town under the rule of the Sakai family. Nearby Sakata was the commercial center for the feudal government. Today, Tsuruoka's population is 100,000, and that of its twin city, Sakata, is 101,000.

Most tourists pass Tsuruoka by, concentrating on Hagurosan, but the city does have a few things to offer visitors with time to spare. Refer to Tohoku Map 21.

While there are some shopping and commercial enterprises near the JR Station (upper right), most of Tsuruoka's downtown is to the south of the Station, centered around the Ginza-dori Arcade (shaded on the map).

Tsuruokajo Castle Grounds 鶴岡城跡

(lower left) (optional). Only the moats remain. The grounds feature Shonai Jinja and Gokoku Jinja Shrines, typical local shrines of no special interest. Hours: dawn to dusk. No admission charge.

Chido Museum 致道博物館 (optional) is near the Castle Grounds. This museum consists of several traditional, historical buildings that have been relocated here from various Sakai territories. The buildings here include the Sakai Family Mansion, the local government office from the Meiji Era (Western style architecture), and merchant and farmer houses. The buildings are laid out in a beautiful garden. Hours: 9:00 AM to 4:30 PM. Admission: 520 yen.

Hotels in Tsuruoka (Refer to Tohoku Map 21)

Tokyo Daiichi Hotel Tsuruoka (upper

MAP 21 Tsuruoka

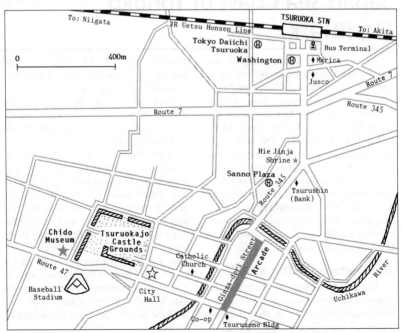

center). Standard. 84 singles (7,000 yen -) & 32 doubles (12,500 yen -). Add: 2-10, Nishi-kicho, Tsuruoka. Tel: (0235) 24-7611.

Tsuruoka Washington Hotel (upper right). Business. 86 singles (6,500 yen -) & 23 doubles (10,500 yen -). Add: 5, Suehiro-cho, Tsuruoka. Tel: (0235) 25-0111.

Hotel Sanno Plaza (middle center). Business. 92 singles (5,500 yen -) & 11 doubles (8,500 yen -). Add: 6-8, Sannocho, Tsu-ruoka. Tel: (0235) 22-6501.

HAGUROSAN　羽黒山

Hagurosan is the premiere tourist desti-nation in the Japan Sea Coast area of Tohoku. For generations, three mountains here have been the principal training grounds for Shinto priests for all parts of Japan. They are: Mt. Hagurosan, Mt. Gassan and Mt. Yudonosan. Even today, many

Japanese make a pilgrimage to these three mountains, making the hard climb to the summit.

Mt. Hagurosan features the Main Shrine, which is dedicated to the gods believed to live on the top of these three venerable mountains. Mt. Hagurosan is also the most accessible of the three sacred mountains. Be forewarned, though, it is still a long walk up the 2,446 stone steps to the top of the mountain.

Buses to Mt. Hagurosan leave from the bus terminal in front of the small JR Tsuruo-ka Station. The bus operates about once every 30-60 minutes. Fare: 590 yen to Haguro Center (upper left, Tohoku Map 22) and 900 yen to Haguro-Sancho (middle right). The bus makes three stops in the Hagurosan area: Haguro Center, Kokumin-Kyukamura (lower right), and Haguro San-cho, the terminal. The ride from Tsuruoka Station to Haguro Center takes about 40 minutes; it's an additional 15 minutes to

MAP 22 Hagurosan

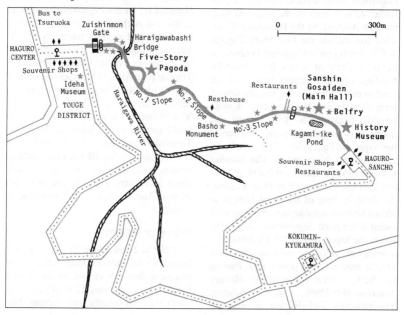

Haguro Sancho. We suggest that you get off at Haguro Center at the bottom of the mountain and make the climb to the top, which will take approximately 90 minutes. If, however, you are not a good walker or not interested in the excellent exercise you'll get climbing to the top of Mt. Hagurosan, you should stay on the bus to Haguro-Sancho stop (the terminal). From there you can walk **down** from the summit. The descent takes about one hour. Most Japanese choose this option, especially on hot summer days.

The area near Haguro Center bus stop has many Shrine accommodations for pilgrims from all over Japan as well as restaurants and souvenir shops. Ideha Museum (upper left) (optional) is a combination meeting center and small museum featuring dioramas and videos that explain the Shinto training process. Hours: 9:00 AM to 5:00 PM. Admission: 400 yen.

Zuishinmon Gate 随神門 is the entrance to the stone steps to the top of Mt. Hagurosan. Many small shrines line the path (indicated with stars on the map). At first, the path descends to the Haraigawa River. Then you will see the **Five Story Pagoda** 五重塔, a 600 year old National Treasure, in the dense forest of cedars. It's a beautiful building; one that camera buffs will not want to miss. After the Pagoda, the first of three slopes begins. The path passes through beautiful thick woods. There is one rest house, after the second slope, that serves beverages and light snacks. There is a broad tableland atop the mountain. **The Sanshin Gosaiden (Main Hall)** 三神合祭殿 is 28 m (93 feet) tall. It was built in 1818. Kagami-ike Pond in front of the Main Hall is so named because many *kagami* (mirrors) were found in the pond. Supposedly, this under-scores the importance of Mt. Hagurosan — women were willing to make sacrifices here of their most precious possessions. Passing the Belfry, you'll come to the **History Museum** 歴史博物館, a modern building. The collection includes statues, religious

training equipment and mirrors from the pond. Hours: 8:30 AM to 5:00 PM. Closed in winter. Admission: 200 yen. This museum is definitely better than Ideha Museum in Haguro Center.

Haguro-Sancho bus stop is just a few minutes walk from the Museum. This bus stop area, too, features restaurants and souvenir shops.

AKITA 秋田

Akita is the largest city in the Tohoku Japan Sea Coast area. It has a population of 298,000. It is the capital of Akita Prefecture, which is known for rice and sake and for the world-famous *Akita* dogs. The area has harsh winters and pleasant summers. It is recommended as a destination for repeat visitors to Tohoku.

Transportation to Akita

Refer to Tohoku Map 1. The JR Uetsu Honsen Line limited expresses connect Tsuruoka and Akita. The trip takes about 2 hours. Limited express trains on the JR Tazawako Line connect Akita with Morioka, the terminus of the Tohoku Shinkansen. The ride from Akita to Morioka takes 1 hour and 50 minutes. These limited expresses, called "Tazawa," operate about once an hour. Please note that **Kakunodate**, a small feudal town described below, is also on the Tazawako Line. Akita is also connected with Aomori by the JR Ou Line. Limited express trains on this Line operate only about once every 2 hours. The trip from Akita to Aomori takes about 2 hours and 30 minutes.

Places of Interest

Refer to Tohoku Map 23. Akita is most famous for its Kanto Festival, during which marchers, about 200 in total, parade through the night, each carrying 12 m (40 foot) tall bamboo frames covered with lanterns. This

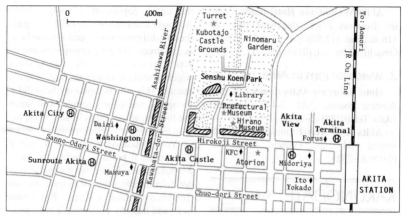

MAP 23 Akita

harvest festival is held in early August on the city's main street, Sanno-Odori Street (middle left). The lanterns on their tall frames represent rice plants rich and full of the precious grain. The parade is a spectacular all-natural light show.

Akita's downtown stretches to the west of JR Akita Station (lower right). Major department stores are located near the Station. Business offices are located on Sanno-Odori Street, across the Asahikawa River from the station area.

Senshu-Koen Park 千秋公園 (upper center) is the former Kubotajo Castle Grounds. The Park is now home to a reconstructed turret and several local museums. **Hirano Museum** 平野政吉美術館 (optional) has a good collection of the works of Tsuguji Fujita, a modern Japanese painter, as well as the works of Western artists, including Cezanne, Van Gogh and Picasso. Hours: 10:00 AM to 6:00 PM (5:00 PM in winter). Closed Mondays. Admission: 410 yen. **Prefectural Museum** 県立美術館 (optional) displays items of local interest. The Turret at the northwestern corner of the Castle Grounds, atop a cliff, was built recently. It houses a local history museum.

Atorion アトリオン (middle center)

(optional) is a new 12-story atrium building that houses a tourism information center and an exhibition hall for local crafts and products (unfortunately, the tourism information is only in Japanese). Atorion features commercial souvenir shops as well. The municipal **Senshu Museum** 千秋美術館 is also located here. This museum displays the works of local artists. Museum hours: 10:00 AM to 6:00 PM. Museum admission: 300 yen. Atorion is open from 8:00 AM to 10:00 PM (No admission charge).

ACCOMMODATIONS
(Refer to Tohoku Map 23)

1. Hotels in Akita

Akita Castle Hotel (middle center). Standard. 93 singles (8,500 yen -) & 79 doubles (17,000 yen -). Add: 1-3-5, Nakadori, Akita. Tel: (0188) 34-1141.

Akita View Hotel (middle right). Standard. 111 singles (8,500 yen -) & 83 doubles (17,000 yen -). Add: 2-3-1, Nakadori, Akita. Tel: (0188) 32-1111.

Akita Terminal Hotel (middle right). Standard. 50 singles (7,500 yen -) & 43 doubles (14,000 yen -). Add: 7-2-1, Nakadori, Akita. Tel: (0188) 31-2222.

Akita Washington Hotel (middle center). Business. 273 singles (6,000 yen -) & 116 doubles (12,500 yen -). Add: 2-2-11, Omachi, Akita. Tel: (0188) 65-7111.

2. Welcome Inns in Akita

Hotel Sunroute Akita (lower left). 113 Western rooms. Add: 3-4-18, Omachi, Akita. Tel: (0188) 65-2111.

Akita City Hotel (middle left). 115 rooms. Add: 2-2-3, Omachi, Akita. Tel: (0188) 63-2525.

KAKUNODATE 角館

Kakunodate was the castle town of the Satake family during the feudal era. Today the city's population is only 16,000. Although Kakunodate's castle is long gone, the city still preserves several samurai houses and streets. Weeping cherry trees line the 300 m (1,000 foot) main samurai street, which is about a 15-minute walk from the Station. This area is especially beautiful in the spring, and is very popular with Japanese tourists, who want to be sure to capture it on film.

You should consider a short stop in Kakunodate if you are traveling the Akita-Morioka route. If you have extra time in Morioka in conjunction with travel to Lake Towadako or Rikuchu-Kaigan, Kakunodate is a good half-day excursion. It takes about 50 minutes to reach Kakunodate from Morioka on the limited express.

JR FARES BETWEEN MAJOR STATIONS IN THE TOHOKU REGION
1. ALONG THE JR TOHOKU SHINKANSEN

To/From	Tokyo	Sendai	Morioka
Koriyama	7,810 yen (226.7 km)	5,130 yen (125.1 km)	9,670 yen (308.6 km)
Fukushima	8,530 yen (272.8 km)	3,510 yen (79 km)	8,330 yen (262.5 km)
Sendai	10,390 yen (351.8 km)		6,160 yen (183.5 km)
Furukawa	10,900 yen (395 km)	1,540 yen (43.2 km)	5,440 yen (140.3 km)
Ichinoseki	12,230 yen (445.1 km)	3,840 yen (93.3 km)	3,840 yen (90.2 km)
Morioka	13,570 yen (535.3 km)	6,160 yen (183.5 km)	

2. ALONG THE YAMAGATA SHINKANSEN

To/From	Tokyo	Yonezawa	Yamagata
Fukushima	8,530 yen (272.8 km)	1,940 yen (40.1 km)	3,050 yen (87.1 km)
Yonezawa	10,000 yen (312.9 km)		2,020 yen (47 km)
Yamagata	10,810 yen (359.9 km)	2,020 yen (47 km)	

3.BETWEEN OTHER MAJOR CITIES (EASTERN HALF OF THE TOHOKU REGION)

To/From	Koriyama	Sendai	Furukawa	Morioka	Hachinohe
Aizu-Wakamatsu	2,720 yen (65.3 km)				
Hon-Shiogama		310 yen (15.8 km)			
Matsushima-Kaigan		390 yen (23 km)			
Yamadera		800 yen (48.7 km)			
Naruko			640 yen (39.1 km)		
Kakunodate				2,520 yen (64.7 km)	
Miyako				1,850 yen (112.3 km)	
Kuji					1,260 yen (71.4 km)
Aomori				5,850 yen (203.9 km)	3,020 yen (96 km)

4. BETWEEN OTHER MAJOR CITIES (WESTERN HALF OF THE TOHOKU REGION)

To/From	Tokyo	Tsuruoka	Akita	Aomori
Tsuruoka	12,640 yen (484.6 km)		4,000 yen (132.3 km)	7,710 yen (318.1 km)
Akita	14,750 yen (606.9 km)	4,000 yen (132.3 km)		5,340 yen (185.8 km)
Hirosaki	16,140 yen (755.3 km)	7,190 yen (280.7 km)	4,310 yen (148.4 km)	1,760 yen (37.4 km)
Kakunodate			2,720 yen (65.7 km)	

BIBLIOGRAPHY

Ashihara, Y. *The Hidden Order: Tokyo Through the Twentieth Century*. Tokyo: Kodansha International, 1989.

Birdsall, D., ed. *The Living Treasures of Japan*. Tokyo: Kodansha International, 1973.

Booth, A. *The Roads to Sata: A 2,000 Mile Walk Through Japan*. Harmondsworth: Penguin Books, 1987.

Brazil, M. *A Bird Watcher's Guide to Japan*. Tokyo: Kodansha International, 1987.

Britton, D., and Sutherland, M. *National Parks of Japan*. Tokyo: Kodansha International, 1981.

Cherry, K. *Womansword: What Japanese Words Say About Women*. Kodansha International, 1988.

Cooper, M. *Exploring Kamakura*. Tokyo: Weatherhill, 1983.

Daggett, J. M. *Along the San'in: A Guide to Unfamiliar Japan*. Matsue: English Guidebook Publishing Committee, 1987.

Dalby, L. *Geisha*. Berkeley and Los Angeles: University of California Press, 1983.

Dower, J. *War Without Mercy: Race & Power in the Pacific War*. New York: Pantheon Books, 1986.

Durston, D. *Old Kyoto*. Tokyo: Kodansha International, 1986.

Durston, D. *Kyoto: Seven Paths to the Heart of the City*. Tokyo: Kodansha International, 1988.

Enbutsu, S. *Discover Shitamachi*. Tokyo: Kokusai Bunken Insatsu Sha, 1984.

Fallows, J. *More Like Us: Making America Great Again*. Boston: Houghton Mifflin, 1989.

Feiler, B. *Learning to Bow*. New York: Ticknor & Fields, 1991.

Gunji, M. *The Kabuki Guide*. Tokyo: Kodansha International, 1987.

Hotta A. and Ishiguro, Y. *A Guide to Japanese Hot Springs*. Tokyo: Kodansha International, 1986.

Hunt, P. *Hiking in Japan: A Detailed Guide to 35 Routes*. Tokyo: Kodansha International, 1988.

Itoh, T. *The Gardens of Japan*. Tokyo and New York: Kodansha International, 1984.

Iwao S., ed. *Biographical Dictionary of Japanese History*. Tokyo: Kodansha International, 1978.

Japan National Tourist Organization. *Japan: The New Official Guide*. Tokyo: JNTO, 1975.

Kennedy, R. *Guide to Good Tokyo Restaurants*. Tokyo: Kodansha International, 1989.

Kinoshita, J. and Palevsky N. *Gateway to Japan*. Tokyo: Kodansha International, 1990.

Melville, J. *The Bogus Buddha*. New York: Fawcett Crest, 1990. This is one of Mr. Melville's delightful Superintendent Otani mysteries, set in Kobe. Others in the series include: *A Haiku for Hanae, The Wages of Zen, A Sort of Samurai, The Chrysanthemum Chain, The Ninth Netsuke, Death of a Daimyo, Sayonara Sweet Amarylis, The*

Death Ceremony, Go Gently Gaijin, Kimono for a Corpse, The Reluctant Ronin.

Miner, E., Odagiri H. and Morrell, R. *The Princeton Companion to Classical Japanese Literature.* Princeton: Princeton University Press, 1985.

Mino, Y. *The Great Eastern Temple: Treasures of Japanese Buddhist Art from Todai-ji.* Chicago: The Art Institute of Chicago, 1986.

Moriyama, T. *The Practical Guide to Japanese Signs (Vol. 1* and *Vol. 2).* Tokyo: Kodansha International, 1987.

Mosher, G. *Kyoto: A Contemplative Guide.* Tokyo: Tuttle, 1986.

Nakamura, M. *Kabuki—Backstage, Onstage.* Tokyo: Kodansha International, 1990.

Nishi, K. and Hozumi, K. *What is Japanese Architecture?* Tokyo: Kodansha International, 1983.

Pearson, R. *Ancient Japan.* Washington: Arthur M. Sackler Gallery, 1992.

Reischauer, E. *The Japanese.* Cambridge: Belknap Harvard, 1977.

Richie, D. *A Taste of Japan.* Tokyo: Kodansha International, 1985.

Richie, D. *The Inland Sea.* London: Century, 1986.

Rimer, J. T., Chaves, J., Addiss, S. and Suzuki, H. *Shisendo: Hall of the Poetry Immortals.* Tokyo: Weatherhill, 1991.

Rimer, J. T. *A Reader's Guide to Japanese Literature.* Tokyo: Kodansha International, 1988.

Roberts, L. *Roberts' Guide to Japanese Museums of Art and Archaeology.* Tokyo: Simul Press, 1987.

Roberts, L. *A Dictionary of Japanese Artists.* Tokyo: Weatherhill, 1986.

Saga, J. *Memories of Silk and Straw.* Tokyo: Kodansha International, 1987.

Saint-Gilles, A. *Mingei.* Tokyo: Heian International, 1983.

Sansom, G. *A History of Japan (3 vols.).* Stanford: Stanford University Press, 1958, 1961, 1963.

Satterwhite, R. *What's What in Japanese Restaurants: A Guide to Ordering, Eating, and Enjoying.* Tokyo: Kodansha International, 1988.

Seidensticker, E. *Low City, High City.* New York: Knopf, 1983.

Shimizu, Y., ed. *The Shaping of Daimyo Culture 1186-1868.* Washington: National Gallery of Art, 1988.

Statler, O. *Japanese Inn.* New York: Random House, 1961.

Statler, O. *Shimoda Story.* New York: Random House, 1969.

Stevens, R. *Kanazawa: The Other Side of Japan.* Kanazawa: Kanazawa Tourist Association, 1991.

Sugiyama, J. *Classic Buddhist Sculpture: The Tempyo Period.* Tokyo: Kodansha International, 1987.

Tsuji, S. *Japanese Cooking: A Simple Art.* Tokyo: Kodansha International, 1980.

Umeda, A., ed. *Tokyo: A Bilingual Atlas.* Tokyo: Kodansha International, 1988.

Walters, G. *Day Walks Near Tokyo.* Tokyo: Kodansha International, 1988.

Weatherly, J. *Japan Unescorted.* Tokyo: Kodansha International, 1986.

Whiting, R. *You Gotta Have Wa.* New York: Macmillan, 1989.

Wild Bird Society of Japan. *A Field Guide to the Birds of Japan.* Tokyo: Kodansha International, 1982.

Yanagi, S. *The Unknown Craftsman.* Tokyo: Kodansha International, 1989.

INDEX

1 STATION 下の電車または地下鉄の駅を教えてください

Where is the following train/subway station?
(Circle either train or subway and fill in the name of the station and the name of the line.)

	Circle either one		路線名 Line Name	駅名 Destination
	Train	Subway		
1	電車	地下鉄		
2	電車	地下鉄		
3	電車	地下鉄		
4	電車	地下鉄		
5	電車	地下鉄		

2 TICKET 下の駅までの運賃を教えてください

How much is the fare to the following station?
(Fill in the name of your destination and the name of the line you want to take.)

	路線名 Line Name	目的駅 Destination
1		SHINJUKU
2		
3		
4		
5		

3 PLATFORM 下の電車の発車ホーム番号を教えてください

What is the platform number for the following train to the destination listed below?
(If the train is a local and does not have a name, write "Donko" in the train name column.)

	路線名 Line Name	電車名 Train Name	目的駅 Destination
1	東海道本線	（普通）	静岡、浜松
2		（快速）	豊橋、米原
3			京都、大阪
4			沼津、大垣
5			

1 STATION 下の電車または地下鉄の駅を教えてください

Where is the following train/subway station?
(Circle either train or subway and fill in the name of the station and the name of the line.)

Circle either one		路線名 Line Name	駅名 Destination
1	Train 電車 Subway 地下鉄		
2	電車 地下鉄		
3	電車 地下鉄		
4	電車 地下鉄		
5	電車 地下鉄		

2 TICKET 下の駅までの運賃を教えてください

How much is the fare to the following station?
(Fill in the name of your destination and the name of the line you want to take.)

	路線名 Line Name	目的駅 Destination
1		
2		
3		
4		
5		

3 PLATFORM 下の電車の発車ホーム番号を教えてください

What is the platform number for the following train to the destination listed below?
(If the train is a local and does not have a name, write "Donko" in the train name column.)

	路線名 Line Name	電車名 Train Name	目的駅 Destination
1			
2			
3			
4			
5			

座席指定申込書
RESERVATION
Application for reserved seats

If you have a Rail Pass, you can request reservations for JR trains free of charge. Show the Pass with this form.
Your Rail Pass cannot be used for private railways.

乗車日 Date of Trip	月 (month)	日 (date)	人数 No. of Psns	大人 ____ 枚 Adults	子供 ____ 枚 Children
出発駅 Departure _____ Station			目的駅 Destination _____ Station		
座席の種類 Class of Seat	(Check either one)	□グリーン車 First Class	□普通車 Coach Class	□禁煙席 Nonsmoking section, if available	
第一希望 First Choice	電車名 Train Name		出発時間 Dep. Time	時 (hour)	分 (minute)
第二希望 Second Choice	電車名 Train Name		出発時間 Dep. Time	時 (hour)	分 (minute)
第三希望 Third Choice	電車名 Train Name		出発時間 Dep. Time	時 (hour)	分 (minute)

座席指定申込書
RESERVATION
Application for reserved seats

If you have a Rail Pass, you can request reservations for JR trains free of charge. Show the Pass with this form.
Your Rail Pass cannot be used for private railways.

乗車日 Date of Trip	月 (month)	日 (date)	人数 No. of Psns	大人 ____ 枚 Adults	子供 ____ 枚 Children
出発駅 Departure _____ Station			目的駅 Destination _____ Station		
座席の種類 Class of Seat	(Check either one)	□グリーン車 First Class	□普通車 Coach Class	□禁煙席 Nonsmoking section, if available	
第一希望 First Choice	電車名 Train Name		出発時間 Dep. Time	時 (hour)	分 (minute)
第二希望 Second Choice	電車名 Train Name		出発時間 Dep. Time	時 (hour)	分 (minute)
第三希望 Third Choice	電車名 Train Name		出発時間 Dep. Time	時 (hour)	分 (minute)

座席指定申込書
RESERVATION
Application for reserved seats

If you have a Rail Pass, you can request reservations for JR trains free of charge. Show the Pass with this form.
Your Rail Pass cannot be used for private railways.

乗車日 Date of Trip	月 (month)	日 (date)	人数 No. of Psns	大人 ____ 枚 Adults	子供 ____ 枚 Children
出発駅 Departure _____ Station			目的駅 Destination _____ Station		
座席の種類 Class of Seat	(Check either one)	□グリーン車 First Class	□普通車 Coach Class	□禁煙席 Nonsmoking section, if available	
第一希望 First Choice	電車名 Train Name		出発時間 Dep. Time	時 (hour)	分 (minute)
第二希望 Second Choice	電車名 Train Name		出発時間 Dep. Time	時 (hour)	分 (minute)
第三希望 Third Choice	電車名 Train Name		出発時間 Dep. Time	時 (hour)	分 (minute)

座席指定申込書

Application for reserved seats

If you have a Rail Pass, you can request reservations for JR trains free of charge. Show the Pass with this form.

Your Rail Pass cannot be used for private railways.

乗車日 Date of Trip	月 (month)	日 (date)	人数 No. of Psns	大人____枚 Adults	子供____枚 Children

出発駅 Departure _____ Station	目的駅 Destination _____ Station

座席の種類 Class of Seat	(Check either one)	□グリーン車 First Class	□普通車 Coach Class	□禁煙席 Nonsmoking section, if available

第一希望 First Choice	電車名 Train Name		出発時間 Dep. Time	時 (hour)	分 (minute)
第二希望 Second Choice	電車名 Train Name		出発時間 Dep. Time	時 (hour)	分 (minute)
第三希望 Third Choice	電車名 Train Name		出発時間 Dep. Time	時 (hour)	分 (minute)

座席指定申込書

Application for reserved seats

If you have a Rail Pass, you can request reservations for JR trains free of charge. Show the Pass with this form.

Your Rail Pass cannot be used for private railways.

乗車日 Date of Trip	月 (month)	日 (date)	人数 No. of Psns	大人____枚 Adults	子供____枚 Children

出発駅 Departure _____ Station	目的駅 Destination _____ Station

座席の種類 Class of Seat	(Check either one)	□グリーン車 First Class	□普通車 Coach Class	□禁煙席 Nonsmoking section, if available

第一希望 First Choice	電車名 Train Name		出発時間 Dep. Time	時 (hour)	分 (minute)
第二希望 Second Choice	電車名 Train Name		出発時間 Dep. Time	時 (hour)	分 (minute)
第三希望 Third Choice	電車名 Train Name		出発時間 Dep. Time	時 (hour)	分 (minute)

座席指定申込書

Application for reserved seats

If you have a Rail Pass, you can request reservations for JR trains free of charge. Show the Pass with this form.

Your Rail Pass cannot be used for private railways.

乗車日 Date of Trip	月 (month)	日 (date)	人数 No. of Psns	大人____枚 Adults	子供____枚 Children

出発駅 Departure _____ Station	目的駅 Destination _____ Station

座席の種類 Class of Seat	(Check either one)	□グリーン車 First Class	□普通車 Coach Class	□禁煙席 Nonsmoking section, if available

第一希望 First Choice	電車名 Train Name		出発時間 Dep. Time	時 (hour)	分 (minute)
第二希望 Second Choice	電車名 Train Name		出発時間 Dep. Time	時 (hour)	分 (minute)
第三希望 Third Choice	電車名 Train Name		出発時間 Dep. Time	時 (hour)	分 (minute)

5 BUS STREETCAR
下の行先の市電またはバス乗場を教えてください

Where is the stop for the streetcar (or bus) going to the following destination?
(Circle either streetcar or bus and fill in the name of your destination.)

Circle either one		目的駅 Destination
	Streetcar	Bus	
1	市電	バス	
2	市電	バス	
3	市電	バス	
4	市電	バス	
5	市電	バス	

6 DESTINATION
私は下の目的地まで行きます
目的地が近づいたら教えてください

I am going to the following place. Please let me know when we near the destination.
(On the train, streetcar or bus)
(Fill in the name of your destination and show the card to a fellow passenger.)

1		6	
2		7	
3		8	
4		9	
5		10	

7 TAXI
下の目的地まで行ってください

Please take me to the following place.
(For a taxi driver) (Fill in the name of your destination.)

1		7	
2		8	
3		9	
4		10	
5		11	
6		12	

5 BUS STREETCAR — 下の行先の市電またはバス乗場を教えてください

Where is the stop for the streetcar (or bus) going to the following destination?
(Circle either streetcar or bus and fill in the name of your destination.)

Circle either one		目的駅 Destination
1	Streetcar 市電 / Bus バス	
2	市電 バス	
3	市電 バス	
4	市電 バス	
5	市電 バス	

6 DESTINATION — 私は下の目的地まで行きます 目的地が近づいたら教えてください

I am going to the following place. Please let me know when we near the destination.
(On the train, streetcar or bus)
(Fill in the name of your destination and show the card to a fellow passenger.)

1		6	
2		7	
3		8	
4		9	
5		10	

7 TAXI — 下の目的地まで行ってください

Please take me to the following place.
(For a taxi driver) (Fill in the name of your destination.)

1		7	
2		8	
3		9	
4		10	
5		11	
6		12	

---

4 RESERVATION	**座席指定申込書** Application for reserved seats	If you have a Rail Pass, you can request reservations for JR trains free of charge. Show the Pass with this form. Your Rail Pass cannot be used for private railways.

乗車日 Date of Trip	月 (month)	日 (date)	人数 No. of Psns	大人 Adults ____ 枚	子供 ____ 枚 Children

出発日 Departure _____ Station	目的駅 Destination _____ Station

座席の種類 (Check either one) Class of Seat	□グリーン車 First Class	□普通車 Coach Class	□禁煙席 Nonsmoking section, if available

第一希望 First Choice	電車名 Train Name		出発時間 Dep. Time	時 (hour)	分 (minute)
第二希望 Second Choice	電車名 Train Name		出発時間 Dep. Time	時 (hour)	分 (minute)
第三希望 Third Choice	電車名 Train Name		出発時間 Dep. Time	時 (hour)	分 (minute)

---

4 RESERVATION	**座席指定申込書** Application for reserved seats	If you have a Rail Pass, you can request reservations for JR trains free of charge. Show the Pass with this form. Your Rail Pass cannot be used for private railways.

乗車日 Date of Trip	月 (month)	日 (date)	人数 No. of Psns	大人 Adults ____ 枚	子供 ____ 枚 Children

出発駅 Departure _____ Station	目的駅 Destination _____ Station

座席の種類 (Check either one) Class of Seat	□グリーン車 First Class	□普通車 Coach Class	□禁煙席 Nonsmoking section, if available

第一希望 First Choice	電車名 Train Name		出発時間 Dep. Time	時 (hour)	分 (minute)
第二希望 Second Choice	電車名 Train Name		出発時間 Dep. Time	時 (hour)	分 (minute)
第三希望 Third Choice	電車名 Train Name		出発時間 Dep. Time	時 (hour)	分 (minute)

<table>
<tr><td>

8
🧳
BAGGAGE

</td><td>

9
🚻
REST ROOM

</td></tr>
<tr><td>

手荷物一時預り所
または
コインロッカーを
教えてください

Where are the coin lockers or
a short-term baggage check room?

</td><td>

お手洗の場所を
教えてください

Where is a rest room?

</td></tr>
</table>

4 ✍ RESERVATION — 座席指定申込書

Application for reserved seats

If you have a Rail Pass, you can request reservations for JR trains free of charge. Show the Pass with this form.
Your Rail Pass cannot be used for private railways.

乗車日 Date of Trip	月 (month)	日 (date)	人数 No. of Psns	大人 ___ 枚 Adults	子供 ___ 枚 Children

出発駅 Departure _____ Station	目的駅 Destination _____ Station

座席の種類 (Check either one) Class of Seat	□グリーン車 First Class	□普通車 Coach Class	□禁煙席 Nonsmoking section, if available

第一希望 First Choice	電車名 Train Name	出発時間 Dep. Time	時 (hour)	分 (minute)
第二希望 Second Choice	電車名 Train Name	出発時間 Dep. Time	時 (hour)	分 (minute)
第三希望 Third Choice	電車名 Train Name	出発時間 Dep. Time	時 (hour)	分 (minute)

4 ✍ RESERVATION — 座席指定申込書

Application for reserved seats

If you have a Rail Pass, you can request reservations for JR trains free of charge. Show the Pass with this form.
Your Rail Pass cannot be used for private railways.

乗車日 Date of Trip	月 (month)	日 (date)	人数 No. of Psns	大人 ___ 枚 Adults	子供 ___ 枚 Children

出発駅 Departure _____ Station	目的駅 Destination _____ Station

座席の種類 (Check either one) Class of Seat	□グリーン車 First Class	□普通車 Coach Class	□禁煙席 Nonsmoking section, if available

第一希望 First Choice	電車名 Train Name	出発時間 Dep. Time	時 (hour)	分 (minute)
第二希望 Second Choice	電車名 Train Name	出発時間 Dep. Time	時 (hour)	分 (minute)
第三希望 Third Choice	電車名 Train Name	出発時間 Dep. Time	時 (hour)	分 (minute)

Bilingual Maps and Atlases from KODANSHA INTERNATIONAL

TOKYO : A Bilingual Atlas
With over 48 bilingual maps, this indexed atlas is the essential survival guide for finding one's way around Tokyo.
Paperback; 154 pp; 151 mm x 215 mm

KYOTO-OSAKA : A Bilingual Atlas
The first bilingual reference for the Kansai region. 36 maps of all major metropolitan areas, transportation, and tourist areas.
Paperback; 96 pp; 151 mm x 215 mm

JAPAN : A Bilingual Atlas
The entire country of Japan is covered, from Hokkaido to Okinawa, in more than 50 color maps.
Paperback; 128 pp; 151 mm x 215 mm

TOKYO RAIL AND ROAD ATLAS : A Bilingual Guide
This bilingual atlas for Metropolitan Tokyo provides clear, detailed maps of all major railways, subways, bus lines, expressways, and international airports.
Paperback; 80 pp; 151 mm x 215 mm

TOKYO: A Bilingual Map
A fold-out wall map of central Tokyo, plus detailed maps of major downtown areas.
Folder: 111 mm x 228 mm, Map: 611 mm x 840 mm

TOKYO METROPOLITAN AREA: A Bilingual Map
A fold-out wall map of the Kanto region, plus area maps of cities outside of central Tokyo.
Folder: 111 mm x 228 mm, Map: 606 mm x 856 mm

KYOTO-OSAKA: A Bilingual Map
A fold-out wall map of the Kansai region, including Kobe, Nagoya and Nara.
Folder: 111 mm x 228 mm, Map: 611 mm x 840 mm

JAPAN: A Bilingual Map
A fold-out national map indicating major travel routes, plus detailed maps of seven major metropolitan areas.
Folder: 138 mm x 264 mm, Map: 770 mm x 1058 mm